LATIN AMERICAN HISTORICAL DICTIONARIES SERIES
Edited by A. Curtis Wilgus

1. Moore, Richard E. *Guatemala*. 1967. (new ed. in prep.)
2. Hedrick, Basil C. & Anne K. *Panama*. 1970.
3. Rudolph, Donna Keyse & G. A. *Venezuela*. 1971.
4. Heath, Dwight B. *Bolivia*. 1972.
5. Flemion, Philip F. *El Salvador*. 1972.
6. Meyer, Harvey K. *Nicaragua*. 1972.
7. Bizzarro, Salvatore. *Chile*. 1972.

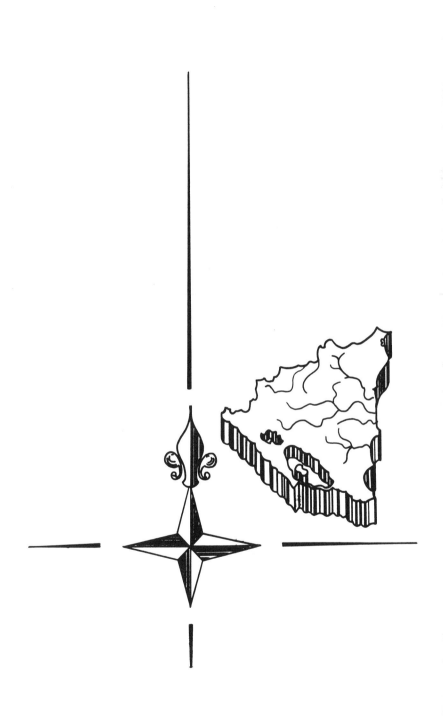

Historical Dictionary of Nicaragua

by

Harvey K. Meyer

Latin American Historical Dictionaries, No. 6

The Scarecrow Press, Inc.
Metuchen, N. J.   1972

Library of Congress Cataloging in Publication Data

Meyer, Harvey Kessler, 1914-
    Historical dictionary of Nicaragua.

    (Latin American historical dictionaries, no. 6)
    1. Nicaragua--Dictionaries and encyclopedias.
I. Title.
F1522.M4   917.285'003   72-2441
ISBN 0-8108-0488-3

All drawings are by the author

Editor's Foreword

        Dr. Meyer has had a colorful life in the United States, Latin America and Europe. Among his many activities he has directed development of university-level television, and has been a silver miner, a building contractor, an electrician, a designer, a carpenter, an air navigator (U.S. Naval Reserve, retired), and, of course, an educator--in both high school and college. From 1946 to 1965 he was a student or staff member at the University of Florida. In the latter year he moved to Florida Atlantic University where he became Associate Dean of Academic Affairs and where he is now Professor of Education. His present academic interests are in higher education as well as Technical education. Honors have come to him from several professional fraternities. He has been active in many professional organizations, lectures widely on his favorite subjects, and has written a number of articles and monographs.

        A number of his vocations and avocations have been related to Central America. In Nicaragua for two and a half years (1955-1957) he was Director of Industrial and Vocational Education and he helped to develop the National Vocational Technical Institute. In 1966 he served as Educational Consultant for the Universidad del Norte, Barranquilla, Colombia. Altogether, his educational work and interests have taken him to 52 countries.

        With his great personal curiosity, his wide-ranging interests in history and geography, his imaginative thinking, and his intense interest in Middle America, Dr. Meyer has undertaken the compilation of this volume about Nicaragua, a country which has played such an interesting role in Central American history and in international relations, especially with the United States and Great Britain. As with other compilers in this Historical Dictionary Series, Dr. Meyer was asked to use his own judgment in selecting material to be included in this dictionary so that a balanced, reasonably comprehensive guide would result.

        As a fellow Latin Americanist and a one-time colleague

iii

at the University of Florida, I am happy that Dr. Meyer could undertake this task, applying his characteristic literary style to its composition and his skillful selection of illustrated material for its overall effectiveness.

A. Curtis Wilgus
Emeritus Director
School of Inter-American Studies
University of Florida

List of Illustrations

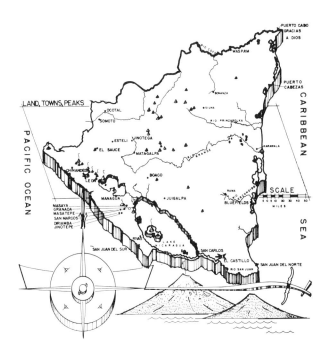

Introduction

This Historical Dictionary of Nicaragua really began in a sojourn of several years in that country by the compiler and his family, and grew in a climate of continued and accelerated interest during 14 years since that time.

Any compilation of elements from Nicaraguan annals must emphasize certain facts and factors which comprehend far more than the mere uniqueness common to all countries. For Nicaraguan history has to a greater extent than that of most small nations been both contributory to and in the grip of major events of world significance. The action has taken place upon a larger stage than Nicaragua's status as a small partially developed tropical country might suggest. Further, there are a number of precedents, military and diplomatic, which have burst from their Nicaraguan origins to prominence on the world scene.

Not only have there been events of global consequence, but men as well whose names have become household words. It may be instructive to cite here some of these as hors d'oeuvres to the main courses of events.

Nicaragua has had in her history a lion's share of men who loomed larger than life. Horatio Nelson, hero of Trafalgar, idol of Great Britain in her "Pax Britannica" heyday, and revered prototype for the officers of the world's navies, was just a stripling (though already captain of a ship) when he stormed "St. John's Fort" on the San Juan River in 1780. Much earlier a dashing Spanish officer was briefly imprisoned in the old San Francisco monastery still standing in Granada. His name was Hernando de Soto; his ultimate grave, the great Mississippi River he discovered.

Bishop Bartalomé de las Casas was one of the first strong voices to be raised in favor of oppressed minorities, and is thus immortally identified with the Indian peoples he sought to liberate. He preached in the extant colonial church in Subtiava.

William Walker, "gray-eyed man of destiny" and a doctor-lawyer-editor, became an exemplar of manifest destiny during the vigorous years of that doctrine. As a filibuster he came to lend his name to the followers of the early freebooters and the forerunners of such as Fidel Castro. He even contributed a considerable chapter to the techniques of rigged elections, becoming a Yankee President of Nicaragua!

Walker's improbable rival was ex-ferryboatman Cornelius Vanderbilt, founder of a financial dynasty, who stubbornly drove a little paddle steamer up the San Juan River to institute the quickest route from New York to the bonanzas of the California gold-fields in the 1850's.

Making the transit via Lake Nicaragua and the San Juan River at a later date--back from "roughing it" in the West-- was another steamer pilot, named Clemens, who may have heard there once again the leadsman's cry of "mark twain!" which gave him his nom-de-plume.

And yet another figure served with Walker and even eulogized him--the poet Joaquin Miller.

Further involved on the storied San Juan was a young Lieutenant Peary, a surveyor of the 1870's working on the canal route, who must have regretted the warmth of the jungle as he stood in later years at the North Pole.

The worlds of transport and war, however, pale before the realm of art and literature when a part-Indian lad who grew up in an obscure Nicaraguan village called Chocoyos became the precursor and the brightest star of modern Spanish literature. No educated Spanish-speaking person is unfamiliar with "Juventúd, Divino Tesoro." Because of Rubén Darío, "Poet" is a title of address in modern Nicaragua.

But when Darío died in 1916, a ferment was in progress which brought to view a vastly different man, César Agusto Sandino, who was destined to be cursed as bandit and hailed as patriot, yet whose significance as a modern guerrilla was not clear during his lifetime. He fought and developed the tactics used ever since from Algeria to Indochina, at the very time another creative guerrillero, Mao, was on his "long march."

Forerunner of Guevara and Giap both in theory and practice, Sandino has had profound influence upon insurrectional movements during the nearly four decades since his death. And the kind of war he brought to prominence has been the bane of world powers.

Less well known than some of these others, the strongman Anastasio Somoza managed to establish a dynasty as caudillo of his country from 1933 to 1956; his two sons both have served as President, through electoral process, in the only such dynastic development in Latin American history, still going in 1972.

Yet spectacular as were these human figures, the ethnological, geographical, and hence historical matrices of the composite Nicaraguan culture are as interesting. Between Point Barrow in Alaska and Tierra del Fuego there is really only one spot where the basic American Cordillera breaks significantly, with bays, lakes, plains, and a river valley broadening the gap. From early days of the conquest, Nicaragua was seen as a site for opening the Atlantic and Pacific oceans to each other. And it was another dramatic feature of Nicaraguan geography, the line of volcanoes, which more politically than physically caused the move of the final isthmus-cutting enterprise to Panama. But throughout its four and a half centuries of post-conquest history, the canal potential of the Nicaraguan lowland was the chief molder of events. Nor has the day ended.

While rich agriculture, of coffee, corn, cane, cotton, cacao, and other crops, and cattle, has matched mineral riches and forest bounties, this melting pot of people (prior to the Spanish era principally speaking Nahuatl and having Mexican origins) has provided a fascinating population. The result is linguistic variety, genetic stimulation, and cultural originality which might well be expected where Mayan, Nahuan, Spanish, and Anglo-Saxon influences all have had their impact, and where hints of Quéchua, Carib, and African overtones are not without substance.

During the two-century thalassocracy of England, she controlled the North and Baltic Seas, the Mediterranean at Gibralter, Malta, and Suez, (as well as Aden), the Indian Ocean and the entry to the Pacific via the Malacca and Makassar Straits; Hongkong, the Falklands, Cape Town at Africa's tip--only in Nicaragua did she fail to have her way of mastering all the ocean entries. The geo-political significance is obvious. England's efforts to master the isthmus were legion, her Mosquito Protectorate being one of the grotesque by-roads of history.

The development of guerrilla warfare during Sandino days found also a number of military firsts--the air-bombing of an open city (Chinandega); medical evacuation by air (Quilalí); tactical air-support, such as bombing of an enemy "fire-base" unsupported by troops (El Chipote), as well as other kinds; first trial use of rotary-wing aircraft in war (the Pitcairn de la Cierva autogiro); dive-bombing, originated not by German Stukas in Spain in the late Thirties, but at Ocotal in Nicaragua in the late Twenties. Comparisons to Viet Nam are evident.

The setting of geography, men, and events sketched above does not truly indicate the nature of this book. There are some details of the dictionary which deserve mention. To begin with, there has been no effort to be exhaustive or even encyclopedic. The choice of entries has been arbitrary and therefore limited and fallible. They have fallen under four loosely defined categories: (1) the Geographical, under which have been considered Departments, Cities, Towns, Rivers, Harbors, Lakes, Regions, Railroads, Highways, Shipping Lines, Air Lines, Islands, Crops, and Mines and Minerals; (2) the Historical, touching Buildings, Battles, Wars, Organizations, Churches, Movements, Labor Groups, Steamboats, Places, Museums, Events, Ruins, Forts, Pirates, etc.; (3) People as Individuals, such as Artists, Bishops, Governors, Presidents, Writers, Poets,

Officials, Engineers, Ministers, Conquistadors, Filibusters, Priests, Friars, "Encomenderos," "Hacendados," and Pirates again; and (4) other Cultural Aspects (broadly interpreted) including: Schools, Tribes, Languages, Dances, Animals, "Coplas," Poetry, Newspapers, Radio and Television Stations, Definitions, Garb, Fiestas, Transport, and so on.

Special mention should be made of the inclusion of a number of "haciendas," cattle ranches, coffee "fincas" (farms or plantations), cane plantations, and mines, in addition to the usual districts (comarcas or territories), departments, and population centers which are pueblos, villas, and cities. In the case of districts, these have particular historical antecedents and special meaning to the inhabitants. Names are from preconquest and colonial sources in the main. An unusual feature is the considerable number of paddle-wheel steamers which used to ply several of the lakes and rivers. Again there is a special significance. Nicaragua has the largest lakes and the longest rivers in Central America, as well as a straight and distinctive march of dormant and active volcanoes.

The general arrangement of the dictionary is alphabetical, with a modicum of cross-referencing for acronyms, spelling variants, further elaborations, pseudonyms, and abbreviations. Names of individuals include not only such obvious entries as governors and presidents, but also a selection, limited though it be, of others who are either significant as individuals or who represent a type of significance as examples. This category can only represent a sampling. The individuals listed are not confined to Nicaraguans, because of the unusual and long-standing foreign involvements hinted at above. Unfortunately, space confines the individual choices to the exemplary rather than the exhaustive, so that many, many people who would have added to the color and significance of the whole have had to be left out.

Gathering of pertinent data has been based upon a two-and-a-half year period of residence in Managua, 1955-57; extensive travels throughout the country during which, by dugout canoe, jeep, outboard boat, airplane, helicopter, auto, train, mountain climbing on foot, and on horseback, the compiler has seen, in one fashion or another, literally all of Nicaragua, a land the size of Michigan or Florida; this background was supplemented by two special fact-gathering journeys, one in 1960 and the last in 1969 with particular reference to this volume.

The bibliography is extensive and ranges from early Spanish materials to little-known but recent Nicaraguan publications. From this listing and its bibliographies in turn may be derived almost all that is in print about Nicaragua. There is considerable local literature in understandably limited editions. General histories, world and otherwise, have a paucity of Nicaraguan references. Incompleteness and frequent inaccuracy of sources is a continuing problem.

Acknowledgment of all who aided would be almost impossible. But special mention must be made of my wife, Jessie; our two sons, Kessler and Matt; and our daughter, Carol--all of whom climbed volcanoes, boated shark-filled waters, rode narrow-gauge railroads, wound down jungle rivers, and flew precariously in single-engined aircraft to learn of our loved foster-country. And no less gratitude goes to our good friends, Rodney and Mireya Jackman, who themselves opened many doors, personal and public, which otherwise would have remained closed. Not least were the hospitable doors of their own home--"mi casa es su casa!"

Among entries the Jackmans provided were those to Jorge Espinosa, whose archaeological findings and dramatic theories of the origin of the word "America" will soon attain more notice; and to Carlos Mantica, whose collection of "antiguos" and linguistic contributions to "Nahoa-Español" evidence the modern scholarship of young Nicaraguans. It should be emphasized that there is a highly regarded intellectual tradition in Nicaragua.

I must mention Armando Argüello and my other early friends and associates of the Instituto Nacional Técnico Vocacional who years ago were a part of the whole; the Wilfred Cross family, who helped so much; the Mahlon Weiss family, who made living especially pleasant on the Sierras; and the memory of Don Crisanto Sacasa, the finest educator I ever worked for: soldier, author, university rector, teacher, diplomat, raconteur and wise octogenarian.

Special appreciation is due Carol Hatcher, Joan Thompson, Lucy Parsons, Lee Wilson, and Frances Malone for their help in preparation of the manuscript.

If there are errors in this volume, as I am sure there are, the burden of responsibility is wholly mine.

Not casually did the early Spaniards name the lovely land of bright lakes and gently breathing volcanoes "El Paraíso de Mahomet"--Mohammed's Paradise.

- A -

ABANGASCA.   Comarca or district of the municipio of León,
    León department.

ABAUNZA, Don Justo.   A lieutenant of colonial troops in
    Masaya in 1800; don Justo's family exists today in
    Masaya.

ABEJAS.   A Nicaraguan political party nickname of the peri-
    od 1821-1830 (early independence and confederation peri-
    od).   See CULUMACOS.

ABRA, EL. Comarca or district in the municipio of Jinotepe,
    Carazo department.

ACADEMIA MILITAR   see CAMPO DEL MARTE

ACADEMIA NICARAGUENSE DE LA LENGUA.   A publisher
    located in Managua.

ACADEMIC YEAR.   The universities open in June and close
    in February, with some variations, such as the School
    of Engineering of the National University, which runs
    from May to March.

ACAHUALINCA.   In the western part of the city of Managua
    is a remarkable archaeological site where footprints of
    man and of extinct animals exist side-by-side, having
    been made in soft material which later petrified, and be-
    ing overlaid with volcanic deposits, was perfectly pre-
    served.   Dr. Earl Flint (q.v.) first brought this site to
    world attention, followed by Dr. S.K. Lothrop (q.v.) in
    1926, and finally in 1941-42 the Carnegie Institute of
    Washington, D.C., sent a group to make excavation.   The
    site has been preserved in good form, and is covered to
    prevent depredations of weather.   Discoveries on the site
    indicate a human population similar to the peoples first
    found in the area by the Spanish Conquistadors.   Most
    significant is that prehistoric bison occupied the area con-
    currently with ancient man.   The bison are long extinct

1

here. Tracks of more than 40 humans have been counted. The people seem to have been nomads, living prior
to the development of textiles and ceramics. It is believed these may be the oldest human evidences to be
found in Latin America. In the area of the tracks, but
at a higher (hence later) level, in a circle of 1800 feet
diameter, over 10,000 pieces of ceramic have been found.
The age of some of the ceramic is 2000 years. The
makers of tracks may have antedated this time by
thousands of years.

ACATL ("cane"). A festival day of the month of this name
celebrated by the Nicaraos.

ACENTE. A territory of the National District, department of
Managua.

ACCESSORY TRANSIT COMPANY. Formed by Cornelius
Vanderbilt in 1850 to take advantage of the gold-rush
traffic to California, the route of this transportation firm
crossed Nicaragua to shorten by 25 days the previous sea
route around Cape Horn, which took at best 51 days. The
Transit Company employed fast seagoing steamers from
New York to San Juan del Norte or Greytown on the Atlantic Coast of Nicaragua. Paddle steamers were spe-
cially constructed to negotiate the shallow, rapid-riven
San Juan River and then Lake Nicaragua. Other ocean
vessels ran from San Juan del Sur on Nicaragua's Pacific
Coast to San Francisco. Across the 12-mile land barrier
between the big lake and the Pacific, a road was built and
coaches in the Nicaraguan colors, blue and white, delivered transit passengers between steamers. Offices,
docks, and staff were all provided. After George Law's
route through Panama was opened, the Nicaraguan route
to California was still the shortest by four days time.
At one time first-class passengers paid only $150 to
reach San Francisco from New York, and steerage passengers $45! By 1852 over 20,000 Americans a month
used this route, among them such notables as Samuel
Clemens. The Accessory Transit Company figured largely in the rise and fall of filibuster William Walker, for
during much of his Nicaraguan adventure, Vanderbilt supported him, but following Walker's high-handed turning
away, was responsible for crushing him.

ACHIAPA. Comarca or district in the municipio of Jinotepe,
Carazo department.

ACHIOTES. A district of the municipio of Yali in the Jino-
tega department.

ACHUAPA. 1) A municipio created in 1870, in the department of León, but on the foothill extensions of the Quibuc
range in the Estelí department. Area: 132 square miles;
population: almost 10,000. Bounded to the north by San
Juan de Limay of Estelí department; south by El Sauce;
east by Estelí; west by Villaneuva of Chinandega department. There are 25 districts. The area is mountainous,
and there are a number of streams. In addition to cattle
raising and general crops, there are some mineral resources, among them semi-precious stones.
     2) A pueblo, San Pedro de Achuapa has only about 200
inhabitants, and is therefore among the least of the cabaceras, in the municipio of the same name, León department. Created in 1870, it has not grown.

ACOTO. A territory of the National District, department of
Managua.

ACOYAPA. 1) Cabacera of the municipio of Acoyapa, department of Chontales, with a population of 1,500. Local
archives indicate it was founded before 1683, it was
designated a city in 1862. In 1858 it was the first
cabacera of the whole department of Chontales. General
Emiliano Chamorro (q.v.), former President and durable
nonagenarian, was born in Acoyapa.
     2) Municipio in Chontales department, second in im-
portance only to Juigalpa, seat of the first Spanish cattle
ranches in colonial days in Chontales. The population
was 9,000 in 1968, with an area of 398 square miles.
Bounded on the north by municipios Acoyapa and San
Pedro de Lovago; on the south by municipio Morrito; and
on the east by Santo Tomas and Villa Somoza.

ACTA NOTARIAL DE LA TOMA DE POSECION DEL GRAN
LAGO DE NICARAGUA. This formal document of possession as executed by Gil González Dávila, is of interest in its careful legality, and also in the archaic Spanish
which (like 16th-century English) shows variants in spelling and use of the Arabic "X". Besides the title, some
examples are "ydalgos," "dixo," "oblygados," "dixesen,"
"posesyon," "dezir," "ynformade," "ynidios," "thesorero,"
"harmada." The act of possession is summarized as follows (translation): "The said captain [González] so states
that in the name of their majesties and heirs of the royal

crown of Castile, he took and hereby takes possession of the said sweet sea, because it is within the limits of conquest of their majesties and it is to be subject to the said royal crown of Castile . . . . " The lake was called "sweet sea" (mar dulce) because it was a large body of fresh water. Not only was the royal flag raised, but the proclamation was cried out three times in a loud voice, and the captain also waded into the lake with drawn sword, taking possession of the land as well as the water. The whole document was signed by the notary San Juan de Salinas. The instrument is in the Archivo General de Indias, in Seville, Spain.

ACTAS DE IMPOSICION DE TRIBUTOS. An act of 1548 concerning levying a tribute and establishing the encomienda system in the Valley of Nicaragua.

ACUERDOS. Executive decrees and rulings which have the force of law, and which can be enacted as decree-laws by the President when congress is not in session or with the concurrence of his Council of Ministers in cases considered to be emergency or public necessity. While exceptional courts are prohibited, special courts for "military crimes" are allowed, and can be applied to civilians when charged with such crimes.

ADELA. A small paddle steamer which ran from the Machuca Rapid on the San Juan River up to El Castillo rapid. The Machuca was impassable in 1900.

ADELAIDA. A gasoline launch (lancha de gasolina) used by revolutionaries in the early 1900's on the San Juan River.

ADELANTADO. Prior to assumption of power by a Viceroy, this official was usually the highest one, being governor in newly acquired territory under the Spanish colonial system (See the various forms: a. del mar, a. fronterizo, a. mayor, a. menor.)

ADELANTADO DEL MAR. When during conquest and Spanish colonial days a commander of an exploring expedition was commissioned to become governor of territory discovered or conquered, this was the title given.

ADELANTADO FRONTERIZO see ADELANTADO MENOR

ADELANTADO MAYOR. A governor with military, judicial,

and administrative power under the Spanish colonial
system.

ADELANTADO MENOR. Also called a "fronterizo," such
a Spanish colonial official held power in frontier outposts essentially as military chieftain, administering
under military law. Since the frontier was frequently
a war zone, this was for the times a usual and practical approach to government.

ADIACT. A cacique of the Subtiava Indians in the area of
León, who was hanged as a result of accusations in relation to his daughter's affair with a Spanish captain.

ADMINISTRATION FOR INTERNATIONAL DEVELOPMENT.
The "AID" organization developed under the Alliance for
Progress and as a successor to FOA, ICA, etc.

ADMINISTRATION, LOCAL. As a unitary political system,
there are in effect no political divisions which share
any power with the national government of Nicaragua.
There are 16 departments and 123 municipios. Each
municipio is further subdivided into comarcas (districts)
and each comarca into cantones. Departments are ad-
ministered by a triumvirate consisting of a political
chief (jefe politico), a military commandant, and a judge.
There is a departmental council elected by popular vote.
The six-member council advises the political chief.
Municipios operate under a mayor (alcalde) with a five-
member council, a judge, a military commander, and
an auditor (regidor). The municipal council, like that
of the department, is elected popularly for four-year
terms. The municipal council is responsible for the
maintenance of local roads and cemeteries and for super-
vising slaughter houses. Local tax revenues are ad-
ministered by these bodies. There is relatively little
local political autonomy, and little political concern in
rural areas.

ADUANAS. A territory of the municipio Del Carmen,
Managua department.

AGATEYTE. 1) Name of the chieftains or caciques of the
Chorotegan region of the same name--two incumbents
(father and son) were identified by Oviedo y Valdez in
1529; also known as Cacique Tegeatega. Such caciques
exercised civil, military, and religious power.

2) Region or chieftaincy of the southwestern part of Nicaragua surrounding Chinandega, at the time of the Spanish conquest. Of Mexican origins in the same manner as others farther to the southeast, Nahua (and Nahuatl-speaking), but bearing names such as Mames, Mangues, Chiapanecans, Chorotegans. The basic migration seems to have been from the area in the present state of Chiapas in Mexico, and occurred about A. D. 596, following the disintegration of the Toltec monarchy. Records indicate that the last migration from Mexico to the area of the Gulf of Fonseca (Gulf of Chorotega) was in 1505, three years after Columbus' last voyage and the discovery of Nicaragua in 1502. When the Spanish arrived later, there were two great divisions of the Chorotegans, the Diriangens and the Nagrandans. The former were called men of the heights, the latter men of the plains or lowlands. The other chieftaincy nearby was that of Subtiava, which was apparently a vassal state to Agateyte. Agateyte was also called Tezoatega.

AGREEMENT OF INTEGRATED INDUSTRIES. This 1959 agreement was a step toward the economic integration of the Central American Common Market.

AGUA AGRIA, EL. A department of Granada hacienda due south of the peaks of dead Mombacho.

AGUA AMARILLA. A district in the municipio of San Ramón, Matagalpa department.

AGUA BUENA. Comarca, valley or district in the municipio of Juigalpa.

AGUA CALIENTE. Comarca, valley, or district in the municipio of Juigalpa.

AGUACATE. 1) A district of the municipio of San Juan de Tola, Rivas department.
    2) A comarca or district in the municipio of Jinotepe, Carazo department.
    3) A mountain lake in Estelí department.

AGUACATE DE LA CRUZ, EL. Comarca or district in the municipio of Diriamba, department of Carazo.

AGUACATE DE LA GUINEA, EL. Comarca or district in the municipio of Diriamba, department of Carazo.

AGUACATE DE LAS MERCEDES, EL.   Comarca or district
in the municipio of Diriamba, department of Carazo.

AGUACATE DE SAN JUAN, EL.   Comarca or district in the
municipio of Diriamba, department of Carazo.

AGUA FRIA.   1) A district in the municipio and department
of Estelí.
2) Comarca or district in the municipio of La Paz,
León.

AGUAN (Steamer).   A ship wrecked on a coral reef while
transporting to Nicaragua in March, 1890, a U. S. government commission of Army and Navy officers, among
them former survey party member (later Admiral) Lieut.
W. I. Chambers.   No lives were lost and the party
landed at Greytown, April 2, 1890.

AGUAS CALIENTES.   A district in the municipio of Muy
Muy, Matagalpa department.

AGUAS THERMALES see HOT SPRINGS

AGUA ZARCA.   A district in the municipio of Sebaco,
Matagalpa department.

AGUA ZARZA.   A district in the municipio of Achuapa,
León.

AGUAY.   Coffee plantation in Pueblo Nuevo municipio of
Estelí department.

AGUEGUESPALA, RIO.   This river, also called Villa Vieja,
passes near the ruins of the church at that site, where
are also found aboriginal rock carvings; in Estelí municipio and department.

AGUERO: PADRE DIEGO DE.   A priest in the expedition
of Gil González Dávila which resulted in the discovery
of Nicaragua in 1522.

AGUILA, ANTONIO DE.   A Recollect (q. v.) missionary who
came to León in 1745; he then was assigned to work out
of Matagalpa.   He established a Carib settlement nearby
San Ramón.   He was associated with Antonio Cáceres.

AGUILAR Y VILLAR, DON JUAN FRANCISCO.   Aguilar y

Villar became rector of the University of Nicaragua in 1822. First rector after independence, he was also the first nonecclesiastical head of the institution.

AGUIRE, LOS. District of the municipio of Masatepe, department of Masaya.

AGUIRRES, LOS. Comarca or district in the municipio of San Marcos, Carazo department.

AID see ADMINISTRATION FOR INTERNATIONAL DEVELOPMENT

AIRCRAFT, MILITARY. The Nicaragua conflict of 1927-32, in which so many military firsts occurred in the application of airpower to warfare, especially in tactical support, found the following types of U. S. aircraft operated in the country by U. S. Marines: DH-4--DeHavilland biplanes (Liberty engines); OL-8--Loening amphibians; O2U--Corsair fighter-bombers (Pratt-Whitney engine); OC-1--Curtiss fighter-bombers (Pratt-Whitney engine); F-4-B--Boeing fighter; and Autogiro de la Cierva (a pioneer rotary-wing craft).

AIRPLANES (first appearance). Four hydroplanes (seaplanes) of the U. S. Marine Corps landed on Lago Xolotlán (Lake Managua) on 15 January 1927, the first of record to appear in the area of Managua.

AIRPORTS. Las Mercedes at Managua is an international airport of entry. Minor strips are also found at Puerto Cabezas (paved), Bluefields, Karawala, La Vijía, Waspam, La Libertad, Matagalpa, Somoto, El Gallo, Vauya, Ocotal, Alamicamba, La Luz, Siuna, Bonanza, San Luis, Pis Pis, and the Corn Islands.

AJONJOLE. This is sesame, whose cultivation has risen in importance in Nicaragua in recent years. Produced in 1961 was a total of nearly 200,000 tons of stalks and almost 400 tons of seeds.

ALA FEMININA. The woman's branch or "wing" of the Partido Liberal Nacionalista, especially active in the elections of 1957 following the assassination of President Anastasio Somoza.

ALALC (Asociación Latinoamericana de Libre Comercio). A free trade commission working in the development of regional agreements, and stemming from the Punta del Este presidential meetings of 1967 in Uruguay. Such organizations as the Mercado Común Centroamericano (MCCA) are involved in regional agreements, and the MCCA is a pattern which might well be extended under ALALC.

ALAMIKAMBA. River port in Zelaya department on the Río Prinzapolka. There is a road south to Makantaka and north as far as Bonanza and Siuna, also connecting with the Puerto Cabezas to Waspam road. This is the only road complex in all Zelaya department, an area nearly as big as West Virginia. There is an airstrip, and downstream, an agricultural colony. The town has been well known for the production of huge dugout canoes or "dories" from the great royal cedar trees available in the high tropical woods nearby.

"ALAMO RANGERS." Since William Walker's advent in Nicaragua was only 20 years after the Alamo, this choice of a name for one of his units in the 1855-57 "National War" seems appropriate.

ALARM (ship) see VIXEN

ALBARDA. A saddle peculiar to Nicaragua and adjacent parts of Central America. The tree, or frame, consists of two cylindrical bundles of reeds tied tightly, and laid parallel to the steed's backbone, with a covering of a single large piece of leather which is often 30" or more from front to rear and the skirts of which may drop 30" on each side. Slender stirrup-straps carry small hooded stirrups which in colonial days were often of brass; such stirrups are now rare and valued antiques. The albarda's great single hide cover and skirts are usually elaborately carved. A single cinch is used. A new albarda is quite imposing, although none is very comfortable for either rider or animal. See also MONTURA.

ALBITEZ, DIEGO DE. Captain Albítez in 1527 was sent by Pedrarias Dávila with a scribe or notary and a magistrate to inform Hernán Cortez against incursions into the territories discovered by Gil González Dávila and populated (sparsely) under the "founder" Hernández de Córdoba in 1524.

ALBIZU. A cattle hacienda in the municipio of Cuidad
Darío, Matagalpa department.

ALCALDE see ADMINISTRATION, LOCAL

ALDEA see COFRADIA

ALEMANIA. A hill (cerro) of the Datanli spur of the Darién
mountains in Jinotega department.

ALGUACIL MAYOR. A Spanish colonial post equivalent to
constable, a position prized and hence frequently purchased.

ALIANZA (lancha). A Lake Nicaragua transport vessel operating in the late 1960's, with a circuit of lake ports including San Carlos and Granada at the terminal points.
A round trip takes three days.

ALLIED STATES. A term applied to Costa Rica, Honduras,
and Nicaragua, when in January, 1839 they signed offen-
sive treaties against El Salvador. They were suspicious
of the leadership of Francisco Morazán there. They invaded El Salvador under Francisco Ferrera in early
1839.

ALMACIGUERA. A district in the municipio and department
of Estelí.

ALMA NICA. A radio station in Managua, call letters
YNWS, power 5000 watts, frequency 900 kilocycles.

ALMENDRO, EL. A district in the municipio of San Isidro,
department of Matagalpa.

ALTAGRACIA. 1) A municipio of the department of Rivas
comprising most of the island of Omotepe in Lake Nicaragua, with an area of 85 square miles and a population
of 8, 300. The limits of this island municipio are entirely the shores of the lake, with the exception of the
small municipio of Moyogalpa on the northwestern coast
of the island. There are 27 valleys or districts in the
area. Coffee and tobacco are principal crops. Cacao
and cattle are also raised.
2) A pueblo, previously known as "Pueblo Grande de
Omotepe, " the present name was confirmed by law in
1871. There are four barrios or sections of the town,

with a population of about 1, 500. Called by aboriginal inhabitants Hastagalpa, Cocinagalpa, or Cuisinagalpa, it was
designated "Pueblo Grande..." in 1752. The first two
aboriginal names represented two "barrios" separated by
a street. The Nahuatl influence is especially strong on
Omotepe Island, as there was a considerable "Aztec"
colony planted there long before the conquest. Several
idols of pre-Columbian days are on display.

ALTAMIRANO, ADOLFO see MEZA, SAMUEL

ALTIPLANO ESTELIANO. There is in the department of
Estelí a series of high tablelands which are unique in
formation. Among them are Moropotente, Tomabú, El
Carao, Miraflor, Las Mesas de la Laguna, Las Mesas
de Arrayan, Las Mesas de Ollanca, Las Mesas de Sabana Larga.

ALTO, EL. Comarca or district of the municipio of Santo
Tomas in Chontales.

ALTOS, LOS. A district of the municipio of Nindirí, department of Masaya.

ALTOS DEL NORTE, LOS. A district of the municipio and
department of Masaya.

ALTOS DES SUR, LOS. A district of the municipio and department of Masaya.

ALVARADO CONTRERAS, PEDRO DE. From 1525 to 1541
a Spanish Governor of the Kingdom (or Chancellorate) of
Guatemala, who succeeded Pedrarias Dávila (also, d'
Avila) in the control of Nicaragua. In 1531 and follow-
ing, he was able to open up transportation along the Río
San Juan from Granada to the Caribbean, and also held
the San Juan River mouth and territory as far as the
Bluefields Lagoon just to the north.

ALVAREZ, DON JONAS. One of the three members of the
first Comite Ejecutive del Distrito Nacional. See DIS-
TRITO NACIONAL.

AMADOR, FRANCISCO see JUNTA DE RECURSOS

AMADORES, LOS. District of the municipio of La Concepción, department of Masaya.

AMALIA. A major sugar refinery in the cane-growing area near Nandaime, Granada department.

AMATAS. A district of the municipio of Jinotega.

AMATITLAN. Comarca or district of the municipio of León, León department.

AMAYITO DE LAS LAJAS. Comarca or district in the municipio of Diriamba, department of Carazo.

AMAYO. Comarca or district in the municipio of Diriamba, department of Carazo.

AMAYO DE APOMPOA. Comarca or district in the municipio of Diriamba, department of Carazo.

AMERIC see AMERICA (def. 3)

AMERICA. 1) Comarca or district in the municipio of La Paz, León.
2) Hacienda in the municipio of La Paz, León.
3) (Origin of name). A recent theory developed by Jorge Espinosa Estrada, in his book Nicaragua, Cuna [cradle] de America, suggests that the name of America may have originated in the name of the mountain range (Amerrique, Amerissque, or Americ) which lies northeast of Lake Nicaragua, rather than in the name of Amerigo Vespucci. Elements of this fascinating speculation are: no major geographical place has been named for the given rather than the surname of an individual; locality names persist through many generations (as ancient Greek Gades, Spain's Cádiz); many place names in Central American Indian dialects end in -ique or -ic, meaning "great" or "prominent"; Columbus stopped at a place on the Nicaraguan Coast called Cariai or Cariay-- perhaps this was "Carcai," home of the Carcas Indians (in the area of the Amerissque range); the Carcas had gold (mines still are in western end of the range) and were also called Cookras--the name as synonym for "golden country" would hence have been known among illiterate seamen in European ports; Columbus would have refrained from using the word in his letter "Rarissima" to Ferdinand the King, if he felt someone had been there before (perhaps Cabot had preceded him on that coast). And so forth; the theory is intricate, and ingenious, interesting to pursue.

AMERICAN ATLANTIC AND PACIFIC SHIP CANAL COM-
PANY. The company of the 1850's which employed the
competent engineer Childs to survey the Nicaraguan canal route. His survey essentially stood the test of
time, and he was the first to locate the whole line
definitely from sea to sea. See also CHILDS.

AMERICAN FRUIT AND STEAMSHIP COMPANY. One of a
number of banana companies shipping fruit from Nicaragua prior to the blights of the 1930's.

AMERICAN TREATY, 1670. Second of the treaties of Madrid
(1667 and 1670) which gave England a "legal" and diplomatic foothold in the Caribbean throughout the following
century. In this treaty Spain not only pledged peace,
friendship, and the suppression of piracy, but also per-
mitted trade, and far more significantly, abandoned her
claim that only she and Portugal had occupation rights
in the New World. To the King of Great Britain was
granted title, in effect, to all the lands he then occupied.
This had later meaning to Mosquitia and Belize even
though the signatory kings were probably not aware of
them as entities at the time.

AMERRIQUE. 1) Comarca, valley, or district in the municipio of Juigalpa.
2) (Also, Amerrisque) mountain range in the department of Chontales, lying between the towns of Juigalpa
and Libertad, parallel to or part of the Cordillera
Chontaleña. It is remarkable in that a number of major
streams have their sources in this range; the Río Grande
de Matagalpa, the Río Blewfields (Escondido), the Ríos
Mico, Artigua, Carca, Comoapa, Mayales, Acoyapa,
Ajocuapa, Oyale, and Terpenoguatapa.
3) See also AMERICA (def. 3).

AMERRISQUE see AMERRIQUE (def. 2); and AMERICA
(def. 3)

AMISTAD, LA. Coffee hacienda in the municipio of San
Marcos, Carazo department.

AMOLONCA. A spring in the southern part of the municipio
of León.

AMORES DEL SOL. Comarca, or district in the municipio
of La Libertad, Chontales.

AMPARO   see   RIGHTS, PROCEDURAL

AMPARO AND EL DESTINO, EL.   Coffee haciendas under one
ownership in the municipio of Yalí, Jinotega department.

AMPHIBIANS   see   FAUNA

AMPIE, JERONIMO DE.   Early encomendero in the area of
Granada following the acts of tribute imposition of 1548.

ANDERSON, FRANK.   A noted veteran of the 1840's war between Mexico and the United States, Anderson was one
of the "Immortals" who joined William Walker in the
filibustering expedition to Nicaragua in 1855.

ANGELES, LOS   1) Cattle ranch in Condega municipio,
Estelí department.
        2) Also called El Nancite; a comarca or district in
the municipio of La Paz, Carazo department.
        3) A district of the municipio of Moyogalpa on Omo-
tepe Island in Lake Nicaragua, Rivas department.   It is
one of the four districts of the municipio which is in effect a village or pueblo.

ANGELES Y ANITA, LOS.   Coffee hacienda in the Jinotega
municipio founded by General Ignacio Chávez of León.

ANGLO-MOSQUITIA.   Term applied to the Mosquito Coast
and the quasi-colony or loose protectorate there maintained by the British during the 18th and 19th centuries.
See also MOSQUITO SHORE.

ANGOSTURA NUMERO DOS.   Comarca or district in the
municipio of Villa Somoza, Chontales.

ANGOSTURA NUMERO UNO.   Comarca or district in the
municipio of Villa Somoza, Chontales.

ANGULO.   District in the Municipio of Altagracia on Omotepe
Island, Lake Nicaragua, in the department of Rivas.

ANGULO, EMILIO.   One of the founders in 1915 of the periodical Iris de la Tarde, a romantic effort which was the
forerunner of a number of similar productions.

ANIHUAS.   A district of the municipio of Jinotega.

ANIMAS.   1) A district in the municipio of La Trinidad,

department of Estelí.

   2) Las Animas, an old Spanish mine near Amatillo
in Nueva Segovia department, with several tunnels and
an appreciable silver yield per ton.   Many small quartz
veins are found in an S-shaped tunnel over 100 feet long.
Near the tunnels are remains of three furnaces used for
reducing the metal, with ore piled near them.   Of archaeological interest concerning the colonial period.

ANSCA.   A cotton gin and processing plant in Télica.

ANTIGUA, CIUDAD   see   CIUDAD ANTIGUA

ANTIMONIO.   Antimony deposits are mined in the Condega
   district of Estelí department.

ANTONELI, JUAN BAUTISTA.   Engineer officer sent to the
   Caribbean in 1585 by Philip II of Spain to investigate the
   state of defense and recommend measures.   He advised
   fortifications and coast guards at Havana, San Juan Ulloa
   (Vera Cruz) San Juan de Puerto Rico, and Portabello.
   It is significant to Nicaragua that he presumed that coast
   guard patrols from these fortified ports could defend the
   long Caribbean coasts of Central America.   This proved
   not to be feasible, and as a result, Nicaragua suffered
   repeated piratical depredations.

ANTONELLI, BATISTA.   An engineer in the service of Philip
   II of Spain, who in the period between 1525 and 1550 was
   given the task of surveying the narrow isthmus of Rivas between Lake Nicaragua and the Pacific Ocean, with a view
   to ascertaining its suitability for a canal to join the two.
   This must have been the earliest such canal survey, but
   was only the prelude to many for the next four centuries.

ANTONIO DE CANDADILLO.   Comarca or district in the
   municipio of El Sauce, León department.

ANZUELO, EL.   A district in the municipio of Matiguás,
   department of Matagalpa.

APANAS.   A district of the municipio of Jinotega.

APANAS, LAGO DE.   Lake Apanas is an artificial lake created on the Tuma River by the Mancotal Dam.

APANTE.   1) A district in the municipio and department of

Matagalpa.
2) A mountain height in the municipio of Matagalpa.
3) Comarca or district in the municipio of Telica,
León.

APANTILLO.   1) A district in the municipio and department
of Matagalpa.
2) A mountain in the municipio of Matagalpa.

APANTILLO DEL SABALAR.   A district in the municipio of
San Ramón, Matagalpa department.

APATACO.   A district in the municipio of San Jorge, Rivas
department.

APATU.   A district of Terabona municipio, Matagalpa department.

APOMPOA.   1) A district in the municipio of Ciudad Darío,
department of Matagalpa.
2) Comarca or district in the municipio of Diriamba,
department of Carazo.

APOMPUA.   1) Comarca, valley, or district in the municipio
of Juigalpa.
2) District in the municipio of Potosí, Rivas department.

APOPOLOTA.   Pueblo or town existing in the valley of Nicaragua during the 16th and 17th centuries.

APOSENTO.   Sleeping room in a ranch-style house.

APOYEQUE   see   ASESE

APOYO, LAGUNA.   Lake Apoyo is a saline lake in a huge
crater, about three miles in diameter, in the Department of Masaya between Masaya and Granada.   From
Nahuatl words "atl" (water) and "poyec" (saline) the
name is derived.   There are thermal springs on the
northeastern shore.   A Spanish word meaning prop,
fulcrum, protection, or patronage is spelled the same
way.

"AQUI FUE GRANADA. "   ("Here was Granada. ")   A mean-
ingful keynote to a bitter bit of Nicaraguan History.
See HENNINGSEN.

ARADO, EL.   1) Comarca, district or valley in the municipio of Acoyapa, Chontales.
2) A district of Terrabona municipio, Matagalpa department.

ARAGON.   Comarca or district in the municipio of Jinotepe,
Carazo department.

ARAMBURO, JOSE   see   LUZ, LA (def. 3)

ARAUZ, BLANCA.   San Rafael del Norte resident who became Agusto Sandino's wife on his 32nd birthday, May
18, 1927.   She accompanied him during several of his
later campaigns, and died June 2, 1933, bearing Blanca
Segovia, their daughter.   Blanca seems to have been a
girl of great beauty and spirit--Sandino wrote a friend
in 1931, saying "She is manly, like Mary the wife of
Joseph was, and all I can do is to permit her to do
everything she likes. "

ARAUZ, DON TRINIDAD.   Patriarch of the San Dionisio area,
whose son is a deputy of the Nicaraguan congress.

ARCHAEOLOGY   see   CITY

ARCHILLAS, LAS.   A district of the municipio of Jinotega.

ARCOS, LOS.   Comarca or district in the municipio of La
Paz, León.

AREA OF NICARAGUA.   The precise area in square miles
is a more elusive figure than might be supposed in modern times, especially after the completion of extensive
surveys under the aegis of the Interamerican Survey of
the 1950's and early 1960's.   One quite recent authority
within the pages of a single volume lists the area in one
place as 48,000 square miles, in another with fascinating if dubious precision as 53,668 square miles!   The
figure of 57,000 square miles was prevalent prior to the
1963 settlement of a boundary dispute with Honduras,
which can possibly account for the lesser figures now
given, but not for their considerable discrepancy.   A
Nicaraguan source gives 148,000 square kilometers as
the size, which upon conversion gives 57,200 square
miles.   The National Geographic Society Atlas of the
World of 1963 gives 57,143 square miles, and the Worldmark Encyclopedia of Nations agrees; Encyclopedia

Americana (c 1969) gives 53, 938. A 1968 release of the
U. S. Embassy in Managua gives 50, 780 square miles,
and again in the same document 49, 000 square miles.
A 1968 volume, apparently thoughtfully researched, gives
the somewhat inexplicable figures of 49, 200 square miles
in 1925 and 57, 143 square miles in 1967, pinning the
variance to dates! Obviously, all we can say with cer-
tainty is that the area is something more or less than
53, 000 square miles. Nicaragua is approximately the
size of Michigan or Florida.

ARENAL. 1) A comarca or district in the municipio of Télica,
León.
2) a cattle ranch in Pueblo Nuevo municipio, Estelí
department.
3) a district of the municipio of Masatepe, department
of Masaya.
4) a district in the municipio and department of Matagalpa.

AREYTOS. A word used in Nicaragua derived from Haitian
dialects of Arawak, meaning a dance.

AREVALO, JUAN JOSE. A President of Guatemala (1945-
51) prior to the Arbenz regime of the 1950's, Arêvalo,
as an intellectual and an exile from his country, wrote
a controversial but significant book, translated into English in 1961, The Shark and the Sardines. This volume
is important to students of the Nicaraguan scene for two
reasons; first, it gives a scathing point of view concerning the United States of America and interventions in
Latin America; second, and specifically, it uses the recent history of Nicaragua (from 1850 to date of publication) as an example of the theme of the book. The language is passionate, even poetic, often extreme. But
the message needs to be understood in order to understand some of the very basic problems in the U. S. -Latin
American relations, and particularly in U. S. -Nicaraguan
relations.

ARGELLO, SOLON. This poet (1880-1920) fled his native
Nicaragua during the turbulent political upheavals of
early 20th-century Central America, and lost his life
by assassination while a member of Emiliano Zapata's
revolutionary forces in Mexico. He had been a follower
of Rubén Darío.

ARGÜELLO, LEONARDO. Distinguished Minister of Education and intellectual who was briefly President in 1947,
under the general aegis of the Somoza regime. Seventy
years old when he took office, he displeased the commander of the National Guard, and lasted in office only
25 days. He took refuge in the Mexican embassy. Benjamín Lacayo Sacasa was made President in the coup.
Dr. Argüello was a respected Minister of Public Instruction in 1925 when at a fete convened to honor him at the
International Club in Managua, a coup d'état took place
which was much more a "golpe cómico" than anything
else. See also RIVAS, GABRY.

ARGUELLO, TORIBIO. Licenciado Argüello was one of the
first faculty members of the University of Nicaragua
when it opened in 1816.

ARIAS, JUAN. A citizen of Diriamba identified in the 16th
century.

ARIAS DE AVILA see PEDRARIAS

ARIRIN. Arawak word meaning "dance"; see AREYTOS.

ARISTOCRACIA, LA. A term for Nicaraguan upper social
levels, somewhat synonymous with la primera, or la
sociedad. This term is, however, more exclusively applied to the old families of Granada, León, Managua,
Masaya, Matagalpa, and even Ocotal (as successor to
Nueva Segovia, a very old town). Such surnames as
Sacasa, Solórzano, Lacayo, Cuadra, Argüello, Navas,
etc. are familiar in this category.

ARKANSAS, U.S.S. This battleship, BB-33, was the first
to carry a unit of the Fleet Marine force, which
stemmed from the oversize detachment kept aboard the
"Rochester" (q.v.) during the Sandino War 1927-33.
This is another example of how action in Nicaragua
during those years permanently altered some military
concepts.

ARLOVI, BENITO GARRET Y. A bishop of Granada who
built a galiot and three pirogues at Granada to provide
a lake patrol against Sambo-Miskito incursions in the
early 1700's. By 1711, this lake patrol force was armed
and manned but was faced down and disgraced in an encounter with the Indian raiders on the lake. The Indians

were able to cut communications between Granada and
the important Fort Inmaculada. Arlovi was humiliated
and removed as a result of the lake fiasco, although his
initiative might have seemed to deserve better.

ARMAS, DON MIGUEL DE. Captain of militia and cavalry
jointly with Juan Montenegro (q.v.) in the 1740-50 period
in the Villa Vieja de Estelí.

ARMENIA. Cattle ranch in the municipio of El Sauce, León
department.

ARRANCABARBA. 1) A pre-conquest name applied to one of
the heights to the east of Sebaco.
2) Mountain complex and pass through the Spanish colonial frontier as used in the years of Sambo-Miskito
confrontation.

ARRAYAN. Comarca, valley or district in the municipio of
Juigalpa.

ARRAYAN, RIO. A stream tributary to the Río Coco on
which the present "Ciudad Antigua" was built in 1611.

ARROYO ADUANA. A ravine in old Granada. See ARROYO
ZACATELIGUA.

ARROYO ZACATELIGUA. One (southernmost) of the two
major deep ravines which surround the old Nicaraguan
city of Granada. They are unusual topographical features and were originally significant in defense. The
ancient town of Jalteva was at a point where the ravines
are only a few hundred yards apart. The present cuartel
is in the same general location. The northernmost ravine is Arroyo Aduana.

ASAMBLEA ORDINARIA DE ESTADO DE NICARAGUA. National legislative body meeting in Granada in the 1835 period, between independence from Spain and full independence.

ASESE. A deep crater lake on a peninsula (Sierra de
Chiltepe) jutting into Lake Managua west of the city and
above Lake Jiloá

ASHEVILLE, U.S.S. American armed ship which appeared
at Puerto Cabezas during the Sandinista guerrilla war
with U.S. Marines to relieve the port which was under

threat from Blandón's forces. The inhabitants of the
port were terrified when the troops at first would not
land, as they felt themselves to be at the mercy of the
guerrilla leader.

ASOCIACION DE ARTISTAS Y ESCRITORES AMERICANOS.
This association of American artists and writers, Mana-
gua-based, is a group promoting intellectual and artistic
activity and expression in Nicaragua.

ASOCIACION DE REPORTEROS DE MANAGUA. A social
and cultural organization of those persons active in newspaper work.

ASOSOSCA. 1) Sugar cane plantation in the municipio of
León, León department.
2) (Laguna), deep crater lake in the Managua area,
used as a city water supply, and with the park "Las
Piedrecitas" on heights above it. The lake is about a
mile in diameter, and ancient Indian paintings are found
on its steep walls. It is one of a series of craters, including Chiltepe, Tiscapa, and Nejapa.

ASSERADORES, ISLA. The coastal island on which the city
and port of Corinto are located. Its ancient Indian name
seems to have been Conchagua. Important early ports
were nearby Realejo and, possibly on the same island,
Puerto de la Posesión, mentioned in a letter to the King
of Spain from Governor Pedrarias Dávila, sent from old
León on March 15, 1529. Pedro de Alvarado here prepared his fleet to go to Perú in 1534. Asseradores was
given to the State in 1858 to establish a custom-house
for the future port of Corinto.

ASTILLERO, EL. One of several unimproved ports or embarkation points on the Pacific Coast of the municipio
San Juan de Tola, department of Rivas.

ASUNCION, LA. Hacienda on the north slopes of the inactive
volcano Mombacho, eight miles south of Granada.

ATENEO DE MASAYA. The organization of an "atheneum"
for Masaya took place on "Día de La Raza," October 12,
1937, with the intent to promote intellectual interchange,
to serve as a vehicle for instruction, to found a magazine as an organ of the association, and to found archives of historical events, Nicaraguan authors, works

of art, etc., and in general to preserve evidence of the historic past and to exchange knowledge of the legends and anecdotes of the people of the area, one rich in historic events and tradition.

ATEXCAPA. Meaning: "place of a pool"; see TISCAPA, LAGUNA.

ATIHUAS. A district of the municipio of Jinotega.

ATILILLO. A drink made from dry corn.

ATL. (Nahuatl: "water.") A very fundamental root-word of the Nahuatl (Nahoa) tongue, both a month festival day and god of the ancient Nicarao have this name. The many combined forms, even of the other named months, show the universal importance of water, from a pantheistic as well as a pragmatic standpoint. (Compare also Tecpatl, Acatl, Ehecatl, Coatl, Magatl, Ozomatl, Malinatl, all q.v. Often used with lan, "place," in the combined form "atlán"; the resemblance to "Atlantic," "Atlantis," "Atlas," etc., is of interest even if coincidental.)

ATLANTICO. A Spanish frigate of 1778. This ship was to set up a trading station for Sambo-Miskitos at the mouth of the San Juan River. The result of the plan was the massacre of the expedition leader, Jeremiah Terry (q.v.).

ATOL. A drink made from green corn.

AUDIENCIA. In Spanish colonial administration the audiencia was a check and balance device, which as an advisory council served in both executive and judicial capacities. It was at once a final court of appeal (the viceroy being "chief justice") and, between terms of viceroys (who often were delayed many months before arrival), was the colonial executive. At any time it had direct access to the Spanish crown--a considerable power. Normally and day-to-day it served as a council of state or cabinet. Needless to say the prestige was great. An audiencia remote from the vice-regal seat was called a "presidencia." During the first Spanish century in America the audiencia was probably the most powerful governmental entity. To understand the modern government of Nicaragua it is useful to have some grounding in the colonial forms which were antecedent.

AUGUSTINIAN RECOLLECTS. A Catholic monastic order
    carrying out charitable and educational enterprises in
    Nicaragua. See also: RECOLLECTS.

AULO. A district in Zelaya department on the Río Tuma.

AUTOGIRO. Invented by Juan de la Cierva, a Spanish en-
    gineer, the Autogiro was the forerunner of the helicopter,
    and was essentially the first practicable rotary-wing air-
    craft. While the rotor was not powered in flight, the
    machine could take off a very short runway, and could
    make a nearly vertical landing. Field tests of the de-
    vice as a military aid in bush warfare were made in
    Nicaragua in the summer of 1932 for the first time any-
    where.

AVENDAÑO, FRANCISCO. The National Guard sergeant who
    killed Adolfo Cockburn (q. v.) on October 3, 1931.

AVILES, FRANCISCO DE DIOS. see BATALLA DE...
    A Captain in command of the third company of Nica-
    raguans at the Batalla [battle] de San Jacinto (q. v.)
    September 14, 1856.

AVILEZ, LEOPOLDO RUIZ DE. A Spanish colonial citizen
    of 1800 in Masaya who has descendants there today.

AVILEZ, MANUEL see AVILEZ, PABLO

AVILEZ, MANUEL ESTEBAN. In his capacity as sub-dele-
    gate of the district (something like lieutenant-governor)
    in 1800, don Manuel was a Spanish official who has de-
    scendants in the same place, Masaya, today.

AVILEZ, MAXIMO. Lieutenant Avilez was stationed in
    Masaya at the turn of the 18th to 19th centuries, and
    his descendants live there today.

AVILEZ, PABLO. One of the several Spanish colonials of
    this name in Masaya in 1800 representing families es-
    tablished there today.

AYAPAL, RIO. A tributary of the Bocay River in Jinotega
    department.

AYERDI, FRANCISCO. Doctor Ayerdi was first rector of
    the University of Nicaragua in 1816 under Chancellor
    Bishop García Jerez.

AYSSA, JUAN DE. Commandant at Fort Inmaculada (St. John's Fort or modern "Castillo Viejo") when the British and Sambo-Miskitos attacked in April, 1780. He sent word to Gálvez in Granada, asking for reinforcements. After an 18-day battle, because of a shortage of water, and because he was cut off from relief by an English force stationed upriver, Ayssa was forced to surrender April 28, 1780. Ayssa's defense had been so gallant that his garrison of 200 remaining men (37 had been killed) marched out of the fort with flags flying, drums beating, to surrender with honor to the force under Captain Polson and his lieutenants pro tem, Despard and Horatio Nelson. Post Captain Nelson had just left, however, too ill from dysentery to see the surrender ceremony. A tragic aftermath was the horror voyage of the transport "Venus," whereon most of Ayssa's men lost their lives. See also: VENUS.

AYUNTAMIENTO DE MANAGUA (1814). This municipal government was formed prior to official independence, under the tacit consent of the royal provincial authorities, especially the Governor, Bishop Nicolás García Jérez, fierce loyalist. The first government was formed by Antonio Benito Medrano, Clemente Silva, Juan Gatica, José Luis Rivas (secretary), Pedro Huete, and Francisco Solís; Huete was mayor.

AZACUALPA. A comarca or district of the municipio of Santa Rosa, León.

AZAMZIBAR. A mountain height in Muy Muy municipio, Matagalpa department, which signifies in the Sumo Indian tongue, a "hill which divides." Another interpretation is "Hill of the Arrows."

AZANCOR. A district in the municipio of San Ramón, Matagalpa department.

AZUCAR DE PILON. Unrefined blocks of brown sugar, in conical form and large size, as produced in Masaya, Managua, and Carazo departments in particular.

AZUCENAL, EL. A district in the municipio of Esquipulas, department of Matagalpa.

AZUL. The collection of lyric poems and short stories published by Nicaragua's world-known poet, Rubén Darió in

1888, at the age of 21. Azul helped to establish that
new style of creative expression in Spanish literature
which came to be called "Modernismo"; the emphasis
is on love of nature and of the exotic, on art and beauty
for their own sake, and upon the listlessness of the human heart. It had a peculiarly predictive quality concerning the latest decades of the 20th century.

AZUL Y BLANCO. A Boaco-based periodical developed during the 1915-37 period.

-B-

BABA. A mountain of the Baba branch of the Isabella range,
Jinotega department, altitude 3960 feet.

BABA, RAMAL DE. Branch of the Isabella Range, between
the Rivers Bocay and Hamaca y Guina.

BABASCA. A district in the municipio and department of
Matagalpa.

BABILONIA. 1) A comarca or district in the municipio of
La Libertad, Chontales.
2) La Babilonia was a gold mine in Chontales owned
by William Smeedle. Begun in 1877, it produced four to
five ounces per ton.

BACA, FRANCISCO (Licenciado) see CABINET OF PA-
TRICIO RIVAS

BAHIA DE BLUEFIELDS see BLUEFIELDS, BAHIA DE

BAHIA PELICANO see PELICANO, BAHIA

BAHIA PUNTA GORDA see PUNTA GORDA, BAHIA

BAILADORA, LA. This great monolith, "the dancer," is
surrounded by legend, and is located in Matagalpa department, in the region of San Pablo.

BAILEY, JOHN. A British engineer who made extensive
surveys on the Pacific side of Lake Nicaragua in 1837,
and on the basis of his work projected a canal route
from Lajas on the lake to San Juan del Sur on the Pacific. The survey results were received with great in-

terest in both the United States and Great Britain.   Mr.
Bailey had been sent by Barclay, Richardson and Company, of England, at an earlier date to survey for the
canal.   He had come to Central America in an armed
brig, and was not only surveying, but arranging concessions.   Bailey stayed on in his own interests, working
for the Central American confederacy.   The U.S. Senate
passed a resolution following a voluminous report on the
project on May 2, 1839, leaving action indefinite.

BALANCE OF TRADE   see   IMPORTS

BALDIZON, DON GREGORIO.   Procurator under the dictatorship of Navas and Vargas in Rivas during the early 18th
century.

BALSAMO, EL.   A district in the municipio of Muy, Muy
Matagalpa department.

BALTODANOS, LOS.   Comarca or district in the municipio
of Diriamba, department of Carazo.

BALUARTE.   A periodical presently published intermittently.

BAMBANA.   Prospecting for copper has been carried on in
this part of the Rosita area.   See   ROSITA, MINA.

BAMBANA, RIO.   A short but fairly large stream in eastern
Zelaya department north of the Río Prinzapolka.

BANCACRUZ, MINE.   This district is in the Pis Pis Area,
the Nueva América Mine being the first under Neptune
Mining Company exploration; 25,000 tons of ore at 0.56
ounces of gold per ton is in reserve.

BANDERAS, LAS.   1) A district in the municipio of Matiguás,
department of Matagalpa.
2) A district of the municipio of Tipitapa, department
of Managua.

BANDOLEON.   A mandolin-type of stringed musical instrument.

BARATA, LA.   Coffee hacienda in the municipio of Yalí,
Jinotega department.

BARBACOA, LA.   Pre-Columbian official residence of the

cacique in the cacicazgo of Agateyte. Also housed the
members of the Council of Elders and top military officers.

BARBA DE TIGRE. A territory of the municipio of San
Rafael del Sur department of Managua.

BARCELONA. Coffee hacienda in the municipio of La Concepción, department of Masaya.

BARCLAY, RICHARDSON COMPANY. A British concern
interested in a cross-Nicaragua canal in the 1830's.
They employed a British engineer who figured in later
negotiations for concessions, and who stayed on to serve
the Central American Confederacy. See BAILEY,
JOHN.

BARQUERO, ANTONIO. A founder of the periodical Iris de
La Tarde, as the initiator of a series of romantic era
publications in Boaco, 1915.

BARRA HONSON. The bar at the southernmost entry to the
Bay of Bluefields.

BARRIO DE LA CRUZ. Comarca or district in the municipio of San Marcos, Carazo department.

BARRIO DE LAS MORAS. Comarca or district in the municipio of Diriamba, department of Carazo.

BARRIO DON FRANCISCO. The section of Granada clustered
about the old monastery and chapel of the same name.

BARRIO EL DOMINGAZO. A far northwestern section of
Granada near the Flor de Caña stadium.

BARRIO EL HOSPITAL. The section of the city of Granada
including several hospitals, in the western portion.

BARRIO GUADELUPE. An eastern section of Granada near
the old cathedral where Henningsen (q. v.) stood siege in
1857.

BARRIO LA CONCEPCION. A section of Granada near the
downtown area.

BARRIO LA ESTACION. A northern section of the city of

Granada, near and including the rail terminus, warehouses, etc.

BARRIO LA MERCED. Section of Granada adjoining the great late colonial church of the same name.

BARRIO LA OTRA BANDITA. A commercial district and area in the northwest of the city of Granada.

BARRIO LAS CAMELIAS. A far southwestern suburb of the city of Granada.

BARRIO LOMA EL MICA. A small suburb in the southeastern portion of the city of Granada.

BARRIO MA JULIA. A section in the southern part of the city of Granada.

BARRIO MONCADA. A district of the municipio of La Concepción, department of Masaya.

BARRIO NUEVO. Comarca or district in the municipio of San Marcos, Carazo department.

BARRIO NUEVO DEL LIMON. Comarca or district in the municipio of Diriamba, department of Carazo.

BARRIO NUEVO SABANAGRANDE. A territory of the National District, department of Managua.

BARRIO PALMIRA. A section of Granada city on the southeast.

BARRIO PUEBLO CHIQUITO. A section of Granada along the Arroyo Zacateliqua.

BARRIO SANTIAGO. A district of the municipio of La Concepción, department of Masaya.

BARRIOS, DON FRANCISCO. One of the Barrios family established in Masaya who was a colonial Spanish resident in 1800. Others were Valerio and Juan Ignacio.

BARRIOS, JUAN IGNACIO. Progenitor of a well-known Masaya family today, Captain Barrios was on record as one of the Spaniards in the same place in 1800.

BARRIOS, VALERIO.   A colonial Spanish resident in Masaya
    around 1800.

BARRO, EL.   1) A comarca or district in the municipio of
    Larreynaga, León.
        2) A district in the municipio of Esquipulas, depart-
    ment of Matagalpa.

BARRUELA, MANUEL.   Recollect friar who was persuaded
    by de Villegas, bishop of Nicaragua, to accompany Col-
    ville Breton (q. v.) in the Spanish effort to gain through
    Breton a foothold of control on the Mosquito Coast.
    See also   RODRIGUEZ MOJICA; and HODGSON, ROBERT.

BASILICA OF THE ASSUMPTION   see   LEON CATHEDRAL

BASTIDE, MARTIN DE LA.   A company was formed by
    Bastide in the late 1700's to build a Nicaraguan canal.
    Under the patronage and encouragement of the Spanish
    crown, this project was to connect Lake Nicaragua with
    the Pacific from the mouth of the Sapoa River (on the
    Lake) to the Gulf of Nicoya.   The Spanish fleet based
    in the Pacific was also ordered to make surveys of the
    route, but the onset of the French revolution created
    such turbulence in Europe that the canal project was
    laid aside.   Spain had other problems, colonial as well
    as peninsular.

BASTILLA, LA.   A height of the Datanli spur of the Darien
    range, Jinotega department.

BASTON, RIO EL.   A stream emptying into the Pacific in
    Rivas department, municipio of San Juan del Sur.   Also
    called Marsella.

BATALLA DE SAN JACINTO.   This engagement was of ma-
    jor importance in the National War because it was the
    first occasion on which the intruding North American
    filibusters under William Walker had gone down to igno-
    minious and crushing defeat.   While only a skirmish in
    terms of numbers engaged, its significance was vast to
    the United Central American armies battling the hated
    invader, and the victory was an encouragement and of
    an inspirational value far beyond its ordinary military
    significance.   The defenders at San Jacinto are revered
    today as Nicaraguan heroes (particularly José Dolores
    Estrada (q. v.), the commanding colonel) and in September

of 1956, a massive centennial celebration took place in
Managua. The meaning of the victory over North Americans is still green in memory and vital in national pride
and integrity.

Facts and factors concerning the battle, which took
place between 7:00 and 11:00 a. m. on September 14,
1856, are as follows: The location was the established
hacienda of don Miguel Bolanos. (The old hacienda
house has been restored as a national monument and
museum.) Approximately 300 filibusters under Byron
Cole and his second-in-command, Marshall, faced 160
Nicaraguans under José Estrada. Estrada's force was
divided in three companies: the first under Captain
Liberato Cisne, the second under Captain Francisco
Sacaza, and the third under Captain Francisco de Diós
Aviles. Captain Bartolo-Sandoval commanded the pursuit
of the rearguard. Patricio Centeno served as Colonel
Estrada's second-in-command with the rank of lieutenant-
colonel. Sergeants were Andrés Castro, Macedonio Gar-
cía, Francisco Estrada, Vicente Vijil and Francisco Gó-
mez (who was killed). Other officers were Ignacio Jarquín (who died); Salvador Bolanos, Venancio Zaragoza,
Abelardo Vega, Carlos Alegría, Juan Estrada, Basilio
Lezama, Espiridión Galeano, and Julián Artola. Lieutenants were Miguel Vélez, Adán Solís, Alejandro Eva,
Manuel Marenco, and José Siero.

The old hacienda house is long and large, adobe-
walled, high-ceilinged, tile-roofed. (See drawing.)
While near hills, it is on a low eminence of a broad
plain. The North Americans were in search of supplies,
principally cattle for meat, and they advanced up the
valley to the northeast from Tipitapa. Warned by Colonel
McDonald in Tipitapa of the strength of the Nicaraguans
in the old manor house, Lieutenant Colonel Byron Cole,
his second, Wiley Marshall, and Major J. C. O'Neal
proceeded on their hunt for provisions. Marshall was
a civilian from Granada, who later died in Tipitapa of
San Jacinto wounds. Early on the 14th, 120 riflemen
under Cole marched toward the fortified house. Estrada's
troops were principally from Granada and Masaya, with
officers who were veterans of the fighting in 1854. The
center of Nicaraguan defense was the hacienda; their
right wing in the walls of a stone corral, the left wing
in a wood corral. Before them extended the broad plains
toward Lake Managua. The filibusters first charged the
left wing, firing their revolvers. The Nicaraguans answered with stones in some cases. The repulse of the

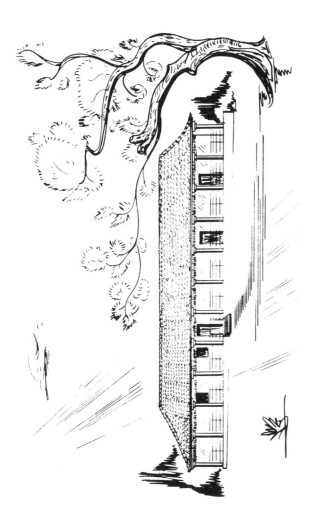

San Jacinto

The old hacienda house where the 1856 battle was fought.

filibusters was such that some, in trying to flee, wound
up in the hands of the Nicaraguans. Byron Cole was one
of these. The filibusters seemed to be terrorized for
the first time. Thirty-five of Cole's men fell and 18
prisoners were taken; 28 were dead and wounded in Estrada's force. The major effect of the battle was not
only to deal the filibuster force a stinging blow--to deny
to it provisions--but to destroy forever the legend of invincibility which had grown up around Walker's forces.
This was the turning point of the Guerra Nacional--from
then on Walker was closer each day to defeat. The strategic meaning of this small battle may be suggested when
it is pointed out that not only did it give new spirit and
the final will to win to the Central American forces, but
if it had not done so, and Walker could have gone on
with his grand design to attach Central America and Cuba
to the Confederate States of America, the change in U.S.
history and the ultimate world repercussions might have
modified the whole march of the 20th century. The battle cries of "Hurrah Walker" and "Viva Martínez" sound-
ed over a little-known and, by the world, forgotten battle, yet one which had that characteristic of being a key,
as well as a keynote, to history.

BATEAU. A French word meaning small light boat, usually
flat-bottomed for use in rivers. In Nicaragua it is used
in a particularized manner to denote a river dugout,
pipante, which has been sawed lengthwise with a wide
plank put in the bottom (to increase the beam to nearly
four feet) and two boards added to the gunwales to increase depth. This makes a solid river scow which is
fast with a big outboard motor, and which will carry
two or more tons. The origin of application of the
French term is obscure, but was probably brought in
by Canadian or French mercenaries who came to Nicaragua in the filibuster wars or by French priests.

BATTLE FOR NICARAGUA. A term applied to the action
which resulted in the capture of Fort Inmaculada on the
San Juan by the British on April 28, 1780, but also in
the abandonment of the fort January 3, 1781. Thus, the
most powerful military force in the world, that of Great
Britain, received one of its few major setbacks in history
and thereby was frustrated in the grand strategic design
of cutting the Spanish colonial empire and at the same
time providing control of an "ocean entry" by cutting a
canal from Atlantic to Pacific waters. This remote

battle, essentially won by fever and the jungle, left
Great Britain with only one entry lacking between major
oceans (the Atlantic and Pacific). She controlled all the
rest. In that sense the battle represents a major strategic element in the geopolitical international relationships of world history.

BEAULAC, WILLARD. Chargé d'affaires of the American
(U. S.) legation in Managua who distinguished himself by
calm and effective service during the absence of the ambassador, Hanna, when the great earthquake (q. v.) struck
Managua on March 31, 1931. The quake lasted only
eight seconds but was tremendously destructive. Fire
followed the quake, with the ultimate destruction of over
30 blocks in downtown Managua.

BEBIDA DE LOS DIOSES see THEOBROMACACAO

BEIBIDEA, DON JOSÉ. A Masaya resident of 1800 who has
descendants there today.

BEISBOL. Baseball, a favorite Nicaraguan game.

BEJUCO, EL. Clear spring in Estelí department.

BEJUCOS. Reeds or pliable vegetable fibres of vines used
by aboriginals of the Matagalpa area in a great variety
of weaving and construction from hats to cables and
houses.

BELEN. 1) A municipio in the department of Rivas, of 33
square miles, and about 8000 inhabitants. It is bounded
on the north by Carazo and Granada departments; on the
south by the municipio of Rivas; east by the municipio
Buenos Aires; and west by Tola municipio. There are
12 districts or valleys.
    2) Plantation in the municipio of Quezalguaque, León
department.
    3) Villa Belén. Founded in 1738, the town (villa)
was based on a "Pueblo del Obraje" in connection with
the hacienda "El Obraje. " In 1862 it became a Villa,
and presently has about 800 inhabitants. The local
school is named "Dr. Pedro J. Quintanilla" for a
prominent son of the area, scion of the family Quintanilla Jarquín, which has had an influential part in
national affairs, especially in education.

BELLAVISTA.   Coffee hacienda in the municipio of El Sauce, León department.

BELLY, FELIX. The Frenchman Belly, a Knight of San Maurice and Lazarus, was one of the major enthusiasts for a Nicaraguan canal route.   He had helped Nicaragua and Costa Rica settle their San Juan River boundary dispute by the Cañas-Jérez Treaty (q. v.) of 1858, and he was further interested in the route surveyed by the Dane, Oërsted (q. v.). Belly made every effort to advance French canal causes in Central America, and wrote a two-volume work on the prospects.   He proposed the canal route be placed under the guarantee of three European powers--England, France, and Sardinia.   He signed a 99-year contract with Nicaragua in May, 1858. Belly and associates were to have the right to construct and operate a canal along Oërsted's route, and French warships were to be stationed at the terminal ports. France would not support Belly's claims to envoy status.

BENEDICTINES.   One of several Catholic orders of a monastic nature established since 1900 in Nicaragua.

BENKS (River) see COCO, RIO

BERLIN.   A territory of the National District, department of Managua.

BERRY, M. S.   Major, U. S. Marine Corps, in contact with Sandino forces in April, 1927.

BETANCOURT, AMBROCIO DE   see NAGUALAPA (def. 2)

BETANZOS, FRAY DE.   The Franciscan missionary who established a convent in the 18th century on the shores of Lake Nicaragua opposite the island of Omotepe, and who gave it the name San Jorge (q. v. , def. 4).

BETULIA.   Comarca or district in the municipio of La Libertad, Chontales.

BIBLIOTECOS MEXICO.   A Mexican information library established in Managua in 1966, which event was followed by a cultural exposition in December, 1966.   Nicaraguan political and cultural ties with Mexico are strong.

BIFTEK see BISTEK

BIJAGUA. A district in the municipio and department of Matagalpa.

BIJAGUA ABAJO. A district in the municipio and department of Matagalpa.

BIJAGUA ARRIBA. A district in the municipio and department of Matagalpa.

BIJAGUE DE JUCUAPA. A district in the municipio and department of Matagalpa.

BIJAO, EL. A district of the municipio of San Ramón, Matagalpa department.

BILAMPI. A district south of the lower Río Tuma.

BILGUAS. A district in the municipio of Matiguas, department of Matagalpa.

BIRDS. In a brief listing, the following Nicaraguan birds may be identified; first, American types of both continents: grebes, cormorants, pelicans, hawks, falcons, ospreys, vultures, herons, ibises, ducks, quail, swallows, fly-catchers, warblers, dippers, vireos, orioles, jays, blackbirds, cuckoos, rails, plovers, gulls, terns, pigeons, owls, kingfishers, swifts, hummingbirds, thrushes, mockingbirds, wrens; second, South American types: tinamous, storks, flamingos, guans, limpkins, sun bitterns, sun grebes, jacanas, parrots, macaws, potoos, trogons, quetzals (arogóns), motmots, puff birds, jacamars, barbets, toucans, tapaculos, ant birds, oven birds, wood hewers, manakins, honey creepers; third, North American types: turkeys, waxwings, creepers, titmice, chickadees.

BISMUNA, LAGUNA. Large coastal lagoon just to the south of Cabo Gracias a Dios, the entrance to the Caribbean being over the Barra de Tukrus. The lake is 12 miles long, nine wide.

BISTEK. "Beefsteak" spelled phonetically. Interestingly, menus have been seen to include "Bistek de Cerdo," hence, "beefsteak of pork"! The word has become a generic term for a way of preparing meat rather than for its animal source. Also spelled "Biftek."

BISTEOT.   (Also, "Huitzteótl" in Nahuatl.)   A Nicarao god
of hunger.   The root "teot" meaning God is interestingly
like "deus" or "dios. "

BIUHKIRA, LAGUNA.   A lake two miles in diameter, five
miles west of Walpasiksa, Zelaya department.

BLACK CARIBS.   An ethnic mix of Antillean Negroes and
Arawakan Indians from the south and east (the Windward
and Leeward Islands).   There are isolated east coastal
Nicaraguan Caribbean communities which still consider
themselves "Careeb. "   Most of these people live on the
shores of Pearl Lagoon.   These are not to be confused,
in spite of phonetic similarities, with Quiribies.   Some
Carib Indians were transported in the 18th century to
the Honduras Bay Islands by the British.   These may be
the basis of the present "Careebs. "

"BLACK LEGEND. "   Credited to Bartolomé de las Casas,
the famous Bishop of the Indians, this widely disseminated account of Spanish colonial cruelty to the indigenous
Americans was circulated throughout Europe as "proof"
of Spanish inhumanity.   Las Casas' intent was to shock
the King of Spain into passing laws to enforce more hu-
mane treatment of Indians.   Such laws were passed in
1542 but the "black legend" persisted in the Anglo-Saxon
Reformation areas of Europe among people anxious to
believe the worst of Catholic Spain.   Las Casas worked
in Nicaragua where treatment of Indians under the cruel
and long governorship of Pedrarias was particularly exe-
crable.

BLACKMAN, M. A.   see   PELLAS, F. A. ; and MARITIME
CANAL COMPANY OF NICARAGUA

BLACK PANTHER.   A "pantera negra, " in Nicaragua more
commonly called "león, " or lion, is sometimes a color
phase of the jaguar.   It was such an animal that was a
200-pound pet of "Tacho" Somoza just before his death
in 1956.   The animal was very dark brown, near-black,
but the vestigial jaguar spots could be seen.

BLACK TIGER MINE.   One of the Bonanza (q. v.) group of
mines.

BLANCA.   A steamer which on at least one occasion ran to
Puerto Limón, Costa Rica, carrying revolutionary troops

on the return to Bluefields. Apparently Captain Cheri Méndez carried famed General Emiliano Chamorro on this trip, as well as a Parrott cannon (of U. S. make and Civil War vintage). This was during the turbulent first decade of the 20th century.

BLANCA, LAGUNA. A small lake due east of Nandaime, in a group of small lakes, of which another is Juan Tallo.

BLANCO, DON LUIS. This lieutenant colonel represented a principal family of Masaya at the outset of the 19th century.

BLANDON, PEDRO. A lumberman in the lower Río Coco lumber camps who became a Sandinista general and whose field of action was the Río Coco valley from the mountains of the Segovias to the sea. In 1931, he was the leader of a group responsible for the murder of Otto Bregenzer (q. v.), Moravian missionary and German citizen. It was he who led the raid on the Puerto Cabezas area. He was killed in the Logtown (q. v.) encounters. See also WOOD, DARRAH.

BLANDON, RAFAEL. Founder of the fincas "Bulbul" and "La Estrella, " he came to the Matiguás area in the decade of the 1850's.

BLASQUEZ, NARCISO FRANCISCO. A Rivas citizen who presented a petition in Madrid in 1779 to redesignate Villa Rivas as a "ciudad. " The petition met royal denial in 1783. He did achieve, however, the continued award of an escutcheon. The coat of arms of the villa included two volcanoes and the imperial crown, and was used previously, so its continuation represented a partial victory for Blasquez and his town.

BLAUVELT, ABRAHAM. Trader of Dutch origin for whom Bluefields, Nicaragua was named (in Anglicized form) and who was one of those who accompanied Captain Cammock of the Providence Company. The bay in Jamaica where he anchored is also named Bluefields. The date of occupation of the Nicaragua port is 1633. This Blauvelt opened contacts with the Rama Indians, a sub-tribe of the Sumus whose descendants still live on Rama Key just south of Bluefields. He was still living at Cabo Gracias a Dios in 1663.

BLAUVELT, WILLIAM. Dutch trader on the Nicaraguan
coast following 1633, who originally accompanied Captain
Cammock of the Providence Company, and who was
doubtless related (probably a brother) to Abraham Blauvelt for whom Bluefields was named.

BLUEFIELDS, BAHIA DE. An extensive coastal lagoon
about 20 miles long and up to eight miles wide. Much
Nicaraguan history has been made in the area, from pirate beginnings in the 1600's to U.S. Marine landings
in the 20th century, with much mayhem and revolution
in between. The port of El Bluff is at the eastern entry,
the city of Bluefields is opposite, to the West. See also
BLAUVELT, ABRAHAM.

BLUEFIELDS, CIUDAD. Cabacera of the department of
Zelaya as well as of the municipio, Bluefields is a departure from familiar Nicaraguan patterns as seen on
the Spanish colonial-influenced west coast of the country.
The buildings are predominantly of frame construction,
the low tropical coast contrasting sharply with the
heights and plains familiar on the Pacific side. Bluefields (named for Dutch freebooter Abraham Blauvelt (q. v.)
has about 9700 inhabitants, over half of those in the entire municipio. There are no roads; hence, very few
vehicles. Grass flourishes in many side streets, transportation is by boat to sea or lagoons, or upriver to
the Rama port and road; or by airplane. There is regular air service from Managua. The port of El Bluff,
several miles across Bluefields Bay, has excellent dock-
age, but the bar to the bay has silted and only very
small ocean-going ships can enter. Bluefields has had
a colorful history of intrigue and revolution, beginning
with pirate occupation in earliest times. On the post-
office in recent years was a sign, "El rifle y el libro
cimienta la paz" (the rifle and the book establish peace).

BLUEFIELDS INFORMATION. Published in León, a weekly.

BLUEFIELDS, MUNICIPIO. Cabacera of the department of
Zelaya, the municipio has 17, 700 population, over half
of them in the "city" of Bluefields. Once the center of
a flourishing banana industry, the blight eliminated that
as a source of revenue. There is now a small commercial fishing industry, with shrimp and oysters the principal products. There are several schools in the area:
the Colegio Moravo, a long-established Moravian school;

and the "La Asunción" and "San José" schools. The
Bluefields waterfront market on the bay edge is unique
and active.

BLUENOS. A district on the upper Río Prinzapolka.

BLUFF, EL. The Bluefields Bay Port, steeped in revolutionary lore, on an eminence near the bay bar and entrance, and flanked to the north by lovely deserted
Caribbean beaches. The Customs-house and docks are
located here.

BOACO. Department located in central Nicaragua, north of
Lake Nicaragua, and adjoining the Lake for a short
frontage. It is bounded on the south by the lake and
the department of Chontales; on the west by the depart-
ments of Managua and Masaya, and in part by the Río
Barco; on the north by the Río Olama and the departments of Matagalpa and Zelaya; and on the east by
Zelaya and the Huapi mountains. It is drained by the
Ríos Tecolostate and Olama, a tributary of the Río
Grande de Matagalpa; and also by two other minor Río
Grande tributaries, the Río Murra and the Las Cañas.
The Cabacera departmental is the town of Boaco, centered in the western sector. The department is approximately 2, 080 square miles in area, with a population of
62, 227 and was established on February 16, 1936, from
a portion of the old department of Chontales. Boaco is
an agricultural and livestock raising region, with
140, 000 head of cattle constantly increasing. Other
products are rice, beans, sugar cane, some coffee,
fruits, and in addition cheeses and meats. Hats are
manufactured. There are minerals largely undeveloped,
although gold was mined in the 16th century and following. The municipios are Teustepe, San José, de los
Remates, Santa Lucía, Boaco, Camoapa, San Lorenzo.

BOATS see PIPANTE; DORI, CANOA; BATEAU; CAYUCA

BOBADILLA, FRAY FRANCISCO DE. The priest who in
1527 first climbed the Volcán de Masaya (Santiago) and
planted a cross on its summit.

BOCANA DE CUISALA. Cattle ranch in Chontales granted
in 1714 to Captain don Francisco González de Urtecho.
Size unknown.

BOCAY. A district of the municipio of Jinotega.

BOCAY, RIO. The Bocay River is a principal tributary of the Río Coco, having a length of 93 miles from its source in the Peñas Blancas massif to its confluence with the Río Coco at the village of Bocay, just across the larger river from Honduras. Its tributaries are the Guina, Hamaca and Ayapal. Navigable by pipantes from El Garrobo to the mouth.

BOCAY, VALLE DE. Between the Bocay and Guina rivers and the Baba and Kilambé mountain complexes, this valley is about 1000 feet above sea level. Gold is found here. Gold prospectors in these dangerous regions are called "guireses" (origin unknown).

BOCAYCITO. A district of the municipio of Jinotega.

BOCAYES. A subtribal group of the Chontales tribe. The Río Bocay and other names derive from this group. Originally of the "Qiribies" (q. v.).

BOHIO. A type of circular thatched hut often attributed to Nicaraguan Indians, but the name and style of which are actually derived from the Caribbean Islands.

BOLAÑOS, DON JOSE GREGORIO. As administrator of the postal service in 1800, don José was a progenitor of Masaya residents of today.

BOLAÑOS, MIGUEL. Owner of the hacienda where the Batalla [battle] de San Jacinto (q. v.) took place.

BOLETIN DE NICARAGUA. Periodical published in León, 1839-1842 (during the first three years of the existence of Nicaragua as an independent nation).

"BOLETIN JUDICIAL. " An important section of the Government Gazette (Gaceta del Gobierno, a continuation of the official government publication of the late 1880's), founded by Gazette Director Jerónimo Pérez of Masaya.

BOLETIN OFICIAL. Published in León in 1854, there is a question if this official bulletin was in supplement to or conflict with the Gaceta Oficial (q. v.) in Managua the same year.

BOLINKY. A district of the municipio of Jinotega.

BOLSA, LA.   1) A district of the municipio of La Concepción, department of Masaya.
      2) A district of the municipio of Yalí in the Jinotega
department.

BOMBARDMENT OF MASAYA, 1912.   On August 11-14,
1912, in the early stages of the U. S. Marine occupation
and involvement, Major (later General) Smedley Butler's
battalion and 100 associated sailors started on a mission
to protect foreigners and to take Red Cross relief to the
hungry populace of Granada.   Near Masaya the train was
fired upon, and the resulting battle and bombardment included the capture of the fortified hills Coyotepe and
La Barranca.

BONANCITA MINE.   One of the Bonanza (q. v.) group of
mines.

BONANZA MINES.   The Bonanza mines are 15 miles north
of the Siuna area, and 65 miles westward from Puerto
Cabezas.   Following the valley of the Pis Pis river,
the mineralized area is 1. 5 x 10 miles in extent.   First
exploitation of the gold-bearing veins was in 1880.   In
1922 the mines were destroyed by revolutionaries, having produced about $12, 000, 000 in gold to that time.
In 1934 the property was acquired by the American
Smelting and Refining Company of New York, in company
with the Honduras Rosario Mining Company.   The Neptune Gold Mining Company was formed, which presently
operates the property.   The Pis Pis area is notable for
the many gold veins; there are three groups: the Nep-
tune-Eden, the Pioneer-Lone Star, and the Constancia.
Mineralization includes galena, hematite, and zinc sul-
fide, in addition to the finely divided gold and silver.
The Bonanza group has 16 mines: Black Tiger, Philadelphia, Luna de Noche, Neptune, Cleopatra, Pioneer,
Highland Mary, Vesubio, San Antonio, Constancia, San
Joaquín, Eden, Culebra, Hidden Treasure, Bonancita
and Morning Star.   In 1939, 35, 130 ounces of gold and
81, 873 ounces of silver were produced.   In 1962,
90, 258 ounces of gold and 122, 216 ounces of silver.
Production of ores is 800 tons daily with the mill a
flotation process served by train.   Some of the mines
are open-pit, others have shafts and tunnels.

BONAPARTE, LOUIS NAPOLEON.   President of the French
Republic in 1849, and later to be Napoleon III, Louis

Napoleon Bonaparte wrote a pamphlet published in London in 1846, entitled "A Project to Connect the Atlantic and Pacific Oceans." This was indeed a proposal for a canal across Nicaragua by the San Juan River and Lake Nicaragua route. The company he suggested was to be called "La Canal Napoleon de Nicaragua." The pamphlet had considerable effect on British opinion. As emperor, he was still interested in the project through his puppet Maximilian of Mexico.

BONETE, EL. 1) A district of Terrabona municipio, Matagalpa department.
2) A mountain in the department of Estelí, La Trinidad municipio, from whose summit may be seen all the Pacific Coastal region of the Republic.

BONETILLO. A district of the municipio of Jinotega.

BONGO see PANGA

BONILLA, JOSE ANTONIO. The first procurador and sindico general of the newly established villa of Rivas in 1720.

BOQUERON. 1) Comarca or district in the municipio of Quezalguaque, León.
2) El Boqueron, a comarca or district of the municipio of Santa Rosa, León.

BOQUITA, LA. Bathing beach in Carazo department on the Pacific.

BOQUITA, RIO LA. A short river flowing from heights near Diriamba into the Pacific Ocean.

BOQUITA Y CASARES, LA. Comarca or district in the municipio of Diriamba, department of Carazo.

BOQUITO. A district in the municipio of Santa Lucia, department of Boaco.

BORAH, WILLIAM E. U.S. Senator from Idaho, who as chairman of the Senate Foreign Relations Committee warned the administration in February, 1927, that he could not support a Central American policy "based... on mahogany and oil...[and] executed by warships and marines." Borah and Senator George W. Norris (q.v.)

were leading opponents of the unpopular Marine expeditionary force in Nicaragua.

BORBOLLON. A spring in the southern part of the municipio of León.

BORDE DE LAS TINAJAS. Comarca or district of the municipio of El Jicaral, León.

BORLAND, SOLON. An agent of the United States sent by
Secretary of State Marcy to Nicaragua in 1854 to attempt to straighten out the tangled diplomatic mess resulting from ambiguities in the Clayton-Bulwer Treaty
concerning Mosquitia and the Bay Islands. Borland was
in Greytown in the home of U. S. Consul Fabens when a
Captain Smith of one of the transit company's river
steamers killed a Negro and precipitated an Anglo-
Mosquito mob action. Borland and Smith escaped to
an American merchant vessel, the Northern Light.
This caused the U. S. sloop Cyane (q. v.) to be sent to
protect transit company interests.

BOSQUE, EL. A cattle ranch in the municipio of Nindirí,
Masaya department.

BOVALLIUS, CARL. A world renowned Swedish archaeologist of the University of Uppsala who travelled in Central America between 1881-1883 and who spoke of the
craft work in shoes, hammocks, ceramics, and so on,
done in Masaya at that time. Author of a rare pamphlet on Nicaraguan archeology.

BRADLEY, J. S. Miner, industrialist, and friend of United
States emissary Ephraim Squier (q. v.) who travelled
Nicaragua prior to 1854.

BRASILITO. Comarca or district in the municipio of Diriamba, department of Carazo.

BRAZIL, EL. 1) Coffee hacienda in the municipio of San
Marcos, Carazo department.
    2) Comarca or district of the municipio of Santa
Teresa, Carazo department.
    3) A territory and hacienda of the municipio del
Carmen, Managua department.
    4) A district of the municipio of Tipitapa, depart-
ment of Managua.

BRAZILES, LOS. 1) A hacienda and dairy farm, essentially
a village in itself, in the municipio of Mateare, Managua
department.
2) A territory of the National District, department of
Managua.

BRAZILITO, EL. 1) Comarca or district in the municipio
of San Marcos, Carazo department.
2) Coffee hacienda in the municipio of San Marcos,
Carazo department.

BREGENZER, KARL OTTO. A Moravian missionary who
was murdered by Sandinista guerrillas in 1931 at Musawas along the Waspuc River in Eastern Nicaragua. The
village and his church were burned to the ground by
forces of Pedro Blandón, who mistook the German citizen for an American. This happened on the same day
much of Managua was destroyed by earthquake and fire--
March 31.

BRENES JARQUIN, CARLOS. Dr. Brenes Jarquín served
briefly as President in 1936, following differences between Anastasio Somoza, General of the National Guard,
and President Juan Batista Sacasa. He was succeeded
by Somoza, who had effective control of Nicaragua for
the next 20 years.

BRETON, COLVILLE. Chief of the Miskitos, south of the
Cabo Gracias a Dios in the late 1700's, Breton was a
tall, muscular, pure-blooded Suma Indian (by this period
a rarity on the coast). He had power over Miskitos and
Caribs from Sandy Bay to Bluefields. He was involved
in the "treaty" with Jeremiah Terry (q. v.). Yarrince,
George II, Terry.) Breton joined the British under
Kemble and in 1782 carried out a reprisal attack on the
Spanish frontier, descending upon Juigalpa, Lavajo and
Lovisicsa. Baptized in 1788, he was given the name
Carlos Antonio de Castilla. After considerable intrigue
during which his marriage to María Manuela Rodríguez
was effected and dissolved, he was murdered by follow-
ers of his nephew, Alparis Delce (q. v.), in 1790. His
death marked the failure of Spanish plans to win over
the Miskitos, and was therefore significant. Following
Breton's death, anarchy was rife. See also GEORGE
II.

BREYERA, LA. 1) Cattle ranch in the municipio of San

Rafael del Norte, Jinotega department.
2) A district or valley in the municipio of San Rafael del Norte, Jinotega department.

BRICIO, PEDRO. Spanish officer who with 500 Nicaraguan militiamen in April 1780 hastily erected a large stockade, 300 feet in diameter, at the place where the San Juan River leaves Lake Nicaragua, now the village of San Carlos. Remains of the old fort and later works on the site still remain. This was done under the leadership of Matías Gálvez (q. v.).

BRIG BAY. A village on the Isla del Maiz Grande (Great Corn Island).

BRISAS, LAS. 1) District in the municipio and department of Rivas.
2) District in the municipio of San Juan del Sur, Rivas department.

BROWN BANK. A village on the southwestern shore of Pearl Lagoon, Zelaya department.

BRYAN-CHAMORRO TREATY. On August 5, 1914, the silver-tongued orator William Jennings Bryan negotiated with President Emiliano Chamorro a treaty essentially identical to the Chamorro-Weitzel Convention (q. v.). This was ratified by the U. S. Senate on February 18, 1916. There was much objection among Latin-American neighbors. Colombia claimed the Corn Islands under an 1803 Spanish decree; and Salvador and Honduras felt that Nicaragua could not so blithely dispose of the Gulf of Fonseca. These matters led to the dissolution of the Central American Court of Justice, when Nicaragua withdrew after judication against her. Chamorro was at the time not only leader of the country but also of the conservative Chamorro family, long a power in the country. He himself as a distinguished soldier-diplomat-President, concluded the treaty which not only gave the United States exclusive rights to construct a canal through Nicaragua (on the basis that an alternative to the Panama route opened that year might ultimately be desirable or necessary), but also a 99-year lease on the two Caribbean offshore "Islas de Maíz" or Corn Islands, as well as a similar lease on a naval base site on the Gulf of Fonseca in Nicaraguan territory. For this Nicaragua was given $3,000,000.

BUCCANEERS, 1665-1685. The particular pirates that affected Central America and with especially notable attention and ferocity the country of Nicaragua, were recruit-
ed from small tobacco farmers, whites who had been
pushed off their land by the development of a slave-
powered sugar plantation economy. Dutch, French and
English, these dispossessed ones banded together in
Jamaica, on the island of Tortuga, and ultimately on
the isthmus coast from Panama to Yucatan, with special bases at Bluefields, Cabo Gracias, and Belize.
They raided the Spanish Pacific coastal interior paying
special attention to the richer towns and mines of Nicaragua. This country bore the heaviest attacks. England,
torn domestically, was unable to enforce treaties. While
Nicaragua was poor compared to Guatemala, it was significant to freebooters because Granada on Lake Nicaragua was a port where precious metals and indigo were
gathered for shipment. Further, Granada was accessible
up the San Juan River and across the big lake. Guatemala was much harder to reach. During this period no
fort protected the interior.

BUENA VISTA. 1) Comarca or district in the municipio of
Diriamba, department of Carazo.
  2) Comarca or district in the municipio of Santa Rosa,
León.
  3) A district of the municipio of Nindirí, department
of Masaya.
  4) One of only two districts in the small municipio of
San Juan de Oriente, Masaya department.
  5) A district of the municipio of San Ramón, Matagalpa department.

BUENAVISTA DEL ARROYO. Comarca or district in the
municipio of La Paz, Carazo department.

BUENOS AIRES. 1) This cabacera of the municipio of the
same name has around 1000 population.
  2) Cattle ranch on Condega municipio, Estelí department.
  3) District in the municipio and department of Rivas.
  4) Municipio in the department of Rivas; the cabacera
having the same name. Area, 37 square miles; population, just under 3000. Bounded on the north by Granada,
south by San Jorge, east by Lake Nicaragua, and west
by Belén. There are six comarcas or districts. Sugarcane and cereals are raised, as well as cattle. There

is a lake coast of ten miles.   Part of this area is a
marsh, near Nocainé.

BUEY, JUSTO.   Celebrated police figure in the history of
    La Concepción, whose cruelty in the pursuit of illicit
    liquor-makers was legendary.

BUEY ACARREADOR.   Water-carrying oxen are used to
    bring water to the people of Alta Gracia and surround-
    ings on Omotepe Island in Nicaragua.   The oxen are
    fitted with wooden water tanks on a pack saddle and the
    water is dipped up from Lake Nicaragua.   Watersellers
    ride the oxen peddling water to the citizenry.

BUITRAGO, PABLO.   Upon the breakup of the United Prov-
    inces, with Nicaragua seceding first in 1838, Licenciado
    Buitrago assumed leadership as director from March 4,
    1841 to April 1, 1843.   Under his administration, the
    founding of the University of Granada, the law book pub-
    lication of Licenciado Benito Rosales, and the develop-
    ment of the newspaper Mentor Nicaraguense all took
    place.

BULLON Y FIGUEROA, ISIDRO MARIN.   The bishop of
    Nicaragua in 1747 who undertook construction of the
    present cathedral in León.   See LEÓN, CATHEDRAL.

BUNAU-VARILLA, PHILIPPE, 1859-1940.   Significant to
    Nicaragua was the man who by his lobbying activities
    was largely responsible for the isthmian canal being
    placed in Panama rather than Nicaragua, in spite of
    U. S. Navy surveys and recommendations as late as
    1902 recommending otherwise.   As agent of the French
    Canal Company, this vigorous and versatile engineer
    designed Panama's flag, promoted the 1903 revolution,
    and helped finance it.   The French plan having failed,
    he forced the sale of the French canal concession to
    the U. S. and was Panama's official representative in
    Washington, and his name is attached to the canal
    treaty with the new republic--the Hay-Bunau-Varilla
    document.   One of his colorful lobbying approaches
    was to send members of the U. S. Senate Nicaraguan
    postage stamps showing an erupting volcano (hence, by
    implication, a threat to that route for the canal).

BUSTAMENTE Y GUERRA, JOSE.   Captain-General of the
    Kingdom of Guatemala from 1811-1818, he was instru-

mental in preventing the effective adoption of the Constitution of 1812 as produced by the Cortes de Cádiz. He
put down an 1811 revolt in León, Nicaragua, and more
brutally dealt with a revolt in Granada in late 1811 and
early 1812. The harsh measures used were a result of
Bustamente's growing fear concerning the revolts in
Mexico under the leadership of Fathers Hidalgo and
Morelos. He further refused advice from the diputaciones provinciales. All of these actions helped to has-
ten independence. "El terror bustamentino" lasted until 1818.

BUTLER, SMEDLEY. U. S. Marine Major (later a well-
known General). See BOMBARDMENT OF MASAYA.

BUTTERS, CHARLES. Owner of the San Albino Mine (q. v.)
who was once an employer and later an early victim of
the Sandino forces.

-C-

CABACERA. The capital of a department or a municipio
(q. v.). A rough parallel to departmental cabaceras
would be state capitals. (The department of Zelaya
is larger than several states of the United States of
America.) The cabaceras of municipios might be considered as tantamount to county seats in United States
usage. The municipio and its cabacera frequently bear
the same name, and in general the cabacera is the
principal population center of the municipio.

CABALLERIA. A measure of land used in old Spanish
grants, amounting to about 33 1/3 (U. S.) acres.

CABALLERO, FRAY VICENTE and Pedro José Caballero.
The doctors Caballero were on the first faculty of the
University of Nicaragua upon its establishment in 1816.

CABEI see CENTRAL AMERICA BANK FOR ECONOMIC
INTEGRATION

CABEZA DE GENTE. Monolith topping a hill of the same
name in the municipio of Juigalpa.

CABEZAS, RIGOBERTO. General Cabezas led an armed
group opposing the presidency of Dr. Roberto Sacasa

in 1893, and in skirmishes at El Cuero and on the Río
Fonseca, several of his men lost their lives.   He and
his associate Moisés Cardoce of Masaya had established
the finca "San Diego" the year before.

CABINET OF PATRICIO RIVAS.   The ministers of the Patri-
cio Rivas government were installed on 13 and 14 Sep-
tember of 1856, when the provisional president appointed
the following: Ministry--Relaciones Exteriores (Foreign
Relations), Incumbent--Licenciado Pedro Cardenal;
Guerra (War), Don Nicasio del Castillo; Hacienda
(Treasury), Licenciado Francisco Baca; Gobernación
(Government), Don Sebastián Salinas.   The time was
critical.   It coincided with the turning-point Batalla de
San Jacinto (q. v.).

CABLE SUMARINO.   In the year 1882, a submarine telegraph cable was laid to connect San Juan del Sur with
the outer world.   This followed the first telegraph
service in the country in 1876.

CABO DE HORNOS.   Comarca or district in the municipio
of La Paz, León.

CACAO (Money).   The use of chocolate beans for money
was well-established among the Nicaraos of the Isthmian
area around Rivas, hence it was termed "money" by the
Spanish.   The cultivation of cacao was a jealously guard-
ed monopoly in the Isthmian area.   It was, in effect, a
"mint. "

CACAO, EL.   1) A comarca or district in the municipio of
Jinotepe, Carazo department.
2) A comarca or district in the municipio of La Paz,
León.
3) A district in the municipio of Ciudad Darío in the
department of Matagalpa.
4) A district in the municipio and department of
Matagalpa.
5) A district in the municipio of Matiguás, department of Matagalpa.
6) A district in the municipio of Santa Lucía, department of Boaco.
7) A comarca or district of the municipio of Santa
Teresa, Carazo department.

CACAQUAT.   The god of cacao or chocolate; an idol representing this god was erected at the time of cacao harvest when the mitote (q. v.) was danced.

CACERES, ANTONIO. Recollect missionary who came to León with Antonio de Aquila in 1745, and who then went to Boaco Viejo, and gathered 200 Caribs in a settlement called San Antonio. In 1749, Cáceres became the only martyr of this particular missionary movement, when a Miskito raid on the settlements of Muy Muy Viejo, Comoapa, Lavajo, and Boaco Viejo resulted in his death with that of many others. Boaco Viejo was then moved 40 miles west, presumably for better protection.

CACHUERCOS. A Nicaraguan conservative political party nickname opposed to Pirujos (q. v.).

CACICAZGO. Chieftaincy, or tribes and territories under the rule of a chief or cacique. Since the word came from Haiti, the general use was probably spread throughout the Caribbean by Spanish conquerors stemming from that island originally. See CACIQUE.

CACIQUE. 1) A word used widely in Spanish America to signify headman or chief. Of Haitian origin, the word came into the Spanish early, and has come to denote through Latin America the influential powers behind the throne of local politics. The system is called caciquismo.
    2) El Cacique, a finca or plantation in Estelí department.

CACM. Central American Common Market.

CADIZ, SPAIN. Ancient "Gades" of the Greeks, tied in the work of some scholars to the lost continent of Atlantis, Cádiz from 1774 was the official Spanish port to which Nicaraguan colonial commerce could be directed. The port was changed from Seville at that time due to the far better harbor at Cádiz.

CAIMITO. 1) A district of the municipio of San Juan de Tola, Rivas department.
    2) El Caimito, a comarca or district in the municipio of Jinotepe, Carazo department.

CALABAZAS, LAS. A district in the municipio of Ciudad Darío, department of Matagalpa.

CALABRIA, LA. A hacienda in the municipio of Rivas.

CALANDRACAS. One of the two major Nicaraguan political
    parties of the 1840's. The opposition party, in 1849,
    it was active in the Southern parts of the country, and
    included Bernabe Somoza, who was providing leadership
    of a revolutionary nature. See also TIMBUCOS.

CALAVERAS. A height in the region of Ciudad Darío mu-
    nicipio, Matagalpa department.

CALCALOTEPE. A district of the municipio of Tipitapa,
    department of Managua.

CALCIUM CARBONATE CALIZA. There are extensive de-
    posits of this mineral in Nicaragua, some of them 99%
    pure, from which high quality lime may be produced.
    Known areas of deposits are El Salto, San Cayetano,
    San Rafael del Sur, Brito Sapoa, San Francisco en
    Rivas, the Valley of the Bocay River, and near Ocotal.
    Nicaragua has a wide variety of minerals, many of the
    nonmetallic ones such as this lime being valuable as
    well as widely distributed.

CALDERA. A geological term for a crater, frequently the
    result of subsidence of the top of a volcanic mountain.
    There are many such in Nicaragua frequently with lakes
    in their depths. Lake Apoyo, a caldera in Nicaragua,
    has over 20 square miles of water surface, about the
    same size as Crater Lake, Oregon. Among other cal-
    dera are Jiloá, Asososca, Tiscapa, Nejapa, Chiltepe,
    and Coseguina.

CALENDAR, NICARAO. The Mexican-derived calendar, used
    by the Nicaraos in southern Nicaragua before the Span-
    ish conquest, had 20 months and a five-day interim peri-
    od each year called Nemonteni. The months are: Acatl,
    Ocelotl, Cuahutli, Cozcauautli, Olín, Tecpatl, Quiahuitl,
    Xochitl, Cipactli, Ehecatl, Cali, Cuetzpalín, Coatl,
    Miquitztle, Mazatl, Tochtli, Atl, Itzcuintli, Ozomatl,
    Malinatl (all q. v.). Each festival name represented a
    God--as tiger, king of the buzzards, iguana, wind, etc.

CALERA, LA. 1) A comarca or district in the municipio of
    Achuapa, León.
        2) A hacienda on the northeast slopes of the dead
    volcano Mombacho, near Granada.

CALI. A word meaning "house," one of the month festivals and gods of the pre-conquest Nicarao tribe around Rivas.

CALICO. A spring in the area of San Dionisio.

CALIFORNIA. 1) Comarca or district in the municipio of La Paz, León.
2) Hacienda in the municipio of La Paz, León.
3) La California, a territory of the municipio of Del Carmen, Managua department.

CALIHUATE, EL. Comarca or district of the municipio of Santa Teresa, Carazo department.

CALLAHAN, CARLOS. In 1856 Administrator of the Customs House in Granada, he was also a correspondent of the New Orleans newspaper the Picayune. He joined the Cole expedition to hunt for food and lost his life on September 14, in the famous Battle of San Jacinto, in the National War.

CALLAO, EL. Coffee hacienda in the Sierras de Managua, of the Distrito Nacional.

CALLE, MARTIN DE LA. Captain in Gil González Dávila's expedition of discovery of Nicaragua in 1522.

CALLE DE ENMEDIO. District in the municipio of Potosí, Rivas department.

CALLE DE LOS BESOS. Comarca or district of the municipio of Nagarote, León department.

CALLE REAL DE TOYAPA. Comarca or district in the municipio of Larreynaga.

CALLEJON DE TICUANTEPE. A district of the municipio of Nindiri in Masaya department.

CALL LETTERS, RADIO (YN for Nicaragua). In each case, see the station name which is cross-referenced. YNAE, Radio Musun; YNAG, Radio Coseguina; YNAJ, La Voz de América; YNAV, Radio Continental; YNAW, Radio Colinas; YNBC, Ondas Segovias; YNBO, Radio Musical; YNC, Radio Capital; YNCA, Radio Atlántico; YNCR, Radio Mongalo; YNCW, Radio Occidental; YNCZ, Radio Progreso; YND, Unión Radio; YNDM, Ondas Sonoras;

YNDN, Radio City; YNE, Radio Femenina; YNG, Radio
Tic Tac; YNGF, Ondas del Sur; YNGR, Radio Zelaya;
YNHC, Radio Hernández; YNHI, Relay for YNP Circuit;
YNJM, Radio Norte; YNKW, Radio Libertad; YNL, Re-
lay for YNP Circuit; YNLL, Radio Masaya; YNLU,
Radio Managua; YNM, Radiofusora Nacional; YNMS,
Radio Phillips, Ondas Populares; YNO, Radio Ivania;
YNOL, La Ondas de Luz; YNOP, Radio Cultural Carazo;
YNOW, Radio Corporación; YNP, Circuito YNP; YNPR,
Radio Centro-Americana; YNQ, La Voz de Victoria;
YNRA, La Voz de Chinandega; YNRC, Radio Católica;
YNRD, Radio Cinco Noventa; YNRM, Radio Alma Latina;
YNRZ, Radio Centenario; YNRPS, Radio Granada; YNRR,
Radio Reforma; YNS, Radio Titania; YNSC, Radio Cen-
tauro; YNTJ, Radio el Eco de las Brumas; YNTS,
Radio Mil; YNTW, Radio Centro; YNTZ, Radio Jinotega;
YNUW, Radio Darío; YNVOZ, Radio Reloj; YNW, Radio
Mundial; YNWA, Radio Mundial/Radio Cinco Noventa;
YNW-1, Relay for Radio Mundial; YNW-2, Radio Mun-
dial; YNW-3, Relay for Radio Mundial; YNWS, Alma
Nica, La Onda del Alegría; YNWW, Radio Sport; YNWX,
Radio Atenas; YNX, Estación X (Juigalpa), Relay for
Estación X (Estelí), Relay for Estación X (Matagalpa),
Relay for Estación X (Chichigalpa); YNXZ, Radio Coci-
bolca.

CALPULES, LOS.   1) District of Pueblo Nuevo municipio,
Estelí department.
   2) An old Spanish mine near Amatillo in Nueva
Segovia department with a tunnel 35 feet long and a
shaft 13 feet deep, as well as some other workings.

CALPULES Y APALI, LOS.   A site given to Francisco
Bellorín in 1903, from aboriginal Indian lands in Estelí
department.

CALPULLI.   An institution something like a town council
which effected local government under the cacique (q. v.)
in a cacicazgo.   The council was concerned with defense,
justice, commerce and trade, as well as related aspects
of government.

CALVARIO, EL.   1) Church in León, completed about 1810,
with some neoclassic influence upon the basic baroque.
Engaged columns replace the older niches for statues,
and classical cornices are evident.
   2) A district of the city of León (with a handsome

colonial church of the same name).
3) A gold mine in the Chontales department opened in 1838, owned by George Edward Chambers.

CAMARON, EL.   District in the department and municipio of Rivas.

CAMARONA, LA.   A comarca or district in the municipio of Santa Teresa, Carazo department.

CAMELOAGATOAZLE.   An aboriginal game of skill and strength practiced by the Managuans and called by modern players, "El Sube y Baja."

CAMMOCK, SUSSEX.   An officer (captain) of the Somers Island Company, which had occupied Bermuda, who was directed to attack shipping or ports anywhere in the Caribbean during the Anglo-Spanish War of 1625. Thereupon in 1629, he discovered San Andrés and Old Providence Islands just off the Mosquito (Nicaraguan) Coast. This led to the formation in 1630 of the Providence Company, all of which had later military and political repercussions in Central America.   The expanded activities of this company led to British occupation of the coast at Cabo Gracias a Dios, and possibly this early also at Bluefields.   Cammock's voyage in 1633 opened up the Mosquito Coast to history.   He moored in the Mosquito Cays, trading with the Sumus on the mainland in small boats.   The shallow coast was destined to be a place where small traders would operate with small sailing craft and various kinds of dugouts.

CAMOAPA.   Municipio in the department of Boaco, second city of the department.   It is ten miles southeast of Boaco.   Historically the city had two other previous seats, the first being destroyed by periodical raids by Sambos, Mosquito, and English in 1749.   The second location was near the monolith of Cuisaltepe.   Now known as Pueblo Viejo, these ruins date from 1752.   In 1768 the present site was chosen, as San Francisco de Camoapan.   The city named Camoapa is the cabacera of the municipio.   The manufacture of straw hats, and the raising of sugar, coffee, and henequen are principal industries.   Population: 16,000; area, 1070 square miles; there are 36 districts.

CAMPAMENTO, EL.   Comarca or district in the municipio

of El Sauce, León department.

CAMPAMENTOS, LOS.   District in the municipio of San
Jorge, Rivas department.

CAMPAÑA, LA.   A cattle ranch in the Tipitapa municipio
of Managua department.

CAMPAÑA DE LA INDEPENDENCIA   see   RIVAS, INDEPEND-
ENCE AND POTOSI, PUEBLO

CAMPAÑON, FRANCISCO DE.   Following close on the heels
of Captain Benito Hurtado (q. v.), in 1526 Captain Campañón crossed the northern part of Nicaragua to take
charge of the "Pueblo de las Minas, " later called Santa
María de la Esperanza, in the region of Juanamostega.

CAMPESINOS POBRES.   "Poor farmers"; essentially landless
country folk, tenant farmers, and day laborers.

CAMPO DEL MARTE.   The "Field of Mars, " or traditional
military compound in Managua, was frequently occupied
by U. S. Marines.   It is presently the site of the Nicaraguan Military Academy, where young officers are
turned out for the effective Guardia Nacional, the sole
armed force (with army, police, air and naval branches).

CAMPOS, LOS.   Comarca or district in the municipio of
San Marcos, Carazo department.

CAMPOS, IGNACIO DE.   Founder of the first Latin school
in Nicaragua in 1838-39, Maestro Campos was active
in Masaya.

CAMPUZANO.   A district of the municipio of Nindiri, department of Masaya.

CAMUSASCA NUMERO DOS.   Comarca or district in the
municipio of Villa Somoza, Chontales.

CAMUSASCA NUMERO UNO.   Comarca or district in the
municipio of Villa Somoza, Chontales.

CANADA, LA.   1) A district in the municipio of La Trinidad, department of Estelí.
     2) Place on the old La Concordia road in La Trinidad
municipio of Estelí department, where many pre-conquest

ceramics and idols are found.

CAÑADA DEL FORDO. An abandoned mine in the area of
   Macuelizo, in the Nueva Segovia department, whose ore
   includes pyrites in quartz, with gold and silver traces.

CAÑADA, RIO LA. A stream in La Trinidad municipio,
   Estelí department.

CAÑADAS. A term for local settlements of San Ramón
   Matagalpa Indians; about 16,000 persons are so identified.
   The term means "ravines"; hence, perhaps "hill-billies."

CAÑA DE CASTILLA. 1) A village six miles southwest of
   Granada.
      2) Comarca or district in the municipio of La Liber-
   tad, Chontales.

CANAL (Technical Data). In April, 1895, a U.S. Commission was appointed to review what was known of the canal route through Nicaragua. as to its ultimate feasibility. The Maritime Canal Company (q.v.) had by this
   time failed. The key to the whole success of a lock
   canal is the summit-level supply of water, which in
   this case is furnished more than adequately by Lake
   Nicaragua. The distance, sea to sea, is 174 miles.
   There are three main divisions: Western, Lake Nicaragua to Pacific; Central, lake and river navigation;
   Eastern, San Juan River to the Atlantic. The Western,
   Lajas to Brito, is 17.7 miles cut through an elevation
   of 154 feet above sea level, 44 feet above the lake.
   Three 30-foot-lift locks and a 25-foot tide lock are
   planned. Waterway in this division is to be 30 feet
   deep. Lajas (on lake) to Fort San Carlos, 56.5 miles.
   Fort San Carlos to Ochoa, 69 miles. (Total lake and
   river, 125.5 miles.) Child's plan was to extend the
   summit level of the lake to Castillo Rapids, 37.3 miles
   from the mouth. Menocal, more boldly, planned a
   great dam 106 feet high at Ochoa, 69 miles from the
   lake. The eastern division below Ochoa would be only
   31.4 miles to Greytown. There would be three locks
   on the Atlantic side, of 40-, 35-, and 31-foot lifts.
   Greytown harbor would be improved by a 1000-foot
   breakwater. Later surveys of the 1930's by Lieutenant-
   Colonel Dan I. Sultan have not vastly modified the
   Childs-Menocal plans. (See drawing.)

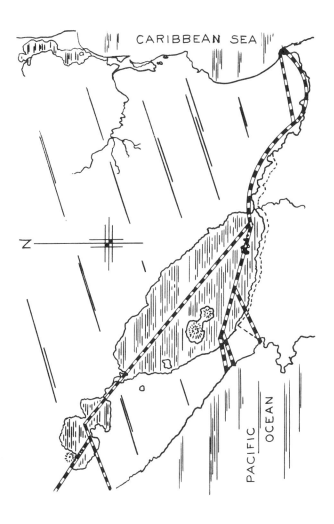

Canal Routes

Westward passage, the "secret of a strait."

CANAL, EL. A coffee hacienda in the municipio of Niquinohomo in the department of Masaya.

CANAL MONCADA. A channel between the Río Silico and
the lower part of Pearl Lagoon, thus opening to small-
boat traffic a direct inland route to Bluefields.

CANALE NAPOLEONE DE NICARAGUA, LA. Proposed
name for a canal company to be formed by Louis Napoleon Bonaparte (q. v.). Bonaparte escaped from the fortress of Ham (where he had been held a political prisoner) on May 25, 1846, proceeding at once to London
where he wrote a famous pamphlet on the advocacy of
a Nicaraguan canal route. He compared Nicaragua to
Constantinople as a meeting point of seas and continents,
and hence as an entrepot of commerce. British interest
was focused on a Nicaraguan route from this time on
(rather than a Tehuantepec or Panama site). The Napoleon canal plan was to proceed across both Lakes
Nicaragua and Managua and down the valley of the Estero
Real to the Bay of Fonseca. It was most grandiose of
all Nicaraguan Canal plans.

CANAS. A district of the municipio of San Juan de Tola,
Rivas department.

CAÑAS, LAS. 1) Comarca or district of the municipio of
El Jicaral, León.
2) A district of the municipio of San Juan de Limay,
Estelí department.
3) Thermal spring in Carazo department, in the area
of Santa Teresa.
4) A district in the municipio and department of
Matagalpa.
5) A district of Terrabona municipio, Matagalpa department.

CAÑAS BLANCAS OCCIDENTALES. Comarca or district in
the municipio of Jinotepe, Carazo department.

CAÑAS BLANCAS ORIENTALES. Comarca or district in the
municipio of Jinotepe, Carazo department.

CAÑAS-JEREZ TREATY. A treaty between Nicaragua and
Costa Rica signed April 15, 1858, settling the boundary
dispute which had arisen in connection with transit concessions eight years earlier. The agreement was facili-
tated by Félix Belly (q. v.).

CANAZ, DON ANTONIO JOSE. Minister to the United
States from the Central American Confederacy after its
formation, who presented upon his arrival in Washington a note to the U. S. State Department concerning the
importance of a canal on the Nicaraguan route. He was
answered by Henry Clay, then U. S. Secretary of State,
concerning the deep interest of the U. S. in the project.
Clay also ordered all possible data to be gathered.

"CANCION DE OTOÑO EN PRIMAVERA. " Most famous,
perhaps, of Darío's (q. v.) poems, and very characteristic of his thought and style, is this poem of "Autumn in
Spring. " It is known well throughout the Spanish-speaking world, beginning: "Juventúd, divino tesoro, Ya te
vas para no volver.... " In free translation: Youth oh
youth--divinest treasure, Now gone, you will give back
no years. When I wish, I weep no measure, But without wishing, I oft drop tears.

CANDIL, EL. One of the periodicals developed in Boaco in
the period 1915-1937.

CANGREJAL. 1) District in the municipio of San Jorge,
Rivas department.
2) Waterfall on the Río Mico in the municipio Villa
Somoza, Chontales.
3) El Cangrejal, a mountain complex along the central
part of the Spanish colonial frontier, a rough line of demarcation between the colonial holdings and the threatening pirates and their Sambo-Miskito allies during the
earlier colonial centuries.

CANGREJITO. Waterfall on the Río Mico in the municipio
Villa Somoza, Chontales.

CANGREJO, EL. Comarca or district in the municipio of
Jinotepe, Carazo department.

CANNON see CANNON Y GROSS

CANNON Y GROSS. A store and drugstore established in
Matiguás in the year 1896, named as a firm for the
proprietors. These men were later executed for their
part in an incident at El Castillo when they attempted
to blow up a steamer on the San Juan River, the El
Diamante. They were summarily executed by the Zelaya
regime, helping to precipitate American intervention in
1912, which led to a long and bitter semi-occupation.

CANOA. A word which seems to have derived from the
eastern Caribbean Arawak tongue, and which from the
time of Columbus has been given to light-weight indigenous craft--in English it became "canoe. " The canoa
of Nicaragua is a specialized vessel, however, and now
quite rare. Relatively small (12' to 16' in length), it
has not the shape or capacity of the other dugout types
such as dori, panga, or pipante (all q. v.). Examples
show a rounded bottom, interior ends rounded off, and
a unique and characteristic deck-like projection at both
ends, not extending over a graceful hull-continuation as
in the pipante, but shelf-like, about 2" to 3" thick and
quite squared-off at the outer extremities. Such vessels
are shown in Egyptian wall-painting hunting scenes of
5000 years ago. Such deck projections are found among
some Pacific peoples and the Florida Seminoles. The
canoa seems to have been planned as a one- or two-
man boat, and was probably paddled, not rowed. Canoas presently in Nicaragua are probably over 100 years
old, and are nowhere in current use as are the pipante
and dori. A canoa viewed as late as 1956 was about
12' long, 2 1/2' wide, and had two projecting platforms,
one each at bow and stern (see drawing). It is especially remarkable that this type of stubby vessel is almost
identical to that pictured in Oviedo's La historia general
de las Indias, published in 1535. The word has been applied as "canoe" to small boats over the world, early to
such variant types as the Ojibway birch bark canoes.

CANOAS, LAS. 1) Cattle ranch in the municipio of Yalí,
Jinotega department.
2) A district of the municipio of Tipitapa, department of Managua.

CAÑO BRAVO. A major channel of the Río San Juan delta,
between the main stream and the Río Colorado.

CAÑO MADRE. The "mother canal" is one name for the
Río Colorado.

CAÑO NEGRO. A channel which empties into the Río Indio
along the east coast above Greytown.

CAÑO WALPASIKSA AWALA. This "canal" is one of the
two major downstream branches of the Río Prinzapolka,
which separates about 18 miles from the Caribbean and
creates an island between its two channels which is as

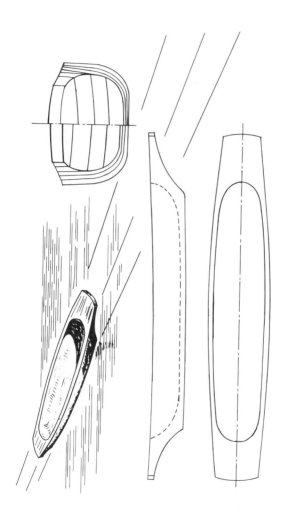

Canoa

An obsolete but still extant type of dugout craft, characterized by shelf-like fore and aft "decks," which is pre-conquest
in origin.

much as eight miles wide; this channel enters the sea at Walpasiksa.

CANTORES DE LA MUSICA SACRA, LOS. These singers of sacred music are one of two major choral groups in Managua.

CANTOS DE VIDA Y ESPERANZA. The fact that Darío could write "songs of life and hope" indicates that possibly his languorous and exotic tropical hedonism was tempered by hope. He considered art a mystical form of revelation, an adventure in which the artist was cast as suffering hero.

CAOBA. The mahogany variety widely distributed in eastern Nicaragua. Swietena macrophylla is essentially the same as "Honduran mahogany" and is a light red tropical hardwood of great strength, stability, and durability. Logs are cut in 12-foot lengths, roughly squared for transport, and often have a section four feet square. Much furniture in Nicaragua is built of this wood. Mahogany does not grow in groves, but as isolated trees which makes it difficult to find and expensive to cut and transport. The Weiss-Fricker lumber interests (Pensacola, Florida) in the 1940's cut a mahogany log 72 feet long, six feet in diameter at the small end and 12 feet in diameter at the butt. Such trees were not uncommon in the primeval and virgin forest.

CAPADO, EL. Comarca or district of the municipio of León, León department.

CAPITALS, DEPARTMENTAL. The name of the city or town is given first, then its department: Boaco (Boaco), Jinotepe (Carazo), Chinandega (Chinandega), Juigalpa (Chontales), Estelí (Estelí), Granada (Granada), Jinotega (Jinotega), León (León), Somoto (Madriz), Managua (Managua), Masaya (Masaya), Matagalpa (Matagalpa), Ocotal (Nueva Segovia), San Carlos (Río San Juan), Rivas (Rivas), Bluefields (Zelaya).

CAPITULACION. Whimsically defined as a "license to steal," this was a royal license of Spanish colonial days permitting a conquistador to appoint officers, exploit land and people, and recruit an army and colonists. In return he gave as tax to the crown the "royal fifth," or 20% of the "take."

CAPTAIN GENERAL. The office of the nominal head of the Captaincy General of Guatemala of which Nicaragua was a part, was very much that of provincial viceroy, other than in matters of very important policy decisions; in effect these Spanish governors ruled with close ties to Spain, in many respects closer than to the viceroyalty.

CAPTAINCY GENERAL OF GUATEMALA. The political entity under the colonial viceroyalty of New Spain which included Nicaragua. The capital was in the old Guatemalan city of Antigua until 1773, when it was moved to the present site of Guatemala City following disastrous earthquakes. The Spanish rule under the captaincy general was not as complete as might be supposed. In effect this political unit--which comprised in addition to Nicaragua the other Central American states and also Chiapas and Belice--was semi-independent of the viceroyalty centered in Mexico, and had close ties to the Council of the Indies and the king.

CAPTAINS-GENERAL OF THE KINGDOM OF GUATEMALA (57). (Includes acting governors. Dates indicate terms of office.)
Alvarado Contreras, Pedro de, 1525-1541.
Cueva de Alvarado, Doña Beatriz de la, 1541.
Marroquín, Francisco, 1541-1542, jointly with
    Cueva, Francisco de la, 1541-1542.
Maldonado, Alonso de, 1542-1548.
Cerrato, Alonso Lopez, 1548-1555.
Quesada, Antonio Rodríguez de, 1555-1558.
Ramírez de Quiñones, Pedro, 1558-1559.
Landecho, Juan Núñez de, 1559-1563.
Briceño, Francisco, 1564-1569.
González, Antonio, 1570-1572.
Villalobos, Pedro de, 1573-1578.
Valverde, García de, 1579-1589.
Rueda, Pedro Mallén de, 1589-1592.
Sande, Francisco de, 1593-1596.
Abaunza, Alvaro Gómez de, 1596-1598.
Criado de Castilla, Alonso, 1598-1611.
Péraza Ayala Castilla y Rojas, Antonio, 1611-1626.
Acuña, Diego de, 1626-1633.
Quiñones y Osorio, Alvaro de, 1634-1642.
Avendaño, Diego de, 1642-1649.
Lara y Mogrobejo, Antonio de, 1649-1654.
Altamirano y Velasco, Fernando de, 1654-1657.
Carrillo de Mendoza, Jerónimo Garcés, 1657-1659.

Mencos, Martín Carlos de, 1659-1667.
Alvarez Alfonso Rosica de Caldas, Sebastián, 1668-1670.
Saenz de Mañosca y Murillo, Juan de Santo Matía, 1670-
   1672.
Escobedo, Fernando Francisco de, 1672-1682.
Augurto y Alava, Juan Miguel de, 1682-1684.
Enríquez de Guzmán, Enrique, 1684-1688.
Barrios y Leal, Jacinto de, 1688-1695.
Escals, José de, 1695-1696
Berrospe, Gabriel Sánchez de, 1696-1700.
Heduardo, Juan Jeronimo, 1701-1702.
Ceballos y Villagutierre, Alonso, 1702-1703.
Espinosa de los Monteros, José Osorio, 1704-1706.
Cosio y Campa, Toribio José de, 1706-1716.
Rivas, Francisco Rodríguez de, 1716-1724.
Echevers y Suvisa, Antonio Pedro de, 1724-1733.
Rivera y Villalón, Pedro de, 1733-1742.
Rivera y Santa Cruz, Tomás de, 1742-1748.
Araujo y Río, Juan de, 1748-1751.
Montaos y Sotomayor, José Vásquez Prego, 1752-1753.
Velarde y Cienfuegos, Juan, 1753-1754.
Arcos y Moreno, Alonso de, 1754-1760.
Heredia, José Fernández de, 1761-1765.
Salazar y Herrea Nájera y Mendoza, Pedro de, 1765-
   1771.
Gonzales Bustillo y Villaseñor, Juan, 1771-1773.
Mayorga, Martín de, 1773-1779.
Gálvez, Matías de, 1779-1783.
Estachería, José de, 1783-1789.
Troncoso Martínez del Rincón, Bernardo, 1789-1794.
Domas y Valle, José, 1794-1801.
González Mollinedo y Saravia, Antonio, 1801-1811.
Bustamente y Guerra, José, 1811-1818.
Urrutia, Carlos, 1818-1821.
Gainza, Gabino, 1821

   The Captains General as listed from 1525 on were in
general charge of Nicaragua from the time of the conquest to 1821, and in combination with the Presidents
of the Confederation of Central American States, the
Spanish Governors of Nicaragua, and the Presidents
of Nicaragua give a complete listing of the executive
power applicable for four and a half centuries.

CAPUCHINS. A monastic Catholic order supporting a seminary in the Caribbean coastal area, as well as churches
   and schools.

CAPULIN, EL.   A district north of Granada.

CARACEÑO.   Resident of the department of Carazo.

CARACOL, EL.   A district of Terrabona municipio, Matagalpa department.

CARACOL, RIO EL.   A stream in Pueblo Nuevo municipio
of Estelí department.

CARACOLES.   Comarca or district in the municipio of
Achuapa, León.

CARAO.   1) A district in the municipio of La Trinidad, department of Estelí.
2) El Carao, a high "altiplano esteliano" in Estelí
department, unique tableland formation at over 4000
feet altitude.
3) El Carao, a district in the municipio and department of Estelí.
4) El Carao, a mountain in the municipio of Estelí;
altitude: 4550 feet.

CARAOS, LOS.   Comarca or district in the municipio of
Achuapa, León.

CARATERA.   A district in the municipio and department of
Matagalpa.

CARAZO.   Established in 1891. this department is bounded
to the north by Masaya, to the south (slightly southwest)
by the Pacific; to the east by Granada and a part of
Rivas, and to the west by Managua.   It is about 36
miles from north to south, and 30 miles from east to
west.   The principal towns are Diriamba, Jinotepe, and
San Marcos.   There are eight municipios: Jinotepe,
Diriamba, San Marcos, Santa Teresa, La Conquista,
La Paz (La Paz de Oriente), El Rosario, and Dolores.
Jinotepe is the cabacera.   While many other crops are
produced, coffee and cacao are principal products.   The
area is one of the best agricultural regions of the country, the Carazo uplands being especially adapted to coffee culture.   One of the principal chieftains or caciques
meeting discoverer Gil González Dávila on April 17,
1522, was Diriangen, who had a considerable army and
much evidence of wealth in the form of gold ornaments.
The population is currently over 82,000.

CARAZO, EVARISTO. President of Nicaragua 1887-1889, Carazo died before the end of his term. He received protests from Costa Rica and Colombia concerning the Cárdenas-Menocal (canal) Treaty (q. v.) signed during that period.

CARBONALES, LOS. 1) A district in the municipio of La Trinidad, Estelí department.
2) Mountain lake in Estelí department.

CARCA. 1) Indian tribe inland in the Chontales region, shown by Squiers on his 1851 map as <u>Cookra.</u>
2) A mountain complex and the pass through it, used in Spanish colonial days on the Sambo-Miskito frontier.

CARCOQUE. A 250-acre grant of a hacienda made to don Juan de Diós Medina in the valley of Estelí, March 3, 1726.

CARDENAL, PEDRO (Licenciado) see CABINET OF PATRICIO RIVAS

CARDENAS. 1) Cabacera of the municipio of the same name, on the south coast of Lake Nicaragua. It is the nearest lake "port" to the Solentiname Islands in the southeastern portion of the lake.
2) A municipio in the department of Rivas, having an area of 104 square miles and a population of 2000. Bounded on the north by Lake Nicaragua, south by the country of Costa Rica; east by Río San Juan department, and west by Rivas and San Juan del Sur. Peñas Blancas, the frontier point with Costa Rica, is in the municipio. There are five districts or comarcas.

CARDENAS, ADAN. President of Nicaragua, 1883-1887; he had to face war with Barrios of Guatemala, who resented Cárdenas' approval of the Freylinghuysen-Zavala Treaty (q. v.). He was also the first governor of the newly created department of Masaya in 1883.

CARDENAS-MENOCAL TREATY. A treaty on canal concessions signed by Menocal, the distinguished U. S. -Cuban engineer and perennial canal surveyor, during the Carazo administration in 1888. The treaty was protested by Costa Rica and Colombia.

CARDOCE, MOISES see CABEZAS, RIGOBERTO

CARDON, EL FARO DE. Lighthouse established at the port of Corinto in the year 1876. The light operated from 6:00 p. m. to 6:00 a. m. It was supported by a tax levied on each vessel entering the port.

CARGAS see CONTLES

CARIBBEAN COAST. Greatly resembling the coastal areas of the states of Florida or Louisiana, the coast of Nicaragua is laced with inshore lagoons and is backed by a large swampy hinterland. Mangrove islands, sluggish rivers, long beaches, and other characteristics are those of tropical or semi-tropical lowlands.

CARIBBEAN FEDERATION. As conceived by the filibuster William Walker in the 1850's, this federation would have consisted of the five Central American countries and the island of Cuba, and would have developed as a significant power in the region, with the possibility of allying itself with the slave-holding states of the U. S.

CARIBBEAN INTRACOASTAL WATERWAY. Two-thirds of the over 300 miles of Nicaraguan east coast are navigable for small, shallow-draft craft in sheltered channels and lagoons, and since prehistoric times these waterways have been used for communication. There is no improvement of these passages, the only man-made additions being portage trails called "haulovers." However, a development similar to the U. S. Intracoastal Waterway would be quite feasible due to the similarity of terrain.

CARIBBEAN LEGION. A loose grouping of scattered armed bands of liberal and radical revolutionaries which developed following World War II, avowedly dedicated to the overthrow of Latin American dictators. Hardly a formal organization, and more a "state of mind" as one writer characterized it, the Legion did take part in the Cayo Confites expedition in 1947, with which Fidel Castro and Alberto Bayo were connected. Bayo, a Spanish Loyalist colonel in the Civil War of the Thirties, lived in Mexico after that war, studied Chinese guerrilla developments, and became an advisor to the Legion. In addition to Cayo Confites, members of this group also fought in Costa Rica in 1948. Nicaraguan legionnaires promoted Bayo to "general" in 1948. Bayo also trained Ernesto "Che" Guevara--part of his written manual for the Legion stated "always remember Sandino." The Legion met during the 1950's in San José, Costa Rica, where the existing government was favorable to them. There was a "Sandino Brigade" of the Legion in the Cayo Confites operation. Guevara and Castro, following Bayo's Legion tutelage, brought Sandino-style guerrilla warfare to Cuba. The Legion was also involved in 1955 hostilities between Nicaragua and Costa Rica.

CARIBBEAN PINE. A significant commercial resource for Nicaragua, growing in the Northeastern part of the country, perhaps stimulated by infertility of soil following "slash-and-burn" or milpah (q. v.) agriculture.

CARIBES DE SOLENTINAME. A pueblo on the slopes of the volcano Madera on Omotepe Island, Lake Nicaragua, in early colonial times.

CARIBICIS see QUIRIBIES

CARIBIES see QUIRIBIES

CARIMAN, ANDRES. A Flemish officer in Spanish service who was named to the post of governor in Jicaro on the Nueva Segovia frontier, which was considered strategic in 1767. He was one of a cadre of 50 officers sent out by Charles III. The plan was to establish a standing colonial army. The problem of "criollos" (q. v.) versus "peninsulares" (q. v.) was hardly understood.

CARMEN, EL. 1) A cattle hacienda in the municipio of Ciudad Darío, Matagalpa department.
        2) Coffee hacienda of the firm of Moisés Baltodano y Hermanos in Diriamba municipio of Carazo department.
        3) A coffee hacienda in the municipio of Niquinohomo, department of Masaya.
        4) A district and hacienda on the northeast coast of Zapatera Island in Lake Nicaragua.
        5) Important finca in the municipio of La Concepción, department of Masaya.
        6) A villa; the cabacera of the municipio del Carmen; the population is 859, smallest among the subdivisions of the department of Managua. Elevated to the status of Villa in 1907, it has not changed greatly since that time.

69

CAROLINAS, LAS. Hacienda and district in the municipio and department of Granada.

CARQUITA. Comarca or district in the municipio of La Libertad, Chontales department.

CARRETA. The typical Nicaraguan oxcart, a heavy, rugged vehicle, capable of carrying two tons or more when drawn by a four-ox team, and about the only form of workable transport in heavy axle-deep mud in certain wet seasons. (It differs greatly from the Costa Rican light-weight, decorated "coffee cart.") The carreta resembles certain Egyptian carvings of carts used by the "sea-peoples" or Philistines in 1200 B.C. It has solid wooden wheels about 4" to 6" in diameter, 4" and more thick, with iron, 1/2" thick segmented iron tires spiked on, and hubs 16" in diameter and 16" to 20" wide. The hubs run on wooden axles, held on by pins; the frame is simple and rugged, the yoke attached by thongs to horns of the oxen, and shaped for their necks. (See drawing.)

CARRETA QUEBRADA. A district of the municipio of Sebaco, Matagalpa department.

CARRILLAL, EL. Comaraca or district in the municipio of Diriamba, department of Carazo.

CARRIZAL, EL. 1) District in the municipio of San Dionisio, Matagalpa department.
2) District in the municipio of San Juan del Sur, Rivas department.

CARRIZAL Y TERRABONA. Cattle hacienda from colonial days in the department of Matagalpa, granted to Manuel and Juan Reyes in 1708; extent, 280 acres.

CARRIZO, EL. Comarca or district in the municipio of Achuapa, León.

CARTER, C. B. A North American who as commandant of the (Marine-supervised) Nicaraguan National Guard, 1925-1927, authored an interestingly titled article, "The Kentucky Feud in Nicaragua" (World's Work, July, 1927). Major Carter was in charge when Emiliano Chamorro's coup of October 25, 1925, took place. He was outgunned and essentially helpless, but stated he would

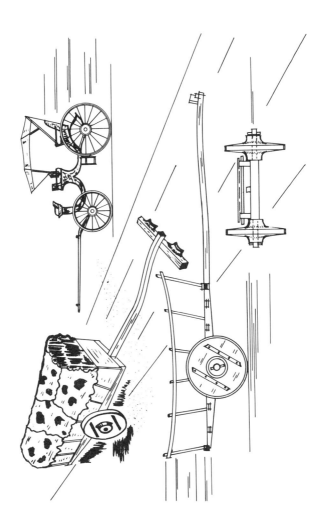

Carreta and Coche

Distinctive in design from the Costa Rican cart, the oxcart is of heavy solid wood construction, rawhide covers. The "coche" is a taxi still in use in several towns.

"take orders from the President" (Solorzano). Chamorro had not only the guns but also political support.
Carter, contrary to Nicaraguan belief that whoever controlled the acropolis fortress "La Loma" in Managua
controlled the country, felt the fort could be taken, and
that if the government had loyal, well-equipped troops
the balance of Nicaraguan politics would not be so affected by the old fort. It was a large "if."

CARTILLA DE SAN JUAN. On March 10, 1790, Intendente
of the province of Masaya Colonel Juan de Ayssa decreed as a first text for scholastic use the Cartilla.
There must have been a school in Masaya at the time,
as indicated by the decree, although there is no other
evidence of it.

CASA COLORADA. A territory of the National District, department of Managua, also a favorite location for second
homes due to its excellent location on top of the Sierras
de Managua. See ZONA MONTAÑOSO.

CASA NUEVA. Comarca or district in the municipio of La
Paz, León department.

CASARES. Bathing beach in Carazo department on the Pacific Ocean.

CASAS VIEJAS. A district in the municipio of Ciudad Darío,
department of Matagalpa.

CASAS VIEJAS, RIO. A stream tributary to the Río Grande
de Matagalpa, in Ciudad Darío municipio.

CASCADE DE ESTANZUELA. A beautiful waterfall in Estelí
department, used as a bathing resort.

CASCAMOPOPO. A waterfall of approximately 100 feet in
height on the Río Guina tributary of the Río Bocay in
Jinotega department.

CASITAS, LAS. A cattle ranch in the municipio of Esquipulas, Matagalpa department.

CASS-IRISSARI. A lake steamer on Lake Nicaragua doubtless named after the January 1, 1958, treaty of that
same name, and captained in 1860 by a man named
Slocum; the chief engineer was named Place.

CASS-IRISSARI TREATY.   One of the many U. S. -Nicaraguan
canal agreements.

CASTAÑEDA, DIEGO DE.   One of Gil González Dávila's
captains in 1522 on the expedition which discovered
Nicaragua.

CASTAÑEDA, JUAN DE.   Captain Castañeda was one of the
first co-disoverers of Nicaragua from the sea.   See
ESPINOSA, GASPAR.

CASTELLANA, LA.   Coffee processing plant in Jinotepe
Municipio, Carazo department.

CASTELLON, DON FRANCISCO DE.   Nicaragua's minister
to France in the 1840's who offered Louis Philippe a
canal route, proposing a French protectorate over the
area.   Rejected by Louis, Castellón turned to Belgian
promoters, and finally formed a Belgian company.   No
financing was effected, however, and meanwhile, there
was another European development.   See MARCOLETA,
M.

CASTILLO, EL.   1) Comarca or district in the municipio of
La Libertad, Chontales.   (Not to be confused with El
Castillo on the San Juan River or with the island of
the name in Lake Nicaragua.)
     2) A district in the municipio of Esquipulas, depart-
ment of Matagalpa.
     3) One of the two districts in the small municipio of
San Juan de Oriente, Masaya department.
     4) A mountain height in the municipio of Esquipulas,
department of Matagalpa.

CASTILLO, DON NICASIO DEL   see CABINET OF
PATRICIO RIVAS

CASTILLO, FRAY BLAS DEL.   A priest who descended
into the boiling crater of Santiago, the Volcan de
Masaya, in 1438, seeking gold there, but finding only
red hot lava.

CASTILLO, RAMON.   A representative of Matagalpa during
the 1855-1856 War.   See JUNTA DE RECURSOS.

CASTILLO VIEJO, EL.   Variously called Castillo del Río
San Juan, St. John's Fort, Castle of Nuestra Señora,

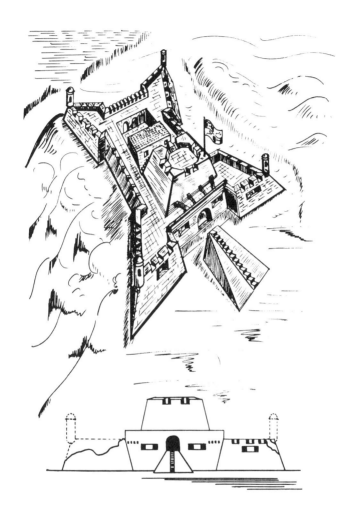

El Castillo Viejo

The storied and now ruined fort on the San Juan River, showing form and general original appearance.   Elevation outline
indicates extant walls.

and Castillo de la Inmaculada Concepción, the full and
original title seems to have been "El Castillo de
Nuestra Señora de la Pura y Inmaculada Concepción. "
It was not the first military post on the present site,
as the Spanish colonial authorities had earlier established
at least a dozen posts, varying from stone forts at
Granada to log stockades down river, on the commercial route through Lake Nicaragua and the San Juan
River to the Caribbean. On a 100-foot eminence nearly
halfway down river, 40 miles from the river-head at
San Carlos, the ancient fort rises today in recognizable
ruins high above a curved rapid in the river, whose
riffles surround the castle eminence on two sides, somewhat reminiscent of several sites on the Rhine River's
castle corridor. The fort is roughly 100 by 200 feet,
with four bastions, and a central tower nearly 60 feet
high. The remains are imposing. Following disastrous
pirate invasions in 1665 by Davis and in 1670 by Gallar-
dillo, action was deemed necessary to fortify the Spanish colonial frontier, and don Fernando Francisco Escobedo was sent to select a site and construct a fortification. He took over in 1672, assigned Maestre de
Campo Vasconcelos as commandant, and chose the site
by the rapids or cascade of Santa Cruz. Actual construction was completed by don Pablo de Loyola in 1675.
Ground-breaking for this fort and the perfectly preserved Castillo de San Marcos in St. Augustine, Florida,
took place in the same year, 1672. Originally equipped
with 36 cannon, the fort also had many musket embrasures and at the foot of the hill by the rapids, a water-
battery of six or eight cannon. There was the "cava-
lier" or tall tower, mounting up to eight cannons, and
"el foso, " the ditch or dry moat surrounding. The
ditch was sometimes lined with sharpened stakes. The
castle saw Nelson's and Despard's attack and capture
in 1780; the William Walker War in the 1850's; the 1912
events, the execution of Cannon and Groce, which led
to the long U. S. Marine occupation of Nicaragua. (See
illustration.)

CASTILLOS, LOS. Comarca or district of the municipio of
Santa Teresa, Carazo department.

CATAGUA, RIO see MATAGULA, RIO

CATALINA MARIA. A stern-wheel paddle steamer wrecked
near the Machuca Rapids in the 1850's near the better-
documented wreck of the Orus.

CATARINA.   1) A municipio of the department of Masaya,
in the southwestern section of an area of less than sev-
en square miles, and with 3, 000 population.   It is bounded on the north by Masaya, on the south by San Juan de
Oriente, on the east by Granada, and on the west by the
municipios Nandasmo and Niquinohamo.   Besides the
Villa de Catarina, the cabacera, the inhabitants live in
the Valle de Pacaya.   The original common lands or
"ejidos" were granted (or given back) to the municipio
in 1875.
    2) Villa de Catarina, cabacera of the municipio of
the same name, was confirmed as villa under President
Moncada.   The location of La Quinta Saratoga (q. v.)
gave a special prominence to the area.

CATHEDRAL, LEON.   The present building in the squat,
strong idiom of "earthquake Baroque" is the fourth cathedral building to stand on this site.   León Santiago de
los Caballeros was established in 1610 after "old León"
near Lake Managua was abandoned following catastrophic
earthquakes and consequent lake floods.   The second
building was burned by the pirate Dampier in 1685, and
rebuilt by an English architect, a prisoner from among
the invaders.   Built of stone with five brick arches,
this structure was narrow and ill-lit, and under Bishop
Isidro Marín Bullón y Figueroa, reconstruction was essayed in about 1747 resulting in the present structure.
The leader in the enterprise was Juan Viléjez y Cabrera,
a native of New Segovia, who as dean and later bishop,
concluded the task.   Consecration of the building came
about in 1780.   Diego de Ponas was chief architect.
The church was dedicated as Basilica of the Assumption
in 1860.   It is an exceedingly massive structure, and
it is told that 10, 000 men and 30 cannon were deployed
on the arched masonry roof during one of the many battles it sustained (about 1823).   Shot marks still pock the
walls.   The plans in the Archive of the Indies, dated
1767, are quite different from the actual building.   (See
drawing.)

"CATHEDRAL FOREST. "   Tall tropical rainforest where
the high canopies of close-spaced large trees have shade-
killed undergrowth.   They usually represent a great variety of species.   Probably 20% of Nicaragua is covered
with such forest, on the Caribbean slopes.

CATHOLIC CENTRAL AMERICAN UNIVERSITY.   Created in

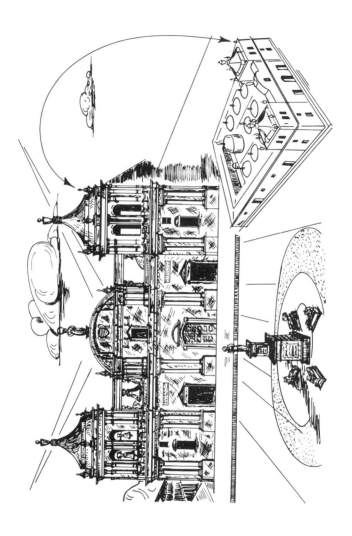

Cathedral in León

The largest in Central America, "earthquake Baroque."

1960, this relatively new institution aspires to be the
social conscience of the nation, to make of Nicaragua
a religious and intellectual center of the whole Central
American region.   It is the first private institution of
higher learning in Nicaragua.   Located in Managua,
there are in the university schools of public administration, law, and engineering.   There are further plans
for schools of veterinary medicine, chemistry, sociology,
teaching, industry, and tropical agriculture.

CATHOLIC CHURCH.   Since the first priest came to Nicaragua with Gil Gonzáles Dávila in 1522, and the first
Franciscan church was founded in Granada two years
later, Nicaragua has been predominantly Catholic.   The
church has great local influence in rural and small-
town parish settings.   Many priests and other workers
are from foreign groups, as there is a shortage of
Nicaraguan clergy.   There is, however, no official
state religion, although the government assists in Catholic educational enterprises.   See   CONCORDAT (of 1862).

CATTLE INDUSTRY.   In the mid-1960's the cattle population
was as follows: cows, 540,000; bulls, 45,000; oxen,
97,000; calves, 146,000; steers, 710,000; for a total of
1,538,000.   Oxen are still used with carts for heavy
transport.   Good breeds, especially Brahman and their
crosses, are more and more prevalent, as beef cattle
especially.

CAUDILLO.   A Spanish word derived from Arabic, meaning
"leader" and virtually synonymous with "dictator."   However, there are frequently caudillos other than single
leaders of the country.   Great political power in the
hands of one person is often called caudillismo.

CAUTY, JOHN.   A British captain, and later colonel, who
in the 1850's was organizing Costa Rica's army under
an aristocratic presidential regime, and who was a bol-
ster of sympathy to the legitimist party of Nicaragua in
opposition to the filibuster William Walker.   Later,
Cauty was a part of Walker's downfall when he invested
a key strong point on the eastern shore of Lake Nicaragua.   Spencer and Cauty in early 1857 seized the key
lake embarkation point of Virgin Bay and thus having
cut the transit route in several places, soon brought
the end for Walker.

CAVENDISH. A blight-resistant strain of bananas being ex-
perimented with in Nicaragua.

CAYALIPU. Lands given to Ensign don Pedro de Lumbi in
1768, in Estelí department. An aboriginal Indian name.

CAYA YELLOW TAIL. A triangular island a mile long in
the north end of Bluefields Bay. (Note the feminine
form "Caya. ")

CAYO ASKIL. One of the Cayos de Perla (q. v.).

CAYO BILL BIRD. One of the Cayos de Perla.

CAYO BUTTONWOOD. One of the Cayos de Perla.

CAYO COLUMBILLA. One of the Cayos de Perla.

CAYO GREAT TREE. One of the Cayos de Perla.

CAYO LITTLE TUNGAWARA. One of the three largest of
the Cayos de Perla (q. v.).

CAYO PIGEON. A small island in the mouth of the Pearl
Lagoon Estuary.

CAYO SCHOONER. Schooner Key is an island in the principal mouth of the Escondido River just north of the
Bay of Bluefields.

CAYO TUNGAWARA. Largest of the Cayos de Perla, Zelaya
department.

CAYOS DE PERLA. A series of over 20 small, named
islands within 15 miles off-shore from Nicaragua's
prominent eastern "nose, " Punta Perlas. The names
are picturesque. None of the islands is so much as a
mile long. They are mangrove "keys. "

CAYOS MAN O'WAR. Tiny keys or islands 13 miles off the
Zelaya department's Caribbean shore, 30 miles south of
Prinzapolka.

CAYOS MISKITOS. Swampy coastal islands 25 miles off the
northeast coast of Nicaragua. Oil exploration has been
carried on in recent years in these shallow waters.

CAYUCA.   A term used for a general-purpose dugout boat
    not found very frequently in Nicaragua.   The type is
    not so well-defined, although it is more related to the
    sea-going dori (q. v.) or to the panga (q. v.).   The term
    is used among the San Blas Indians of Panama.   (See
    illustration.)

CEBADILLA.   A district in the municipio of Matiguás, de-
    partment of Matagalpa.

CECLA.   Acronym for "Comisión Especial de Coordinación
    Latin Americana. "

CEDRO.   1) The cedar, Carapa nicaragüense, is a tropical
    aromatic hardwood--the Spanish cedar or "cigar-box-
    wood" which is light pink, light in weight, but stable
    and durable.   It is used for furniture, canoes, and
    building material throughout the areas of growth.   Ma-
    jor stands are on the east coastal area.   In appearance
    the Spanish cedar closely resembles mahogany, although
    the cedro is much softer.
       2) El Cedro, a district of the municipio of Jinotega.

CEDRO GALAN.   A territory of the National District, de-
    partment of Managua.

CEDRO REAL (Royal Cedar)   see   CEDRO

CEDROS, LOS.   1) A district of the municipio of Jinotega.
       2) Mountain of the Isabella Range, Jinotega depart-
    ment, altitude 3870 feet.   .

CEIBA, LA.   1) Comarca or district in the municipio of
    El Rosario, Carazo department.
       2) Comarca or district of the municipio of León,
    León department.
       3) Comarca or district of the municipio of Santa
    Teresa, Carazo department.
       4) A district of Terrabona municipio, Matagalpa de-
    partment.

CEIBA CHACHAGUA.   Comarca or district in the municipio
    of Quezalguaque, León.

CEIBA MOCHA.   Comarca or district of the municipio of
    Nagarote, León department.

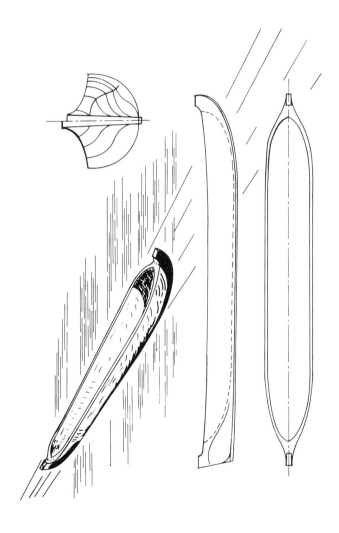

Cayuca

A type of dugout craft partaking of characteristics of both
the panga and the pipante.

CEIBA TREE. Any one of several very large tropical trees of the genus ceiba, the silk-cotton or "kapok" tree being perhaps best known. Characterized by huge buttress roots, as much as 50 feet in span. Ceiba is probably an Arawak word.

CEIBITA, LA. A district of the municipio of San Juan de Limay, Estelí department.

CEMLA. Acronym for the "Centro de Estudios Monetarios Latino-Americanos," a regional organization whose principal function is to effect and advance matters related to monetary and fiscal aspects of the region. A special committee worked on Central American regional credit mechanisms in 1968.

CEMPONALLI. A month of 20 days used by the tribes in the Managua area. The year consisted of ten months. See FESTIVAL DAYS, ABORIGINAL.

CEMPUAL see CEMPONALLI

CENSO, EL. Comarca or district of the municipio of El Jicaral, León.

CENTENO, GENERAL PATRICIO. One of the heroes of the Walker War of the 1850's, Patricio Centeno was born in Jinotega November 14, 1814. He became executive officer of an expeditionary column under General José Delores Estrada, and in this capacity as captain and second-in-command fought in the Batalla de San Jacinto (q. v.) September 14, 1856, when for the first time Walker's North American troops were routed. He was made Brigadier General in 1889, and died in Jinotega in April, 1890. As colonel, he was Military Commandant in Jinotega following 1856.

CENTRAL AMERICA. 1) Nicaragua is the largest and least populated of the five Central American countries, the others being Guatemala, El Salvador, Honduras, and Costa Rica. In the Organization of American States (q. v.) these five small nations bear a weight, due to their numbers (nearly 1/4 of the total membership), somewhat disproportionate to both their area (1/100 the total) and their population (1/40 the total).
    Geographically, Central America constitutes that portion of the isthmian area of Meso-America or Mid-

dle America between the two continents of the hemi-
sphere--the area between the isthmus of Tehuantepec
and the Darien area of Eastern Panama: this would
include besides the five nations mentioned, British
Honduras (or Belize); the states of Chiapas, Tabasco,
Yucatan, Campeche, and the territory of Quintana Roo
in Mexico. All the Americas stretch from 55° south
latitude to 85° north. The five small nations occupy
latitude bands between 8° and 18° north. The longitude
range is also 10°, from 82° 30' to 92° 30' west. The
measure between extremities is 900 miles. The land
between Pacific Ocean and Caribbean Sea is only 250
miles at its widest. Culturally, the five nations are
part of Middle America. Politically, each is sovereign.
They are now associated in the Central American Common Market, as well as the OAS and the United Nations.
Total population is about 11,000,000.

Geologically, during the Tertiary period a large part
of Central America is believed to have been an island
although prior to that time (60,000,000 years), there
seems to have been a land bridge. Then the link was
broken, and South America developed separately. The
antedeluvian "island" probably included Mexico's Chiapas,
Guatemala, Honduras, and most of Nicaragua, with other
islands smaller and nearby. The land bridge may have
been broken in accordance with the modern theory of
"continental drift." Nicaragua has a flora and fauna
partaking of both continents.

2) A shallow-draft paddle steamer wrecked in the
1850's at the mouth of the Savolo (Tarpon) River.

CENTRAL AMERICAN AND UNITED STATES ATLANTIC
AND PACIFIC CANAL COMPANY. Under authority of
the Federal Congress of Central America, permission
was granted in June, 1826, to this company to construct
a canal for "vessels of the largest burden possible, "
and a contract was ratified on June 14 of that year with
American capitalists who had formed the company.
Among the entrepreneurs was DeWitt Clinton, Governor
of New York, who had the pertinent experience of building the Erie Canal; Monroe Robinson, president of the
Bank of the United States and Stephen Van Renssalaer
were other well-known members of the company. No
money could be raised from private sources for this
company and the U.S. Congress would not provide funds.

CENTRAL AMERICAN BANANA FLEET see SPECIAL
SERVICE SQUADRON

CENTRAL AMERICAN BANK FOR ECONOMIC INTEGRATION.
The bank, created in 1961, was a final pragmatic step
in the creation of a Common Market in Central America.

CENTRAL AMERICAN CONFEDERATION. A league of three
states created by delegates from El Salvador, Honduras,
and Nicaragua under a constitution drafted at Chinandega,
Nicaragua, in 1845 when Honduras and El Salvador attacked Nicaragua. José León Sandoval took over the
government, and two years later (1847) again, under an
amended constitution, the three states united. This nation was dissolved in 1853.

CENTRAL AMERICAN TELEVISION NETWORK see TELE-
VISION

CENTRAL AMERICAN TRANSIT COMPANY. A reconstitution
of the American Canal Company, under William H. Webb
and associates in 1857. The Felix Belly (q. v.) contract
spoiled these plans. Strong representations by the
United States caused abrogation of Belly's essentially
private contract. This was a company authorized by
Nicaragua between the Belly efforts on behalf of the
French, and the appearance of Michel Chevalier (q. v.).
On March 20, 1861, Webb and his group secured the
former monopoly of steam navigation on Nicaraguan
waters. In 1863 there was informal ratification of a
transfer of canal rights to this company. The old
rights of the American Atlantic and Pacific Ship Canal
Company were thereupon transferred to Mr. Webb and
his associates in the 1870's.

CENTRAL HIGHLANDS. A geological as well as geographical subdivision which is part of the basic American cordillera that extends throughout Middle America; this
particular portion is anchored in Mexico's Chiapas and
continues through Costa Rica to Panama.

CENTROAMERICANA, EL. A daily paper published in León,
traditional liberal capital.

CENTRO AMERICANO, EL. In Granada in the 1880's and
following, this periodical presented more continuity than
some of the earlier efforts.

CEPEDA, CASIMIRO. Recollect missionary sent in 1746 to
help Cáceres in the Boaco Viejo and Acoyapa area.

CERAMIC TRAITS. The characteristics of ceramic finds in archaeological sites in Central America as elsewhere are: polychrome paint, negative painting, pedestal bases, white-on-red pottery, tripod bases, zoned red paint, zoned hatching, rocker stamping, stirrup sports, and others. In Nicaragua, combinations of low-relief sculpture and painted panels on the same pot are frequently found. This seems to be a mode of Mayan derivation. There are many private collections in Nicaragua with an incredible variety of ceramics.

CERDA y ARGÜELLO. The War of Cerda and Argüello occurred in 1826, when Nicaragua decreed a constitution on April 8 of that year terminating the Cerda-Argüello administration which had been essentially reactionary. Civil War broke out, with León and Granada adhering to Argüello, Managua and Rivas to Cerda. Six months of fighting ensued. Cerda lost.

CERECEDA, ANDRES DE. Treasurer of the expedition of Nicaraguan discovery headed by Gil González Dávila in 1522.

CERRITOS, LOS. Comarca or district in the municipio of Larreynaga, León department.

CERRO COLORADO. 1) Coffee hacienda in the municipio of El Sauce, León department.
    2) A district of the municipio of San Ramón, Matagalpa department.
    3) A district in the municipio of Santa Lucía, department of Boaco.
    4) Laguna de Cerro Colorado, a lake near the town of Yalí, in Jinotega department in the crater of a peak of the same name. Legends surround its origin.

CERRO DE CARACOL. With three waterfalls and natural bathing pools, this is an unusually beautiful natural setting of Terrabona municipio.

CERRO DE COYOTEPE. A pronounced height just north of Masaya, site of the fort of the same name--a turreted, battlemented fortification from the late 1800's and early 1900's, now (since April 5, 1964) turned over to the Boy Scouts of Nicaragua as a center and museum. The fort was garrisoned into the 1950's and has a considerable collection of arms and other military memorabilia.

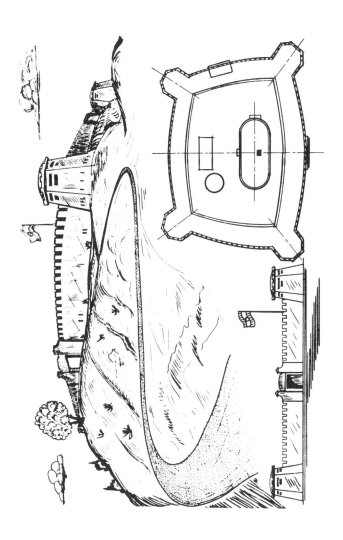

Cerro de Coyotepe

The Masaya hilltop fort now a museum and Boy Scout Center.

It was the scene of a battle during the "Guerra de Mena" of 1912, when General Benjamín Zelodón of the defending forces distinguished himself as a Nicaraguan hero. The events around the old fort are celebrated in Nicaraguan song and story. The view from the summit is a commanding one, and it is one of the more dramatic scenic and historical attractions of the country. (See drawing.)

CERRO DE LA CRUZ. 1) A height of the Guasguali spur of the Darién range of mountains in Jinotega department.
2) A mountain height in the municipio of Matagalpa.

CERRO DEL CABALLO. A district in the municipio of Muy Muy, Matagalpa department. During the Constitutionalist Revolution of 1926, a significant battle took place in this area.

CERRO DEL DIABLO. A height of the Datanli spur of the Darién Mountains in Jinotega department.

CERRO DEL MUSUN. A mountainous section of the municipio of Matiguás, Matagalpa department. Deep forest, high waterfalls, and wild animals contribute to the natural beauty and inaccessibility of the area.

CERRO DE TORO. A mountain height in the municipio of Matagalpa.

CERRO DEL PADRE. 1) A district in the municipio of Esquipulas, department of Matagalpa.
2) A mountain height in the municipio of Esquipulas, department of Matagalpa.

CERRO DEL VENTARRON. Heights of Terrabona municipio.

CERRO DOMINICO. Mountain of the Isabella Range, Jinotega department, altitude 4270 feet.

CERRO GRANDE. 1) A district in the municipio of Santa Lucía, department of Boaco.
2) A height so named ("big hill") in Carazo department.

CERRO KUKRA. Kukra or Cookra Hill is a prominent landmark, the highest natural eminence for many miles in radius, about 15 miles north of Bluefields. The Kukra village and airstrip are adjacent.

CERRO LA ZOPILOTA.   This "buzzard hill" is a low complex of sierras north of the lower Río Tuma.

CERRO NEGRO, VOLCAN.   First appearing in the 1840's
during the visit of American Minister E. G. Squier to
Nicaragua, and recorded by him, this "black hill" volcano is now over 600 feet above the general level of its
base, and has erupted on numerous occasions during recent decades.   The volcano is a simple cone with no
vegetation, black and with a central crater as well as,
on occasion, several supplementary vents.   A few miles
from Leon, it frequently rains cinders upon that city.
Lava flows 1,000 feet wide have been observed moving
at 12 feet per hour.   The cloud of cinders frequently
rises to 1,600 feet or higher during each explosion.
The "newest" of the volcanic peaks in the range of Los
Marabios, Cerro Negro is an excellent working "laboratory" for the study of volcanology, especially in its
close relationship to other live (but not so active) volcanoes, and to numerous "dead" ones in the area.
Eruptions in 1968 and 1971 were especially violent, the
latter sending up flame and cinders to 10,000 feet and
smoke and fumes to 40,000 feet.   (See illustration.)

CERRONES, LOS.   A district of the municipio of Jinotega.

CERROS, LOS.   District in the municipio and department
of Rivas.

CERROS DE LA LAPA.   Mountain heights of Terrabona municipio.

CERROS Y SAN ANTONIO.   Comarca or district in the municipio of La Libertad, Chontales.

CERRO TILBA.   One of the rare heights in the savannahs
west of Puerto Cabezas in Zelaya department.

CERRO TUNGLA.   One of the few heights in northeastern
Nicaragua, on the Río Wawa, 900 feet elevation.

CESAR, DON JOSE DOLORES.   Sub-prefect of Masaya in
1870, under Governor don Fernando Guzmán.

CESAR, JULIO.   Doctor César was an 1872 Licentiate in
Medicine from the University of San Carlos in Guatemala, and became a professor in the Universidad

Cerro Negro

Volcano near León in 1968 eruption.

C. G. T. see CONFEDERACION GENERAL DEL TRABAJO

C. G. T. I. see CONFEDERACION GENERAL DEL TRA-
BAJO INDEPENDIENTE

CHACALAPA. A district in the municipio of Belén, Rivas
department.

CHACALAPITA, RIO. A stream in the municipio of Belén,
Rivas department.

CHACARA SECA. Comarca or district of the municipio of
León, León department.

CHACARAS, LAS. Comarca or district of the municipio of
León, León department.

CHAGUE, EL. Comarca or district of the municipio of
León, León department.

CHAGUITE, EL. A district in the municipio of La Trinidad,
department of Estelí.

CHAGÜITE BLANCO. A district in the municipio of La
Trinidad, department of Estelí.

CHAGÜITE GRANDE. 1) A district of the municipio of
Jinotega.
2) A district of Terrabona municipio, Matagalpa department.
3) A mountain height in the district of the same name.

CHAGÜITES, LOS. A district of the municipio of Jinotega.

CHAGÜITILLO. A district of the municipio of Sebaco,
Matagalpa department.

CHAGÜITON. A coffee plantation in Pueblo Nuevo municipio,
Estelí department.

CHAMBER OF DEPUTIES see LEGISLATURE

CHAMORRISTA. Adherents of the Chamorro family and
faction--traditionally conservatives, and over a long
period of time representative of the opposition party
(essentially since 1933).

CHAMORRO.   1) A Nicaraguan family with many distinguished
     members, one of the dozen most prominent families from
     the earliest times of Nicaraguan independence.   (See
     specific entires.)   Emiliano Chamorro (q. v.) died a non-
     agenarian, one of the best-known of the clan and a for-
     mer President.   Pedro Joaquín Chamorro Cardenal edits
     La Prensa
          2) El Chamorro, a comarca or district in the mu-
     nicipio of La Libertad, Chontales.
          3) El Chamorro, a mountain in La Libertad, munici-
     pio of Chontales.

CHAMORRO, DIEGO M.   Fourth Chamorro to be President
     of Nicaragua (Fruto, 1853-54; Pedro Joaquín, 1875-79;
     Emiliano, 1917-20), Diego served from 1921-23.   He
     died in office, October 23, 1923, and was succeeded by
     Martínez to finish the term.

CHAMORRO, EMILIANO, 1871-1966.   One of the truly re-
     markable men of a distinguished family was the old dip-
     lomat and warrior who died of a heart attack at age 95
     on February 26, 1966.   Known, with reason, as the
     Lion of Nicaragua, Chamorro was President of Nica-
     ragua from 1917 to 1921.   As Nicaraguan representative
     to the United States in 1916, he was a signatory to the
     Bryan-Chamorro treaty which was another in a series
     of treaties, giving the United States the right to con-
     struct an inter-oceanic canal.   Chamorro was president
     for life of Nicaragua's Conservative Party, the chief op-
     position to Somoza rule.   Chamorro was only 22 when
     in 1893 he began his political career against the govern-
     ment of José Santos Zelaya, which fell 17 years later.
     General Chamorro is credited with organizing and being
     active in many of the 17 revolutions which were mounted
     against the Zelaya regime.

CHAMORRO, FRUTO.   Legitimist leader who had forced his
     way to the Presidency with help from wealthy ranchers
     and the clandestine aid of the British government to pre-
     cipitate the crises which led to William Walker's (q. v.)
     advent in 1855.

CHAMORRO, PEDRO JOAQUIN.   The first but not last of
     this name, Chamorro, of the distinguished old Granada
     conservative family, was President of Nicaragua (1875-
     1879).   There was a conflict with Germany over consu-
     late matters during his administration and it was also a

period of turbulence in relation to canal concessions.
De Lesseps was getting up steam for the Panama Canal
project, and Chamorro was left in a kind of limbo on
that important matter, with France, England and the
United States pulling Nicaragua in several directions.

CHAMORRO-WEITZEL CONVENTION. On February 8, 1913,
    just following the first U. S. Marine intervention in Nica-
    ragua, George T. Weitzel, U. S. Minister, and General
    Emiliano Chamorro met and signed the pact which gave
    the U. S. the right "in perpetuity" to construct a canal
    through Nicaragua and in order to protect the existing
    Panama Canal, to hold renewable 99-year leases on the
    Corn Islands, Nicaraguan islands off-shore in the Carib-
    bean.   Further, the right to construct a naval base on
    the Gulf of Forseca was granted.   The price was to be
    $3,000,000.

CHANAL, EL.   1) Comarca or district in the municipio of
    Diriamba, department of Carazo.
        2) Comarca or district in the municipio of La Paz,
    León.
        3) Hacienda in the municipio of La Paz, León.

CHANCELLORATE OF GUATEMALA. see KINGDOM OF
    GUATEMALA.   The English term frequently applied to
    the area of the Vice-Royalty of New Spain which in-
    cluded the Intendancy of Nicaragua (following 1542).

CHANNEL 8 TELEVISION.   This Managua channel is owned
    by Television of Nicaragua, S. A.

CHANNEL 6 TELEVISION.   This Managua channel is owned
    by Television of Nicaragua, S. A.

CHANNEL 3 TELEVISION.   This Managua channel is owned
    by Mariano Valle Quintero.

CHANNEL 12 TELEVISION.   This Managua channel is owned
    by Television Comercial.

CHANNEL 2 TELEVISION.   see   TELEVICENTRO DE
    NICARAGUA

CHAPARRAL, EL.   1) A district of the municipio of San
    Pedro, Chinandega department.
        2) A comarca or district of the municipio of Santa
    Rosa, León.

CHAPERNO, EL. Mountain in the municipio of El Jicaral, León department.

CHAPIOLLOS. A Nicaraguan political party Nickname. See SAPELCOS.

CHAPOLTEPE see CHILTEPE. [Note similarity to "Chapultepec," the Mexican height and fortress just west of the center of the city of Mexico. The word and meaning, Nahuatl in origin, are the same.]

CHAQUITILLO. Comarca or district in the municipio of Villa Samoza, Chontales.

CHARCO, EL. 1) A cattle hacienda in the municipio of Ciudad Darío, also known under the ancient name of Moyoa.
2) A cattle ranch in the Tipitapa municipio of the department of Managua.
3) A spring in Estelí department.

CHARCO DE GENIZARO see TISMA, LAGUNA DE

CHARCO DE TISMA see TISMA, LAGUNA DE

CHARLES MORGAN. A shallow-draft San Juan River paddle steamer used on both Lake Nicaragua and the River. Used by Spencer, leader of the Costa Ricans in the 1957 filibuster battle at El Castillo, this vessel once carried a band to Granada, undoubtedly a rare enough event for the place and time.

CHARTER OF SAN SALVADOR. A renewed effort for isthmian political organization and unity put forth on October 8-14, 1951, when the foreign ministers met in San Salvador. Part of the language of the charter follows: "Considering that the Central American republics, disjoined parts of a single nation, remain united by indestructible ties which ought to be utilized and strengthened for the common advantage ...." The Charter was the basis for the ADECA (q. v.); not a federation, but a joint organization.

CHASCHITE. Sun dial or clock, similar to sun-dials in Europe, found in the cacicazgo of Ogateyte. It was erected in the central plaza, a sort of "town" clock, and was in use in the pre-conquest era near Chinandega.

CHAVARRIA, LOS. Comarca, valley or district in the municipio of Juigalpa.

CHEPEÑOS, LOS. A district of the San Rafael del Sur municipio, Managua department.

CHEVALIER, MICHEL. An able lieutenant of the Emperor Napoleon III, who sent him to Nicaragua to assure the emperor's rights there, as Napoleon had continued his interest in a canal project. Napoleon in the 1860's was also establishing a short-lived Mexican empire under Maximilian. Nicaragua embraced Chevalier and without annulling previous charters, accepted Chevalier's proposals. But as Napoleon's star rapidly set, the plans came to nought, especially as Lee's surrender at Appomattox brought the U.S. again into the picture. The battle of Sedan and Napoleon III's fall ended French designs upon a Nicaraguan canal route forever.

CHIBCHA. South American Indian language group spoken by early Nicaraguan indigenes. The Chibchan language is related to Sumu--probably the latter is a residual dialect. The tribe other than Sumu which is of Chibcha origin is the Rama--a remnant of 275 remain, located on Rama Key near Bluefields.

CHICHA. A fermented liquor, made from corn, known widely in Central America and northern South America, the name seeming to be also widely disseminated over regional and linguistic boundaries. The cry of "la chee-ee-chah!" is a familiar one at remote rail stations and similar spots in Nicaragua. Sometimes fruit is added to the drink. It varies from place to place and country to country. In the ancient manner of preparing it, the corn is chewed and spit into kettles by women, the saliva speeding fermentation. Modern "chicha" has a greater variety of ingredients, however (and is perhaps of more sanitary origins).

CHICHIGUALTEPE. A territory of the National District, department of Managua.

CHICHIGUAS, LAS. A cattle ranch in the municipio of La Concordia, department of Jinotega.

CHICOYATONAL. A cacique in the Rivas area baptized during Gil Gonzáles Dávila's incursion in 1528, by Padre Bobadilla, with the Spanish name Don Alonso de Herrera.

CHILAMATE. 1) A cattle ranch in the municipio of Nindiri
Masaya department.
2) Comarca or district in the municipio of Villa
Somoza, Chontales.
3) A district in the municipio and department of
Matagalpa.

CHILAMATILLO. A cattle ranch in the Tipitapa municipio
of Managua department.

CHILDS, C. W. An eminent engineer, Colonel Childs, who
in 1850 went to Nicaragua in the employ of Cornelius
Vanderbilt to make a detailed survey of a trans-isthmus
canal route following the valley of the San Juan River,
across the southern part of Lake Nicaragua, and cutting
the 12-mile isthmus between the Lake and the Pacific
Ocean at San Juan del Sur. Childs ran into difficulties
when he found five rapids thought not passable by steamer. Vanderbilt himself later dispelled this objection (to
his own satisfaction) by "driving" a steamer all the way
up the river. Colonel Childs had been the chief engineer of the New York State canals and his survey is significant in that it was the first to be done across the
entire isthmus with scientific accuracy. The canal
route as laid out by Childs has continued to the present,
with only slight modification, as the best of the several
proposed routes through Nicaragua, and up to the very
time of building the Panama Canal, it was considered
by many experts the best route through the isthmus.

CHILE, EL. A mountain height in the municipio of Matagalpa.

CHILE DOS. A district in the municipio and department of
Matagalpa.

CHILE UNO. A district in the municipio and department of
Matagalpa.

CHILIBEES see QUIRIBIES [a variant form used in the
19th century].

CHILOTES. Little ears of green corn (often boiled very
immature and eaten cob and all).

CHILTEPE. This ancient name for the area of Managua is
still born by the crater on the peninsula of the name

which juts into Lake Managua from the south-central
shore.   The older spelling (in the Nahoa idiom) is
Chapoltepet.

CHIMBORAZO.   1) A mountain which at 5538 feet is the
eighth highest in Nicaragua.   Located in Jinotega department, four miles east of the town of Jinotega.
      2) El Chimborazo, a coffee hacienda in the Jinotega
department.

CHINANDEGA, BATTLE OF.   Fought during early February,
1927, between insurrectionist and government forces in
the town of Chinandega, the battle almost destroyed the
town.   Hundreds of Nicaraguans died, most of them non-
combatant women and children.   Two American pilots,
Brooks and Mason, formed a "Nicaraguan Air Force"
with two Laird-Swallow biplanes powered by OX-5 Cur-
tiss engines.   They flew over Chinandega dropping hand-
made dynamite "bombs," the fuses lit by cigars.   The
effect was to stampede the Liberal (insurrectionist) forces into giving victory to the Conservatives.   The historical meaning lies in the early use of tactical air support and in the first bombing from the air of civilians
in an "open" city.

CHINANDEGA, DEPARTMENT.   In the far northwestern
Pacific coastal area of Nicaragua adjoining the Gulf of
Fonseca (q. v.), Chinandega has an area of 1800 square
miles and a population of 125, 000.   As a major cotton-
growing area, there is some migration of labor, causing
a fluctuation in population figures.   There are 13 municipios, and the Villa Salvadorita.   Known as the
"granary of Nicaragua, " the department raises an abundance of cereals, especially corn.   There are also coffee, cattle, cotton, and sugar cane agricultural areas.

CHINANTLAN.   Ancient village or town at the site of the
present city of Chinandega.

CHINCHARON CON YUCA.   A tasty dish--frequently and
traditionally served by street vendors on a neat square
of banana leaf--consisting of deep-fried pigskin with the
root vegetable yuca, tasting somewhat like a boiled potato.   Always served with a little slaw.

CHINEGRITOS, BAILE DE.   A traditional dance traced to
the Mangues or Chiapanecans.

CHINEGRITOS A CABALLO.   Dance of the Chinegritos done
on horseback, and in masquerade--a traditional dance.

CHIPOTE, BATTLE OF.   The air attack on Sandino's (q. v.)
fortress of El Chipote (q. v.) began January 14, 1928,
and on January 26th of that year ground forces reached
the guerrilla's headquarters in that elusive spot.   As a
"battle" it is significant in that it is the first time in
history that an aeroplane attack was mounted against a
fortified position unsupported by ground troops.   Four
"Corsair" aircraft carried out the attack with fixed and
free machine guns, 50-pound demolition bombs, and 25-
pound shrapnel bombs.   An estimated 1500 defenders
were routed from their mountain fortress.   The exact
location of the battle is difficult to determine from maps
and published information, but is probably either "Cerro
Chachagua" or "Cerro Burbusco" each about 14 miles
in a generally north-easterly direction from Quilalí, the
northernmost being Burbusco, with "Chachagua" 8 miles
further east.   Both are "vee-shaped mountains of around
4, 000 feet altitude, " which is the description of El
Chipote.   (As to difficulty of location, as late as 1960
some geographical features in Nicaragua were found to
be 10 miles from the previously mapped position.)

CHIPOTE, EL.   A base used by Sandino and his forces in
1927 and 1928.   A Vee-shaped mountain several thousand
feet high, El Chipote had been turned into a considerable
fortress near Honduras, just north of Quilalí, and due
east of Ocotal.   The base was strategically located.
First considered mythical (el chipote may be translated
"the myth"), the fortified mountain was discovered by
aviation Major Rowell in November, 1927; on January
14, 1928, the air action began with new 50-pound demolition bombs.   On January 26, 1928, Major Young
and his men reached El Chipote to find it deserted.
Sandino had his men gather huge brush and wood piles,
so that Marine bombing would start fires that would
cover his withdrawal.   This was one of the earliest
instances of tactical air bombardment in the history
of warfare, and apparently the first unsupported by
ground troops.   (Regarding the etymology of "Chipote, "
it should be noted that the Spanish words for myth are
mito, fábula, ficción alegómica--none resemble chipote.
Since "ote" is a familiar Nahuatl (Aztec) ending, it is
presumed that this is one of the many Indian words
commonly used by Nicaraguans as "Spanish. "   El
chipote may also be translated as "back-handed slap. ")

CHIQUILISTAGUA. A territory of the National district, department of Managua.

CHIQUINAUT. God of the Winds of the Nicaraos (also, "Chiconahuitlhecatl"). Also can be translated as God of the Nine Winds.

CHIRINO. District in the municipio of San Jorge, Rivas department.

CHISCOLAPA. A district in the municipio of Santa Lucía, department of Boaco.

CHOCOLATA, LA. District in the municipio and department of Rivas.

CHOCOYOS, LOS. A district of the San Rafael del Sur municipio, Managua department.

CHONCA, LA. Comarca or district in the municipio of La Conquista, Carazo department.

CHONDALES see CHONTALES

CHONTALEÑO. A citizen of Chontales.

CHONTALES. A tribal subgroup of Quiribies (q. v.), which occupied south central portions of Nicaragua at the coming of the Spanish, speaking a language for which they were named, "chontal" or "chondal. " This group was defeated by Chorotegans in A. D. 600's and retreated from their previous dominance from Caribbean Sea to Pacific, to the isthmus at Rivas, the islands of Lake Nicaragua (Solentinames) and ultimately to the wild country north and east of Lake Nicaragua, now designated "Chontales. " There is a reason to believe that the group may have originated in California, Oregon, and northern Mexico.

CHONTALLIS see CHONTALES

CHORRO, EL. Waterfall of great natural beauty in the municipio of San Juan de Limay.

CHORUTEGAN (Language). The Mexican-derived language of the original emigrants from Nahuatl-speaking regions to Nicaragua, as much as 1500 years ago. As a lan-

guage, the Mangue dialect and other Chorutegan are closely related to Chiapaneco (from the Mexican state of
Chiapas).

CHORUTEGANOS. The "choruteganos" were a numerous
tribe of Indians found in the North Central part of Nicaragua in pre-conquest times. Of Mexican origin the
original group apparently occupied the islands of the
Gulf of Fonseca, and then moved on into adjacent territories to the Northeast. The word "chorutega" means
"place of refuge." The migration of these "nahuattaca"
or "nahua" or "Nahoa" groups continued from about A. D.
596 until 1505. It is probable they moved up stream-
beds into the area they finally settled in, principally in
Jinotega and Matagalpa departments. Many Nicaraguans
today call themselves "Choruteganos." The Choruteganos may have originated in the area now covered by
the Mexican state of Chiapas. Some authorities ascribe
the Chorutegan influx this far south as related to the
Pipil migration following A. D. 650. The origin of the
culture as transmitted was the great Mexican center of
Teotihuacán. See also PIPILES.

CHRISTIAN BROTHERS. This famous French teaching order
maintains several excellent Catholic schools in the country.

CHRISTMAS, LEE. A former railway man from Louisiana,
"General" Christmas was a soldier of fortune with activities all over Central America. Reputed to have four
wives, and embroiled in myriad revolutionary activities,
Christmas was involved with the Zelaya period activities
in Nicaragua, when in 1908 he led an invasion of Honduras from El Salvador which soon involved Nicaragua
and Guatemala as well. This gave the Central American court its first international case. War was finally
prevented.

CHUNCHI. A "thing"; a "whatchamacallit"--frequently used
slang.

CHURCHES OF MANAGUA. In addition to La Catedral
Metropolitana, the Managua cathedral, there are a number of Catholic churches in the city. Among these are:
San Antonio (from 1927 - 37 period); El Carmen (1959
and later); San Sebastián (1959 and later); El Redentor
(1959 and later); Santa and Cristo del Rosario; Nuestra

Señora de Alta Gracia; San Francisco; Santa Rosa; Santa María de Achualinca; San Luiz; and Santa Fe. (All these are earlier, from 19th century). There are also a First Baptist Church, a First Church of the Nazarene, a Church of Latter Day Saints, a Moravian Church, and a number of other protestant chapels. A number of historic churches have disappeared with time; among them: Candelaria, Veracruz, Parroquia de Santiago de Managua, San Mateo, and San Miguel.

CHUSCADA, LA. Hacienda on the northwest slopes of the dead volcano Mombacho.

CICI-BOLA. A variant spelling used by some 19th-century writers for the name Cocibolca, the pre-conquest name for Lake Nicaragua which is still in more or less frequent use.

CIES. Initials and acronym for the Consejo Inter-Americano Económico y Social. This economic and social council is a special organization of the CECLA and the objective is to present a unified Latin American policy on international commerce and economic development in relation to UNCTAD. See CECLA and UNCTAD.

CIGAR CUT. A Sandinista guerrilla practice from the 1927-32 war whereby a dead enemy's penis would be amputated and placed in his mouth. See CORTES (for other cuts).

CILAMA, LA. Comarca or district of the municipio of Nagarote, León department.

CINCO ESTRELLAS. A Lake Nicaragua transport vessel ("launch") in the late 1960's providing service to San Carlos from Granada, with stops at Moyogalpa on Omotepe Island, at Mérida, and at San Miguelito and Colón.

CINEMA. There are 104 cinema houses in Nicaragua, several of those in Managua being large, modern, air-conditioned units. In 1963 there were 7,500,000 admissions, or 4.9 per capita. A curious feature of cinema attendance is that while the theatres are seldom full on any ordinary day of the year, New Year's Day has become a traditional time for movie attendance, and long lines form.

CINTA VERDE. A district in the municipio of Esquipulas, department of Matagalpa.

CIPALTONAL. One of the creators of the heavens, the earth, and the stars in the Nicarao pantheon. The other was Tamogostad (q. v.). They were major gods and the authors of creation--a duo equal to the Yahweh of the Hebrews in original function and responsibility for creation.

CIPE. Acronym for the Centro Interamericano de Promoción de Exportación, stemming from the 1968 Punta del Este meeting of presidents. The purpose is aid to Latin American countries in specialized information designed to promote development and diversification of exports.

CIPOCTLE. Meaning a lizard, probably a large one like an iguana, this was one of the month festivals of the preconquest Nicaraos.

CIPRESES, LOS. A district in the municipio and department of Estelí.

CIRCUITO YNP. A radio station in León, power 500 watts, 1530 kilocycle, call letters YNP.

CIRCULO DE ESTUDIOS JURIDICOS Y SOCIALES. An organization of students in León whose demands for university autonomy as initiated in 1953 resulted in the designation of the Universidad Nacional Autónoma de Nicaragua in 1958 by President Luis Somoza.

CIRCUM-CARIBBEAN. A single cultural area which comprises the Indian peoples of Nicaragua, Costa Rica, Panama, Colombia, the islands of the West Indies and the northern part of Venezuela. This is particularly significant in that Nicaragua and the rest of Central America plus part of Colombia are considered an Intermediate Area which lay between the high civilizations of the Central Andes and Meso-America, and which received cultural influences from both the areas--a meeting ground. Compared to Middle America and the Andean area, little is known of this Circum-Caribbean area. Definitive archaeological and ethnological research is yet to be accomplished.

CIRCUM-CARIBBEAN INDIANS. An arbitrary grouping of
   indigenes by geographical region which is used to include all Indians of Nicaragua, Panama, Colombia, Costa Rica, the West Indies, and northern Venezuela. Less
   is known of this group than of the Middle American (Mexi-
   can-Mayan) or the Ecuadorean-Andean groups. In Nicaragua immigrants from Middle America included Choru-
   tegas of the Macro-Otomangean "superstock" and Nahuatl-
   speaking Nicaraos and Siguas, southernmost of the Utaztecan language family. The earliest Circum-Caribbean
   peoples seem to have been hunters over 10, 000 years
   ago, in the Pre-Projectile Point stage of development.
   Manioc cultivation began 3, 000 to 7, 000 years ago, and
   pottery and organized agriculture arose around 5, 000
   years ago. By A. D. 600 to 800 in Nicaragua there
   was interregional trade.

CISNE, LIBERATE. A captain in command of the first company of Nicaraguans at the Battle of San Jacinto (q. v.),
   September 14, 1856.

CITALAPA. A territory or district of the municipio of San
   Rafael del Sur, department of Managua.

CITELPANECA. Original name of Telpaneca (q. v.), coming
   from Nahuatl sources.

CITIZENSHIP. Citizens in Nicaragua include: (1) persons
   of either sex who are at least 18 and possess an academic degree ("bachillerata, " mark of secondary gradu-
   ation); (2) persons at least 18 who are married and can
   read and write; (3) all others at least 21 years of age.
   Citizens may vote, hold office, and petition. Women's
   suffrage became effective in 1955.

CITY (Archeological discovery). Within the past two years
   a major achaeological site has been discovered on the
   east coast of Nicaragua near Monkey Point, north of
   San Juan del Norte. Found by Jorge Espinosa on air
   photographs after his research in the diary of Columbus'
   son who spoke of buildings near the shore, the site is
   thought to have been originally a community of as many
   as 100, 000 persons. There are indications that the site
   was settled by people from South America (perhaps of
   Inca origin). The whole matter relates to Espinosa's
   theory of the naming of America (q. v. , def. 3). It is
   too early to report definitive results, but the potential

of showing Nicaragua as a meeting point of the great
cultures to north and south is an exciting prospect.

CIUDAD ANTIGUA.   To the east of Ocotal is the second
site of the town of Nueva Segovia, first established yet
farther east near Quilalí in 1524.   The present town
has a venerable and distinguished colonial church.   The
population removed to the present site of Ocotal in 1759
to escape further depredations of pirates, Miskitos, and
Sambos, who attacked up the Río Coco.   Present Ocotal
is above several protective falls and cascades on the
river.   There are presently 400 inhabitants of Ciudad
Antigua.

CIUDAD DARIO.   1) A municipio of the department of Matagalpa; area 272 square miles, population 23, 000.   Bounded on the north by the municipios of San Isidro, Sebaco,
and Terrabona; on the south by the municipios of San
Francisco de Carnicero and Tipitapa of Managua department; on the east by Terrabona and by part of Boaco
departments San José de los Remates; and on the west
by the León municipios of El Jicaral and Santa Rosa.
There are 13 comarcas or districts.   Pursuits are agricultural with a great variety of grains and vegetables,
and about 9000 acres under cultivation.   Sorghum is a
major crop.   During the last decades of the colonial
period, the area was a major source of tobacco.
   2) The present town became Ciudad Darío on May 26,
1920, "Because here was born Rubén Darío, ... poet
of worldwide fame, prince of Spanish letters, symbol of
the highest national glory" (to quote the decree).   The
population now is about 4400, and the house where Darío
was born on January 18, 1867, is preserved as a national shrine.   The two previous names of Darío's birthplace were Metapa and Chocoyos.   The latter is an affectionate nickname bestowed upon the town even earlier
than 1687, when there was a record of it.   The name
Metapa comes from "Metlapan" and was known by the
year 1600, by which time sugarcane plantations and cattle ranches dotted the fertile area.   For defense against
the "Caribes" of the east coast, whose depredations
were already beginning, a company of militia was stationed there.   The official name of the town was "San
Pedro de Metapa. "   By 1751, some 125 years following
the establishment of the Reducción Mercedaria, Bishop
Morel de Santa Cruz reported two companies of militia
with their captains, totalling 440 men, "muy pocas

armas. " With "very few arms" it was hardly a formidable force. There were at that time 59 cattle ranches and 66 sugar plantations in the region.

CIUDAD DE LAS FLORES. A romantic title given to the city of Masaya by the Nicaraguan poet Rubén Darío and Baroness Wilson.

CIUDAD PINEDA. Third name given to the port of San Juan del Sur (q. v. , def 2) replacing San Juan de la Concordia. An act of the assembly under the governorship of Licenciado Pineda, 1851-1852.

CLARENCE, CHIEF see REVOLUTION AT EL BLUFF 1894

CLARIN DEL EJERCITO. Periodical published in León, 1844.

CLARK, C. H. Second lieutenant of U. S. Marines in the Nueva Segovia area who entered an engagement near Pasa Honda in February, 1932. He was responsible for routing Umanzor's (q. v.) band and capturing a large amount of Sandinista equipment and supplies.

CLAYTON-BULWER TREATY. This document of April 19, 1850, a treaty between the United States and Great Britain, agreed that neither nation would seek exclusive control of a transit route, anywhere through Middle America, nor would they colonize, settle, or fortify in Central America in such a way as to interfere with any canal route. Further, they would support the Atlantic and Pacific Steam Navigation Company in efforts to provide a transit route through Nicaragua, with free ports at both terminals. The hand of Commodore Cornelius Vanderbilt was evident here. The representatives were U. S. Secretary of State John M. Clayton and British Ambassador to the U. S. Sir Henry Upton Bulwer. In general, the treaty was principally to the advantage of England. The questionable Mosquito Protectorate remained essentially unimpaired, as did British influence in Belize (British Honduras). As of 1971, British Honduras is about to win independence, with Guatemala's claims still unanswered.

CLEOPATRA MINE. One of the Bonanza (q. v.) group of mines.

CLINTON, DEWITT   see   CENTRAL AMERICAN AND
    UNITED STATES ATLANTIC AND PACIFIC CANAL
    COMPANY

C. N. T. D.   see   CONFEDERACION GENERAL DEL TRABAJO
    DEMOCRATICA NACIONALISTA

COAL   see   HULLA

COATL.   This word, meaning snake, is especially familiar
    among the Nahuatl words in the combined form "Quet-
    zalcoatl. " This title applies to a month festival in the
    Calendar used by the ancient Nicarao from around
    Rivas.

COBANO, EL.   1) Comarca, valley or district in the mu-
    nicipio of Juigalpa.
       2) District in the municipio of San Dionisio, Mata-
    galpa department.

COCAL, EL.   District in the municipio of Buenos Aires,
    department of Rivas.

COCHE.   A horse-drawn taxicab still in use in several
    towns.   (See illustration, p. 70).

COCIBOLCA.   Ancient name of Lake Nicaragua, still fre-
    quently used and well-known.   The lake was early called
    Mar Dulce ("sweet sea') as well as Gran Lago ("big
    lake").

COCINAGALPA   see   ALTOGRACIA PUEBLO

COCKBURN, ADOLFO.   A Sandinista collaborator and liberal
    member of the Nicaraguan Congress, secretly commis-
    sioned a general by Sandino in 1931.   A native of Grand
    Cayman, Cockburn was English and Miskito.   A huge
    man, he was chief of the Indians of the lower Río Coco
    valley in the area of Sacklin.   The fact Rivera's (q. v.)
    men took the Kisalaya garrison typewriter figured in the
    later revelation that he was a Sandinista.   Cockburn was
    killed when a U. S. Marine lieutenant showed him that
    the serial number on the typewriter he had in October,
    1931 was that of the stolen machine.   Cockburn was shot
    as he drew a pistol on the officer.   See also SUPREN-
    ANT.

COCKBURN, JOHN. An Englishman who travelled in Central America in 1730, and who wrote about what he saw, especially in describing the Indians.

COCO PATROL. A force established on June 28, 1928, when Captain Merritt Edson was asked to lead an expedition 400 miles up the Coco River and take Sandino's headquarters. For a month the marines under Edson proceeded upriver in dugout canoes (pipantes, q. v.) with immense difficulty. On August 7th a battle was fought at Ililihuas with losses on both sides. Edson captured supply trains and finally took Sandino's reputed headquarters, Poteca, but the quarry had flown.

COCO, RIO. The longest river in Central America, this stream rises in highlands near San Marcos de Colón, Honduras, and winds across the widest part of the isthmus between Guatemala and Panama to empty into the Caribbean near Cape Gracias a Dios. For a great portion of its lower course it is the border between Nicaragua and Honduras, although until recently this matter was in dispute, the territories "in litigio" being north of the river. Navigable for several hundred kilometers by shallow draft vessels, the upper reaches of the river are strewn with falls, rapids, and cascades. It has been a highroad of history for pirates, priests, colonists, and rebels. There are 21 different names applied to the river, seven deriving from its (probable) original Indian name, Huancs (variously rendered Wanks, Benks, Vankes, Wanx, Wonks, and Río Huanqui). Five further names derive from popular "Río Oro" (gold is still found in the rapids)--Yoro, Yore, Yari, Gold. It is also called Río del Encuentro, Great Cape River, and Pantasma and Telpaneca, the latter being tributaries, and their application to the whole stream probably simple error. Steamers and launches have plied the river, the latter pushing barges, but most travel now is by outboard powered bateaux or pipantes (both q. v.).

CODINA, JOSE. A friar who was sent by Bishop Villegas in 1789 to attempt to establish missions in Mosquitia. He went in February with Colville Breton and his bride María, and was accompanied by Cristóbal Novarro down the Wanks (Coco) River. By May the friars had to return to León in defeat.

COFRADIA (or ALDEA). A district of the municipio of Nindirí in the department of Masaya.

COFRADIA RURAL. A district of the municipio of Nindirí
in Masaya department.

COINAGE. Nicaragua does not have an intricate numismatic
history, but some stages of development relate to the
unusual history of the country. Original currency among
the indigenous Indian population was the cocoa bean.
First metal currencies in the area were the cobs and
later coins of the Mexico City mint, when Nicaragua was
part of the Captaincy General of Guatemala under the
viceroyalty of New Spain. First coin identified with
Nicaragua was a commemorative or "proclamation" one-
real piece struck for the city of León de Nicaragua on
the occasion of the coronation of Ferdinand VII in 1808.
Prior to this time, coinage from the mint in Antigua,
Guatemala, was in circulation. In 1821, Iturbide became Emperor of Mexico briefly and another commemorative was struck for León at this time. From 1845 on
to 1859, U.S. cents circulated freely, due to the gold-
rush-bound traffic across Nicaragua. In the latter year,
León issued a copper centavo which might be thought of
as the first national emission. As a Republic from 1838
on, Nicaragua abandoned the Spanish real (eight to the
peso) and adopted 100 centavos to one peso, changing
the latter to córdoba in 1912. It is of interest that in
the mid-20th century in the markets of Nicaragua illiterate market women still spoke of "peso, " "reals" (counting one real as ten centavos, rather than 12 1/2), and
"shilín, " or shilling, with four "shilín" to the córdoba.
This resulted from the English influence on the Caribbean or Miskito coast. During the U.S. Marine invasions between 1912-1933, U.S. money circulated freely.
Following 1880 there were a number of hacienda tokens
issued privately, in brass, silver, copper, and zinc.
Most interesting of Nicaraguan coins, and rarest, are
the ones issued by Agusto César Sandino, minted of
gold from the San Albino mine in 1927. They bore his
picture, and were "diez pesos oro" issued in behalf of
Sandino's "Republic of Nueva Segovia" with capital at
Jicaro (renamed Ciudad Sandino). There was also an
even rarer coin of lead and silver; there are known in
existence only three of the gold and two of the lead-
silver Sandino coins.

COLE, BYRON. A wealthy, ambitious and sophisticated
young New Englander who in the San Francisco of the
Gold Rush era, bought control of a conservative news-

paper, the Commercial-Advertiser. He asked Walker
(q. v.) to edit it, and also got Walker interested and involved in Nicaragua. Cole's business interests in Honduras caused him to work out a "colonization" agreement which was the proximate cause of William Walker's
appearance on the Nicaraguán scene. (See Honduras
Mining and Trading Company.) Cole returned to Nicaragua later as a combatant, and was killed in the Battle
of San Jacinto on September 14, 1856. He commanded
the small band which was defeated at the old hacienda
house. The man who killed Cole is recorded as Faustino
Salmerón, who thereby became a hero. The Nicaraguans
considered it poetic justice that Cole, who had initiated
the contract bringing the invading filibuster Walker to
their shores, should have been the one to command the
first defeated Walker force at the San Jacinto battle.

COLEGIO DE LA UNION. Inaugurated in February of 1877
as Masaya's own university, the colegio offered not only
primary and secondary studies, but also canon and civil
law, medicine, and natural sciences, as well as French
and English. It was founded by Licenciado don Jerónimo
Ramírez and Bachiller don José Torres.

COLEGIO DE MASAYA. Inaugurated in October, 1871, this
academy was founded by Rosálio Cortez and Jerónimo
Pérez, with the following studies: philosophy, rhetoric,
political economy, civil and canon law, and medicine.

COLINAS, LAS. 1) Plantation of the municipio of Quezalguaque, León.
2) Coffee hacienda and cattle ranch in the municipio
of Yalí, Jinotega department.

COLINAS, LOMA DE LOS. A height in the municipio of
Quezalguaque, department of León.

COLINDRES, JUAN GREGORIO. Sandinista general of the
early 1930's in charge of the Fourth Column. See
DEFENDING ARMY ....

COLOCONDO. A district of the municipio of San Juan de
Limay, Estelí department.

COLON. 1) A district of the municipio of Cárdenas, Rivas
department.
2) A district in the municipio and department of Estelí.

COLON, CRISTOBAL see COLUMBUS

COLONIA, LA. Coffee hacienda in the municipio of La
Concepción, department of Masaya.

COLONIAL FORMATIVE. A period of Formative (q. v.)
cultures which extends from about 3000 B. C. to about
1200 B. C. ; a period of wide ceramic distribution in the
Americas, probably by seaborne colonies. (This term
colonial is not in any way related to the much later
Spanish colonial era.) See also THEOCRATIC FORMA-
TIVE.

COLONIAS DE MANAGUA, LAS. 1) The capital city has
many residential suburbs, among them certain ones
erected by the Instituto Nacional de Vivienda. These
are: La Salvadorita, Maestro Gabriel, Tenderi, Nicarao,
Quatorce de Septiembre. All of the above are east of
the city, plus Managua (southwest of the city), and Centroamérica (also southeast). See INSTITUTO NACIONAL
DE VIVIENDA.
    2) A number of Managua suburbs have been erected
by private enterprise, with hundreds of entirely modern,
spacious homes. Such colonias are: Mantica, Somoza,
Pereira, El Carmen, Militar de la Explanada, Militar
de la Aviación, Dambach, Chico Petón, Los Robles.

COLORADO, RIO. The Río Colorado is one of the mouths
of the San Juan River, entering the Caribbean Sea over
the Barro Colorado, at the southeasternmost tip of Nicaragua.

"COLOSSUS OF THE NORTH. " For decades a most frequently used term applied to the United States of America by
Nicaraguans (as well as some other Central Americans)
to indicate the dominance of the North American giant
as well as to express their displeasure at policies which
were interventionist in nature.

COLUMBUS. A mine near Cerro el Callao 40 miles west
of Puerto Cabezas.

COLUMBUS, CHRISTOPHER, 1435-1506. Cristóbal Colón,
Genoese-born discoverer of America, reached the continental mainland for the first time in 1502, his fourth
voyage. On September 14th of that year he discovered
Nicaragua when he rounded Cabo Gracias a Dios, giving

it that name. This northeasternmost corner of Nicaragua is a flat, swampy area ill-matched to its imposing
title of "thanks to God," but the admiral had just spent
a month of bucking headwinds and was grateful for a fair
wind and a southward-trending shoreline. In a river-
mouth which was either the Río Grande or the Bluefields
estuary, two of his sailors were drowned when a small
boat swamped in surf over the bar. During a sail of
approximately one week along the coast, other features
were named--"Cabo de Rojas" with its red cliffs probably is modern Monkey Point.

COMALCAPA. Comarca or district of the municipio of
    Santa Teresa, Carazo department.

COMANDITA, EN. Term applied to a limited collective
    partnership.

COMARCA. A territory or district. In Nicaragua such
    areas are named for ranches, coffee fincas, or natural
    features within the territory and are identified within a
    municipio. The usage is somewhat like that of a rural
    township. It is also used to represent a "territory" as
    in the United States. It is a significant political and
    geographic unit in Nicaragua, partly because of the co-
    lonial hacienda heritage, partly because of the rugged
    mountain isolation of some of the districts, and also be-
    cause of the nomenclature and position of the areas de-
    scribed.
        It will be noted that frequently several comarcas or
    districts of different municipios in the same department
    will have the same name--either through popularity or
    because of some natural land feature (a prominent moun-
    tain) or some old Spanish grant which causes the name
    to have multiple application. Such repetition is of itself
    significant, and shows pattern development. It is also
    of interest that stream access (by canoe) or stream
    water supplies had a part in the nomenclature.

COMARCA SOMOZA. A district of the municipio San Rafael
    del Sur, department of Managua.

COMARCA SUR. District of Pueblo Nuevo municipio, Es-
    telí department.

COMEDIA NACIONAL DE NICARAGUA. Founded in 1965,
    this group directed by César Sobrevallos is a dramatic
    enterprise.

COMEJEN, EL. A district of the municipio and department of Masaya.

COMERCIO, EL. A Managuan-based newspaper of the late 1920's, as intervention and internecine conflict were building up during the Solórzano regime. 1925 proved to be a critical year for this paper.

COMEYAGUA. A district of the municipio of San Juan de Limay, Estelí department.

COMITE EJECUTIVO DEL DISTRITO NACIONAL. This executive committee of the national district, is composed of three members who exercise executive power, and who take turns in presiding over the group. The first Comité met January 1, 1930, and was composed of don Jonas Alvarez, don Francisco Fixione, and don Constantine Pereira. The committee was superseded by the Ministry of the National District on December 15, 1939, whose first minister was Don Hernán Robleto.

COMMERCIAL COMPANIES. There are six commonly applied types. See SOCIEDAD ANÓNIMA; SOCIEDAD CO-OPERATIVA; SOCIEDAD EN COMANDITA; SOCIEDAD EN COMANDITA por ACCIONES; and SOCIEDAD EN NOMBRE COLECTIVO. See also LIMITADA.

COMMUNIST PARTY. Before 1947 the labor sector of the Nicaraguan electorate was divided between the Partido Liberal Nacionalista and the Partido Socialista Nicaragüense (both q.v.). The Communists essentially controlled the Workers' Confederation of the country, which used the usual techniques of strikes and agitation to put pressure on governmental decisions. Declared illegal in 1947, the Party did not go underground so much as that it simply died out. By 1956 it was declared by the government that "there were only six Communists in Nicaragua, and we know who they are." The original Workers' Confederation of Nicaragua and the Somoza Popular Front (F.P.S.) superseded the Party in function, and most of labor entered into the PLN orbit of activities. This was one of the effective moves of the Anastasio Somoza regime.

COMMUNITY DEVELOPMENT PROJECTS. The Río Coco area, under the Ministry of Education, is conducting courses in health education, home economics, agricultural techniques, primary literacy, the Spanish language, and so forth. Basic to this effort, was the earlier work (1950's) of the "Educación Fundamental" activities of CREFAL (q. v.) under UNESCO auspices, in the Río Coco Pilot Project.

COMPADRAZGO. Relationships between a child's parents and godparents. Where family ties are stronger than churches, clubs, and other organizations, this pattern has special significance. Padrino (godfather) and Madrina (godmother) are both part of compadrazgo in the relationship of a child's parents and godparents. It is a ritual kinship, but important, and a tremendously respected pattern in Nicaragua. Sometimes these friend-relatives are used to build loyalties toward furtherance of political or economic careers.

COMPAÑIA DE TRANSITO DE NICARAGUA. Organized in Nicaragua by some capitalists from the northern United States, this company signed a contract with the Nicaraguan government on March 17, 1849 to provide a quick transit route across the country. This helped to call attention to the aggressive British actions at San Juan del Norte in 1848. See also VIXEN.

COMPAÑIAS DE CONQUISTA. Companies organized in 1711 in Matagalpa and nearby pueblos to defend the residents against incursions of the Caribes and other invaders from the eastern Part of Nicaragua. These groups lasted for many years, but later fell into persecution of the very tribes (Chorutegans) which they were organized to defend.

COMPASAGUA. A district in the municipio of Muy Muy, Matagalpa department.

COMPASAGUA, RIO. A river in the Muy Muy municipio of Matagalpa department.

COMPUERTA, LA. Cattle ranch in the municipio of San Juan del Sur, Rivas department.

COMUNIDADES. Large tracts of land granted by the Spanish Crown in the 18th century to Matagalpa Indians. In 1877 these lands were divided by legislative order. Legal status of such lands has been varied in a pendular swing since that time. As late as 1934 there was allocation of

100, 000 acres to the Creole community of Bluefields.
An ancient pattern of communal land-holdings was current through Meso-America, and the confiscation of such
lands was a proximate cause of revolutionary developments by such leaders as Emiliano Zapata in Mexico in
1910.

CONCEPCION, LA. 1) Comarca or district in the municipio
of La Paz, León.
2) A district in the municipio of La Trinidad, department of Estelí.
3) A district in the municipio of Moyogalpa on Omotepe Island in Lake Nicaragua, Rivas department. It
is one of the four districts of the municipio which is in
effect a village or pueblo.
4) Municipio of the department of Masaya, area 22
square miles, totally in cultivation, with about 10, 000
population, over 8000 of them rural. Known popularly
by the nickname "La Concha." Bounded on the north
by Nindirí; south by San Marcos, of the department of
Carazo; east by Masatepe; and west by Managua department. There are 17 comarcas or districts. San Juan
de la Concepción has become in essence a barrio of the
Villa Concepción. Sugar cane, cereals, bananas, plantains, all are agricultural products. "Azúcar de pilón"
(q. v.) is a specialty of the area. There are also a
number of coffee haciendas. The valley of San Juan de
la Concepción is also called popularly "San Juan del
Dulce." There are two coffee beneficios, San Antonio
and San José.

CONCEPCION DE MARIA. Comarca or district in the municipio of San Marcos, Carazo department.

CONCEPCION VOLCANO see OMOTEPE (def. 3)

CONCHA, LA see CONCEPCION, (def. 4)

CONCHAGUA, LA. A district in the municipio and department of Rivas

CONCHITAS, LAS. 1) A hacienda along the Pan-American
Highway just southeast of Nandaime.
2) Coffee plantation in Pueblo Nuevo municipio of
Estelí department.

CONCORDAT (of 1862). An agreement with the Vatican

obligating Nicaragua to support the Catholic Church,
(terminated by legislation under the Zelaya regime following 1894). The church regained power later as the
conservative party triumphed, but the anticlerical legislation remained and succeeding Nicaraguan constitutions
(the latest: 1950) have taken the same position, that the
state has no official religion. It also guarantees freedom of religion. In practice, however, the Catholic
Church has certain privileges, and diplomatic relations
with the Vatican are maintained.

CONCORDIA, LA. 1) Municipio of the department of Jinotega, a small area of 63 square miles, with a population
of 550. Bounded on the north by the municipio of Yalí,
on the south by Estelí department and the municipio of
San Rafael del Norte, and on the west by Estelí. There
are four districts or valleys in the municipio.
2) A pueblo; the original name was San Rafael, but
when that name and the population were transferred to
Chagüite Largo in 1851, La Concordia remained as a
village under the present name. The town is losing
population.

CONDAMINE, LA. A famous French astronomer who was
sent to Central and South America by his government
on an international scientific expedition, with the immediate purpose of measuring an arc of the meridian
on the plain of Quito, Ecuador. La Condamine made
instrumental surveys along the isthmus, and his con-
clusions included strong support for a canal through
Nicaragua to join Atlantic and Pacific waters. He presented a brilliant paper on this subject to the Academy
of Sciences in Paris in 1740. Spanish companions of
La Condamine--Antonio de Ulloa, a renowned Spanish
scientist, and Jorge Juan, a naval officer--were on the
same expedition, and added much knowledge concerning
the topography of the country. This being during a
period of war with the English, no practical results
could be carried out.

CONDEGA. 1) This municipio of Estelí department has an
area of 183 square miles and 13,000 inhabitants.
Bounded on the north by the municipios Telpaneca and
Palacaguina; on the south by Estelí; and on the east by
municipios San Sebastián and Yalí and the west by Pueblo Nuevo. There are 11 districts and a number of
mountain heights. Two lakes, Los Patitos and Venecia,

are within the area, and the Estelí, Yalí, Piré, and
Jocote rivers as well. Coffee culture and cattle raising
are principal activities. There is one gold mine.
2) A pueblo, and cabacera of the municipio of that
name, this is one of the aboriginal population centers
of the department of Estelí. The pueblo is named in the
Chorutegan language, "Village of the Potters." The making of ceramics is an age-old endeavor, as is evidenced
by findings in the area of "guacas" as well as ceramic
utensils. The pueblo being a part of the encomienda
awarded in 1548 to Juan Gallego, there is a record of
tribute paid by the inhabitants to the encomendero. In
1586 Fray Alonso Ponce came through Condega en route
to the convent of El Viejo. He found that the aboriginal
town had declined to eight houses. In 1751 the population was of mulattos, cultivating cotton. There was at
that time a mounted company of 75 militiamen armed
solely with lances, but by this time there were 55
houses. In 1854 the North American miner J. S. Brad-
bury, an associate of Ephraim Squier, testified to the
beauty and progress in Condega. In 1962 the town was
designated Ciudad. There are 3500 inhabitants. A
fiesta of the Patron Saint, San Isidro Labrador, is a
feature of the year.

CONDEGA, RIO DE. A principal stream of Estelí department, the Condega flows by the city of that name and
into the Río Estelí.

CONDEGA RURAL. A district of the municipio of Condega,
Estelí department.

CONFEDERACION GENERAL DEL TRABAJO (C. G. T.). The
"general federation of labor" is one of four labor organizations (q. v.) which are "official" in that they are
registered with the Labor Ministry.

CONFEDERACION GENERAL DEL TRABAJO DEMOCRATICA
NACIONALISTA (C. N. T. D.). One of the four labor organizations (q. v.) in Nicaragua recognized and registered
by the Ministry of Labor, this organization is a general
union and essentially adheres to the liberal party.

CONFEDERACION GENERAL DEL TRABAJO INDEPENDIENTE
(C. G. T. I.). This nonregistered labor union is generally
recognized to be Communist in affiliation. While there
is relatively little Communist activity in the country,

this union and the Sandinista front (see P. S. N.) are among the far leftist organizations.

CONGO, EL. A district of the municipio of San Ramón, Matagalpa department.

CONGRESS: THE COMMISSIONS. Under the two chambers of the Nicaraguan Congress a number of Special and Permanent Commissions operate, as well as a staff to provide administrative and general services.

CONGRESS, OF CENTRAL AMERICA, FIRST NATIONAL. In February, 1825, under the Constitution of 1824, the Congress met, the issue of representation being a burning one as the outlying areas did not wish Guatemala City to have undue influence or to be the capital. One of the tactics was to create a new state from the area around Quetzaltenango--Los Altos. With a delegates-at-large policy, this could help to minimize Guatemala City's influence. The return of Chiapas was also expected. Deputies were distributed as follows: Guatemala, 18; El Salvador, 9; Honduras, 6; Nicaragua, 6; Costa Rica, 2. The optimism of the 1825 meeting was ended by the outbreak of a three-year civil war, 1826-1829.

CONQUISTA, LA. Municipio in the department of Carazo, bounded by Santa Teresa on the east, Jinotepe to the west and south, and Santa Teresa and Jinotepe on the north. It is a small municipio of 19 square miles and 3, 000 population, on the rivers Grande and Ochomogo.
    2) A pueblo; this small town in Carazo department is the cabacera of the municipio of the same name and has 1, 200 inhabitants.

CONSEJO DE UNIDAD SINDICAL (C. U. S.). This "council of unity" is not registered with the Ministry of Labor, but has extra-territorial affiliation.

CONSEJO DISTRITORIAL DE MANAGUA. The National District has a District Council, popularly elected, presided over by a Minister of the district appointed by the President. Begun under the reformed constitution of 1950.

CONSEJO SUPERIOR UNIVERSITARIO CENTROAMERICANO. This Higher Council of Central American Universities organized in 1948 comes under a Central American

Agreement for the Basic Integration of Education, providing for collaborative effort by the five Central American Republics for text book improvement and teacher exchange programs.   There has been particular interest
in improving university education, and in studying the
educational systems.   Special problems of university
education in the region include: lack of laboratory ex-
periences; paucity of discussion sessions; emphasis on
traditional professions such as law (there is a great
surplus of lawyers); neglect of natural sciences, applied
engineering, etc.; part-time professional staffs; inade-
quate or nonexistent laboratories; low professional sala-
ries.

CONSERVATORIO NACIONAL DE MUSICA.   This national
musical conservatory has a choral ensemble (see Coro
del Conservatorio) as well as three chamber ensembles:
Orquesta de Cámara (a chamber orchestra); Quienteto
Pro-Música Antigua (a quintet devoted to historic and
ancient music); and Duo Pireteau (for violin and piano).

CONSTANCIA.   1) A district of the municipio of Yalí in the
Jinotega department.
      2) La Constancia, a coffee hacienda in the municipio
of Yalí.
      3) Gold-bearing veins in the Pis Pis mining district.
See also   BONANZA MINES.

CONSTANCIA MINE   see   BONANZA MINES

CONSTITUTION OF 1812.   Produced by the Cortes de Cádiz,
the 1812 Constitution was an astonishing document of
imperial reorganization, and might have retained the
Spanish colonial empire if other matters had not intervened.   The Kingdom of Guatemala was to elect 12
deputies to the Spanish parliament.   Further, there
were to be two regional bodies; one at León, Nicaragua,
the other in Guatemala City.   These "diputaciones provinciales" were something like modern development cor-
porations.   The reforms failed but Spain's willingness
to give her subjects a more representative form of
government is worth noting.   This constitution was the
basis for the national governments which came later in
Central America.   Both system and terminology were
adopted.

CONSTITUTION OF 1824.   On November 22, 1824, a Cen-

tral American constitution was promulgated which was a
compromise that attempted to reconcile the sharply differing political desires of aristocrats, liberals, and
others, especially the major conflict between Serviles
and Radicals. Based on the Cádiz Constitution of 1812,
and to some extent on the United States Constitution of
1789, there were also in use the Colombian, Portuguese,
and French plans and codes. The major organ of sovereignty was a Chamber of Deputies, elected by propor-
tional representation of the people. Executive and judicial branches were under legislative control. The
Senate had both executive and advisory functions. The
executive was almost powerless. State level government was similar. The states were "free and independent" in their interior administration. This cause provided later difficulties; whether this constitution established a unitary republic or "federation" on the one hand,
or whether it was a league of states or "confederation"
on the other, is hard to assess. It was statesrights
controversy based on this point which led to the final
breakup of the Republic.

CONSTITUENT ASSEMBLY, 1858. During the administration
of Tomás Martínez, and just following the National War
of 1855-1857, a new constitution was promulgated by this
assembly which met for the purpose. Martínez held
power under the Assembly. The 1863 revolution of
Máximo Jérez and Fernando Chamorro broke out because of discontent at Martínez' reelection.

CONSTITUTIONALISTS. Nicaraguan government party ousted
in 1925-1926, and opposed by the United States with the
general result of a renewed Marine occupation. The
Marines landed in Bluefields on August 27, 1926,
avowedly to protect property of American and foreign
residents.

CONSUELO, EL. 1) Comarca or district in the municipio
of Achuapa, León.
2) Coffee plantation in Pueblo Nuevo municipio of
Estelí department.

CONTARINI, G. M. Author of a world map which was en-
graved in 1506 by Rosselli, and which showed Cuba and
Haiti very recognizably, as well as the north coast of
South America, but in the Central American area only
ocean was indicated, with a large island in the general

position of Yucatan. The point being, that there seem
to have been no published maps of the Nicaraguan mainland this early, though Columbus had been there four
years previously. A manuscript world map of 1508
shows a blob of land with the island of Guaneca (off the
Honduras coast) indicated. Apparently Columbus' charts
had reached the press by this time.

CONTINUISMO. "Continuation" or the technique of staying
in power through quasi-legal means but without any real
referendum to the people, has been a recurrent theme
in Central America, especially since 1930. Cuadillos
ruled in Guatemala and El Salvador, 1931-1944. In
Nicaragua the regime started later and lasted longer.

CONTLES. A unit of counting cacao beans as money in
aboriginal Nicaragua, derived from the area of Masaya.
A contles was 400 beans. A xiquipil, 20 contles, and
una carga, three xiquipiles. Note the vigesimal system
--20 and "20 twenties" (400)--no doubt derived from the
same sources as the Maya numerical system.

CONVENTO, EL. Comarca or district of the municipio of
León, León department.

COOKRA see CARCA AND KUKRA

COOKRA. A tribe of Indians on the east coast of Nicaragua,
living on the banks of rivers emptying into Pearl Lagoon
and as far north as the Huahuashan (Wawa shaan) River.
They were almost extinct by the early 1820's when Orlando Roberts commented on them. The tribal name
persists in an eminence of the region called Cookra Hill,
but no tribal characteristics are extant.

COOLIDGE COROLLARY TO THE MONROE DOCTRINE. In
April of 1927 President Coolidge of the United States
stated that the "United States recognized responsibility
towards the Governments of the countries this side of
the Panama Canal that did not attach to other nations"
and further expressed U. S. determination to discourage
revolutions and to encourage peaceful elections as a
method of settling political differences. In spite of its
general irrelevance to the Monroe Doctrine, this was
hailed as a "Coolidge Corollary. "

COLLIDGE MESSAGE TO CONGRESS. On January 10, 1927,

President Coolidge of the United States of America sent
to the U. S. Congress a message on the Nicaraguan situation.   Following the Theodore Roosevelt corollary to
the Monroe Doctrine, Coolidge avertised that the U. S.
was in a position of special responsibility to Nicaragua,
due to American investment, the existing Panama Canal,
and the potential of a Nicaraguan Canal.   While the U. S.
did not desire to intervene, the interests of the U. S.
could not allow indifference.   Threats to Nicaraguan
stability would result in taking steps necessary to protection of American lives and property.   (That same
day a Marine expeditionary force landed at Bluefields,
Nicaragua.)

COOPERATIVA AGROPECUARIA DE YALI.   An agricultural
cooperative complete with a store for members, in the
town of Yalí, Jinotega department.   Such socio-economic
institutions are centers of development for backward or
remote communities.

COOPERATIVES.   In the late 1960's, Nicaraguan cooperatives included 64 credit unions, 12 consumer savings
groups, 14 transportation societies, 8 for agricultural
producers, 2 building societies, and one each of market-
ing and rural electrification cooperatives; a total value
of capitalization, over $1, 000, 000 U. S. , with almost
10, 000 membership.   See SOCIEDAD COOPERATIVO.

COPAITEPE.   Comarca or district of the municipio of
Nagarote, León department.

COPELAR, RIO.   River in the municipio of Santo Tomás
and noted for the falls of La Porfía.

COPLAS.   The couplet, or short verse, is a favorite form
in poetry-conscious and verse-fertile Nicaragua.   It is
a means of transmitting folk wisdom such as is found
in the Biblical Book of Proverbs, and is also a vehicle
for clever sallies, sly satire, and veiled or doubled
meanings.   Typical is the opener from Alfonso Cortés'
collection:
                    La historia la hace la guerra,
                    la Patria la hace el honor,
                    la Religión el fervor,
                    y todo lo que hay la Tierra.

A free translation follows:

> History is made by War;
> Homeland is by Honor made;
> Religion stems from pure fervor--
> And all from how the land is laid.

And a copla with a strictly Nicaraguan setting:
> "Al Xolotlán el Momotombo, un día
> que en chanza bajo el sol amanecieron,
> le dijo: 'Si tu gloria está en la mía,
> en ambos son los siglos que antes
>   fueron.'"

Another free translation:
> To Mount Momotombo said Lake
>   Xolotlán,
> When a new day dawned under the sun,
> 'If your own glory in mine once began,
> In both are the centuries already run.'

CORAL.   Comarca or district in the municipio of Villa Somoza, Chontales.

CORAZON DE JESUS.   Object of a "cuadra" and of saints' day reverence frequently found in home shrines.   (A cuadra is a picture, usually a print of some well-known painting.)

CORCUERA.   Sugar cane plantation in the municipio of León, León department.

CORCUERITA.   Sugar cane plantation in the municipio of León department.

CORDILLERA DARIENSE.   The Darién range partially in the department of Jinotega lies between the Tuma and Grande de Matagalpa Rivers.   There are two branches, the Ramal of Guasguali and the Ramal of Detanli.

CORDILLERA ISABELLA.   The Isabella range crosses the northern part of Nicaragua largely in Jinotega department, and parallel to the Pantasma and Coco Rivers.

CORDILLERAS   see   CENTRAL HIGHLANDS

CORDOBA.   Monetary unit named for the Spanish discoverer of Nicaragua, under the Monetary Law of March 20, 1912.   The córdoba was divided into 100 centavos and when established was valued on a par with the U.S. dollar. In 1934, the córdoba was devalued to 90 cents U.S., in 1937, to 50 cents; in 1938, to 20 cents; and in 1950, to .05 cents. Since that time it has been valued at between 14 cents and 15 cents official rate. A discount black market flourished in the 1950's, but the official exchange of seven córdobas to $1.00 U.S. is now fairly well established, and has in fact remained fairly stable for two decades (to 1970). The silver córdoba minted at Birmingham, England, in 1912, showed a portrait of Córdoba on the face and five Nicaraguan volcanoes on the reverse, with the sun peering over, as well as the motto "En Díos Confiamos." The face gave the date and simply "República de Nicaragua"; content was 90 per cent silver and 10 per cent copper, weighing 25 grams with a diameter of 38 mm. Succeeding coinage of all denominations (five centavos, ten centavos, 25 centavos, and 50 centavos) has the same design. The modern coins are 75 per cent copper and 25 per cent nickel.

CORDOBA, FERNANDO HERNANDEZ DE. Conquistador Hernández de Córdoba was sent to Nicaragua in 1524 by Pedrarias Dávila after Gil González had disappointed Dávila by taking a quantity of Nicaraguan gold to Santo Domingo upon his return thereto. Córdoba himself collected 258,000 pesos, most of which went to himself, the members of his expedition, and Dávila. Searching for a port of communication with the northern sea, Córdoba's expedition ran into officers of Hernán Cortez. They became friends, which angered Pedrarias so that he later beheaded Córdoba in the plaza of León. He founded the cities of León and Granada in 1524.

CORDOBAS, LOS. A district of the San Rafael del Sur municipio, Managua department.

CORDONAZO. A Pacific tropical cyclone; these tend not to have much effect upon Nicaraguan weather.

CORINTO. 1) Coffee hacienda in the Jinotega department.
    2) Principal port city of Nicaragua in the department of Chinandega, Ciudad Corinto is a successor to the colonial port of El Realejo, farther up the estuary. Corinto was connected by rail to Chinandega in 1881, and thereby to Managua. The movement of the customs house in Punta Icaco in 1858 marked the establishment

of the port. The present population is 9200. During a
hundred years of commercial activity duties received
have totalled over 400 million dollars.

CORINTO TREATY. In 1902, President Zelaya of Nicaragua
called a session in Corinto which was attended by four
Central American presidents and in which they prepared
a treaty accepting arbitration as a principle and establishing a regional tribunal. Rivalry between Zelaya and
others doomed the plan.

CORN ISLANDS. These islands are not only a tropical
"paradise" but have been concerned in international affairs since the U.S. took a lease on them in the past
century to serve in protecting the projected entrance of
a cross-Nicaraguan canal. Pronounced "Karn" islands
in the Jamaica-flavored dialect of the Caribbean east
coast of Nicaragua, these islands reentered the lime-
light in early 1972 when billionaire Howard Hughes went
to Nicaragua in February of that year, reputedly at the
invitation of President Anastasio Somoza, to reside for
a time and to discuss development of the Islands as a
resort. See ISLAS DEL MAIZ.

CORNETA, LA. 1) A district in the municipio and department of Matagalpa.
2) A mountain height in the municipio of Matagalpa.

CORNETA, CERRO DE LA. Part of the Guasguali branch
of the Darién range of mountains in Jinotega department.

CORO DEL CONSERVATORIO. This Conservatory Choir is
an ensemble from the National School of Music.

COROZO, EL. 1) A district in the municipio of Muy Muy,
Matagalpa department. Known for the fight which took
place during the Constitutionalist Revolution of 1926, in
the "Muralla Circular, " or Muralla de el Corozo, a
natural formation (see latter reference).
2) A district of the municipio of Niquinohomo, Masaya
department.
3) A district in the municipio of San Dionisio, Matagalpa department.
4) A district in the municipio of San Ramón, Matagalpa department.

CORRAL DE PIEDRA. A district of the municipio of Jinotega.

CORRAL, POINCIANO. Legitimist general and Minister of War in the Patricio Rivas government, who made peace with Walker in Granada in 1855, but who then as Minister of War wrote a letter to the new dictator of Honduras, which was in effect treason under the existing peace agreements. When Walker captured the letter, Corral was summoned and in spite of much pleading from both sides of the Nicaraguan political fence, Corral was executed November 8, 1855. Walker's ruthlessness was thereby established.

CORREGIDOR. 1) A Spanish colonial official having judicial as well as administrative power. Named by the viceroy until 1678, corregidors were designated by the Council of the Indies after that date. Probably because of the power to collect tribute and draft Indian labor, these officials were petty despots with great local power. Caudillismo and caciquismo may have their origins in this frequently abused office.
    2) A spring near León.

CORREGIMIENTO DE MATAGALPA. An extended region which included the present region of Nueva Segovia to the San Juan River and bounded on the east by the lines of the Frontiers. The time was 1570 to 1573. By 1743 much of this territory had become part of the Province of Matagalpa and Chontales. To the east was the province of "La Tologalpa."

CORREO DEL ISTMO. A periodical published in León, 1849, 1850, 1851.

CORTE DE ... see also CIGAR CUT AND TIE CUT

CORTE DE BLOOMERS. One of the horror tactics employed in the 1920's by Sandinista guerrilleros, in administering "justice." The victim's legs were chopped off at the knees, bringing slow and painful death through bleeding. See also CORTE DE CUMBO AND CORTE DE CHALECO.

CORTE DE CHALECO. The "vest cut" used by Sandinista guerrilla forces during the 1927-1932 War in Nicaragua. An enemy's head was cut off with a machete, after which both arms were also cut off at the shoulders and a design slashed on the chest. This gruesome technique was adopted especially by the guerrilla chieftain Pedro

Altimirano Pedrón.   See also   CORTE DE CUMBO and
CORTE DE BLOOMERS.

CORTE DE CUMBO.   The "gourd cut" was like other barbarous guerrilla tactics and was possibly most cruel of
the several murderous "cuts" in common use during the
Sandino War of 1927-1932.   An expert machete-wielder
would slice off a portion of the victim's skull, leaving
the brain exposed with consequent loss of equilibrium
and hours of convulsions and terrible agony before death.
This was considered an instrumentation of Sandinista
justice and was commented on by Sandino who said in
1931 "liberty is not conquered with flowers; for this
reason we must resort to the cortes of vest, gourd,
and bloomers. "   See also   CORTE DE BLOOMERS and
CORTE DE CHALECO.

CORTES, ALFONSO.   Born in 1889, this follower of Rubén
Darío, who is a fascinating Central American poet, has
been in a mental hospital for years.

CORTES DE CADIZ.   Spanish government during the Napoleonic Wars.   Enacted liberal constitution of 1812,
which was rejected by Ferdinand VII in 1814.   In 1820
Colonel Rafael Riego rebelled and compelled Ferdinand
to restore the 1812 document.   These events were of
significance to Hispanic America, including Nicaragua,
because they helped to set the stage for independence.
In Central America the tussle over Ferdinand strained
relations between peninsulars (Iberian-born) and criollas
(colonial-born Spaniards).   Note that Indians and the
mixed "mestizos" did not count much.

CORTEZ.   District in the municipio of San Jorge, Rivas
department.

CORTEZ, HERNAN.   A Conquistador who needs no introduction, but whose connection with Nicaragua lies in his
epic overland trek as far as Truxillo, Honduras (whence
he returned to Mexico, in April 1525 to quell an uprising).   The purpose of Cortez' southeastward-bound journey through the formidable Petén jungles of Guatemala
was to secure Lake Nicaragua, the "Sweet Sea, " from
control by Pedrarias.   He had also lost faith in his
earlier emissary Christóval Olid (q. v.).   Cortez' 1524
march was an immense feat but he did not succeed in
preventing Pedrarias Dávila from securing the lake.

Córdoba and Olid lost their lives for their treachery in the matter.

CORTEZAL. 1) Comarca or district in the municipio of La Paz, León.
2) El Cortezal, a district of the municipio of San Pedro, Chinandega department.

CORTEZAS, LAS. District in the municipio of Tisma, department of Masaya.

COSCUILO. A district in the municipio of Esquipulas, department of Matagalpa.

COSEGÜINA, VOLCAN. Volcano at the northwesternmost tip of Nicaragua, on the Cosegüina Peninsula jutting into the Bay of Fonseca. An explosive eruption on January 20, 1835 ranks with the explosion of Krakatoa in the East Indies as one of the major volcanic events of recorded history. According to calculations the volcano was originally about 6,000 feet in altitude, and half of that elevation was blown off in the eruption. Cinders reached Mexico and Colombia, and are believed to have covered 1,400,000 square miles as they fell. The sound was heard across the Caribbean in Jamaica. Now a rich cattle-ranching area, the sleeping giant has a lake in its large, relatively low crater, and thermal springs on its slopes. It is presently 2820 feet high.

COSMATILLO. Comarca or district in the municipio of La Libertad, Chontales.

COSTA, LA. A district in the municipio of Altagracia on Omotepe Island in Lake Nicaragua, department of Rivas.

COSTEÑOS. East-coast dwellers in Nicaragua, self-identified as distinguished from the ladinos.

COUNCIL OF MINISTERS see MINISTRIES OF GOVERNMENT

COYOL. 1) A district of the municipio of San Juan de Tola, Rivas department.
2) El Coyol, a district of the municipio of Condega, Estelí department.
3) El Coyol, a comarca or district in the municipio of Jinotepe, Carazo department.

COYOLAR.   1) A district in the municipio and department
of Matagalpa.
2) A district of the municipio of Yalí in the Jinotega
department.
3) El Coyolar, a district of the city of León.

COYOLITO.   1) A district in the municipio and department
of Estelí.
2) A drink, one of the tastiest of Nicaraguan "refres-
cos, " made from coyol fruit, and of a light red color.
3) El Coyolito, a district in the municipio of Ciudad
Darío, department of Matagalpa.
4) El Coyolito, a district of the municipio of San
Pedro, Chinandega department.

COYOTEPE.   Sugar cane plantation in the municipio of León,
León department.

COYOTEPE, FORTALEZA DE   see   CERRO DE COYOTEPE

COYOTERA, LA.   Comarca or district of the municipio of
León, department of León.

COYUAGALPA.   Pueblo or town existing in the valley of
Nicaragua during the 16th and 17th centuries.

COZCACUAUTLI.   This month and festival as celebrated by
the Nicarao tribe meant "king of the buzzards. "

CRAD, JOSEPH.   A pseudonym for Edward Clarence Trelawney-Ansell who was a mercenary under Agusto Sandino
during the famous guerrilla's activities in the Segovias
in the late 1920's and who authored a book I Had Nine
Lives--Fighting for Cash in Mexico and Nicaragua.

CRAMER   see   YSASI

CRATER, EL.   A hacienda located in pit of the old crater of
spectacular dead volcano Mombacho near Granada.

CREDO DE JUVENTUD NICARAGÜENSE.   The creed of Nicaraguan youth, by historian Julian N. Guerrero C., was
composed in 1933.   Translation: "I believe in the glorious future of Nicaragua, bound by geographic destiny to
be a passage between the worlds.
"I believe in her great future through the constant labor
of her sons, forcing from the land her riches.
"I believe in the best future through the talent, valor,
patriotism, and daring of the youth, following in the

footsteps of Goyena, Estrada, Cabezas, and Rafael Herrera.
"I believe in the renewal of the fruitful and effective work of the home where each father will be a patriot, each son a commander of liberty, and each mother a priestess of virtue, and where shines as in a sanctuary the lamp of the rebellion against slavery and social corruption.
"I believe in the new Nicaragua, where each Nicaraguan takes patriotism for a motto, work for a shield, talent for his banner, and for honor a fatherland sovereign and free. "

CREFAL. Acronym representing Centro Regional de Educación Fundamental para la América Latina. A function of the UNESCO (q. v.) with home office in Pátzcuaro, Mexico, and of particular interest to Nicaragua due to a special fundamental education project on the Río Coco. The home office of UNESCO's fundamental education endeavors on a worldwide scale is in Paris.

CREMA DE ALMENDRA. A delicious "refresco" or mixed refreshing drink made from almonds and milk with other flavoring. One of many delicious such drinks made in Nicaragua.

CRESTONES. A Nicaraguan political nickname of the 1887-1893 period. See also PAPERONES.

CROCKER, TIMOTHY. Captain Crocker was one of William Walker's "falange" in 1855, and was well-known for his courage. An aide who had accompanied the paranoid little Tennessean on his abortive Sonora expedition in Mexico, Crocker joined the Nicaraguan adventure and was a spirited and loyal aide, until his early death in the battle of Rivas on June 29, 1855, when during the first few minutes of fighting he and Major Achilles Kewen were among the first six to fall.

CROSSMAN (Commander). Ill-fated commanding officer of a survey expedition to Nicaragua in 1872, Crossman was drowned as his ship's boat capsized in surf. His second in command Chester Hatfield took over. (See INTER-OCEANIC CANAL COMMISSION)

CRUCERO, EL. Coffee hacienda in the municipio of Masatepe, department of Masaya.

CRUCES, LAS. Comarca or district of the municipio of
Santa Teresa, Carazo department.

CRUCITAS, LAS. A district of the municipio of Niquinohomo, Masaya department.

CRUZ, LA. 1) Height near the town of San Juan de Limay,
Estelí department.
2) Name on some maps of a supposed (and possibly
disappeared) colonial settlement at the mouth of Pantasma River. Old Spanish mines are reputed to be in the
area, just across the Coco River from the grass airfield "La Vigia. "

CRUZ, CERRO DE LA. An eminence of the Guasquali spur
of the Darién range of mountains in Jinotega department.
A large cross is placed on the highest part of the spur,
easily visible above Jinotega.

CRUZ BOLQUE, LA. District in the municipio of Altagracia on Omotepe Island in Lake Nicaragua, department
of Rivas.

CRUZ DE ESPAÑA, LA. District in the municipio and department of Rivas.

CRUZ DE RIO GRANDE, LA. Village on the Río Grande in
Zelaya department.

CRUZ DIVISORA. A cross marking the divides placed by
early Spanish surveyors in Nicaragua in the 16th century.

CSUCA see CONSEJO SUPERIOR UNIVERSITARIO CENTRO-
AMERICANO

CUA ABAJO. A district of the municipio of Jinotega.

CUACAS, LAS. Comarca or district in the municipio of
Jinotepe, Carazo department.

CUADERNOS UNIVERSITARIOS. Its major concern being
in the social sciences and the humanities this publication of the National University is one of few professional
intellectual journals indigenously produced.

CUADRA. A recent genealogical study developed over 1, 600
names as part of this particular family, which is one of

a dozen or so distinguished Nicaraguan families, furnishing presidents and other leaders since independence. (See Sacasa, Chamorro, etc.)

CUADRA, PABLO ANTONIO.   Contemporary literary figure involved in publishing El Pez y la Serpiente, and is its editor.   He is poet and novelist as well.

CUADRA, VICENTE.   President of Nicaragua 1871-1875, of a distinguished and numerous family, Cuadra had to deal with conflicts with President Tomás Guardia of Costa Rica, including temporary closing of the frontier.   At this time also Justo Ruffino Barios became President and dictator of Guatemala, threatening war against his neighboring republics.   The canal surveys first handled by A. G. Menocal came during this period.

CUADRO.   A picture of a saint, found in nearly every Nicaraguan home and often in a setting of flowers and special decoration indicating a revered status.   Sometimes the number of "cuadros" in a home is taken as an index of social status.

CUAHUTLI.   A festival day of a month as celebrated by the pre-conquest Nicaraos, the calendar being derived from Mexico.   The word means "eagle."

CUAJACHILLO ARROYO.   A territory of the National District, department of Managua.

CUAJACHILLO FILO.   A territory of the National District, department of Managua.

CUAJACHILLO PLANO.   A territory of the National District, department of Managua.

CUAJINAQUILAPA, RIO.   A stream tributary to the Río Grande de Matagalpa in the municipio of Ciudad Darío.

CUAJINIQUIL.   A district in the municipio of La Trinidad, department of Estelí.

CUAPA.   Comarca, valley or district in the municipio of Juigalpa.

CUAREZMOS, LOS.   A territory of the National District, department of Managua.

CUARTEL MILITAR DE METAPA. In Metapa [see Ciudad Darío], General Tomás Martínez established a military post prior to marching to Masaya to unite the armies of Central America against the forces of William Walker (1856).

CUASCOTO. A district of the municipio of San Juan de Tola, Rivas department.

CUASTOMA. Comarca or district in the municipio of Jinotepe, Carazo department.

CUATRO ESQUINAS. 1) District in the municipio of San Jorge, Rivas department.
    2) A territory of the National District, department of Managua.
    3) Las Cuatro Esquinas, a comarca or district in the municipio of Diriamba, department of Carazo.
    4) Las Cuatro Esquinas, a comarca or district in the municipio of Jinotepe, Carazo department.

CUATRO PALOS. 1) Comarca or district in the municipio of La Paz, León.
    2) Hacienda in the municipio of La Paz, León.

CUCHILLAS, LAS. 1) Comarca or district in the municipio of Diriamba, department of Carazo.
    2) District in the municipio of Altagracia on Omotepe Island in Lake Nicaragua, department of Rivas.
    3) District in the municipio of San Dionisio, Matagalpa department.

CUERO, EL see CABEZAS, RIGOBERTO

CUESTRA, LA. 1) Comarca or district in the municipio of La Conquista, department of Carazo.
    2) District in the municipio of San Juan del Sur, Rivas department.

CUETZPALIN. Meaning: "small lizard." One of the month festivals of the ancient Nicarao, near Rivas.

CUEVA DE LA MOCUANA, LA. A cave in the area of Esquipulas, Matagalpa department.

CUEVA DE LAS VENTANOS, LA. Natural cave in the hacienda Yapali, municipio Concordia, department of Jinotega.

CUEVA DEL DUENDE. This cave in the Cerro de Pedernal, between Terrabona and the valley of Ojo de Agua, is one of the unusual sites in the area of Terrabona.

CUEVAS, LAS. An old mine in Granada southwest of Nandaime.

CUGES. A subtribal group of the Chontales tribe. Originally from the "Quiribies" (q. v.).

CUICUINITA. This placer mining area in the northeast mining districts is considered to have an average value of $3. 75 in gold per cubic yard.

CUISIANGALPA see ALTAGRACIA (def. 1)

CULEBRA, MINA. One of the Bonanza (q. v.) group of mines.

CULHUA. A dialect of the Chorutegan language, spoken in the area of Condega, department of Estelí. Also known as Ülua. Also, a tribe speaking the dialect. (See WOOLWAS.)

CULUMUCOS. A Nicaraguan political party nickname. This party followed independence, during the tragic era 1821-1830. (See ABEJOS.)

CUMAICA. 1) Coffee hacienda in the municipio of Esquipulas, Matagalpa department.
2) A district in the municipio of Esquipulas, department of Matagalpa.
3) A mountain height in the municipio of Esquipulas, department of Matagalpa.

CUMPLIDA, LA. A district in the municipio and department of Matagalpa.

CURANDEROS. Local curers of disease who often operate without license of any sort, and in remote and rural areas.

CURINAGUA. A height of the Guasquali branch of the Darien range of mountains in Jinotega department.

CURVA, LA. A district in the municipio of Niquinohomo, Masaya department.

C. U. S.   see   CONSEJO DE UNIDAD SINDICAL

CUSCAGUAS. A district of the municipio of San Ramón, Matagalpa department.

CUSILES. A district in the department of Matagalpa, municipio of Matiguás.

CUSUSA. Illicitly distilled aguardiente, or "moonshine. "

CUYALI. A district of the municipio of Jinotega.

CYANE (Sloop of War). This U. S. Naval vessel was sent to Greytown (San Juan del Norte) in 1854 as a result of the disturbance there surrounding Smith and Borland (q. v.). Captain Hollins could obtain no satisfaction from the town officials, and no answer from the British commander of a small sloop of war. He then proceeded to shell the town on July 9, 1854, after due warning. A force of Marines was then landed to burn the remainder of the town. Hollins immediately formed a provisional government for the port. The incident had understandably international repercussions.

-CH-

All entries beginning CH will be found in the appropriate place under C.

-D-

DALLING, JOHN. Governor of Jamaica, 1777-1781, during which time there took place the abortive expedition to cut Spanish America in two on the San Juan River--Lake Nicaragua Axis. Dalling had a "Western Design" (like Oliver Cromwell before him) which included not only the bisection of the Spanish empire, but ultimately the opening of a canal from Caribbean to Pacific, and hence one more control of an ocean entry by Great Britain. The plan was strategically attractive even if militarily unsound, as it proved to be. To carry out his plans he had such men as the brilliant young Captain Horatio Nelson, an Irish visionary and engineer named Despard, and other active and effective officers. Dalling's great plan failed in the fever-ridden jungles of the San Juan

River, and his dream was never realized by England in
spite of recurrent efforts during more than a century.

DAMPIER, WILLIAM. Celebrated pirate leader and historian who was one of those instrumental in the greatest
buccaneer action ever carried out in colonial Central
America, when in late 1685, he commanded a force of
over 400 freebooters that landed in the Estero Doña
Paula near Realejo on the Pacific Coast (now near Corinto) and marched to the capital, León, whose cathedral,
churches, and convents were by that date already lux-
uriously well-established. The city was sacked; the
cathedral, La Merced Convent, and the hospital fell to
the flames. León thus became the only provincial capital of Central America ever to be captured by an enemy
during the colonial period. An interesting sidelight of
this event was that one buccaneer captured by the Spanish was an English architect who helped to rebuild the
cathedral. William Dampier figured further in one of
the principal adventures of the age, when Captain Woodes
Rogers, later of Nassau gubernatorial fame, led a round-
the-world expedition of Privateers. Dampier as "Pilot
of the South Seas" was apparently master of one of the
two vessels commanded by Rogers, the Duke and the
Duchess, and by internal evidence in Rogers' journal
account, seems to have lost his life on this expedition.

DANCE TO THE SUN. Simple melodic music continued as
a tradition from pre-conquest times and played on occasions of illness, death, birth, marriage, and harvest.
The Hymn to the Sons of the Moon is another traditional
and similar piece of music, based on a pentatonic scale.

DANCES, CURRENT AND POPULAR. While popular music
from the United States gains favor among middle- and
upper-class Nicaraguan youth, still the most frequently
used dances among the people of all ages are the cumbia,
the merengue, tangos, boleros, and rumbas, all from
Latin-American cultural origins, with the waltz and fox-
trot also popular.

DANOS, LOS. Mountain height in the municipio of Pueblo
Nuevo, Estelí department.

DANTA, LA. 1) Coffee hacienda in the municipio of Esquipulas, Matagalpa department.
2) A hacienda on the Lake Nicaragua shore just opposite Zapatera Island.

DARAILI. Coffee hacienda in Condega municipio, Estelí department.

DARIEN MOUNTAINS see CORDILLERA DARIENSE

DARIO, CIUDAD see CIUDAD DARIO

DARIO, RUBEN. A pseudonym which became world famous because of the poetry of its bearer, Félix Rubén García Sarmiento born January 18, 1867, in the village of "Chocoyos" (or Metapa) which is now known as Ciudad Darío. The legitimate son of Manuel García and Rosa Sarmiento, the poet changed his name, or rather had it changed for him, in that his family became known as "los Daríos," because of family prominence of his great-grandparents; even his father did business as "Manuel Darío." See under GARCIA SARMIENTO for complete entry.

DARRAH, CLYDE. Lieutenant in charge of the garrison at Puerto Cabezas at the time of the Logtown (q. v.) engagement, April 11, 1931, when Sandinista forces under Pedro Blandón attacked the railroad. Darrah took initiative and with 30 National Guardsmen and 30 armed civilians took a train toward the Logtown area. On April 12th, when returning, the train was ambushed. Loening Amphibian aircraft from Managua appeared and attacked the entrenched guerrillas. The men proceeded on foot toward Puerto Cabezas. (See also WOOD, JOHN C.)

DATANLI, COMARCA DE. A district of the municipio of Jinotega.

DATANLI, RAMAL DE. Branch of the Darién range, which includes the eighth highest mountain of Nicaragua, Chimborazo near Jinotega. Principal heights of the range; Olemania, Dolores, Las Nubes, Volcán Grande, Cerro del Diablo, La Bastilla.

DAVILA see "PEDRARIAS"

DAVILA, GIL GONZALES. Generally understood to be the European discoverer of Nicaragua by land, although he was not the first to have sighted the terrain, Dávila first heard of the splendid and powerful cacique Nicarao from the cacique Papagayo, in what is now Costa Rican

territory.   Authorized to use the fleet of Núñez de Balboa, Dávila abandoned the fleet and proceeded by land in
early 1522, when he reached the lands of Chief Nicoya
(now Costa Rica) and then went on to the Rivas isthmus
of Nicaragua where he met the Chief Nicarao and spent
eight days with that powerful and intelligent cacique.   He
planted the Cross of Spain in the Rivas area.   On April
17, 1522, there was a battle when the Spanish under
Dávila were attacked by troops of Chief Diriangen, and
were forced to withdraw.   Gil Gonzales Dávila was the
discoverer of the Mar Dulce, Lake Cocibolca, now Lake
Nicaragua.   He covered 224 leagues by land, baptized
32, 264 Indians, and collected 112, 524 pesos of gold (according to report).   Later his right of primacy in the
area was removed when he returned to Santo Domingo
with the gold.   Governor Pedrarias (q. v.) Dávila then
sent Hernández de Córdoba.

DAVIS, CAPTAIN CHARLES H.   see   ST. MARY'S

DEBATE, EL.   A periodical of a political-romantic nature
developed in Boaco in the 1915-1937 period.

DEBAYLE, LUIS H.   Paris-trained eminent Leonese physician
and surgeon, poet and scientist; known in Europe and
America for his wisdom and skill.

DE CASTILLA, JOSE MARIA.   Son of Colville Breton (q. v.),
who was sent to Spain to be educated in 1788.

DE CASTILLO, CARLOS ANTONIO   see   BRETON, COL-
VILLE

DECLARATION OF PANAMA (of 1939).   As a precursor to
World War II, the declaration, following a meeting of
representatives from all the American republics, stated
that while the signatory nations maintained neutrality
their waters would be kept free of hostile acts by non-
American nations.   Close on the heels of Hitler's invasion of Poland, the purpose and impact was obvious.

DECLARATION OF PANAMA (of 1956).   Held July 21-22,
1956, this meeting of all American Presidents was held
following the First Panama Congress in 1826.   The declaration, unanimously signed, dealt with fiscal, political,
and economic concerns of the American Nations.   As a
result there was some strengthening of the Organization
of American States.

DEFENDING ARMY OF THE NATIONAL SOVEREIGNTY OF
NICARAGUA. "Official" title of the Sandino Guerrillas
in the early 1930's. There were eight "columns" of 75
to 150 men each as follows: the first, under Pedrón,
based in southern Jinotega department; the second, under
Salgado, on the Mosquito Coast; the third, under Irías,
in Northern Jinotega; the fourth, under Colindres, in
Nueva Segovia and to the east in the rain-forest; the
fifth, under Díaz, in Estelí, León, and Chinandega; the
sixth, under Rivera, on the Mosquito Coast (Coco Val-
ley--the northern area); the seventh, under Peralta, in
Estrelí, León, Chinandega, (but separate from Díaz);
and the eighth, under Umanzor, in Nueva Segovia.

DEFENSOR DE ORDEN, EL. Published in Granada in 1854,
the title of this "defender of order" denotes the parlous
trend of the times just prior to William Walker's (q.v.)
coming.

DEL CARMEN. A municipio in the southeasternmost part
of Managua department with an area 276 square miles
and 550 population--an essentially rural area. Bounded
on the north by Mateare and Managua, on the south by
the Pacific Ocean, on the east by the municipios San
Rafael del Sur, and on the west by León department.
There are five districts. It is a zone of cattle and
other agriculture, with a variety of crops. There is
a sugar refinery, Santa Rita, and several large haciendas.

DELCE, ALPARIS. Called "Admiral, " this Miskito-Carib
chieftain of Pearl Lagoon held sway during the mid-18th
century and was a contemporary of Carlos Yarrince.
He signed a treaty of peace and friendship with Spain
in 1768, under the aegis of the Indian agent Jeremiah
Terry. Delce in 1780 was allied with Miskito King
George, Duke Isaac of the Cape, and Colville Breton
(q.v.), in joining the British for their fateful expedition
up the San Juan River to Fort Inmaculada. Though he
was a nephew of Colville Breton, Delce's followers finally assassinated Breton. He became a joint leader with
King George II (Sambo King) in 1790 as anarchy took
over and thereby dashed Spanish hopes for a docile Mosquito coast. In that sense the Miskitos were an instrument of defeat for the English and Spanish.

DELEGATES TO THE CORTES OF CADIZ (Central American). In 1810 six municipalities in the Captaincy-Gen-

eral of Guatemala were asked to provide delegates in
accord with the Cádiz 1812 Constitution, to help decide
on the government to be created by the Cortes of Cadiz.
León provided the delegate from Nicaragua.

DELGADILLO, IRENEO   see   TELEGRAFO, EL

DELGADILLO, LUIS A.   A native of Managua, born 1887,
    a composer of classical music and hundreds of songs,
    he studied in Milan, Italy, and was a teacher at the
    Mexican conservatory from 1921-1925, and since 1943
    in the Panamanian National Conservatory.   A pianist
    and conductor as well as prolific composer, he repre-
    sents Central American culture at the highest level.

DELICIAS, LAS.   1) Coffee hacienda in the Sierras de
    Managua, National District.
        2) Hacienda up the north slopes of Mombacho, the
    dead volcano just south of Granada.

DE LOS RIOS, CAPTAIN DON FRANCISCO.   Surveyor and
    judge of measurements in Sebaco and Chontales in 1677
    who surveyed the land holdings in the Juigalpa area at
    that time.

DENNIS, LAWRENCE.   The United States chargé d'affaires
    in Nicaragua during the Civil War of 1926.   The confer-
    ence over which he presided ended in failure October 26,
    1926.   Dennis resigned from the foreign service, and
    later was known as "the dean of American intellectual
    fascism. "   Only 32 when he went to Nicaragua, a Har-
    vard graduate and American Expeditionary force veteran
    of World War I, he had already had foreign service ex-
    perience in Europe and Latin America.   He is the offi-
    cial who called for war vessels at Bluefields and Cor-
    into.   The Chamorro government felt he was interfering
    in the public peace, and thereby pushing Nicaragua to-
    ward anarchy.

DENVER.   The U. S. warship on which a truce conference
    was held by U. S. chargé d'affaires Lawrence Dennis
    (q. v.) on October 1, 1926, in an attempt to end the
    Civil War between Chamorro and Sacasa forces--respec-
    tively, Conservatives and Liberals.

DEPARTMENTS OF 1838 (Nicaragua).   (1) Department of
    Oriente--districts of Granada, Masaya, and Jinotepe;

(2) Department of Occidente--districts of León and
Chinandega; (3) Department of Setentrión--districts of
Segovia and Matagalpa; (4) Department of Meridional--
district of Rivas.

DEPARTMENTS OF 1858 (Nicaragua). Created by the electoral law of August 24, 1858; on August 30th the State
of Nicaragua was divided into seven departments:
Chinandega, León, Nueva Segovia, Matagalpa, Chontales, Rivas and Granada.

DEPARTMENTS OF 1971 (Nicaragua). The 16 departments
of Nicaragua correspond to state divisions in Mexico,
Brazil, or the United States. See facing page for map.
(Note that the previous "Comarca del Cabo" has been
incorporated into Zelaya since the recent boundary settlement with Honduras.)

DERECHO DE ALMIRANTAZGO. A payment during colonial
days to the descendants of Christopher Columbus, who
as "Admiral of the Indies" received this admiral's tax
of five silver reales on all vessels using the port of
Seville.

DERECHO DE ALMOJARIFAZGO. This duty on imports and
exports of colonial products was in effect during the
Spanish colonial centuries and in combination with the
Derecho de Avería (following entry) made a very heavy
tax drain on the colonies, as it was 15% to 20% on all
exports from colonies to Spain, and 7% to 10% on Spanish goods for the colonies. Combined with the other
taxes, colonial products could bear as much as 50%
taxation.

DERECHO DE AVERIA. This "average" was a tax imposed
on all products exchanged between Nicaragua and other
Spanish colonies and the mother country, this traffic
being either with Seville or Cádiz. The tax was 5% on
exports to the colonies and 21% on imports from the
colonies. The purpose of the tax was avowedly to maintain Naval fleets of galleons to protect the commerce.

DESIGNATO see VICE-PRESIDENCY

DESNUDOS. A Nicaraguan political party nickname in the
period of 1847-1849, under José Guerrero. The "shirt-
less ones"--a poor peoples' party. (See also MECHUDOS.)

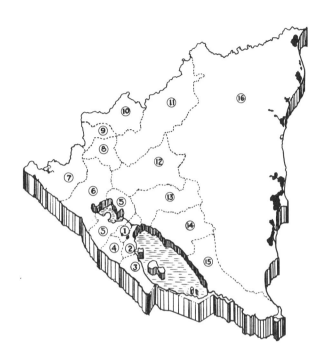

Departments of Nicaragua

1.	Masaya	9.	Madriz
2.	Granada	10.	Nueva Segovia
3.	Rivas	11.	Jinotega
4.	Carazo	12.	Matagalpa
5.	Managua	13.	Boaco
6.	León	14.	Chontales
7.	Chinandega	15.	Río San Juan
8.	Estelí	16.	Zelaya

DESPARD, EDWARD MARCUS. Irish visionary and engineer lieutenant of the 79th regiment who was in command of forces investing El Castillo Inmaculada in 1780, with the cooperation and active help of young Horatio, later Lord Nelson. Then Colonel Despard later, in 1803, was involved in a treasonous plot which led to his disgrace and execution, but in his Nicaraguan adventures of 1780, he was as much of a hero as Nelson.

DESPOBLADO. Comarca, valley or district in the municipio of Juigalpa.

DIABLITOS, BAILE DE. A traditional dance, traced to the Mangues or Chiapanecans.

DIAMANTE. 1) A San Juan River steamer remembered because two American engineers and soldiers of fortune attempted unsuccessfully to blow her up near El Castillo in 1909. Cannon and Groce were executed as a result of the affair, and in turn their execution triggered U. S. intervention in 1910 which continued for 23 years, and had world-wide reverberations. The guerrilla war of 1927, continuing to 1933, was indirectly triggered by the Diamante affair.
2) Name of a rapids in the San Juan River, between the Castillo and Machuca Rapids.
3) El Diamante, a hacienda in the municipio of La Paz, León.

DIARIO NICARAGÜENSE, EL. A daily paper published in Granada, 1884 and following.

DIAZ, LOS. Comarca or district in the municipio of Diriamba, department of Carazo.

DIAZ, ADOLFO. As President of Nicaragua, 1911-1916, Díaz was leader during an extremely controversial period. The rival generals Luis Mena and Emiliano Chamorro began a struggle for power, and the U. S. ambassador, Weitzel, became involved. The intervention of U. S. Marines in 1912 was a principal factor, the battle and sacking of Masaya being a crucial event. The country was humiliated and bankrupt and came under a species of military occupation as a result. Díaz won again in January, 1913. He founded the National Bank of Nicaragua, but the railroad interests were in effect turned over to U. S. bankers. On August 5, 1914, the

Bryan-Chamorro Treaty was negotiated in Washington,
General Emiliano Chamorro being the Díaz minister to
the U.S. Díaz was succeeded by Chamorro in January,
1917. Meanwhile, the European War (World War I) had
begun.

DIAZ, JOSE LEON. Sandinista general of the early 1930's
in charge of the Fifth Column. (See DEFENDING
ARMY ....)

DIAZ, RUY. A captain under Gil González Dávila (q.v.)
when Nicaragua was discovered in 1522.

DICKINSON, ANDREW B. Abraham Lincoln's envoy to Cen-
tral America in relation to inter-ocean transit projects.
Author and negotiator of the Dickinson Ayón Treaty in
June, 1868.

DICKINSON-AYON TREATY. In June, 1868 a treaty was
prepared by the Nicaraguan Minister of Foreign Affairs,
Señor Ayón, and Andrew Dickinson (see reference). It
was similar to the Squier and Cass-Yrisarri Treaties,
and was a general arrangement, granting U.S. rights
but not exclusive rights. The 1868 Treaty was one
more in a long series of international negotiations concerning canal rights in Nicaragua. There was guarantee
of Nicaraguan territorial sovereignty, and prohibition of
unilateral construction of a trans-Nicaragua canal by any
international power, Great Britain and the United States
of America being the principal aspirants.

DIEZ NAVARRO, LUIS. Lieutenant and military engineer,
this native of Málaga, Spain, was ordered to Central
America from New Spain in October, 1741. With experience in Africa and on the construction of forts at
Cádiz and Gibralter, Díez Navarro had also worked on
the giant fort San Juan de Ulúa at Vera Cruz, Mexico.
Generally recognized as a distinguished military engineer, Díez Navarro had also done work on churches
and hospitals and on a new mint in Mexico. In 1744,
he made the only complete survey of Spanish Colonial
defenses in Central America (the captaincy-general of
Guatemala) which was ever carried out during the Colonial era. He served as castellano of Fort Inmaculada,
as well as governor of Costa Rica, and in addition to
the reworking of Inmaculada ("El Castillo") and San
Felipe forts, planned Fort Omoa after selecting its

site.   He wound up a distinguished career as a brigadier
general and as master military engineer on the captaincy-
general.   At Inmaculada he recommended building an
outer wall and deepening the shallow moat.   He also
planned strategic defense of the area from the maraud-
ing Sambo-Miskitos.

DILLY, ADMIRAL.   An Indian chieftain, of the Mosquito
tribe, during dealings with the British in 1740 (as reported by Robert Hodgson).

DIPILTO.   A municipio of the department of Nueva Segovia,
population 400.   Due north of Ocotal, the departmental
cabacera, and very near the border with Honduras.

DIPUTACION PROVINCIAL.   A form of representative regional body planned by the Spanish Constitution of 1812,
and upon which Nicaragua and other Central American
governmental patterns were later based.   Under a jefe
polftico, one of these regional groups was to be centered
in León, Nicaragua, to deal with the areas now in modern Costa Rica and Nicaragua.   The other, in Guatemala, would be the senior one with a jefe polftico superior.

DIRECCION GENERAL DE CARTOGRAFIA.   Central map-
service in Managua which handles the publication of a
number of map series in such scales as 1:10,000,
1:250,000, etc.   Map availability for Nicaragua is now
very good, a major contrast to 1955 and previously.
U.S.-made maps for Marine activities in the 1920's
were the best previously available, but yet quite limited.
See Map List following the Bibliography at the end of
this book.   (See also SERVICIO GEODESICO INTER-
AMERICANO.)

DIRIA.   A municipio of the department of Granada, just
north of Diriomo and a few miles southwest of Lake
Apoyo.   Population, 3200.   Rice and tobacco are major
crops and there is a considerable ceramic industry.

DIRIAMBA.   1) Cabacera of the municipio of Diriamba in
the department of Carazo, at 1750 feet altitude, located
eight miles from Jinotepe on the Panamerican Highway,
and with 40,500 inhabitants.   Named for the chief
(cacique) Diriangen who was undoubtedly the ruler of
the Carazo area at the time of the conquest and who

battled Gil Gonzáles Dávila in 1522, the city was probably the seat of his ancient capital or in the near environs
thereof.   The name comes from the Chorutegan language:
Diri, "hills," and mba, "large."   Here is located the
Instituto Pedagógico, a normal school, as well as secondary schools (colegios) La Asunción, La Inmaculada,
La Dinna, Pastora, and San José.   It is considered an
educational center throughout Central America.
   2) Municipio in the department of Carazo, 135 square
miles, population 27,000.   Bounded to the north by San
Marcos, south by the Pacific Ocean, eastward by Jinotepe and westward by the department of Managua.   There
are 11 miles of seacoast in the department; of which
7 1/2 are in the municipio.   Second to Jinotepe in size
in the department, like that municipio it extends from
the central tableland of Carazo to the coast.   Coffee is
the principal industry, but corn, beans and cereals are
also cultivated.   Before 1900, sugar was the principal
product.   The climate is cool in these Carazo uplands.

DIRIAMBINOS.   Residents of Diriamba, or of the region
   thereabouts; in the 16th century, followers and tribesmen of Diriangen, the cacique.   Also called Diriangénes.

DIRIANES.   1) Indians occupying the following sites in the
   pre-conquest era (names still used today):   Jalteva
   (Granada), Diriomo, Niquinohomo, Jinotepe, Diriamba,
   Masatepe, Masaya, Nindirí, Managua, Tipitapa, Mateare.
   (In other words, the plains area between the two big
   lakes and on their southern shores.)
      2) A tribe of pre-conquest times, basically Choru-
   tegan in derivation, led by the Chief Diriangen, and living in the area of modern Carazo department.   They
   were the first tribesmen to be contacted by Spaniards
   in the Pacific regions of Nicaragua.

DIRIANGÉNES   see   DIRIAMBINOS

DIRIOMO.   A municipio of the department of Granada, population 9000, an old Indian town of great importance in
   pre-conquest days.   In the area tobacco and beans are
   major crops.   It is just south of Dirfa, north of Nandaime, and near Lake Apoyo.

DIRITAS.   A district of the municipio of Nindirí in Masaya
   department.

DISTRITO NACIONAL DE MANAGUA. The National District,
comprising the geographical seat of national government
in the capital city area, was created on October 31,
1929, under the government of President José María
Moncada. It represented an organized municipal government, and ranks as a municipio. It took the place of
the municipio of Managua from a governmental standpoint. There was an executive committee of three which
exercised the power over the district until 1939, when
the power was taken over by a ministry (see Comité
Ejecutivo del Distrito Nacional). Presently, the district
operates under the minister and a council. The national
district (as a municipio) is limited to the north by Lake
Managua, to the south by the departments Masaya and
Corazo, to the east by Tipitapa and to the west by
Mateare, el Carmen, and San Rafael del Sur. It has
226 square miles, and about 280,000 population (most
of them in the city of Managua). The principal agriculture is coffee raising. A number of huge hacienda holdings are involved and cattle and cotton are also significant.

DIVISIONES DE CUA. A district of the municipio of Jinotega.

DOBLE, EL. Coffee hacienda in the Sierras de Managua,
of the National District.

DOCTRINERAS. A women's Catholic religious order founded
during the last two decades.

DOLLAR DIPLOMACY. A phrase used to denote the policy
initiated by U.S. Secretary of State Philander C. Knox,
under President William Howard Taft. The basic plan
was to force foreign interests inimical to the U.S. to
withdraw from strategic areas by application of economic
pressure on Latin American governments. North American capital would fill the gap, backed by U.S. arms.
Defense was primary, economics secondary. The bold-
ness of the catch phrase elicited an understandably un-
desirable reaction throughout Latin America. The application of the policy was especially painful during the
1927-1933 Sandino War in Nicaragua.

DOLORES. 1) Coffee hacienda in the Jinotega department.
2) A district of the city of León.
3) A municipio of the department of Carazo now a

legal fiction, as the population is part of the neighboring
Jinotepe and Diriamba, approximately 1, 500 people.
    4) Cerro Dolores, a hill of the Dantanlí spur of the
Dariên Mountains in Jinotega department.

DOLORES (Pueblo)   see   MUNICIPIO DOLORES

DOMAS Y VALLE, JOSE.   Governor of the Kingdom of
    Guatemala, 1794-1801 succeeding Troncoso y Martínez
    (see latter) and who was in his nineties when appointed.
    A further sign of Spanish weakness upon which the arro-
    gant and recalcitrant denizens of the Mosquito coast
    capitalized.   The Spanish Colonial empire was two dec-
    ades from its end at the end of this governor's incum-
    bency.

DONAIRE, DON JUAN ANTONIO.   Chief ensign of the Villa
    de Estelí in the 1740's.

DORADO, EL.   This placer mining area of gold-bearing
    gravels assays out to an average value of $3. 75 per
    cubic yard indicated.   This is part of the northeast
    mining district.

DORI (Also, doree.)   A specialized dugout vessel planned
    for seagoing use and found in such saltwater bays and
    estuaries as that of Bluefields, Nicaragua.   The name
    doubtless derived early from English "dory" but is pro-
    nounced with accent on the second syllable.   Original
    doris were modelled with rounded bottoms and were
    double-ended, making a very seaworthy craft.   Made
    of one royal cedar log as much as 40 feet long, the
    dori often has a beam of 4 feet and a hull depth of 3
    feet.   The hull is cut out very thin, often down to one
    inch or less, and auxiliary frames are introduced every
    four to five feet the length of the craft, each frame
    being unconnected "knees" laid in parallel pairs from
    each gunwale along the insides of the hull just onto
    the opposite bilge, or turn of the hull, of the boat.
    Rudders are often swung on gudgeons and pintles.
    Large doris occasionally have low cabins and inboard
    engines installed.   Modern practice chops off the stern,
    builds in a transom, and installs a large outboard mo-
    tor.   Some doris could carry ten-ton loads.   They are
    used for coastal passages and for such offshore trips
    as the 40 miles to the Corn Islands.   The dori differs
    greatly from the river types of dugouts.   (See illustra-
    tion.)

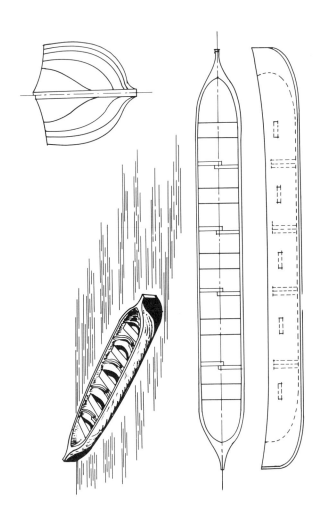

Dori

A seagoing round-bottomed dugout canoe used on Nicaragua's east coast.

DUBUQUE. A vessel of the U.S. serving intelligence applications during the 1909-1912 conflicts in which the U.S.
became involved with Nicaragua and following which the
long U.S. Marine series of involvements took place, until 1933.

DUCUALI, RIO. A stream whose floods caused the removal
of the original town of Pueblo Nuevo (q.v., def. 1) from
a site on its banks to the present one.

DUKE ISAAC. A Sambo-Miskito chieftain, and "governor"
of the Cabo Gracias a Dios area who was allied with
the British for the 1780 expedition up the San Juan
River. (See Dalling, Delce, etc.)

DULCE NOMBRE. 1) Comarca or district in the municipio
of Diriamba, department of Carazo.
2) El Dulce Nombre, comarca or district in the municipio of Jinotepe, Carazo department.
3) El Dulce Nombre, comarca or district in the municipio of San Marcos, Carazo department.

DUTCH CANAL CONTRACT, 1830 see WERWEER

-E-

EARL OF WARWICK. Sailing under a British letter of
marque and reprisal, the Earl seized the island of
Santa Catalina, called Old Providence by the British,
just off the Nicaraguan coast. The Old Providence
Company under the Earl established a trading station
at Cape Gracias a Dios, thus helping to assure the
British foothold on the Mosquito coast which was in
effect for over two centuries. From here the English
freebooters (with their comrades the Dutch) could prey
on traffic from the San Juan River mouth. The 1600's
found the freebooters in their heyday.

EARTHQUAKE (at Managua). The March 31, 1931, quake
was a great natural and national disaster; 1450 Nicaraguans lost their lives. Anastasio Somoza, at that
time Deputy Minister of Foreign Affairs, and later
President, took charge coolly during the disaster, which
with the fire which followed destroyed 30 blocks in downtown Managua. The surveying party of U.S. Army Engineers then working on a canal survey under Major

Dan I. Sultan rendered valuable service. Medical supplies were flown in from American bases in the Canal Zone and Cuba. Lt. Leslie R. Groves put the Managua reservoir and water pumps back in order. Many Managuans still remember the great "temblor" vividly and searingly.

EAST COAST (in 1908). An atlas of 1908, in German, by Moravian missionaries, shows the area of their work with a number of names familiar today (Karawalla, Walpasiksa) and some which seen to have dropped out of use since then, such as: Matina Bay, Awultara, Auastara, Uland, Sharon, Magdala, Bethany, Man of War Cay. Some of the names are, it will be noted, Biblical.

EASTERN REGION. Large in geographical extent but low and scattered in population, the part of the Caribbean littoral which is represented by a number of scattered settlements at river mouths of the Mosquito Coast. Bluefields might be designated as "capital" of this area.

EBACISO TASBAPAUNI. A village near Alamikamba, upstream on the Río Prinzapolka, Zelaya department.

ECHEVERRIA, DON LEONCIO. A Spanish colonial of 1800 in Masaya, whose family is still established there.

ECO NACIONAL, EL. A daily newspaper from León.

EDEN, EL. 1) A district of the municipio of Granada, on the banks of Lake Apoyo.
2) A territory of the National District, department of Managua.

EDEN MINE. One of the Bonanza (q.v.) group of mines.

EDITORIAL .... The following seven publishers, all located in Managua, have "Editorial" as the first word of their name: Alemana, Lacayo, Recalde, Robelo, San Enrique, San José, and Unión.

EDUCATION see STUDENTS

EDUCATION BUDGETS. The national budgets for education have been moving upward rapidly in recent years, in 1966 the total being 87,500,000 córdobas ($12,500,000), which amounts to about 16.5 percent of the national budget, where the similar percentage in 1960 was only 12. 8.

EHICATL. A month festival of the ancient Nicarao. The meaning is "wind" or "air. "

ELECTORAL POWER. Organized in addition to the Executive, Legislative and Judicial branches of government, this unusual fourth branch dealing with elections is an autonomous part of government under the 1950 constitution, set up to deal with overseeing the national elections, preventing electoral fraud, recognizing legally constituted political parties, and declaring the winners. Their Electoral Tribunal, like the Supreme Court of Justice, is composed of five magistrates chosen by congress. There are also 16 departmental electoral tribunals, and municipalities have electoral boards as well. The Supreme Tribunal is essentially a majority partisan body. It also presides over a Control Bureau of Certification and the Certificate Archives, as well as a store of electoral supplies.

ELENCO ESTABLE DE TELEVISION DE NICARAGUA. A social and cultural organization of people involved in broadcasting and related television activities.

"EL GENERAL" see "GENERAL, EL"

ELIZABETH. A San Juan River steamer during the post-filibuster-war period, owned by a Mr. Hollenbeck; wrecked on a sunken rock in 1871 or 1872.

ELOTES. Large ears of green corn.

EMPRESA NACIONAL DE LUZ Y FUERZE. The national monopoly on light and power has had a sales growth of 23 percent per annum since 1958, the installed power capacity having risen from 78 megawatts in 1963 to 156 megawatts in 1967. The budget of ENALUF is 106 million córdobas, or over $15 million U.S. Average utilization of installed capacity in 1966 was low-- 30. 5 percent, but better in 1967--42. 7 percent. Power rates are highest among Central American Common Market Countries.

"EMPTY LANDS" REGION. The one of four major Nicaraguan regions which is essentially uninhabited--a rainforest and pine barrens area, east of the central highlands and on the Caribbean slope. It also includes much of the low, pestilential, waterlogged Caribbean Coastal Plains area.

ENALUF   see   EMPRESA NACIONAL DE LUZ Y FUERZA

ENCANTO, EL.   1) Coffee hacienda in the Sierras de Managua, of the National District.
2) A hacienda five miles north of Nandaime.

ENCOMENDERO   see   ENCOMIENDA

ENCOMIENDA.   One of the most significant institutions of the early days in colonial Spanish America, this was a system of forced labor, parading under the guise of "Christianizing" the native peoples.   The encomenderos became very powerful, so that attempts at reform in the mid 1500's failed.   Not until 1720 was progress made in ending the system which frequently included cruelty and was in effect a feudal form of slavery, masquerading as conversion.

ENCUENTROS, LOS.   1) Comarca or district in the municipio of Jinotepe, Carazo department.
2) Comarca or district of the municipio of Santa Teresa, Carazo department.
3) A district of the municipio of Sebaco, Matagalpa department.

ENEA, LA.   A district in the municipio of Esquipulas, department of Matagalpa.

ENRAMADAS, LOS.   Comarca or district in the municipio of La Conquista, Carazo department.

ENSALADA.   A medley of songs and or dances, very popular in Nicaragua, especially in the traditional fiestas such as "Toros Venados" in Masaya.

ENSENADA DE CALAYSA, LA.   District in the municipio of Altagracia on Omotepe Island in Lake Nicaragua, department of Rivas.

ENSENADA DE TICHANA, LA.   District in the municipio of Altagracia on Omotepe Island in Lake Nicaragua, department of Rivas.

ERMITA LA ENCARNACION.   A colonial Rivas church
which has disappeared.

ERMITA DE GUADELUPE.   A church and cemetery in
Rivas, near what is now known as the "Río de Oro"
(not related to the Coco River).

ESCALANTE, PUERTO DE.   A sea-port on the Pacific
coast of Carazo department, created as a port in 1858,
but now abandoned because of its exposed position and
unsuitability for deep draft ocean-going vessels and also
its lack of interior transportation facilities; it is used
only by small craft.

ESCALANTILLO.   A district or valley in the municipio of
Belén, Rivas department.

ESCALERAS, LAS.   A district in the municipio and department of Matagalpa.

ESCAMECA GRANDE.   Cattle ranch in the municipio of San
Juan del Sur, Rivas department.

ESCAMECA, RIO.   River in the municipio of San Juan del
Sur, Rivas department, emptying into the Pacific.

ESCAMEQUITA.   Cattle ranch in the municipio of San Juan
del Sur, Rivas department.

ESCAMEQUITA, RIO.   Stream in San Juan del Sur municipio, Rivas department, emptying into the Pacific.

ESCANDOLO, EL.   A Chontales gold mine owned by Etienne
and Wells, founded in 1871.   A relatively high level of
production of two to four ounces per ton was maintained.

ESCOBAR PEREZ, JOSE BENITO.   Identified as chief of a
guerrilla group operating in Northern Nicaragua in 1970,
Escobar was among those arrested in the September,
1970, student uprisings in Nicaragua.   It was supposed
that he was part of the Sandinista front (F. S. L. N.).

ESCOBEDO, DON FERNANDO FRANCISCO DE.   Captain-
general of the Kingdom of Guatemala following Mencos--
1672-1678.   Promoted from the governorship of Yucatán,
a general of artillery of the Kingdom of Jaén, he was
ordered to proceed personally to Nicaragua and select

a site for a new frontier fort. The 600-mile arduous
journey from Santiago de Guatemala (now Antigua) was
the first visit of any Captain-General to a province outside Guatemala, and represented a step in the aware-
ness of far-away Madrid that there were defense needs
in the Central American provinces. Escobedo went to
the province and chose the site where the Fort Inmaculada Concepción was built high above a rapids midway
along the San Juan River between Lake Nicaragua and
the sea. This fortification stopped buccaneer depredations along the San Juan River route, and turned them
instead to Fort San Felipe in Guatemala. (See also
CASTILLO VIEJO.)

ESCONDIDA, LAGUNITA DE. Mountain lake in Estelí department.

ESCONDIDO, RIO. A river on the eastern slope of Nicaragua, emptying into the Caribbean. Called by early
English pirates, traders, and settlers the "Blewfields"
River, as its estuary is the Bay of Bluefields. Long
an artery of traffic for crossing Nicaragua, the river
has as a principal upstream port the town of Rama,
which is now connected by an all-weather road to Managua. This river-road combination is the first fully
satisfactory cross-Nicaragua transportation artery since
Vanderbilt's steamers of the 1850's (up the San Juan)
or the Spanish galleons plying from Cádiz to Granada
before the river was damaged in an earthquake in the
17th century.

ESCUELA DE LATINIDAD. The first Latin School (a private school) in Nicaragua was founded in 1838-1839, in
Masaya, by Maestro don Ignacio Campos.

ESCUELA DE MUSICA DE LA PUREZA, LA. One of two
schools of music or conservatories located in Managua.

ESCUELA INTERNACIONAL DE AGRICULTURA Y GANA-
DERIA DE RIVAS. In Rivas is located the school of
agriculture and cattle raising which has been developed
in part through the Alliance for Progress. The building and surrounding farm lands were donated by the
Malinano family. A total of over 300 students had
graduated by 1968.

ESCUELA NACIONAL DE BELLAS ARTES. This national

school of fine arts, located in Managua, has graduated
most of Nicaragua's leading artists. It has had much
influence in such undertakings as the founding of the
Galería Praxis, organized in 1962.

ESCUELA PUBLICA DE MASAYA. In 1832 the state established the first public school in the Masaya area. Its
operations were suspended during the war days of 1854-
1856; in 1858 two schools were reestablished.

ESFUERZA, EL. A gasoline launch (lancha de gasolina)
used by revolutionaries in the early 1900's on the San
Juan River.

ESHORT-STOP. "Short-stop" in Nicaraguan baseball.

ESK (Ship) see FAYSSOUX, CALLENDAR

ESLABON, EL. A hacienda in the southwestern tip of
Granada department.

ESMERALDA, LA. Hacienda on the eastern slope of dead
Volcano Mombacho overlooking Lake Nicaragua just
south of Granada.

ESPERANZA, LA. 1) Cattle ranch in the municipio of Esquipulas, Matagalpa department.
2) Large "finca" or farm in the municipio of El
Sauce, León department.

ESPINAL. A district in the municipio of La Trinidad, department of Estelí.

ESPINO, EL. A customs and immigration point of entry on
the Inter-American Highway, and at the northern frontier bordering on Honduras, 143 miles from Managua.
Facilities are modern.

ESPINO, PADRE FRAY FERNANDO. In the late 1600's
this native of Nicaragua's Nueva Segovia was the Superior of Franciscans in the Order of Guatemala. It
was he who sent missionaries to the Pantasma region
for the first time following the murder of two missionary priests in 1612.

ESPINOSA, GASPAR. "Licenciado" Espinosa and his Captain Juan de Castañeda were the European discoverers

of the southern part of Nicaragua at the Gulf of Nicoya
in early 1519 or 1520.   Apparently they did not land,
the land expedition of Gil Gonzáles Dávila being credited
with the actual discovery two or three years later.

ESPINOSAS, LOS.   A district of the San Rafael del Sur municipio, Managua department.

ESQUINAS Y SANTA CLARA, LAS.   Comarca or district in
the municipio of San Marcos, Carazo department.

ESQUIPULAS.   1) Comarca or district in the municipio of
La Paz, Carazo department.
    2) Ciudad Esquipulas had a population of 2000 in 1967,
and is the cabacera of Esquipulas municipio, Matagalpa
department.
    3) A municipio of Matagalpa department, generally
considered the richest area of the department because
of cattle, coffee, and other agricultural productivity,
these highlands are especially good for coffee.   Area,
83 square miles; population 8000.   Bounded on the north
by Matagalpa municipio; on the south by San José de
Los Remates (of Boaco); on the east by Muy Muy, and
on the west by San Dionisio and Terrabona municipios.
The Río Grande de Matagalpa curves throughout the area.
Nearly 40, 000 acres are in pasture lands, and almost
4000 acres in coffee.   There are some important coffee
and cattle haciendas, and in addition there is production
of corn, sorghum, etc.   There are 17 districts.
    4) A district of the municipio of Moyogalpa on Omo-
tepe Island in Lake Nicaragua, Rivas department.   It is
one of the four districts of the municipio which is in effect a village or pueblo.
    5) A territory of the National District, department
of Managua.   A built-up suburban area.

ESQUIRIN, EL.   A district in the municipio of Muy Muy,
Matagalpa department.

ESTACION X.   A series of radio stations owned by the
Somoza family with call letters YNX and relays as follows: Chichigalpa, 1000 watts, 640 kilocycles; Estelí,
1000 watts, 1370 kilocycles; Juigalpa, 1000 watts, 1400
kilocycles; Matagalpa, 1000 watts, 810 kilocycles.   The
home station in Managua has a power of 10, 000 watts
and a frequency of 750 kilocycles.

ESTADIO SOMOZA. This huge stadium within the city limits
of Managua, is used not only for the prevalent baseball
and spirited soccer but also for fairs and exhibits. The
seating of the open oval is about 100, 000. A decade
ago, when games were played under lights at night, the
power demands for lighting tended to dim the city.

ESTADO IN SITIO   see   STATE OF SIEGE

ESTADO LIBRE DE NICARAGUA. The "Free State of Nicaragua" under the agreements of April 30, and December
21, 1838, related to the Federation of Central America.
(See NUEVO PACTO.)

ESTADOUNIDENSE. A very convenient Spanish word which
has no English counterpart. If it had one, it would be
"United-Statsian, " which would be an adjective of broad
utility. "American" is obviously generic, and is incon-
siderate when used patently to mean "of the United
States. " "Northamerican, " while not precise for this
use, is preferable to "American. " Estadounidense is
both accurate and melodious.

ESTANCIA, LA. A district of the municipio of Sebaco,
Matagalpa department.

ESTELI.   1) One of the departments of Nicaragua, area 845
square miles, population 72, 000. Bounded on the north
by the departments of Madriz and Nueva Segovia; on the
south by Matagalpa department; on the east by Jinotega
and Nueva Segovia departments; and on the west by
Madriz, Chinandega, and León. There are five municipios: Estelí, Condega, Pueblo Nueva, La Trinidad,
and San Juan de Limay. Estelí is unique among the departments of Nicaragua in its history of "nace, muere,
y resucita" (birth, death, and resuscitation). "Born"
first on December 8, 1891, it disappeared on November
15, 1897, under the Zelaya administration, and it was
reinstated over Zelaya's veto on March 1, 1900 (see
Meza, Samuel). The department was originally "sup-
pressed" by decree of October 9, 1897, ostensibly because the relatively new department had not produced
sufficient funds for its own support, but there is some
reason to suppose the act was retaliatory for subversive
movements in the Segovias against the Zelaya regime.
The department is rugged, mountainous, in part a big
plateau (the "altiplano esteliano"). There are several

mountain lakes at altitudes of over 3500 feet above sea
level.   There is also a series of big springs, although
there are no thermal or medicinal waters.   The department is essentially out of the active volcanic zone as
represented by the line of Los Marabios (the volcanoes).

2) Municipio in the department of the same name,
area of 319 square miles, population about 30,000,
largest municipio in the department.   Bounded on the
north by Condega, south by San Nicolás, east by La
Trinidad, La Concordia, and San Rafael del Norte, and
west by Achuapa (of León) and San Juan de Limay.
There are 21 districts.   There are several mountains
of 4,000-5,000 feet altitude.   The lakes La Tunosa and Santa Clara are in the department.   Origin of the name
"Estelí" seems to be from Chorutegan Indian sources,
Exteli or Extelli, or more precisely, Ixcotelli: one
source gives the Mexican origin of the word as "river
of obsidian" (itztetl signifying obsidian).   Another suggests "current of red blood, " from extli (blood) and li
(current).   Ix signifies "eye" and telli, a plain or field.
Hence, Ixcotelli might signify a plain or field before the
eyes, a panorama.   Still others suggest "river of red
jasper. "   Since the Conquistadors later termed the area
the "Valley of Estelí, " it would seem that the conception
of a "panorama" best fits the subject.

3) The present city of Estelí, cabacera of the municipio of the same name, is called the "metropolis of
the Segovias, " and is located in the extensive Estelí
valley.   A center of agriculture, cattle, and light industrial development, it was known during colonial days
as the "district of haciendas. "   The population is around
15,000 and the city is the commercial and cultural center
of this whole area.   Originally called San Antonio de
Estelí, (1778), the original town was not in the present
location, but near the Río Agueguespala.   In 1823, the
Valley of Mochiguiste was chosen, in the larger valley
of Estelí, for the town seat.   Hospital, banks, clubs,
commercial enterprises, and schools all attest to the
significance of this regional center.   The Normal School
is an especially significant national enterprise located
here.

ESTELI, RIO DE.   Rising in the mountains of Tisay and
emptying into the Río Coco to the east of Telpaneca,
this is the most important stream of Estelí department.

ESTERO DE EL LIMON.   Receiving the rivers Atoyo, El

Viejo, Chiquito, and Acome, or Chinandega, this is an important estuary.

ESTERO DE EL REALEJO. Mouths of the rivers Ameya and Cosmapa, La Chorrera and Telica, are found in this estuary, historic in nature because it was the early colonial seaport on the Pacific for the region.

ESTETE, MARTIN. Lugarteniente or deputy of Pedrarias (q. v.) Dávila in Nicaragua. Sent by Pedrarias in 1529 to conquer Cuzcatlán, in the region of Nequeipo. An establishment of "La Cuidad de los Caballeros" under Estelí in the Salvadorenean area of Perulapan was short-lived. In the year 1528, 22, 000 pesos and in 1529, 30, 000 pesos of gold went to the Spanish crown from the Segovias.

ESTRADA, JOSE DOLORES. General Estrada led the Nica-raguan forces at San Jacinto (q. v. , Batalla de ...) into immortality for them and for himself on September 14, 1856. As a colonel of the 160 men fortified in the old hacienda house a few miles north of Tipitapa, his leadership in the resounding defeat of the filibuster Walker's North Americans under Byron Cole was a hero's part not only in the matter of a battle won, but in the legend of Walker invincibility once and for all destroyed; in the new spirit given to Central American forces which led them on to victory; and in the example of courage and fortitude which has inspired generations of Nicaraguans since. Estrada was born in Nandaime on March 16, 1792, his parents being Timoteo Estrada and doña Gertrudis Vado. An interesting postscript is that in continuing civil war following the Walker menace, General Estrada (with Generals Fernando Chamorro and Máximo Jérez) was reduced to a soldier's rank and branded as a traitor by his government, on April 24, 1863 at El Castillo.

ESTRADA, JUAN JOSE. Briefly President in 1911, Estrada was forced from power by events and by Adolfo Díaz, who then took over.

ESTRECHO EL BOQUERON. The narrow (half-mile wide) strait between Zapatera Island and the Granada department mainland, where a point juts out toward the Island.

ESTRECHURA, LA. A district in the remote foothills north of the lower Río Tuma.

ESTRELLA, LA.   A romantic periodical developed in Boaco in the era of 1915-1937.

ETHNIC COMPOSITION.   The ethnic composition of Nicaragua represents an assimilated Indian population with the exception of some Mosquito Indians and some tribal Sumos on the upper Río Coco.   Most of the population, about 85 percent, is Mestizo, or mixed Indian-white. About 10 percent are mixed Indian-Negro-white, most of this group living on the East or Caribbean Coast. The white population constitutes three to five percent of the whole, not only Spanish, but some German and English of long-standing in the country.   Tribal Indian groups are of negligible numbers.   There is a similarity to Honduras and El Salvador, and a marked difference in comparison to near-white Costa Rica and to Guatemala, which is two-thirds tribal Mayan.

EVA, ALEJANDRO.   A lieutenant at the Battle of San Jacinto (q. v., Batalla de ...) September 14, 1856, who later gave an account of the battle which was used by historians.

EVA, RAMIREZ.   Former head of Construcciones Nacionales who distinguished himself on September 21, 1956, by pouncing on President Anastasio Somoza's assassin, Rigoberto López, and throwing the young gunman to the floor just before guards pumped 70 bullets into López. Eva's friends pulled him away barely in time to escape the fusillade.

EVOLUCION, LA.   One of the spate of periodicals of a romantic and political nature originating in Boaco in 1915-1937.

EXCELENTISIMO SEÑOR PRESIDENTE DE LA REPUBLICA GENERAL DE DIVISION.   Full title given to President Anastasio Somoza García in the mid 1950's just prior to his assassination.   As general of division his uniform carried five stars in line on the epaulet straps.

EXIMBANK.   Acronym for the Export-Import Bank established in 1934 and modified in 1945 to provide and promote the financing of United States exports.   Active in Nicaragua to the amount of $5,000,000 U.S. in 1968.

EXPORTS OF NICARAGUA.   On the facing page, principle

Nicaraguan Exports, by Commodity by Year (in Millions of U.S. Dollars)

	1961	1962	1963	1964	1965	1966	1967
Cotton	18.3	31.3	39.8	51.5	66.1	56.8	56.0
Coffee	17.4	15.4	17.5	21.2	15.3	21.8	21.2
Meat	4.1	6.0	8.4	7.5	6.7	10.2	12.5
Copper	2.9	3.7	4.0	4.5	6.1	7.2	7.7
Cottonseed	2.6	4.6	5.2	6.6	8.7	8.2	5.6
Gold	7.7	7.7	7.1	6.9	5.4	5.2	5.2
Shrimp, lobster	--	1.6	1.6	1.7	2.1	3.8	4.7
Wood	2.9	2.7	2.2	2.1	1.9	2.5	2.1
Sugar	2.8	4.5	6.0	5.7	5.5	2.1	5.9
Sesame seed	2.4	2.0	2.2	2.3	2.1	2.0	2.5
Cottonseed oil	--	--	--	--	0.3	1.5	2.3
Bananas	0.1	0.8	1.4	2.1	0.8	0.9	3.3
Soluble coffee	2.2	3.7	3.7	4.0	2.3	1.4	0.4

exports are shown in tabular form for a seven-year
period. Note that in dollar value cotton is not only
first, but the one with greatest increase. Export items
include cotton, cottonseed, coffee, fresh meat, copper,
gold, shrimp and lobster, sugar, and lumber. Where
cotton products have held for ten years at well above a
third of total exports, gold has dropped from 10% in
1957 to 3% in 1967, with copper displacing it at 5%,
and seafood equalling it at 3%. Coffee has dropped
from 40% in 1957 to 14% in 1967, and lumber from 5%
to 1%. Coffee and cotton accounted for $77,000,000
(U. S.) in exports in 1967. Gold dropped also in dollar
volume. Meat has shown a dramatic increase, due in
part to improvement of breeding practices.

EXTRA. A weekly journal presently published in Managua.

-F-

FAJARDO, CORNELIO. One of the founders of a periodical
"Iris de La Tarde" (q. v.) in Boaco in 1915.

FALANGE AMERICANA, LA. The "American Phalanx" was
the name given to William Walker's (q. v.) party of 58
filibusters and their leader when they arrived in Nicaragua in 1855. Walker spoke of his men as the "Falange." See also GUERRA NACIONAL.

FALANGES ESPAÑOLES. Groups found to promote sympathy to
and cooperation with the Franco Regime in Spain. In some
countries of Latin America they have met with repression.

FALANGISMO. Falangismo is hispanicism with a heavy
stress on political objectives. See HISPANISMO.

FALSO BLUFF. An eminence and coastal projection, "false
bluff," 15 miles north along the Caribbean Coast from
Bluefields' "El Bluff."

FAN, EL. A commonly used abbreviative nickname for the
F. A. N., Fuerza Aérea Nicaragüense, or Nicaraguan
Air Force, part of the national guard military establishment. In the 1950's a number of P-51 pursuit planes
were purchased from Sweden. Transport craft were
also part of the force, with miscellaneous supporting
aircraft. Pilots built up flying hours by flying LANICA
commercial air routes.

FANDANGO. A Spanish dance which became popular in León in 1765.

FARALLONES DEL RIO DE OLAMA. This cleft through which the stream roars in Muy Muy municipio, Matagalpa department, is narrow enough to be leaped across by travelers.

FARFANA. A ranch, also known as Miraflores, which in 1756 in the area of the hill of Chiltepe was a subject of topographic survey efforts to clear titles.

FASHION (Ship). The steamer which cleared for Nicaragua in 1857 from Mobile Bay with William Walker and a number of his trusted lieutenants aboard in a futile attempt to land once again and recoup his Nicaraguan losses.

FAUNA. Nicaragua has in addition to a variety of birds (q. v.) a large variety of reptiles, some amphibians, relatively few fishes: <u>reptiles,</u> turtles (three families); lizards (iguanas, skinks, geckos, etc.); snakes, seven-- boas, worm snakes, coral snakes, pitvipers, etc. ; <u>amphibians</u>, caecilians, salamanders, frogs and toads (six families); and <u>fishes</u>, characins, gymnotid eels, catfish, minnows, killfishes, cichlids, gar-pikes, mud-eels, sea catfish, sharks (the freshwater variety unique to Lake Nicaragua), sawfish (a shark relative also in Lake Nicaragua), and tarpon (abundant in Lake Nicaragua, also freshwater adapted).

FAYSSOUX, CALLENDAR. Commander of William Walker's "navy, " this talented officer was in charge of the armed schooner <u>Granada</u>. Fayssoux had been a member of the ill-fated Narciso López expeditions to Cuba a few years earlier. When Sir Robert McClure of the <u>Esk</u> challenged the <u>Granada</u>, "flying a flag unknown to any nation, " Fayssoux refused to come aboard the <u>Esk</u> and when threats were made to sink his ship he did not budge. McClure later was dumbfounded by Walker's insistence on an apology. There is no doubt Fayssoux was the favorite among Walker's officers due to this incident, which occurred just offshore from San Juan del Sur. Then, later in 1856, a well-armed brig from Costa Rica appeared off San Juan del Sur and the <u>Granada</u> engaged her in a seafight, with two guns and 28 men; Fayssoux sunk the brig, and then rescued half her crew of 114.

Fayssoux stuck with Walker through thick and thin, arranging Walker's last trip on the schooner Taylor. He later had a distinguished career in the U. S. Civil War as a Confederate officer. Fayssoux was also a favorite among his fellow officers, a rare matter.

FEDERACION DE CENTRO AMERICA, LA. One hundred years after the original union, once again in July, 1921, a constituted assembly met to prepare a constitution for Central American Union, four states having signed the initial pact on January 19, 1921. Nicaragua walked out because the others would not accept the Bryan-Chamorro Treaty (q. v.). The plan of union began to fall apart when Costa Rica voted against joining and when a revolutionary government took over Guatemala, whose capital, Guatemala City, was to have been the federal capital. Many Central Americans consider that the U. S. sabotaged this movement toward union, the open act being recognition of the revolutionary government in Guatemala. The Federation ended February 7, 1922. Central American union remains a dream, paradoxically, in each of the five countries.

FEDERACION DE OBREROS DEL VOLANTE. One of the four registered labor organizations (q. v.) in Nicaragua.

FEDERACION DE OBREROS Y CAMPESINOS. This group is of Communist persuasion and links workers and peasants. It is one of two Communist worker organizations, the other being the Confederación General del Trabajo Independiente.

FEDERACION DE TRANSPORTADORES UNIDOS DE NICARAGUA (F. T. U. N.). The "teamsters union" of the country, this labor organization (q. v.) is registered with the Ministry of Labor, one of four so recognized.

FEDERACION SINDICAL DE MAESTROS DE NICARAGUA (F. S. M. N.). This teacher's group partakes somewhat of a professional as well as a labor organization. It is not registered under the Ministry of Labor.

FELAND, LOGAN. U. S. brigadier general of Marines, who commanded the Marine forces in Nicaragua following March 7, 1927. At that time there were 2, 000 men under his command. His principal task soon became the long difficult guerrilla war with Agusto Sandino.

FERROCARRIL A LOS PUEBLOS. The railroad section
which was opened in 1898 under the Zelaya administration and which served Masaya, Jinotepe, Diriamba, and
other towns, has been closed due to highways newly
available and motor vehicular traffic.

FESTIVAL DAYS, ABORIGINAL. In the Managua area, the
pre-conquest Mexican-derived tribes kept the following
festival days, some of which were names of animals:
Agat, Ocelot (same animal name now used), Oate, Cas-
caguate, Olín, Tepecat, Quianit, Sochet, Cipat, Acat,
Cali, Quespal, Coat, Misiste, Macat (deer), Toste (rabbit), At, Isquindi, Ocomate, Malinal, and Acate.

FILA ALTA. District in the municipio of Yalí in Jinotega
department.

FILIBUSTER. The word filibuster is anglicized from several sources, but originates in Holland Dutch as "vry-
bruiter": from vry, "free, " and bruiter, "booty, " or
spoils, taken in battle. "Freebooter" is the English
form of the original. The Spanish "filibusteros" in
Nicaraguan annals is applied to both the pirates of the
colonial centuries and the adherents of William Walker
in the 1850's. Buccaneers of the Caribbean were also
called filibusters.

FINCA MODELO. A "model farm" installed by the Nicaraguan government in the "Zona de Riego, " Rivas department. This experiment station for irrigated crops
is experimenting with a strain of bananas which is
blight resistant.

FINCAS DE CAFE. Coffee plantations.

FINQUERO. A rural farmer, owner of a finca.

FISH   see   FAUNA

FLAG, NICARAGUAN. Consists of three broad horizontal
stripes, equally divided along the hoist. The upper and
lower ones are blue and the middle one, white. The
great seal of Nicaragua is superimposed and is centered
on the white stripe. The seal is geometrically a triangle within a circle. Established at the time Nicaragua became a nation at the break-up of the Central
American Confederation, 1839.

FLEET MARINE FORCE   see   ARKANSAS.

FLEET SYSTEM, VENETIAN.   Adopted in 1543 by Spain
   under pressures of French piracy, this system replaced
   the old pattern of individual ship sailings to America,
   and was essentially an armed convoy plan.

FLINT, EARL.   Dr. Flint of the U.S., in 1878 discovered
   the remarkable archaeological site of Acahualinca (q.v.).

FLOR, LA.   1) Cattle ranch in the municipio of León,
   León department.
      2) Cattle ranch in San Juan del Sur minicipio, Rivas
   department.
      3) Comarca or district in the municipio of Achuapa,
   León.
      4) A district of the municipio of Moyogalpa on Omo-
   tepe Island in Lake Nicaragua, Rivas department.
      5) A district of the municipio of San Juan de Limay,
   Estelí department.

FLOR, RIO LA.   Stream in the Rivas department, municipio of San Juan del Sur, emptying into the Pacific.

FLOR BLANCA.   District in the municipio of Buenos Aires,
   department of Rivas.

FLOR DE CAÑA.   A locally produced rum in various grades,
   popular in the country by comparison with imported
   rums.

FLOR DE PIEDRA.   Comarca or district in the municipio
   of La Paz, León.

FLORA.   Isthmian plant families as found in Nicaragua are
   derived from both continents, to the North and to the
   South.   Among them are: tree fern, podocarp (conifer),
   pine, pondweed, sedge, palms, aroids, pipewort, spider-
   wort, amaryllis, iris, oxalis, malpighia, soapberry,
   dillenia, cacli, mallows, sterculia, myrtle, primrose,
   melastoma, heaths, dogbane, morning glory, figwort,
   bignonia, madder, gourds, pineapple, lily, cauna, orchids (a great variety), custard-apple, poppy, saxifrage,
   witch hazel, rose, legumes, spurges, sapodilla, logania,
   borages, vervain, mint, potato, gesnaria, and acanthus.

FLORES, LAS.   A district of the municipio and department

of Masaya.

FLORES, JOSE DOLORES. A representative of Chontales
     during the 1855-1856 War.   (See JUNTA DE RECUR-
     SOS.)

FLOYD, JOHN B. Secretary of War of the U.S. in 1858
     under the Buchanan administration.   He favored expedi-
     tions of conquest in Nicaragua, Mexico, and even the
     incitement of war with Spain so as to annex Cuba.   See
     HENNINGSEN.

FM STATIONS   see   FREQUENCY MODULATION.

FOA   see   FOREIGN OPERATIONS ADMINISTRATION.

FOAM (Tugboat).   On a voyage from New York to San Diego
     in 1926, this tug loaded arms and Nicaraguan revolution-
     aries at a Mexican port, was taken over by these bel-
     ligerent passengers, and was instrumental in the bom-
     bardment of towns along the Mosquito Coast.   The tug
     finally grounded, the captors left, and the crew then
     sought U.S. help.   The episode is reminiscent of the
     Jacksonville filibuster tugboat Three Friends and its
     Cuban adventures a generation earlier.

FONSECA, GOLFO DE.   One of the largest bays or gulfs
     in the South Pacific, affording one of the finest harbors
     in the world.   At the extreme western edge of Nica-
     ragua it is bounded also by Honduras and El Salvador.

FONSECA, JUAN.   A sub-lieutenant at the Battle of San
     Jacinto (q. v.), September 14, 1856.

FOREIGN OPERATIONS ADMINISTRATION.   The U.S. inter-
     national assistance agency after World War II.   The
     name was changed to International Cooperation Adminis-
     tration in 1956.   The succession of agencies had agri-
     cultural, military, educational, and other enterprises
     in Nicaragua.

FORMATIVE.   A term applied by archaeologists to the ear-
     liest appearance of sedentary village life based on agri-
     culture.   Throughout Central America evidential infor-
     mation has been assembled as to when and where for-
     mative life occurred, including such ceramic studies
     as those of Lothrop and others in the Nicaraguan-Costa-
     Rica area.

FPS.   see   FRENTE POPULAR SOMOSISTA

FRANCISCAN OBSERVANTS. Order of missionary priests
    who entered Nicaragua in 1706 from earlier work just
    to the north in the Pedro Sula-Yoro regions of Honduras;
    the movement was weak and difficult.   Franciscans felt
    at this time that servitude, use of armed force and
    mass baptisms were valid instruments of Christianiza-
    tion.   They did not devote the manpower or the effort
    in Nicaragua to support these policies, which were in
    effect conquest and enslavement.

FRANCISCANS.   1) The original group of a monastic order
    tracing their Nicaraguan origins to the colonial period.
        2) The women's order of this name, currently serv-
    ing in Nicaragua, their work is in hospitals and educa-
    tion in orphanages, etc.
        3) A Spanish religious order serving in churches,
    schools, etc.; established during the 20th century.

FRENCH CAY.   A tiny island off the Caribbean Coast of
    Zelaya department just 19 miles south of El Bluff.

FRENCH, PARKER H.   An officer of William Walker's who
    was appointed as Nicaraguan minister to the U.S. in
    1855.   Colonel French was not recognized, and in his
    fury at this rebuff Walker seized the Accessory Transit
    Company's steamers and assets.   Since this was de-
    fiance of Cornelius Vanderbilt, it was the beginning of
    Walker's downfall.

FRENTE POPULAR SOMOSISTA.   The FPN developed in the
    1947-1956 era to handle the problem of communistic
    tendencies in the labor force, and did so with success.
    (See   COMMUNIST PARTY.)

FRENTE SANDINISTA DE LIBERACION NATIONAL (FSLN).
    The Sandinista front of national liberation takes its name
    from the guerrilla leader of 1927-1933, César Agusto
    Sandino, who was a prototype for Castro and Guevara,
    and who has assumed the proportions of a folk-hero in
    some Latin American quarters.   The party is distinctly
    clandestine, dedicated to the violent overthrow of regu-
    larly constituted government and continues to harass
    from both rural and urban hideouts.   Eight Sandinistas
    were killed in a tank-battle in Managua streets in 1969.

FREQUENCY MODULATION RADIO (FM). There are 13 FM
stations in Nicaragua, as follows: Las Nubes, 94 megacycles; León, 90.06 megacycles; and Managua, respectively, 89, 92, 93, 94.3, 95, 96, 97, 97.5, 102, and
104, 178 megacycles. One station (93) is owned by the
Catholic Church and one (94.3), by the Nicaraguan Cultural Association. Two (94 and 96) are owned by the
Somoza family and one (97), by National Radio.

FREXIONE, DON FRANCISCO. One of three members of
the first executive committee of the Distrito Nacional
(q. v.).

FREYLINGHUYSEN, FREDERICK T. U. S. Secretary of
State under President Arthur who was involved anew in
diplomacy in regard to the Clayton-Bulwer Treaty, and
whose name is attached to the Freylinghuysen-Zavala
Treaty (q. v.) with Nicaragua in 1884.

FREYLINGHUYSEN-ZAVALA TREATY. A treaty between
U. S. and Nicaragua drawn up by Commissioner Zavala
of Nicaragua and U. S. Secretary of State Freylinghuysen
and sent to the U. S. Senate for ratification in December, 1884. It provided that the U. S. Government should
construct, operate, and maintain a canal through Nicaragua, maintaining also exclusive control. Nicaragua
would provide right-of-way 2 1/2 miles wide, and would
receive from the U. S. a guarantee of territorial integrity
and $4,000,000 for public improvements; the canal would
belong jointly to the U. S. and Nicaragua. Nicaragua
ratified the F-Z convention as it was written. The U. S.
Senate balked, due to the implications of trouble with
Great Britain and by 32 ayes to 23 nays, the treaty
failed of the necessary 2/3 vote for ratification. This
left the unsatisfactory Clayton-Bulwer Treaty with England and the equally inconclusive Dickinson-Ayón Treaty
with Nicaragua still in effect.

FRISBIE, GRANVILLE K. A U. S. Marine Captain who discovered a Sandinista camp near "El Chipote" (q. v.) on
December 26, 1931, when leading his patrol. The camp
and several others were destroyed.

FRONT OF REVOLUTIONARY YOUTH. One of several student political organizations thought to have Communist
orientation.

FRONTERAS, LAS.   Used in the Nicaraguan context, "the Frontiers" were the part of the country separating the known areas along the Pacific Coast from the vast jungle unknown of the eastern two-thirds of the country, inhabited by hostile tribes and for as many as 200 years not penetrated by the Spaniards.   Their "conquest" was in Nicaragua confined by hostile rainforest mountainous jungle and the indigenous human enemy.   The frontiers extended from the River San Juan head to the north between the modern departments of Boaco and Matagalpa. Even today this same belt of territory represents a well-defined zone of demarcation between the populous, settled, cultivated Pacific Coastal area and the wild rainforest in the east, sparsely populated and difficult to reach, the two means of access being aircraft and dugout canoes.

F. S. L. N.   see   FRENTE SANDINISTA DE LIBERACION NATIONAL

F. S. M. N.   see   FEDERACION SINDICAL DE MAESTROS DE NICARAGUA

F. T. U. N.   see   FEDERACION DE TRANSPORTADORES UNIDOS DE NICARAGUA

FUENTE, LA.   Comarca or district in the municipio of La Paz, department of León.

FUENTE, PADRE DE LA.   First president of independent Rivas under the abortive rebellion of 1811.

FULTON (Ship).   American naval war vessel involved in the capture of William Walker's second expeditionary force to Nicaragua in 1857.   (See   HORNSBY.)

FUMAROLAS DE AGUAS CALIENTES.   These volcanological phenomena occur along the banks of the Río Grande de Matagalpa in Muy Muy municipio of Matagalpa department.

FUNDADORA, LA.   1) Coffee hacienda in the Jinotega municipio founded by General Ignacio Chávez, originally from León.
    2) A district of the municipio of Jinotega.

-G-

GACETA, LA.   Official publication of the Nicaraguan government which publishes legislative enactments, government
statistical and other reports of an official character, and
presidential decrees, which have the force of law.

GACETA DEL GOBIERNO SUPREMO DEL ESTADO DE
NICARAGUA.   A periodical of an official nature in
this compromise capital (between León and Granada),
Managua, in 1848 and 1849.

GACETA OFICIAL DE NICARAGUA.   This "official gazette"
was published in Managua in 1854.

GAGOS, LOS.   A district of the San Rafael del Sur municipio, Managua department.

GALIA, LA.   Coffee hacienda in the Jinotega department.

GALISTEO, DON MANUEL.   A Spanish surveyor who in
1781 made a report on a Nicaraguan canal project, and
who followed up work of Ysasi (q. v.) and others.   He
found the lakes to be 133 feet above sea level.   Locks
were not well understood, and Galisteo gave a discour-
aging report because of his feelings that the differences
in level of 133 feet from lakes to the sea 12 miles
away made the canal task too difficult.   It is strange
that Galisteo did not know of the locks built in Sweden
in 1607 at Lilla Edet on the Gota River; by 1800, Lake
Vanern had been connected with the sea through the
Trollhatten locks.

GALLEDO, JUAN.   Comendador of Condega (q. v. , def. 2)
in 1548.

GALVAO, ANTONIO.   Portuguese governor of Ternate in
the Moluccas, who published in 1555 a book called The
Discoveries of the World, and therein placed in print
for the first time the conception of a canal through the
Middle American isthmus.   He attributed the idea to
Alvaro de Saavedra, a cousin of Hernán Cortez.   Saavedra went to the Moluccas from Mexico in 1528.   Saavedra mentioned four of the feasible routes considered to
this very day: the present Panama route, the Panama
route farther east to the Pacific Bay of San Miguel, the
Isthmus of Tehuantepec, and the San Juan River/Lake

Nicaragua route. Galvao's translator gave San Juan as Xaquatur (q. v.). It is worthy of remark that the idea in this detailed form of feasible alternates originated during the first four decades of the post-conquest period, and was finally realized on one of the originally suggested routes, at least 386 years after the proposal.

GALVEZ, MATIAS DE. As lieutenant general, highest ranking commission ever granted by Spain in Central America, this officer later became viceroy of New Spain following his initial posting to Central America in 1778. Brother of José Gálvez, Minister of the Indies, he was an experienced and thorough man who toured his new command through Nicaragua, an unusual move for the times, and one difficult to effect. He had heard rumors of an impending British expedition to seize the San Juan River and Lake Nicaragua. He toured León and Granada and presumably all the defenses, and named Ignacio Maestre sergeant-major of the Navy at Granada, charged with the building of a fleet on Lake Nicaragua. (It was at about this same time that similar naval and fortification activities were being carried out on a similarly strategic lake-river complex in North America--Lake Champlain; the parallel of the two frontier endeavors makes a fascinating historical comparison.) Gálvez, however, in ordering the arrest of Carlos Matías Yarrince (q. v.), probably precipitated the massacre of Terry (q. v.) at the San Juan mouth. He was also responsible for developing the defense of Fort Omoa in Honduras during the ensuing war with England, and recaptured the fort in 1779. Gálvez seems to have been at Granada in 1780 when the British attacked El Castillo Viejo (q. v.), and may have given the orders which caused the hasty erection of Fort San Carlos (q. v. , def. 2) and the ultimate "wearing out" of the British in their fever-ridden conquest of El Castillo.

GAMALOTE, EL. Comarca or district in the municipio of La Libertad, Chontales.

GAMBRINO'S. A hotel-restaurant considered the best in Managua in the late 1920's and frequented by U. S. Marines of the occupying forces.

GAMERO, LUIS. This priest was one of the Jesuits expelled from Guatemala in 1871. Coming to Rivas with Felipe M. Gardella and Ignacio Toboada, also priests,

the men were instrumental in education and hospital
work in that city. This Jesuit priest also organized
the first band in the city of Rivas in 1875 and 1876,
he himself being a musician and composer. The pro-
ceeds from band concerts went to support the Catholic
Church and the Hospital of Rivas.

GARCIA, LAS. A district in the municipio of Santa Lucía,
department of Boaco.

GARCIA JEREZ, NICOLAS. Bishop of Nicaragua and first
chancellor of the University of Nicaragua in 1816.

GARCIA SARMIENTO, FELIX RUBEN. The real name for
Nicaragua's immortal poet, Rubén Darío, born in Chocoyos or Metapa, January 18, 1867, and destined to
revolutionize Spanish literature with his "modernism."
Living abroad much of his life, as literateur, bon vivant,
and diplomat, Darío lent a particular note to his writings which has influenced the Spanish style ever since.
His works include the following: La Iniciación Melódica,
done in 1880-1886; Epístolas y Poemas, 1885; Abrojos,
1887; Canto Epico a las Glorias de Chile, 1887; Otonales,
1887; Azul, 1888 and 1890; Prosas Profanas y Otros
Poemas, 1896 and 1901; Cantos de Vida y Esperanza,
Los Cisnes, y Otros Poemas, 1905; El Canto Errante,
1907; Canto a la Argentina y Otros Poemas, 1914; and
Del Chorro de la Fuente, in 1886-1916. Widely travelled in South America and Europe, Darío lived abroad
much of his life, yet had a passionate love for his
homeland, Nicaragua. Over his grave in the cathedral
in León is a marble lion.

GARDELLA, FELIPE M. see GAMERO, LUIS

GARDNER, GEORGE E. U. S. Marine second lieutenant in
command of a detachment which helped drive off guerrilla forces under Colindres and Umanzor (see DEFEND-
ING ARMY...) near El Sauce in November, 1931.

GARITA, LA. 1) Coffee hacienda in the municipio of Yali,
Jinotega department.
    2) A district in the municipio and department of
Matagalpa.

GARRISON, CORNELIUS K. see VANDERBILT, CORNELIUS

GARROBO GRANDE. Comarca or district in the municipio
    of Villa Somoza, Chontales.

GATEADA NUMERO DOS. Comarca or district in the mu-
    nicipio of Villa Somoza, Chontales.

GATEADA NUMERO UNO. Comarca or district in the mu-
    nicipio of Villa Somoza, Chontales.

GDP see GROSS DOMESTIC PRODUCT

"GENERAL, EL. " A term applied with considerable affec-
    tion to Anastasio Somoza García during the many years
    he was virtual ruler of Nicaragua: from 1933 to the
    time of his assassination in 1956. On the part of the
    campesino or countryman, the word was used with respect
    and frequently with adoration. Somoza was the general.
    (Five stars in a row on his shoulders.) While Somoza
    had vigorous opposition, he was revered by many of the
    common people who viewed him as the rallying symbol
    of their aspirations. During his incumbency the order,
    peace and prosperity relative to the century immediately
    preceding was a matter for gratitude which expressed it-
    self in both the affectionate diminutive "Tacho" (q. v.)
    and the more formal, but often equally affectionate,
    "The General. " There was during Somoza's terms in
    office little chance of the sort of popular uprisings which
    took place in Mexico under Zapata and Villa.

GENERAL DE DIVISION. Highest rank in the Nicaraguan
    Guardia Nacional (Armed Force), and so far held only
    by Anastasio Somoza García (several times president of
    Nicaragua 1933-1956) and his son, West Point graduate
    Anastasio Somoza Debayle, presently (1971) President
    of Nicaragua. The rank insignia, worn on the shoulder,
    is five stars in a row.

GENERAL SOMOZA. A motor vessel on the Lake Nicaragua
    circuit in the 1950's, making a two-day round trip be-
    tween Granada and San Carlos. In 1969, the Somoza
    lay a stranded wreck on one of the isletas near Granada.

GENERAL TREATY ON CENTRAL AMERICAN ECONOMIC
    INTEGRATION. This 1960 agreement finally established
    a Common Market among the five Central American
    countries, and the benefits have persisted in spite of
    the war between Honduras and El Salvador in 1969,

which shut off a great deal of commercial traffic across
the Pacific shores of Honduras.   A Salvador-to-Nicaragua
ferry has taken up some of the slack.   Signed in Managua on December 13, 1960, the treaty provided for a
Central American Bank of Economic Integration and a
quadripartite common market to be set up within five
years.   Only Costa Rica seemed reluctant.

GENERAL TREATY OF PEACE AND UNITY.   Signed by all
the Central American States in 1907, the treaty provided
for compulsory adjudication of disputes between signatories and prohibited political intervention by any state
in the internal affairs of another.   A corresponding act
of 1907 was the creation of the Central American Court
of Justice, which was to decide disputes.   In 1918,
Nicaragua abrogated this treaty due to dissatisfaction
over disputes and rulings in connection with Costa Rica
and El Salvador.

GENIZARO, CHARO DE   see   TISMA, LAGUNA DE

GENTE DECENTE ("decent people")   see   ARISTOCRACIA,
LA

GENTE PEQUENE ("humble people")   see   ARISTOCRACIA,
LA

GEOGRAFIA DE NICARAGUA.   Published in 1909, the work
of Dr. Jorge Bravo, this text was used at the primary
level in Nicaraguan schools.

GEORGE II.   King of the Sambos on the Mosquito Coast in
1776 and following.   As Prince George he had visited
George III of England in 1775.   A handsome mulatto,
he became a cruel despot following the war of the 1780's
and was finally assassinated.   He joined Colville Breton
and "Admiral" Delce in the Jeremiah Terry (all q. v.)
fiasco of 1778.   He regarded Carlos Yarrince (q. v.) as
his vassal.   He never was entirely won over by the
Spanish even though they made every effort to achieve
his support on the coast.   The Spanish "Indian policy"
in eastern Nicaragua never jelled, as it was too depend-
ent upon questionable and rapacious allies in a vast and
dangerous tropical wilderness.

GIGANTE, EL.   1) A mountain in Terrabona municipio,
Matagalpa department.

2) Thermal Spring in Carazo department, between Santa Teresa and La Conquista.
3) Unimproved embarkation point or small port on the Pacific coast of municipio San Juan de Tola, Rivas department.

GIL GONZALES, RIO.   A stream in the municipio of Belén, Rivas department.

GIL GONZALEZ.   District in the municipio of Potosí, Rivas department.

GILIGUA.   A district in the municipio of Muy Muy, Matagalpa department.

GILIGUA, RIO.   A river in the Muy Muy municipio of Matagalpa department.

GIRON RUANO, MANUEL MARIA.   Trusted lieutenant of Agusto Sandino, a well-educated middle-aged Guatemalan, Girón was probably the most able officer to serve under Sandino.   In April of 1928 he seized the La Luz and Los Angeles gold mines, owned by a Pittsburgh company working in Nicaragua since 1901.   He fought in the Río Coco and Río Bocay jungles, and won a significant engagement in May of 1928.   Captured by U. S. Marines in February, 1929, Girón, who was ill, was summarily tried by a court-martial under volunteer "General" Juan Escamilla, a Mexican.   Girón was executed, the only important Sandinista chief to be made prisoner by either the U. S. Marines or the Nicaraguan National Guard.

GLORIA, LA.   Quinta, or country house in the vicinity of Niquinohomo.

GOLD (River) see   COCO, RIO.

GOLFO, EL.   A district of the municipio of Jinotega.

GOLFO DE CHOROTEGA.   Aboriginal name given by the Nahuatl-speaking Chorutegans to the Gulf of Fonseca (q. v. , under Fonseca).

"GOLPE DE CUARTEL. "   A "barracks stroke"--in other words, a coup d'état effected by the military element. An excellent example is the Emiliano Chamorro coup of October 25, 1926 (see Carter, C. B.).

GOMEZ, LOS. Comarca or district in the municipio of La
Conquista, Carazo department.

GOMEZ DE VALDIVIESO, DON RODRIGO. The first Alcalde
de Segunde voto (vice-mayor) of the new villa of Rivas
in 1720.

GORRION, EL. 1) A district in the municipio of Esquipulas,
department of Matagalpa.
2) District in the municipio of Yalí in Jinotega department.
3) A mountain height in the municipio of Esquipulas,
department of Matagalpa.

GORRIONA, LA. A hacienda just opposite the Isla Zapatera
on the Granada department shores of Lake Nicaragua.

GOTTEL, ENRIQUE H. see PORVENIR DE NICARAGUA,
EL.

GOVERNMENT, NICARAGUAN. Based on the Constitution
of 1950, Nicaragua is "a unitary, free, sovereign, and
independent state," its government being republican and
democratically representative. A residual hope for Central American union lies in the constitutional provision
that such union may take place in spite of the indivisible
and unalienable character of the nation. The Constitution also permits canal treaties. The opposition party
is guaranteed one-third representation in Congress. By
this provision, third parties are given legal denial--
only two parties are "legal" under the strictest construction of the Constitution. However, several more or less
clandestine parties flourish.

GOVERNMENTAL STRUCTURE. Nicaragua is a republic
with a unitary form of governmental structure, which
is divided for administrative purposes into 16 departments, one territory (or comarca: Cabo Gracias a
Dios), one national district (distrito nacional) of Managua, and 123 municipalities, corresponding roughly
to U.S. counties. See also ADMINISTRATION, LOCAL.

GOYENA. Cattle ranch in the municipio of León, León department.

GOYENA, INSTITUTO RAMIREZ. A major governmental
secondary school in Managua, named for a distinguished

Nicaraguan.   Most students are studying on scholarships
(or "becas"), and the usual pattern of part-time ad hoc
instruction is carried out.

GRANADA. 1) The city of Granada, located at the northwest
corner of Lake Nicaragua, is understandably colonial in
appearance and to some extent in character for it is the
oldest Spanish city in the Central American isthmian
area to have been in one location since its founding in
1523 by Francisco Hernández de Córdoba.   In 1523 he
commanded the construction of the San Francisco monastery.   While reconstructed several times, the basic
building is still there.   It was used as a hospital by the
filibuster William Walker, and as a school in recent
years.   Granada has a remarkable cemetery, a city of
marble, which gives much history in its epitaphs.   There
is a march of events from pirate attacks in the 17th
century to the revolutionary activities of the 20th.
Granada was a major port of the Spanish colonies from
the early 1500's, until in the late 1600's an earthquake
made shallows in the San Juan River which curtailed
galleon traffic.   Up until that time the lake port of
Granada was in direct contact with the Spanish port of
Cádiz, or the Guadalquivir River and its port of Seville.
There was a fort in Granada, the ruined remains of
which are still the base for the present dock buildings,
and this 16th-century castillo or fortaleza was the first
of a series of 12 fortifications which defended the San
Juan River and Lake Nicaragua route.   On a nearby
"isleta" in sight of Granada is a ruined fort or battery
which was the second post in the chain (see Isla El Castillo).   Granada suffered its greatest trauma when
burned by William Walker's General Henningsen (q. v.)
in 1857, following the epic siege sustained by the filibusters.   Rebuilt after the holocaust, Granada has many
buildings with marks of the fire evident, such as the
La Merced church.   Built on the site of an ancient Indian town, Xalteva or Jalteva, Granada has a cuartel
(fortified barracks), a pentagonal crenellated battlement
with five towers which still bears the name, "El Jalteva. " It is situated where two deep ravines, the Arroyo Peladientes and the Arroyo Aduana nearly meet in the
western edge of the city.   The city site due to the ravines
was adapted for defense.   (The Arroyo Peladientes is a
tributary of the southernmost protective ravine, the Arroyo
Zazateligua.) Granada bears much of the aspect of a Spanish colonial city with the Guadelupe, La Merced, San Fran-

cisco, and other churches. There are a number of barrios
or sections of the city long established. There is a large
modern stadium for baseball, the "Flor de Caña."
Granada has many old mansions on the Spanish patio
pattern, drawn from earlier Greek origins. In the environs to the south is the looming dead volcano, Mombacho, and down-lake from the foreshore may be seen
the perfect cone of Volcán Concepción on Omotepe Island. Granada is still the principal lake port, and the
terminus of the railroad to Corinto.

2) The department of Granada is equally divided in
extent north and south by its ancient cabacera, the city
of Granada, which with León was one of the first two
Spanish colonial cities to be established in Nicaragua,
4 1/2 centuries ago. The department has an area of
545 square miles, and a population of over 40,000 persons. Originally the Department Oriental, or eastern
department, Granada took up a third of the whole country. The present department includes the large island
of Zapatera in Lake Nicaragua, and the remarkable
"isletas" or little islands, composed of heaps of volcanic rock lodged offshore, and presumed to have been
ejected in geologic times from the long-dead crater of
nearby Mount Mombacho. Another huge crater is the
caldera filled by Lake Apoyo a few miles east of Granada. Bounded on the north by the departments of Boaco
and Managua, on the west by Carazo and Masaya, on
the south by Rivas and on most of the east by the Lake
Nicaragua Coast, the department includes the municipios
of Nandaime, Diriomo, and Diría, as well as the ruins
of old Nandaime. The whole area is steeped in Nicaraguan history, particularly with the pirate depradations
of the colonial centuries and burning of the city of Granada by William Walker's General Henningsen in 1857.
There are extant colonial buildings still standing in the
department. The pursuits of the population are agricultural and similar to those in much of the rest of Nicaragua. The whole department is well-known for the
many varieties of fruits raised.

3) Partido de Granada, one of the nine districts of
the country under the Constitution of April 8, 1826,
when it was one of the United Provinces of Central
America. (See PARTIDOS DE NICARAGUA.)

4) This armed schooner was William Walker's "navy"
in 1856. It figured in several spirited encounters under
the command of Callendar Fayssoux (q. v.).

5) A steamer (Lake Nicaragua and San Juan River)
of the post-filibuster war period, 1860-1880.

GRANADILLA, LA. A hacienda to the southwest of the dead volcano Mombacho in Granada department.

GRANADILLO. A district in the municipio and department of Matagalpa.

GRANADIÑO. A citizen of Granada.

GRANDE, ISLA. Island in Lake Nicaragua off the Chontales shore.

GRANDE, RIO. 1) With the Río Tola, part of a projected canal route for Nicaragua, this stream is in the municipio of San Juan de Tola.
2) One of the Pacific-flowing streams of Carazo department, with several tributaries: El Magua, La Chorrera, La Conquista, San Gregorio, El Nance, and Achuapa.

GRANDES PROPRIEDADES. A land-holding classification of properties from 200 to 1000 manzanas, or about 350 to 1750 acres.

GRANDEZA, LA. Comarca or district in the municipio of Diriamba, department of Carazo.

GRANERO DE LA PROVINCIA. Term applied to Masaya and environs as the "granary" of the province in the colonial era.

GRANERO DE NICARAGUA. A term applied to the department of Chinandega, as the "granary" of the country.

GRANJA, LA. District on the shores of Lake Nicaragua opposite the Isletas de Granada.

GRANJA, SALVADOR DEL AGUILA. One of the first officers of the new Villa of Rivas in 1720, as Alfarez Mayor. Also one of the two who presented the request for Villa status in Guatemala; July, 1717.

GRANT, ULYSSES S. A U.S. post-Civil War President, Grant wished to pursue a vigorous isthmian canal policy. He used the strong phraseology: "...I commend an American canal, on American soil, to the American people." Grant appointed an Interoceanic Canal Commission (q.v.). He did his utmost during two terms to put the canal project on a sound basis. The diplomatic and political situations, partly due to the spectre of the Clayton-Bulwer Treaty, were worse than ever. Grant agreed to lead the roster of American canal promoters upon the formation of the Provisional Interoceanic Canal Society (q. v.).

GRAY, EARL T.   An aggressive second lieutenant commanding National Guard patrols against Pedrôn in early 1932, in the Pis Pis district.

GREAT CAPE RIVER   see   COCO, RIO; and CABO GRACIAS A DIOS

GREAT LAKE STEAMER COMPANY (Compaña de Vapores del Gran Lago).   This company had the one steamer, the old Victoria (q. v.) of 180 tons, which made a Lake Nicaragua circuit to all ports eight times a month, during the late 19th and the first third of the 20th centuries.

GREAT RIFT.   A major depression in the basic American Cordillera which in Nicaragua contains broad plains and the two large lakes, Managua and Nicaragua.   Most of the great rift drains to the Caribbean via Lake Nicaragua and the San Juan River, in spite of the fact that only a low 12-mile isthmus separates the lake from the Pacific Ocean.   It is at this point of all the Americas that Atlantic and Pacific waters most nearly join.

GRECIA, LA.   1) A district of the municipio of San Juan de Limay, Estelî department, known for mining activities early in this century.
    2) Abandoned gold-silver mine in the Limay municipio of Estelî department.

GREYTOWN BAY   see   PUNTA GORDA, BAHIA

GRIFFIN, R. G.   Captain commanding guardsmen in second phase of action near El Sauce, occupying Santa Isabela in November, 1931.   (See GARDNER and HENRICH.)

GRINGO.   A nickname given to North Americans in much of Latin America.   Not used very often in Nicaragua, by comparison with some of the other countries.

GROSS   see   CANNON Y GROSS

GROSS DOMESTIC PRODUCT.   For a five-year period, the
GDP was as follows, with tax revenues also shown:

Year	Dollars GDP	Cordobas GDP	Tax (córdobas)
1963	$446, 500, 000	3, 125, 300, 000	316, 200, 000
1964	475, 000, 000	3, 323, 900, 000	335, 700, 000
1965	587, 500, 000	4, 162, 600, 000	364, 100, 000
1966	616, 500, 000	4, 315, 800, 000	420, 000, 000
1967	658, 200, 000	4, 617, 300, 000	438, 300, 000

However, as a basis for comparison, Nicaragua's GDP
for recent years is as follows (in millions of dollars,
U. S.) according to a different source.   This statement
is more conservative but agrees for the 1963-1964 years:
1961, 376. 2; 1962, 415. 8; 1963, 446. 5; 1964, 474. 8;
1965, 549. 1; 1966, 566. 3; and 1967, 590. 7.

GROSS NATIONAL PRODUCT (GNP)   see GROSS DOMESTIC
PRODUCT

GROVES, LESLIE R.   A lieutenant subordinate to Major Dan
Sultan of the U. S. Army engineers who directed repair
of the Managua reservoir and water pumps following the
1931 earthquake.

GUABILLOS.   Comarca or district in the municipio of Jinotepe, Carazo department.

GUACALITO, EL.   One of several embarkation points or
small ports on the Pacific coast of municipio San Juan
de Tola, Rivas department.

GUACAS DE CERAMICAS.   "Guacas" or little idols of ceramic are found in many places such as "El Jocote" in
the municipio of Condega.   This term is used widely,
particularly in Panama and Costa Rica.

GUACHIPILIN.   1) District in the municipio and department
of Rivas.
2) El Guachipilin, a comarca or district in the municipio of Jinotepe, Carazo department.

GUADALUPE.   1) A district of the municipio of San Ramón,
Matagalpa department.
2) A flowing spring in the municipio of San Ramón,
Matagalpa department.

3) Barrio Guadalupe a district of the city of León named for a small church which was dedicated to the Virgin of Guadelupe by Fray José Ramón de Jesús María in about 1820. One of the older districts of the city.

4) One of the old Spanish mines, an open pit prospect hole, found between Las Calpules and Amatillo in Nueva Segovia. A low yield is indicated. This dig is part of the La Misericordia group.

GUADALUPE NUMERO DOS.   Comarca or district of the municipio of León, León department.

GUADALUPE NUMERO UNO.   Comarca or district of the municipio of León, León department.

GUAILO, EL.   A district of the municipio of San Juan de Limay, Estelí department.

GUALAN.   Mountain of the Kilambé complex, altitude 4040 feet, Jinotega department.

GUALISES, LOS.   Coffee hacienda and cattle ranch in the municipio of Yalí, Jinotega department.

GUAMBLAN.   Mountain of the Kilambé complex, altitude 3, 760 feet, Jinotega department.

GUAMBLAN ABAJO.   A district of the municipio of Jinotega.

GUAMBLON, VALLE DE.   Surrounded by the Kilambé mountain complex and the rivers Coco, Guamblón, and Yacalguas, this valley approximately 1000 feet above sea-level is in part impenetrable and all forested.

GUAMBLONCITO.   A district of the municipio of Jinotega.

GUANABANA, LA.   1) A cattle ranch in the municipio of La Concordia, department of Jinotega.

2) The largest of the Granada "islets," or small volcanic islands.

GUANACASTE, EL.   1) A district in Granada department five miles due south of Lake Apoyo.

2) A comarca or district in the municipio of Diriamba, department of Carazo.

3) A comarca or district in the municipio of San Marcos, Carazo department.

GUANACASTILLO.   1) Comarca, valley or district in the
municipio of Acoyapa, Chontales.
2) A district of the municipio and department of
Masaya.

GUANACASTON.   A district of the municipio of San Juan de
Limay, Estelí department.

GUANACOS.   Nickname ("apodo") given to natives of the Republic of El Salvador.

GUANAGUANA.   A district in the department of Matagalpa,
municipio of Matiguás.

GUANAGUAS.   A district in the municipio of Matiguás,
Matagalpa, department.

GUANEXICOS.   Aboriginal tribal group in the mountains of
the Segovias, speaking "Chondal."

GUAPINOL.   1) A district in the municipio of Jinotega.
2) Mina El Guapinol, an old Spanish mine near the
mouth of the Macualizo River in Nueva Segovia department of which a tunnel ditch and prospect holes remain.
A quartz vein exists of a thickness of ten feet, 150 feet
long.   Ore is gold and silver.
3) El Guapinol, a district of the municipio of Niquinohomo, Masaya department.

GUAPOTAL.   A district of the municipio of San Ramón,
Matagalpa department.

GUARDIOLA, SANTOS.   A Honduran general noted in Central American annals for his cruelty, who was in command of a Legitimist Army in Rivas on the occasion of
William Walker's (q. v.) first battle in Rivas on June
29, 1855.   Walker's Nicaraguan allies fled, leaving his
55 Americans opposed to over 500 of the enemy under
Guardiola, who had earned his appelation of "the butcher."
Incredibly, the Walker force, though decimated, put some
of the Legitimists to flight, but had to retreat to their
schooner, the Vesta, and sail again to Realejo, regain-
ing their courage and treating their wounds.

GUARUMO.   1) Comarca or district of the municipio of
Santo Tomás in Chontales.
2) Mountain in the municipio of Santo Tomás, Chontales.

3) El Guarumo, comarca or district of the municipio of Santa Teresa, Carazo department.
4) El Guarumo, comarca or district in the municipio of Villa Somoza, Chontales.

GUASACA. A district in the municipio and department of Matagalpa.

GUASACA ABAJO. A district in the municipio and department of Matagalpa.

GUASACA ARRIBA. A district in the municipio and department of Matagalpa.

GUASGUALI. A district in the municipio and department of Matagalpa.

GUASGUALI, RAMA DE. Branch of the Darién Range, departments of Jinotega and Matagalpa. Heights near Jinotega. Major heights are Saraguasca, Curinagua, Ocotal de la Contera, Cerro de la Cruz, El Matazano.

GUASIMAL, EL. Comarca, valley or district in the municipio of Juigalpa.

GUASIMOS, LOS. Comarca or district in the municipio of Achuapa, León.

GUASLALA. A district in the municipio and department of Matagalpa.

GUATEMALA. Important finca in the municipio of La Concepción, department of Masaya.

GUAYABAS, LAS. 1) Cattle ranch in the municipio of Yalí, Jinotega department.
2) Comarca or district of the municipio of El Jicaral, León.
3) District in the municipio of Yalí in Jinotega department.

GUAYABO. 1) Comarca or district in the municipio of Larreynaga, León department.
2) El Guayabo, coffee hacienda in the municipio of El Sauce, León department.

GUAYABO DE LA PIEDRA. A district of the municipio and department of Masaya.

GUAYACAN, EL. Comarca or district in the municipio of
Diriamba, department of Carazo.

GUAYALO, EL. Comarca or district in the municipio of
Achuapa, León.

GUAYUCALI. A district of the municipio of Condega, Estelí department.

GUERERO, JOSE MARIA. Doctor Guerero was one of the
first faculty of the University of Nicaragua in 1816.

GUERGUERO, EL. A district just east of Siuna.

GUERNICA. The bombing and destruction in 1937 of this
Spanish town is considered an archetypical case of aerial
bombardment. However, the first such action occurred
in Nicaragua in February 1927 in the Battle of Chinandega (q. v.).

GUERRA "CERDA Y ARGÜELLO. " War in 1825 between
political factions is remembered for the massacre on
the Lake Nicaragua Island "La Pelona. "

"GUERRA DE MENA. " The "Mena War" of 1912 included
a siege of Masaya, which lasted 26 days following September 8th. Ostensibly the cause was the opposition of
the conservative forces to the presidency of the Republic,
which had been assigned him by constituent assembly.
It was the participation of U. S. Marines in the capture
of the forts "El Coyotepe" and "La Barranca" that has
been deeply resented by Nicaraguans since as unjustified
intervention. The 1912 events ushered in 21 years of
U. S. Marine involvement in Nicaragua. The forces of
General Emiliano Chamorro, opposed to Mena, were
those which took over the city, burning a part of it.
This was also called the "War of 1912. "

GUERRA NACIONAL. The "National War" of Nicaragua
which began on June 29, 1855, as filibuster William
Walker's (q. v.) 58 "Immortals, " the American Phalanx
(Falange) advanced on Rivas, and which ended, oddly
enough, in the same town, on April 11, 1857, when the
last battle was fought there between Walker's dwindled
forces and General Zavala's besieging Central American
Armies. In that battle Zavala had nearly 2000 men and
Walker only 332 fit for duty. Even so, 700 of the at-

tacking force were casualties, as against only nine of
Walker's tough supporters.   The siege and illness wore
them out so that Walker's surrender came on May 1,
1857, when Walker surrendered to U.S. Naval Commander Charles N. Davis.   The high point of the war from
the Nicaraguan standpoint was the defeat of Walker's
raiding party under Byron Cole in the Batalla de San
Jacinto (q. v.) on September 14, 1856.   One of the many
key events was the destruction of Granada under General
Henningsen and the latter's dramatic postscript "Aquí
fue Granada. "   Perhaps most significant of all, from
the time of the 1839 breakup of the several members
of the Central American Federation until the recent
years of the Central American Common Market, this
was an outstanding example of cooperative effort among
them.   Central American forces were estimated to total
17, 000 during the conflict.   Walker's men had totalled
2500, of whom 1000 died of wounds or disease, 700 deserted, 250 had been discharged, and 80 captured.   An
estimated 5800 Central Americans were battle casualties.
(See also SPENCER, CAUTY, HENNINGSEN, CORRAL,
BATALLA DE SAN JACINTO, and ESTRADA.)
   The Walker filibuster war of 1854-1857 was the only
major enterprise to unite the five countries between the
1839 breakup of Central America and the economic cooperation now current.   The action was centered in
southern Nicaragua and a little in Northern Costa Rica.
Troops from all five republics gathered to a total of an
estimated 17, 000 to repel Walker.   Costa Rica furnished
most of these men, doubtless due to poor overland communications from the other countries.   While the five
small countries are very nationalistically minded as individuals, this unity against the invading Walker was
Central American in character, and it is interesting
that as such it has been dubbed the "national" war.
There is still much feeling for union in spite of the
separatist events of the past century and a half.
   A list of the Presidents of Central American countries involved at the outset of the war (September 12,
1856) is given: Nicaragua, Don Patricio Rivas; Guatemala, General Rafael Carrera; El Salvador, Don Rafael
Campos; Honduras, General Santos Guardiola; Costa
Rica, Don Juan Rafael Mora.

GUERRA DE 1912   see   GUERRA DE MENA

GUERRERO, JOSE.   This director was elected by provi-

sional assembly in 1846 to follow Sandoval (q. v.).
There was still great unrest, with continued persecution
of the followers of Morazán, and refusal to admit the
Salvadorean diplomat Nicolás Angulo, which became an
issue between the countries.

GUERRERO, LORENZO. President pro tem of Nicaragua
following the death in office in 1967 of René Schick
Gutiérrez, President since 1963, following Luis Somoza's
term.

GUERREROS, LOS. Comarca or district in the municipio of
Diriamba, department of Carazo.

GUILIQUE. A district in the municipio of Matiguás, Matagalpa department.

GUILITO. A district in the municipio and department of
Matagalpa.

GUILLEN, ASILIA. Best known of Nicaragua's primitive
artists, she took up painting at the age of 61 under the
urging of Rodrigo Penalba. By the time of her death
in 1964, aged 78, her works had become well-known
and in great demand. One might call her the "Grand-
ma Moses" of Nicaragua--her work was not dissimilar
from that of the doughty New Englander.

GUINA. A district of the municipio of Jinotega.

GUINA, RIO. A tributary of the Bocay River in Jinotega
department.

GUINEA, LA. A hacienda on the south coast of Zapatera
Island in the department of Granada.

GUINEO, EL. District in the municipio of Altagracia on
Omotepe island in Lake Nicaragua, department of Rivas.

GUINES, LA. Coffee hacienda in the municipio of Jinotepe,
Carazo department.

GUIRESES. Word of unknown origin applied to gold prospectors in the Bocay region of Nicaragua.

GUISISIL. A volcano with an altitude of 3600 feet in the
municipio of Ciudad Darío, Matagalpa department.

GUISISIL, CUEVA DE. This cave played an important part in Nicaraguan history when during the 1855 National War (the William Walker period) "Democratic" forces pursued three leaders of resistance against the filibusters and they took refuge in it. These men were Jeronimo Pérez, Don Fernando Guzmán (both q.v.), and don Agustín Avilez.

GUISQUILAPA. Comarca or district in the municipio of Jinotepe, Carazo department.

GUISTE. Comarca or district in the municipio of Jinotepe, Carazo department.

GUSANERAS. A district of the municipio of Jinotega.

GUTIERREZ, LOS. Comarca or district in the municipio of Diriamba, department of Carazo.

GUTIERREZ, FRANCISCO. Encomendero from León, following the Acts of Importion of Tribute on the peoples of the valley of Nicaragua in 1548.

GUTIERREZ, LORENZO GUERRERRO. The one among three Nicaraguan vice presidents who was designated as provisional president upon the death of President René Schick in 1966. Gutiérrez was also incumbent Minister of Interior, and Vice President of the Liberal Party.

GUTIERREZ, PERFECTO. Sandinista officer in February, 1932 in the Peña Blanca area responsible for action against guardsmen of the government forces.

GUTIERREZ NORTE, LOS. A district of the San Rafael del Sur municipio, Managua department.

GUTIERREZ SUR, LOS. A district of the San Rafael del Sur municipio, Managua department.

GUTIERREZ Y LIZAURZABEL, DON AGUSTIN. Mayor of Rivas in 1811 when the city joined 5000 rebels against the Spanish crown, and declared independence. A commission of government was organized. In 1812 the Rivas rebellion was quelled by troops from Cartago. This was one of the first uprisings for colonial independence from Spain in the whole viceroyalty.

GUZMAN, DON FERNANDO. A caudillo of the resistance against William Walker in 1855, operating in the Cantón Yucul of Matagalpa (see Cueva de Guisisil). He was a citizen of Metapa (Ciudad Darío) and was President of the Junta de Recursos (q. v.) which was a major focus of resistance against the filibusters.

GUZMAN, FERNANDO [no relation to the above]. President of Nicaragua from 1867-1871, his administration was marred by insurrectional activities in behalf of Martínez, and in 1869 with General Jérez. He was succeeded by Vicente Cuadra in 1871.

-H-

HACIENDA DE CACAO DEL VALLE MENIER. A cacao plantation in Nandaime municipio, department of Granada, basic to the manufacture of chocolates by Menier in Paris.

HACIENDA DE CAFE, MANAGUA DEPARTMENT. There are in the Managua hills a number of coffee haciendas, around 155. The 15 million trees of the area are a major part of the national coffee production.

HACIENDA SYSTEM. Based on the plantation or "hacienda," the hacienda system was essentially feudal in character, although as has been pointed out by Mario Rodríquez, it was also partly capitalistic. It is the blend which has enabled it to persist, for there are modified haciendas to this day. It was self-sustaining. In bad times this meant it would persist--in good times, it was a source of exports and profits. Monoculture was the pattern-- thus there were separate haciendas for cacao, indigo, coffee, cattle, and other products. Food often had to be imported. Productivity from a natural standpoint was not great, but the "hacendado" benefited greatly.

HAJACHIQUE, EL. A district of the municipio of Niquino-homo, Masaya department.

HAMACA, RIO. A tributary of the Bocay River in Jinotega department.

HAMACAS. Comarca or district in the municipio of Villa Somoza, Chontales.

HAM, CLIFFORD D.   Colonel Ham as collector of customs
in the American interventionist period following 1909,
reduced the foreign debt of Nicaragua from $32,000,000
to $9,000,000.   In 1924 the córdoba was on a par with
the U.S. dollar; in 1971, the ratio is seven córdobas to
one dollar.

HANDYSIDE, COMMODORE.   A British Naval Officer who
during the blockade of Admiral Lord Anson along the
west coastal colonies of South America, laid siege in
1739 to Corinto and Puerto Realejo, the Nicaraguan
ports on the Pacific side.   The siege seems to have
been in the form of a tight blockade.

HASTAGALPA   see   ALTAGRACIA (def. 2).

HATFIELD, CHESTER.   Captain Hatfield took over the Nicaraguan canal survey of 1872 when his commanding officer
was drowned.   (See CROSSMAN and INTEROCEANIC CA-
NAL COMMISSION.)

HATILLAS.   Comarca or district of the municipio of Santo
Tomás in Chontales.

HATILLO.   Comarca or district in the municipio of Telica,
León.

HATILLO, EL.   1) Comarca, valley or district in the municipio of Juigalpa.
2) Comarca or district of the municipio of Santa
Rosa, León.
3) A district of Terrabona municipio, Matagalpa department.

HATILLOS, LOS.   1) District in the municipio of Altagracia
on Omotepe Island in Lake Nicaragua, department of
Rivas.
2) District of Pueblo Nuevo municipio, Estelí department.

HATIO [HATO] DE SAN BUENAVENTURA.   Cattle ranch
near Juigalpa in Chontales, granted in 1660, and owned
by Don Juan de San Juan, Escribano Público.   Size,
six cabellarías, 200 acres.

HATO, EL.   A district of the San Rafael del Sur municipio,
Managua department.

HATO GRANDE. 1) Comarca or district of the municipio of
León, León department.
2) Comarca, valley or district in the municipio of
Juigalpa.
3) Also called San Juan de Buenavista, a cattle ranch
in Chontales, belonging to the descendents of Don Diego
Chamorra--a "latifundia" of 70 caballeriôs, or about
2400 acres, the grant being made in 1640.

HATO VIEJO. Large "finca" or farm in the municipio of
El Sauce, León department.

HECAT. "God of the Winds, " a Nicarao diety, sometimes
thought to be combined with chiquinaut (same function).

HENDY OF BLUEFIELDS. A stern-wheel steamboat which
nearly a century ago made the run from Bluefields up
the Río Escondido to Rama. Owned by the firm of Wilson and Belanger it was one of several boats used during the period of the Mosquito government. It was noted
for the cuisine aboard.

HENNINGSEN, CHARLES FREDERICK. Among the many
remarkable men to have any connection with the filibuster William Walker was Henningsen, Swedish-born
soldier of fortune. George Law (q.v.) persuaded Henningsen to help Walker. Henningsen at age 40 had been
a chief officer and friend of the Hungarian revolutionary
Kossuth, and had also distinguished himself in warfare
in both Russia and Spain. He was author of several
books on military strategy, and was also a novelist, a
journalist, and allied by marriage to a Georgian lady of
beauty, wealth, and aristocratic antecedents. Henningsen warmed to the chance to fight in Nicaragua, and his
first act was to procure Minié rifles, the most advanced
arm of the time. Arriving in October, 1856, Henningsen
soon had reorganized and retrained the whole Walker
army. Walker made him a Major General. Henningsen
gave high praise to the courage and intellect of Walker's
men. They discussed Aeschylus and Euripides, translated Dante in 1856 and received 137 wounds for each
100 men, according to Henningsen. Henningsen was with
Walker at the end in Rivas in May, 1857, and ate mule
meat while under siege by the Costa Ricans. Henningsen's most famous utterance, however, was just three
words, "Aquí fue Granada, " ("Here was Granada").

Soon after Henningsen's arrival, Walker was plunged
into a two-front war with 600 men against about 5,000
United Central Americans, recently reinforced by a
strong Costa Rican contingent. An epidemic of disease
was added to the attrition of war in Masaya and Granada, and it was necessary to abandon Granada. Walker
and Henningsen decided to destroy that city rather than
let it fall to the Central Americans who already had
the other traditional capital, León. To Henningsen fell
the grim task of destruction. Marks of Henningsen's
"scorched earth" policy still scar Granada 115 years
later. Capturing the strong point of the city, Guadelupe
cathedral, Henningsen guided an almost epic defense under siege. With less than 200 fighting men, and encum-
bered by scores of women and children in the stronghold, he held out although Zavala's capture of the docks
meant no food could reach the beleaguered defenders.
When Zavala broke off the attack, Henningsen went
ahead with the burning of Granada, leaving the "Here
was Granada" message on a streamer stuck to a lance
thrust into the ruins. Somehow Walker had infused
Henningsen and others with the belief that "manifest
destiny" was to be worked out in Nicaragua. Henningsen was helping Walker to raise funds again in late 1857
for a second attempt. Incredibly, U.S. Secretary of
War Floyd sought to involve Henningsen in a Mexican
revolution in 1858, and also to provoke war with Spain
so that Cuba might be annexed to the United States.
Henningsen did later go to Mexico to offer his services
to the revolution.

HENRICH, CHARLES. Second lieutenant who with a patrol
of six Nicaraguan military academy cadets and ten aux-
iliaries encountered guerrillas near Mayacundo and were
driven into El Sauce in November, 1931. (See GARD-
NER.)

HENRY BULWER. A shallow draft stern-wheel paddle
steamer on the San Juan River which in 1860 lay a
wreck near the mouth of San Bartolomeo creek. Under
the command of a Colonel Fernández during the filibuster
war, 1855-1857, this vessel was captured at El Castillo
Viejo during a battle there in 1856. The steam machinery was still in the wreck in 1860.

HENRY, THOMAS. Colonel Henry was one of the legendary
original "Immortals" who landed with filibuster William

Walker in Nicaragua in 1855. He returned to Nicaragua with Walker on the Fashion in late 1857, and again in the final abortive descent on Truxillo, Honduras, in the schooner Taylor in early 1860. Henry met a particularly horrible death. Setting out from the fort at Truxillo with a Honduran guide he scouted several days, and on his return, fortified with a few drinks and somewhat pugnacious, an argument with a lieutenant over Henry's lighted cigar in the fort's powder magazine, caused the young man to shoot Henry in the jaw at close range with a pistol. The lower part of his face was shot away, and he could not speak to give the news of his scouting venture, although he attempted to write a message on a slate. Henry's suffering with his now-gangrenous wound was ended when Walker left a cup of morphine near him. Henry was able to swallow it for release and death. This is an example of the strong, strange loyalties men had for Walker.

HERBIAS RIVER see COCO, RIO.

HERMANOS CRISTIANOS see CHRISTIAN BROTHERS.

HERNANDEZ, DANIEL. Sandinista officer in the area of Peña Blanca in February, 1932, responsible for sorties against National Guardsmen.

HERRARA. In his History of America, Vol. IV, page 14, this historiographer to the King of Spain writes of the events of 1527, and mentions four routes for an interoceanic canal, one of them being the Lake Nicaragua / San Juan River route.

HERRERA, DIONISIO. Honduran president of the Central American Federation 1830-1834, a period of relative calm during which Nicaragua assumed the liberal look and attitude then prevalent on the isthmus. This was only a prelude however, to her secession in 1838, the first to leave the Provincias Unidas.

HERRERA, RAFAELA. First among Nicaraguan heroines, the 19-year-old Rafaela took charge of El Castillo Viejo (Fortaleza Inmaculada) in the year 1762 when the Governor of Jamaica sent a 2000-man English force against that stronghold. Her father, the Castellano of the fort, having died as the attackers approached, the doughty Rafaela manned the cannon and rallied the defenders.

She also at night sent burning rafts of grass downriver
to confuse the enemy. The attackers having lost many
of their boats as well as their soldiers as casualties,
broke off the attack and retreated downriver, not to return for 18 years.

HERVIAS, GABRIEL DE. Lieutenant colonel who was appointed Chief Spanish Commissioner for the Miskito
coastal area following British defeats of 1780-1782.
He was in contact with Miskito King George and others.
He skillfully handled the old Sumu Chief Colville Breton (q. v.). (See VALLEJO and HODGSON.)

HIDALGO REYES, ELEUTERIO see MEZA, SAMUEL.

HIDDEN TREASURE MINE. One of the Bonanza (q. v.)
group of mines.

HIGHLAND FRONTIER REGION. Centered on Matagalpa,
this growing frontier area is moving eastward toward
the mountainous rainforest areas, principally by the ex-
tension of agriculture. This is one of the four major
regions at present.

HIGHLAND MARY MINE. One of the Bonanza (q. v.) group
of mines.

HIGHWAYS. All-weather highways were scarce prior to
World War II, but in the early 1950's a program was
begun and the central government, through the Departmento de Carreteras, has built highways until there are
over 4000 miles of usable road, with over 2000 being
all-weather and about 1, 100 miles paved--this from 93
miles paved in 1950 and 675 paved in 1960.   There is
a paved highway through the country from the Honduran
to the Costa Rican border, much of it first-rate both
as to engineering and surface. The system has revolu-
tionized transportation patterns in the last two decades:
ox-carts are barred from Managua streets! (Not so in
1956.)

HIJAS DE MARIA. These "daughters of Mary" represent
church welfare groups which are essentially drawn from
upper class ranks. They are single women.

HISE, ELIJAH. An agent for the U. S. appointed in 1849 by
the James Knox Polk administration, to go to Nicaragua

and investigate the highhanded British actions at the San Juan River mouth (see Vixen). Hise became enthusiastic on arrival in Nicaragua, and exceeded his instructions by drawing up a treaty dated June 21, 1849, with the eager help of the Nicaraguan government, and aided by their appointee don Buenaventura Selva. The treaty provided for an exclusive right to build a transitway, as well as to establish fortifications and to provide free ports at each end. The U.S. government would in turn recognize Nicaraguan sovereignty from sea to sea (a slap at the British pretensions in Mosquitia). The treaty was never formally submitted to the U.S. Senate for ratification, but it became widely known and was applauded by many North Americans enamored (just following the War with Mexico) with the glamour and profit of "manifest destiny."

HISE-SELVA CONVENTION. In June, 1849, Elijah Hise and Buenaventura Selva were parties to a convention between the United States and Nicaragua, giving the United States or any corporation it favored exclusive rights to passage across the country. This was to counteract British moves to control the Mosquito Shore coast of the Caribbean and the mouth of the San Juan River. This convention was followed by treaties later affected by Ephriam George Squier. The final result was the Clayton-Bulwer Treaty of 1850, still a thorn in U.S.-Latin American relations.

HISPANICISMO see HISPANISMO

HISPANIDAD see HISPANISMO

HISPANISMO. Hispanicism in Latin America, fostered in Spain following the formation of the Union Ibero-Americana in Spain and the 1941 formation of a Consejo de Hispanidad (Council of Hispanicism), which was formed by government decree in Madrid.

H. H. HUNT. A San Juan River shallow-draft river steamer of the 1860's and 1870's. Only the name survives.

HODGSON, ROBERT. 1) Captain Hodgson was sent by Governor Edward Trelawney of Jamaica to the Miskito area at the outbreak of the War of Jenkins Ear in 1739. He was first Superintendent of the Shore and was instructed to take over the colony as a British protec-

torate.   The superintendency lasted half a century.
2) His son, also Robert Hodgson, took over on his
retirement in 1759, but did not have such a firm hold
on the Sambo-Miskitos as had his vigorous father.   To
this day, a considerable percentage of the coastal population is named Hodgson, related to some of the less
official activities of the two superintendents.

HOJA PARROQUIAL, LA.   A periodical of Boaco in the
1915-1937 era.

HOJACHIQUE.   1) A coffee hacienda in the municipio of
Niquinohomo in the department of Masaya.
2) El Hojachique, a comarca or territory in the municipio of Villa Somoza, Chontales.

HOLIDAYS.   Official Holidays of Nicaragua are New Year's
Day, January 1; Air Force Day, February 1; "Semana
Santa, " Easter Week; Labor Day, May 1; Army Day,
May 27; Patron Saint's Days (Santo Domingo), August 1
and August 10; Anniversary of the Battle of San Jacinto,
September 14; Independence Day, September 15; Colum-
bus Day (Día de La Raza) October 12; All Saints' Day,
November 1; Immaculate Conception, December 8;
Christmas, December 25.

HOLLENBECK.   A river steamer of the early 1900's on the
San Juan River which figured in the mine-planting episode of Cannon and Groce.   (See also   DIAMANTE, EL.)

HOMEN, DIEGO.   Mapmaker of the well-known Portuguese
family of mapmakers who in 1558 produced a map which
is the first to show California as a peninsula--not to be
so "discovered" again until Fray Eusebio Kino's maps
150 years later.   In this 1558 map the great San Juan
River and Lake system of Nicaragua are clearly shown,
except that while the general outlines are correct, Lakes
Managua and Nicaragua are shown as one.   It is interesting that the slightly earlier map by his relative Lopo
Homen (q. v.) is more accurate on this count.

HOMEN, LOPO.   A Portuguese mapmaker whose world map
of 1554 shows both Lake Managua and Lake Nicaragua
in a very recognizable Central America.   Florida, Cuba
Haiti, Jamaica, Lake Maracaibo, and other features are
also very clear.   (The present location of the map is
the Bibliothèque Nationale in Paris.)   It is believed he

lived from 1497-1572. It is worth remarking that many later maps were not as geographically accurate about the isthmian area as was this one.

HONDURAS MINING AND TRADING COMPANY. Significant to Nicaragua in that Byron Cole (q. v.) owned a share, and that events of the Legitimist and Democratic struggles in Nicaragua led him to attempt to protect his interest by working out an agreement with rebel Democratic leader Francisco de Castellón to assist the rebel forces. Cole agreed to send a 300-man army. Under a trumped-up "colonization" agreement to circumvent U. S. neutrality laws, it was Cole who finally sent Walker (q. v.) to Nicaragua, thus precipitating events which over a century later are still having their repercussions.

HORCONES, LOS. A district of Terrabona municipio, Matagalpa department.

HORIZONTE, EL. Comarca or district in the municipio of Jinotepe, Carazo department.

HORMIGA, LA. Comarca or district in the municipio of La Conquista, Carazo department.

HORMIGUERO, EL. "The Anthill, " an old-prison-fort in the center of Managua, across Roosevelt Avenue from the Campo del Marte, and at the foot of La Loma. Crenellated walls, machine gun towers, and a history of coups and insurrections all add lustre to the dull grey stones.

HORNILLO Y EL TAMARINDO, EL. District in the municipio of La Trinidad, department of Estelí.

HORNO, EL. 1) A district of the municipio of Jinotega.
2) A district in the municipio and department of Matagalpa.
3) A district of the municipio of San Juan de Limay, Estelí department.
4) A district of the municipio of San Ramón, Matagalpa department.

HORNSBY, C. C. Colonel Hornsby as one of William Walker's trusted associates in the 1855 "Falange" had fought in the war between the United States and Mexico, and was thus experienced. He was one of the faithful to

Walker who survived the Nicaragua campaign and who tried to return in late 1857 on the steamer Fashion. Upon the landing at San Juan del Norte, their camp was blocked by two British men-of-war and the American Naval vessels, the frigate Wabash and the Fulton. Under Commodore Paulding on the Wabash, a detachment of Marines landed, and the Walker forces were forced to surrender, in spite of the fact that Hornsby and Fayssoux (q. v.) had earlier protested the moves to Paulding.

HORQUETAS, LAS.   A district in the municipio of La Trinidad, Estelí department.

HOT SPRINGS.   In the region of Managua are many hot springs, best known being those of Tipitapa. There are, also the Infiernillos of Jiloá (q. v.); springs in Lake Nejapa and Las Positas, Cinco Tubos, and at the head of the Río Teocinal, in the Valle of las Maderas.

HOYA, LA.   A district of the municipio of San Pedro, Chinandega department.

HOYADA, LA.   Comarca or district in the municipio of Jinotepe, Carazo department.

HUACUCAL, EL.   Comarca or district in the municipio of La Paz, León.

HUAHUASHAN   see   WAWASHAN

HUANCS   see   COCO, RIO

HUASPUC, RIO   see   WASPUK, RIO

HUCHERETE.   Bathing beach in Carazo department on the Pacific.

HUEHUETE.   Comarca or district in the municipio of Jinotepe, Carazo department.

HUELLAS DE ACAHUALINCA   see   ACAHUALINCA

HUERTA QUEMADA.   Comarca or district in the municipio of Diriamba, department of Carazo.

HUGHES, HOWARD.   Semi-legendary in his own lifetime,

reputed billionaire, cinematic producer, entrepreneur, aircraft pilot and builder, Hughes is another of the long line of unusual and remarkable foreigners to go to Nicaragua. The 66-year old Hughes was often involved in storms of controversy, the most recent prior to his going to Nicaragua being the arrested publication of an "authorized biography" by Clifford Irving that was branded as false by Hughes. While Hughes aids reserved the top floor of the new Maya-styled Intercontinental Hotel in Managua, the Hughes visit was imbued with all the mystery attendant to the movements of the eccentric recluse since the mid-1950's. Hughes had recently spent some time in the Bahamas. Nicaragua has sought foreign development, especially from the United States, ever since favorable laws were drafted in the late years of the first Somoza, in the 1950's--the present Anastasio Somoza regime had been in recent contact with Hughes in regard to investment and development, with particular reference to the Corn Islands off the Caribbean coast of Nicaragua, a palm-clad pair of "South Sea" islands ripe for tourist development. Official communiques of the Somoza government made it clear Hughes was in Nicaragua upon the invitation of President Somoza. (See also ISLAS DEL MAIZ and SHELTON, TURNER.)

HUITZILOPICHTLI. God of War of the ancient Mexicans (Nahuatl) which was corrupted by the Nicaraos into "Orchilobos."

HUITZTEOTL see BISTEOT

HULLA. This hard coal or pit coal is mined in the areas of El Carao, La Laguna, and Pueblo Nuevo in Estelí department.

HUNGRIA. A cattle ranch in the municipio of La Concordia, Jinotega department.

HURTADO, BENITO. A "lugarteniante" or officer attached to Captain Francisco Hernández de Córdoba, Captain Hurtado was sent in pursuit of Gil Gonzáles Dávila who had gone on to Honduras from Nicaragua in search of the elusive strait between Atlantic and Pacific. Captain Hurtado on this expedition founded in early 1525 a settlement on the waters of the Río Jicaro now known as "Ciudad Vieja," but then the first of several locations of Nueva Segovia, a town which was moved several times to its present site (Ocotal) because of pirate and

Moskito-Sambo depredations from the Caribbean Coast.

HURTADOS, LOS. A district of the San Rafael del Sur municipio, Managua department.

HYMN, NATIONAL. Words by Salomón Ibarra Mayorga; composer unknown (composed before 1821).
Salve a tí, Nicaragua! En tu suelo
Ya no ruge la voz del cañón
Repeat [Ni se tiñe con sangre de hermanos
Tu glorioso pendón bicolor

Brille hermonsa la paz en tu cielo
Nada empañe tu gloria inmortal
Repeat [Que el trabajo es tu digne laurel
Y el honor es tu enseñe triunfar

(A free translation follows):
Hail to you, Nicaragua! In your land
No longer sounds the cannon's lusty roar
Nor does blood by any brother's hand
Stain your glorious bi-color any more

Peace reigns in beauty bright beneath your sky
Immortal glory bears no mark of soil
Your laurel earned is honorable toil
And honor is the standard that you fly.

[Note: The "bicolor" of the flag is blue and white.]

HYMN TO THE SONS OF THE MOON   see   DANCE TO THE SUN

-I-

IACHR see ORGANIZATION OF AMERICAN STATES

IACI see ORGANIZATION OF AMERICAN STATES

IACW see ORGANIZATION OF AMERICAN STATES

IADB see ORGANIZATION OF AMERICAN STATES

IA - ESOSOC see ORGANIZATION OF AMERICAN STATES

IAGS									200

IAGS   Initials for the Servicio Geodésico Interamericano (q. v.)

IAIAS   see   ORGANIZATION OF AMERICAN STATES

IAII   see   ORGANIZATION OF AMERICAN STATES

IAN   see   NATIONAL AGRARIAN INSTITUTE

IAPC   see   ORGANIZATION OF AMERICAN STATES

IBARRA, MANUEL.   Nicaraguan contemporary composer specializing in religious music.

ICA   see   INTERNATIONAL COOPERATION ADMINISTRA-TION

ICARUS   see   SALMON, WALKER

ICAYAN.   Lands in Estelí department originally belonging to the aboriginal community of Somoto, and granted in 1769.

IIAA   see   INSTITUTE OF INTERAMERICAN AFFAIRS

ILILIHUAS.   A district of the municipio of Jinotega.

"IMMORTALS. "   The filibuster William Walker (q. v.) was able to gather about him for his venture into fame and ultimate death in Nicaragua, a remarkable group of men.   Dr. Jones, officers Kewen, Hornsby, Anderson and Crocker, and others made up the adventurous band of 58 men who came to be called the "Immortals. "

IMPORTS.   In 1967, Nicaragua imported $204,000,000 (U.S.) of goods.   A fourth of this was raw material and products for industry.   Construction materials and capital goods for agriculture and industry made up another fourth.   Nondurable consumer goods added to durable goods made up another fourth.   There was a trade deficit of about $52,000,000 (U. S.).   Only in 1959, of the last decade, did Nicaragua have a trade surplus ($5,000,000).   Heavy dependance on coffee and cotton exports is one of the trade balance problems.

INALI.   An original communal ownership of land by Indians in Estelí department, disputed by don Francisco Guete in 1696.   An aboriginal Indian name.

201 201 Inali, Rio.

INALI, RIO. A river in the department of Madriz, a short
    southern tributary of the upper Río Coco.

INCAE see INSTITUTO CENTROAMERICANO DE ADMINIS-
    TRACION DE EMPRESAS.

INCEI see INSTITUTO NACIONAL DE COMERCIO EX-
    TERIOR Y INTERIOR.

INCOME TAX. There is an income tax on income of in-
    ternal origin; that is, earned on property and assets,
    from services rendered and business operations within
    the country. (See also TAXATION.) The scale is as
    follows:

Taxable Income (in Córdobas)			Tax Rate
0 -	50,000	($7,143 U.S.)	4%
50,000 -	60,000		5%
60,000 -	100,000		10%
100,000 -	200,000	($28,570 U.S.)	15%
200,000 -	300,000		20%
300,000 -	400,000		25%
400,000 -	500,000	($71,430 U.S.)	30%
500,000 -	and more		35%

INDE. Initials of the Instituto Nicaragüenese de Desarrollo
    (Nicaraguan Development Institute).

INDEPENDENCE, SPANISH COLONIAL. The sequence of
    the final moves for independence of the Spanish colonial
    empire from Mother Spain is summarized here in that
    it is a part of the matrix of Nicaraguan history.

Revolt in New Granada (Colombia) under Miranda and Bolívar.	1811
Colombia established as republic, comprising New Granada, Venezuela, Ecuador.	1821
Guatemala, (and all Central America)	September 15, 1821
Mexican intervention under Iturbide	January 5, 1822
Mexican power established in Guatemala	November 4, 1822
Santa Anna and insurgents topple Iturbide (and end the empire)	April 23, 1823

Central America then formed the Federal Republic of
United Provinces, putting forth a charter in April, 1826
(with Chiapas adhering to Mexico). Nicaragua was first
to secede from this federation as an independent entity
on April 30, 1838, and first to write a constitution providing for separate governments in November, 1838.

INDEPENDENCE MOVEMENT, RIVAS. In 1811 the Villa of
Rivas and surrounding neighborhoods of the Valley of
Nicaragua, under initiative from San Jorge and with an
adherence of 5000 persons, declared independence from
Spain.   They elected a temporary government of "criollos. " The purpose was to end taxes and duties which
were burdensome. This was no doubt stimulated by the
earlier American and French revolutions.   The attempt
was put down by Spanish colonial troops sent from Cartago in April of 1812, but there is no question that this
act was one of those significant in the development of
the independence which was finally gained in Guatemala
on September 15, 1921, and that it was one of the earliest of such uprisings in the entire viceroyalty.

INDEPENDENT LINE. A steamship line organized by Cornelius Vanderbilt to divert passengers from the Nicaragua
cross-isthmian line to Panama, in the hope of ruining the
entrepreneurs Morgan and Garrison who had cheated the
doughty ex-ferryboatman.   Fares on this line fell as low
as $100 first-class, New York to California, and $30
steerage.

INDIA, LA (mine). Developed by a U.S. engineer, Spencer,
who searched for a gold property from California to
Nicaragua in the early years of this century, this mine
was extremely productive for its discoverer and owner
and only shut down its operation in the 1960's.   It is
located northwest of Lake Managua in a mineral district
completely removed from and separate from the northeast (Zelaya) and Nueva Segovia mineral areas.   Presumably the vein is now depleted.

INDICES DEL ARCHIVO DE TIERRAS DE NICARAGUA. A
record of lands and persons engaged in agricultural
enterprise in Nicaragua; all lost during the earthquake
and fire in the capital city in 1931.

INDIGO. An 18th-century Central American cash crop, not
so important in Nicaragua.   Used as dyestuff, the textile revolution of the 1700's created the demand.

INDIO, RIO. The "Indian River" of Nicaragua is very like
    the coastal lagoon on the eastern part of Florida which
    bears the same name. The Río Indío is a narrow la-
    goon parallel to the Caribbean coast for 12 miles north-
    east of San Juan del Norte. It also comes from inland,
    however, and is an authentic river as far as Loma la
    Cucaracha.

INDIOS NABORIOS. Indians who were free during Spanish
    colonial days in Nicaragua, but who were nevertheless
    in service.

INDITAS, LAS. Traditional dance seen occasionally during
    the festival of San Jerónimo. Masked dancers in couples
    move to strains of Marimba and guitar.

INFONAC. Acronym for the Instituto de Fomento Nacional,
    the development institute which deals with foreign and
    domestic enterprise, gives information for investors:
    data on crop exports, trends, industrial development,
    the common market, etc. It is a governmental agency
    which deals with all phases of agricultural and industrial
    development.

INGENIO, EL. District in the municipio and department of
    Rivas.

INLAND WATERWAYS. For much inland transport the
    waterways are still essential in spite of the rapid
    growth of truck transport (q. v.). Navigable rivers
    include the San Juan, the Coco, the Prinzapolka, the
    Escondido, and the Río Grande. Upper reaches are
    navigable only by small boats such as dugouts. There
    are almost no connecting roads or ocean port facilities
    for these rivers, all of which flow toward the Caribbean.
    Water transport on Lakes Managua and Nicaragua played
    a much larger part before development of the road and
    rail nets. There are 25 or more lake ports, and about
    160 water craft of about 600 aggregate tonnage, essen-
    tially negligible in a modern transport context. Lake
    freight costs . 721 córdobas (ten cents U. S.) per ton
    mile, or double the cost of truck transport, with 30
    córdobas ($4. 30 U. S.) per ton for terminal handling
    due to poor port facilities.

INSS see INSTITUTO NACIONAL DE SEGURIDAD SOCIAL

INSTITUTE OF INTERAMERICAN AFFAIRS. A Latin-American research segment of the University of Florida, U. S.,
established in 1927; also the title of the early predecessor agency to modern AID.

INSTITUTO AGRARIO DE NICARAGUA. This agrarian institute, charged with carrying out agrarian reform, instituted operations in 1964. Transformation of Indian communities into agricultural cooperatives is one of the
goals. Regional development programs in such areas
as Zelaya department are also planned activities.

INSTITUTO CENTROAMERICANO DE ADMINISTRACION DE
EMPRESAS. The Central American Institute of Business
Administration conducts management seminars as there
is as yet a general lack of trained business personnel.
Such training is industrially as well as commercially
oriented. The location is on the outskirts of Managua.

INSTITUTO DE FOMENTO NACIONAL DE NICARAGUA.
Ever since world bank studies on the Nicaraguan economy were carried out around 1950, the development
institute has played an important part in the business
and industrial progress which has taken place. Courses
of training for managerial personnel are among the many
activities of the Institute. The Institute has as its prime
function operations as a National Development Bank.

INSTITUTO NACIONAL DE COMERCIO EXTERIOR Y IN-
TERIOR. This National Institute for Foreign and Domestic Commerce operates under the executive branch
of government, and has a board of directors consisting
of three of the ministers of government, and one member of the principal opposition party.

INSTITUTO NACIONAL DE SEGURIDAD SOCIAL. Social
Security is a growing function of Nicaraguan government which has been increasing coverage and benefits
rapidly. It is broadly patterned after the successful
Mexican prototype.

INSTITUTO NACIONAL DE VIVIENDA. This National Housing Institute is engaged in erecting low-cost homes for
workers, soldiers, and government functionaries who
have reason to need homes in the National District
area, where most of the activity is taking place.

INSTITUTO NACIONAL TECNICO VOCACIONAL. The national vocational technical institute developed as a result
of World Bank recommendations in the 1950's. Begun
by the Foreign Operations Administration of the United
States, as that organization changed to International Cooperation Administration, a contract was awarded to the
University of Florida at Gainesville for opening and operation of the Institute. This was accomplished during
1955-1957 by a university team of technicians under Dr.
Harvey K. Meyer, functioning as Director Técnico de
Artes Industriales y Educación Vocacional within the
Nicaraguan Ministry of Education. Such shops and laboratories as machine, plumbing, automotives, electronics,
diesel, electricity, air conditioning, and welding were
established.

INSURRECTION, 1967. On January 22, 1967, a revolt broke
out in Managua in relation to the presidential elections
then in prospect. Hostages were held in the Gran
Hotel in downtown Managua until tanks were brought up.
Reports varied of killed and injured, some as high as
40 deaths and over 100 injuries. Opposition candidate
Agüero was credited with leading a bloody clash with
National Guardsmen.

INTENDENCIA DE NICARAGUA. By royal decree from
Madrid, December 23, 1786, the Intendencia of Nicaragua was formed. The first intendent was Colonel
Juan de Aysa, who as Governor of Nicaragua had exercised full command.

INTERAMERICAN PEACE COMMITTEE. Empowered to act
in case of any dispute between American nations, this
group was activated in 1959, following certain portions
of the Rio de Janeiro Treaty of 1947. At any given
time the group has a membership from several American nations.

INTERMEDIATE AREA. A sub-region of the Circum-
Caribbean Indian peoples, comprising those in Colombia,
Western Venezuela, and Central America. This intermediate area seems to have been a meeting place of
the Andean and later Inca cultures from the south, and
of the Maya and Nahuatl from the north.

INTERNATIONAL COFFEE ORGANIZATION. A group established among 15 coffee-producing nations to stand-

ardize policies in coffee merchandising by the member nations, essentially centered on price stabilization and attendant control of production.

INTERNATIONAL COOPERATION ADMINISTRATION. The U.S. Aid Agency successor to the Foreign Operations Administration in 1956.

INTERNATIONAL SCIENTIFIC CONGRESS. Assembled in Paris, May 15, 1879, with 136 delegates, 74 of them French in support of Suez Canal builder de Lesseps. The subject was a decision concerning an isthmian canal. Menocal and others stood for the Nicaragua route. Sub-committees were appointed to study both locks and tide-level canals. The latter plan was rejected, and Nicaragua was unanimously chosen by the two committees as the most feasible route. The cost of a Nicaraguan canal was projected at $143,000,000; a Panama Canal, at $208,000,000. Moves by de Lesseps' group arbitrarily cut the Panama estimate to $140,000,000 to gain their point. The Congress voted (with many abstentions) to choose Panama, on May 29, 1879. The ultimate disaster to both de Lesseps and the French Canal Company as a result of the ill-informed decision is well-documented. All France was embroiled in the debacle.

INTEROCEANIC CANAL COMMISSION. Apointed on March 13, 1872, by U.S. President Grant, this commission was to gain all available knowledge of interoceanic communication between Atlantic and Pacific waters. The group included Chief Army Engineer General A. A. Humphreys, Supt. of Coast Survey C. P. Patterson, and Chief of the Bureau of Navigation Admiral Daniel Ammen. The latter as a young man had taken great interest in the canal question. The Commission completed a thorough check of the Atrato River routes in Colombia for the first time; they checked also the Darién isthmus route and the Tehuantepec route. By elimination, the Nicaragua route finally occupied primary attention once more. In 1872, a survey expedition set out. Commander Crossman, the leader, was drowned in a surf landing, and Captain Chester Hatfield went to the western shore of Lake Nicaragua to begin a systematic examination of passes through the low coastal hills. Child's previous Lajas-Brito route was verified. A hydrographic survey party was left to study the lake. In the fall of 1872, Captain Lull came out to take charge of the survey with Lieutenant A. G. Menocal as chief engineer. They examined all passes from lake to ocean near Brito, and also checked the Lake Managua route favored by Napoleon III. Child's views were again confirmed. They planned to use dams to make the San Juan River navigable as far down as El Castillo, or farther. Lull and Menocal also checked the Panama route and decided these two were the only feasible ones, with similar locks to be necessary in each. The surveys were completed by 1875, and a report to the President by the Commission, dated February 7, 1876, unanimously chose the Nicaraguan route.

INVIERNO. The winter season, although since Nicaragua is in the northern hemisphere it is actually summer time. This "winter" is so called because of the lowered temperature due to the frequent rains which fall for a six-month period. Rains in Nicaragua start almost like clockwork on May 15 and the dry-brown land suddenly turns emerald in a dozen brilliant tints and shades of green.

IPLAN. A district on the lower Río Tuma.

IRIAS, J. Miguel. Colonel Irias was one of two people who, around the turn of the 19th century, stimulated the growth of the fledgling community of Ocotal.

IRIAS, PEDRO ANTONIO. Sandinista general of the early 1930's, in charge of the third column. (See DEFENDING ARMY ....)

IRIS DE LA TARDE. A weekly periodical appearing in 1915 in Boaco, started by a small but active group of local intellectuals; in the romantic style. This production initiated a spate of such publications.

IRMA. A shallow-draft river steamer which ran in the 1900 period from Greytown to the Machuca Rapids on the lower San Juan River. She was owned by the canal company then operating and connected with the Norma or the Adela which ran further upstream.

ISIQUI. A tributary stream of the Río Viejo.

ISLA DE ASERRADORES. The island on which the significant seaport of Corinto is located. It parallels the

Pacific Coast, is north of the Bahía de Corinto and west
of the Estero Realejo, which estuary used to lead to the
colonial port of Realejo.

ISLA DE JESUS GRANDE. A tiny islet off the north coast
of Zapatera Island in Lake Nicaragua.

ISLA EL ARMADA. The "armed" island is one of several
islets off the north coast of Zapatera Island in Lake
Nicaragua.

ISLA EL CARDON. Island just to seaward of the Isla Asseradores (q.v.), port of Corinto, and location of the lighthouse of the same name.

ISLA EL CASTILLO. An island in Lake Nicaragua, near
and in sight of the city of Granada, on which is located
a ruined fortification, one of the chain which was constructed to protect the city against incursions of pirates
and Sambo-Miskitos. Apparently of the period early
16th century, the semicircular fort is in a low battery
form with embrasures for eight cannon, and there are
clearly discernable remains of a central tower structure
which probably served as powder magazine and lookout.
Not to be confused with the district of the same name in
Chontales or with El Castillo Viejo (both q.v.). The
island is inhabited by an Indian family, and is about one
acre in extent. (See illustration.)

ISLA EL MUERTE. This grimly named "Island of Death"
just off the north coast of Zapatera Island in Lake Nicaragua is onlyaa half-mile across, but is known for the
archaeological finds originating there, including idols
and ceramics.

ISLA EL VENADO. A ten-mile long island which bounds
the eastern side of Bluefields Bay from the Caribbean.
It is about two miles wide, and extends from the El
Bluff bar to the Barra Honsôn.

ISLA GRANDE. One of three islands in a group in the
northwest part of Lake Nicaragua. (See ISLA RE-
DONDA.)

ISLA KISUDAKRI. A small island in the northernmost end
of Pearl Lagoon.

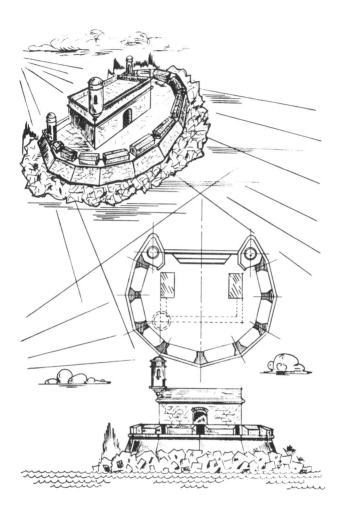

Isla el Castillo Fort

Near Granada; present plan and probable original elevations
shown.

ISLA LA CABEZAS. A district 20 miles up the Prinzapolka
River from Alamikamba.

ISLA MAIRNKAYASKA. A coastal island near the Páhara
Lagoon, several miles north of Puerto Cabezas.

ISLA MUERTE. One of a group of three islands in the
northwest part of Lake Nicaragua. (See ISLA RE-
DONDA.)

ISLA REDONDA. An island in the northwest part of Lake
Nicaragua of basaltic formation, and wooded. Water
and wave marks 30 to 50 feet above present level of
the lake indicate that the waters have lowered that
much from their original level. This is an island
group, the other two being Isla Grande and Isla Muerte.
The origin is obviously volcanic.

ISLA SALAMON. An island in the Río San Juan main channel, 15 miles above the mouth.

ISLA SAN PIO. A small island in the delta of the Río Coco
at Cabo Gracias a Dios.

ISLA ZAPATERA. The "lady shoemaker" island, second
only to Omotepe in size among Lake Nicaragua's islands. Almost rectangular, four by six miles, the island is famed for the idols, ceramics, and other archaeological treasures which abound there. The highest
point is almost 2,000 feet above the lake. Zapatera
seems to have been an especially sacred place among
the aboriginal inhabitants. It still is somewhat remote
and known to relatively few people.

ISLAS DEL MAIZ. There are two "Corn Islands" off the
Nicaraguan coast, about 40 miles from El Bluff, the
port on the bay of Bluefields. Typical tropical isles
with waving palms and broad beaches, these islands
are beginning to be sought as tourist attractions by
Nicaraguans. The inhabitants number around 2,000.
The larger island is a bit more than three miles long,
and has an airport. Treaty agreements giving the U.S.
fortification rights on these islands to protect the mouth
of the nonexistent projected Nicaraguan canal, are largely fallen into limbo. The February, 1972 visit of Howard Hughes (q.v.) to Nicaragua in connection with these
islands is of special interest. (See map.)

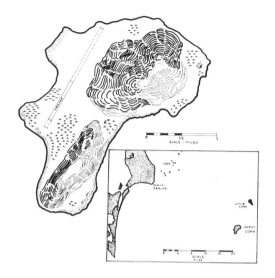

Islas del Maíz

A pair of typical tropical "paradise" islands 40 miles east of Bluefields in the Caribbean Sea, consisting of "Great Corn" and "Little Corn. "

ISLETAS DE GRANADA, LAS.   Tiny islands in Lake Nicaragua just southeast of Granada.   They number 523 in all, some of them under a quarter-acre in extent, all seemingly based on great piles of basalt chunks.   A curious aspect of the vacation homes on many of the islands is that swimming places have to be netted-in like swimming pools because of the freshwater sharks in the lake.

ISPANGUAL.   A district in the municipio of Ciudad Darío, department of Matagalpa.

ISQUIERDO, JUAN.   Moyogalpa was the encomienda of Isquierdo following the tribute acts of 1848, and produced corn, beans, cotton, salt, chickens, and cloth.

ITALIA.   Coffee hacienda in the Sierras de Managua, National District.

ITIPITAPA   see   TIPITAPA

ITURBIDE, AGUSTIN DE (Emperor of Mexico).   Iturbide was for a period the monarch of all Meso-America. Central America, following the Plan of Iguala, was annexed to the Mexican empire briefly, from January 5, 1822 (relatively soon after the Day of Independence, September 15, 1821), until June 24, 1823.   The geographical and social fragmentation of Central America, as well as the colonial heritage, helped to make any union short-lived.   An army was sent by Iturbide to parts of El Salvador, Honduras, and Nicaragua, to help enforce his authority.   This force was under Brigadier Vicente Filísola.

ITZCUINTLE.   A month-festival god, and fiesta day, of the pre-conquest Nicarao.   Meaning, "dog. "

IYAS, RIO.   A major tributary of lower Río Tuma.

-J-

JABALI.   A gold mine in Chontales, scene of a spectacular Sandinista raid by Pedrón on July 18, 1931, when he also occupied Santo Domingo.   It was here that two Germans were captured and mistreated.   There was much looting.   (See   PFAEFFLE.)

JABILLITO, EL.   A hacienda in southwestern Granada department.

JACKSON, ANDREW.   As U.S. President, Jackson took a great interest in the Nicaragua Canal question, first pursuing with vigor the matter of getting stock in the Holland Canal Company (see Werweer) and then on U.S. Senate action March 3, 1835, opening negotiations for a canal with the Central American Federation.   While Jackson seemed opposed to plans for national progress at home, he dispatched a special agent, Charles Biddle, to collect data on this faraway but intriguing developmental enterprise.   Biddle went only to Panama, and his partial report and personal machinations were in part responsible for the vagueness of a Senate resolution and the resultant static situation on the canal which persisted through Jackson's administration.

JALAPA. Second town in size in Nueva Segovia department, Jalapa has a population of 1800 and is in the far northern section only five miles from the Honduran border.

JALTEVA. Ancient Indian town on the site of modern Granada, and still the name of a section of Granada and of the fortified national guard post there.

JAMAICA. A district in the municipio and department of Matagalpa.

JAMES DIETRICH. A very shallow-draft sternwheel steamer on the Río Coco in 1905. Upriver trips were made as far as Sachín. Fitted with electric lights, searchlight, fans, good cabins, water filters, shower bath, and good dinnerware, she was captained by a riverman from Pittsburgh.

JARQUIN, ANDRES see NUESTRA SEÑORA DEL ROSARIO

JARQUIN, CARLOS BRENES see BRENES JARQUIN, CARLOS

JARQUIN, IGNACIO. Considered a hero and martyr of the national war, Jarquín of Matapa took command of troops on the left wing on September 14, 1856, in the crucial battle of San Jacinto. He fell dead after giving the order to fire.

JAVILLO, EL. A district in the municipio of Santa Lucia, department of Boaco.

JAVIO, EL. Comarca or district of the municipio of Santa Teresa, Carazo department.

JEFE POLITICO. Political chief of a department. (See ADMINISTRATION, LOCAL.)

JEREMY. Son of "King" Oldman, Jeremy was sent to Jamaica in 1687 to beg that Mosquitia be taken under the protection of the King of England. Referring to the Earl of Warwick's Old Providence Island enterprise and "King" Oldman's fealty to Charles I, a group of the coastal settlers accompanied Jeremy to make his plea.

While the confirmation of Jeremy's status as royalty
was proceeding, Jeremy climbed a nearby tree in the
British major's uniform which had been given him by
his sponsors. The Earl of Albemarle, Governor of
Jamaica, is supposed to have granted the request. By
1701 a regular English factory for trade was established
on the coast. A second trip by Jeremy further confirmed the arrangement on June 25, 1720, by Act of
the Assembly of Jamaica, and Jeremy was sent back
in a British sloop with a generous supply of rum.
Miskito royalty seems to have been a kind of tincture
from that day on.

JEREMY I, KING (1687-1723). This Miskito Chief was
crowned "King" by the Duke of Albemarle of the New
Providence Company, and was given the first "treaty
of friendship" to bind Anglo-Miskito relationships.
This Miskito "reign" was to last nearly 200 years and
to be a great source of trouble between Spain and England, as well as between England and the United States.
The puppet kingdom maintained under the direction of
British Governors of Jamaica was essentially a geo-
political subterfuge to retain for Great Britain the canal
rights which would result in her ultimate command of
all ocean entries once a canal was dug.

JESUITS. One of the earliest of the Catholic monastic orders to come to Nicaragua in colonial times, the Jesuits
operate schools and churches and carry out humanitarian
projects.

JESUS. Mountain a mile north of Nicaraguan-Honduranian
border, five miles northwest of Jalapa. The altitude
of the mountain's Nicaraguan portions are 5857 feet,
which makes it Nicaragua's third highest mountain even
though the crest is in Honduras. The high point is in
the department of Nueva Segovia.

JESUS DIVINO OBRERO. A religious order which runs a
Managuan reformatory.

JICARAL, EL. 1) Municipio of León department, area 63
square miles, population of 4000. Bounded on the north
by Santa Rosa, south by La Paz Centro and San Francisco del Carnicero (of Managua department) and east
by Ciudad Darío, Matagalpa and El Sauce. There are
eight districts or valleys in the area.

2) A pueblo on the ancient road from the Segovias to León, this tiny village has only fifty houses. As a cabacera of a municipio, it is minimal. There are two stores.

JICARAL, RIO. A small river originating in San Nicolás municipio and crossing El Jicaral, León department.

JICARITO. Comarca or district in the municipio of Telica, León.

JICARO. A gourd which grows in unusual places on tree trunks and limbs of the thorny calabash tree. The "jicaros" are made into drinking cups and used in other craft fashions.

JICARO, EL. 1) Comarca or district of the municipio of Santo Tomas in Chontales.
2) A district or valley in the municipio of Belén, Rivas department.
3) A district in the municipio of Ciudad Darío, department of Matagalpa.
4) A district in the municipio and department of Estelí.
5) A district in the municipio of La Trinidad, Estelí department.
6) A district of the municipio of San Ramón, Matagalpa department.
7) On the river of the same name, this municipio of Nueva Segovia department has 1200 population. It is about 37 miles east of Ocotal, in a mining and cattle-raising region.

JICARO, RIO EL. A tributary from the northern part of Nueva Segovia to the Río Coco. Quilalí is on the Jicaro, and in the rugged area of the eastern part of the department.

JICOTE, EL. Comarca or district of the municipio of Santa Rosa, León.

JILGERO, EL. A mountain in Condega municipio, Estelí department.

JILOA. A recreational lake near Managua, in a crater several miles west of the city along the Lake Managua shore. Hot sulfur springs are found on the northwest

shore. Water-skiing is a favored pastime, and many
Managuans visit the lake. The hot springs are called
"infiernillos. "

JINOCUAO. Comarca or district in the municipio of Larreynaga, León department.

JIÑOCUAO. Nahuatl name for a tree called the eternal tree,
a sacred tree among the Nahua people. The name of
Jinotega is derived from this word plus Tecatl, signifying the peoples of the region.

JINOTEGA. 1) A cacicazgo or chieftaincy of pre-conquest
Chorutegans which gave its name to the present town,
municipio, and department. It covered the total southwestern portion of the present department from the Pantasma and Tuma Rivers on the east, the Yalí on the
west, the Coco on the north, and the Viejo to the south.
The cacicazgo was governed by a cacique and a council
of old men or principal chiefs, and a general elected
by this council.
2) The present "city" of Jinotega has about 8000
population. Schools, banks, churches, market, hospital,
and social clubs perform its function as the mercantile
and governmental center of a huge and nearly inaccessi-
ble area which comprises much of the municipio and
department of which it is cabacera and capital. Subject
to pillage by pirates and coastal Indians in the 16th,
17th and 18th centuries, and to destructive acts during
revolutions of the 19th century, Jinetega was also involved tragically in the Sandino War of the 1930's.
Elevated to villa status in April, 1851, and to city
status in February, 1883, Jinotega has been in a frontier situation for many of the years since its establishment.
3) Municipio in the department of the same name.
Of 330 square miles the population is about 9500. To
the north and east the municipio is essentially the same
as the department, and comprises four-fifths of that
unit. To the west it is bounded by the municipio of
San Rafael del Norte. Because of its large size, Jinotega comprises 79 districts, widely distributed.
4) The present department of Jinotega was created
on October 15, 1891, upon petition from the town council of Jinotega and allied towns. Previously Jinotega
had been part of the department of Matagalpa and earlier of the Matagalpa district of the 1838 department of

Setentrión. There have been territorial changes, such
as the removal of San Isidro to the department of Estelí when that entity was created in 1892. In 1894 the
district of Bocay was added, which tripled the original
area. The department has four municipios: Jinotega,
San Rafael del Norte, Yalí, and La Concordia (San
Rafael de la Concordia). Area of the department, 4700
square miles. Population, approximately 60,000; 7,000
of these in the town of the same name. Bounded to the
northwest by the departments of Madriz and Nueva Segovia and by Honduras, on the southeast by the territory
of the Cape and by the departments of Matagalpa and
Zelaya, much of Jinotega department is mountainous,
with some of the highest ranges in Nicaragua. Marine
sediment comprises many of the heights. The Isabella
range parallels the department. Products are: pine,
hardwood, coffee, grain. There are two zones, the
southeast and the northern. The latter has the climate
of the Atlantic Coast of Nicaragua, the former that of
the Pacific Coast. Average temperatures are 20º F.
lower in the mountainous cool northern part. There
are five zones of activity in the department. The agricultural areas are those of coffee, cattle, and general
agriculture of sugar, bananas, etc. Flowers are raised
to a great extent, especially lilies. The forested area
has a potential of lumbering. The gold-bearing areas
have been worked in a modest way for a long time.

JINOTEGA ANTIGUA. There is some uncertainty as to the
exact place of establishment of the old city, but the date
seems to be 1603, and the place either Liginaguina or
in the southeastern part of the Valley of La Tejera.
By the time of the visit of Bishop Morel de Santa Cruz
in 1752, the town had 743 inhabitants.

JINOTEPE. 1) Cabacera of the department, municipio, and
judicial district, the population of this town is 18,000,
with a rural population in the immediate region of 6,000.
The name according to some authorities, is derived from
the Nahuatl xilotl and tepetl, the first meaning "chilotes"
or immature corn, the second usually translated "hill."
A normal school is located in the town, also the Hospital Santiago. There are three major churches, the
principal one being over 100 years old. There are
several schools. The elevation is 1,700 feet.
   2) Municipio in the department of Carazo; population
24,000; area, 131 square miles. On the highest part

of the Carazo plateau, it is bounded by the department of Masaya to the north and by the Pacific Ocean to the south. Eastward are the municipios of El Rosario, La Paz, Santa Teresa, and La Conquista; to the west, Diriamba and San Marcos. Coffee is the principal product, but corn, rice, beans, other cereals, and sugar cane are also grown. Along the coast are some small cattle ranches. There are 39 districts, as the area is closely settled.

3) In 1889, the sub-prefecture of Jinotepe was established with adherence to Granada. This was under the department of Granada.

JINOTEPELENSES see JINOTEPINOS

JINOTEPINOS. Residents of Jinotepe or of the region thereabout.

JIQUELITE. A district of the municipio of Jinotega.

JIRON, EUFRASIO. A resident of Nueva Segovia who made mineral strikes in the Depilto area in 1840.

JIRONES, LOS. Comarca or district of the municipio of Santa Teresa, Carazo department.

J. L. WHITE. A Lake Nicaragua or San Juan River steamer of 1860-1880 period.

J. M. CLAYTON. A shallow-draft sternwheel river steamer captured by Cauty in San Juan del Norte during the filibuster war.

J. N. SCOTT. A shallow-draft sternwheel steamer on the San Juan River, its chief claim to fame being its destruction by a spectacular explosion in 1857. The Scott was taking part in the Lockridge Expedition against El Castillo, the Spanish fort guarding the rapids of that name. Following the failure of Colonel Titus' attack on El Castillo, the steamer was going downstream with the beaten filibusters when ignorant handling caused her to explode. A participant, C. W. Doubleday, reported 20 killed; he himself was seriously burned in the accident. The small accompanying steamer Rescue transported the survivors on to Greytown.

JOCOMICO. 1) A district valley in the municipio of Belén,

Rivas department.
2) A district of the municipio of Jinotega.

JOCOTE, EL. A district of the municipio of Condega, Estelí department.

JOCOTE DULCE. 1) A sweet fruit of the jocote tree, much
favored by Nicaraguans to eat as a between-meals snack.
Fruit about the size of a small plum.
2) A territory of the National District, department of
Managua.

JOLATA. An aboriginal settlement, since disappeared, near
Nandasmo.

JOME, DON ANDRES. One of the Spanish colonial families
established in Masaya by 1800 and extant today.

JONES, ALEXANDER. A physician who joined William Walker for the Nicaraguan adventure in 1855 and who was one
of the 58 original "Immortals." Jones had already sav-
ored danger venturing on a treasure hunt in the Indian
Ocean.

JONRON. Phonetic "home-run." Baseball is a favorite
Nicaraguan game.

JORA, LOS. A district of the San Rafael del Sur municipio,
Managua department.

JORDAN, EL. Coffee hacienda in the Sierras de Managua,
of the National District.

JORNADA. One of several periodicals presently published
with limited circulation.

JOVITOS, LOS. A district of the municipio of Santo Tomás,
Chinandega department.

JUAN, JORGE see LA CONDAMINE, LA.

JUANAMOSTEGA see CAMPAÑON, FRANCISCO DE.

JUAN DAVILA. A district of the municipio of San Juan de
Tola, Rivas department.

JUAN NAGUAS. Comarca or district in the municipio of
Jinotepe, Carazo department.

JUAN TALLO, LAGUNA.   A small lake due east of Nandaime.

JUCUAPA.   A mountain height in the municipio of Matagalpa.

JUCUAPA ABAJO.   A district in the municipio and department of Matagalpa.

JUCUAPA ARRIBA.   A district in the municipio and department of Matagalpa.

JUDICIARY.   Consists of the Supreme Court of Justice, the
Superior Labor Court, and five Courts of Appeal (in
León, Granada, Matagalpa, Bluefields, and Masaya).
In addition there are departmental courts, municipal
courts, and several local courts--juez de mesta, juez
de cantón.   The Supreme Court sits in Managua, with
five magistrates chosen by Congress.   There is no comprehensive judicial review of legislative acts.

JUEZ DE CANTON.   A court at cantón or village level, beneath that of Juez de Mesta (q. v.).

JUEZ DE MESTA.   A court at the comarca or district level
in each municipio (hence the local importance of the
"comarca" designation), something like "justices of the
peace, " or perhaps it might be thought of as a position
something between judge and sheriff.

JUIGALPA.   1) Cabacera of the municipio Juigalpa and of
the department of Chontales, population 9200 in 1968.
Altitude, 385 feet.   Noted in 1742 by Corregidor don
Francisco de Pasada, Juigalpa was also mentioned in
1752 by Brother Augustín Morel de Santa-Cruz, and in
1869 by Pablo Levy, when he observed 3000 inhabitants.
Thomas Belt, the naturalist and resident mine manager
stated that in 1872 it was a principal city of the province of Chontales, near the river Mayales and at the
feet of the Amerrisque Mountains.   A Normal Institute
is located here, and a National Institute or Secondary
School as well.   The Colegio San Francisco de Asís is
a modern school.   A museum and a zoological garden
are also features.   The name Juigalpa originates in
Nahuatl--xuctli, "small black snail"; calli, a place or
house; and pan, an adverb of place; hence, originally
Xuctli-calli-pan.
          2) Municipio in the department of Chontales; area

675 square miles, population (1968) 22,670, largest in
the department, second in density to La Libertad.
Bounded on the north by the municipio of Comoapa in
Boaco; on the south by Lake Nicaragua; on the east by
the municipios of Acoyapa, San Pedro de Lavago and
La Libertad; and on the west by Comolopa and the Lake.
More than 9200 of the inhabitants live in the cabacera
of Juigalpa.

JULIA, TOMAS DE. This Spanish captain, on December 31,
1780, led 200 men from Fort San Carlos at the foot of
Lake Nicaragua toward the Fort Inmaculada (see El Castillo) then held by the British. Cautiously approaching
the fort, he shelled it on January 3, 1781, only to discover that Despard and the British had slipped away.
The recovery of the big frontier fort was a strategic
success far beyond its seeming tactical importance, for
the British twin hope, to sever the Spanish colonial empire and to provide a passage from Atlantic to Pacific,
was, as the events later spun out, thus forever thwarted.
Juliá was later made commandant at Black River in
Honduras, to hold the gains made on the Spanish frontier.
He was defeated and taken prisoner by Despard at Black
River in 1782. But while in this sense he lost the battle, at El Castillo he won the war.

JUMAIQUI. 1) A district in the municipio and department of
Matagalpa.
    2) A mountain height in the municipio of Matagalpa.

JUMAYLI. Property of don Leondro Delgado, granted in
Estelí department in the early 18th century. An aboriginal Indian name.

JUNTA, LA. 1) Comarca or district in the municipio of
Diriamba, department of Carazo.
    2) A district of the municipio of San Juan de Tola,
Rivas department.

JUNTA DE MINERIA. A council formed by the chief officer
of the army, General Muñoz, on March 14, 1846, following mineral strikes in Depilto, Macuelizo, and Santa
María. The purpose was to prevent improper exploitation of mineral resources.

JUNTA DE RECURSOS. An action committee established in
Metapa (see Ciudad Darío) during the national war.

President of the junta was Fernando Guzmán and the secretary, Francisco Amador; Ramón Machado represented Nueva Segovia, Ramón Castillo represented Matagalpa, and José Dolores Flores represented Chontales. The purpose was to assist with logistical support of the forces opposed to William Walker (q. v.).

JUNTA NACIONAL DE ASISTENCIA Y PREVISION SOCIAL. A public welfare organization headed in 1970 by doña Hope Portocarrero de Somoza, wife of the President of Nicaragua.

JUNTA NACIONAL DE TURISMO. Increasingly aware of the tourist potential of their beautiful and unspoiled country, Nicaraguans are attempting by such devices as this Tourist Board to both develop and control tourism. Freshwater tarpon fishing, the unique lakes and volcanoes, the fairly undeveloped archaeological riches, all are considered. Adequate hotels are being added slowly. The junta has such publications as a colorful information map and brochure, "Welcome to Nicaragua. "

-K-

KAKABILA. A village on the southwestern shore of Pearl Lagoon.

KAMA, RIO. A tributary of the Río Escondido, entering that stream just to the west of Bluefields.

KARATA, LAGUNA. One of twin coastal lagoons just south of Puerto Cabezas. The other is Laguna Yulu.

KARAWALA. A village in the Caribbean coastal area just to the north of the Río Grande estuary. Lanica Airlines used to make a stop in this village on an air strip down the main "street. "

KEARSARGE, U. S. S. Dispatched to help settle a Nicaragua-Honduras dispute in 1893, the doughty old steam sloop which had distinguished herself by defeating the famous Confederate blockade runner Alabama off the French coast, while yet new following her 1861 christening, was lost on a Caribbean reef, and thereby left a free hand to British forces arriving in late February to land Marines and reassert British implicit sovereignty over the Mos-

quito reserve. However, the U. S. government forced
the British to pull back.

KEMBLE, STEPHEN. Lieutenant colonel Kemble had been
    leading troops against the colonists in the American
    Revolutionary War when he was sent in 1780 to assist
    in the invasion of the Spanish empire in Nicaragua. An
    American-born native of New Brunswick, New Jersey,
    this model soldier, a bachelor, was a very able man.
    In charge of San Juan Harbor, he ascended the river in
    May after Polson with Nelson's help took Fort Inmacula-
    da. While awaiting reinforcements, he reconnoitered
    between the fort and the lake, presumably looking to-
    ward the seizure of Lake Nicaragua and then of Granada
    and León. It turned out that 500 Spanish troops were
    guarding the lake at Fort San Carlos, precluding further
    advance by Kemble without reinforcement. By the end
    of July only 70 of Kemble's men were still on their
    feet. He transferred to Bluefields. By January 3,
    1781, the fort was evacuated by the decimated English
    and Kemble's command was a final failure. The Kem-
    ble Papers (New York Historical Society) are a major
    and fascinating source on this period and its events.
    (See CASTILLO VIEJO, EL.)

KEWEN, ACHILLES. An officer under William Walker in
    1855 like Fayssoux, Kewen had fought with Narciso Ló-
    pez earlier in Cuba, and was a professional soldier of
    fortune. His brother Edward was prominent in Californ-
    ia politics of the Gold Rush era. As a Major, Kewen
    was with Walker in León, during his early encounters
    with his allies Muñoz and Castellón. During the first
    few minutes of fighting in the first battle of Rivas on
    June 29, 1855, Kewen was killed, as was Crocker,
    another chief Walker aide.

KILAMBE. Mountain complex, a branch of the Isabella
    range comprising Mount Kilambé, Guamblón, and Gua-
    lán, on an old volcanic crater and Nicaragua's fourth
    highest mountain at 5742 feet; location: 22 miles due
    east of Quílalí, in the department of Jinotega. Kilambé
    is characterized by a well-wooded and fertile crater
    like a round amphitheatre, a mile or more in diameter,
    tipped toward the north. It lies between the Coco and
    Bocay Rivers.

KILAMBE Y CAMALIONA. A district of the municipio of
    Jinotega.

KINKAJOU. A relative of the raccoon found widely in Nicaragua, generally in forest or jungle areas.

KIRIBIES see QUIRIBIES.

KNOX, PHILANDER C. From 1909, when Knox took over as U.S. Secretary of State under President William Howard Taft, policy toward Central America, Nicaragua in particular, was that of the "big stick." While ostensibly the purpose was to maintain order, the policy of "dollar diplomacy" (q.v.) seemed more calculated to attain markets, monopolies, and in general, economic advantage for the U.S. Knox was not familiar with Latin America, and was especially opposed to Nicaragua's Zelaya. Policy centered on offshore naval forces, landings of Marines, preference for conservative governments, insistence on financial reforms backed by such matters as collection of customs duties. It was during such periods of insensitivity that much of present-day mistrust and unrest was bred.

KOSSUTH. Hungarian revolutionary who influenced William Walker (q.v.), who wore a black, broad-brimmed "kossuth hat." Henningsen (q.v.), later Walker's chief lieutenant, had fought with Kossuth in his liberation of Hungary from Russia in 1848. He was a man symbolic of the turbulent mid-century, and in indirect ways influenced the coming crucial events in Nicaragua following 1850.

KUKALAYA. A village in Zelaya department up the Kukalaya River from Laguna Wounta.

KUKRA. Village with an airstrip 18 miles north of Bluefields and near the prominent landmark Kukra Hill.

KUM. Village on the Río Coco, 12 miles below Bilwaskarma. There is an air strip.

KUM KUM, RIO. A stream of the department of Zelaya, tributary to the Río Kurinwas west of Pearl Lagoon.

KUSKAWAS. A district on the lower Río Tuma.

-L-

LABERINTO, EL. Coffee plantation in Pueblo Nuevo municipio of Estelí department.

LABOR ORGANIZATIONS. There are nine labor union
groups in the country, four of which are registered
with the Ministry of Labor, as follows: Confederación
General del Trabajo Democrático (C. N. T. D.); Confederación General del Trabajo (C. G. T.); Federación de
Transportadores Unidos de Nicaragua (F. T. U. N.); and
Federación de Obreros del Volante. The others are
essentially to the political left of those recognized by
the Ministry of Labor. Casas del Obreros, or labor
halls, are in every major population center. The organizations are quite active.

LABORIO, BARRIO. A district of León since the 17th century, it was known as "San Nicolás de los Laborios. "
It was early peopled by Indians used as servants.

LABRADOR, SAN ISIDRO. Patron Saint of Condega; a festival to him is an annual event in May.

LABRANZA, LA. A district of the municipio of Condega,
Estelí department. There is a mountain height of the
same name.

LABU, RIO. A tributary of the Río Prinzapolka.

LACAYO FARFAN, ENRIQUE. Leader of an attempt to un-
seat President Luis Somoza in 1959. Based in Costa
Rica, the rebel forces entered Nicaragua by land and
by air. President Mario Echandí of Costa Rica refused
to support the "invasion, " and it came to naught. Lacayo Farfan, himself an Independent Liberal, was not
anti-liberal (the Liberal Party being in power) but anti-
Somoza. The affair fizzled. Nicaraguan exile groups
remain strong in Costa Rica.

LACAYO SACASA, BENJAMIN. President of Nicaragua
briefly in 1947, following Leonardo Argüello (q. v.).

LADINO. A term used in Nicaragua, as elsewhere, to denote hispanicized people of mixed Indo-European blood.
There are some interesting innovations to this term in
this particular country, such as "Nica-Chinos" (Nica-

raguans of part Chinese ancestry). The term ladino is
basically nonethnic, referring to assimilation of Spanish culture. It also has bearing upon social stratifica-
tion.

LADINOS, LOS. A territory of the National District, department of Managua.

LAGARES, FRAY PEDRO. Missionary priest of the Franciscan order who entered the Pantasma region in 1674
and established two towns, San Francisco Nanaica and
San José Paraca, with the plan to develop churches,
schools, and hospitals for the tribes of the region.

LAGARTA, LA. A district in the municipio of Belén, Rivas department.

LAGARTO COLORADO. A district in the municipio of
Matiguás, department of Matagalpa.

LAGEROSO. Comarca or territory in the municipio of
Villa Somoza, Chontales.

LAGUNA, LA. 1) A district of the municipio of Condega,
Estelí department.
2) A district in the municipio and department of Estelí.
3) A district of the municipio and department of
Masaya.

LAGUNA DAKURA. A coastal lagoon just north of Punta
Gorda on the northeast Caribbean coast of Nicaragua.

LAGUNA DE LOS MISTERIOS. A lake in the summit of
Cerro Padre, Esquipulas municipio, Matagalpa department.

LAGUNA DE MOYOA. A lake in the Ciudad Darío area
which in its dried-up state indicated through findings
of antique silver coins and by other objects, that some
cataclysm had here destroyed an ancient pueblo.

LAGUNA DE PAHARA. A large lagoon with access to the
Caribbean Sea over the "Barra Sanawala" bar, 20 miles
north of Puerto Cabezas. It is surrounded by a 20-
mile sector of swamp laced with streams.

LAGUNA DE PERLAS. A coastal lagoon nearly 30 miles
    long extending from 18 miles north of Bluefields on
    Zelaya's Caribbean coast to within five miles of the
    Río Grande estuary. There is canoe travel all through
    these shallow lagoons. This one in particular was a
    pirate haunt during the 17th century.

LAGUNA GRANDE. A coastal lagoon which is part of the
    frequented inland waterway between Bluefields and La-
    guna de Perlas.

LAGUNA VERDE. A district in the municipio and depart-
    ment of Matagalpa.

LAGUNILLAS DE ARINCE. Small lake in the department of
    Estelí.

LAJAS, LAS. 1) Coffee hacienda in the municipio of San
    Rafael del Norte in Jinotega department.
        2) A district of the municipio of Tipitapa, depart-
    ment of Managua.
        3) Hacienda in the municipio of Rivas.

LAKIATARA. Aboriginal name for Rivas, signifying "Star
    of the Morning" (possibly referring to the planet Venus).

LANA ABAJO. A district of the municipio of Jinotega.

LANA ARRIBA. A district of the municipio of Jinotega.

L. A. N. I. C. A. Lineas Aéreas Nicaragüense is the Nica-
    raguan airline affiliated with the Pan American system.
    Local flights are on regular schedule to Bluefields,
    Puerto Cabezas, the gold mines at Bonanza and Siuna,
    the Río Coco ports of Waspam and Bilwaskarma, and
    to the Corn Islands. International jet schedules are
    maintained to Miami and Mexico. Miami to Managua
    is a flight of two and a half hours. Since Nicaraguans
    are often called "Nicas, " the acronym also has a nicety
    of meaning in the form "La Nica. "

LANZABOMBAS. Name given to U. S. Marine divebombers
    by Sandinista partisans in 1927. These planes were
    armed with 30-calibre machine guns and 17-pound bombs.
    They were of Boeing manufacture, fabric-covered bi-
    planes, powered by Wright radial engines. Their sig-
    nificance lay in the fact that the Nicaraguan divebomb-

ing was the first used in warfare, presaging the Stuka
bombers used in Spain's Civil War of the thirties, and
by Germany in World War II. (See OCOTAL, BATTLE
OF.)

LAPAN. A remote village in the swampy coastal area of
Zelaya department, 25 miles west of the Barra de Wawa.

LARIOS, LOS. A district of the San Rafael del Sur municipio, Managua department.

LARREYNAGA. 1) Municipio in the department of León;
area, 322 square miles; population, 19,000. Bounded
on the north by El Sauce and Villanueva, and the department of Chinandega; on the south by La Paz Centro;
on the east by El Jicaral and La Paz Centro; and on
the west by León and Télica. There are 23 districts,
three of them semi-urban in Larreynaga. The agriculture is almost exclusively devoted to cotton and sugar
cane. There are two villages other than the town of
Larreynaga; El Limón (a mining town), and Mineral de
Santa Pancha.
    2) The pueblo, at present cabacera of the municipio
of the same name, was named for the hero of Nicaraguan
independence in 1821. The pueblo dates, however, only
from 1936. About 20 miles from León, 400 feet above
sea level, the population is 5500.

LARREYNAGA, MIGUEL. Distinguished Nicaraguan whose
name is identified with the independence movement which
was reaching a climax on September 15, 1821. On May
9, 1821 came the cry of independence in Guatemala,
and then the Act of Independence. Larreynaga was a
steadying influence in the Junta Provisional Consultiva
which was formed immediately following the act, when
the Mexican Plan of Iguala was being considered.

LAS CASAS, BARTOLOMÉ DE. Born in Seville in 1474, a
graduate of the famous university at Salamanca, he first
came to America in 1502. Ordained in Spain in 1510,
he soon returned to the Americas. Known later as Protector of the Indians, he fought the cruel encomienda
system of semi-slavery for Indians. He made frequent
trips back and forth to Spain in these difficult times, in
behalf of the Indians. The introduction of Negro slaves
in place of the Indian slavery was not a long-range
solution. Later, he was Bishop of Cuzco, Peru; he

became Bishop of Chiapas yet later, and died in Spain in 1566 at 92 years of age. Las Casas is also known for his major historical work, Historia General de Las Indias. He was one of the great figures of the dramatic century of such giants as da Vinci, Machiavelli, Cellini, Cervantes, Michelangelo and a host of others.

LATIFUNDIOS. A land holding classification representing over 1000 manzanas (or 1750 acres). The department of Chontales, for example, has about 30 such holdings. It is the problem of large holdings such as this which finally precipitated the Mexican peasant revolution of 1910.

LATIMER, JULIAN L. U. S. Navy Commander of all U. S. forces in Nicaragua in 1926-1927. Admiral Latimer was relieved as commander of the Special Service Squadron and was replaced by Rear Admiral David F. Sellers.

LAULO. A district in the municipio of Matiguás, department of Matagalpa.

LAURA FRANCES. A shallow-draft San Juan River paddle steamer concerning which more than usual information is available because in 1860, British Commander Bedford Pim went up-river on her. She was of three-foot draft, 100 tons, 75 horsepower, six knots speed. Captain, G. F. Holton; Mate-Pilot, Mr. Carman; Clerk, Mr. Dickson. Later sold to New Granada (Colombia) as a gunboat, the sale price was $5000, for a vessel which cost new $13,000 and $50 per day to run.

LAUREL GALAN. A district of the municipio of San Francisco, Managua department.

LAVADERO, MINA. One of the Misericordia groups of Old Spanish mines near Amatillo in Nueva Segovia department. Schistose ores show low gold and silver yields. Old tunnels are blocked.

LAVAS, LAS. District in the municipio of Altagracia on Omotepe Island in Lake Nicaragua, department of Rivas.

LAW, GEORGE. The multi-millionaire Law, known as "Liveoak," was a Panamanian shipping magnate of the 1850's, and a rival of the powerful Cornelius Vander-

bilt (q. v.); believing that filibuster William Walker (q. v.)
in Nicaragua could give him support and the privileges
of the transit across that country, Law gave Walker
secret support in 1857.   His principle contribution was
getting the interest and support of Charles Frederick
Henningsen (q. v.), one of the remarkable figures of the
century.   Law bought arms, but in the end his contributions came to naught.

LAWIRA, RIO.   This tributary of the lower Prinzapolka is
short but carries a large volume of water from its
swampy headwaters.

LEANARDOS, LOS.   A district of the San Rafael del Sur
municipio, Managua department.

LECHECUAGOS.   Comarca or district of the municipio of
León, León department.

LEGAL SYSTEM.   Judicial decisions must rest upon the
constitution, organic law, decree-laws, and acuerdos
(q. v.).

LEGATION GUARD.   A force of 100 U. S. Marines left in
Nicaragua to "guard" the U. S. Embassy there following
withdrawal of larger Marine forces in 1913, upon election of Adolfo Díaz as President; the guard remained
until August, 1925.   In effect, this guard prevented the
capture of Managua by revolution, which fact resulted
in the continuance of the Conservative Party in power.
The withdrawal was followed soon by a coup by Emiliano
Chamorro.   By 1926 civil war had broken out, and then
President Díaz called for U. S. Marines again.   The
Sandino War followed.

LEGISLATION.   In the legislative process, most bills are
presented by the President.   Members of Congress may
introduce bills, but in general they tend to present ideas
rather than formulated bills.   All legislation is introduced in the Chamber of Deputies.   It takes a two-
thirds Senate majority to kill a Chamber Bill.   The
Legislature has legislative, constitutive, electoral, and
judicial functions.   Under the second they may formulate
or amend constitutions.   In electoral capacity, they may
select an interim president from one of the vice-presidents, when such selection becomes necessary.   In judicial capacity, they may impeach--investigating charges

against a national public official, and issuing an indict-
ment if the charges are substantial.   The resultant trial
is in the Senate.   The electoral function is unique and
relates to the supervised conduct of elections.   In practice, there is presidential-congressional concurrence in
policy, as a result of the two-thirds majority of the incumbent party.   In effect the executive has the strength.

LEGISLATURE.   The structure of Nicaragua's Legislature
(Congress) is bicameral, with two representative bodies,
the Senate and the Chamber of Deputies.   The Senate is
made up of elected Senators, one for each of the 16 national departments, and senators-for-life who are ex-
Presidents of the country, and a senator who was presidential runner-up in the last national elections.   (He
has a four-year term.)   One third representation of the
major opposition party is guaranteed in both houses.
In 1968 there were 18 senators.   All of the Chamber
of Deputies is composed of representatives popularly
elected at large, with one representative for each
30, 000 citizens; in 1968, there were 28 majority and
14 minority deputies for a total of 42.   A deputy must
be a citizen, secular, and at least 25 years of age.

LENCAS.   A subtribal group of the Chontales tribe, which
in turn derived from the "Quiribies. "

LEON.   1) Traditional "Liberal" Capital of Nicaragua, Ciudad León, was its first capital, in the old site on Lake
Managua.   (See also León Viejo.)   Established there in
1524 and moved to its present site in 1610, the city
shares with Granada the mantle of Nicaraguan leadership over the colonial centuries and is today an extant
gem of colonial city planning and architecture.   The
great cathedral (see Leon Cathedral) is the largest
structure of its type in Latin America.   Founded as a
ciudad or city, from the start, León was destined to
leadership first under the vigorous and cruel Governor
Pedrarias (q. v.) Dávila and went on to become the symbol of liberal views and the seat of liberal parties
through the independence era and until today.   It also
became the capital of one of the four original departments of separately independent Nicaragua on April 30,
1838 (Nicaragua or Rivas, Granada, Segovia, and León).
A present population of over 50, 000, at an altitude of
360 feet above sea level, occupies the site on the broad
plains of León, in full sight of the line of volcanoes,

Los Marabios, the most recently active of which, Cerro Negro, is nearby; it rained cinders on León in 1971. The town is almost three miles square. While recent construction has taken away some of the colonial appearance, there are still many structures such as the massive cathedral (1747-1816), the churches La Merced (q. v., 1615), San Francisco (1639), and La Recolección (1788), as well as the great bridge, Puente de Guadelupe, which evidence the colonial heritage. And the nearby suburb of Subtiava (built in about 1548) attests to the energy of early ecclesiastics. The history of the city of León with its revolutions, the incursions of the filibuster, William Walker, and the ebb and flow of political influence and excitement, would fill two volumes.

2) The municipio of León has an area of 328 square miles and is second in size among the divisions of the department of the same name. The population is 75, 000 and it is bounded on the north by municipios Larreynaga and Telica; on the south by the Pacific Ocean; on the east by La Paz Centro; and on the west by Posoltega and Chichigalpa. There are 28 districts. The department and municipio are distinguished as the seat of the old liberal capital, León, a historical spot. The range of the Marabios is a scenic skyline to the north, the beaches of Poneloya on the Pacific to the south and west.

3) Partido de Leon, one of the nine districts of the country under the constitution of April 8, 1826, when it was one of the United Provinces of Central America. (See PARTIDOS DE NICARAGUA.)

LEON, BARRIOS OF. San Felipe, Subtiava, Laborio, Guadalupe, San Juan, Dolores, San Sebastián, Zaragoza, El Calvario, San Luis, La Pila de Agua, Lomas de Veracruz and El Coyolor are among the 20 districts of the modern city of León.

LEON, SANTIAGO DE LOS CABALLEROS. The old city of León was established on the shores of Lake Managua (Lago Xolotlán), in 1524, by Captain Francisco Hernández de Córdoba, on the day Domingo de la Santísima Trinidad of 1524, June 19. The location was on the site of an Indian town, in the Nagrandan province or district of Imabite. There lived in the vicinity 15, 000 people. Old León is now an archaeological site being developed. (See León Viejo.) For 86 years the city remained on this site and then was moved following earthquakes in the year 1610. The old city was capital

of Nicaragua as a province of the Kingdom of Guatemala.
Moved on March 20, 1610 to its present site, adjacent
to the ancient and important pre-conquest Indian town of
Subtiava, the city was called variously Ciudad de Santiago de León, León de los Caballeros, and Santiago de
León de Los Caballeros. This city of "St. James of the
Gentlemen" is so recorded in Guatemala and Costa Rican national archives. There seems to be some question
as to the legality of these romantic titles. Captain Córdoba seems to have used simply the title "City of León."

LEON CATHEDRAL. The magnificent late-baroque cathedral of León is said to have the "earthquake baroque"
style because it lies in a tremor-prone fault zone, and
the low towers and massive construction are calculated
to preserve it. The cathedral was established in 1610
when the capital city of Nicaragua was moved to its
present site. However, the present structure is the
fourth to occupy the same site. The second was burned
in 1685 by pirates under Dampier, and the third was
erected shortly thereafter under the supervision of an
English architect who was captured from among the
invading pirates. The building thus produced was described as a fine stone building with brick arches and
a wood roof, but the interior was dark and narrow.
Bishop Isidro Marín Bullón y Figueroa began the new
and present structure in 1747, which was destined to
be the greatest structure of its kind in Central America,
and one of the largest in the hemisphere. Diego de
Porras was chief architect, Bishop Vilchez y Cabrera
of Nueva Segovia, chief "expediter." The building was
consecrated in 1780, and dedicated as Basílica of the
Assumption in 1860. Built of cut stone and on a low
platform, the structure is vast, a full city block long,
and has withstood earthquakes and cannon fire for two
centuries. The facade and towers are a five-part composition. Great buttresses support the lateral walls.
There are added aisles each side in the interior. It
was used as a fortress due to its massive strength.
In 1823, thirty cannon were mounted on its vaulted
masonry roof. Within the cathedral is buried Rubén
Darío. (See illustration, p. 76.)

LEON THEATRE. A magnificent theatre of colonial days
remained in relatively good repair until a fire in the
1960's destroyed much of it. The building was of an
unusually attractive design. The existence of a theatre
indicated the somewhat sophisticated life attendant to the

city's status as a colonial capital, as was also evidenced by the magnificent extant cathedral.

LEON VIEJO. "Old León" was the municipality originally
established under the name in a site differing from that
now occupied by León. Founded by Francisco Hernández de Córdoba, June 15, 1524, the old city was in the
province of Imabite, on a plain near the shores of Lake
Xolotlán, (now Lake Managua), and about six miles
across an arm of the lake from the Volcano Momotombo. In the neighborhood lived about 15,000 Nagrandan
Indians at the time. De Córdoba was acting as a lieutenant to Pedrarias Dávila. There is some reason to
believe that the founding may actually have occurred in
1523. The town was immediately provided with a fort
and a major church. There was a problem of getting
fresh water. By the early 1600's there was recorded
a cathedral. The houses of the town probably extended
from the city center, as marked by this church, toward
the lake, just to the east. The first mayor, probably
named by de Córdoba, was don Sebastián de Belelazar.
The city was abandoned just after a disastrous earthquake on January 11, 1610, and moved to the present
site. Old León is presently in the hands of archaeologists who have unearthed a number of foundations of
major buildings. The site of the fort on a nearby crest
has been identified but not yet excavated. León was
capital of the Province of Nicaragua under the governorship of Pedrarias Dávila. Among other bloody deeds,
Pedrarias beheaded Hernández de Córdoba in the public
plaza of León in June of 1526. He was also, at an earlier time (1519) in Panama, responsible for the death of
Balboa, discoverer of the Pacific.

LEONESA, LA. Mine in the area of San Ramón's (q. v.)
pueblo; now no longer operating.

LEONESE. A citizen of León.

LEUIRE. The "spirit of the waters, " a passed from the
Miskitos to the Bocay-Pantasma group of Chorutegans,
in post-conquest times.

LEYENDA NEGRA see BLACK LEGEND

LIBERTAD, LA. 1) Cabacera of the municipio of La Libertad, 2000 population. Beginning as a mining camp about

1852, known then simply as "La Mineral." Named, it is said, by a gambler named Conrado who, pursued by police, said "Let us go to Mineral--there, there is freedom [libertad] to play, drink, and anything else." The name stuck.

2) A municipio in the department of Chontales since 1855 having 69 square miles and a population of 8000 (it has the highest density in the department, with 109 persons per square mile). Bounded on the north by municipio Comolapa in Boaca; on the south by San Pedro de Lavago; on the east by Santo Domingo, and on the west by Juigalpa.

3) A periodical developed in Boaco in the period 1915-1937.

LIBRERIA SIGLO EDITORIAL. A book publisher located in Managua.

LICOROY. 1) A district in the municipio of La Trinidad, Estelí department.

2) A mountain height of Condega municipio, Estelí department.

LIGINAGUINA. Possible location of first establishment of the town of Jinotega.

LIGUISTIGUES. One-hundred foot waterfall on the Río Guina, tributary of the Río Bocay, Jinotega department.

LILIAM. A quinta (country mansion) in the environs of Masaya.

LIMAS, LAS. 1) Comarca or district of the municipio of Nagarote, León department.

2) A district in the municipio of Matiguás, department of Matagalpa.

LIMAY. A comarca or district of the municipio of San Nicolás, León.

LIMBASNA. Waterfall on the Río Hamaca tributary of the Bocay, Jinotega department.

LIMITADA. A collective partnership similar to North American limited liability companies, which in this case limits liability of each partner to the amount of his contribution--hence "limitada" (or "Ltda.") is added following the company name, with the same significance of "Inc. "

LIMON. 1) A district of the municipio of San Juan de Tola, Rivas department.
2) El Limón, a comarca or district in the municipio of Jinotepe, Carazo department.
3) El Limón, a district in the municipio and department of Estelí.
4) El Limón, a spring in the southern part of the municipio of León.

LIMONAL. District in the municipio of Buenos Aires, department of Rivas.

LIMONES, LOS. 1) A comarca or district of the municipio of San Nicolas, León.
2) A district in the municipio and department of Matagalpa.

LIMOSNA. Offering of a small monetary nature given to a statue of a saint on the occasion when the statue is brought to homes, left for one day, and passed to another house for the next day. Prayer sessions accompany the visit and the offering. This is a highland, non-church observance.

LINCOLN, ABRAHAM. The U. S. President of the turbulent 1860's found time to deal in his message of December 4, 1864, with the trans-isthmian canal question: "At the request of Costa Rica and Nicaragua, a competent engineer has been authorized to make a survey of the River San Juan and the Port of San Juan.... We could not exaggerate either the commercial or the political importance of that great improvement. " A little known plan of Lincoln's was to settle freed slaves in the better agricultural portions of the isthmian area, such as the Chiriquí region of Panama. Lincoln had dispatched as a minister to Central America, Andrew B. Dickinson.

LINDIRI see NINDIRI

LION OF NICARAGUA see EMILIANO CHAMORRO

LIPULULO. A district of the municipio of Jinotega.

LIQUIA. A district in the municipio of Matiguás, department of Matagalpa.

LIRA, GENARE AMADOR. Born in 1910 in Managua, and a
student in Mexico in 1935, Lira founded the National
School of Fine Arts as a branch of the National University in 1941. Sculptor in stone and plaster, he frequently uses animals as subjects. With Penalba he has
had a great influence in developing other Nicaraguan
artists.

LIZAURZABAL, DON BENITO. One of the three elected
junta members of the independence movement in Rivas
in 1811. A pioneer venture in Spanish colonial independence.

LLANAS DE PALMERA. A low plateau area adjacent to
Alamikamba, site of the airfield.

LLANITO, EL. A district in the municipio of Santa Lucia,
department of Boaco.

LLANITOS, LOS. Comarca or district in the municipio of
Achuapa, León department.

LLANO DE ALAMIKAMBA. A low plateau just north of
Alamikamba.

LLANO GRANDE. 1) Comarca, valley or district in the
municipio of Jinotega.
2) A district of the municipio and department of
Masaya.
3) A district in the municipio and department of
Matagalpa.
4) A village on the railroad between Granada and
Masaya.

LLANO ISNAWAS. A savannah north of Alamikamba in
Zelaya department.

LLANO LARGO. 1) Comarca or district in the municipio
of La Libertad, Chontales.
2) A district in the municipio of La Trinidad, department of Estelí.

LLANO LUNBAIKA. A low plateau north of the Río Prinzapolka and east of Alamikamba.

LLANO RAYA TARA. A plain of pine savannahs just north
of Puerto Cabezas on the northeast coast in Zelaya department.

LLANOS DE BUTKO.   Piedmont uplands northwest of Puerto Cabezas.

LLANOS EL DORADO.   Plains in northern Rivas department, just west of Isla Zapatera.

LLANOS MAKANTAKA.   A tableland between the Río Grande de Matagalpa and the Río Prinzapolka, adjacent to and south of Alamikamba in Zelaya department.

LLAVES, LAS.   A territory of the National District, department of Managua.

LOCALISMO.   This feeling of "localism" or special provincialism in Nicaragua has been heightened by several factors; initially, perhaps, because Nicaragua's population (because of the wide plains areas of the Rift) was settled in a more urban pattern than occurred elsewhere in Central America.   Devotion to the old conservative center of Granada and the liberal one of León transferred itself to an equally local feeling in the newer capital of Managua and such towns as Matagalpa.   The local feeling is not as segmented, however, as in the more isolated mountain valleys of the Maya regions of Guatemala.

LOCKRIDGE, S. A.   Colonel Lockridge was one of William Walker's most trusted officers, and was particularly involved in events on the San Juan River.   Lockridge was stymied by the British at Greytown in 1857 when he attempted to give aid to defeat Spencer and Cauty in their river operations which were denying Walker needed supplies.

LOGTOWN.   Scene of a battle between Sandinista and U. S. Marine forces on April 11, 1931.   Sixty miles from Puerto Cabezas, the place was on the Standard Fruit Company rail line which extended to Cuyu Tigni.   (See DARRAH.)

LOGWOOD.   The cutting of Logwood and other dyewoods along the Mosquito Coast of Nicaragua went on from the earliest accession of English freebooters in the area, in the first decades of the 17th century.   Sir T. Modyford, governor of Jamaica, reported this activity as taking place at Cape Gracias a Dios and "Mosquito, " as well as other places.   He said a dozen vessels were engaged in the trade in 1670.

LOMA, LA. 1) Comarca or district in the municipio of
Larreynaga, León department.
2) A district in the municipio of La Trinidad, department of Estelí.
3) "La Loma," the hill or crater of Tiscapa in the
center of Managua. "Who holds The Hill holds Nicaragua" was a byword during the revolutions in the past
century.

LOMA AZUL. A district of the municipio of Jinotega.

LOMA DE ABAJO. A territory of the Mateare municipio,
department of Managua.

LOMA DE ARRIBA. A territory of the Mateare municipio,
department of Managua.

LOMA DEL ZACATE. A prospector's mine of little production or consequence in the area of Macuelize in the
Nueva Segovia department.

LOMA LA CUCARACHA. A hill 200 feet high where the
Río Indio moves to become a coastal lagoon, on the
southeast coast of Nicaragua. Only eminence in the
general area.

LOMA NEGRA. A district of the municipio of La Concepción, department of Masaya.

LOMAS, LAS. 1) Comarca or district in the municipio of
Jinotepe, Carazo department.
2) A district of the municipio of Jinotega.

LOMAS DE VERACRUZ. A district of the city of León.

LOMAS KRASA DAKURA. The only hill in northeastern
Nicaragua, Zelaya department, for a radius of 20 miles
or more in a swampy area north of Laguna de Pahara.

LONGHORNS. Littleknown by most Nicaraguans is the fact
that a number of wild longhorn cattle, with twisted widespread horns in best Texas style, still roam the prai-
ries and uplands of Boaco and Chontales on the fringes
of civilization and in the wild eastern forest region.

LOPEZ, DON JOSE AVARADO Y. A leader, who in the

valley Nombre de Jesús established in 1855 a cantón
militar to provide for the forces arrayed against William
Walker.

LOPEZ, ELVIRA   see   LOPEZ, MIGUEL

LOPEZ, JUAN   see   LOPEZ, MIGUEL

LOPEZ, MIGUEL.   One of three citizens of Jinotepe (other
    two: Juan López and Elvira López) identified as early
    as 1548, as being under the jurisdiction of the city of
    León in Nicaragua; this fact also established the exist-
    ence of Jinotepe.   It is evident that these men (pre-
    sumably brothers) were awarded encomiendas.

LOPEZ, NARCISO.   A Venezuelan living in New Orleans
    who had prepared on several occasions for an expedition
    against Cuba, with the avowed purpose of freeing it from
    Spain and (hopefully) attaching it to the United States.
    López and his "gallant fifty-one" lost their lives.   This
    episode is of Nicaraguan interest because of the relation-
    ship to Nicaragua's near-nemesis William Walker (q. v.),
    who early in his career inveighed loudly against the Ló-
    pez expedition in his newspaper The Crescent (most un-
    popularly, considering the contemporary mood in New
    Orleans).   But by the time, within five years, that he
    was organizing and carrying out two similar expeditions
    in Sonora, Mexico, and in Nicaragua, Walker had not
    only changed his views on the maintenance of neutrality,
    but had also employed two of López' effective associates
    in adventurism, Calendar Fayssoux (Walker's intrepid
    "admiral") and Achilles Kewen.   Further, the mood of
    the whole United States being one of "manifest destiny, "
    the López expedition lent a preliminary air of verisimili-
    tude to an otherwise rash and unconvincing enterprise.

LOPEZ, PASCUAL.   Doctor López was a member of the
    first faculty of the University of Nicaragua upon its
    establishment in 1816.

LOPEZ DE LA PLATA, MANUEL.   Doctor López was a mem-
    ber of the first faculty of the University of Nicaragua upon
    its establishment in 1816, and was its second rector, 1818.

LOPEZ PEREZ, RIGOBERTO.   Young assassin of Anastasio
    Somoza García, President of Nicaragua, September 21,

1956.   The President lingered a week before dying.
López was shot dead on the spot.   (See EVA, RAM-
IREZ.)

"LORD OF THE BLUEFIELDS SETTLEMENTS. "   Robert
Hodgson (q. v. , no. 2) the Younger assumed this title,
self-awarded.   Following war with England, Spain appointed him governor of Bluefields.   He was quite remote from Spanish control.   His wealth was considerable for the late 1700's--he had 200 Negro slaves, several plantations, and a fleet of ships.   As agent of the
Spanish crown, he was as an Englishman in an understandably anomalous position.   The Spanish hoped vain-
ly to secure the lawless coast by this means of appointing an Englishman to govern, but loyalties were too
divided and rapacity too rampant among the Sambo-
Miskitos for the strategy to work.

LOTHROP, SAMUEL K.   Author of Ceramics of Costa Rica
and Nicaragua (1926) and a significant authority on archaeology of the region.   He was also involved in the
considerations of Acahualinca (q. v.).   Lothrop's work
is considered standard and definitive, although much
has been discovered since his activities in the area.

LOURDES.   Cattle ranch in the municipio of El Sauce, León
department.

LOVAGO.   A pass at the head of the river of the same name
on the Spanish colonial frontier with the Sambo-Miskitos.

LOVAGO, RIO.   A river on the central Spanish colonial
frontier.

LOVIGUISCA see MOLLEJONES, LOS

LOYOLA, DON PABLO DE.   Governor of the province of
Nicaragua in the Kingdom of Guatemala during the period (1672-1681) of the erection of the Fort Inmaculada
Concepción now known in ruins as "El Castillo Viejo"
(q. v.).   He was responsible for the actual construction
of this major bastion, and for some of its features such
as the moat, which was unusual since the fort crowned
a hilltop.   It was he who completed the work in essentially its present form, in the year 1675.

LUBBEROUGH, "PRINCE. "   Pirate who took the first Fort

San Carlos (q. v., def. 1) on the San Juan River in 1670 and went on to sack Granada again. (This is not the San Carlos presently sited at the head of the San Juan, but much lower down the river.)

LUKU, RIO. A tributary of the Prinzapolka from the west of Alamikamba.

LULL, CAPTAIN. Leader of the second 1872 survey party in Nicaragua, the civil engineer being Lieutenant A. G. Menocal (of Cuban extraction). (See INTEROCEANIC CANAL COMMISSION.)

LUNA DE NOCHE MINE. One of the Bonanza (q. v.) group of mines.

LUZ, LA. 1) Cattle ranch in the Tipitapa municipio of the department of Managua.
    2) Comarca or district of the municipio of León, León department.
    3) A periodical developed in Boaco following 1915.
    4) The La Luz Mines, Ltd., has been in operation in Nicaragua for several decades, near the town of Siuna. Extensive workings carry shafts to depths of 1300 feet. The goldbearing deposits were discovered originally by Spanish prospectors and on a small scale the mine was worked by José Aramburó in 1896. In 1909 it was incorporated as La Luz and Los Angeles Mining Company. The workings were destroyed in 1928 by the revolutionaries, after 523,000 tons had been taken out valued at $2,675,000. Ventures Ltd. acquired the property in 1938, operating the mine until 1962 when it became part of the Falcon Bridge Complex, a Canadian group. The extensive working is in a body of ore assaying about 0.10 to 0.22 ounces of gold per ton. Nearly 2,000 tons a day are mined. In 1958, 65,916 ounces of gold and 25,161 of silver were recovered. Galena, Pyrite, and other minerals are part of the available ores. Four million tons are calculated to be in reserve.

LYNCH, SIR THOMAS. Governor of Jamaica from 1681-1684 who is best known for his suspension of sometime pirate chieftain Henry Morgan from his official duties and for enforcing laws against piracy, thereby stopping the depredations, many of which had been aimed at Nicaragua. The last of these pirate efforts took place

anti-climatically "post-Lynch" in 1689, when some mining towns in Nueva Segovia were raided. Three centuries of pirate raids aided by the Sambo-Miskitos were
a continual thorn in the flesh of the colonial authorities
and the hapless residents of the embattled colony.

-LL-

All entries beginning with a double l will be found in the
appropriate place under L.

-M-

McCLURE, SIR ROBERT.   Captain of the British man-of-
    war "Esk. "   (See   FAYSSOUX.)

MACDONALD, COLONEL.   English superintendent at Belize
    who was appointed on February 25, 1826, as regent
    over Mosquito-land by Robert Charles Frederick, nomi-
    nal king of Mosquitia in that year.   He was, however,
    being held a virtual prisoner in Belize.   It was Mac-
    Donald who determined to constitute Belize a regular
    British colony, and to this end he gathered an assembly
    of white settlers (less than 300) who declared formal
    independence from Spanish America on March 14, 1835.
    In 1841, he occupied the Island of Roatan and in the
    British frigate Tweed (q. v.), proceeded to Greytown,
    Nicaragua, to force Nicaragua to recognize the independ-
    ence of Mosquitia.   (See Quijano.)   Such high-handed
    acts caused his recall by 1845, but much that he did
    persisted as Belize became a crown colony and the
    British continued for another half-century their pro-
    tectorate of Mosquitia.

McGHEE, WILLIAM H.   see   POWER, LESTER

MACHADO, RAMON.   A representative of Nueva Segovia
    during the 1855-1856 War.   See   JUNTA DE RECUR-
    SOS.

MACHISMO.   Masculinity is much valued in Nicaragua, es-
    pecially since the male and female roles are sharply
    differentiated.   The man represents dominance, asser-
    tiveness, drive; the female--submissiveness, devotion,
    dependence.   Man is free, woman is homebound.   Sexual

prowess is a major factor in machismo. Women's liberation is antithetical to this element of the culture, and yet, women are not mistreated.

MACHO RATON. Alternate title of the Nahuatl-Spanish Güegüence comedy drama.

MACHUCA. A small paddle steamer on the San Juan River, named for the explorer who also gave his name to the Machuca Rapids. Burned during the 1857 action at El Castillo, the Machuca had been captured previously by the Britisher Spencer, leader of Costa Rican forces at that time.

MACHUCA, DIEGO. In 1529 Captain Diego Machuca, then living in Granada, essayed to explore Lake Nicaragua, and probably was the first European to traverse the entire San Juan River, although there is a modern theory which postulates that Columbus may have come partway up the San Juan in 1502. Machuca projected a colony at the river mouth. The Port of San Juan was later the 12th and last of a series of Spanish military stations on the river.

MACHUCA RAPIDS. One of several major rapids in the San Juan, located below the Castillo rapids, and named for the generally acknowledged European discoverer of the river, Diego Machuca.

MACUELIZO. 1) An old Spanish mine within 400 yards of the Village of Macuelizo in Nueva Segovia department. A tunnel 22 feet long follows minor quartz veins.
2) Far west in the department of Nueva Segovia, this municipio has only 160 population.

MADERAL, EL. Cattle hacienda converted to cotton culture in the municipio of Nindrí, Masaya department.

MADERAS, LAS. A district of the municipio of Tipitapa, department of Managua.

MADRIGALES, LOS. A territory of the National District, department of Managua.

MADRIZ, DEPARTMENT OF. In the northwestern corner of Nicaragua lies the small department of Madriz, bounded on the east by Jinotega, west by Honduras,

south by Chinandega and Estelí, and north by Nueva
Segovia.   Area, 530 square miles; population 44,000.
Originally peopled by the pre-conquest immigrants from
the Mexican area, the inhabitants retain much of their
heritage if not their language.   There are still Indian
communities in the department living on their own communal lands.   The department was created from the department of Nueva Segovia in August of 1936, and named
for Dr. José Madriz, former President of Nicaragua,
1909-1910.

MADRIZ, EMILIANO.   Taking over from Manuel Pérez
under the attacks by Santos Guardiola and Francisco
Malespín in the 1840's, Madriz completed an agreement, following which Montenegro was chosen director.

MADRIZ, JOSE.   President of Nicaragua 1909-1910, following the long and troubled regime of Zelaya, Dr. Madriz
found the revolution was continuing.   In a battle at Tisma, the rising and able young General Emiliano Chamorro took part, with the result the Madriz armies had
to retreat to the mountains and ultimately to the coastal
town of Bluefields.   Under U.S. urging, a peace was arranged, Madriz resigned, and Juan José Estrada became
President.

MADRONO, EL.   Comarca or district in the municipio of
Larreynaga, León.

MADROÑO, EL.   A district of the municipio of Tipitapa,
department of Matagalpa.

MADRONO, RIO EL.   A small river in the municipio of
Larreynaga, León department.

MAESTRE, IGNACIO.   Sergeant-major of the Navy in Granada, 1778 and following.   (See GALVEZ.)

MADERAL.   A cattle hacienda in the municipio of Nindirí,
Masaya department.

MAHOGANY see CAOBA

MAHOGANY, RIO.   1) A tributary of the Río Wawashan in
Zelaya department, named for the principal product of
the area.
2)A southern tributary of the Río Escondido, presumably named for the same reason.

MAIZ.   Corn--a basic and essential staple, native to the
Middle American area.

MAIZE CULTURE.   The development of corn cultivation
seems to have begun about 8000 B. C. with domestication
occurring possibly 5000 B. C., as indicated by studies
by MacNeish in the Valley of Tehuacán, in Pueblo,
Mexico.

MAKANTAKA.   Village at the end of the southerly road
branch from Alamikamba in Zelaya department and just
north of a major "haul-over" on the Río Grande.

MALACAGUAS.   A district in the municipio of Matiguás,
department of Matagalpa.

MALACATOYA, RIO.   1) A river to the north of the Laguna
de Tisma, and the northeast boundary of Granada department, with Boaco on the other side.   The Malacatoya empties into Lake Nicaragua through a grassy
delta several miles northeast of the Río Tipitapa mouth.
2) Stream in the municipio of El Sauce, León department.

MALINATL.   Meaning: "herb," or grass (as in pasture);
one of the month festival days, and gods, of the ancient
Nicarao.

MALPAISITO.   District in the municipio of Masatepe, department of Masaya.

MAL PASO.   A district in the municipio of Muy Muy, Matagalpa department.

MAMENIC.   An acronym for Marina Mercante Nicaragüense
which is the shipping line that carries most Nicaraguan
sea-borne exports and imports.   Owning six vessels in
the late 1950's, a number of others were leased by the
line.   The principal ports visited are the Pacific ports
of Nicaragua.   The Presidential family Somoza has a
major interest in the line.

MANAGUA.   1) The city of Managua is the capital of Nicaragua, cabacera of the National District, commercial
and industrial center of the nation, and political and
social heart as well.   Chosen as a compromise capital
between the two traditional capitals of León and Granada,

Managua was the site of an old Indian town which
stretched for many miles along the Xolotlán lake front,
and which was first visited by Hernández de Córdoba in
1524. Following major destruction by the earthquake of
1931, the city has rebuilt with many attractive modern
structures, one rising to 18 stories. The new Intercontinental Hotel is one of several architectural gems.
"La Loma" and the presidential palaces are a majestic
acropolis in the heart of the city. Many "colonias" and
"barrios" represent various sections of the city, new
and old. The National Palace, (the seat of the government), the Presidential House, the Municipal Palace,
the Stadium, plus markets and other public buildings
are joined by the Metropolitan Cathedral and many other
churches in gracing the city with imposing edifices.
Parks and esplanades are frequent. The population is
around a quarter of a million.

In Oviedo's History (see Oviedo y Valdez) it is affirmed that Pedrarias Dávila reported to Toledo in 1525
that Managua was a city extending three leagues (seven
to eight miles) along the lake front, and that the language was Chorutegan; that there were 40,000 people,
10,000 of them "indios de arco y fleches," hence an
army of archers of that size. The discovery and description were by Hernández de Córdoba in his 1524
visit. By five years later, one of Pedrarias' lieutenants
affirmed the Chorutegans to be the "worst people in the
world." The Spanish reported the population was decimated through the "waste of war," but it would seem
that cruelty and forced enslavement must have had some
part to play. In 1548 under the encomienda system the
Managua area was given to Francisco Téllez, and to
Cristóbal de San Martín. Later encomenderos were
Diego de Pastrana and Luis de la Rocha. There is a
considerable gap of information of over two centuries
concerning events in the Managua-Lake Xolotlán (south
coast) area from Mateare to Tipitapa. Not until the
first independence movements of 1811 do we hear more
about it. Apparently, the encomienda system wreaked
havoc with the population in this region. The great
aboriginal city of Managua mentioned in the mid-1500's,
by the end of that century was dispersed.

As noted, a gap from 1550-1811 exists in data on
Managua. But during the first movements for independence, 1811-1814, Managua maintained its loyalty under
Padre Yrigoyen's Monarchist direction. Ferdinand VII
in 1819 designated the town "Leal Villa de Managua,"

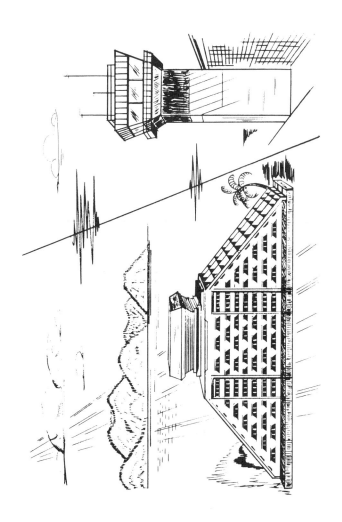

Modern Managua

A hotel and the Las Mercedes Airport control tower.

an act published in León on April 21 of the year 1820.
This was a move toward consolidation of such loyalty
as was remaining during that penultimate year of colonial independence.   In 1824, the townspeople joined
monarchists Padre Yrigoyen, Bishop García Jérez and
don Pedro Chamorro in opposing the independence leader
and Caudillo Cleto Ordóñez.   Again in 1833, following
independence, Managuans kept alive a royalist movement
in support of Ferdinand VII, in the hope of restoring the
Spanish colonial empire, under the urging of secret
agents from Madrid.   Managua was under a judicial
district of Managua, department of the East, one of
the four extant in 1849.   In that year it became a sub-
prefecture, responsible direction to the national government.   In 1867, it became the District of Managua.

On July 24, 1846 the Managua municipality was elevated to the status of ciudad under an interim government headed by Senator don José María Sandres, who
deserves the credit for its change from the colonial
status of "villa. "   The official name as then given is
"Ciudad de Santiago de Managua, " following the villa
title, simply "Santiago de Managua, " of 1819, effected
in the capital León.

2) Managua Department, in spite of the historical and
traditional significance of León and Granada, respectively the liberal and conservative capitals of Nicaragua and
hotbeds of much fratricidal conflict, is doubtless the
most important in the nation because of the location of
the capital, the National District, the considerable population, and the political, economic, and social power engendered by these considerations.   In some sense over
the years Nicaragua has been a "city-state, " and when
it is said "Quien tiene La Loma tiene Nicaragua" (who
has "the hill" owns Nicaragua), there is perhaps a bit
more truth than poetry, since the "hill" of Tiscapa with
its acropolis-like position on an eminence above Managua
(its palaces, fortifications, etc.), is in some sense the
"high city" developed by the Greeks and their forebears.
Becoming a "Distrito Judicial" on June 23, 1849, Managua's judicial district was a separate political entity
from that time on, uniquely responsible only to the chief
of state.   Finally, on March 11, 1875, the department
of Managua was created, under don Isidro López, Minister of Government.

The department is bounded on the north by the departments of Boaco and Matagalpa; on the south by the
departments of Masaya and Carazo, and by the Pacific

Ocean; on the east by the departments of Boaco, Granada, Masaya, and Carazo; and on the west by León department, and again by the Pacific. The municipios include the National District, Tipitapa, San Rafael del Sur, El Carmen, Mateare, and San Francisco del Carnicero. The ancient Valle de Colama also contains a special dispensation to the Pueblo de Colama. The area (aside from the area in the lake) is over 1330 square miles. The population is over 330,000, about 250,000 of these living in the city of Managua. The department has just over 20% of the total population of Nicaragua; the city, about 17%. (Athens, Greece, has one-third of that nation's population). There are two zones, the Zona Montañosa and the Zona de las Llanuras (both q. v.). Managua is the economic center of the nation in all respects and is the fountainhead of commerce and industry. In days earlier in the century, Managua was a lake port. Now it is a center of rail, highway, and air transportation. The department has six municipios including the Distrito Nacional.

3) Partido de Managua, one of the nine districts of the country under the consitution of April 8, 1826, when it was one of the United Provinces of Central America. (See PARTIDOS DE NICARAGUA.)

4) A steam vessel on Lake Nicaragua during the 20th century, 120 tons. The Managua was used above the Tipitapa River, which was not navigable to Lake Nicaragua.

MANAGUA, RIO see entries under Managua def. 's 1 and 2, and XOLOTLAN, LAGO.

MANAGUA, TREATY OF. In 1880 by this document Great Britain ceded to Nicaragua all claims to the eastern (Caribbean) coast of that country. However, the local autonomy of the Mosquito government continued for 14 years until surrendered by the Indians, when in 1894 they were incorporated into the department of Zelaya. Mosquito separatism, however, was responsible for their support of Sandino in 1927-1933. Physical separation of and transportation difficulties to and within the Mosquito Coastal area have perpetuated a separate and even a prejudiced relationship. Signed by Nicaragua and England on January 28, 1880, it was one of three treaties made by Great Britain to assure her foothold in Central America. It provided for her withdrawal of a protectorate over the Mosquito Indians, giving the Mosquito Shore to Nicaragua, but in this way Nicaragua was forced to recognize something she had previously denied --that England had any Mosquito rights whatever! The treaty provided a hands-off policy on Mosquitos, Britain relying on her continued influence with her Indian "allies." Greytown was to remain a free port.

MANAGUA ABORIGINALS. Tribes of Mexican origin which came into Nicaragua and particularly the Managua area around the A. D. 500's were called by these names: Mames, Mangues, Chiapanecas, Totonecas, Chorotegas. Ancient Managua was on the lake coast, extending for about nine miles as far as Tipitapa, as indicated by Hernández de Córdoba in 1524.

MANAGÜENSES. People of Managua, also applied in particular to the large aboriginal population which lived in the area prior to the Spanish conquest.

MANAGÜITA. A district of the municipio of San Juan de Tola, Rivas department. (Also sometimes called "Managua.")

MANCHESTER. Cattle ranch in the municipio of León, León department, named for a British consular agent of the mid-1880's.

MANCOTAL. 1) A district of the municipio of Jinotega.
2) Name of the recent hydro-electric dam on the Río Tuma near Jinotega. The dam is 158 feet high. The generators have a capacity of 25, 000 kilowatts. The tunnel to the generators is 9, 200 feet long.

MANGA, LA. Comarca, valley or district in the municipio of Acoyapa, Chontales department.

MANGAS, LAS. Mountain in the municipio of Acoyapa, Chontales.

MANGON, EL. One of the Granada isletas, small volcanic islets; this one is sometimes termed the "best, " because of a bay of clear water in the center.

MANGUE. A dialect of Nahuatl derivation, from the basic Chorutegan (q. v.) language. The origin is generally thought to be Mexican. Mangue is closely related to the Chiapanecan dialects. Carlos Mantica has estab-

lished and demonstrated the relationship to the Aymará
of Peru, but not necessarily to the Nahua of Nicaragua,
which is a matter ripe for further research.

MANIWATLA. A village with an air landing strip in northern Zelaya department, 22 miles west of Puerto Cabezas.

MANTUDOS, LOS. An ancient traditional Nicaraguan dance
which has disappeared.

MANZANA. A land measurement equal to 10,000 square
varas (100 varas (q.v.) on a side) or 1.72 acres. One
square mile equals 372.09 manzanas. The word is also
used in the sense of "city block" in giving directions
and expressing ownership.

MANZANILLO. A district of the municipio of San Juan de
Tola, Rivas department.

MANZANO, EL. A district of the San Rafael del Sur municipio, Managua department.

MANZERAS. A district in the municipio of Matiguás, department of Matagalpa.

MAPS. Maps of Nicaragua take a variety of forms and an
even greater variety of degrees of accuracy. A great
deal of mapping of the New World took place in the early 1500's; because of the prominence of Nicaragua's two
large lakes, they were easily identified, and because
from high eminences they could be seen in entirety, they
were fairly accurately represented. The sharp identifi-
cation of Cabo Gracias a Dios on the Caribbean coast
was possible too. However, there was much inaccuracy
as late as 1960, in relation to mountain heights, exact
stream locations, etc. The Interamerican Survey of the
1950's and 1960's (see Servicio Geodésico Interamericano)
provided accurate information for the first time. The
Dirección General de Cartografiá (q.v.) in Managua has
excellent maps now available.
    Bagrow's great work on the history of cartography re-
counts that in 1520 Hernán Cortés described to his Emperor (Charles V) how Montezuma sent him "a chart of
the whole coast," painted on cloth. Drawn and painted
on a material woven from agave fibre, or on fig-bark
paper or prepared skins, these maps were systematically
destroyed with other native documents by Spanish church-

men. In 1526 envoys of Tabasco and Xicalango drew for
Cortés "a figure of the whole land, whereby I calculated
that I could very well go over the great part of it";
this map extended almost to Panama, and guided him in
his overland journey to Honduras. This is the first recorded map of the area covered by Nicaragua.

MAQUIMA, RIO LA. A stream flowing into the Pacific in
southern Carazo department.

MARAÑONAL. Comarca or district in the municipio of
Télica, León.

MARAVILLAS. Mountain in the municipio of Santo Tomás,
Chontales department.

MARBLE. There are significant deposits of light gray, dark
gray, and black marble in the department of Nueva Segovia around Ocotal, Mosonte, San José de Jalapo and
Estelí.

MARCELINO. Comarca or district in the municipio of La
Libertad, Chontales.

MARCOLETA, M. Nicaraguan chargé d'affaires in Belgium
in the 1840's who hard upon the heels of Castellón's
(q.v.) canal plan attempted to get the attention of Louis
Napoleon Bonaparte (q.v.), then a political prisoner.
Marcolete succeeded, and Bonaparte's famous pamphlet
on the Nicaraguan canal question was the result.

MAR DULCE. The "Sweet Sea," an alternate name for Lake
Nicaragua or "Cocibolca." It was so called because of
its fresh water and its vast extent.

MARENCO, DON GREGORIO. One of the Spanish colonial
families established in Masaya by 1800 and extant today.

MARENCO, MANUEL. A lieutenant at the Battle of San
Jacinto, September 14, 1856.

MARENEO, DON MANUEL. One of three elected "junta"
members of the independence movement in Rivas in 1811.

MARIA (Wood). This wood, often called "Santa María," is
a handsome striped open-grained tropical hardwood,
Claphyllum basiliense. It is used in panelling and construction.

MARIAS, LAS. Comarca or district in the municipio of Télica, León.

MARIBICHOAS   see   MARIBIOS

MARIBIOS.   Prehistoric tribe occupying the area of the volcanic line in Nicaragua, now called "los Marabios." Language spoken, Chondal.

MARIMBA, LA.   Comarca or district in the municipio and department of León.

MARINA MERCANTE NICARAGÜENSE   see   MAMENIC.

MARIPOSA.   A very small steamer, not much more than a flat-bottomed steam launch, on the San Juan River in 1885, when Engineer Menocal used her for survey work. Their upstream progress averaged about one mile per hour.

MARITIME CANAL COMPANY OF NICARAGUA. This is the formal organization of the Provisional Interoceanic Canal Society, which was somewhat abortive since the concession which had been granted to the Society lapsed in September, 1884, and the French Panama Canal project was by then well launched.   The company instituted important surveys (q. v.) by Menocal and others in the early 1880's but essentially it died with the failure of ratification of the Freylinghuysen-Zavala Treaty (q. v.). As a result of a second Provisional Association the Maritime Company was finally incorporated under U. S. law on February 20, 1889, and was duly organized with $150, 000, 000 in 50% bonds and $100, 000, 000 in ordinary stock.   Mr. Hiram Hitchcock was elected president, and the concessions were transferred.   This company then began operations as a private undertaking.   A. G. Menocal was retained as chief engineer.   May 26, 1889, a construction party proceeded to Nicaragua.   The canal line was laid out, storehouses and wharfs and dwellings built, hospital services organized, and without the fanfare attendant upon the French Panama project, but with much determination, the work was begun, with railroad and telephone lines along the route's eastern section. The real test was to be in fund-raising.   Warner Miller was elected President of the construction company. Rights problems arose with Sr. F. A. Pellas (q. v.) as well as with M. A. Blackman who claimed residual rights of the Accessary Transit Company.   In spite of great U. S. national support, as evidenced by the National Nicaragua Canal Convention of 1892, the U. S. Congress would not appropriate canal funds, and the Maritime Company was thrown back upon private resources. The financial panic of 1893 suspended payments and the canal work ground to a halt, about $6, 000, 000 having been spent.   The company went into receivership August 30, 1893.   It should be recorded that the Maritime Company had a powerful enemy in the complex of U. S. coast-to-coast railroads, who considered the canal a dangerous rival.   (See CANAL.)

MARIVIO.   A dialect of Nahua or Nahoa that is Mexican in origin, derived from the Chorutegan (q. v.) language.

"MARK TWAIN. " Samuel Clemens crossed Nicaragua in 1857, and was then put ashore in Key West, Florida, when two deaths from cholera beached passengers there. The major transit days were over, but the experience of crossing Nicaragua was one the doughty ex-river pilot and westerner found of interest.

MARMOLES.   Marble (q. v.) quaries are found in Estelí department in the Miraflores section.

MARQUECES, LOS.   Comarca or district in the municipio of San Marcos, Carazo department.

MARRABIOS, LOS.   A mountain range which is unique in its straightline array of active and inactive volcanoes.   Running from northwest to southeast and roughly paralleling the Pacific Coast of Nicaragua at a distance averaging about 20 miles inland, within a span of 100 miles from Cosegüina, the northernmost volcano, to Momotombito, the island cone farthest south, there are a dozen cratered mountains shown on official maps as volcanoes, as well as ten "hills" ("lomas" and "cerros"), which go as high as 2500 feet.   The highest volcano, San Cristóbal ("El Viejo") is 5726 feet.   The most famous by far, lauded in poetry by Rubén Darío and Victor Hugo, is Momotombo--"nude and bald colossus, " 4200 feet in altitude.   Los Marrabios are part of a 500-mile long ridge of volcanic mountains which stretches from Mexico to Panama, and along which there are dozens of peaks no more than five miles from a straight line.   In 1968 and 1971 Volcán Cerro Negro, near León, was erupting

vigorously.   The 1971 eruptions sent fiery lava 10,000
feet in the air and smoke clouds over 30,000 feet, and
left layers of ash for 20 to 30 miles around.   In the
1830's Cosegüina blew-up with a bang heard in Jamaica.
In 1902 Momotombo erupted within weeks of the disastrous eruption of Mt. Pelee.   Not counted as part of the
Cordillera Los Marrabios, but in the same line extended
are the other Nicaraguan volcanoes of Mombacho, Omotepe (Concepción), Masaya (Santiago) and Maderas, as
well as the volcanic crater lakes of Asososca, Xiloa,
Apoyo and Masaya, as well as many smaller hills and
craters.   This chain constitutes an area of volcanic activity unmatched on the planet.

MARSELLA, RIO see EL BASTON

MARTA VIEJA, RIO.   A river in the municipio of San Pedro
de Lovago, Chontales department.

MARTINEZ, LOS.   A district of the municipio of La Concepción, department of Masaya.

MARTINEZ, BARTOLOME.   The second Martínez to serve
as President, he completed the Diego Chamorro term
from 1923-1924.   His attempt to be elected on his own
failed, and Solórzano succeeded him.

MARTINEZ, TOMAS.   President of Nicaragua from 1859-
1867, in the difficult reconstruction period following the
National War, Martínez provided considerable leadership
in the enactment of laws (some of which still exist) in
the development of the Constitution of August, 1858; and
in dealing with the involved diplomacy of canal concessions and the continuing border disputes with Costa Rica.
The first legal document in retrieval of the Mosquito
Coast for Nicaragua from British protection was the
convention signed in January, 1860.   His reelection precipitated a civil conflict when he was supported against
General Fernando Chamorro.   There was further support
for Martínez against Guzmán in 1869, and a brief civil
war resulted.

MASACHAPA.   A district of the San Rafael del Sur municipio,
Managua department.   This is a Pacific beach area much
frequented by Managuans, and there is quite a pueblo.

MASAPA, RIO.   A short river in the western part of Carazo
department, flowing directly into the Pacific Ocean.

MASATEPE. 1) Cabacera of the municipio of the same
    name in Masaya department, this Ciudad Masatepe is
    one of the oldest towns in Nicaragua, a seat of the
    tribe known as Dirianes, who are of the Chorutegan
    groups.   The name Masatepe comes from mázatl, "deer,"
    and tépec, "hill," or "place." Again, this is the basic
    Mexican idiom of the Chorutegans.   At 1500 feet altitude,
    the climate is excellent, and since 1900 the community
    has developed considerably with commensurate public
    buildings and services.   José María Moncada, President
    of the republic in the 1930's, and Dr. Hildebrando Cas-
    tellón, who studied at the Sorbonne in Paris, as well as
    several deputies and diplomats, were citizens from
    Masatepe.   There are two ancient barrios--de Arriba,
    where ladinos lived, and de Abajo, where Indians lived;
    now there are the barrios de La Estación, Centro Ur-
    bano, Jalata, and Veracruz.
       2) A municipio of the department of Masaya, area 21
    square miles, population 18,000.   Bounded on the north
    by Nindirí, on the south by Carazo department, on the
    east by the municipios Nandasmo and Niquinihomo, and
    on the west by La Concepción municipio.   There are
    eight comarcas or districts.   The land is fertile and
    nearly all under cultivation, with a number of significant
    coffee haciendas and also plantings of tobacco, corn,
    rice, beans, plantains, and other fruits and vegetables.

MASATEPINOS.   Citizens of Masatepe (cabacera, municipio,
    all in the department of Masaya).

MASAYA. 1) Cabacera of the department of the same name,
    Ciudad de Masaya is one of the significant and charac-
    teristic cities of Nicaragua.   A population of over 24,000
    is located at 770 feet above sea level.   As temporary
    provincial capital it was the residence of several gover-
    nors and of the high ecclesiastics of the León diocese.
    It was the country's capital in 1845 and the National
    Legislative Assembly met here in 1846.   It was briefly
    the capital again in 1855 and in 1939.   There are four
    sections or barrios which date from the 18th century:
    Diriega, Monimbó, Don Sebastián, and Don Guillén.
    Modern barrios added are San Jerónimo, San Juan La
    Estación, San Miguel, La Parroquiá Magdalena, Palo
    Blanco, and La Reforma.   A famous and historical mar-
    ket is located in Masaya, where the many unusual in-
    digenous industrial and craft products of the city are
    displayed. The title of "city" was awarded in 1839, under

the chief of state Joaquín de Cosío. Masaya was the
site of battles during the William Walker troubles in
the 1850's and during the "Mena War" of 1912 which
brought U.S. Marine intervention in Nicaragua. The
Coyotepe Fort was a center of the action. There are
several distinguished colonial churches and a number of
industrial plants. For more on general Masaya history
see MASAYA, PUEBLO COLONIAL.

2) The present department of Masaya is made up in
the main of territory which was in the predecessor
Partido de Masaya, one of the nine partidos in which
the State of Nicaragua was divided in April, 1826. When
on August 30, 1858, the Constituent Assembly divided the
country again, Masaya was not one of the seven, and in
fact the pueblos of Nindirí, Tisma, and Masaya were not
even mentioned. However, the political and judicial control seems to have been in Managua during this period.
In 1870, the political sub-prefecture of Masaya was reestablished. The department itself was created March
10, 1883, the first governor being Dr. Adán Cárdenas.
The department included Masatepe, Nandasmo, Nindirí,
and the Cantons of Tisma and Tismita. The present department is bounded on the north by the department of
Managua, on the south by Carazo, on the east by Granada, and on the west by Managua again. The cabacera
is Masaya, and in addition to the original pueblos of the
department, Catarina, Niquinohomo, San Juan de Oriente,
and La Concepción are included. The population is over
80,000, about half of these living in towns. The highest
elevation is 1700 feet; the area, 210 square miles.
General agriculture, cattle raising and cotton and coffee
culture are chief concerns. Other products are "yuca,"
cacao, corn, beans, sugar cane, tobacco, rice, wheat,
sorghum, vegetables, and fruits such as mango, pineapple, etc. Coffee is in first place, cotton is second.
The railroad serving Masaya was completed in 1898 under
the Zelaya administration. It has since ceased operations
due to highway availability. Masaya is a center of craft
industry of the whole nation, based on pre-Columbian activities of the industrious Indians who lived there. Ceramics, leather saddles, etc., are all part of a great
variety of products. The department has a number of
heights better known for historical or other reasons than
for altitude. The "Volcán Masaya," or Santiago, is
about 2100 feet with huge craters, both live and dead.
Until the last decade it was in continual activity. It
was first climbed by Fray Francisco de Bobadillo in
1527.

3) The municipio of Masaya has the departmental
capital, Masaya, which is also the municipal cabacera.
The area is 65 square miles, the population 34, 500.
Bounded on the north by Managua department, on the
south by Catarina municipio, on the west by Nindirí municipio, and on the east by Granada department and municipio.   There are 15 districts or comarcas.   The municipio has lands which are the possession of the Comuni-
dad Indígena de Masaya, lands pertaining to the descendants of the Diriangen Indians of the Chorotegan race.
The lands were given (or returned) to the people by the
King of Spain, and a law of February 16, 1906, established rules for determining the quality of indigenous
ownership.   There are two areas for these granted
lands.   The rural areas are devoted to agriculture, and
the town of Masaya is famous for its indigenous industry.

4) Partido de Masaya, one of the nine districts of
the country under the constitution of April 8, 1826, when
it was one of the United Provinces of Central America.
(See PARTIDOS DE NICARAGUA.)

5) Laguna de Masaya, a lake nearly six miles long
and two and one-half miles wide, between the town and
volcano of Masaya, has an area of over three square
miles.   It is a volcanic crater depression.   In 1529,
the Spanish chronicler Oviedo y Valdez reported the
waters to be hot.   Originally a tortuous trail led down
cliffs to the water's edge, from which people of the vicinity carried their needed water supplies.   Present day
Masaya water supplies are pumped from the lake.

6) The M. S. Masaya was operated as a fast shallow-
draft banana carrier in the 1920's and 1930's.   It had
been converted from a "four-piper" U. S. destroyer and
could carry 25, 000 stems of fruit at 16 knots, and could
go a distance up Nicaraguan and other Central American
rivers.   Originally the Dale as DD-290, the ship was
taken back in service with her sister ship Matagalpa
(formerly Osborne, DD-295).   Both ships were put back
in U. S. service and loaded as blockade-runners to the
Philippines at the outset of World War II, but Bataan
fell before they sailed.   The Masaya was manned with
an Australian crew to serve MacArthur's forces, and
was sunk at Oro Bay, New Guinea, in 1943.   The Matagalpa burned in Sydney, Australia, late in 1942.

7) Volcán de Masaya, also called Santiago, this low
but large volcano near Masaya (2100 feet) has been an
object of fear and reverence since pre-Columbian times.
Eruptions were recorded in 1772, when an extensive lava

field was laid down and when the original crater and
summit was changed in shape; in 1858 and 1904 when
some coffee fincas in the Sierras de Managua were
ruined. There were also eruptions in 1926 and 1927.
The activities of a German chemist and engineer in 1927
aimed at harnessing the heat-power of the volcano, was
followed by the 1926-1927 activities. The people of the
country at large generally attributed the disastrous earthquake of March 31, 1931 in Managua, to the closing of
the vents in Santiago by the two hapless Germans. A
Nicaraguan historical author states, "The colossus did
not seem to sympathize with the work of the German
scientists." The volcano was further active following
1946. The first crater is 2000 feet in diameter and
800 feet deep. The second is 580 feet deep and 1100
feet in diameter.

MASAYA FIESTAS. The city and general area of Masaya
are noted as the center of particular folklore observances,
during the fiestas of San Jerónimo, around September 30;
San Lázaro, during Holy Week; and Toros Venados in
October. Traditional dances are Toro Venado, Toro
Guaco, La Yegüita, Los Negritos, Las Inditas, Los
Bailantes. Coplas and Ensaladas are also very popular.

MASAYA, PUEBLO COLONIAL. The present city of Masaya
occupies the same site as the colonial pueblo which in
turn was based on pre-Columbian beginnings several centuries or more before the conquest. The present industrious character of the inhabitants is a pattern which
has come down in direct line from those pre-Columbian
days. It is the oldest industrial culture of a continuous
nature in the republic of Nicaragua. The name of
Masaya is thought by some to be related to the word
"deer," or mazatl, in the basic Nahuatl-derived idiom.
Yan or lan means "place," hence a place of deer. But
the nearness of the volcano of Masaya makes the translation of Spanish chronicler oviedo y Valdez in 1529
plausible--"Mountain that Blazes." Since the dialect
Tacacho was used in the area, and since Chorutegan
was often a corrupt Nahuatl, this is possible. It is
known that the inhabitants in early colonial days wore
the characteristic dress--huipils, or short shirt-like
dresses--which would have been found in Mexico. Masaya was the "Granero de La Provincia" and as granery,
provided food for the garrison of the Castillo de La Inmaculada Concepción, which was a frontier bastion of

the Spanish colonial empire.   There was also in Masaya during colonial days a battalion of militia and of artillery. Many families still prominent in Nicaragua were established in Masaya in colonial days.   In 1728 the Partido de Masaya was formed with its cabacera in the city of Masaya itself.   It included the pueblos of Nindirí, Catarina, San Juan, Niquinohomo, Nandasmo, Jalata, Masatepe, Jinotepe, and Diriamba.   Masaya had a history of rebellion against the Spanish crown, which arose sporadically during the colonial period, partly because Masaya was forced to furnish logistical support for so much of the Spanish military effort.   A leader of some Irish descendancy was José Gabriel de O'Horan, who in 1811 and 1812 was involved in several acts of insurrection, and whose release from prison was demanded by people in arms.   (One of his descendants was Irene O'Horan, who figured as one of William Walker's familiars during the 1850's.)   The O'Horan 1811 affair was one of the early movements for independence in Central America.

MASAYA, VILLA FIEL DE SAN FERNANDO DE.   On December 12, 1812, the Ayuntamiento de Masaya (q. v.) was sought and renewed.   Petitions were presented in 1814 and 1815.   Finally the request was granted with the title "Villa Fiel...."   This took place seven years following the initial request, that is, in 1819.

MASCOTA, LA.   Coffee hacienda in Jinotega department.

MATA DE CAÑA.   A district in the municipio of Belén, Rivas department.

MATA DE TULE.   A hacienda in southwestern Granada department.

MATAGALPA.   1) Known as the "pearl" of the northern area (Perla del Setentrión), Ciudad Matagalpa is a city at about 2300 feet elevation, of 18, 000 population.   The setting is within a beautiful mountain perimeter.   The area was mentioned as "the region of Matagalpa" in the Acta Notorial de Teotecacinte of 1603, and the pueblo was recognized as a village of ladinos in 1751 by Bishop Morel de Santa Cruz.   Probably there was a pre-conquest village of Calpulli aborigines on the site.   Known as "San Pedro de Matagalpa" from 1751 on, the town was again noted in 1873 by the English naturalist and miner, Thomas Belt.   Cabacera of the department, modern Matagalpa is a commercial center for an extensive area of the Segovias to the north; Titled villa in 1851, the town became ciudad on February 14, 1862 under the Martínez administration.

2) A district in the municipio of Buenos Aires, department of Rivas.

3) The department of Matagalpa is fourth in size among Nicaragua's major subdivisions, with 2550 square miles. It is 120 miles across from east to west and 80 miles, north to south. To the north it is bounded by the departments of Jinotega, Estelí, and Zelaya; to the south by Boaco and Managua; to the east by Zelaya; and to the west by León. Only the departments of Zelaya, Jinotega and Río San Juan (all "frontier" areas) are larger. There are 172,000 inhabitants, about 30,000 of them urban, the rest rural. There are ten municipios; Matagalpa, Ciudad Darío, Esquipulas, Matiguás, Muy Muy, San Dioniso, San Isidro, San Ramón, Sebaco, and Terrabona. The population has quadrupled since 1906. There are three zones of cultivation and agricultural activity in the department--those of coffee, cattle, and general farming. The coffee is of a special high grade, called "Matagalpa Coffee" in international markets. Coffee culture is carried on particularly in the municipios of Matagalpa, San Ramón, and Esquipulas. The cattle areas are Muy Muy, Matiguás, Ciudad Darío, and in part of Matagalpa municipio. Other agricultural products are: sugar cane, corn, potatoes, onions, rice, beans, cotton, and tobacco. There was navigation by small boats on the rivers Grande de Matagalpa, Saiz, Paigua, Guanaguas, and Tule. (The first Ford cars reached Matagalpa in April 1919.)

4) One of seven departments of Nicaragua established by the 1858 constitutional revisions, Matagalpa included the towns of Jinotega, San Rafael and La Concordia in present Jinotega, in addition to the area of present-day Matagalpa.

5) The district of Matagalpa under the 1838 federating act comprised the following towns or settlements: Matagalpa, Jinotega, San Rafael, Sebaco, Metapa (now called Ciudad Darío), Terrabona, San Dionisio, Esquipulas, Muy Muy, and San Ramón.

6) For the M. S. Matagalpa, see MASAYA (def. 6).

7) This municipio, with an area of 730 square miles, has a population of about 73,000, the city of Matagalpa being the cabacera and principal trading center of the whole area, with about 18,000 persons. There is a

great variety of terrain, from mining mountains to great agricultural plains. Bounded on the north by Jinotega department, on the south by the municipios San Ramón, Esquipulas, San Dionisio, and Muy Muy, and on the west by Sebaco and Terrabona. There are two small lakes, Susumá and La Joya. The Río Grande de Matagalpa is the most significant stream in the area. The Río Tuma is in the northern section and several smaller tributaries such as the Salalar, Bijao, and Babasca cross it. Communal lands in the municipio received royal title in 1722 and 1823, under colonial authorities. Coffee is a particularly important crop, as well as cattle. Other usual Nicaraguan crops are produced to the north. Many flowers are grown near Santa María de Ostuma.

8) Partido de Matagalpa, one of the nine districts of the country under the constitution of April 8, 1826, when it was one of the United Provinces of Central America. (See Partidos de Nicaragua.)

MATAGALPEÑO. A citizen of Matagalpa.

MATAGUA, RIO. A river in the municipio of San Pedro de Lovago in the department of Chontales. Sometimes called "Río Catagua."

MATAPA. A shallow-draft stern-wheel steamer noted in 1860 as a wreck above the Toro Rapids of the San Juan River.

MATAPALO. 1) Comarca or district in the municipio of Achuapa, León.
2) A district of the municipio of San Ramón, Matagalpa department.

MATASANO. 1) A district in the municipio and department of Matagalpa.
2) A mountain height in the municipio of Matagalpa.

MATEARE. 1) A district in the municipio of San Juan de Limay in the department of Estelí.
2) A municipio of the department of Managua to the northwest along the shores of Lake Managua; area 154 square miles, population 3,000. A small rural municipio, it is bounded on the north by the lake and León department; on the south by the municipio El Carmen; on the east by the lake and by Managua; and on the west by the lake and León again. Dairy farming and cotton

are principal agricultural pursuits.   Fishing is a long-
established commercial enterprise.

3) A pueblo, and a small cabacera of the municipio
of the same name, it has a population of 1, 500.   It was
in existence from pre-conquest times, and was mentioned
in the writings of Oviedo y Valdez. At that time "Matiari"
had 1, 000 archers, and over 2, 000 population.

MATETULE (or El Llano).   Comarca or district of the municipio of Santa Teresa, Carazo department.

MATIARI.   Old form of the modern name Mateare (q. v.) for
the cabacera and municipio.

MATILDINA.   A cattle ranch and plantation in the municipio
of Masaya.

MATRONAS.   Church welfare group drawn from the upper
class and dedicated to church welfare activities.

MATUS, DON FRANCISCO ESTEBAN.   One of the Spanish
colonial families established in Masaya in 1800 and extant today.

MAUNICA.   A district in the municipio of Ciudad Darfo, department of Matagalpa.

"MAYPOLE. "   A species of Saturnalia held for a month
(early April) on the east coast of Nicaragua, as late
as the 1930's.   The festivities were characterized by
erotic dances held around certain chosen big trees, after
a pattern established by pagan Britons in ancient times.
The Mosquito Indians with various shades of blood mix
were the chief participators, and the resultant festivities
had a high positive effect on the birthrate.

MAZATL.   One of the month festival days (and gods) of the
ancient Nicarao.   Meaning: "deer. "

MAZORCA, LA.   A game of aboriginals of the Managua
area, in which cobs of corn are thrown in the air and
shot with arrows, catching the grains as they fall.

MEASURES   see   WEIGHTS AND MEASURES

MECATEPE.   A district near Laguna Blanca south of Granada and the Mombacho Volcano.

MECHAPA. A district in the municipio of La Trinidad, department of Estelí.

MECHAPA, RIO. A stream in La Trinidad municipio, Estelí department.

MECHUDOS. A Nicaraguan political party nickname (meaning "many-locked," or "hairy") of a group in opposition to Desnudos (q.v.), in the 1847-1849 period. Party of the "establishment."

MEDIA UNIVERSIDAD MERIDIONAL. Founded by D. Alejo Mayorga in 1872, there were studies carried on in anatomy, physiology, hygiene, pathology, and therapeutics. The location was Rivas.

MEDIANA PROPRIEDAD. A land-holding classification of farms ("fincas") from 50 to 200 manzanas, or 88 to 350 acres approximately.

MEDIO MUNDO. 1) Comarca or district in the municipio of Villa Somoza, Chontales.
2) The "half world" is a district and hacienda near Diría in Granada department.

MEJIANOS. Known historically to be one of the names applied to Mexican tribes who settled Nicaragua, among them Chorutegans, Nahuas, or Nahuatlacas. The groups around Estelí were of this type.

MELERO. A monolith near Cuapa in the municipio of Juigalpa.

MENA, DON IGNACIO. "Professor" Mena was the first to open a private school in Masaya in 1820.

MENCO, EL. A district in the municipio of Buenos Aires, Rivas department.

MENCOS, MARTIN CARLOS DE. Captain-General of Guatemala, 1659-1668, and first military officer to hold the post in lieu of lawyer-presidents. Formerly General of the Armada, he extended his concern to all of Central America where previous governors had confined themselves to local matters. When the attack of Morris on Granada in 1665 was reported, he not only authorized a militia, but began to explore sources of funds to build a

fort on the vulnerable Nicaraguan River-Lake route.
Guatemalan merchants, sorely hit by the freebooters,
agreed to an export tax to cover the cost of a fort.
Mencos ordered de Salinas to survey the San Juan
River for a fort site.

MENDIETA, SALVADOR. Born in Diriamba, where he died
in 1958, Dr. Mendieta was founder of the union party,
Partido Unionista de Centroamérica. He was notable as
a writer, lawyer, and as cabinet minister.

MENOCAL, A. G. Perennial canal surveyor, this competent
engineer of Cuban origin was involved in several of the
canal surveys from the 1870's on, as well as in such
enterprises as the Maritime Canal Company and the
Nicaraguan Canal Construction Company. His project
for a great earthworks dam at Ochoa was one of the
more daring and brilliant of the many canal engineering
plans over the years. His son later became president
of his native Cuba following its independence.

MENTOR NICARAGUENSES. A newspaper which appeared
under the Buitrago administration in Nicaragua, soon
after secession, and during the period 1841-1843. Fruto
Chamorro was the entrepreneur of this periodical and
was later President.

MERCADOS DE MANAGUA. Managua has several large markets in the Central American pattern, the old "Mercado
Central" being in the very heart of the city. Built in
1881, it was destroyed in the fire and earthquake in
1931, with considerable loss of life. The "Mercado el
Boer, " constructed by the National District, is in the
northern part of the city. The "Mercado Oriental" is
in the barrio of El Calvario. Certain peripheral markets are also planned. There are seven "supermarkets"
on the North American pattern in various parts of the
city, but these serve largely the well-to-do upper sector
of the population, and are developed by private enterprise, this having occurred since 1958.

MERCED, LA. 1) A cattle ranch in the area of San Ramón,
Chontales, granted to the Convent of La Merced, in
Granada, in the year 1635. Size: 28 caballerías, or
about 900 acres.
    2) A church in the city of León, constructed in 1615,
soon after the city was established in its new location.

La Merced Church in Granada

As restored following the 1856 destruction by Walker forces.

3) Church and convent in Granada, which shows the classical tendency of the 18th century in the layout and decor, although Baroque is still in evidence. Completed around 1781, it was extensively damaged in the Walker filibuster war of 1856, but was restored in great measure in 1862. Marks of the fire still are in evidence. (See illustration.)

MERCEDES.   Cacao plantation in the municipio of Nandaime, Granada department.   Many fruits are raised also.

MERCEDES, LAS.   1) Coffee hacienda in the municipio of La Concepción, department of Masaya.
2) Coffee plantation in Pueblo Nuevo municipio of Estelí department.
3) A district of the municipio of Jinotega.
4) Comarca or district in the municipio of El Sauce, León department.
5) Comarca or district in the municipio of La Paz, León.
6) Comarca or district in the municipio of Quezalguaque, León.

MERCEDES, RIO LAS.   Stream in the municipio of El Sauce, León department.

MERCEDES Y SAN ANTONIO, LAS.   Cattle haciendas in the valley of Sebaco, 180 acres granted in 1711 to Sergeant Luis Bautista Díaz, a Spanish colonial soldier.

MERIDIONAL, DEPARTMENTO.   One of the four departments created by the first constituent assembly of the free state of Nicaragua by the law of December 21, 1838, founded by the district of Rivas.

MESA DE LOS ESPEJOS see MOCUANA

MESA DE ALANCA.   A district in the municipio of La Trinidad, department of Estelí.

MESAS, LA.   Mountain height at altitude of 4300 feet, Pueblo Nuevo municipio Estelí department.

MESAS, LAS.   Comarca or district in the municipio of Santo Tomás in Chontales.

MESAS, LAGUNA DE LAS.   Lake in the municipio of La Concordia, Jinotega department.

MESAS DE ACICAYA, LA. A district of the municipio of
Tipitapa, department of Managua.

MESAS DEL ARRAYAN, LAS. One of Estelí department's
high tablelands or "alti-planos estelianos" of a general
3,900 foot altitude.

MESAS DEL GARABATO, LAS. Heights in the area of the
municipio of San Juan de Tola, Rivas department.

MESAS DE LA LAGUNA, LAS. One of Estelí department's
high tablelands, at 3,900 feet altitude.

MESAS DE OLLANCA, LAS. One of the tablelands in Estelí
department, lowest of eight at a general altitude of
2,600 feet.

MESAS DE SABANA LARGA, LAS. One of the high and
unique tablelands of Estelí department, general altitude
around 4,000 feet.

MESETA DE LA CUCHILLA. Mountain of the Isabella range,
Jinotega department, altitude 3,840 feet.

MESETA MOMBACHITO MADIGUE, LA. Between Boaco
and Comoapa, this high plateau is surrounded by sharp
peaks, volcanic intrusions. Like many other geological
features of Nicaragua, the tableland is both unique in
character and beautiful in surroundings.

MESITAS, LAS. A district of the municipio of Jinotega.

MESO-AMERICA. A geographical area encompassing central
and southern Mexico, the peninsula of Yucatán, Belíze
or British Honduras, Honduras, El Salvador, and Nicaragua. Costa Rica and Panama might also be considered
as part of the area. The sub-regions are the Valley of
Mexico, the area of Oaxaca, the Gulf Coast Huastec region, the southern part of the Gulf Coast, western Mexico, the Mayan Highlands, the southern and western lowlands, the Guatemalan Pacific Coast and Chiapas, flat
northern Yucatán, the Honduran and Nicaraguan Highlands, etc.

MESON DE GUERRA. Cuartel, "fort" or base of the William
Walker forces in the battle of Rivas, April 11, 1856.
Rivas houses still bear traces of the cannonading.

METALLURGY (Pre-Conquest). There is much evidence of
    inter-regional trade in metalwork, principally jewelry,
    in the area of Nicaragua, Panama, and Costa Rica
    around A. D. 600-800. Work was also done in semi-
    precious stones.

METAPA see CIUDAD DARIO

METATE (Metatl). The word found in several variants de-
    rives from Nahuatl (metatl) and denotes a milling stone,
    with a concave surface, usually three legs, and a double
    tapered stone roller. Such mills are sold in Nicaraguan
    markets to this day, although of simpler and cruder
    form than the works of art frequently found in ancient
    times and now preserved in museums. (See illustra-
    tion of a metate.)

MEZA, SAMUEL. Doctor Mezá was born in Estelí and is
    considered a significant poet of the Segovias, and is
    given credit for the re-establishment of the department
    in 1900, unique in Nicaraguan annals. This re-estab-
    lishment, over the veto of President Zelaya, was also
    supported and effected by Mezá's associates, Doctor
    Eleuterio Hidalgo Reyes and Doctor Adolfo Altamirano.

MICA, LA. Comarca or district in the municipio of La Paz,
    León department.

MIDDLE AMERICA see "MESO-AMERICA"

MILLER, JOAQUIN, 1839-1913. American western poet who
    came through Nicaragua during the days of the Accessory
    Transit Company, and who wrote of the filibuster William
    Walker as having "a piercing eye, a princely air, a
    presence like a chevalier. " Miller served briefly under
    Walker and followed up Walker's execution in Honduras
    by interviewing the priest who last spoke to Walker.
    Miller's real name was Cincinnatus Hiner Miller.

MILLER, WARNER see MARITIME CANAL COMPANY OF
    NICARAGUA

MINA, LA. District in the municipio of San Jorge, Rivas
    department.

MINAS QUISILALA. Abandoned mines in the east coast area
    northwest of Rama.

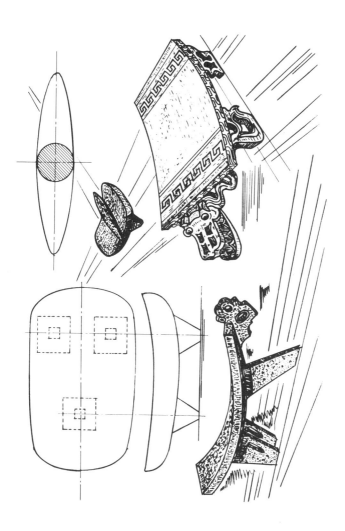

Metate

Three milling stones, or metatls.

MINERALS. In general the mineral industry of Nicaragua contributes about two percent to the Gross Domestic Product (q. v.). A typical production year exported over 200, 000 troy ounces of gold, twice that weight of silver, and 8, 000 tons of copper. Mineralization, of ores and other substances, is widespread, with antimony oxide, pyrite, quartz, stibnite, malachite, azurite, mica, cuprite, chrysocolla, chalcocite, borite, alaskite, monzonite, hematite, magnetite, pyrrhotite, and other minerals among those available. Nonmetallic mineral production totals 1. 6% of all Nicaraguan industrial production.

MINES (Spanish). The existence of many old Spanish mines, dating from earliest times of the conquest on through the colonial years, has been well established in several locations in Nicaragua, particularly in the "Segovias" in the region of present-day Ocotal, which was the third location chosen for "Nueva Segovia. " The incursions of pirates up the navigable Río Coco was in part because of the placer gold known to come from this area (still a placer source) and also because of the old Spanish hardrock mines of the area, where tunnels, shafts, refining furnaces, dams, and water channels all exist in ruined form and attest to the considerable activity of early colonial days, which was principally aimed at the extraction of gold and silver. Modern mining has been an important industry in Nicaragua for nearly a century in the northeastern mining area, which was not penetrated by the Spaniards. The mines abound--one is within two or three miles of La Vigía at the junction of the Río Pantasma with the Río Coco, to the north of Jinotega.

MINIFUNDIOS. A classification of landholding still used in Chontales signifying from one to 20 manzanas, approximately 1. 75 to 35 acres. (There are 970 such holdings in the department.)

MINISTRIES. The cabinet branches of the executive power, vested in the President and his Ministers of Government, who form a consultative Council of Ministers: Interior, Foreign Affairs, Economy, Finance, Education, Development and Public Works, War, Navy and Air Force, Agriculture, Public Health, Labor, and National District. Presided over by the President of the republic, the ministries above operate as a cabinet, in their membership in the Council of Ministers.

MINITA, LA.   1) Coffee hacienda in the municipio of El
    Sauce, León department.
        2) A tunnel near the Macuelizo River, in connection
    with old Spanish workings, water filled.   It seems to
    have been aimed at a vein of pyrite.

MINITAS, LAS.   1) A district in the municipio and depart-
    ment of Matagalpa.
        2) A district in the municipio of Matiguâs, department
    of Matagalpa.

MIQUITIZTLI.   A month festival of the pre-conquest Nicarao
    tribe in the region of modern Rivas.   Meaning: "death."

MIRAFLOR.   1) Mountain lake in Estelí department.
        2) At 4, 300 feet general level, the highest of Estelí
    department's unique tablelands or "altiplanos estelianos."

MIRAFLORES   see   FARFANA,

MIRAGUAS.   A district in the municipio of Esquipulas, de-
    partment of Matagalpa.

MIRIAM.   Cattle ranch of Colonel Ernesto A. Artola in
    Diriamba municipio of Carazo department.

MISERICORDIA, LA.   One of a close group of old Spanish
    mines near Amatillo in Nueva Segovia department.   A
    rudimentary mill existed at the site.   Old tunnels are
    fallen in.   Schist and quartz show small amounts of
    gold and silver.   The site is more interesting archaeo-
    logically than mineralogically.

MISIONERAS CATEQUISTAS LUMEN CRISTE.   An indigenous
    women's religious order of the last 20 years; Catholic,
    and giving service to health and mind.

MISKITO COAST   see   MOSQUITO SHORE

MISKITO (Language).   Spoken all along the Río Coco Valley,
    up several of the eastern jungle rivers like the Prinza-
    polka, the Grande, and the Escondido, this Indian-de-
    rived tongue has a sound all its own, a whining sing-
    song--nakh-sahn (a greeting); mairen kampura ("beautiful
    woman"); ay-sa-veh ("good-bye").   Signs on the east
    coast are often in three languages: IN CASE OF FIRE;
    EN CASO DE INCENDIO; PAUTA AMBIA KAKA (Miskito).

Origins probably are with Quiribies and Sumus (both q. v.). The early tongue may even have come north from the South American mainland. The Miskito tongue has suffered corruption over the centuries but it still has an unusual sound. A few examples follow: "Close your mouth, " Bilam praks; "Give me a knife, " Kishura kum aid; "Take care of him, " Witin remaind kaika; "Did a Snake bite you?" Piuta mai Saman?; "I lost all my money, " Lalaki sut tikri; "Divide it in half, " Bakriki kat baiks; "My stomach hurts, " Biaira klauhisa; "Where's my gun?" Roksi anira sa?

MISSIONARIES OF THE SACRED HEART. Foreign Catholic Missionary order of women serving in Nicaragua, in teaching, hospitals, orphanages, etc.

MITOTE (Mitotl). A dance of worship among the Chorutegans of Tezoatega, at the time of gathering cacao. The ceremony was held in the plaza, numerous costumed, masked and painted dancers taking part. A painted idol, "Cacaguat, " was a central figure in the dance. Mitotl is Nahuatl for "dance. "

MIXCOA. A god of commerce of the Nicarao tribe, "serpent of the clouds" from mixtli, "clouds, " and coatl, "serpent. "

MOBILITY, SOCIAL. Generally difficult though not impossible. There is little mobility from laboring or farm worker classes to the middle class (see "Segundos"). It is, however, possible, and depends on educational opportunities. The leap from middle to upper classes has the same dependency but is even harder. Usually marriage is an entree, but the decision is made by the elite. Land possession is still an important criterion for social position, hence "family. "

MOBILIZACION REPUBLICANA. A pro-Castro political party; therefore, outlawed (only two parties are "legal").

MOCA, LA. Coffee hacienda in the municipio of Jinotepe, Carazo department.

MOCHIGUISTE. Valley to which the town of Estelí (q. v. , def. 3) was transferred in 1823.

MOCOTON. A mountain on the Nicaraguan-Honduras border 11 miles northwest of Ocotal which, according to best

survey information, is the highest mountain in Nicaragua
at 6, 913 feet.   Up until a decade ago, Mt. Saslaya (q. v.)
was reported as the highest at altitudes up to 8, 500.
Mocotón is in Nueva Segovia.

MOCUANA (or Mesa de los Espejos).   A district in the municipio of La Trinidad, department of Estelí.

MODAL, ARTURO JOSE.   A distinguished native Nicaraguan
pianist living in Chile.

MODERNISMO.   A movement in Spanish literature which
spread from Central America throughout the Spanish-
speaking world about the end of the 19th century.   Rubén
Darío, Nicaraguan poet, was the leader of this literary
movement which was a reaction to naturalism, the stilted
literary standards, and the conformity of the late Vic-
torian era.   Relying on free verse, the modernistic
movement emphasized internal rhythm, individualism,
and creativity.

MODYFORD, SIR T.   Governor of Jamaica in 1670.   (See
LOGWOOD.)

MOJARRA, LA.   Comarca or district in the municipio of
La Paz, León.

MOJON, EL.   Comarca or district in the municipio of Jinotepe, Carazo department.

MOJON DE VERACRUZ, EL.   A district of the Granada department near Isla Zapatera.

MOJONES OCCIDENTALES, LOS.   Comarca or district in
the municipio of El Sauce, León department.

MOJONES ORIENTALES, LOS.   Comarca or district in the
municipio of El Sauce, León department.

MOLENDEROS.   The "mills" used with metates (metlates or
metatls) to prepare the corn for tortillas, with channels
for the escape of the water used in preparation.   Archae-
logical pieces of this nature often found, are elaborately
and beautifully carved, even though made of hard and
rather coarse stone.

MOLINA, LOS.   Comarca or district in the municipio of
San Marcos, Carazo department.

MOLINO, EL.   Major cattle ranch in the municipio of San
Rafael del Norte, Jinotega department.

MOLINO NORTE.   A district in the municipio and department of Matagalpa.

MOLINO SUR.   A district of the municipio of Sebaco, Matagalpa department.

MOLLEJONES.   1) A flowing spring in the municipio of San
Ramón, Matagalpa department.
   2) Los Mollejones, a comarca or district in the municipio of Santo Tomás in Chontales.   In this district
are ruins of pyramidal sacred sites used by the aboriginal tribes of Chontales, as well as the abandoned town
of Loviguisca.

MOMBACHO.   Dead volcano six miles south of Granada,
4,010 feet high.   The isletas de Granada, scenic isles
of great volcanic boulders, are presumed to have been
cast into the lake following some prehistoric explosion
of the volcano.   Only half or less of the crater crest
of Mombacho remains, lending credence to the story of
the isletas origin.   A projection of the slopes to a hy-
pothetical peak would extrapolate a mountain cone of
9,000 to 10,000 feet.   (See illustration.)

MOMOTOMBITO.   Wooded volcanic cone (constituting an island) in Lake Managua, a companion to its "father, "
Momotombo (q.v. , def. 3).

MOMOTOMBO.   1) Comarca or district in the municipio of
La Paz, León.
   2) A poem by Rubén Darío concerning Nicaragua's
best-known peak.   He speaks of the mountain as "father
of fire and stone. "   The poem is historical not only in
that it relates to this symbol of the nation, but also in
that Victor Hugo's comments as well as the part of
others in discovery are woven into the poem.
   3) Volcán Momotombo, best-known of Nicaragua's volcanoes, this 4,400-foot perfect cinder cone in tints of
red is on a peninsula thrust into Lake Managua, and is
accompanied by the little companion cone, the round island Momotombito.   There are many legends about
Momotombo--among them that no one has ever climbed
it and lived to tell the tale.   (This compiler has done
so, however.)   Sung in poetry by Victor Hugo and Rubén

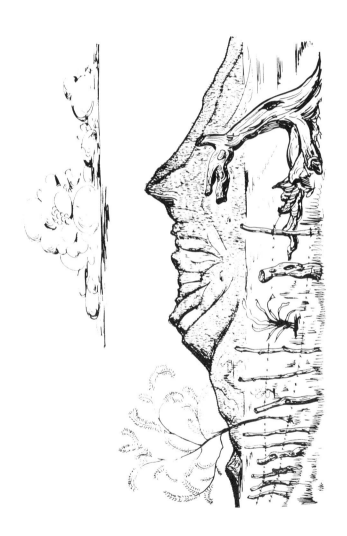

Mombacho

The dead crater south of Granada.

Darío, an untimely eruption in 1902 had a great deal to
do with the rejection of Nicaragua as a site for an isthmian canal.   Momotombo is mildly active, with several
eruptions recorded.   The crater is about 300 yards in
diameter, and a great lava channel runs straight down
its northern slope.   (See illustration.)

MONAGALPA.   Pueblo or town existing in the valley of
Nicaragua during the 16th and 17th centuries.

MONCADA, JOSE MARIA.   Leader of the revolution supporting the presidency of Juan Batista Sacasa and opposed to
the coup and takeover by Emiliano Chamorro in 1923,
Moncada was involved in the dealings with Henry L.
Stimson, U. S. President Coolidge's emissary, which
resulted in the Tipitapa agreements.   Moncada laid down
his arms and only Sandino of his nominal followers refused to do so.   Moncada became president in 1928.
He was instrumental in the building of the Lake-Ocean
railroad, San Jorge-Rivas--San Juan del Sur, and the
León-El Sauce spur.   He was able to redeem the custom
collections at Corinto and to nationalize the National
Bank.   During his administration (1931) occurred the
disastrous earthquake at Managua, as well as the latest
complete canal survey under U. S. Army engineer Dan I.
Sultan.

MONGALO Y RUBIO, MANUEL.   Generally considered a
hero of the battle of June 29, 1855, in Rivas against the
forces of William Walker, Mongalo y Rubio was also a
poet and teacher of Rivas.

MONIMBO.   1) The Indian "barrio" in the suburbs of Masaya,
which retains the flavor of an ancient indigenous culture
(named for the sub-tribal group still residing there).
2) A residual Indian group living near and in Masaya,
nevertheless Spanish-speaking and otherwise considered
Ladino.

MONOLITO DE SAN RAMON, EL.   A hugh monolith, 75 feet
high and 40 feet diameter, in the municipio of El Sauce.

MONROE DOCTRINE.   Honored almost as much in the breach
as in the observance, and subject to errors in both cita-
tion and interpretation, this "doctrine" was simply a
part of U. S. President Monroe's message to Congress
on December 2, 1823.   Threats of the Holy Alliance to

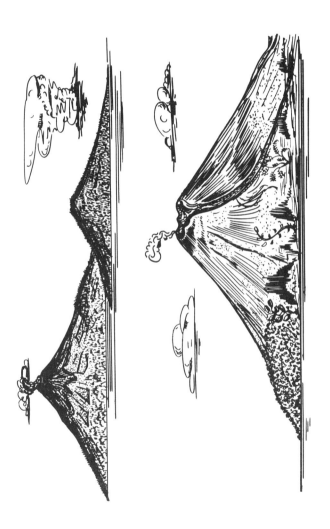

Momotombos

Active volcano Momotombo and volcanic isle, Momotombito,
upper sketch from the lake, lower showing lava channel from
the north.

reconquer rebellious Spanish colonies, as well as North American incursions by Russia, added to a general distrust of Great Britain, were a portion of the proximate causes for the pronouncement. The crux was that European intervention in either of the continents could not be viewed "... in any other light than as the manifestation of an unfriendly disposition toward the United States." The doctrine also disavowed intention to interfere in European wars and excursions. Aimed at Europe, the mistaken notion has persevered in Latin America that the Doctrine was a blueprint for hemispheric intervention.

MONTAÑA, LA.   1) A district in the municipio of Belén, Rivas department.
2) A comarca or district of the municipio of San Nicholás, León.

MONTAÑA DECA.   A mountain height in the municipio of Ciudad Darío, Matagalpa department.

MONTAÑA GRANDE.   A district of Terrabona municipio, Matagalpa department.

MONTAÑITA, LA.   1) A district in the municipio and department of Estelí.
2) District in the municipio of Tisma, department of Masaya.

MONTEAGUDO, FRAY JUAN DE.   Missionary priest who was killed by Indians in the Tologalpa area in 1612, at the same time Fray Esteban Verdelete was assassinated.

MONTE CARMELO.   1) A district including the Village of Rosita.
2) In the Pis Pis mining area of northeastern Nicaragua there are several mineral bodies of iron ore near the River Sang Sang Was.   The ore is micaceous hematite.   Low in phosphorus, the iron content is around 65% with estimated tonnage of as much as 25,000,000. Around four to eight million tons seem assured.   Minor percentages of copper are also found.

MONTECRISTO.   A cattle ranch and plantation in the municipio of Masaya.

MONTE FRESCO.   Also called Santa Rita, a district of the Del Carmen municipio, Managua department.

MONTE GRANDE. A district of Terrabona municipio, Matagalpa department.

MONTE GRANDE DE SAN MIGUEL. Comarca or district of
the municipio of Santa Teresa, Carazo department.

MONTEMAR. Cattle ranch in the municipio of San Juan del
Sur, Rivas department.

MONTENEGRO, DON JUAN. Captain of militia and cavalry
in the Villa Viejo de Estelí in the mid-1700's. Defense
of the sparsely-populated region was difficult because of
its exposed frontier status.

MONTENEGRO, JOSE. Between 1843-1845, Buitrago, Orozco,
Pérez, and Madriz (all q.v.) had served Nicaragua as
provisional directors. After an agreement with Francisco Malespín, Montenegro was chosen provisional director, to be followed soon by Selva and Sáenz.

MONTE VERDE. A district of Terrabona municipio, Matagalpa department.

MONTURA. A saddle which in contrast to the more prevalent albarda resembles the "Western saddle" of the
United States except that there is no prominent saddle
horn, as the use of the lariat (la reata) is generally by
"tail-dally, " meaning it is tied to the horse's tail.
Horses are trained to set their feet in relation to the
strain on the tail-dallied lariat rather than to pull back
as with the saddle-horn-dallied lariat. See also AL-
BARDA.

MORA, LA. A district or valley in the municipio of the
La Concordia, department of Jinotega.

MORA Y SUS ANEXOS, LA. A cattle ranch in the municipio
of La Concordia, Jinotega department.

MORALES, ARMANDO. Nicaragua's best known contemporary
painter. He was born in Granada in 1927, and from
1941-1945 attended the National School of Fine Arts. As
a Guggenheim Fellow in 1959, he developed his skill and
has exhibited widely in the U.S. and Latin America.
His work, generally abstractions, is in the Museum of
Modern Art in New York and elsewhere.

MORAN, EL. A height of the area of Terrabona municipio.

MORAVOS, LOS. "The Moravians," a religious sect which established mission work in Nicaragua in the 1840's. After Prince Karl of Prussia investigated Nicaragua in 1841 because a British sea captain tried to sell him some land which he had received from Miskito King Robert Charles Frederick, another German prince became interested. He decided Nicaragua needed missionaries more than settlers, and persuaded the Moravians to act. Two missionaries went to Bluefields from Jamaica. Under encouragement by the British Consul (the Miskito Coast being a British protectorate), the Miskito Council passed a resolution asking the Moravians to begin mission work. In March, 1849, the work began with the organization of a school, first for Creoles, then for the Indians on Rama Key. In 1881 the work greatly expanded and in 1896 medical work was established. Following 1925 a station was established up the Waspuk River. Here in 1931, a band of Sandinos' rebels killed Karl Bragenzer, missionary, and burned the village of Musawas and its church. In 1933 Doctor A. D. Thaeler established a clinic. Now Bilwaskarma's mission hospital is visited by 5,000 patients a year; Puerto Cabezas also has a school and hospital, and well in its second century the Bluefields school is still vigorous. Catholic and Moravian cooperation on the east coast of Nicaragua is outstanding.

MORCILLO, EL. A district in the municipio of San Juan de Limay in the department of Estelí.

MOREL DE SANTA CRUZ, AGUSTIN. This Nicaraguan Bishop in 1752 recognized the temporary hopelessness of the missionary movement in Nicaragua, when he said, "How can we consider supporting missions, especially when the Indians either die in them or run from them?" This was in special reference to the Recollect Mission. As a priest he visited and reported on the territory of Carazo (Diriamba and Jinotepe) in the 1750's. He reported great misery among the inhabitants, and the decline of the wealth which the Spanish conquerors found there. Jinotepe, he found, had only 280 inhabitants, and following a disastrous earthquake of 1739, little had been rebuilt by 1850, over a century later.

MORGAN, CHARLES see VANDERBILT, CORNELIUS; for the paddle steamer, see CHARLES MORGAN

MORNING STAR MINE.   One of the Bonanza (q. v.) group of
    mines.

MORO, EL.   Mountain height in the municipio of Pueblo
    Nuevo, Estelí department.

MOROPOTENTE.   1) Altiplano or high mesa in Estelí de-
    partment, of a general level of 3, 600 feet.
        2) A district in the municipio and department of Es-
    telí.
        3) A significant hacienda granted to Antonio de Ruga-
    ma y Alvarado on December 15, 1719, consisting of 50
    caballerías (1, 400 acres) located in the extensive Valley
    of Estelí.
        4) Mountain in the municipio of Estelí.

MOROPOTO.   A hacienda of 40 cabellerías (1, 120 acres)
    granted to Don Diego de Avila on January 23, 1724, in
    the rich valley of Estelí.

MORRILLO.   A village near the mouth of the Río Consuelo
    on the north shore of Lake Nicaragua between San Mig-
    uelito and San Carlos.

MORRIS, JOHN.   Leader of a piratical attack on Granada on
    June 30, 1665, under authorization of Sir Thomas Mody-
    ford, Governor of Jamaica.   Captain Morris had help
    from Henry Morgan.   They attacked in broad daylight,
    having sneaked up to the environs of the city with Sambo-
    Miskito allies in dugouts.   They took away 6, 000 pesos
    and some slaves.   This was one of the final straws
    which led to the building of El Castillo (q. v.).

MORRITO.   A municipio of the Río San Juan department,
    just south of the Río Oyate and on the north shore of
    Lake Nicaragua.   The area is agricultural, with cattle,
    rice, and other cereals.   Lumber is also produced.

MOSAN   see   MOVIMIENTO SINDICAL AUTONOMO DE
    NICARAGUA.

MOSCOES.   A variant term for the Caribbean Coastal tribe
    found from Bluefields north along the Nicaraguan Carib-
    bean Coast.   (See   MISKITOS or MOSQUITOES.)

MOSKITO-KUSTE.   Moravian terminology (German) in a
    1908 Missionary Atlas, showing the Nicaraguan coastal

area as it was then developed. (See EAST COAST in 1908.)

MOSKITO RESERVE. The whole area of Eastern Nicaragua which following the British protectorate period was a special reservation for the multi-racial tribesmen.

MOSKITO STATE. The political entity recognized by Great Britain in the 18th and 19th centuries as a "Kingdom, " which was in effect a British creation and wholly a protectorate.

MOSQUITO COAST   see   MOSQUITO SHORE

MOSQUITO PROTECTORATE (Great Britain). The end of this longstanding involvement (since the logwood cutters and pirates of the 16th and early 17th centuries) came in 1894. (See REVOLUTION AT EL BLUFF.)

MOSQUITO SHORE. Loosely, the geographical area between Belize (now British Honduras) and Bocas de Toro (in Western Panama), which was occupied by the British following 1700, when the Spanish power in Yucatán had forced the British to abandon the coast in the Campeche area as well as the Panamanian Coast near and west of Porto Bello. The Mosquito Coast proper extends from about Cape Gracias a Dios to the Río Maiz, just north of the San Juan River. This included settlements at the Cape and at Bragman's Bluff (modern Puerto Cabezas) as well as at Punta Gorda (mouth of the Rama River) and at Bluefields. It is likely that all the coastal settlements during this period contained fewer than 1, 500 Englishmen. These outposts on the English-Miskito side of the Spanish frontier accounted for at best a few thousand persons versus over a million in the Spanish parts of Central America by the end of the 1700's.

MOVIMIENTO SINDICAL AUTONOMO DE NICARAGUA (MOSAN). Of Social-Christian political affiliation, this labor group is not one of those registered by the Ministry of Labor. It is in that sense like the minority political parties.

MOYOA   see   CHARCO, EL

MOYOGALPA. This municipio is the smaller of the two located on Omotepe Island in Lake Nicaragua, in the de-

partment of Rivas. Area 31 square miles, population of
4, 400 persons. There are eight districts. The special
fertility of the volcanic soil on the slopes of the active
volcano Concepción gives a special impetus to the raising of cereals. Further, the soils are just right to
raise the light burley tobaccos such as are found in the
U. S. states of Virginia and Kentucky. A tobacco ware-
house and handling center is a feature of the department.
Cacao and cattle are also raised.

MOZO. Local term for temporary harvesters, migrant type
agricultural labor.

MOZONTE. A municipio of 300 population in Nueva Segovia
department.

M. R. see MOBILIZACION REPUBLICANA

MUELLE DE LOS BUELLES. The "oxen-dock" is a river
port below Rama on the Río Escondido.

MUERTO, ISLA EL. Island in Lake Nicaragua off the Chontales shore.

MUESTRO see YSASI

MUHAN NUMERO DOS. Comarca or district in the municipio
of Villa Somoza, Chontales department.

MUHAN NUMERO UNO. Comarca or district in the municipio of Villa Somoza, Chontales department.

MULA, LA. A district of the municipio of San Ramón,
Matagalpa department.

MULTILATERAL TREATY OF 1958. A treaty basic to the
establishment of the Central American Common Market.
Nicaragua has been a major exponent of the concept of
economic integration among the five states.

MULUKUGUAS. A district of the municipio of Jinotega.

MULUKUKU. A district at the junction of the Río Iyas with
the Río Tuma, Zelaya department.

MUNA, LAGUNA. A ring-shaped ox-bow lake cutoff from
the main Río Coco near Saynika and 30 miles from Cabo
Gracias a Dios.

MUNDO, EL. A daily paper published in Granada, traditional conservative capital.

MUNICIPAL COURTS. At the level of municipios, these courts operate somewhat as "county courts" might in the United States of America.

MUNICIPIO. A segment of a department, as used in Nicaragua. If the department is considered equivalent to a "state" (as in Mexico, Brazil, or the United States), then the municipio might be paralleled to a "county," although it also partakes of the idea of "township." However, the municipio always has a principal town or cabacera which is like a U.S. county seat in central location and local governmental function. Municipios vary widely in size depending upon the degree to which the country or region is settled, which also varies widely in Nicaragua.

MUÑOZ, DON MANUEL. One of the secretaries of the independence movement in Rivas in 1811.

MUÑOZ, JOSE TRINIDAD. General-in-Chief of the Nicaraguan Army at the time of Walker's coming to Nicaragua, native of Granada, he commanded troops who caught up with the rebel Bérnabe Somoza. Muñoz had served with Santa Anna in Mexico.

MURALLA DE EL CORAZO. A natural rock formation which may be the hollow plug remains of ancient volcanic action, in the municipio of El Corazo. The rocks are 900 feet above the valley and have a total elevation of 1,500 feet above sea level with an interior area of half a square mile and a diameter of 3/4 of a mile, the bottom being only 150 feet above the general surrounding plain. It is also thought that the area may represent the impact crater of a meteorite, since the whole formation resembles so nearly a moon crater.

MURIELAGO. 1) District in the municipio and department of Rivas.
    2) A district in the municipio of San Juan de Tola, Rivas department.

MURRA. 1) A municipio and cabacera on the river of the same name, about 12 miles from the Honduran border in northern Nueva Segovia department.

2) A river-head pass between Spanish colonial Nicaragua and the Sambo-Miskito enemy to the east of the frontier.

MURRA, RIO. A tributary of the Río El Jícaro to the north of Quilalí in Nueva Segovia department, one of the important demarcations of the central Spanish colonial frontier.

MUSICAL INSTRUMENTS. 1) Aboriginal: pre-conquest musical instruments used by many of the Nicaraguan tribes (originating in the Mexican Nahua groups) were: flutes of clay and wood, trumpets of wood and bamboo, marine shells ("conch" shells or "trumpet shells"), drums and "tom-toms, " and whistles of wood and clay as well as reeds. While some authors also claim the marimba was used in Nicaragua, early chroniclers do not record it.

2) Colonial: the Spanish introduced guitars, mandolins, and violins. It is possible that the marimba was also introduced at this time, and that farther north it was an aboriginal instrument. It seems to have been long established in southern Mexico.

MUY MUY. 1) A municipio of Matagalpa department, area 147 square miles, population 5, 800. Bounded north by San Ramón and Matiguás municipios, south by Esquipulas and by Boaco of Boaco department, east by Matiguás, and west by Esquipulas and Matagalpa. There are ten comarcas or districts. The principal activity is cattle raising. The Nestlé Company has built a good road through the area.

2) A pueblo, the present town (see Muy Muy Viejo) was founded in its current location in 1748. The population, now 1, 000, handles considerable commercial trade as it is in a relatively remote cattle raising area.

MUY MUY VIEJO. 1) A district in the municipio of Matiguás, department of Matagalpa.

2) This ancient pueblo was in the high westernmost part of the Caribbean Valley of Guanaguás which trends eastward down the Caribbean slope; the site is today in the municipio of Matiguás. Near the Río El Cacao, a tributary of the Río Tuma, the navigable stream (by Pipantes and other light craft) brought invasion to the town three times from the Atlantic Coastal savages. In 1748, the town was transferred to its present site.

3) Not only a town, but also a mountain pass in colonial frontier days between Spanish-held and Sambo-
Miskito dominated territory.

-N-

NACASCOLITO. Comarca or district of the municipio of
Nagarote, León department.

NACASCOLO. Cattle ranch in the municipio of San Juan del
Sur, Rivas department.

NACATAMALES. A Nicaraguan food dish usually prepared
as a very large "tamale," with a cornmeal dough exterior up to one-half inch thick, and the interior prepared of a variety of meats, often raisins, bits of very
hot pepper, etc. In pre-conquest times, it was prepared with a great variety of ingredients. Baked in a
banana leaf and served very hot, it is a delicacy. It is
the custom among some Nicaraguans to break fast on
Sunday with Nacatamales. The cornmeal dough used is
somewhat the same as that used for preparing tortillas,
and is called "masa."

NACATIME. The cacique Nacatime was the last free and
sovereign leader of the pre-conquest people of Nindirí,
the Diriangens. He and his subjects became part of the
encomienda of Captain Diego Machuca, who later was
one of the explorers of the San Juan River. Prior to
this time the encomienda had been assigned to Pedrarias
Dávila and his followers. The encomienda system
caused a major reduction of the Nicaraguan population
during early years of the 16th century.

NAFI see NALI

NAGAROTE. Municipio in the department of León, 12,000
population, 223 square miles in area. Bounded on the
north by Lake Managua and on the south by the Pacific;
on the east by the municipios Mateare, Managua, and
El Carmen, and on the west by La Paz Centro. There
are 15 valleys or districts. Within the municipio is
Puerto Somoza developed during the last two decades.

NAGULAPA. 1) Cattle ranch in the municipio of León, León
department.

2) Early hacienda granted to Ambrocio de Betancourt in 1714, in the area of Rivas; of five cabellerías (140 acres).

NAHOA. The form used in Nicaragua to indicate the basic Mexican mother-language, more properly known as Nahuatl (q. v.). Similar usage farther north is "Nahua," but in Nicaragua the "u" sound became "o. "

NAHUATL-SPANISH. A dialect prevalent in Nicaragua up until the end of the last century. The comedy-ballet "Gueguence" originating in Nicaragua was set down in this dialect by a D. G. Brinton in 1883. The derivation of Nahuatl is Mexico. The modern writer and scholar Carlos Mántica Abaunza has done a great deal to revive the cultural and linguistic aspects of this blended language called more commonly in Nicaragua, "Nahoa-Español. "

NALI. Lands granted to don Vicente Avendaña y Guzmán in 1747 in Estelí department; an aboriginal Indian name.

NAMANJI. A district or valley in the municipio of San Rafael del Norte, Jinotega department.

NAMASIGUE, BATTLE OF. Nicaraguan troops invaded Honduras as a result of Honduran troops violating Nicaraguan soil in a revolutionary gambit in 1906. Fought March 18, 1907, the battle toppled the Manual Bonilla government. In this battle machine guns made their first appearance in Central America.

NANAICAS. A sub-tribal group of the Chontales branch of the "Quiribies. "

NANCE, EL. Comarca or district in the municipio of Jinotepe, Carazo department.

NANCE DULCE. Comarca or district of the municipio of Santa Rosa, León.

NANCIMI. A district of the municipio of San Juan de Tola, Rivas department.

NANCIMI, RIO. A stream in the municipio of Belón, Rivas department.

NANCITE DULCE.   District in the municipio and department
of Rivas.

NANDAIME.   A municipio in the department of Granada, of
14, 000 population.   The birthplace of national hero José
Dolores Estrada as well as of former president Diego
Manuel Chamorro, Nandaime has a remarkable colonial
church and a long and spirited record of events since
pre-colonial days.   It was a principal center of the Diriangens.   The local plantations concentrate on cacao but
also raise many fruits, such as various citrus, mangoes,
Zapote, etc.   Sugar cane is also raised.

NANDAPIO.   Pueblo or town existing in the Valley of Nicaragua during the 16th and 17th centuries.

NANDASMO.   1) The smallest municipio in Masaya department, with 2, 300 population and an area of less than
four square miles, with the Lake of Masaya to the north;
to the south is Niquinohomo and Masatepe; east, Masaya
and Catarina; and west, Masatepe municipio.   Half the
small population is rural, the rest live in the cabacera
of the same name.   There are three districts or comarcas.
2) A pueblo, cabacera of the very small municipio of
the same name.   The name in the Chorutegan (Nahuatl-
based) tongue means "near the arroyo (or ravine. ")   The
present site has been inhabited since pre-conquest days,
the pueblo of Jalata being part of the area in aboriginal
times.   The population is about 1, 100.

NANDAYOSI.   A territory of the National District, department of Managua.

NAPAZ, MINA.   One of the La Misericordia group of old
Spanish mines in the Amatillo area of Nueva Segovia department.   An old tunnel and shallow shaft shows a low
gold and silver yield.

NARANJAL, EL.   A district in Zelaya department 30 miles
southwest of Alamikamba.

NARANJITA, LA.   A district in the municipio and department of Estelí.

NARANJITO.   Comarca, valley or district in the municipio
of Juigalpa.

NARANJO, EL. 1) Comarca or district in the municipio of
El Rosario, Carazo department.
2) A district of the municipio of Jinotega.
3) Cattle ranch in the municipio of San Rafael del
Norte, Jinotega department.
4) A district in the municipio of San Juan de Limay
in the department of Estelí.

NARANJO, RIO EL. A stream entering the Pacific in the
municipio of San Juan del Sur, Rivas department.

NARANJOS, LOS. Comarca or district in the municipio of
Diriamba, department of Carazo.

NARVAEZ, LOS. A district of the San Rafael del Sur municipio, Managua department.

NATIONAL AGRARIAN INSTITUTE. This autonomous cor-
porate body has the broad responsibility of arranging a
more favorable pattern of land distribution and tenure
than obtained under the old hacienda system which was
the basis of present plantations and fincas. It also
deals with loans for rural housing and the development
of rural schools. Further functions are the planning
and execution of agricultural settlement projects, action
in cooperation with the Institute for Internal and External Trade in minimum price establishment, and supervision of credit to settlers. Hampered by lack of funds,
it operated on 10.1 million córdobas in 1967 (about
$1,430,000). A total of 78,700 acres of land has been
redistributed under the program.

NATIONAL CONGRESS OF NICARAGUA see LEGISLATURE
and LEGISLATION.

NATIONAL DEVELOPMENT BANK see INSTITUTO DE
FOMENTO NACIONAL DE NICARAGUA.

NATIONAL INSTITUTE FOR FOREIGN AND DOMESTIC COM-
MERCE see INSTITUTO NACIONAL DE COMERCIO
EXTERIOR Y INTERIOR.

NATIONAL NICARAGUA CANAL CONVENTION. The continued involvement for more than a century and a half
of the U.S. in Nicaragua concerns in perhaps best epito-
mized by this convention held in St. Louis, Missouri,

in June, 1892. Three hundred representatives from 30
states and territories of the U.S. were present, and
resolutions were adopted seeking congressional aid in
the canal construction. Plans were made for a follow-
up convention later on. Since both free-trade and re-
ciprocity favored interoceanic communication, the Nicaragua canal project did not become a political football
in that election summer of 1892. The result was a
genuinely national endorsement for the canal project.

NATIONAL PLAN FOR SOCIAL AND ECONOMIC DEVELOP-
MENT. This 1965-1969 plan under the National Economic Council was the country's first venture in systematic planning at the overall national level. The plan
includes expanding and improving the economic and social infrastructure of the nation, to plan for private initiative in industry and agriculture (and to make it possible), to promote industry within the Central American
Common Market framework, and to provide such services as to raise labor productivity. A goal is a seven-
percent annual average rate of increase in the gross domestic product. To do this, it was hoped that expansion
of imports could be reduced to 9.5 percent annually with
a corresponding increase of exports to 10 percent annually, with investment at 17 percent GDP, two-thirds
of this from the private sector. The plan has not
achieved all its goals but has reached some of them,
including a fixed investment level; however, most of
this comes from the private sector.

NATIONAL SCHOOL OF AGRICULTURE AND MINING. One
of the three university-level institutions in Nicaragua,
obviously specialized.

NATIONAL SCHOOL OF MUSIC   see   CONSERVATORIO NA-
CIONAL DE MUSICA

NATIONAL TOURIST BOARD   see   JUNTA NACIONAL DE
TURISMO

NATIONALISM. A strong tradition, sometimes ascribed to
Rubén Darío, much-loved literary figure of Latin America, who in his writings propounded a strong, somewhat
mystical nationalism, cradle of a unique human nature.
Resentful of foreign intervention in all Caribbean affairs,
Darío envisioned a unique Nicaragua as an epitome of
the free human spirit. His literary heirs and many of
his countrymen share this view and vision.

NAVARACA. A district in the municipio of Matiguás, Mata-galpa department.

NAVARRETES, LOS. A district of the San Rafael del Sur municipio, Managua department.

NAVAS, DON MARCOS DE LAS. Depositorio general of the new Villa of Rivas in 1720, and one of those who pre-sented the request for Villa status in Guatemala in July, 1717. One of two men who established an oligarchical government significant as the first such in Nicaragua. (See also VARGAS.)

NEJAPA. A territory of the National District, department of Managua.

NEJAPA, LAGUNA. A crater lake near Lake Asososca (q.v.) about 600 feet beneath the general level. The waters are medicinal, having many dissolved salts. It is a favored haven for ducks, especially teal. The old site of the Managua Country Club was nearby.

NELSON, HORATIO. Few men have had their lives so com-pletely examined and recorded as has the hero of Tra-falgar, Britain's best-known and perhaps best-loved na-val hero. His significance to Nicaragua (and Nicaragua's to him) is one of the lesser-known passages of his histo-ry, as it is one of the earliest. Fulfilling the prime ambition of a Georgian naval officer, Nelson was "posted" as captain of the Hinchinbrooke, 32-gun frigate, on June 11, 1779, destined while in that command to engage in a major amphibious operation as Great Britain attempted to cut the Spanish colonial empire in Nicaragua. Nelson was only 21, but he had the year before commanded the brig Badger off the Nicaraguan Coast, engaged in pro-tecting the Mosquito shore and the Bay of Honduras from privateers. Between these commands he had also com-manded the batteries in Port Royal, Jamaica. In Janu-ary 1780, Nelson and his ship accompanied the expedi-tion to Nicaragua against "St. John's Fort" (now El Cas-tillo Viejo, q.v.). He went upstream with the attacking troops, "boarded" the island of Bartolo near the fort, helped in establishing and firing the batteries which pounded the fort into surrender. But the tolls of fever and dysentery were so high that the victory over the fort's Spanish garrison was indeed hollow. After an increasingly disastrous sojourn, the British had to abandon both the fort and their grand strategic design of dividing new Spain. Before the surrender of the fort even, however, Nelson had to return to his ship. Of the 200 men who went up the San Juan River with him from the Hinchinbrooke, only 10 lived, and young Nelson himself was ill for a year, a direct result of the jungle campaign. One of the best (and the earliest) of Nelson portraits is that by John Francis Rigaud, who portrays the short, slender young man in a proud pose with a very creditable rendition of the Nicaraguan fort in the background. There is also an extant sketch of "Fort San Juan" from downriver, which was probably made by Nelson himself. It shows not only a very recognizable representation of the structure, but also the battery of the British attackers on a nearby eminence, which is still called "Nelson's Hill. " It also shows the water battery at the river's edge, and the surrounding rapids.

NEMBITHIA. A male god of the Matiari Indians, pre-conquest.

NEMONTENI see CALENDAR, NICARAO

NENQUITAMALI. A female mother-god of the Matiari Indians, pre-conquest.

NEOTROPICAL SPECIES. Most Nicaraguan animals either are South American species or belong to Nearctic groups which have followed the highlands south. Of the latter are the white-tailed deer, the raccoon, the turkey, and the puma; the northward moving neotropical animals are such as the opossum, parrots, armadillos, peccaries, and termites.

NEPTUNE EDEN. Gold-bearing veins in the Pis Pis mining district. (See also BONANZA.)

NEPTUNE MINE. One of the Bonanza (q. v.) group of mines.

NEREBGYE. A popular dance rhythm.

NERVO, AMADO. A Mexican poet, 1870-1919, related to Nicaraguan annals in the sense that he is generally considered second only to Rubén Darío (q. v.) as a poet in the modern movement of Spanish literature. It is particularly significant that both men were of Spanish American origin, rather than "peninsular" Spaniards.

NEW GRANADA. Spanish colonial name for what is now the
  Republic of Colombia, it is significant to Nicaraguan
  history in that a Spanish royal order of November 20,
  1803, transferred the entire isthmian shore from the
  Chagres River in Panama to Cape Gracias a Dios, to
  New Granada authority. This decree seems never to
  have been carried out, however, and was obviated by
  the advent of peace between Spain and England soon
  after. The committee on Fortifications of the Indies
  had made the recommendation.

NICARAGUA. 1) Cacicazgo or chieftaincy centered in pre-
  conquest times in the area around the modern city of
  Rivas.
     2) Partido de Nicaragua, one of the nine districts of
  the country under the constitution of April 8, 1826, when
  it was one of the United Provinces of Central America.
  (See   PARTIDOS DE NICARAGUA.)

NICARAGUA (General). One of the smaller nations of the
  Western Hemisphere, centrally located in the Middle-
  American isthmus which links the continents, relatively
  low in population density, and neutral ground between
  the great Indian cultures of Mexico and of South America, Nicaragua is relatively unknown. And while it is
  not unknowable, data is sparse, scattered, and frequently unreliable. As an example of the latter problem, in
  1957 maps and published data all agreed on the highest
  mountain in Nicaragua (see Saslaya). In the sixties,
  more accurate mappong and geology of the Interamerican
  Survey established it as the tenth highest--a considerable
  error in earlier data. In 1956, the Village of Rama was
  found to be ten miles from its mapped position. And in
  1970, a handbook published by the U. S. Superintendent
  of Documents has two different figures for the area (q. v.)
  of Nicaragua which differ by nearly 6, 000 square miles--
  a 12 percent discrepancy. Among the oddities of fact-
  gathering on Nicaragua is that one of the best descrip-
  tions of the cultural milieu is a work (by Squiers) published in 1852. With the above as an introduction it may
  still be said that a great deal is known of Nicaragua and
  that the dramatic and globally significant historical mile-
  posts are far beyond what might be expected from a
  small and underdeveloped nation. Nicaragua is a constitutional republic, the official name being República de
  Nicaragua. It has been a sovereign independent national
  state since 1838. It is a member of the OAS and the

UN, as well as the Central American Common Market.
The current basic organ of law is the Constitution of
1950, which provides for a strong executive leadership.
However, there are four major branches of government--
the Executive, Legislative, Judicial, and Electoral. The
legal code is derived from the Code Napoleon and other
19th century French legal practice, as well as from an
earlier base in Spanish colonial law and administrative
patterns.   Chilean codes of 1850 also have had an effect.

The area is similar in size to that of the State of
Michigan (or Florida), and is variously listed as from
48, 000 to over 57, 000 square miles.   Arable land is 12
percent, or about 6, 000 to 7, 000 square miles. There
are two major regions: the first, the fertile Pacific
lowlands and the accompanying rift valley which cuts
the American Cordillera and contains two great lakes
(Managua and Nicaragua); and the second, the eastern
two-thirds of the country which is rugged, drained by
jungle rivers to the Caribbean lowlands and into that
sea, and covered with rain forest, lowland jungle and
savannahs, and some coastal swamps and lagoons. A
major feature of the Pacific side is the majestic line of
volcanoes, some active, which border the coastal plains
and extend through the lakes.   Three climatic regions
are the eastern rain-forest, the cool and mild tropic
highlands, and the warm western lowlands, subject to
major wet-dry seasonal change.   The rainy season starts
in May, and lasts half the year; on the Pacific slope the
months November through April are dry and dusty.
Earthquakes are common and mild volcanic action is
continuous in such peaks as Momotombo and Concepción.
Major cataclysms are on historical record; the explosion
of Cosegüina in the early 1800's being the best example.
Cerro Negro, a low cinder cone near León, is the volcano with the most recent and violent eruption record
(1968-1971).

The (official) language is Spanish, but it is laced
with many Indian words of Nahuatl (Mexican) origin.
Up until the mid-1800's "Nahua-Spanish, " a lingua franca
was spoken.   The East Coast, with Negro blood infusion,
is tri-lingual; English (Jamaica variety), Spanish, and
Miskito (q. v.).   Some few tribal Sumos speak that language.   Ten percent of the people speak other than Spanish.   The population in 1967 was about 1, 800, 000--an
average density of 32 persons per square mile.   Education has improved in recent years, from about 25% in
1955 to an announced 49% in 1963.   The literacy rate in

1965 was estimated at 50%. Higher education is confined to the public National University and the private
parochial Central American Catholic University. There
are 16 departments (see map, page 139) subdivided into
"municipios" ("counties" or townships) and further into
districts (comarcas). See also POPULATION.

The economy, expressed in percentages of the gross
domestic product in 1967, is as follows: agriculture,
30%; commerce, finance, 23%; industry, 17%; services,
14%; transport, communication, 5%. Of the labor force,
60% is agricultural, 15% industrial, 14% in service and
10% in commerce and transportation. An export summary (1966) indicates: cotton, 40%; coffee, 15%; fresh
meat, 7%; cottonseed oil, 6%. Gold and bananas do not
have the significance they did a half century ago. Re-
cipients of exports show Japan, 30%; United States, 22%;
West German, 15%; the rest of Central America, 13%.
Based on 1967 figures, the per capita GNP (GDP) was
about $400. Principal imports are food, pharmaceuticals,
clothing, automobiles, and trucks. Newspaper circulation is over 100,000. Radio receivers, 200,000; TV receivers, about 25,000.

Transportation is now heavily on highways. Good
roads have increased greatly in the last decade. There
are 217 miles of railroad, over 1,100 miles of paved
road. Oil pipelines, 50 miles; navigable water, the two
lakes, the Rivers Coco, Grande, Escondido, and San
Juan. Ports: Corinto, Puerto Somoza, San Juan del
Sur, Puerto Cabezas, Puerto Isabel, El Bluff. Las
Mercedes in Managua is the international airport, modern and well served by jets of TACA, LANICA, Pan
American. The Merchant Marine is owned in Nicaragua
(see MAMENIC). The armed force ("Guardia Nacional")
combines police, army, and air force functions, and
numbers 11,000 with a military budget of 11% of the
governmental total.

The history of Nicaragua has been controlled in great
measure by five circumstances: the ancient Indian cultures; the Spanish colonial centuries; the favored site
for a passage between Atlantic and Pacific; the theatre
of (official) inter-American intervention; the target of
thrusts toward varied forms of "manifest destiny." Two
additional factors should be mentioned: the vital and
friendly people and the awesome natural beauty of the
land. See also POPULATION.

NICARAGUA (POPULATION OF YOUTH.) 1) Enrolled in
    schools--elementary: 1965, 188, 100; 1980, 242, 000;
    secondary: 1965, 10, 300; 1980, 16, 100; university:
    1965, 1, 100; 1980, 2, 100.   The attrition rate is obvious
    as the educational ladder is scaled.   The predictions
    are consistent with total population and other data.
        2) By age groups--seven to fourteen: 1965, 323, 200;
    1980, 415, 800; fifteen to nineteen: 1965, 146, 500; 1980,
    229, 900.   Total for 1965:   1, 666, 000; total for 1980:
    2, 791, 000.

NICARAGUA CANAL   see   CANAL (Technical Data)

NICARAGUA CANAL CONSTRUCTION COMPANY.   A com-
    pany formed on the basis of a provisional association in
    1887, to institute final canal surveys.   Mr. A. G. Meno-
    cal (q. v.) was sent again to Nicaragua to make a final
    location of the canal line.   The canal promoters got in
    touch with U. S. Secretary of State Bayard under Presi-
    dent Cleveland.   He encouraged them, but political revo-
    lution in Guatemala intervened.

NICARAGUA, RIO DE.   In De Bry's America published in
    Frankfurt (1590), the map which shows Middle America
    labels the whole complex of Lake Managua, Lake Nica-
    ragua, and the San Juan River as the "River of Nica-
    ragua. "

NICARAGUAN INSTITUTE OF SOCIAL SECURITY.   Principal
    channel of the Nicaraguan government to offer social
    benefit to both worker and employer, this is an autono-
    mous body, initiated in 1957, and comes under the Ex-
    ecutive Council of the National Social Assistance and
    Welfare Board.   The program is very comprehensive,
    including: compensation for accidents at work and occu-
    pational illness; nonoccupational medical care; maternity
    benefits; pensions for nonwork-related disabilities; death
    and survivor benefits.   By 1967, still only 14% of the
    work force was covered, but the program is being ex-
    tended.   Employers contribute 7 1/2%, employees 3%,
    the government 3%, of the various pay levels.   For old
    age pension, age must be 60 or over, and at least 750
    weekly contributions must have been made.   Benefits
    are 30% of last five years of pay, plus 1. 5% for each
    50 weeks of social security contributions over 150; the
    maximum rate is 80% of base pay.

NICARAGUAN TELEVISION ASSOCIATION see ELENCO
ESTABLE DE TELEVISION DE NICARAGUA

NIEBEROWSKY, DON JOSE. Of the Misioneros Paulinos
order, and curate of Boaco in 1916, Padre Nieberowsky
was accused as a spy in the service of Germany in 1918.
under the Emiliano Chamorro administration. The parroquial church in Boaco was burned in 1922 because of
feelings of injustice engendered by the charges against
the Padre.

NILA MAIRENA. An alternate form of "La Niña Irene, "
the part-Irish woman, Irena Ohoran, who was a favorite
of William Walker's in Nicaragua, 1855-1857.

NIMBOJA. District of the municipio of Masatepe, department of Masaya.

NIÑA IRENE, LA see OHORAN, IRENA

NINDIRI. 1) This village of 1, 500 population has a distinguished pre-colonial history, although as present principal town (cabacera) of the municipio of the same name
it is relatively inconspicuous. There is a museum
which has archaeological treasures of the area, founded
by don José María Gutiérrez. It is one of the best collections of pre-Columbian ceramics. Also called Lindirí
or Tenderí, the town was noted by Spanish writers as
early as 1551. Many fruits are grown in the area, and
it was formerly the site of the cacicazgo of the cacique
Nacatime and his forebears. The chieftaincy extended
from Tipitapa to Granada and to Masatepe. Ephraim
Squier, the envoy and writer of Nicaragua around 1850,
spoke in enraptured terms of the beauty and Acadian
pastoral tranquility of Nindirí.
2) A municipio of the department of Masaya of 45
square miles and 7, 600 inhabitants. Bounded on the
north by Managua department, on the south by municipios La Concepción and Masatepe, on the east by Masaya, and on the west by the National District of Managua.
There is still a question as to whether the Valle de
Ticuantepe pertains to the municipio. There are 13
districts or comarcas, with Ticuantepe as essentially
a pueblo. There are four major valleys or areas--
Buena Vista, El Raizón, Piedras Azules, and El Portillo. There is a great variety of cultivation: grains,
rice, beans, wheat, sorghum, yuca, quequisque. There

are also several cattle ranches or haciendas, and some converted to cotton plantations. There are old "ejidos" or common lands assigned, with landmarks from El Ventarrón to La Barranca to La Pelota, Guanacastello, Cerro Grande de Veracruz, and then to the Sierra de Managua, Presa de Agua, and back to the start. The ancient town of Nindirí was the seat of the Cacique Nacatime of colonial days.

[EL] 93. A small steamer at Granada on Lake Nicaragua, used as a gunboat, and named for the year of its launching (1893). A quick-firing small cannon (possibly a Gatling gun) was mounted on the bow of El 93. An extant photograph shows the little gunboat being transferred to Granada by rail, during the "Revolution of the Lake," when the old steamer Victoria had been commandeered by General Emiliano Chamorro. The locomotive in the photo, Number 9, had the flared stack of mid 1800's vintage.

NIÑO, ANDRES. Pilot and discoverer of the Bay of Corinto in 1522. Commissioned by the Spanish crown, Andrés Niño prepared a map of the expedition showing the whole Central American Coast from the Pearl Islands off Panama to the Mexican region of Tehuantepec. The Bay of Corinto and the Gulfs of Fonseca and Nicoya are shown on the charts. This Spanish pilot in 1522 also discovered the charming bay and port of San Juan del Sur, while on a search for a strait through the isthmian area.

NIQUINOHOMO. 1) In the extreme southeastern corner of Masaya department, this municipio has an area of only 15 square miles, and a population of 5,400. Bounded on the north by Nandasmo, south by Carazo department, east by San Juan de Oriente, and west by Masatepe and a part of Carazo. There are nine districts or comarcas, several important coffee haciendas, and a variety of agricultural pursuits, especially the raising of fruits such as oranges, lemons, mandarin oranges and local types, with the citrus fruits predominating.

2) The name of Ciudad Niquinohomo is derived from the Chorutegan language (of Mexican origins): neck, "warrior," and nahome, "valley"--hence, the "valley of the warriors." This is an interesting name in view of this town being the birthplace of the controversial Nicaraguan guerrilla warrior, César Agusto Sandino. The area was under the cacicazgo of Chief Diriangen at the

time of the conquest. The present town, cabacera of the municipio of the same name, became villa in 1870, and ciudad in August, 1962. The population has changed little in 200 years. The chief business is coffee and the area is well known for its citrus fruits.

NIRATIA. Pueblo or town existing in the Valley of Nicaragua during the 16th and 17th centuries.

NISPERAL, EL. Coffee hacienda in the municipio of La Concepción, department of Masaya.

NISPERO, EL. A district in southwestern Granada department.

NOCARIME, LAGUNA. A lake in Rivas department along the Lake Nicaragua Coast, and connected at La Bocana.

NOGUERA Y REBELLEDO, GONZALO. Commander of Fort San Carlos (the first one on the Río Pocosól) when it was taken by Prince Lubborough while that buccaneer was on his way to sack Granada.

NOMBRE DE JESUS. A district in the municipio of Ciudad Darío, department of Matagalpa. Especially known for its role as a "cantón militar" established by José Avarado y López (q. v. , López) during the 1855-1856 War.

NOQUERA, DON CAYETANO. A Spanish colonial resident of 1800 representing an established Masaya family.

NORMA. A flatbottomed shallow-draft sternwheel river steamer which around 1900 ran from the Machuca to the Castillo Rapids, continuing a run begun by the Irma (q. v.) on the lower San Juan River up as far as the Machuca. The Norma was owned by the canal company then operating.

NORMAL DE ESTELI, LA. This center for teacher education was established under cooperative work of the Ministry of Education and the Servicio Cooperativo Interamericano de Educación Pública, and was opened in October, 1956. Under the original direction of Doctor Raul Quintanilla, the studies are developed along modern educational patterns, adapted to Nicaraguan conditions. There is a staff of 23 and there are around 400 students served; about 60% are young women.

NORRIS, GEORGE W. U.S. Senator in strong opposition to
   the Nicaraguan intervention of 1926-1927. He stated
   that it was a "blot on the national honor ... [;] shocking
   to every peace-loving citizen in civilization. " With
   Senator Borah of Idaho, he led a vigorous opposition in
   Congress, aided by strong press opposition. The parallels to U.S. involvement in Viet Nam in the 1950's to
   1970's are obvious. U.S. intervention in Nicaragua
   lasted from 1911-1933.

NORTHERN LIGHT (Ship). This merchant vessel was involved in the 1854 disturbances in Greytown. (See
   BORLAND and CYANE.)

NOTICIA, LA. A Managua newspaper of the late 1920's era--
   it reported much of the activity as U.S. intervention
   built up again in 1926.

NOTICIERO, EL. One of the group of periodicals of a romantic nature developed in Boaco following 1915.

NOTICIOSO, EL. Periodical published in León, 1847.

NOVARRO, CHRISTOBAL. Friar who accompanied José
   Codina (q.v.) on a 1789 mission to Mosquita.

NOVEDADES. The News, a daily paper published in Managua, and the traditional government-oriented organ of
   the Somoza regimes. Strongly pro-administration and
   hence an organ also of the Liberal party. (See PARTIDO
   LIBERAL NACIONALISTA.)

NOVENA. A ceremony and prayers offered at the time of a
   death, usually on the first night following the death, and
   attended by friends and relatives. Refreshments are
   prepared for the mourners, and frequently the gathering
   is a social one involving family members who see each
   other at infrequent intervals. In Nicaragua this serves
   as a special bond of family friendship.

NOVIOS, LOS. A district of the municipio of Tipitapa, department of Managua.

NUBES, LAS. 1) A district in the municipio and department
   of Matagalpa.
      2) A height (cerro) of the Datanli spur of the Darién
   mountains in Jinotega department.

NUESTRA SEÑORA DE LAS DOLORES DE YOSICA. A pueblo founded in 1732, since disappeared, in the present area of Matagalpa department. The founder was don Juan Santos, and the founding documents are to be found in the General Archives of Guatemala.

NUESTRA SEÑORA DEL PILAR DE LOS CHONTALES. Cattle ranch in Chontales granted in 1736 to Captain Don Juan Alvarez, surveyed by ensign don Alonso Aldana de Meneses; size--eight caballerías, or 267 acres.

NUESTRA SEÑORA DEL ROSARIO. An early hacienda grant of 1714 to Andrés Jarquín, in the area of Rivas, of 12 cabellerías, or 335 acres.

NUEVA JAEN. Among the "new" cities of Nicaragua named for Spanish cities, this one has entirely disappeared. (Only Granada is in its original site, since 1523. León, established in 1523, moved to its present site in 1610. Nueva Segovia (Ocotal) is in its third location.) Nueva Jaén was just north of the headwaters of the Río San Juan as it left Lake Nicaragua, but there seems to be no trace of the establishment left.

NUEVA REDUCCION DE OCOTAL. The 1767 name given to the Nueva Reducción de Segovia, finally confirmed as a city in 1791. (See OCOTAL, def. 1.)

NUEVA SEGOVIA. 1) This northern department of Nicaragua takes its name from the magnificent city northwest of Madrid--the haunt of El Cid. At least three sites in Nicaragua were chosen for "New Segovia," but pirates of the early colonial centuries drove the inhabitants farther and farther west. The present site of New Segovia was founded soon after the founding of León and Granada in 1524. This department is in the section of Nicaragua known as "El Setentrión," which it shares with Matagalpa and Jinotega. The present departmental population is about 46,000. It was originally a rich mining region. It is also one of the major haunts of the legendary Sandino. The department is bounded on the north and west by Honduras, on the southeast and east by Jinotega department, and on part of the south by Madriz department.
    2) República de Nueva Segovia, formed by Agusto Sandino on June 18, 1927, this short-lived political entity of the Sandinista guerrillas was one of the sev-

eral moves toward autonomy taken under Sandino's direction.   Francisco Estrada was named the political
leader, or "jefe político. "   The town of El Jicaro was
renamed Ciudad Sandino as the capital.   Sandino also
coined money.

NUEVAS HORIZONTES.   A periodical of a cultural emphasis
by Paul Steiner and María Teresa Sánchez.   The New
Horizons is devoted to intellectual and literary ends.

NUEVO PACTO.   The "new pact" or agreement was a state-
ment in the first article of the "Federation of Central
America" of April 30, 1838.   The pact was one of
"true federalism. "   In December of that year the Estado
Libre de Nicaragua was divided into four departments--
Oriental, Occidental, Setentrión, and Mediodía.

NUÑEZ.   A quinta in the environs of Masaya.

-O-

O. A. S.   see   ORGANIZATION OF AMERICAN STATES

OBLATE SISTERS OF DIVINE LOVE.   Catholic Women's
order serving in Nicaragua, with emphasis on orphans,
the sick, and education.

OBRAJE, EL.   An early hacienda grant in the Rivas area
to don Francisco de Ugarte, of 50 cabellerías (1, 400
acres).

OBREGON.   A district just to the north of the city of Granada, near the airfield.

OBREROS.   Laborers, working-class people.   (See SE-
GUNDOS.)

OBSERVADOR, EL.   A Catholic weekly periodical presently
published in Managua.

OCALCA.   1) A district in the municipio and department of
Matagalpa.
2) A flowing spring in the municipio of San Ramón,
Matagalpa department.
3) A mountain height in the municipio of Matagalpa.

OCATULU.   Waterfall on the Río Bocay just above its mouth.

OCCIDENTE.   One of the four departments created by the first constituent assembly of the free state of Nicaragua by the law of December 21, 1838--formed by the districts of León and Chinandega.

OCELOTL.   A festive day marking a month of the Nicarao calendar (derived from Mexico).   Note that as the meaning is "tiger," the little spotted tiger-cat of Middle America, the ocelot, gets its name from this word.

OCHOMBA.   Pueblo or town existing in the Valley of Nicaragua, Rivas area, during the 16th and 17th centuries.

OCHOMOGO, RIO.   A stream flowing from heights of Carazo department north into Lake Nicaragua.

OCONWAS-ROSITA.   This mining district in the Oconwas Valley near La Luz is a prospect area as yet undeveloped. (See   LA LUZ.)

OCOTAL, EL.   Comarca or district in the municipio of El Sauce, León department.

OCOTAL.   1) Cabacera of Nueva Segovia department, Ciudad Ocotal has a population of 4,300.   Formed in 1759, by citizens emigrating from the earlier locations of Nueva Segovia to the eastward.   The first name of the town was Nueva Reducción de Segovia (q.v.) and finally it reached the status of a city in 1791, with the name Nueva Reducción de Ocotal (q.v.).   In 1810 the first municipal government was organized, and it thus became the valid successor to the ancient locations of Nueva Segovia.   At an altitude of 3,050 feet, Ocotal on its cool plateau, has as a principal activity the raising of cattle.   In 1927, the Battle of Ocotal (next entry) opened new chapters in warfare because of the dive-bombing attack.
    2) The principal municipio in the department of Nueva Segovia; population, 6,900.   On the Río Coco, but above the easily navigable section, Ocotal is just across the southern departmental line from Madriz department.   The name is from Nahuatl ocote ("pines") and tlan ("place")-- hence, a place of pines, which is accurately descriptive. The natural setting of the surrounding hills is attractive.

OCOTAL, BATTLE OF.   At 1:00 a.m., on July 16, 1927,

Agusto Sandino's rebel force of about 300 "Sandinistas" attacked defending U.S. Marine Captain G. D. Hatfield and his force of 38 Marines and 49 Nicaraguan National Guardsmen, who were ensconced in buildings about the central plaza of Ocotal. Three furious attacks were mounted before 8:00 a.m. Demands to surrender were rejected by Hatfield, who said, "Marines never surrender." Two Marine planes appeared on patrol, one that landed briefly escaping under fire. Five Marine dive bombers then attacked, and after 30 minutes of bombardment, the attackers raised the siege. This battle has military significance far beyond the theatre or the force employed as an early example of successful tactical air support, and an early application of the dive-bombing technique. It has been stated that this Ocotal engagement represents the very first use of dive bombers in warfare. In any event, it is the first time that the relief of a beleaguered town was accomplished by air power.

OCOTAL DE LA CANTERA. A height of the Guasguali spur of the Darién Range of mountains in Jinotega department.

OCOTE, EL. District in the municipio of San Dionisio, Matagalpa department.

OCOTILLO. 1) Comarca or district of the municipio of Santa Rosa, León.
2) El Ocotillo, a district of Terrabona municipio, Matagalpa department.

O. D. E. C. A. see ORGANIZACION DE LOS ESTADOS CEN-TRO AMERICANOS

OERSTAD, ANDREAS. Doctor Oerstad was a Danish engineer who surveyed a canal route through Nicaragua, a route which was to leave Lake Nicaragua at the mouth of the Río Sapoa and go from there to the Bay of Salinas on the Pacific, a plan quite different from those having San Juan del Sur or Brito as termini. It was his survey which influenced Louis Napoleon Bonaparte.

OFIR. Coffee hacienda in the municipio of Jinotepe, Carazo department.

OGDEN. A shallow-draft paddle steamer on the San Juan River and Lake Nicaragua in the 1850's regarding which only the name has survived.

OHORAN, IRENA. Nicknamed "La Niña, " this dimunitive
    lady of Granada was a friend, confidant, and legitimist
    ally of filibuster William Walker (q. v.) when he first
    arrived in that conservative capital. There was gossip
    about them, though it is hard to know how deep their
    relationship became. Her name appeared in later writ-
    ings about Walker as a sort of mystery woman named
    "nila Mairena. " Irene was able to introduce Walker to
    the techniques of political warfare in the Central Ameri-
    can manner. Granada was a city of aristocratic heritage,
    and like the addition of the aristocratic Marina to Cortez'
    cortege in Mexico, the friendship and "know-how" of
    Doña Irene must have been of great help to the outward-
    ly staid, strait-laced, and repressed Walker.

O'HORAN, JOSE GABRIEL see MASAYA, PUEBLO CO-
    LONIAL

OJOCHAL. 1) Comarca or district in the municipio of Jino-
    tepe, Carazo department.
        2) Comarca or district in the municipio of Télica,
    León.
        3) A mountain height in the municipio of Ciudad Darío,
    Matagalpa department.

OJOCHE DE AGUA ABAJO. Comarca or district in the mu-
    nicipio of San Marcos, Carazo department.

OJOCHE DE AGUA ARRIBA. 1) Comarca or district in the
    municipio of Diriamba, department of Carazo.
        2) Comarca or district in the municipio of San Marcos,
    Carazo department.

OJO DE AGUA. A district of the municipio of Santo Tomás,
    Chinandega department.

OJO DEL PUEBLO, EL. The "Eye of the People, " a peri-
    odical published in Granada, 1843-1844.

OJOS DE AGUA. Stream in the municipio of El Sauce, León
    department.

OLAMA. A district in the municipio of Muy Muy, Matagalpa
    department.

OLAMA, RIO. A river in the Muy Muy municipio of Mata-
    galpa department. The famous "Farallones" (q. v.) are
    on this stream.

OLDMAN, CHIEF. A chief of the Mosquitoes whose son had been taken to England, and who was later crowned and commissioned as King Oldman (see next entry) of Mosquitia by Charles II (purportedly). The settlers had arranged this in 1685 to effect their control over the land.

OLDMAN, KING. Son of the old Mosquito chief who was "crowned" (with an old cocked hat) by English freebooter settlers on the coast, and who presumably turned over sovereignty of his nation to Charles II (1680's).

OLID, CHRISTOVAL. Sent by Hernán Cortez in 1524 from Mexico to oust Gil Gonzáles Dávila following the latter's discovery of the "Sweet Sea" (Lake Nicaragua), Olid was charged to take over for Cortez the whole isthmian area as far south as Panama, to be annexed to Cortez' Mexican possessions, now assuming almost the character of an empire. Olid met Hernando do Soto, who had been sent from Córdoba's (q. v.) mistaken landing on the Honduran Coast to go south and secure the big lake for Córdoba, preventing Gil Gonzáles Dávila's party from pushing on south. A great confusion reigned, with the result that each of the three men schemed to shake off control of his master and grab a part of the land and riches for himself. Cortez lost faith in Olid, and finally set out himself to straighten things out, and personally to become Master of the Sweet Sea. Thus, it was Lake Nicaragua as a prize that stimulated Cortez' epic march to northern Honduras. Olid died having been disposed of by Dávila and Cortez' Lieutenant Francisco de las Casas.

OLIN. A word simply meaning "movement, " one of the month festivals as observed by the Nicarao tribe preconquest.

OLLANCA. 1) A district in the municipio of La Trinidad, department of Estelí.
2) A mountain in La Trinidad municipio, Estelí department--3, 300 feet altitude.

OLOCCI. Properties owned by don Felipe Moreno, granted to him in 1709 in Estelí department. An aboriginal Indian name.

OLOMEGA. An ancient cacicazgo or chieftaincy cited by Fray Alonso Ponce in A. D. 1575, long since disappeared. Possibly near the present El Viejo, since it seemed the population transferred to that location.

OMEYATEITE. Father of the rain or water god of the tribe
of Nicaraos in southern Nicaragua at the time of the conquest. (See also QUIATEOT.) It is also interesting to
compare this word with the early British name for the
most famous island in French Oceania, Otaheite.

OMEYOCIHUATL. Mother of the water god in the Nicarao
pantheon.

OMEYOTECUHTLI see OMEYATEITE

OMOTEPE. 1) Island in Lake Nicaragua, located in the department of Rivas. Approximately 19 miles long and
ten wide, the island is the largest in Nicaraguan territory, and is distinguished by the two volcanoes, one active and one inactive, Concepción (see def. 3, this entry) and Maderas. A number of small communities on
the island include the largest, Moyogalpa; the next, Alta
Gracia, as well as San Marcos, Los Angeles, San José
del Sur, Mérida, and others. The island was a seat of
the Toltecan--Aztec culture which was a strong influence
in Nicaragua during the century just preceding the Spanish conquest. (See drawing.)
2) A shallow-draft paddle steamer which operated on
the lower San Juan River and which in the early 1900's
was used by General Estrada for a revolutionary sortie
from Bluefields.
3) Volcán Omotepe, at an altitude of 5, 282 feet,
while shown on air charts as "Omotepe, " is better
known as Vol Concepción. Located on Omotepe Island
in Lake Nicaragua, it is an active volcano which has
had an eruption period of as short as 20 minutes. In
1956 the eruptions of Concepción at that frequency
reached 12, 000 to 15, 000 feet above the cone. There
has been no major lava outflow in recent times--the
island on which it is located has at the very base of
the mountain, a considerable population in several small
towns. A twin cone on the island is Madera, which has
been inactive in recent times. The 11th highest mountain in Nicaragua, Omotepe is a classic cinder cone,
similar to Momotombo. It is in the department of Rivas.

ONDA DE LA ALEGRIA, LA   see ALMA NICA

ONDAS DE LUZ. A Managua radio station under the auspices
of the Nicaragua Cultural Association, call letters YNOL,
power 15, 000 watts (one of the three most powerful in the
country) and frequency 825 kilocycles.

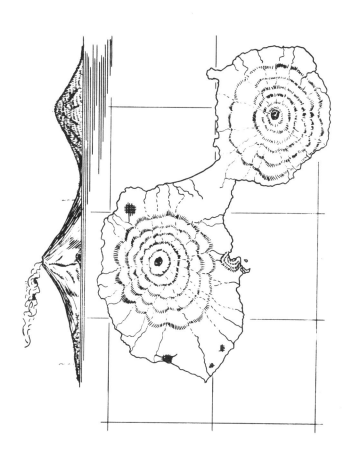

Omotepe Island

Plan and profile showing active Concepción Volcanco and inactive Madera.

ONDAS DEL SUR. A radio station in Jinotepe, call letters YNGF, power 250 watts, frequency 1360 kilocycles.

ONDAS POPULARES. Also known as Radio Phillips, this radio station has call letters YNMS, power of 500 watts, and frequency of 540 kilocycles.

ONDAS SEGOVIAS. A radio station in Estelf, call letters YNBC, power 1000 watts, frequency 1150 kilocycles.

ONDAS SONORAS. A Managua radio station, call letters YNDM, 500 watts power, 1340 kilocycles frequency.

ORCAL, EL. Coffee hacienda in the municipio of San Marcos, Carazo department.

ORCHILOBOS see HUITZILOPICHTLI

OREGANO, EL. A district in the municipio of Santa Lucfa, department of Boaco.

ORGANISMOS ASESORES. Advisory agencies in Nicaraguan foreign affairs, in the areas of economy, finance, and public credit.

ORGANIZACION DE LOS ESTADOS CENTRO AMERICANOS. Since 1955, the five small states of Central America (q. v.) have been united in this organization, which is a voluntary grouping of sovereign states rather than a federation, the last of such affecting Central America being the Provincias Unidas del Centro de América (q. v.) in 1823-1838.

ORGANIZATION OF AMERICAN STATES. Nicaragua is an active member of the OAS, which is the world's oldest international organization. It has united the 21 western hemisphere republics in a community of nations dedicated to peace, security, and prosperity for all citizens. The idea was first conceived by the South American liberator, Simón Bolívar, in 1826, but the present agreement originated on April 14, 1890, when the International Union of American Republics became a reality. Then, in 1948, a charter was adopted giving the OAS its present name with the Pan American Union as its permanent secretariat. Objectives of the OAS are carried out by the Inter-American Conference, meetings of consultation by Foreign Ministers, the Council of the OAS, the Pan

American Union, and various specialized organizations and conferences. Peace and security, common action against aggression, solution by discussion of political, juridical, and economic problems, and the promotion of social, economic, and cultural development of member nations, are among the major purposes. International law, good faith, and American agreement, as well as social justice, economic cooperation, individual rights, and spiritual unity are among the principles. There are many specialized sub-organizations of OAS. Some are: IACI, The Interamerican Children's Institute; IACW, The Interamerican Commission of Women; IA-ECOSOC, The Interamerican Economic and Social Council; IACHR, The Interamerican Commission on Human Rights; IADB, The Interamerican Defense Board; SCCS, The Special Consultative Committee on Security; IAPA, The Interamerican Peace Committee; PAIGH, The Pan-American Institute of Geography and History; PAHO, The Pan-American Health Organization; IAIAS, The Interamerican Institute of Agricultural Sciences; IAII, The Interamerican Indian Institute. The OAS has successfully handled a number of international conflicts (such as the El Salvador-Honduras War of 1969).

ORGANIZED WORKERS OF NICARAGUA. A labor organization in opposition to the Communist Party (q. v.) influenced Worker's Confederation, sponsored by the P. L. N.

ORIENTACION POPULAR. A weekly periodical published with small circulation relative to the dailies. It is considered by the government to be an illegal pro-Communist newspaper.

ORIENTE. One of the four departments created by the first constituent assembly of the free state of Nicaragua by the law of December 21, 1838--formed by the districts of Granada, Masaya and Jinotepe.

ORILLA, LA. A hacienda north of Nandaime.

ORINOCO. A Carib village on the western shore of Pearl Lagoon, also spelled Orinooco.

O. R. I. T. see ORGANIZACION REGIONAL INTERAMERICANA DE TRABAJO

ORO (River) see COCO, RIO

OROPENDOLA. 1) Mountain in the municipio of Santo Tomás, Chontales.

2) La Oropendola, a comarca or district of the municipio of Santo Tomás in Chontales department.

OROSI. A district in the municipio of Cárdenas, department of Rivas. (Also the name of a famous inactive volcano nearby in Costa Rica, part of the basic Central American cordillera.)

OROZCO, JUAN DE DIOS. A senator who took over power as director of Nicaragua following Buitrago in 1843. He was soon followed by Pérez.

ORTELIUS. In Ortelius' Theatrum of 1587, is a printed map which shows in distorted but clear fashion Lake Nicaragua and the Gulf of Fonseca, as well as a fair representation of the general shape of both coasts.

ORTEZ, MIGUEL ANGEL. Sandinista general who in May, 1931, commanded a crack guerrilla outfit of over 100 men. Many were Hondurans. This force attacked the National Guard barracks at Palacaguina on the night of May 14-15. There was quite a battle. Ortez was killed in the encounter. He was considered by his enemies as one of Sandino's best officers, valiant and disciplined. As a guerrilla, he was less successful than illiterates like Pedrón, who would not expose themselves, and hence lived to "fight another day. " This self-preservation has become classic in guerrilla tactics.

ORUS. A stern-wheel shallow-draft river steamer, also known as the Oras, and which was possible named at one time the Nicaragua. This vessel was the first one to enter the Taura mouth of the San Juan River (now the Barro Colorado) and was also the first one wrecked on that river, in the early 1850's. In 1860 a British observer, Captain Pim, noted that the wreck of the steamer covered with vegetation, helped to obstruct the Machuca Rapids as a permanent island. The Orus had a colorful history prior to her death in Nicaragua, for she was originally the first gold-rush steamer on the Chagres River of Panama, having paddled down from New Orleans in 1849 laden with gold-seekers. In this way she pioneered both the major routes to the California gold-rush. (See illustration.)

314

Paddle-Steamers

As used on Nicaraguan rivers, especially the San Juan, 1850-
1910.

OSORIO, DON DIEGO ALVAREZ DE. Actual first Bishop of
Nicaragua, 1532, following Zúniga who died before leaving Spain.

OSORNO, DON FERMIN see OSORNO, LUIS

OSORNO, DON LUIS. One of the brothers established in
Masaya in 1800 as Spanish colonials, whose descendants
are there to this day.

OSTIONAL, EL. District in the municipio of San Juan del
Sur, Rivas department.

OSTIONAL, RIO EL. A stream entering the Pacific San
Juan del Sur municipio, department of Rivas.

OVIEDO Y VALDEZ, FRANCISCO GONZALO FERNANDEZ,
1478-1557. Historian of the Spanish New World, author
of the Historia general y natural de las Indias, Oviedo
records the discovery of Nicaragua, and many events
contributing and subsequent thereto. He is a substantial
and contemporary chronicler and authority, and a base
of information for both pre- and post-conquest data on
indigenous inhabitants as well as their customs, numbers,
etc.

OYATE, RIO. A river flowing into Lake Nicaragua from the
north, which is the boundary line between Chontales and
Río San Juan departments.

OZOMATL. A month festival day, and god, of the pre-conquest Nicaraos, in the region of Rivas. Meaning:
"monkey. "

-P-

PACAYA. 1) A cattle hacienda in the municipio of Ciudad
Darío, Matagalpa department.
2) Comarca or district in the municipio of San Marcos,
Carazo department.
3) A district of the municipio of La Concepción, department of Masaya.
4) A district in the municipio of La Trinidad, department of Estelí.

PACHECO, FRANCISCO. In 1527, following Captains Campañón and Huitado by one and two years respectively, Captain Pacheco instituted a search for further gold mines in the province of Chorutega. The "Segovias" were a principal early source of gold.

PACIENTE. Comarca or district in the municipio of Quezalguaque, León.

PAC LI. Also written "Pacli, " a grant in Estelí department of aboriginal Indian lands given to Eusebio Ortiz in 1872.

PACK-OXEN. Still useful in remote places where the oxen can plod through mud which will stop horses. Pack-oxen used to meet scheduled aircraft to transfer loads at Siuna in Northeast Nicaragua.

PACT OF CHINANDEGA. An instrument of international unity signed by Nicaragua, Guatemala, El Salvador, and Honduras in 1842. This was to establish the "Confederación de Centroamérica. " A reaction against the "George Washington of Central America, " Francisco Morazán, it ceased to be in effect in 1845. The original agreement resulted from the move of Superintendent Macdonald of Belize in action at San Juan de Nicaragua (del Norte). (See CENTRAL AMERICAN CONFEDERATION.)

PADILLA, FRANCISCO DE see TELEGRAFO, EL

PADUCAH. A dispatch and intelligence vessel used by the U. S. on the Caribbean Coast of Nicaragua during the events of 1909-1912 which led to the long U. S. involvement (1912-1933).

PAHO see ORGANIZATION OF AMERICAN STATES

PAIGH see ORGANIZATION OF AMERICAN STATES

PAIQUA. A district in the municipio of Matiguás, Matagalpa department.

PAISAGUA. A district in the municipio of Matiguás, Matagalpa department.

PAJARITO, EL. Comarca or district in the municipio of Achuapa, León.

PAJARO, EL. A district in the municipio and department of Matagalpa.

PALABRA, LA. One of the dozen or more periodicals developed from 1915 to 1937 in Boaco.

PALACAGUINA. A small town in Madriz department, five miles east of Yaltagüina.

PALACIO, EL. Coffee hacienda in the Jinotega municipio, founded by General Ignacio Chávez of León.

PALACIO DEL DISTRITO NACIONAL DE MANAGUA. A Greek revival structure of severe and classic Doric lines which was constructed in 1927 to house the administration of the National District.

PALANCAS, LAS. Comarca or district in the municipio of Larreynaga, León.

PALCILA. A district in the municipio and department of Matagalpa.

PALENQUE. 1) A district in the municipio and department of Masaya.
2) El Palenque, a district in the municipio of San Jorge, Rivas department.

PALERMO. 1) Cattle ranch in the municipio of San Juan del Sur, Rivas department.
2) Sugar cane plantation in the municipio of León, León department.

PALESTINA. 1) Coffee hacienda in the Jinotega department.
2) Coffee hacienda in the municipio of La Concepción, department of Masaya.

PALMA, LA. 1) Comarca or district in the municipio of La Paz, León.
2) District in the municipio of Altagracia on Omotepe Island in Lake Nicaragua, department of Rivas.

PALMAR. 1) Mountain in the municipio of Santo Tomás, Chontales.
2) El Palmar, a comarca or district in the municipio of Santo Tomás, Chontales.
3) El Palmar, a district in the municipio of San Juan de Limay in the department of Estelí.

PALMARCI. A district of the municipio of San Juan de Tola, Rivas department.

PALMERA, LA. Coffee hacienda of Dr. José Ignacio Gonzáles in Diriamba municipio, Carazo department.

PALMIRA. 1) A cattle ranch in the municipio of Esquipulas,
Matagalpa department.
2) Coffee hacienda in the municipio of Yalí, Jinotega
department.

PALO, EL JUEGO DEL. A game of skill whereby aboriginal
inhabitants of the Managua area would turn a log on their
feet, while shoulders were on the ground. Great speed
and agility were necessary.

PALO BLANCO. A district of the municipio of San Pedro,
Chinandega department.

PALOS NEGROS. District in the municipio and department
of Rivas.

PALO SOLO. Also called Palo Seco, a district of the municipio of La Concepción, department of Masaya.

PALSILA. A mountain height in the municipio of Matagalpa.

PANAL. 1) Comarca or district in the municipio of Télica,
León.
2) El Panal, a district of the municipio of San Pedro,
Chinandega department.

PANALAYA. One of four river steamers belonging to the
transit company on San Juan River in 1858. Drawing
three feet of water, she carried 400 passengers and 20
tons of cargo.

PANALES, LOS. Comarca or district in the municipio of
El Sauce, León department.

PANAMA. 1) Comarca or district in the municipio of Jinotepe, Carazo department.
2) A district of the municipio of San Juan de Tola,
Rivas department.
3) A district of the municipio of Tipitapa, department
of Managua.
4) El Panamá, a comarca or district in the municipio
of El Rosario, Carazo department.

PANAMA CONFERENCE. An 1826 meeting called by the

South American liberator, Simón Bolívar, who saw the
desirability of Pan-Americanism, and who hoped to bring
the Western Hemisphere nations into an accord against
external (European) attack, as well as to promote joint
action. A practical failure, the Conference had representation from only a few nations, and even among those,
national pride and attendant jealousies precluded agreement or any persisting joint action. Almost a century
passed before relatively stable and effective Pan-Americanism became a reality, with such approaches as the
Pan American Union and the Organization of American
States.

PANCAZAN. A district of the municipio of San Ramón,
Matagalpa department.

PANGA. (Variant spelling, "bongo.") A boat used in Central America and Panama, being a dugout, but not a
"canoe" in form. Cut from large logs of "cedro real"
(royal cedar), mahogany, guanacaste or similar wood,
these boats were relatively large, wide-beamed in relation to their length, stocky, planned for several oars-
men or paddlers, often equipped with a "chopa" or shelter aft, and covered with boards, thatch, or hides.
There were benches for rowers or "marineros." A narrow deck astern of the "chopa" is the pineta, a place
for the steersman-captain. Modern "pangas" on Lake
Nicaragua in general do not have the shelter. Panama
used these during California gold rush days, and there
they were called "bongos." The pangas were sometimes
equipped with masts and sails. Some were all-dugout,
others partly built, and could carry as much as eight to
ten tons. A round trip from Granada to San Juan del
Norte (170 miles each way) took about 20 to 30 days in
the mid-1800's. The panga is often flat-bottomed and
sometimes has a wineglass-shaped transom stern. (See
drawing.)

PANGIL. A Carib chieftain noted for his gross obesity,
who sacked Camoapa in 1767, and who was captured
and delivered in chains to Governor Cabello in León,
by "Captain" Carlos Antonio Larrince (himself a considerable scourge of the Spanish in colonial times).

PANORAMA, EL. Coffee hacienda in the Sierras de Managua,
National District.

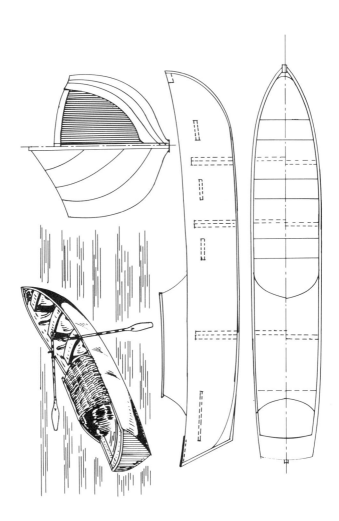

Panga

Used on lakes and rivers, frequently with a shelter aft.

PANSACO. 1) District in the municipio of Potosí, Rivas department.
2) A district of the municipio of San Juan de Tola, Rivas, department.

PANTASMA, LAGUNA DE. Small lake in the valley of the Río Pantasma, Jinotega department.

PANTASMA, NUESTRA SEÑORA DE LA ASUNCION DE. An ancient townsite established by Fray Pedro Lagares in 1678, in the Pantasma Valley, possibly near its mouth. The town has entirely disappeared. The nearest point is probably the present La Vigía airfield, across the Coco from the Pantasma mouth.

PANTASMA, RIO. The Río Pantasma flows into the Río Coco near La Vigía, just where the Coco turns north past the Kilambé massif to the east. (Pantasma has sometimes been mistakenly used as a name for the whole system including Río Coco.)

PANTASMA, VALLE DE. A valley of the Jinotega department, 1, 000 feet above sea level, on the east side of the Río Coco and between the Pantasma and Gusaneres tributaries. In this valley were established the missionary towns Asunción de Pantasma, San Francisco Nanaica, and San José Paraka, all by now having disappeared. There are old Spanish mines reported in the area, but not confirmed.

PANTASMAS. Sub-tribal group of the "Quiribies, " or Chontales, identified by Fray Francisco Vasques in 1691.

PAPAGAYO. When in winter months cold polar air occasionally pours into Central America, the results are termed papagayo, "parrot storms. "

PAPALONAL, EL. 1) Cattle ranch in the municipio of León, León department. Departure point (horseback) for climbing Nicaragua's famous and formidable volcano "Momotombo. "
2) Comarca or district in the municipio of La Paz, León.
3) Large hacienda holding to the north of the volcano Momotombo in municipio of La Paz, León. About 18, 000 acres.

PAPEL SALLADO. While not unique to Nicaragua, the policy of selling "sealed paper" to record transactions such as sales, is a simple form of taxing widely practiced in Latin America. For example, a "papel sellado" for the sale of a horse costs 50 centavos (about 7. 5 cents U. S.) plus an extra tax stamp of 10 centavos. In round numbers, the tax on the transaction would be a U. S. dime.

PAPERONES. Nickname of a Nicaragua political party in opposition to Crestones (q. v.). Supporters of Dr. Roberto Sacasa, 1887-1893.

P. A. R. see PARTIDO ACCION REVOLUCIONARIA

PARAISO, EL. 1) A cattle ranch in the municipio of Nindirí, Masaya department.
2) Coffee hacienda of Dr. Buenaventura Rappaecioli in Diriamba municipio, Carazo department.
3) Coffee hacienda in the municipio of La Concepción, department of Masaya.
4) Sugar cane plantation in the municipio of León, León department.

PARAJON, FRANCISCO. General of Nicaraguan Liberal Forces in 1926-1927, who led forces in the bloody battle of Chinandega in January, 1927.

PARDO, CAPTAIN FRANCISCO MELENDEZ. Captain Meléndez went with Fray Pedro Lagares to the Segovias in 1674 to interpret and to help in the uplift and Christianization of the tribes of the Pantasma area.

PARTIDO ACCION REVOLUCIONARIA. A successor party to the Partido Renovación Nacional (q. v.) which arose in 1963, but was disbanded after the elections of that year to be reactivated in 1966 for the 1967 elections. It supported the Unión Nacional Opositora (q. v.) candidate.

PARTIDO CONSERVADOR DE NICARAGUA (P. C. N.). One of the two legal and recognized political parties in Nicaragua. In general, the conservatives have been on the outside as far as presidential elections are concerned for nearly four decades. Principal conservative family name is Chamorro--also, Arellanas, Cuadras, Solórzanos, and others.

PARTIDO DE ESTELI. . Title of the province or district of Estelí as declared by the Captaincy General in Guate- mala in 1788, adding "its districts and haciendas. " When the sub-delegation of Nueva Segovia was created in 1795, Estelí, Condega, and Pueblo Nuevo were in- cluded. This attachment lasted until independence in 1821, confirmed finally on July 1, 1823.

PARTIDO LIBERAL INDEPENDIENTE (P. L. I.). One of several minority parties which have little force politi- cally in elections where the two legally recognized par- ties (P. C. N. and P. L. N.) are the prime contenders. These minority parties are to an extent clandestine.

PARTIDO LIBERAL NACIONALISTA (P. L. N.). One of the two legal and recognized political parties in Nicaragua. Further, this is the party of incumbency under the Somozas, many Sacasas, Lacayos, and others.

PARTIDO RENOVACION NACIONAL. A non-Communist po- litical party of opposition to the P. L. N. which was formed in 1953, but was disbanded in 1962. It was succeeded in function by the Partido Acción Revolucion- aria (q. v.).

PARTIDO SOCIAL CRISTIANO (P. S. C.). This party, simi- lar to Christian and Social Democratic parties in some European countries, is a minority group carrying little weight in the elections which are dominated by the two legal political parties, especially the one in power (P. L. N.).

PARTIDO SOCIALISTA NICARAGUENSE (P. S. N.). One of the minority party groups, this socialist party is of a leftist nature, but not extreme.

PARTIDO UNIONISTA. Formed in 1904, this "Union Party" gained support and adherents in all five of the Central American countries, reviving the old Morazanista ideas and ideals. In essence this movement developed from the 1898 failure of union and helped to shape leaders in all the countries. President Zelaya of Nicaragua again sought unionism in 1902.

PARTIDO UNIONISTA CENTROAMERICANO. A new party of union for the five countries, set up as a party of revolution to make a fundamental change in the social, political, and economic structure, not alone to simply change the ruling oligarchies. It was founded by Diriamba native Dr. Salvador Mendieta.

PARTIDOS DE NICARAGUA. The term partido in this sense is used as it is in Spain, as one of the districts of a province. On April 8, 1826, Nicaragua was divided into nine such districts, when Nicaragua was one of the five states of the Federación de las Provincias Unidas del Centro de América. These were: Nicaragua (Rivas today), Granada, Managua, Matagalpa, Masaya, Segovia, León, Subtiava, El Realejo.

PARTNERSHIPS see SOCIEDAD EN NOMBRE COLECTIVO and SOCIEDAD EN COMANDITA ...

PARUNDO, CAYO. A small island in the northern end of Pearl Lagoon.

PASLE. A cattle hacienda in the municipio of Ciudad Darío, department of Matagalpa.

PASLE, RIO. A small stream in the municipio of Ciudad Darío, Matagalpa department; tributary to the Río Grande de Matagalpa.

PASO BONITO. Comarca or district in the municipio of Télica, León.

PASO DE CENIZAS. Comarca or district in the municipio of Diriamba, department of Carazo.

PASO DE LAS LAJAS. Comarca or district in the municipio of Télica, León.

PASO DE PIEDRAS. District in the municipio of Potosí, Rivas department.

PASO DEL MANGO see PASO DEL MENGUE

PASO DEL MENGUE. District in the municipio of San Jorge, Rivas department (also called "del Mango").

PASO HONDO. 1) A cattle ranch in the municipio of Esquipulas, Matagalpa department.
2) A district of the municipio of Santo Tomás, Chinandega department.

3) Sugar cane plantation in the municipio of León, León department.

PASO REAL. 1) A district of the municipio of Jinotega.
2) A district in the municipio of Matiguás, Matagalpa department.

PASO REAL DE OCHOMOGO. A district in the municipio of Velén, Rivas department.

PASO REAL DE SAN FRANCISCO. Comarca or district in the municipio of Diriamba, department of Carazo.

PASTOR, EL. Comarca or district in the municipio of Jinotepe, Carazo department.

PASTOREO, EL. A district in the municipio and department of Estelí.

PASTRANA, DIEGO DE. An encomendero of the Managua area, mid-sixteenth century.

PATASTE. The seventh highest mountain in Nicaragua, 5,676 feet in altitude. It is in Estelí department about twelve miles south of Somoto.

PATASTULE. A district in the municipio of Matiguás, Matagalpa department.

PATOS REALES. A large duck, of a localized species.

PATRIOTIC YOUTH. A student political organization thought to be under Communist influence.

PAVAS, LAS. 1) Comarca, valley or district in the municipio of Acoyapa, Chontales.
2) Comarca, or district in the municipio of Villa Somoza, Chontales.
3) A district in the municipio of Muy Muy, Matagalpa department.
4) Mountain in the municipio of Acoyapa, Chontales.

PAVON, EL. Cattle ranch in the municipio of El Sauce, León department.

PAVONA, LA. District in the municipio of Yalí in Jinotega department.

PAVONA ABAJO. A district of the municipio of Jinotega.

PAVONA ARRIBA. A district of the municipio of Jinotega.

PAYACUCA. A district of Terrabona municipio, Matagalpa department.

PAZ, LA. 1) Coffee hacienda in the municipio of San Rafael del Norte in Jinotega department.
2) Municipio in the department of Carazo, smallest of all with a bit over two square miles in the northeastern corner of the department, bordered by Masaya to the north, Santa Teresa to the south, Granada to the east, and El Rosario to the west. There are four districts, 1, 800 population.
3) Also called La Paz Central or La Paz Centro, this is a municipio of León department, originally "La Paz Vieja" with the name San Nicolás de Naborios. Largest in the department, the area is 336 square miles, with 13, 500 population (third in population). Bounded on the north by Larreynaga and El Jicaral; on the south by Nagarote; on the east by Lake Managua and the municipios of Mateare and San Francisco de Carnicero or Managua; and on the west by León and Larreynaga municipios. There are three short but significant rivers--El Tamarindo, El Sinecapa, and Las Lajitas. There is a Lake Momotombo in the volcano of the same name and Lake Tigre at the foot of the Asososca Volcano. The most famous volcano in Nicaragua, Momotombo--Victor Hugo's "bald, nude colossus"--is in this department; also El Hoyo and Asososca. Principal activity is agriculture, especially cotton and cattle. It is a prime cotton-raising area, on large holdings. The making of ceramics and tile is also a principal industry; the soft pink tiles (roof and floor) and the equivalent bricks of La Paz Centro being both charming and prevalent throughout the Pacific coastal area of the country.
4) A pueblo (Villa de la Paz), the cabacera of La Paz municipio in León department was, according to tradition, founded when adjacent León Viejo was abandoned. Founded by Nicolás de la Torre in January of 1610, it was first called "San Nicolás de Momotombo, and also "San Nicolás de los Naborios. " Also known as "Pueblo Nuevo" it attained its present name "Villa de la Paz" in 1869. The pueblo has 1, 400 inhabitants. Apparently a site of prehistoric cemeteries. In excavation many pre-Columbian ceramics have been found.

PAZ VIEJA, LA. Comarca or district in the municipio of
La Paz, León.

P. C. N. see PARTIDO CONSERVADOR DE NICARAGUA

PEARL LAGOON see LAGUNA DE PERLAS

PEDERNAL, EL. 1) A district in the municipio of San Juan
de Limay in the department of Estelí.
2) Comarca or district of the municipio of Santa
Teresa, Carazo department.

PEDERNAL Y TAGUA. Comarca or district in the municipio of La Libertad, Chontales.

PEDRARIAS, 1441-1531. Pedro Arias Dávila (d'Avila) was
a major figure in early Nicaraguan history as the first
governor of that province of the Kingdom of Guatemala
in the viceroyalty of New Spain. From an old family
of that stark Roman-walled native city of St. Teresa's,
Avila, in Spain, Pedrarias early distinguished himself
as a General against the Moors of Granada, and in an
expedition to Africa. Brother of a count (de Puño en
Rostro) and married to a countess (de Moya), who was
a good friend of Queen Isabella, Pedrarias was by birth,
military prowess, and politics a man of his time and
destined for notice. Governor of Darién in 1514, he
arrived in Panama with a coterie of ruined nobles seeking their fortunes. He directed the conquest of Nicaragua and Costa Rica. The murderer of Balboa (in
1519), Pedrarias was noted life-long for unscrupulous-
ness and cruelty. He sent Gil Gonzáles of his home
city on the expedition to discover Nicaragua. Pedrarias
was Governor of Nicaragua from 1526 until his death in
1531, at the age of 90. He is credited directly and indirectly with the death of nearly 2, 000, 000 Indians as
well as of some Spaniards.

PEDREGAL, EL. A district in the municipio of Santa Lucia,
department of Boaco.

PEDREGOSA. Comarca or district in the municipio of Télica, León.

PEDRONES, LOS. District in the municipio and department
of Rivas.

PEGON, EL. District in the municipio and department of Rivas.

PELICANO, BAHIA. A bay on Isla del Maíz Pequeña (Little Corn Island).

PELLAS, F. A. An Italian-born resident of Greytown, Pellas received from Nicaragua on March 16, 1877, the concession to a monopoly of steam navigation on Nicaraguan inland waters which had been hopelessly entangled in: the original 1850 grant of the Accessory Transit Company to Cornelius Vanderbilt, the William Walker annulment of the charter, the French involvement with Belly and Chevalier, and the rights of Webb. A. L. Blackman, a resident of Kansas, objected on the basis of residual rights and pursued the matter in the U.S. House of Representatives attempting to void the Maritime Canal Company's rights. These rights were confirmed on August 30, 1890, voiding Blackman's claim. The effect of this imbroglio was to push the U.S. government toward a more definitive ownership of the canal enterprise.

PELONA, LA. Island in Lake Nicaragua off the Chontales shore.

PEÑA DE LA LUNA. A mountain height in the municipio of Esquipulas, department of Matagalpa.

PEÑA MORDIDA, LA. A great monolith 1,000 feet high and 350 in diameter, in the Cerro de las Mesas, municipio of Terrabona, Matagalpa department. It is of a reddish color, and legends have grown up concerning its crevices and tunnels--aboriginal worship of a male goat, sounds of drums and bugles from its interior, and so on.

PEÑACHOS, LOS. Coffee hacienda in the Sierras de Managua, National District.

PENALBA, RODRIGO. Expressionist painter and contemporary leader in the founding and work of the Escuela Nacional de Bellas Arts. He returned to Nicaragua in 1947 after studying and working in the United States, Mexico, and Italy, when he was appointed director of the Escuela Nacional de Bellas Arts. Born in León in 1908, he studied at the Chicago Academy of Fine Arts in 1926, and later in the Academy of Fine Arts of San

Carlos in Mexico and the San Fernando Academy of Fine
Arts in Madrid. In 1941 he graduated from the Royal
Academy of Fine Arts in Rome. His impressionistic
paintings include figures, still life, and landscapes, and
have been widely exhibited in galleries on three continents.

PEÑAS, LAS. A territory of the Mateare municipio, department of Managua.

PEÑAS BLANCAS. 1) A district of the municipio of Jinotega.
2) Mountain of the Isabella range, a considerable massif 25 miles northeast of Jinotega, fifth highest in Nicaragua, in the department of Jinotega. Altitude 5,726
feet.

PEÑASCOS, LOS. A mountain height in Condega municipio,
Estelí department.

PENCA, LA. A district in the municipio of Belén, Rivas
department.

PENCAS, LAS. A district in the municipio of La Trinidad,
Estelí department.

PENDERGRASS, "PAT." A U.S. Army engineer who headed
the Inter-american Survey in Nicaragua in the 1950's.
A classmate of Anastasio Somoza DeBayle's at West
Point, Captain Pendergrass welded a Nicaraguan and
U.S. Army team into a mapping group that produced
most of the data for the present excellent maps availa-
ble for Nicaragua. He was awarded honorary wings in
"El Fan," the Fuerza Aéreo Nacional, or Nicaraguan
Air Force.

PENINSULARES. During Spanish colonial days, natives of
the Iberian Peninsula were thus designated. Peninsulares
usually took precedence over criollos, or colonial-born
Spaniards.

PEÑITAS, LAS. Comarca or district of the municipio of
León, León department.

PEÑON, EL. Comarca or district in the municipio of Jinotepe, Carazo department.

PEORESNADA, MINA. An old Spanish prospect mine working in schist, with a dump of material from the working. The tunnel is fallen.

PEQUEÑA PROPRIEDAD. A land holding classification used to indicate 20 to 50 manzanas (approximately 35 to 88 acres).

PERALTA, ISMAEL. Sandinista General of the early 1930's in charge of the Seventh Column. (See DEFENDING ARMY ....)

PEREIRA, DON CONSTANTINO. One of three members of the first executive committee of the Distrito Nacional (q. v.).

PEREZ, JERONIMO. Distinguished Nicaraguan lawyer and historian of Masaya, born there, September 30, 1828. With a bachelor's title in philosophy from Granada in the Casa de Estudios, he began a political career in 1853. He was mayor of Masaya during the Civil War of 1854 and at the outset of the National War of 1856. His memoirs cover an interesting period when he was aid to Colonel Tomás Martínez during the fratricidal warfare in the Segovias. In 1875 he directed La Tertulia, a periodical. In the political realm he served as mayor of Masaya, chief of the Tobacco Factory, director of the Government Gazette, Minister of Interior, Deputy to the National Congress, and Secretary of the Diplomatic Missions. He founded the Boletín Judicial as an official organ. He died on October 14, 1884.

PEREZ, MANUAL. In the mid-1840's, Pérez as provisional director of the Nicaraguan independent state less than a decade old, had to face the "butcher" Santos Guardiola and Francisco Malespín. He resigned in favor of Senator Emiliano Madriz.

PEREZ DE NOVOA, DON JUAN ANTONIO. The first Alcalde Ordinerio (Mayor) of the Villa of Rivas in 1820.

PERLA DEL SETENTRION. Term applied to the city of Matagalpa. Such appellations as "pearl of ... " are frequently used today.

PERSONALISMO (Spiritual Value). Part of the Catholic and Hispanic heritage is the intense individualism which is expressed as "personalismo. " As a consequence, Nica-

raguans are not too interested in the everyday routines
of commerce and government. Scholarship and artistic
or literary creativity are marks of the ideal or "upper-
class" man, rather than business powers. The individual
soul is more important than pragmatic or technical
achievements. This becomes a fundamental point to help
illumine differences in cultural, social, business, and
governmental relationships as compared to countries with
Anglo-Saxon antecedents.

PESCADO, EL. Coffee hacienda in the Sierras de Managua,
National District.

PETEN, FORT. Frontier fortress in the formidable Petén
jungle of northern Guatemala established somewhat anti-
climatically between 1699-1714, related to Nicaragua in
that it was the northwestern bastion of a frontier line
loosely held by Spain and anchored in the southwest by
the great Fort Inmaculada (El Castillo, q.v.) on the San
Juan River, maintained in the center by Fort San Felipe
near the Guatemalan coast. The line was incredibly far-
spaced, but had nevertheless effect disproportionate to
its scanty strength, as the British discovered to their
sorrow just after 1780.

PEZ Y LA SERPIENTE, EL. A literary magazine published
in Managua.

PFAEFFLE, W. Captured, with his son Otto, by Pedrón's
Sandinista troops on July 18, 1931, and dragged around
as purported "yankees" until Pfaeffle's protests that
they were German citizens were finally listened to. The
German was employed at a gold mine near Santo Domingo. (See JABALI.)

PHILADELPHIA MINE. One of the Bonanza (q.v.) group of
mines.

PIARISTS. One of a number of Catholic monastic orders in
the country.

PICACHO, EL. 1) Comarca or district of the municipio of
Santa Rosa, León.
2) Mountain in municipio La Libertad of Chontales.

PICA PICA. A plant, growing several feet in height, and
whose tiny seedspines penetrate clothing and cause instant

and prolonged pain, as if of an acid injection. Pica pica "burns" have been known to cause extended distress, itching, and recurrent eruption for over a year.

PICADO, CAPTAIN ARTURO. Director of the National Guard Band of Nicaragua, and composer of the "Celeste Esperanza" overture, the operetta "Canta del Guís" and various intermezzos, sonatas, and dance music. Native of Chinandega.

PICHE, EL. District in the municipio of Potosí, Rivas department.

PICHES. A Nicaraguan species of duck, very large, principally black.

PICHICHA, LAGUNA DE. A small lake on the Granada department mainland just opposite the north end of Zapatera Island.

PIE DEL GIGANTE. A district of the municipio of Niquinohomo, Masaya department.

PIEDRA COLORADA. 1) A district in the municipio and department of Matagalpa.
2) A mountain height in the municipio of Matagalpa.

PIEDRA DE CUAPA. Monolith near Cuapa in municipio Juigalpa, 500 feet above the general level--a volcanic plug.

PIEDRA DEL DIABLO, LA. A district on the lower Río Grande de Matagalpa, Zelaya department.

PIEDRA GRANDE. A district in the municipio of Esquipulas, department of Matagalpa.

PIEDRA GORDA. Comarca or district in the municipio of Achuapa, León.

PIEDRA LARGA. 1) A district of the municipio of Condega, Estelí department.
2) District in municipio of San Dionisio, Matagalpa department.

PIEDRA LUNA. A district in the municipio and department of Matagalpa.

PIEDRA MENUDA. A district of the municipio of Nindirí in Masaya department.

PIEDRA PINTADA. Comarca, valley, or district in the municipio of Juigalpa.

PIEDRAS, LAS. 1) District in the municipio of Buenos Aires, Rivas department.
2) District in the municipio and department of Rivas.

PIEDRAS GRANDES. 1) Comarca, valley, or district in the municipio of Juigalpa.
2) A district of Terrabona municipio Matagalpa department.

PIEDRAS PINTADAS, LAS. Stones covered with low-relief carvings of picturesque aboriginal figures, found in the San Roque area of Estelí municipio.

PIEDRECITAS, LAS. Cattle ranch in the municipio of San Rafael del Norte, Jinotega department.

PIJIVALLE. A palm, also called supa (q. v.).

PIJIVALLE DE LAS BRISES. Comarca or district in the municipio of La Libertad, Chontales.

PIJIVALLE DEL PARLAMENTO. Comarca or district in the municipio of La Libertad, Chontales.

PILA DE AGUA, LA. A district of the city of León.

PILAS, LAS. 1) Cattle ranch of don Gilberto Briceño in Diriamba municipio of Carazo department.
2) Comarca or district in the municipio of Diriamba, department of Carazo.
3) Comarca or district of the municipio of Nagarote, León department.
4) District in the municipio of Altagracia on Omotepe Island in Lake Nicaragua, department of Rivas.
5) A district of the municipio of San Juan de Tola, Rivas department.
6) Hacienda in the municipio of La Paz, León.
7) A territory of the National District, department of Managua.

PILAS OCCIDENTALES. A district in the municipio and department of Masaya.

PILAS ORIENTALES. A district of the municipio and department of Masaya.

PILON, EL. 1) Cattle ranch in the municipio of El Sauce,
León department.
2) Cattle ranch in the municipio of León, León department.

PINEDA, LA. Coffee hacienda in the municipio of Esquipulas, Matagalpa department.

PINEDA, LAUREANO. This talented jurist became Chief of
State of Nicaragua only to fall victim of a military coup
during the period of Guardiola. Pineda was forced to
deal with revolutionary opposition, with General José
Trinidad Muñoz who had served with the brutal armies
of Malespín and Guardiola, as well as with hostile bishop
Jorge Vitery Ungo, who had been consecrated by the
Pope as bishop of Nicaragua.

PINEDA, LICENCIADO see CIUDAD PINEDA

PINETA. Small platform at the stern of a "panga" or lake
boat, where the captain, or patrón, stays.

PINOL. The mixed, dry ingredients of pinolilla (q. v.)

PINOLERO. Drinker of pinolilla (q. v.).

PINOLILLA. The "national drink" of Nicaragua, made of
"massa" meal (fine cornmeal) and dry chocolate, mixed
with some sugar in water. It has to be continually
whirled or stirred to prevent the meal from gathering
in the bottom. A Nicaraguan is sometimes called a
"verdadero pinolero" or "true drinker" of pinolilla, to
indicate his genuineness as a native of the land.

PINTADAS, LAS. One of several large springs in the department of Estelí.

PINTURA SAN CARLOS. Comarca or district in the municipio of Diriamba, department of Carazo.

PINUELAR, EL. Comarca or district in the municipio of
Larreynaga, León.

PINUS CARIBEA see CARIBBEAN PINE

PINUS COCARPA. North American pines which grow down into Nicaragua from the countries to the north, but which are found no farther south than about the Central Atlantic Coastal area of the country.

PIO DOCE. A district of the municipio of Nandasmo, in Masaya department.

PIO XII. District of the municipio of Masatepe, department of Masaya.

PIONEER-LONE STAR. Gold bearing veins in the Pis Pis mining district and one of the Bonanza (q. v.) group of mines.

PIONEER MINE. One of the Bonanza (q. v.) group of mines.

PIPANTE. A dugout canoe found only in this part of Central America, one of four or more distinct types. The pipante is a narrow, flat-bottomed, shallow, very graceful dugout, usually made from cedro real, or royal cedar ("Spanish" cedar), an aromatic wood often called in the U. S. "cigar-box wood. " This light, mahogany-like wood is very strong and durable. A 20-foot dugout is often under 150 pounds weight, the thickness being under an inch at the gunwales. The bow usually has a 3-inch square mortise cut through it to enable the pipante to be moored by thrusting a pole through the opening into the stream-bed. The size averages 20 inches beam, 25 foot length. It is estimated there are 20, 000 or more pipantes used on the Río Coco and other rivers of Nicaragua emptying into the Caribbean. These light vessels were used to carry knocked-down mining machinery deep into the gold country of northeastern Nicaragua. (See illustration.)

PIPILES. The Pipiles were Nahuas, who, following the fall of the Nahua-influenced Teotihuacán north of Mexico City in around A. D. 650, began a major migration to the southeast. The Pipiles were "nobles" or "princes" who established themselves on the north side of the Isthmus of Tehuantepec, and then continued on in the same direction to settle in southern Guatemala, all of El Salvador, and in limited numbers in and beyond the Gulf of Fonseca in Nicaragua. A few Pipiles reached Colombia (on the Pacific side) and down as far as northern Peru. The settling of Nicaragua was a result of pursuit by

336

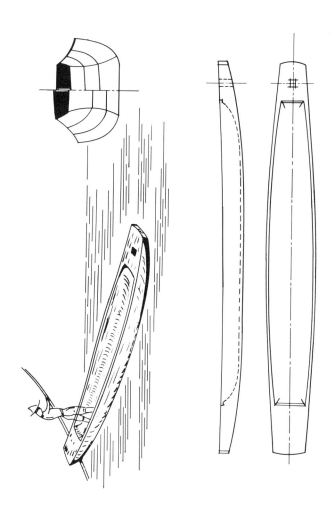

Pipante

A flat-bottomed dugout canoe especially designed for shallow
river use.

the Olmecs of the Tehuantepecan isthmus.   Torquemada
wrote in 1590-1615 of the Pipil-Nicaraos.   Such words
as Matagalpa, Totogalpa, Tagucigalpa are of Pipil derivation.   It is remarkable that an early location of the
Pipils was in Xolotlán on the northern Tehauntepec
Coast, and that Xolotlán was the name (still often used)
of Lake Managua.   The similarity is more than coincidental.   Atlán means a place of water, atl being the
root for "water."   These "Indios pipiles," the tribe of
"Nahuatlaca" origin, who seem to have been a group of
nobles working down from Mexico over centuries, peopled northern Nicaragua, their descendants being known
as Chorutegans.   The vigorous and creative aristocratic
nature of these princes has seemed to transmit itself
down the ladder of heredity to modern times.   A parallel
is the development of the Venetians from the Roman de-
bacle.

PIPISCAYAN   see   TIPISCAYAN

PIRE.   A district of the municipio of Condega, Estelí de-
    partment.   There is a mountain height of the same
    name.

PIRE, RIO DE.   A river in the Estelí department, Condega
    municipio.

PIRERE.   One of the heights to the east of Sebaco bearing
    a very old pre-conquest name.   This was a very heavily
    settled area prior to the coming of the Spanish.

PIRUJAS.   A liberal Nicaraguan political party nickname,
    opposed to the Cachurecos (q. v.).

PITA, LA.   1) A district in the municipio of Esquipulas,
    department of Matagalpa.
        2) A district of Terrabona municipio, Matagalpa de-
    partment.
        3) Mountain in the municipio of El Jicaral, León de-
    partment.
        4) Comarca or district in the municipio of Jinotepe,
    Carazo department.
        5) Comarca or district of the municipio of Santa
    Teresa, Carazo department.
        6) A hacienda on the line between southern Granada
    department and Carazo.
        7) A height of the sierra in Carazo department.

PITA DEL CARMEN, LA. A district of the municipio of Jinotega.

PITAL, EL. A hacienda southeast of Nandaime.

PITAS, LAS. Comarca or district of the municipio of El Jicaral, León.

PITAYA, LA. Comarca or district of the municipio of Santa Teresa, Carazo department.

PITPAN   see   PIPANTE

PLAN GRANDE. District in the municipio of San Juan del Sur, Rivas department.

PLAN OF IGUALA. This project of Iturbide proposed the establishment of a Mexican empire headed by one of the Bourbon dynasty in Spain. This appealed to Central America. Provincianos hoped to shake off the control of Guatemala City. Chiapas joined--it is now part of Mexico. The alternative was a Central American republic. León, Nicaragua, declared for the Plan of Iguala on September 28, 1821, but Granada opposed León on this. If the plan had gone through, the isthmus area from Tehuantepec to Colombia might have been part of a single empire extending from California to the southern continent. Geography was a major deterrent to union.

PLANES BILAN, LOS. A district of the municipio of Jinotega.

PLANTEL, EL. 1) Cattle ranch in the municipio of San Juan del Sur, Rivas department.
    2) Coffee hacienda in the municipio of San Rafael del Norte in Jinotega department.

PLANTELES DE MACUELIZO. Among the Spanish mineral works in the vicinity of Macuelizo, Nueva Segovia department, is an ancient "plantel" for the handling of gold and silver ore. [Note: the Spanish word for such a plant is not "plantel," which means a nursery garden or a training school, but here obviously it is used to mean "physical plant" the Spanish word for which would be "planta"--and the plural "plantas."] Among the remains are several dams, a water-bearing flume over a kilometer in length, storage tanks for water, a furnace for burning lime, another for refining metals (much ore remains in the area), and two small mills. Ore near the mills assays from 523 to 750 grams of silver per ton, with traces of gold. It is believed by modern mineralogists that the Spanish were able to refine ores containing from 300 to 750 grams per ton, which would make many of these existing Macuelizo mines profitable.

PLATANAL, EL. 1) Comarca or district of the municipio of León, León department.
2) Comarca or district in the municipio of Quezalguaque, León.

PLATANALES DE SAN ANTONIO, LOS. A district in the municipio of San Juan de Limay, in the department of Estelí.

PLATANAR. A spring near the city of León.

PLATANO, ISLA DEL. A small island in Lake Nicaragua between Isla Zapatera and the mainland of Granada department.

PLAYA, LA. District in the municipio of Tisma, department of Masaya. (Also called La Placer.)

PLAYITAS, LAS. A broad expanse of shallow lakes near Ciudad Darío, known for wild fowl hunting.

PLAYONES, LOS. Comarca or district in the municipio of Achuapa, León.

P. L. N. see PARTIDO LIBERAL NACIONALISTA

POBRES, LOS. Simply, "the poor"; the term used by the people themselves. See CAMPESINOS POBRES.

POCHOCUAPE. A territory of the National District, department of Managua.

POCHOTE, EL. 1) A district of the municipio and department of Masaya.
2) Famous spring near León. In one of the most popular of Nicaraguan songs (known throughout Central America), "Viva León!", there is a line: "El Pochote, su fuente Castalia ...."

POCHOTES, LOS.   Hacienda in the municipio of Rivas.

POCITOS, LOS.   1) A district of the municipio of Niquinohomo, Masaya department.
2) A spring in the southern part of the municipio of
León.

POETA.   A title of address in Nicaragua, largely because
of the international renown of (and local regard for)
Rubén Darío (q.v.).   Literary people in Nicaragua are
national figures in a manner not so pronounced in some
other small countries.   (Perhaps Iceland may be an interesting European parallel.)   There is a strong intellectual tradition among the leading families.

POLITICAL DIVISIONS, 1838.   When Nicaragua became a
separately independent nation in 1838, the country was
divided into four departments: Oriental, Occidental,
Setentrión, Mediodía.

POLITICAL DIVISIONS, 1858.   When the Constitution of 1858
was adopted by the National Legislative Assembly in
1858, Nicaragua was divided into seven departments:
Chinandega, León, Nueva Segovia, Matagalpa, Chontales,
Rivas, and Granada.

POLITICS.   Where in earlier years such issues as separation of church and state took precedence as political issues, both major parties (see Liberal and Conservative)
tend today to stress social reform; economic development in industry, commerce, and agriculture; and improvement in educational opportunities.   Their differences lie in approaches to these general goals.   The Liberals seek more centralization of authority and state direction of economic development.   In recent years elections have been the chief route of political power--coups
d'état and revolutionary or insurrectionist efforts have
had little success, undoubtedly due to the strong centralization and well-organized and armed Guardia Nacional
which has supported the government and in particular
the strong executive.

POLVAZAL, EL.   Comarca or district in the municipio of
Jinotepe, Carazo department.

POLVON, EL.   Sugar cane plantation in the municipio of
León, León department.

PONS. (Also called Ponce). One of the Spanish colonial
    families established in Masaya by 1800 and extant today.

PONZOÑA, LA. A district in the municipio of Matiguás,
    Matagalpa department.

POPOYUAPA. 1) District in the municipio and department
    of Rivas.
        2) Pueblo or town existing in the Valley of Nicaragua
    during the 16th and 17th centuries.

POPULATION. Growing at the rapid rate of about 3 to 3.5
    percent annually, a 1967 estimate places the Nicaraguan
    ·population at 1,800,000. There are a few more women
    than men. The population is young--48.2 percent were
    in the 0-14 year age group in 1963. Average age of all
    Nicaraguans in that year was 15.8 years. Birth rates
    per 1000 population hover around 44; deaths, around 8.
    Since 1955 (to 1967) infant mortality per 1000 live births
    has been cut astonishingly from 72.7 to 45.4. Catholics
    make up 96 percent of the population; 3.8 percent is
    Protestant (most of the latter on the Atlantic Coast).
    The rural population is decreasing. Estimated composi-
    tion is: 71% mestizo; 17% white; 9% Negro; 3% Indian
    (pure). The Hispanicized population (white and mestizo)
    lives in the main in the Pacific Coastal areas, with the
    Pacific Zone accounting for 58%, the Central for 35%,
    and the other 7% on the Atlantic side. The population
    of Nicaragua is now (1971) probably about 1,950,000 and
    57 percent of the population is rural, much of it engaged
    in subsistence agriculture. Probably 14-16% of the popu-
    lation lives in the capital city, Managua. (Compare to
    Athens, where 2,000,000 or 25% of 8,000,000 Greeks
    live in the capital.) See also NICARAGUA (Population
    of Youth).

POPULATION, 1850's. Nicaragua's population was static at
    250,000 in this period, with the interesting ratio of
    three women to two men, in some villages women out-
    numbering men five to one. This condition occurred be-
    cause of continual conscription of males into the inter-
    necine conflicts of the area and the times. There was
    valid comparison to the terrible Paraguayan War of the
    1860's, when a preponderance of that country's males
    were killed.

POPULATION, 1920. To compare with the pre-conquest

mid-1800's, and present populations, it is instructive to view the 1920 population: all Nicaragua: 638, 119; León: 38, 318; Managua: 27, 839; Granada, 18, 066. While the population has tripled by 1971, the population of Managua has increased tenfold. In this sense Nicaragua is a "city-state."

PORRAS, DIEGO DE. Chief architect of the final and present structure of the León cathedral (q. v.), built from 1747-1780.

PORTELLO, RIO EL. Stream in the municipio of El Sauce, León department.

PORTILLO, EL. 1) A district of the municipio of Nindirí in Masaya department.
   2) A district of the municipio of Niquinohomo, Masaya department.
   3) A district of the San Rafael del Sur municipio, Managua department.
   4) Height above San Juan de Limay, in Estelí department.

PORTILLOS, LOS. Comarca or district in the municipio of La Paz, León.

PORTOBANCO. Cattle ranch in the municipio of León, León department.

PORTOCABECEÑOS. Residents of Puerto Cabezas in the department of Zelaya.

PORTOCARRERO, PEDRO. Doctor Portocarrero was one of the first faculty members of the University of Nicaragua in 1816 when it opened. The surname is still a significant one in Nicaraguan leadership and society.

PORVENIR, EL. 1) Coffee hacienda in the Jinotega department.
   2) Coffee hacienda in the municipio of San Marcos, Carazo department.
   3) District in the municipio of San Jorge, Rivas department.
   4) Prospecting for copper has been carried on in this part of the Rosita area. Copper is a relatively new important Nicaraguan export. See ROSITA MINE.

PORVENIR DE NICARAGUA, EL. A nineteenth century periodical established in Rivas, founded by Enrique H. Gottel in 1865.

POTONA. A dialect of Nahuatl which was a corruption of the basic Mexican idiom spoken in parts of El Salvador and down into Nicaragua.

POTOSI. 1) Municipio of the department of Rivas, population 4,500 persons, area 37 square miles. Bounded on the north by Granada, south by Rivas, east by Buenos Aires, and west by Belén, it is an area of cattle raising, sugar cane culture, and general agriculture. There are nine comarcas, valleys, or districts.
     2) Pueblo Potosí, cabacera of the municipio of the same name, has about 800 inhabitants. It is distinguished by a church named "Campaña de la Independencia" for the insurrection mounted in the department of Rivas in 1811, anticipating by a full decade Central American independence in general. Birthplace of Laureano Pineda, martyred in Guardiola days of the 19th century.

POTRERILLOS, LOS. 1) Comarca or district of the municipio of Santa Teresa, Carazo department.
     2) A district of the municipio of Condega, Estelí department. There is a mountain height of the same name.
     3) A district in the municipio of San Isidro, department of Matagalpa.
     4) A district or valley in the municipio of San Rafael del Norte, Jinotega department.

POTRERO DE OLLANCA. A district in the municipio of La Trinidad, department of Estelí.

POTRERON, EL. Comarca or district in the municipio of La Paz, Carazo department.

POTREROS, LOS. A district in the municipio of Esquipulas, department of Matagalpa.

POWER, LESTER E. National Guard captain (U.S. Marine) who as commander of a guard patrol in June, 1931, was killed near Embocaderos. His second-in-command, Lieutenant William H. McGhee, was also killed, and the patrol fled, having lost its officers.

POZA AZUL. A district in the municipio of Belén, Rivas department.

POZAS, LOS. A district of the municipio of Sebaco, Mata-galpa department.

POZO, EL. Plantation in the municipio of Quezalquaque, León.

PRADO, EL. A coffee hacienda in the municipio of Niquino-homo in the department of Masaya.

PRENSA, LA. Daily paper published in Managua, presently with the largest circulation in the country under the editorship of intellectual, exile, and scion of a famous family, also revolutionary, Pedro Joaquín Chamorro Cardenal. An organ of the Conservative party, vigor-ously anti-administration. It is a living example of relative freedom of the press. At times it has pub-lished when the editor-publisher was under house arrest or in exile.

PRESIDENCIA see AUDIENCIA

PRESIDENCY. The President of Nicaragua under the present (1950) constitution is elected by direct popular vote for a five-year term. He must be born in Nicaragua, of Nicaraguan parents, and cannot be a relative of the in-cumbent president "to the fourth degree of consanguinity." He must be a full citizen and 40 years of age or more. The President has considerable military power as Com-mander-in-Chief of the National Guard, and he appoints all guard officers with the approval of Congress. Mili-tary service is voluntary, but the President can institute compulsory service, or a "draft." He must preserve internal order and protect against external aggression, and to do so may issue decrees which have the force of law. (See ACUERDOS.) He may in emergency suspend all constitutional guarantees. He is head of the National Administrative Organization and appoints and removes all Ministers. He also has, through decrees, considerable legislative power and function. He introduces most bills in Congress.

PRESIDENTS OF CENTRAL AMERICA. (Dates indicate terms of office): Gabino Gainza, 1821-1822; Vicente Filísola, 1822-1823; Manuel José Arce, 1823-1828;

Mariano Beltranena, 1828-1829; José Francisco Barrundia, 1829-1830; Francisco Morazán, 1830-1839.

PRESIDENTS OF NICARAGUA.   (Dates indicate terms of office.   There are certain discrepancies.   Two examples: William Walker was "President," illegally, during the 1850's; Anastasio Somoza was in actual control 1933-1956.)   Fruto Chamorro, 1853-1854; José María Estrada, 1855-1859 (Filibuster War); Tomás Martínez, 1859-1867; Fernando Guzmán, 1867-1871; Vicente Cuadra, 1871-1875; Pedro Joaquín Chamorro, 1875-1879; Joaquín Zavala, 1879-1883; Adán Cárdenas, 1883-1887; Evaristo Carazo, 1887-1889; Roberto Sacasa, 1889-1893; José Santos Zelaya, 1893-1909; José Madriz, 1909-1910; Juan José Estrada, 1911; Adolfo Díaz, 1911-1916; Emiliano Chamorro, 1917-1920; Diego M. Chamorro, 1921-1923; Bartolomé Martínez, 1923-1924; Carlos Solórzano, 1925-1926; José María Moncada, 1929-1932; Juan Bautista Sacasa, 1933-1936; J. Carlos Brenes, 1936; Anastasio Somoza García, 1937-1939 and 1939-1947; Leonardo Argüello, 1947; Benjamín Lacayo Sacasa, 1947; Víctor M. Román y Reyes, 1948-1950; Anastasio Somoza, 1951-1956; Luis A. Somoza DeBayle, 1957-1963; Rene Schick Gutiérrez, 1963-1967; Anastasio Somoza DeBayle (hijo), 1967-present.

PRIMAVERA.   1) A cattle hacienda in the municipio of Ciudad Darío, Matagalpa department.
    2) Prospecting for copper has been carried on in this part of the Rosita Mine (q. v.) area.

PRIMERA, LA.   Term used for "the leaders," the upper stratum of Nicaraguan society.

PRINZAPOLKA.   A Zelaya department community at the mouth of the River of the same name, the principal activity being a sawmill.   There is an airstrip.

PRINZAPOLKA, RIO.   A major river of the eastern coast of Nicaragua, in the central portion of that Caribbean Coast.   (See   RIVERS.)

PRISIONERO.   A district of the municipio of Jinotega.

P. R. N.   see   PARTIDO RENOVACION NACIONAL

PROGRESO, EL.   1) Coffee hacienda in the municipio of

Masatepe, department of Masaya.

2) A passenger steamer which in the 1890's and early 1900's plied between Granada and San Carlos on Lake Nicaragua, there connecting with river steamers which continued down river to Greytown.

PROMETHEUS. This ocean-going steam vessel was built by Cornelius Vanderbilt to initiate the service of the Accessory Transit Company across Nicaragua in 1850. Its first voyage for this purpose found the doughty Commodore aboard and likewise in tow a small river steamer, the Director, which Vanderbilt later personally piloted up the San Juan River. Prometheus also initiated the first passenger voyage in mid-1851. First class passengers paid $400.00 to go to San Francisco, but later competition brought the price down to $150.00 with steerage passengers able to take the long journey for $45.00. This compares to much longer, more expensive, and more dangerous routes across the great plains. The time was usually considered as four or five weeks, New York to San Francisco.

PROPERTY RIGHTS. Article 63 of the Nicaraguan Constitution of 1950 gives the right to own property and to maintain it against governmental expropriation. However, Article 65 adds that social institutions, by law, may limit the amount, nature, and extent of property. This permits, in effect, agrarian reform; to abolish latifundios and to permit small rural holdings. There has to date been no such reform on any extended scale, although some progress has been made.

PROSAS PROFANAS. This Profane Prose was published by Rubén Darío (q. v.) in 1896 and sets the exotic and somewhat hedonistic note found in much of his work. (See AZUL.)

PROTECTORATE. Some analysts state baldly that following United States acquisition of the Virgin Islands, Puerto Rico, and the Canal Zone, protectorates were established over Nicaragua (subsequent to 1912), Haiti, and the Dominican Republic "frequently by the use of armed intervention. " Whatever the terminology, there is little question these were de facto protectorates.

PROTOCOL OF 1960. A step beyond the Multilateral Treaty of 1958 and the Agreement of Integrated Industries, to-

ward the economic integration of Central America;
strongly advocated and supported by Nicaragua.

PROTOCOL OF 1964.   A protocol of further agreement (see
Protocol of 1960) subsequent to the General Treaty of
Economic Integration of Central America.

PROVIDENCIA.   1) Hacienda in the municipio of La Paz,
León.
2) La Providencia, a coffee hacienda in the municipio
of San Marcos, Carazo department.
3) La Providencia, a district in the municipio and department of Rivas.

PROVINCIAS UNIDAS DEL CENTRO AMERICA.   A federation established after secession from Mexico, proclaimed
by a constituent assembly in Guatemala on July 1, 1823.
Included the states of Nicaragua, Guatemala, El Salvador,
Honduras, and Costa Rica.   Civil War came soon after,
with the result that Francisco Morazán was made President in 1830.   His Liberals proposed a liberal program.
The Confederation, known as the United Provinces of
Central America, persisted for a period of 16 years,
1823-1839.   A league of confederated states rather than
a federal republic with strong central government, the
period of the union was riddled by civil war and the
union itself was made tenuous by inherited social ills,
a strong residual caste system, the hacienda pattern,
agricultural monoculture, civil war, and factional strife
of several sorts.   Under the "George Washington of
Central America, " Francisco Morazán, and while he
was President (1830-1839), the administration in spite
of conflict and vicissitudes was able to promote public
education, reorganize the administrative aspects of government, and within the limits of time and geography,
to develop industry and commerce.   He was instrumental
in getting Central America to adopt the criminal code
originally drafted by Edward Livingston for Louisiana.
The capital of the Republic was moved to San Salvador
in 1835.   Guatemalan forces under the strong leadership
of Rafael Carrera were responsible for the collapse of
the Confederation on May 18, 1838, when civil war broke
out again.   Morazán met defeat at the hands of Carrera,
and the Confederation ended when Morazán resigned in
February, 1839.   Nicaragua and the four other states
have since then been independent nations.   Central American unity is a dream widely praised but little pursued in
all the countries.

PROVISIONAL INTEROCEANIC CANAL SOCIETY. Organized as an American answer to the French high-handedness in the International Scientific Congress (q. v.) of 1879, the society accepted Menocal's recommendations for a route. Captain S. L. Phelps, as President, and people such as Captain E. S. Crowninshield, George Riggs, A. G. Menocal, and Admiral Daniel Amman all sought former President Grant to head their group of canal promoters as a name to rival that of the Frenchman de Lesseps. Menocal was sent to Nicaragua to negotiate concessions and was able to do so with the difficult proviso that canal work should begin by May 22, 1880.

P. S. C.   see   PARTIDO SOCIAL CRISTIANO

P. S. C. N.   The coalition social-Christian party (also known as P. S. C.) which arose in 1957, and which has joined the UDCCA (q. v.).   See   PARTIDO SOCIAL CRISTIANO.

P. S. N.   see   PARTIDO SOCIALISTA NICARAGUENSE

PUEBLA, LA.   District in the municipio and department of Rivas.

PUEBLO CHIQUITO.   District in the municipio of Altagracia on Omotepe Island in Lake Nicaragua, department of Rivas.

PUEBLO DE COLAMA see   MANAGUA, def. 2

PUEBLO GRANDE DE OMOTEPE   see   ALTAGRACIA, def. 2

PUEBLO NUEVO.   1) Founded in 1652, the town of Pueblo Nuevo has had two locations.   Composed of indios naborios, who were free Indians in service, and who were given their own separate town by the Governor Arbieto. The original name was "Pueblo Nuevo de la Santísima Trinidad de Pliego. "   In 1861, there were 248 villagers, all naborios.   Because of floods of the Dacuali River, the town was moved to the present site in 1745-1750. By 1751 the population had no free Indians--all were ladinos.   The town now is well-known for the examples of aboriginal ceramics.
       2) A municipio in the department of Estelí, only 68 square miles in area, with 10, 500 inhabitants.   Bounded by the municipios of Somoto, Yalaguina, and Palacaquina

(all of Madriz department) on the north; on the south by
San Juan de Limay of Estelí; on the east by Condega;
and on the west again by Madriz, the municipios of San
Lucas and Las Sabanas.   There are six districts.
Mountain heights are El Moro, Los Llanos, La Mesa
and San Francisco.   Rivers are El Caracol, El Rosario,
and San José.   Coffee and cattle are raised.
     3) District in the municipio of San Jorge, Rivas de-
partment.
     4) District in the municipio of San Juan del Sur,
Rivas department.

PUEBLO NUEVO, RIO DE. A stream flowing in the environs
     of the town of that name, and into the Río Estelí.

PUEBLO NUEVO DE LA SANTISIMA TRINIDAD DE PLIEGO
     see   PUEBLO NUEVO (def. 1)

PUEBLO NUEVO SUR.   District of the municipio and de-
     partment of Rivas.

PUEBLO REDONDO.   Comarca or district in the municipio
     of Télica, León.

PUEBLO VIEJO. A district in the municipio and depart-
     ment of Matagalpa.

PUEBLOS NAMOTIVOS. A term given at the beginning of
     the Spanish colonization to people in the region of Cata-
     rina, department of Masaya.   This was an area of
     heavy aboriginal population.

PUERCO, CAYO.   An island over two miles long in the
     Pearl Lagoon estuary, Zelaya department.

PUERTO CABEZAS.   Northernmost town of significance on
     the Nicaraguan east (Caribbean) coast, Puerto Cabezas
     no longer has the lumbering activity which made it blos-
     som early in the century.   There is a long paved air-
     port runway built by the U.S. Air Force during World
     War II, and used to launch bombers for the ill-fated
     "Bay of Pigs" invasion of Cuba in 1961.   The Catholic
     Bishop of Zelaya department resides in the town.   There
     is also a Moravian hospital recently developed.   The
     long dock extends toward the open roadstead for shipping.
     A good road runs to Waspam, but is essentially isolated
     from the rest of the country.   Travel to the Pacific

Coast of Nicaragua would be by sea through the Panama Canal, or by sea and land to Bluefields, up the Río Escondido to Rama, and across the Rama road to Managua. Otherwise, travel is by air and inland by dugout canoe. The huge Zelaya department is a complex of rain-forest mountains and wet tropical lowlands.

PUERTO DE GRACIAS. District in the municipio of Altagracia on Omotepe Island in Lake Nicaragua, department of Rivas.

PUERTO DE LA INDEPENDENCIA. Name given to the present port of San Juan del Sur in 1830, under the Central American Federation. (It had originally been called Puerto en el Mar del Sur, or San Juan en el Mar del Sur.)

PUERTO DIAZ. Comarca, valley or district in the municipio of Juigalpa.

PUERTO ISABEL. An open roadstead port in Zelaya department just south of the Prinzapolka River mouth. There is a long pier, and the principal traffic is in copper from upstream mines opened in the last decade.

PUERTO SOMOZA. Comarca or district including the port of the same name, within the municipio of Nagarote, León department; at the mouth of the Río Tamarindo.

PUERTOS DE LA FRONTERA. Passes in the mountains of the "frontier" under Spanish rule were to be found in the following spots: Yasica, Muy Muy Viejo, the mountains of "El Cangrejal, " the heads of the rivers Murra, Quisaura, and Lóvago, and the mountains of Carca and Arrancabarba.

PUL Y LA POLONIA, EL. District in the municipio of Altagracia on Omotepe Island in Lake Nicaragua, department of Rivas.

PUMICE. There are extensive deposits of this light-weight porous volcanic stone between Granada and Nandaime and near Granada on the road to Managua.

PUNTA ARENAS. Comarca or district in the municipio of Quezalguaque, León.

PUNTA BARRA. Southern point at the entrance to Pearl Lagoon from the Caribbean (Zelaya department).

PUNTA DEL CHILAITE. A prominent point on Omotepe Island in Lake Nicaragua which is one end of the line of
demarcation between the municipios of Altagracia and
Moyogalpa, as decreed by President Martínez in June,
1862.

PUNTA DE SAN SILVESTRE. District in the municipio of
Altagracia on Omotepe Island in Lake Nicaragua, department of Rivas.

PUNTA GORDA, BAHIA. The great crescent-shaped bay of
the Caribbean on the east coast of Nicaragua, south of
Monkey Point, and from that promontory to the place
where the coast again tends south (Laguna Taura). The
bay extends 48 miles and its depth (east to west) is
over 15 miles. It is sometimes called Greytown Bay.

PUNTA MASAYA. A point on the Bay of Bluefields at the
western edge adjacent to the airfield of the town.

PUNTA MOSQUITO. Northern point at the entrance to Pearl
Lagoon from the Caribbean (Zelaya department).

PUNTA PERLAS. Most prominent cape on the eastern (Caib-
bean) coast of Nicaragua, it projects on the map like a
"nose" (very similar in shape to Cape Canaveral, Florida).

PUNTA SET NET. Northernmost point of the "nose" pro-
tuberance of eastern Nicaragua which is terminated by
Punta Perlas. For six miles south the beach is ab-
solutely straight and due north and south, an unusual
geographical feature.

PUNTA TAQUISAPA. District in the municipio of Altagracia
on Omotepe Island in Lake Nicaragua, department of
Rivas.

PURISIMA CONCEPCION DE MARIA, LA. A subject for
home shrines and saint's day observance as well as
daily reverence.

-Q-

QUEBRACHAL, EL. A district of Terrabona municipio,
Matagalpa department.

QUEBRACHITO. A district in the municipio of La Trinidad,
department of Estelí.

QUEBRADA DE HONDA. A tributary stream of the Río Viejo.

QUEBRADA GRANDE. A cattle ranch in the municipio of
Esquipulas, Matagalpa department.

QUEBRADA HONDA. 1) A district of the municipio and department of Masaya.
2) A district in the municipio and department of Matagalpa.
3) A district of the municipio of Tipitapa, department
of Managua.

QUEBRADA HONDA Y RIO DE CUISALA. Cattle ranch in
Chontales granted in 1719 to Ensign (Alfárez) Don Juan
de Sierra, of the city of León. Size: 40 cabellerías or
about 1, 300 acres.

QUEBRADA SECA. Comarca or district of the municipio of
León, León department.

QUEBRADA SECA, RIO. Stream in the municipio of El
Sauce, León department.

QUEBRANTADERO, EL. Comarca, valley or district in the
municipio of Juigalpa.

QUEQUISQUE. A purplish root plant, edible and nutritious,
which is known in English as "dasheen." Used in soups
and stews, it is a delicious tropical vegetable.

QUEZALGUAQUE. 1) Comarca or district in the municipio
of Quezalguaque, León.
2) Smallest of the municipios of León department, this
one with the distinguishing indigenous name is of less
than 19 square miles in area, with a population of 3, 000.
Bounded on the north by Posoltega and the department of
Chinandega, south by León, east by Télica, and west by
Chichigalpa, the municipio has nine districts. Principal
products are agricultural: cattle, cotton, and sugar cane,

plus some grains.

3) Pueblo de Quezalguaque is very old. Under the cacicazgo of Subtiava in earliest colonial times, from 1529 on it was an encomienda under the "Protector of the Indians" don Diego Alvarez de Osorio, later first bishop of Nicaragua. Later it was an encomienda under Alonso de Segovia and later yet it was given by Governor Contreras to his son Pedro. The name is derived from the Nahuatl quetzal, denoting the bird well known as the national bird of Guatemala, and guaca, which signifies abundance or place of abundance--hence, "a place of many quetzal birds." There are records of tribute from the town in 1554 and in 1664. By 1774, a visit from Bishop Morel de Santa Cruz found 36 families, Mestizo and Indian, and a large parish church. By 1792 there were only 150 people, and in 1854 it was annexed to Télica. The present town has a colonial church with unusual jewels and icons.

QUEZALGUAQUE, RIO.   Stream in the municipio of the same name.

QUEZALSA.   A cotton gin processing plant in Télica, León department.

QUIABUC.   Mountain in the municipio of Estelí.

QUIAHUITL.   A Nicarao month festival as practiced pre-conquest.   Meaning: "rain."

QUIATEOT.   A god of rain and water of the Nicaraos.

QUIBUC.   A mountain range in Estelí department.

QUIJANO, LIEUTENANT.   A strong-minded Nicaraguan officer of the port of San Juan del Norte at the mouth of the San Juan River who on August 19, 1841, indignantly refused to recognize the "Mosquito King" as an ally of Great Britain.   English officials and men of the British frigate Tweed then carried off the brave customs officer, left him ashore on a lonely stretch of coast, to make his way back as best he could.

QUIJONGO.   A musical instrument formed of a bow of wood about five feet long, with a jar affixed at one-third the length of the bow, and strings from the extremities of the bow to the base of the jar.   By opening or closing the mouth of the jar with the left hand, a limited number of notes are made.

QUILALI. On the Río El Jícaro, this town has 450 population, and is the cabacera of the municipio of the same name. The air evacuation of 1927 was a principal event.

QUILALI, BATTLE OF. Following ambushes near the town on December 30, 1927, forces of U.S. Marines with 30 wounded men met in this village, which became the scene of a heroic episode when Lieutenant Christian F. Schilt (q.v.) effected the evacuation of the wounded by flying repeatedly into Quilali during January 6-8, 1928, under enemy fire. The airstrip had been improvised by demolishing 250 feet of buildings along one side of the village's main street.

QUILAMBE, RAMAL DE see KILAMBE

QUIMUMA, RIO. A river in the municipio of San Pedro de Lovago, Chontales department.

QUINAL, EL. Comarca or district of the municipio of Santa Teresa, Carazo department.

QUINOÑEZ, FRANCISCO and MATIAS. The Doctors Quiñóñez were among the first faculty members of the University of Nicaragua when it opened in 1816.

QUINTA SARATOGA. Located in the municipio Catarina of Masaya department, this "country house" (quinta) was a favorite haunt of diplomats and visitors during the Zelaya government, and was the site of elaborate entertainment and both political and social events of significance. The site is presently in a partially ruined state. Rubén Darío was inspired there in 1907 to compose his "Canto a Masaya."

QUINTA ZOILA. A country house in the vicinity of Niquinohomo.

QUIRIBIES. Tribal groups which came into the Middle American area in about the fourth century B.C. Often confused due to name similarities with Caribs of the eastern Caribbean.

QUIRRAGUA. 1) A district in the municipio of Matiguás,

Matagalpa department.

2) A mountain height to the northwest of the pueblo of Matiguás in the municipio of the same name, Matagalpa department.

QUISAURA. 1) Comarca or district in the municipio of La Libertad, Chontales.

2) A river-head pass between Spanish colonial holdings and the Sambo-Miskito enemy and their pirate allies to the east.

QUISAURA, RIO. A river along the Spanish colonial frontier.

-R-

RADICALES. A party in opposition to the Serviles at the time of the establishment of the United Provinces of Central America. They favored a federal republic and abolition of abuses and privileges that were the province of the conservative classes. This faction had their greatest adherence in outlying areas such as Nicaragua, León being the principal "liberal" center, as it is today a century and a half later.

RADIO. Radio is a major means of communication in Nicaragua, more significant than newspapers and certainly more widespread. The reasons are considerable illiteracy, making speech a better medium than the written word: rugged terrain, with few other communication media in some areas; and the recent prevalence and availability of inexpensive transistor radios from Oriental manufacturing sources. Because of the significance of radio, in this collection a list of call letters has been provided, as well as a brief treatment of location, power, and frequency of each broadcast unit. There are nine 10,000 watt stations in Nicaragua and three of 15,000 watts. There were by 1966 about 150,000 radio receivers in the country.

RADIO A   see   VOZ DE AMERICA, LA.

RADIO ALMA LATINA. A radio station in Estelí, call letters YNRM, power 2000 watts, frequency 1350 kilocycles.

RADIO AMERICANA. A radio station in Granada; call letters YNXW, also under letters called "Radio Sport"; power

1000 watts, 915 kilocycles. Radio Sport frequency is
650 kilocycles.

RADIO ATENAS. A radio station in León; call letters YNWX,
power 2500 watts, frequency 1270 kilocycles.

RADIO ATLANTICO. A radio station in Bluefields; call letters YNCA, power 150 watts, frequency 6120 kilocycles.

RADIO CAPITOL. A Managua station; call letters YNC,
power 500 watts, frequency 1200 kilocycles.

RADIO CATOLICA. A Managua radio station; owned by the
Catholic Church, call letters YNRC, power 10,000 watts,
1130 kilocycles frequency.

RADIO CENTAURO. A radio station in Managua; call letters
YNSC, power 10,000 watts, frequency 700 kilocycles.

RADIO CENTENARIO. An inactive radio station in Matagalpa;
1000 watts power, 5975 kilocycles, YNRZ call letters.

RADIO CENTRO. A radio station in Granada; call letters
YNTW, 170 watts power, 1070 kilocycles.

RADIO CENTROAMERICANA. A Managua radio station; 250
watts power, 1560 kilocycles frequency, call letters
YNPR.

RADIO CINCO NOVENTA. A radio station in Managua; call
letters YNRR, power 3500 watts, 570 kilocycles frequency.

RADIO CINCO NOVENTA. Power, 1000 watts; frequency,
5965 kilocycles. (Compare with the larger station,
same name, same ownership). (See RADIO MUNDIAL.)

RADIO CITY. A Managua radio station; call letters YNDN,
power 1000 watts, frequency 1450 kilocycles.

RADIO COCIBOLCA. A radio station in Granada; call letters
YNRPS, power 2000 watts, frequency 1285 kilocycles.

RADIO COLINAS. A radio station in Jinotega; call letters
YNAW, power 1000 watts, frequency 1590 kilocycles.

RADIO CONTINENTAL. A radio station in Managua; call
letters YNAV, power 10,000 watts, and frequency 850
kilocycles.

RADIO CORPORACION.   A radio station in Managua; call
   letters YNOW, power 5000 watts, 540 kilocycles.

RADIO COSEGUINA.   A radio station in Chinandega; power
   2000 watts, 1475 kilocycles, call letters YNAG.

RADIO CULTURAL CARAZO.   A radio station in Jinotepe;
   call letters YNOP, power 500 watts, frequency 1220
   kilocycles.

RADIO DARIO.   A radio station in León; call letters YNUW,
   power 1000 watts, frequency 1180 kilocycles.

RADIO EL ECO DE LAS BRUMAS.   A radio station in Jinotega; call letters YNTJ, power 500 watts, frequency
   1460 kilocycles.

RADIO EL MUNDO.   A Managua radio station; call letters
   YNSV, power 1000 watts, frequency 1240 kilocycles.

RADIO FEMENINA.   A Managua radio station, call letters
   YNE, 2500 watts power, 1580 kilocycles frequency.

RADIOFUSORA NACIONAL.   A government radio network in
   Managua, of variable frequency; call letters YNM, power
   10,000 watts, 615 kilocycles listed frequency.

RADIO HERNANDEZ CORDOBA.   A radio station in Ocotal;
   call letters YNHC, power 400 watts, frequency 6100
   kilocycles.

RADIO IVANIA.   A radio station in Managua; call letters
   YNO, power 1000 watts, frequency 800 kilocycles.

RADIO JINOTEGA.   An inactive radio station located in
   Jinotega; 100 watts power, 9550 kilocycles.

RADIO LIBERTAD.   A radio station in Managua; call letters
   YNKW, power 10,000 watts, and frequency 885 kilocycles.

RADIO MANAGUA.   A radio station located in the capital;
   call letters YNLU, power 1000 watts, frequency 965
   kilocycles.

RADIO MAR.   Puerto Cabezas radio; call letters not available, 9560 kilocycles.

RADIO MASAYA. A radio station in Masaya; call letters YNLL, 250 watts power, 1050 kilocycles.

RADIO MIL. A Managua radio station; call letters YNTS, power 15,000 watts (one of the only three thus powered in Nicaragua), and frequency 1000 kilocycles, hence the name.

RADIO MONGALO. A radio station in Rivas; call letters YNCR, power 250 watts, frequency 980 kilocycles.

RADIO MUNDIAL. "Worldwide" radio station; call letters YNW, located in Managua, power 10,000 watts, 930 kilocycles. There are relays as follows: León, YNW-1, 1000 watts, 875 kilocycles; Matagalpa, YNW-2, 1000 watts, 775 kilocycles; Estelí, YNW-3, 1000 watts, 1025 kilocycles; Managua, YNW-4, 1000 watts, 5965 kilocycles.

RADIO MUSICAL. A radio station in Masaya; call letters YNBO, power 1000 watts, frequency 1000 kilocycles.

RADIO MUSUM. A radio station in Matagalpa; call letters YNAE, power 250 watts, frequency 1090 kilocycles.

RADIO NORTE. A radio station in Somoto; call letters YNJM, power 1000 watts, frequency 6200.

RADIO OCCIDENTAL. A radio station in Chinandega; power 5000 watts, frequency 1035 kilocycles, call letters YNCW.

RADIO PHILLIPS see ONDAS POPULARES

RADIO PROGRESO. A radio station in León; call letters YNCZ, power 500 watts, frequency 1515 kilocycles.

RADIO REFORMA. A radio station in Managua; call letters YNRR, power 3500 watts, 570 kilocycles.

RADIO RELOJ. A Managua radio station with the interesting call letters YNVOZ ("voice"); power 3000 watts, frequency 1015 kilocycles.

RADIO SPORT. See RADIO AMERICANA. Also, an inactive station in Granada call letters YNWW, power 500 watts, frequency 6140 kilocycles.

RADIO TIC TAC. A radio station in Chinandega; power 1000 watts, frequency 555 kilocycles, call letters YNG.

RADIO TITANICA. A radio station in León; call letters
   YNS, power 1000 watts, frequency 725 kilocycles.

RADIO ZELAYA. A radio station in Bluefields; call letters
   YNGR, power 500 watts, frequency 5955 kilocycles.

RAIDS, MISKITO. The Miskito Indians tended to raid west
   and south from their bases on Tuapi, Pearl, and Bluefields Lagoons. Their main track into the interior of
   Nicaragua was by the Bluefields and Rama River route.
   The Miskitos knew the "haul-overs" or canoe portages
   on this route. Their first attacks were made in 1705,
   several years after the first Sambo attacks (see following entry), and the area attacked was the gold mining
   town of Muy Muy Viejo, and on Acoyapa and other villages of Chontales near Lake Nicaragua. The attacks
   were repeated at almost annual intervals. It is probable
   that the Nicaragua attacks were more frequent than those
   of record.

RAIDS, SAMBO. The Sambo raids on the Nicaraguan Spanish
   frontier were carried out from Cabo Gracias a Dios, and
   in general up the Wanks River (Río Coco, etc.). The
   frontier towns of Nueva Segovia were the principal victims. The first known raid was in 1701, and they occurred sporadically after that. Those the Sambos captured were made slaves; those who resisted were killed.
   The Sambos were better armed than the defenders of
   the small frontier villages, who had few firearms. The
   Sambo raids were distinguished from the Miskito raids
   (q. v.) in both personnel and location. However, the
   whole coastal population of the time was frequently
   blanketed under the term "Sambo-Miskito. "

RAINFALL. The Atlantic (Caribbean) Coast of Nicaragua is
   one of the high-rainfall spots of the world. Selected
   annual readings for an average of recent years: San
   Juan del Norte, 237 inches; Bluefields, 166 inches;
   Puerto Isabel, 150 inches; Puerto Cabezas, 129 inches;
   El Castillo, 129 inches; Río Kukra, 146 inches; Siuna,
   80 inches; Bonanza, 110 inches; Bilwaskarma, 107 inches; San Miguelito, 107 inches; San Carlos, 73 inches.

RAITAPURA. A village at the southern tip of Pearl Lagoon,
   Zelaya department.

RAIZON, EL. A district of the municipio of Nindirí in
   Masaya department.

RAMA.   1) Municipio of the department of Zelaya, population 17, 000, along the Río Escondido, terminus of the Rama Road, important east-west link and only such road in the country, nearly 30 years in the building.   Communication with Bluefields is by river.   Fairly large barges and river craft can negotiate the deep lower Río Escondido.

2) An Indian tribe once numerous on the East Coast of Nicaragua just south of Bluefields.   In 1820 there were fewer than 500.   Fishermen, tortoise-shell collectors, and excellent boatmen, the Rama built "dories" and canoes more seaworthy than those of neighboring tribesmen.   The Rama River commemorates this group, which still has a small nucleus on Rama Key near Bluefields.

3) Ciudad Rama, population 700, cabacera of the municipio of the same name, is situated at the confluence of three rivers--the Mico, Siquía, and Rama.   It is the terminal for the Rama road and Escondido River traffic to Bluefields.   Nearby is the agricultural experiment station, El Recreo.

RAMA CAY.   A series of small islands in the lower end of Bluefields Bay occupied by the Rama Indians, a remnant of a Sumu group which may have originated in South America.

RAMAKEY   see   RAMA CAY (an alternate form)

RAMIREZ, JERONIMO   see   COLEGIO DE LA UNION

RAMIREZ, NORBERTO.   A Director of Nicaragua whose term, which ended on March 31, 1851, was distinguished by the Treaty of Commerce signed with U. S. Minister Ephraim Squier (q. v.).   There was continued agitation for a reestablishment of the federation, which had dissolved by Nicaragua's secession 13 years before.

RAMOS, LOS.   A district in the municipio of Altagracia on Omotepe Island in Lake Nicaragua, department of Rivas.

RANCHITOS, LOS.   Comarca or district in the municipio of Quezalguaque, León.

RANCHO DE PAJA.   A simple shelter or dwelling, usually with a thatched roof and wattle walls, deriving from the aboriginal form of dwelling in Central America.   (See illustration.)

Rancho de Paja

A typical small indigenous dwelling.   The clay oven is characteristic.

RANCHO GRANDE. A district in the municipio and department of Matagalpa.

RANCHONES, LOS. A hacienda on the lower southeast slope
of Mombacho, a dead volcano in Granada department.

RANCHOS, LOS. 1) Comarca or district of the municipio of
León, León department.
2) District in the municipio and department of Rivas.
3) An imaginative restaurant with an excellent cuisine
in modern Managua. The "ranchos" are separate
thatched-roof pavilions like modest "campesino" homes.
Nicaraguan steaks are a specialty, various native dishes
available.

RAPIDO CABACERA DE TILBA. One of the Tilba groups of
rapids on the shallow-draft navigable portion of the Río
Coco.

RAPIDO JUANA BAY. A rapid on the Río Waspuk (q. v.)
and a water route to the Bonanza goldfields.

RAPIDO KADAL. A major rapid on the Río Waspuk (q. v.)
and an avenue to the Bonanza goldfields.

RAPIDO KAIRASA. A River Coco Rapid on the Tilba group,
near R. Pistal Kiton.

RAPIDO LUMBU. A major rapid on the Río Waspuk (q. v.).

RAPIDO PARAWAS. A Río Waspuk (q. v.) rapid.

RAPIDO PISTAL KITAN. A rapid with a typical Miskito
name on the Río Coco.

RAPIDO PAUNKA KITAN. A cascade of the Río Waspuk
(q. v.). Note: the Miskito name typical of the northeastern region of Nicaragua.

RAPIDO TILBA. A major rapid on the light-draft navigable
portion of the Río Coco, above Carrizal.

RAPIDO TILBA LUPIA. A rapid on the Kukalaya River in
the Caribbean rainforest area of eastern Nicaragua.

RAYTI. A district of the municipio of Jinotega.

REAL DE LA CRUZ. 1) A cattle hacienda in the municipio
of Ciudad Darío, department of Matagalpa.
2) A district in the municipio of Ciudad Darío, department of Matagalpa.

REAL DE LA CRUZ, RIO. A stream in Ciudad Darío,
tributary to the Río Grande.

REALEJO, PARTIDO DE EL. In the area of modern Corinto,
one of the nine districts of the country under the Constitution of April 8, 1826, when it was one of the United
Provinces of Central America. See PARTIDOS DE
NICARAGUA.

REBELLION OF THE GREAT LAKE. This colorful revolt
during the Zelaya regime was characterized by the capture of the old Lake Steamer Victoria (which was still
a hulk in the 1960's). Occurring in 1905, the revolution
was short-lived, but was one of many attempts against
Zelaya, and left the Victoria bullet-pocked. The gunboat El 93 (q. v.) was also prominent in the fracas.

RECOLLECION, LA. This ornate church in León has a
grouping of columns similar to the unique Subtiava (q. v.)
parish church. It was built in 1788 under the bishopric
of Juan Félix de Villegos. The church is very much in
original condition, the last extensive work on it being
done in 1795. A later baroque work, it shows some
neo-classic influence, and is a good example of the tran-
sitional architecture between the older baroque and the
neo-classical which became popular at the opening of the
19th century.

RECOLLECTS. (Or, Recolectos.) The missionary order
that first planned work in Nicaragua during the terrible
buccaneer attacks of 1685, but were unable to do much
about it at that time. By 1706, the Crown of Spain ap-
proved a Recollect Convent in Granada, but this soon became principally a supply depot for Fort Inmaculada, the
major defense work of the Spanish south-eastern frontier.
These monks were frequently called the "Propaganda
Fidei" due to their zealous activities in behalf of the
poverty-stricken. During mid-18th century they were
highly active in Central Nicaragua, but the raids of 1749
resulting in Cáceres' death was the start of a rapid decline so that by 1765 they shifted their work to Panama.
The missions were essentially defunct in Nicaragua by

1762, when the Mission of Guadalupe near Apompuá was destroyed.

RECOPILACION DE LEYES DE LAS INDIES. The Spanish colonial experience was a remarkable burgeoning of administrative technique, with obvious imperfections and stifling bureaucratic overtones, but nevertheless unequalled both in challenge and response by any similar event or condition since. The first important publication of laws and regulations pertinent to the Indies was in 1567, with several versions during the next century. In 1680 a "final" and definitive edition was published which lasted until 1805, almost the remainder of the colonial period, and which covered all aspects of the colonial government and life, property, ecclesiastical matters, servitude and slavery, and fiscal and related policy. Not lacking in humanitarian emphasis, it was nevertheless a compilation so complex that enforcement proved to be if not impossible at least highly improbable and ineffective.

REDEMPTORISTS. A Catholic monastic order established in Nicaragua during the 20th century.

REDONDA, ISLA. Island in Lake Nicaragua off the Chontales shore.

RED STAR GUARDS. Many units who fought with William Walker in 1855-1857 in the "National War" chose colorful names such as this one.

REDUCCION MERCEDARIA. Founded in Metapa in 1627 for a place of defense against Carib raiders. (See CIUDAD DARIO.)

REFORMA. A quinta in the environs of Masaya.

REFORMA, LA. 1) A coffee hacienda in the municipio of Masatepe, department of Masaya.
2) A district of the municipio of Jinotega.
3) A district of the municipio and department of Masaya.

REGENERADOR NICARAGUENSE, EL. Periodical published in Managua, 1847.

REGIDOR see ADMINISTRATION, LOCAL

REGISTRO OFICIAL. A newspaper founded by Manual Blás
    Sáenz in January, 1845. Sáenz was a provisional di-
    rector. It was published from 1845 through 1847 in
    Masaya and Managua.

REIS, PERI. A Turkish hydrographer and mapmaker whose
    fragment kept in the Topkapu Soray of Istanbul shows the
    Atlantic and the New World, with coastal outlines which
    might be considered to represent Nicaragua. Reis stated
    that he copied it from a chart obtained from an Italian
    seaman who had been on three voyages with Columbus
    and who was captured by the Turks in 1497. There was
    at this time no knowledge on Columbus' part of the Cen-
    tral American Coast. The possibilities are intriguing--
    among them that either the "sailor" or Reis lied. How-
    ever, by 1513 the knowledge of that coast did exist. In
    the meantime, there have been theories of other pre-
    1502 visits, among them the remote possibility that one
    of the Cabots, Venetians sailing for England, made a
    landfall in Central America.

REPARTIMIENTO. The encomienda system of forced labor
    was used to provide workers for mining and plantation
    activities in the Spanish colonial era. The repartimiento
    was either a distribution or assignment of Indian laborers
    for this purpose, or was also used to mean a forced sale
    of goods to the Indian natives. This distribution or as-
    signment system was also used to carry out public enter-
    prises, drafting artisans or farmers accordingly.

REPARTO ADELITA. A modern subdivision to the south of
    the city of Granada.

REPARTO BILBAO. A Granada subdivision near the lake-
    shore, and south of the docks.

REPTILES see FAUNA

REPUBLICA DE NICARAGUA see NICARAGUA (General).

REPUBLICA MAYOR. This "Greater Republic" of Central
    America was a loose confederation of the three states,
    El Salvador, Honduras, and Nicaragua. Under the Bri-
    tish blockade of Corinto in 1895, and with the strong
    leadership of Nicaraguan President José Santos Zelaya,
    who was the strongest of Central American presidents
    in this period, there was an impetus toward union.

Essentially aimed to represent the three governments in external and diplomatic relations, the union was short-lived, dying when El Salvador withdrew in 1898.

REPUBLIC OF CENTRAL AMERICA. A project for the elusive Central American Union of 1893, which resulted in war between Honduras and Nicaragua in 1894, when Honduran troops crossed the border at Cape Gracias a Dios. Nicaragua occupied Bluefields (Mosquitia) on February 11, hauling down the Mosquito Flag. Chief Clarence of the Mosquitoes protested.

REQUERIMIENTO. A bit of legalization used in Spanish colonial times to justify war and the conquest of native peoples, this document was read to the native victims, and contained a description of the Papacy and Christian history, and the word of the Pope in assigning the helpless victims and their territories to the Spanish crown--hence, since the natives were on crown lands they owed not only allegiance but taxes and labor to the crown.

RESCUE. The very small paddle-steamer on the San Juan River which after the Titus fiasco of 1857 during the filibuster war, transported survivors of the J. N. Scott disaster down river. (See J. N. Scott and Lockridge.)

REVENTION, EL. A territory of the National District, department of Managua.

REVOLUTION AT EL BLUFF, 1894. Following the Nicaragua-Honduras conflict of 1893, in which Britain intervened, an abortive attempt was made by two Americans, 12 Britons and native Mosquito police to attack Nicaraguan forces at El Bluff, across the Bluefields Bay. Two Nicaraguan soldiers were killed, others wounded. The effect was that American citizens were interfering with Nicaragua's sovereignty. A ticklish political-diplomatic situation resulted. A Captain O'Neil, naval officer in command of U.S. forces in the area, diplomatically offered his services to the Nicaraguan commander in restoring order. American Marines landed. Nicaragua was aroused, troops were sent to chase Miskito Chief Clarence and his mulatto allies to Jamaica, and Bluefields was occupied. The rebel "Council of State" was ordered to appear. The culprit British and Americans were sent to Managua. The whole party was banished. Nicaragua soon lifted the ban on the American exiles,

and the Mosquitoes were persuaded to become Nicaraguan
citizens. On November 24, 1894, the Indians themselves
under Chief Clarence decided to become Nicaraguan citizens and be incorporated. Thus ended the long-standing,
frequently explosive, and highly questionable Mosquito
protectorate of the British. The area became in due
time the Nicaraguan department of Zelaya.

REVOLUTION OF 1909. In this year revolt against Zelaya
rose again, beginning at Bluefields under General Juan
J. Estrada. Among the latter's supporters were Adolfo
Díaz and General Emiliano Chamorro (each of whom
later served as president). Zelaya's capture and the
execution of two Americans, Cannon and Groce (both
q. v.), who attempted to plant a dynamite bomb to destroy a steamer at El Castillo, precipitated the arrival
of American Marines. When Zelaya attempted to blockade Bluefields, a U. S. warship intervened. As a result
of peace and of the expulsion of Zelaya, Estrada became
President and Díaz, Vice President.

RIBEIRO, DIOGO. A Portuguese cartographer in the service
of Spain whose world map of 1527 is probably the earliest to show clearly both coasts of Nicaragua. There
are tantalizing indications on other maps, but none as
clear as on this Mercator-type projection. It is an extremely competent world chart considering the extent of
knowledge at that time, especially in its accurate pro-
portioning of the vast extent of the Pacific Ocean.

RICA ABAJO. A district in the municipio of Yalí in Jinotega
department.

RICA ARRIBA. A district in the municipio of Yalí in Jinotega department.

RICOS see ARISTOCRACIA, LA

RIEGO, EL. A district in the municipio of Santa Lucía, department of Boaco.

RIEWE, FRED. This U. S. Marine, lieutenant of the National Guard commanding the barracks at Rama (far
from the usual Sandinista theatres), counter-attacked
when guerrillas briefly occupied the barracks by a ruse
in July, 1931. Half the guerrillas were local residents
of Rama, which provided what has become known as a
classic guerrilla situation.

RIGHTS, PERSONAL. Constitutional personal rights include freedom of conscience and religion, right of assembly, freedom of speech, and individual liberty. These may, however, be suspended by the President when "public tranquillity is threatened. "

RIGHTS, PROCEDURAL. The constitution of 1950 guarantees equality before law, public trial, trial by jury, habeas corpus, right of counsel, protection against self-incrimination, and "amparo, " which is the right of any citizen to apply to the courts for legal redress if he thinks an act of a public official or a law impairs his rights. Frequently illiterate mozos or campesinos go directly to the Presidential Palace for aid--and are listened to!

RINCONADA, LA. Cattle ranch in the municipio of El Sauce, León department.

RINCON DE DIABLO, EL. A spring in the Ciudad Darío area.

RINCONES, LOS. District of the municipio of Masatepe, department of Masaya.

RINCON LARGO. A district in the municipio of La Trinidad, department of Estelí.

RIO ABAJO. District of Pueblo Nuevo municipio of Estelí department.

RIO ARRIBA RODEITO. Comarca or district in the municipio of Achuapa, León.

RIO BLANCO. 1) Comarca or district in the municipio of Santa Teresa, Carazo department.
2) A district in the municipio of Matiguás, Matagalpa department.

RIO BLEWFIELDS see ESCONDIDO, RIO

RIO COCO see COCO, RIO

RIO DE DON GASPAR, EL. Comarca or district in the municipio of Jinotepe, Carazo department.

RIO DE LAS MARIPOSAS. Poetic name for the Río de Limay.

RIO DEL CABO   see   COCO, RIO

RIO DEL ENCUENTRAS   see   COCO, RIO

RIO FRIO   see   FORT SAN CARLOS

RIO GRANDE.   1) Comarca or district in the municipio of
    La Paz, León.
        2) A district of the municipio of Jinotega.
        3) District in the municipio and department of Rivas.
        4) The "Río Grande de Matagalpa" at its headwaters
    in the region of El Sauce.   A major stream, partly
    navigable.
        5) A stream in Carazo department.
        6) A district or valley in the municipio of San Rafael
    del Norte, Jinotega department.
        7) Hacienda in the municipio of La Paz, León.

RIO HUANQUI   see   COCO, RIO

RIO MICO.   1) Comarca or district in the municipio of La
    Libertad, Chontales.
        2) A principal river in the municipio of San Pedro
    de Lavago, Chontales department.

RIO NEGRO.   Coffee hacienda in the municipio of San Rafael
    del Norte in Jinotega department.

RIO NUEVO.   A district of the municipio of Sebaco, Mata-
    galpa department.

RIO SAN JUAN.   Formed from a part of the department of
    Chontales as well as the territory of San Juan (Comarca
    de San Juan) the present department was elevated to that
    status in July of 1949.   Bounded on the north by Zelaya
    and Chontales; on the south by the Costa Rican Border;
    on the east by the Caribbean Sea; and on the northwest
    by Chontales department, the most important geographi-
    cal feature is the San Juan River, running along the
    southern edge of the departmental territory.   Area 2, 850
    square miles; population 15, 400.   It is the department
    with the smallest population of any in the country.
    Principal products of the department are hardwood tim-
    ber such as mahogany; also cacao, bananas, and chicle.
    The department also contains the Lake Nicaragua archi-
    pelago of Solentiname.

RIO SICO. Comarca or district in the municipio of Diriamba, department of Carazo.

RIO VIEJO. A district in the municipio of San Isidro, department of Matagalpa.

RISITO, EL. Comarca or district in the municipio of Villa
Somoza, Chontales.

RIVAS, LOS. A district in the municipio of Santa Lucía,
department of Boaco.

RIVAS, ALFREDO. Brother-in-law of President Solórzano
in 1925, and commander of the fortress La Loma in
Managua in that critical year.

RIVAS, CIUDAD. 1) Ciudad Rivas has one of the most stirring
and ancient histories of any in Nicaragua. As "Nicaragua,"
the capital of the tribe under a cacique Nicarao, the
town was well established as an Indian capital for many
years before Columbus. Probably the name was Nicara-
ocalli, a "place" of the tribe (calli meaning location).
The 1966 population was about 8400; the altitude, approximately 250 feet above sea level; the location, five miles
from Lake Nicaragua and about 12 from the Pacific
Coast, in the center of the isthmus area between the
lake and the ocean. There are in the present town several barrios or extended suburban areas, known as La
Puebla, Obrero, Somoza, Mongalo and San Martín.
There is a distinguished colonial parish church. The
chieftaincy there established gave Nicaragua her name.
The first Spanish discovery by Gil Gonzalez Dávila occurred here. The present city centered around a church
of San Sebastián in 1657, although in 1607 Bishop Pedro
de Villareal had attempted to erect a church. Fifty
years later the San Sebastián Church was the heart
around which clustered the town. The aboriginal population and their descendants were in the environs.
    By 1717 there were about 3,000 inhabitants and in
that year Rivas became a villa, on the request of Salvador Granja and Marcos de las Navas. The former
name, "Pueblo del Valle de Nicaragua," was changed
to the name of "Villa de la Pura y Limpia Concepción
de Rivas de Nicaragua" named for Captain-General Rodríguez de Rivas, then incumbent in Guatemala. In 1743
the Captain-General had a report from engineer Luis
Díez Navarro, and in 1752 the Bishop Augustín Morel

de Santa Cruz visited Rivas. At this time the Villa had
over a hundred houses. Already many of the aboriginal
population had disappeared. Cattle, sugar cane, coffee,
and salt were the principal products. In 1773 a petition
was presented to change the status from villa to ciudad
but was denied. In 1811 an abortive rebellion was begun
in Rivas. (See Independence Movement.) It was crushed
in 1812, but was a forerunner of final colonial independence in 1821, and as such of great historical meaning to
the hemisphere. In 1835, partly because of this independence activity earlier, Rivas was finally designated a city.
An 1844 earthquake destroyed much of the town. In
1855-1857, Rivas was attacked by William Walker, and
it was here he fought his final Nicaraguan battle. Modern Rivas still bears the marks of Walker cannonading
in some of the older houses.

2) The present state or department of Rivas has as
its capital the city of Rivas and lies between the Great
Lake Nicaragua and the department of San Juan to the
east. To the west is the Pacific Ocean; to the north,
the departments of Carazo and Granada; and to the south,
the republic of Costa Rica. It is the farthest south of
Nicaragua's Pacific coastal departments. The area is
about 830 square miles. It is almost 45 miles long,
and 27 wide--at the narrowest part between Lake Nicaragua and the Pacific, only 11. 5 miles, the narrowest
isthmus between the waters of Atlantic and Pacific from
Alaska to Cape Horn. There is a long "pan-handle"
about two miles wide which extends down the lake shore
to the department of San Juan. A major feature is the
great Island of Omotepe in the lake, with its two volcanoes, one active, one inactive.

There are over 70, 000 inhabitants of the department,
over 20, 000 in urban areas. There are ten municipios:
Rivas, San Juan del Sur, San Jorge, Moyogalpa, Alta
Gracía, and Cárdenas among them. The area is generally flat with the exception of some coastal hills and the
volcanoes on the island. The streams run into both the
Pacific and the lake, which is on the Caribbean side.
Hence, the narrow and relatively low isthmus is a continental divide. There is major attention to agriculture
with cattle ranches a significant element. Sugar cane
is the second most important product and coffee third,
with over 1, 000, 000 coffee trees. In addition, corn,
beans, rice, and many fruits are raised. Cheese, and
other products are produced, as well as refined sugar.
Salt is evaporated from the sea. There are two ports,

San Juan del Sur on the Pacific, and San Jorge on Lake
Nicaragua. Between lake and ocean once ran Cornelius
Vanderbilt's blue and white coaches of the "Accessory
Transit Company," shortest trip (in time) from New
York to California in the gold rush days of the 1850's.

RIVAS, DAMASO. Doctor Rivas studied in the United States
and Europe, and is known for his work in parasitology.

RIVAS, GABRY. Conservative political leader who was the
center of a comic-opera coup on August 28, 1925, when
he led a slightly inebriated and motley band of insurgents
into the International Club in downtown Managua. In
boots, spurs, and ten-gallon hat Rivas fired into the
air, and after much shouting made off with the Minister
of Finance, Dr. Román y Reyes, and General José Moncada (both later presidents). The U.S. Ambassador
Charles Eberhardt was among those present. Rivas was
decrying the overly-liberal influence around President
Solorzano.

RIVAS, INDEPENDENCIA DE (1811) see INDEPENDENCE
MOVEMENT, RIVAS

RIVERA, ABRAHAM. One of Agustin Sandino's lieutenants
who in the early years of the Sandino revolt had been a
merchant in Bluefields. He carried out guerrilla activities around Bocay in 1931. Colonel Rivera also
plotted with Cockburn (q.v.) to capture Cabo Gracias a
Dios. Rivera occupied the Cape as a colonel with 40
guerrillas coming down the river in small boats from
Bocay. He contacted Cockburn at his Sacklin hacienda,
and took possession of the Cape without a battle on
April 15, taking over the customs-house and sacking
it. The Cape stores were also ransacked. A manager
of the Standard Fruit Company's Tropical Radio Station at
the Cape was saved from capture because he was spend-
ing the night aboard his yacht in the harbor. The town
was bombed by American planes in the afternoon. Rivera had charge of Sandino's sixth column. (See DE-
FENDING ARMY....)

RIVERA, JUAN MARIANO DE. Presbyter in Ocotal who
helped, with Colonel J. Miguel Irias, to attract people
and to develop the community.

RIVERS. The longest river in Central America is the Río

Coco (it may also possess the greatest variety of names!).
A summary of principal (and navigable) streams follows:
Río Coco, 200 miles long, 16 feet deep and 600 feet
wide; Río Prinzapolka, 100 miles long, 10 feet deep,
300 feet wide; Río Grande de Matagalpa, 120 miles long,
25 feet deep, 300-1000 feet wide; Río Curinwas, 10
miles long, 14 feet deep, 100 feet wide; Río Wawashon,
5 miles long, 10 feet deep, 60 feet wide; Río Escondido,
80 miles long, 25 feet deep, 1000-4000 feet wide; Río
Indio, 26 miles long, 10 feet deep, 40 feet wide; Rio San
Juan (including the lake), 215 miles long, 10-18 feet deep
(i. e., 105 miles below lake), 1200-1400 feet wide; Río Estero Real (Pacific), 20 miles long, 30 feet deep, 1000-4000
feet wide. The craft commonly used on lakes and rivers
vary from the several forms of dugout canoes (see pipantes, canoas, pangas, doris) to motor launches and
barges carrying up to 50 to 200 tons. On the Coco,
Escondido, and Río Grande, tugs and barges of shallow
draft operate. Small seagoing vessels are held out of
deeper rivers by the bars, as at Bluefields.

RIZOS, LOS. A district of the San Rafael del Sur municipio,
Managua department.

ROADS see HIGHWAYS

ROBERTS, ORLANDO W. Known for his only literary
work, Narrative of voyages and excursions on the east
coast and in the interior of Central America (1827),
Roberts was a trader on the Mosquito Coast for many
years, and his career began with command of a brig in
Kingston, Jamaica, in 1816. He had many trading adventures from Panama to Honduras, but in 1822 was
"captured" by Spanish authorities and taken to León, the
basis for his highly informative book and the excellent
map accompanying it, whereon most major features of
Nicaragua are shown with surprising accuracy. Roberts
is an interesting example of the broadly educated "practical" man of the 19th century.

ROBINSON, "GENERAL." A Sambo chieftain under Miskito
King George II, at or about the time of George's as-
sasination in 1795.

ROBLEDALITO. 1) A district of the municipio of Condega,
Estelí department.
    2) A mountain height in the same area.

ROBLES, LOS. 1) Clear spring in Estelf department.
2) A district of the municipio of Jinotega.

ROBLETO, HERNAN. Author of Sangre en el tropico (blood
in the tropics), a novel concerning the long United
States intervention in Nicaragua, and also one of the
founders of a series of local romantic periodicals in
Boaco in 1915.

ROCHA, LUIS DE. An encomendero of the Managua area,
mid-16th century.

ROCHA, LUIS DE LA. Early encomendero in the area of
Granada following the acts of imposing tribute, 1548.
He was given the Island of Omotepe in Lake Nicaragua.

ROCHESTER, U.S.S. This cruiser of the U.S. Navy was
flagship of the Special Service Squadron (q. v.) during
the period of the Sandino War in Nicaragua. The 105-
man Marine detachment was the largest afloat--it was
essentially a landing force. Home-port of the "CA-2"
was Balboa, Canal Zone. The Marine force was the
forerunner of the "floating battalion" (see Arkansas).
A landing force went ashore from the Rochester for a
three-month stay to supervise elections, and there was
a one-day excursion of Marines ashore in Cabo Gracias
a Dios to chase "bandits" in 1931. Nickname of the
ship was, inevitably, "Rocky. " She was also distinguished by having had three names--first, the New York,
then the Saratoga.

RODEO, EL. 1) A district in the municipio and department
of Estelf.
2) A district three miles southeast of Diriomo, Granada department.

RODRIGUEZ, DON NESTOR. Subprefect of Jinotepe upon
establishment of the subprefecture in 1889, prior to
formation of the department of Carazo in 1891.

RODRIGUEZ MOJICA, MARIA MANUELA. A ladino girl
captured by Colville Breton (q. v.) in 1782 at Juigalpa.
She gave the old Sumu chief of the Miskitos religious
instruction and he became a converted Catholic as a
result. Her marriage became a political matter of
considerable importance. She wished to break her

promise, but the whole Spanish presence on the Miskito Coast seemed to depend on her. They were married (she at age 15) but later a priest removed her from her unhappy bargain.

ROGACIONES. Prayers for specific acts by God or by a saint, frequently seeking rain or cures for illness. A priest and special Mass are usually involved, and frequently processions as well.

ROGATIVAS see ROGACIONES

ROMAN, DON J. A. A Nicaraguan senator appointed in 1890 to examine the work of the Maritime Canal Company and verify that terms of the concession had been met. The report was favorable and was concurred in by Román's associate, don Maximilian Sonnenstern.

ROMAN Y REYES, VICTOR M. President of Nicaragua under the aegis of the Somoza regime in 1948-1950. (See also RIVAS, GABRY.)

RONCHOUD. A French promoter authorized by Nicaragua in the 1840's to conclude an agreement with French capitalists for a canal or transit-way in Nicaraguan territory.

ROOSEVELT COROLLARY OF THE MONROE DOCTRINE. Having tremendous repercussions during the Nicaraguan interventions by U.S. Marines between 1912-1933, this corollary assumed United States' right to intervene in countries where internal order was breaking down or where there were threats of external interference. Elihu Root attempted to implement this policy as Theodore Roosevelt's secretary of state 1905-1909.

ROSALES, BENITO see TERAN, TORIBIO

ROSARIO, EL. 1) Comarca or district in the municipio of Jinotepe, Carazo department.
2) District in the municipio and department of Rivas.
3) Important finca in the municipio of La Concepción, department of Masaya.
4) A municipio in the department of Carazo, smallest in the department, slightly over three and a half square miles, with 2,100 population. Bounded on the north by Masaya, south by Santa Teresa, east by La Paz, and

west by Jinotepe. There are four districts. The area is known for the richess of artifacts from pre-Columbian times, particularly ceramics.

5) A pueblo brought into being in 1848, the small town has 1, 000 inhabitants and is the principal place in the municipio of the same name.

ROSARIO, RIO EL. A stream-bed in Pueblo Nuevo municipio of Estelí department.

ROSARIO ABAJO. A district in the municipio of La Trinidad, department of Estelí.

ROSARIO ARRIBA. A district in the municipio of La Trinidad, department of Estelí.

ROSITA. A village in the mining region of Zelaya; there is an airstrip.

ROSITA MINE. Also known as Santa Rita, it is in the northeast mining zone in the Tunkey district 30 miles northeast of La Luz. From 1906 to 1912, it was worked for gold by the Eden Mining Company. In 1916 it was acquired by the Tonapah Mining Company; in 1949, by Venture Ltd. (the La Luz group); and in 1962, by Venture's successor, Falcon Bridge of Canada. Copper explorations were carried out in 1931 to 1955. The copper is in the form of malachite, azurite and other cuprous minerals, with some oxide. There is also hematite. In 1957, reserves of copper sulfate at 5. 00% copper were estimated at 200, 000 tons, and of carbonates, 3, 582, 000 tons at 2. 91%. Copper has become a fairly important Nicaraguan export.

ROSQUILLAS. A dish prepared from corn and cheese.

ROTA. Comarca or district in the municipio of Larreynaga, León.

ROUTH. A shallow-draft river steamer which figured in the filibuster war during an incident at Punta Arenas in May, 1853.

RUICES DE ABAJO, LOS. A district of the municipio of La Concepción, department of Masaya.

RUICES DE ARRIBA, LOS. A district of the municipio of La Concepción, department of Masaya.

-S-

SAAVEDRA, ALVARO DE. First man of record to conceive
a canal through Nicaragua by the San Juan River/Lake
Nicaragua route. The conception antidated 1528. (See
GALVAO and XAQUATUR.)

SABALOS. A district in the municipio of Cárdenas, department of Rivas.

SABANA, LA. District in the municipio of Altagracia on
Omotepe Island in Lake Nicaragua, department of Rivas.

SABANA GRANDE. 1) Comarca or district in the municipio
of El Sauce, León department.
2) District in the municipio of Potosí, Rivas department.
3) A territory of the National District, department
of Managua. (Actually a suburban area with characteristics of a town.)

SABANA LARGA. A district in the municipio of La Trinidad, Estelí department.

SABANAGRANDE. A district or valley in the municipio of
San Rafael del Norte, Jinotega department.

SABANETAS, LAS. A comarca or district in the municipio
of Larreynaga, León.
1) Las Sabanetas, a comarca or district in the municipio of La Paz, León.

SACACLI. A district or valley in the municipio of San
Rafael del Norte, Jinotega department.

SACASA. A distinguished Nicaraguan family, among whom
were many leaders (see following entries).

SACASA, DON CRISANTO, 1774-1824. Ancestor of the
Crisanto Sacasa who was the first rector of the National
University and later (1950's) Minister of Public Education, this distinguished Nicaraguan was the son of Roberto Sacasa and Paula Parodi. Married early to An-
gela Méndez, his descendants were and are numerous
and distinguished.

SACASA, FRANCISCO. A captain in command of the second

company of Nicaragua at the Battle of San Jacinto,
September 14, 1856.

SACASA, GUILLERMO SEVILLA. A news release of 1971
quoted U.S. President Nixon as saying that as ambassador from Nicaragua and as dean of the diplomatic corps
in the U.S., Sacasa had "lived through six presidents,
nine chiefs of protocol, nine secretaries of state ...
four speakers [of the House] and four chief justices.
Any man who can survive that long has got to be quite
a man." Dr. Sevilla Sacasa is the brother-in-law of
Nicaragua's current President, Anastasio Somoza hijo.
The Sevilla Sacasas are famed for their qualities as
diplomatic hosts.

SACASA, JUAN BATISTA. Sacasa was the proclaimed legitimate successor to deceased Diego Chamorro in 1923,
when Emiliano Chamorro seized power. Becoming President after Moncada, he served from 1933 to 1936, and
signed a peace treaty with Sandino who was killed, however, allegedly by members of the Guardia Nacional.
He built the Banco Hipotecario de Nicaragua and opened
the National Pawn Shop. During the Sacasa regime the
strong man of the country was Anastasio Somoza García,
General and head of the National Guard.

SACASA, ROBERTO. President of Nicaragua from 1889-
1893, Sacasa's term was terminated early by revolution,
which began in León on July 11, 1893, and was headed
by General José Santos Zelaya. Zelaya took over and
remained in power 16 years.

SACUANJOCHE. Frangipani, the national flower of Nicaragua. It is native and profuse; the name is Indian.

SAENZ, MANUEL BLAS. Following Silvestre Selva and José
Montenegro (q.v.) in the 1845 period, Sáenz was provisional director of Nicaragua. He founded the newspaper
called Registro Oficial in 1845.

ST. FERDINAND. This parish church of Masaya was begun
in the late 17th century, enlarged in the 18th and given
a facade in 1800, with further work in 1833. Remarkable for its three entrances, it is stylistically related to
Granada. Pilasters have a series of upright and inverted
urn forms.

ST. MARY'S (Corvette).   The U. S. Naval vessel which was
    lying in the harbor of San Juan del Sur under command
    of Captain Charles H. Davis when William Walker's last
    defense in Rivas was sputtering out.   Walker surrendered
    to Davis on May 1, 1857, and he and his surviving band
    were taken to Panama, thence to be sent to the United
    States for trial as neutrality-law violators.

SAIZ.   A district in the municipio of Matiguás, Matagalpa
    department.

SAHSING LAYA, LAGUNA.   A small lake just off the Río
    Prinzapolka near Alamikamba.

SAKIANG.   A district in Zelaya department along the Makan-
    taka road south from Alamikamba.

SALALE.   Comarca or district in the municipio of El Sauce,
    León department.

SALAZAR, CANONIGO REMIGIO.   Writer, orator, wise lead-
    er, Salazar was one of the most refined and educated
    personages of Nicaragua during the middle 1800's.   A
    resident of El Viejo in 1849, he was noted for his vir-
    tues and philanthropies by Squier (q. v.).

SALCEDO, DIEGO LOPEZ DE.   Captain Salcedo was named
    by the governor of Honduras in 1527 to proceed to Nica-
    ragua and take possession as far as the lakes.   There
    is reason to believe Salcedo killed many inhabitants of
    the country along the route.   Imprisoned in the recently
    established fortification of León (now León Viejo, an
    archaeological site), Salcedo finally returned to Hon-
    duras in 1529 with a soldier escort, but took with him
    381 Indian slaves from Nicaragua.   This was the first
    and last campaign of Indian enslavement in the history
    of the country, although under Pedrarias and within the
    encomienda system there was a decimation of the Indian
    population.

SALESIANS.   A Catholic order, often emphasizing vocational
    education, which has schools and engages in other active
    aid to the people of Nicaragua.

SALGADO, ANGEL.   Born in 1894, this literary follower of
    the poet Rubén Darío died of tuberculosis in 1920, one
    of several Darío disciples who met tragic ends.

SALGADO, CARLOS. Sandinista general of the early 1930's in charge of the Second Column. (See DEFENDING ARMY....)

SALINAS, LAS. A district of the municipio of San Juan de Tola, Rivas department.

SALINAS, DON SEBASTIAN see CABINET OF PATRICIO RIVAS

SALINAS, JUAN DE. Scribe attending the expedition of discovery of Nicaragua in the Rivas Isthmian area in 1522, headed by Gil Gonzáles Dávila.

SALINAS, JUAN FERNANDEZ DE. Governor of Nicaragua, 1665-1672, overlapping the captain-generalcy of Mencos, Maestre de Campo de Salinas surveyed the San Juan River for a fort site, and chose the mouth of the Pocosol River on the Costa Rican side. He built there a stockade, the first Fort San Carlos (not to be confused with the one now in ruins at the head of the river). Seventy musketeers were assigned, and four light cannon provided. (See SAN CARLOS, def. 1.)

SALINAS GRANDES. Comarca or district of the municipio of León, León department.

SALITA. Living room in open "rancho" style houses.

SALITRE, EL. Comarca or district in the municipio of El Sauce, León department.

SALITRE, RIO EL. Stream in the municipio of El Sauce, León department.

SALMERON, FAUSTINO. The man who killed Byron Cole (q.v.), commander of filibuster Walker's forces at the Battle of San Jacinto, first major defeat for the North Americans. Salmerón became a central American hero thereby. He was also credited with first reporting the onset of the American column.

SALMON, NORVELL. Captain Salmon of the British warship Icarus delivered William Walker (q.v.) to the Hondurans in September, 1860. Walker was then executed by a firing squad.

SALT. Salt production in Nicaragua is primitive but considerable, using a series of tanks in locations along the
Pacific Coast where the sea water may be evaporated.
These evaporating pans produce a product 85% to 90%
sodium chloride, whereas a similar but more refined
process should achieve 99. 4%.

SALTO, EL. 1) A clear spring in Estelí department.
2) A district of the San Rafael del Sur municipio,
Managua department.

SALTO DE CARNERO. Falls and rapids on the Río Grande
de Matagalpa in the Muy Muy municipio, Matagalpa department.

SALTO DE ESQUIRIN. A falls on the Río Grande de Matagalpa, where are found many pictographs and archaeological pieces such as ceramics and idols.

SALTO DE ESTANZUELA see CASCADA DE ESTANZUELA

SALTO DE LA OLLA, EL. A district in the municipio of
Matiguas, Matagalpa department.

SALTO NEGRO. Waterfall on the Río Bulum in the municipio Villa Somoza, Chontales.

SALTO YAHU. A major cascade on the Río Waspuk (q. v.).

SAMARIA, CERRO DE. Mountain of the Isabella Range in
Jinotega department, altitude 5, 500 feet.

SAMBO-MISKITOS. The mixed-blood inhabitants of the Mosquito Coast who emerged as early as the mid-1600's as
a blend of white, Negro, and Sumu Indian. The Sumus
were indigenous, the whites were early traders, and the
blacks were brought in as slaves to work plantations and
to cut timber; their number was further augmented by
the wreck of a Cartagena-bound Portuguese slave-ship
in 1641. The Sambo-Miskitos allied themselves with the
buccaneers who appeared in numbers in the late 1600's,
and who led raids on the Spanish frontier to the westward in the Segovias. In the 18th century they proved
warlike at every opportunity. It is also useful to regard
Sambos and Miskitos as separate, for there were differences (see appropriate references).

SAMULALI. A district in the municipio and department of Matagalpa.

SAN AGUSTIN. A district of Terrabona municipio, Matagalpa department.

SAN ALBINO MINE. Butter's gold mine at San Albino figured in the Sandino War of 1927 and years following. Sandino's first operation on his own was to occupy the mine where he had once been employed. This occurred in June of 1927. The owner, Charles Butters of Oakland, California, appealed to the U.S. Marines for aid. The mine valued at $700,000 was the largest single foreign investment in Nicaragua. Later, the Sandinistas used the mine and its shop equipment as an armory where they manufactured trench mortars from iron pipe and bombs from rawhide bags of dynamite mixed with stones, glass, and iron. They apparently minted coins here also.

SAN ALEJANDRO. Hacienda in the municipio of Rivas.

SAN ANDRES. A district in the municipio of San Isidro, department of Matagalpa.

SAN ANDRES DE AYOTEPE. A territory of the municipio of Del Carmen, Managua department.

SAN ANDRES DE LA PALANCA. A territory of the Mateare municipio, department of Managua.

SAN ANDRES DE LOS SANCHEZ. A territory of the National District, department of Managua.

SAN ANDRES DE TOTUMBLA. A cattle hacienda of 130 acres, granted to don Pedro de Tórrez in Matagalpa department in 1717.

SAN ANTONIO. 1) Cattle ranch in the municipio of Yalí, Jinotega department.
2) A coffee "beneficio" in the municipio of La Concepción, department of Masaya.
3) Coffee hacienda in the municipio of La Concepción, department of Masaya.
4) Comarca, valley or district in the municipio of Juigalpa.
5) Comarca or district in the municipio of La Paz, León.

6) A district in the municipio and department of Estelí.

7) A district of the municipio of Jinotega.

8) Comarca or district of the municipio of Nagarote, León department.

9) District of Pueblo Nuevo municipio, Estelí department.

10) A district of the municipio of Yalí in the Jinotega department.

SAN ANTONIO DE ABAJO. Comarca or district in the municipio of Diriamba, department of Carazo.

SAN ANTONIO DE ARRIBA. Comarca or district in the municipio of Diriamba, department of Carazo.

SAN ANTONIO DEL NORTE. Comarca or district in the municipio of Achuapa, León.

SAN ANTONIO DE PIRE. A hacienda of 195 acres granted in the Valley of Estelí to José, Ambrosio, María Dionisia and Jacoba Benavídez in 1742.

SAN ANTONIO MINE. One of the Bonanza (q. v.) group of mines.

SAN ANTONIO NUMERO DOS. Comarca or district of the municipio of León, León department.

SAN ANTONIO NUMERO UNO. Comarca or district of the municipio of León, León department.

SAN BARTOLO. A district of the San Rafael del Sur Municipio, Managua department.

SAN BENITO. 1) Coffee hacienda in the municipio of Esquipulas, Matagalpa department.
2) Comarca or district of the municipio of León, León department.

SAN BUENAVENTURA. Comarca or district in the municipio of La Libertad, Chontales.

SAN CARALAMPIO. A district of the municipio of La Concepción, department of Masaya.

SAN CARLOS. 1) The first protective fortification established on the Río San Juan, Fort San Carlos, a wood stockade, was completed in 1667, manned by 70 musketeers, and equipped with four light cannon and their crews. Far downstream from the other later, better known Fort San Carlos (see def. 2), this stockade did not last long, and nearly 200 miles from Granada was almost impossible to support. A freebooter called Prince Lubberough took the fort with 200 men from old Providence Island in 1670. The garrison had only 37 effectives--the rest were ill or dead. Lubberough went on to sack Granada again.

2) Hastily erected in early 1780 by Bricio under the orders of Gálvez (see Pedro Bricio and Matías Gálvez), the fort named for Charles the III of Spain was a second line of defense on the colonial frontier, intended to· back up Fort Inmaculada 40 miles down the San Juan River, under attack at the time by a large British expeditionary force. The earthworks of this fort still exist, and a small clay airfield and dingy stilt-perched river port (see def. 4) commemorate the name San Carlos. The site is a commanding one at the point where the San Juan, a large stream, flows out of Lake Nicaragua and toward the Caribbean, and where a hundred yards from this outlet the deep Río Frío flows into Lake Nicaragua from origins in the Costa Rican highlands.

3) This side-wheel paddle-steamer was named for the fort and town (see def. 2 and 4) at the southeastern end of Lake Nicaragua and at the head of the San Juan River, and was the largest vessel on the Lake during the Walker era. Filibuster control of the two lake steamers La Virgen and San Carlos gave an edge to Walker over Costa Rican General Mora.

4) The present location of the town of San Carlos was based on the hasty fortification of 1780 (see def. 2). On a slight eminence just north of the headwaters of the Río San Juan, the town is still based around the old fort, remains of which are evident; there is an airstrip, and there are numerous docks. The location is famous for tarpon fishing; and April brings most fishermen from Managua and elsewhere. There is boat service on the lake and a weekly launch downstream to San Juan del Norte. The population is 1,550, making it the largest town in Río San Juan department, of which it is also the cabacera.

5) Coffee hacienda in the municipio of Masatepe, department of Masaya.

6) Comarca or district in the municipio of Diriamba, department of Carazo.

SAN CAYETANO. A district of the San Rafael del Sur municipio, Managua department.

SANCHEZ, LOS. 1) A district of the municipio of La Concepción, department of Masaya.
2) A district of the municipio of San Juan de Tola, Rivas department.

SANCHEZ, VICTORIA DE. A school in San Isidro del Guayabal named for a functionary of the Servicio Cooperativo de Educación Pública during the 1950's. Mrs. Sánchez gave leadership in elementary education.

SANCHEZ DEL NORTE, LOS. A district of the San Rafael del Sur municipio, Managua department.

SANCHEZ DEL SUR, LOS. A district of the San Rafael del Sur municipio, Managua department.

SAN CRISTOBAL. 1) A cattle ranch in the municipio of La Concordia, department of Jinotega.
2) A district of the San Rafael del Sur municipio, Managua department.
3) Volcano in the range of Los Marabios, tied for fifth highest in the country with Peñas Blancas at 5,726 feet. Reported over 6,000 feet until recent times. Mildly active in the period since the conquest. Better known locally as El Viejo, it is in the department of Chinandega. The last volcanic activity was reported in 1685. The crater is between 600 and 900 feet deep in various portions.

SAN DIEGO. Comarca, valley or district in the municipio of Juigalpa.

SANDINO, AGUSTO CESAR. Guerrilla leader in Nicaragua (1927-1933). Variously called bandit, patriot, hero, and villain, Sandino has been considered by some scholars to be the first of the modern guerrilla organizers of a "people's army." Born May 18, 1895, the "natural" (i.e., pre-marriage) son of don Gregorio Sandino (from a wealthy family) by Margarita Calderón, a servant girl. He early went by the name of Agusto Calderón. Later, living with his father, who had a sizable library, the boy, who was also a lover of classics, began to be Agusto C. Sandino, the "C" standing for "César." He studied in a Granada high school, later worked in his home town of Niquinohomo,

and after a time left to work for Vaccaro Brothers and
Company (later Standard Fruit) in Honduras at La Ceiba.
He also worked in Guatemala and Tampico, Mexico.
Mexican nationalism appealed to him and he became pos-
sessed by a mysticism and a messianic sense of mission
about Latin American nationalism.   Returning to Nicaragua in 1926, he worked for the San Albino gold mine
in Nuevo Segovia.   Here he lectured mine workers on
injustice, and discovered his power of leadership.   From
Honduras gun-runners, he raised arms to equip a band
of 29 men.   Failing in an attack on the Jícaro garrison,
he led his band to the Caribbean Coast and joined the
Constitutionalists under Moncada.

When the peace of Tipitapa was signed, Sandino did
not lay down his arms.   For the next six years he carried on a guerrilla war which became a classic pattern
for such "guerrilleros" as Castro and Guevara.   The
principal opponent was the U.S. Marine expeditionary
force; a principal tactic, terror; a principal strategy,
following his contemporary Mao Tse Tung's dictum of
being a "fish" in the water represented by the common
people.   His first major engagement was at Ocotal,
where a pitched-battle with Marines under Captain G.
D. Hatfield was fought on July 16, 1927.   Among his
strongholds was the famous fortified mountain "El
Chipote."   Sandino was in Managua for a peace conference when he was seized and shot on February 21, 1934,
allegedly by members of the National Guard.   His name
lives on in "Sandinista" movements, one of which was
active in Nicaragua in 1969, involving a battle in which
tanks were used in Managua streets.   Sandino has been
the subject of considerable revolutionary literature, including fiction.   Carleton Beal's assessment of Sandino
in 1965 bears repeating (The Nation, September 20,
1965, "In Quest of Sandino, Imperialism Still Rides"):

Throughout the vast Latin-American world, this century's
outstanding popular hero is Agusto C. Sandino who for
six years (1927-1933) fought for the independence of
Nicaragua against foreign invasion by the most powerful
military nation in history--the United States.   His David-
Goliath exploits are the theme of songs and ballads.   He
is celebrated in articles, biographies and novels.   His
ghost has haunted every Pan-American reunion and every
good-will emissary from Hoover to Nixon.   His fame
reaches far beyond Latin America....

SAN DIONISIO. 1) A municipio of the department of Matagalpa, this area is distinguished by being in the form of a
miniature map of Nicaragua, of about 40 square miles
with 3,700 population. Bounded on the north by Matagalpa; on the south by Esquipulas and Terrabona; on the
west by Terrabona again; and on the east by Esquipulas
and part of Matagalpa. Some of the mountains of the
department are nearby, such as Susuli and Piedra Colorada; there are two rivers, the San Dionisio and the Los
Limoes. The usual food crops are raised plus some
sugar cane and bananas, but coffee and cattle are the
major enterprise. There are seven districts or comarcas.
2) Pueblo San Dionisio, cabacera of the municipio of
the same name in Matagalpa department, was founded
in 1830 and has about 800 inhabitants presently.

SANDOVAL, BARTOLO. A Captain of Nicaraguan forces
who commanded close pursuit of the enemy rear-guard
at the September 14, 1856, Battle of San Jacinto.

SANDOVAL, JOSE LEON. Elected director of the new nation by the Nicaraguan legislative assembly by decree
of April 4, 1845, Sandoval served during the period
when the chief events were the insurrectional activities
of the several caudillos--Valle, Bernabe Somoza, and
Gallardo. He was succeeded by Licenciado José Guerrero.

SANDOVAL, LUIS BELTRAN. Leader of liberal troops in
May, 1926, who attacked and captured the town of Bluefields, taking into custody the departmental governor and
the director of police, as well as the National Bank and
its funds of $161,642.00. These liberals also captured
the customs house, and soon controlled a major sector
of the east coast; Rama, La Cruz, Río Grande, and
Bragman's Bluff (Puerto Cabezas). Emiliano Chamorro
declared a state of war on the basis of this action.

SANDY BAY SIRPI. Village on the Caribbean Coast five
miles north of the Río Grande mouth.

SAN ESTEBAN. 1) Comarca, valley or district in the municipio of Juigalpa.
2) A district of the municipio of Jinotega.

SAN ESTEBAN DE LA SUCESION. Hacienda in the municipio of Rivas.

SAN FELIPE. 1) Hacienda in the municipio of Rivas.
    2) Barrio San Felipe, one of the seven districts of
the city of León as identified in 1811, it was founded in
1651, under the name "San Felipe de Austria." At that
time it was largely peopled by mulattos and mestizos as
well as free Negroes.

SAN FERNANDO. 1) An airfield near Lomo El Naranjo,
Boaco department.
    2) A municipio in Nueva Segovia department with 480
population. In the northwest of the department near
Nicaragua's highest mountains, the Mogotón on the Honduran border.

SAN FRANCISCO. 1) A municipio of the department of Managua, area 220 square miles, population 5,800. It was
only a comarca or district until after 1900. Bounded on
the north by Matagalpa department; south by Lake Managua; east by Tipitapa; and west by León department;
it is a broad plain on the "other side of the lake" from
Managua. There are only three districts.
    2) Coffee hacienda in the municipio of La Concepción,
department of Masaya.
    3) Coffee hacienda in the municipio of Jinotepe, Car-
azo department.
    4) Coffee hacienda in the municipio of Masatape, de-
partment of Masaya.
    5) Coffee hacienda in the municipio of San Marcos,
Carazo department.
    6) Coffee plantation in Pueblo Nuevo municipio of
Estelí department.
    7) A district in the municipio of La Trinidad, Estelí
department.
    8) A district of the municipio of Nindirí in Masaya
department.
    9) District of Pueblo Nuevo municipio, Estelí depart-
ment.
    10) Mountain height in the municipio of Pueblo Nuevo,
Estelí department.
    11) A church built in León in 1639 under Fray Pedro
de Zúñiga, first bishop of Nicaragua.
    12) An ancient church in Granada, the original fortress
on the site probably being older than the Subtiava Church
(q.v.) although its nonsecular construction post dates
that of the "oldest church." In any event, construction
on the site is from the first half of the 16th century.
Here in the adjacent Franciscan monastery, Hernando

de Soto, explorer of Florida and discoverer of the Mississippi River, once was imprisoned, and Bartolomé de
Las Casas, Protector of the Indians, preached here:
the mid-16th century fortress was intended to be a
stronghold for treasure. The present facade was restored in 1862 after the Walker War. An open-arch bel-
fry is distinctive. During the Walker War of the 1850's
the building was used as a hospital, and in the 1950's as
industrial arts and homemaking shops for schools. Fort,
treasury, prison, monastery, church, hospital, shop,
school--the old adobe buildings have had perhaps the
most varied history of any in the country. The walls
are three-feet thick in places, of adobe, with an overlay
of thin hard lime plaster.

SAN FRANCISCO DEL CARNICERO. Cabacera of the municipio of Managua department just north of Lake Managua, the village has a population of 800. There is
commerce across the lake to the city from the local
dock. There is a coal mine in the area, mined under
concession by Carlos F. Goddard who was given this
right in 1907.

SAN FRANCISCO DEL COYOL. Comarca, valley or district
in the municipio of Junigalpa.

SAN FRANCISCO DEL CUAPAN see SITIO DE CAUPA

SAN FRANCISCO DEL GAMALOTE. Comarca, valley or
district in the municipio of Juigalpa.

SAN FRANCISCO NANAICA. An old townsite established in
1678 by Fray Pedro Lagares in the Pantasma valley
area, eastward of the Río Coco at that point. The town
has entirely disappeared.

SAN FRANCISCO Y EL CONGO. District in the municipio
of Altagracia on Omotepe Island in Lake Nicaragua, department of Rivas.

SAN GABRIEL. 1) Comarca or district in the municipio of
La Paz, León department.
    2) A district or valley in the municipio of San Rafael
del Norte, Jinotega department.

SAN GREGORIO. A gold mine opened in 1868 in Chontales,
owned by "Jackson and Marenco." Production was not
sufficient to support the enterprise.

SAN GREGORIO DE LOS ANGELES. Comarca or district in the municipio of Diriamba, department of Carazo.

SAN GREGORIO DE LA ERMITA. Comarca or district in the municipio of Diriamba, department of Carazo.

SAN IGNACIO. 1) Comarca, valley or district in the municipio of Acoyopa, Chontales.
2) A district of the municipio of La Concepción, department of Masaya.
3) Comarca or district in the municipio of Larreynaga, León.
4) A district of the municipio of San Juan de Tola, Rivas department.

SAN ILDEFONSO. 1) Cattle ranch in the Tipitapa municipio of the department of Managua.
2) Comarca or district in the municipio of Larreynaga, León.

SAN ISIDRO. 1) Comarca or district of the municipio of León, León department.
2) District in the municipio and department of Rivas.
3) The smallest municipio of Matagalpa department, of an area 36 square miles and population 6,500 persons. Bounded on the north by La Trinidad of Estelí, south by Ciudad Darío, east by Sebaco, and west by San Nicolás of León, the municipio has six districts or comarcas. Recently cotton culture has been a principal concern as this is the northwesternmost part of the valley of Sebaco. The Río Viejo is the only continuous stream. There are cattle raised as well as cotton, with other familiar Nicaraguan crops.

SAN ISIDRO DE BOLA. A territory of the National District, department of Managua.

SAN ISIDRO DE LA CRUZ VERDE. A territory of the National District, department of Managua.

SAN ISIDRO DEL GUAYABAL. Cabacera of the municipio of San Isidro in Matagalpa department, the name was given to the pueblo under President Martínez in 1862. The present population of 2,000 serves the agricultural countryside.

SAN JACINTO. 1) Cattle ranch in the Tipitapa municipio of

the department of Managua.
2) Comarca or district in the municipio of Télica, León.
3) A cotton gin and processing plant in Télica, León department.
4) A hacienda in southernmost Granada department.
5) Sugar cane plantation in the municipio of León, León department.

SAN JACINTO, BATTLE OF   see   BATALLA DE SAN JACINTO

SAN JERONIMO.   1) Coffee hacienda in Condega municipio, Estelí department.
2) Comarca or district of the municipio of Santa Teresa, Carazo department.
3) Mountain in the municipio of La Libertad in Chontales.

SAN JOAQUIN.   1) A district in the municipio and department of Estelí.
2) A district and hacienda on the western slope of the dead Volcano Mombacho, south of Granada.

SAN JOAQUIN MINE.   One of the Bonanza (q. v.) group of mines.

SANJON DEL SANTO CHRISTO.   Comarca or district in the municipio of Télica, León.

SAN JORGE.   1) With a population of 3, 300, the municipio of San Jorge is on the shore of Lake Nicaragua bounded on the north by the municipio Buenos Aires, on the south by Rivas, on the east by the lake, and on the west by Rivas municipio also.   The land is flat and good for cultivation.   Cattle and sugar cane are principal crops. There are several small streams, emptying into the lake.
2) Elevated to city status in 1931, the Villa of San Jorge had a turbulent political history in earlier years. The name originated in the mid-1500's, and the area was known, following the coming to the region of Fray Pedro de Betanzos, as "Provincia Franciscana de San Jorge de Nicaragua. "   The present town became a villa in 1852.   It figured in the Walker War, and represents the successor to an aboriginal town and an early colonial Indian town, now both disappeared.   The "Cross of

Spain" near San Jorge commemorates the place where tradition indicates Gil González Dávila and the Cacique Nicaragua had their historic first meeting. The place as a community, "Barrio de España" has also disappeared.

3) A district of the municipio of La Concepción, department of Masaya.

4) District in the municipio and department of Rivas.

SAN JOSE. 1) Cattle ranch in the municipio of San Juan del Sur, Rivas department.

2) A coffee "beneficio" in the municipio of La Concepción, department of Masaya.

3) Coffee hacienda of Dr. Alejandro Castro in Diriamba municipio, Carazo department.

4) Coffee hacienda in the municipio of La Concepción, department of Masaya.

5) District of the municipio of Masatepe, department of Masaya.

6) A stream bed in Pueblo Nuevo municipio of Estelí department.

SAN JOSE BOCAY. A district of the municipio of Jinotega.

SAN JOSE DE GRACIAS. Comarca or district of the municipio of Santa Teresa, Carazo department.

SAN JOSE DEL CARDON. Coffee hacienda in the Sierras de Managua, of the National District.

SAN JOSE DE LA MONTAÑA. A district of the San Rafael del Sur municipio, Managua department.

SAN JOSE DE LEON. Cattle ranch in the municipio of San Juan del Sur, Rivas department.

SAN JOSE DEL NORTE. District in the municipio of Altagracia on Omotepe Island in Lake Nicaragua, department of Rivas.

SAN JOSE DEL RIO DE LOS MONOTES. A cattle ranch in Chontales, granted to Don Domingo de Verganza in 1643; size, 5 caballerías, or about 165 acres.

SAN JOSE DEL SUR. 1) District in the municipio of Altagracia on Omotepe Island in Lake Nicaragua, department of Rivas.

2) A district in the municipio of Moyogalpa on Omotepe Island in Lake Nicaragua, Rivas department; one of
the four districts of the municipio which is in effect a
village or pueblo.

SAN JOSE DEL TRIONFO see   TRIONFO DE LA CRUZ.
One of the towns which has "disappeared" in northwestern Jinotega department.

SAN JOSE DE TECOLOSTOTE.   Cattle ranch in Chontales
granted in 1739 to the heirs of Don José Ramírez; size,
10 caballerías, or 334 acres.

SAN JOSE DE UMURE.   A district in the municipio and department of Matagalpa.

SAN JOSE MINE.   Old Spanish mine between Macuelizo and
Amatillo in Nueva Segovia department, showing a quartz
vein eight or nine feet in depth.   There are three old
tunnels, only one of which can be traversed.   Gold and
silver ore was produced.

SAN JOSE MONTEVIDEO.   Coffee hacienda in the Jinotega
department.

SAN JOSE PARAKA.   An ancient townsite established in
1678 by Fray Pedro Lagares in the Pantasma valley
area.   The town has entirely disappeared.

SAN JOSE, RIO.   Stream in the municipio of El Sauce,
León department.

SAN JOSE YAPALI.   A district or valley in the municipio
of La Concordia, Jinotega department.

SAN JUAN.   1) Cattle ranch in the Tipitapa municipio of the
department of Managua.
2) Coffee hacienda in the municipio of Masatepe, department of Masaya.
3) Barrio San Juan, a district of the city of León
which during colonial days was peopled with "free Indians. "   It was organized as a pueblo prior to 1797.

SAN JUAN DE BUENAVISTA.   1) See   HATO GRANDE.
2) Another cattle ranch of the same name as the alternate name for "Hato Grande, " but granted in 1719 to
Captain don Fernández del Valle, near Juigalpa.   Three
caballerías, or 100 acres.

SAN JUAN DE COCOLISTAGUA. About 90 acres granted as
a cattle hacienda, near Terrabona in Matagalpa department. Grant given in 1715 to Antonio, Bárbara and
Catalina de Rivas. (See following entry.)

SAN JUAN DE COCOLISTAGUA Y LA PICOTA. Granted title in the years 1715-1720, this Spanish cattle hacienda
was also a sugar plantation, granted to Antonio, Bárbara,
and Catalina de Rivas originally of León. The town of
Terrabona developed on the hacienda site. Ruined hacienda structures still exist on the site.

SAN JUAN DE LA CARIDAD. A gold mine in Chontales begun in the year 1858, owned by José León Avendaño.
Production, 1 1/2 ounces per ton.

SAN JUAN DE LA CONCEPCION. Valley, comarca, district,
and near-barrio of La Concepción (cabacera), in the municipio of La Concepción of Masaya department. (Also
called San Juan de la Concha.)

SAN JUAN DE LA CONCHA see SAN JUAN DE LA CON-
CEPCION.

SAN JUAN DE LA CONCORDIA. Second official name of the
port of San Juan del Sur (q. v., def. 2), in 1840 replacing "Puerto de la Independencia. " It lasted as a name
for ten years. (See CIUDAD PINEDA.)

SAN JUAN DEL DULCE. Popular name of the Valley of
San Juan de la Concepción in La Concepción municipio
of the department of Masaya, because of the great production of sugar in the valley.

SAN JUAN DE LIMAY. 1) A municipio of the department of
Estelí, area 185 square miles, population 10, 400.
Bounded on the north by Pueblo Nuevo, Las Sabanas,
and San José de Cusmapa of Madriz department; and
on the east by Estelí and by Achuapa, León department.
There are 16 districts. The area is mountainous, and
there are several streams. Two lakes, Lagunas Negros,
are in the Colocondo Valley. The mineral district of
La Grecia is within the municipio. Cattle and general
agriculture are the principal economic activities.
   2) A town of 2, 400 inhabitants, this cabacera of the
municipio of the same name is located in an especially
lovely deep bowl-like valley surrounded by mountains.

SAN JUAN DE LIMAY, RIO DE. One of the principal
streams of Estelí department, a principal tributary of
the Río Negro.

SAN JUAN DEL MONTE. District in the municipio and department of Rivas.

SAN JUAN DEL NORTE. Known as Greytown during many
years of British influence, this port at the mouth of the
San Juan River on the Caribbean Sea has had a history
of conflict and importance greatly disproportionate to its
size. The bay was once a port for ocean-going vessels
in the 18th and 19th centuries. It was the portal to the
San Juan River and hence to the only feasible cross-
Nicaragua route for centuries. It saw the forces under
Despard and Horatio Nelson (both q. v.) as well as those
under William Walker (q. v.). The present population is
under 400, and there are only a few signs of former activities. Giant dredges still rust in the mouth of the
only canal ever dug on this route--a short beginning
made in the 1890's. There was even a railroad parallel
to the canal. In 1908-1910, the population was over
2, 000. The principal product is copra. There is weekly launch service upriver. The port is a municipio of
Río San Juan department. Greytown is known for the
remarkable longevity of its sparse population. Several
nonagenarians live there.

SAN JUAN DEL SUR. 1) A municipio in the department of
Rivas, second in importance in the department, a light-
erage port and a favorite Nicaraguan resort area because of its crescent Pacific beach. The port is third
in importance in the country. Area, 110 square miles,
with a population of 5, 000, almost half of them in the
cabacera of the same name. It is a curious fact that
San Juan del Sur, the port, is actually north of San
Juan del Norte, another port of the Caribbean Coast.
Both were named for the seas which wash them rather
than for their geographic relationship to each other.
The municipio is bounded on the north by Rivas, on the
south by the Pacific and the Republic of Costa Rica, on
the east by the municipios of Rivas and Cárdenas, and
on the west by the Pacific again, with a 20-mile stretch
of coast. There are several rivers, emptying into the
Pacific, and several heights, the low range running from
north to south. Part of the southernmost coast is on
the Bay of Salinas, much of which is bordered by Costa

Rica.   Cattle raising and fishing are characteristic economic activities.   There are also salt mines and quarries.
There are seven districts.

2) The little town of San Juan del Sur is both historic
and picturesque, with two jutting points sheltering a perfect crescent of beach over a mile long.   Bays, islands,
and streams enhance the adjacent Pacific Coast.   It is a
resort area which is a favorite of upper-class Nicaraguans,
and many maintain vacation homes there.   As a lighter-
age port, it used to have a considerable traffic, especially
when from the 1930's until the late 1950's, a narrow-
guage train ran from the beach of San Juan to San Jorge
nearby on Lake Nicaragua.   A lighthouse marks the port
on an extended point, and on a crest above the light are
the ruins of an early 19th-century fortification.   It was
the terminus of the Accessory Transit in the 1850's
when Commodore Vanderbilt's blue and white coaches
carrying the Nicaraguan crest came from his lake steamers at La Virgen over a good road (part of which is extant) to the Pacific port where other vessels cleared for
San Francisco and the California Gold Rush.

Discovered by Andrés Nino in 1522, the bay became
a port in about 1830, following independence, and was
designated "Puerto de La Independencia"--later, in 1840,
it was called "San Juan de la Concordia, " and then in
1851-1852, "Ciudad Pineda. "   But in the late years of
the 19th century its name reverted to the original "St.
John of the South [Sea]. "   It became a customs port of
entry in 1859 under the Tomás Martínez administration,
and a "Puerto de Depósito" in 1885.   International cables
come ashore at this point.   There are over 2,000 inhabitants, and there are four barrios--Chino, Auxiliadora,
La Planta, and Holmann.   The fishing industry, in addition to sport fishing in nearby teeming Pacific waters,
has increased in recent years.

SAN JUAN DE ORIENTE.   1) Less than five square miles
in area, this municipio is the least populated in the department of Masaya, with less than 1,000 inhabitants,
over 600 of them living in Pueblos of San Juan de Oriente.
To the north in the municipio of Catarina; to the south,
the department of Granada; to the east, also Granada;
and to the west, Niquinihomo municipio.   There are only
two comarcas or districts.   There is in addition to the
usual agricultural pursuits considerable ceramic work
done, of a good quality, an industry inherited from aboriginal forebears.

2) Cabacera of the small municipio of the same name, this pueblo has changed little since the 18th century. San Juan is near Catarina; both are spread over irregular terrain.

SAN JUAN DE TOLA. 1) This municipio of the department of Rivas, known popularly as "Villa de Tola, " has 210 square miles, largest in the department. There are approximately 9, 000 inhabitants. It is bounded on the north by Carazo and Belén, south by Rivas, east by Rivas and Belén, and west by the Pacific Ocean. There are 20 miles of Pacific Coast. The municipio has 21 districts.

2) The pueblo name comes from Nahuatl or Mexican origins, and means "land of the Toltecs, " signifying sacred land, hence it is of very ancient pre-Columbian beginnings. The present village is of about 800 persons. It was the first place upon which William Walker and his 58 "Immortals" descended when they invaded the area on June 27, 1855. Several Nicaraguan soldiers were killed and others wounded in the skirmish.

SAN JUAN, PORT OF ENTRY. In 1791, following an advantageous treaty with England in 1786, the Spanish established a port of entry at the mouth of the San Juan River--San Juan del Norte--and a customs house which was a further effort to confirm the recent and tenuous hold they had over the Caribbean Coast.

SAN JUAN VIEJO. A district in the municipio of Belén, Rivas department.

SAN LAZARO. A district of the municipio of Moyogalpa on Omotepe Island in Lake Nicaragua, Rivas department.

SAN LORENZO. 1) A district in the municipio of La Trinidad, Estelí department.

2) A district in the municipio of San Juan de Limay in the department of Estelí.

3) A district of the San Rafael del Sur municipio, Managua department.

4) Large "finca" or farm in the municipio of El Sauce, León department.

SAN LUCAS. Comarca, valley or district in the municipio of Acoyapa, Chontales.

SAN LUIS.   1) A district of the city of León.
   2) Important finca in the municipio of La Concepción,
department of Masaya.

SAN LUIS and EL PORTAL.   Coffee haciendas under one
ownership in the municipio of Yalí, Jinotega department.

SAN MARCOS.   1) Municipio in the department of Carazo,
of 50 square miles and 11,500 population, on the high
central tableland.   Bounded to the north by Masaya,
south by Diriamba and Jinotepe, and west by the department of Managua, the municipio is in the northeastern
part of Carazo.   The principal activity is coffee culture,
with cattle raising and honey production also important.
Served by the railroad "de los Pueblos," there are also
road connections to the departmental capital, Masaya,
and other points.   There are 14 districts.
   2) This cabacera of the municipio of San Marcos,
Carazo department, has 6,000 population.   Originally
in the department of Granada, San Marcos was founded
by several families: the Campos, Martínez, García,
and Rojas families, originally of Jinotepe.   By 1820 it
had status as a pueblo.   It was made a villa in 1905,
and a ciudad in 1916.   It is known as a place of origin
of the presidential Somoza family.   It is likewise a significant coffee merchandising center.   A girl's normal
school is located here, for the preparation of elementary
teachers.
   3) A comarca or district in the municipio of San Nicolás, León.
   4) District in the municipio of Altagracia on Omotepe
Island in Lake Nicaragua, department of Rivas.
   5) A district in the municipio of Belén, Rivas department.
   6) Cattle ranch in the municipio of San Rafael del
Norte, Jinotega department.
   7) A district in the municipio and department of Matagalpa.

SAN MARTIN.   1) District in the municipio and department
of Rivas.
   2) A traditional Nicaraguan dance which has disappeared.

SAN MARTIN, CRISTOBAL DE.   Encomendero of the Managua
area following 1548.

SAN MIGUEL.   1) Cattle ranch in the municipio of Nindirí,

department of Masaya.

2) District in the municipio of Altagracia on Omotepe
Island in Lake Nicaragua, department of Rivas.

3) The first gold mine to be worked in Chontales according to record, in the year 1854, by "Gago y Jiménez
y Compañía, " located near the municipio of La Libertad
and Santo Domingo.   Production, two ounces gold per
ton.

SAN MIGUEL DE RIO GRANDE.   Comarca or district in the
municipio of Jinotepe, Carazo department.

SAN MIGUELITO.   1) Comarca, valley or district in the municipio of Juigalpa.

2) Comarca or district of the municipio of Nagarote,
León department.

3) A municipio of the department of Río San Juan, a
lake port on the north shore of Lake Nicaragua.   There
is a long pier, and cattle as well as lumber are principal ventures.   Large plantings of rice are nearby.
The population is about 900.   There is boat service on
a regular schedule twice a week.   Somewhere in the
hinterland to the east is the site of Nueva Jaén (q. v.),
now long disappeared.

SAN NICOLAS.   1) Municipio in the department of León,
area 81 square miles, population 4, 300, bounded to the
north by Estelí, to the south by Santa Rosa, to the east
by La Trinidád of Estelí department and San Isidro of
Matagalpa department, and to the west by El Sauce.
There are four districts or valley areas.

2) Cabacera of the municipio of the same name, it is
a place of small population and no business ventures,
awaiting road connection to Estelí to evade extinction.

3) Cattle ranch in the municipio of León, León department.

4) Comarca or district in the municipio of Achuapa,
León.

5) A district in the municipio and department of Matagalpa.

SAN NICOLAS DE MOMOTOMBO see PAZ, LA (no. 4)

SAN NICOLAS DE LOS NABORIOS see PAZ, LA (nos. 3
and 4)

SAN PABLO.   1) Comarca, valley or district in the munici-

pio of Acoyapa, Chontales.
2) A district of the municipio of San Ramón, Matagalpa
department.

SAN PEDRO. 1) A municipio of the department of Chinandega, just over 30 square miles in area, with 3,200
population. On the northeast and west the area is bounded by Honduras, and south by the municipios Cinco Pin-
os, San Francisco, and Santo Tomás. There are seven
districts.
2) Coffee hacienda in the municipio of Masatepe, department of Masaya.
3) Coffee hacienda in the municipio of San Marcos,
Carazo department.
4) Comarca or district of the municipio of El Jicaral,
León.
5) Comarca or district in the municipio of Quezalguaque, León.
6) A district in the municipio and department of Estelí.
7) A district in the municipio and department of Matagalpa.
8) A district of Terrabona municipio, Matagalpa department.
9) A large spring in Estelí department.

SAN PEDRO BUCULMAY. A district of the municpio of
Jinotega.

SAN PEDRO DEL NORTE. A district along the lower Río
Grande where the Río Tuma enters Zelaya department.

SAN PEDRO DE LOVAGO. Municipio in the department of
Chontales; population 7,800 in 1968, 148 square miles.
Seventh in size, and sixth in population in the department, the municipio is bound on the north by the municipios Juigalpa, La Libertad, and Santo Domingo; on
the east by Santo Tomás; Juigalpa again on the west;
and on the south, Acoyapa and Santo Tomás.

SAN PEDRO E ISABEL. Sugar cane plantation in the municipio of León, León department.

SAN PIO. A corvette, Spanish ship under command of Captain Gonzalo Vallejo (q.v.) in 1786.

SAN RAFAEL. 1) Coffee hacienda in the municipio of Jinotepe, Carazo department.

2) Comarca or district of the municipio of León,
León department.
3) District in the municipio and department of Rivas.
4) Plantation in the municipio of Quezalguaque, León.

SAN RAFAEL DEL NORTE. 1) Second municipio in size in
the department of Jinotega, this one has an area of 173
square miles and a population of 6, 370. It is bounded
on the north by Nueva Segovia, on the south by Estelí
(department), on the east by the municipio of Jinotega,
and on the west by the municipios of Yalí and La Concordia. There are nine "comarcas" districts, or valleys
in the municipio. Important for coffee culture; cattle
raising and general agriculture are also practices. Sugar
cane is among these products. Ceramics, weaving, and
sugar production are carried on.
2) The town of San Rafael is the cabacera of the municipio of the same name in the department of Jinotega.
Population, 1, 300. The present site was not the first,
that being, until 1848, where the present town of La
Concordia stands. The move caused conflict among two
factions, lasting until 1851.

SAN RAFAEL DEL SUR. 1) Cabacera of the municipio of
the same name, Pueblo San Rafael del Sur has 2, 500
population. Located on the low Pacific littoral of the
department of Managua, it is close to the beaches--
Masachapa and Pochomil. The cement plant is a major
industry nearby. President José María Moncada was
born here; also don Rodrigo Sánchez, linguist.
2) This is a municipio of Managua department, area
120 square miles, 17, 000 population. Bounded on the
north by Managua municipio; on the south by the Pacific
Ocean (it lies between the Sierras de Managua and the
Pacific); on the east by Carazo and by Managua municipio; and on the west by El Carmen, and again the
Pacific. Several beaches are used a great deal by Managua residents, as they are the closest sea beaches to
the city. A great cement plant, the "Fábrica Nacional
de Cemento, " is in the area. A sugar refinery, Monte-
limar, is also here. There are many limestone and
other quarries. There are 31 districts.

SAN RAFAEL DE OCHOMOGO. District in the municipio of
Potosí, Rivas department.

SAN RAMON. 1) A municipio of the department of Matagalpa,

of 298 square miles in area and 21, 500 inhabitants.
Bounded on the north and west by the municipio of Matagalpa, on the south by Muy Muy, and on the east by
Matiguás municipio.   Cattle, hogs, and coffee are the
agricultural production of the area, as well as chickens
and various food crops.   The Nestlé Company has interests in the area.

2) Cabacera of the municipio of the same name in the
department of Matagalpa, the pueblo of about 500 inhabitants was established around 1800 by the missionary
priest Fray José Ramón Rojas de Jesús María, of León.
While the "La Leonesa" mine operated, about 2, 000
workers lived in the area early in this century.

3) Comarca, valley or district in the municipio of
Juigalpa.

4) District in the municipio of Tisma, department of
Masaya.

SAN RAMON MINE.   This mine is located in the Pis Pis
district near the Bonanza group "Constancia" mine.   A
20, 000 ton reserve has a value of 0. 21 ounces per ton
of gold and 0. 57 ounces of silver.

SAN ROQUE.   1) Comarca or district of the municipio of
León, León department.

2) A district in the municipio and department of Estelí.

3) District in the municipio of Potosí, Rivas department.

4) A district of the municipio of San Francisco, Managua department.

SAN SALVADOR.   1) A district in the municipio and department of Matagalpa.

2) A mountain height in the municipio of Matagalpa.

SAN SEBASTIAN.   1) A district of the city of León.

2) A Rivas church which has disappeared, but which
was in ruins in 1871.   It was from the ruins of the
church that the hero Juan Santa María sallied against
Walker's men in the Battle of April 11, 1856.

SAN SEBASTIAN DE LA RICA.   Coffee hacienda in the municipio of Yalí, Jinotega department.

SANTA ANA.   1) A cattle ranch and plantation in the municipio of Masaya.

2) A district in the municipio of Esquipulas, department of Matagalpa.

3) A district in Zelaya department along the upper
Río Prinzapolka.

4) Hacienda on the northwest slopes of volcano Mombacho, dead giant south of Granada.

5) Quinta or country house in the vicinity of Niquinohomo.

SANTA ANA MINE.   The area known as Santa Ana includes
an old mine with a tunnel nearly 100 feet long, cut
through quartz and gravel deposits partly timbered.
The River Jícaro flows nearby, and the area is near
the confluence with the Murra River.

SANTA BARBARA.   1) Cattle ranch in the municipio of El
Sauce, León department.

2) A district of the municipio of Jinotega.

SANTA BULA.   Monolith in the Amerrique range, a volcanic
plug, municipio of Juigalpa.

SANTA CASIMIRA.   Hacienda in the municipio of La Paz,
León.

SANTA CECELIA.   Coffee hacienda of the family of Dr.
José Rodríguez Blán in Diriamba municipio in Carazo
department.

SANTA CLARA.   1) Comarca or district in the municipio
of Villa Somoza, Chontales.

2) Mountain lake in Estelí department.

SANTA CRUZ.   1) Comarca or district in the municipio of
Achuapa, León.

2) Comarca or district of the municipio of Santa
Teresa, Carazo department.

3) A district in the municipio and department of
Estelí.

4) District in the municipio of Tisma, department
of Masaya.

5) Large "finca" or farm in the municipio of El
Sauce, León department.

6) Mountain in the municipio of Estelí.

SANTA CRUZ DE CHONTALES.   A cattle ranch in Chontales,
granted to ensign (alfárez) don Leandro López Jorge of

Granada in 1719.   Size, nine and a half cabellarías, or about 316 acres.

SANTA CRUZ DEL NARAJAL.   A cattle ranch granted by the Spanish crown to don Miguel Mateo in 1606, located in the department of Chontales.   In the region of the Achoapan River; size, four caballerías, or about 134 acres.

SANTA ELENA.   Cattle ranch in the municipio of Tipitapa, department of Managua.

SANTA ENRIQUETA.   Coffee hacienda in the Jinotega department.

SANTA FE.   A district of the municipio of Jinotega.

SANTA GERTRUDIS (o Los Gomez).   Comarca or district of the municipio of Santa Teresa, Carazo department.

SANTA ISABEL.   1) Hacienda on the shores of Lake Nicaragua just south of the Isletas de Granada.
    2) Spring in the department of Estelí.
    3) Sugar cane plantation in the municipio of León, León department.

SANTA JUANA.   1) Coffee hacienda in the municipio of Masatepe, department of Masaya.
    2) Comarca, valley or district in the municipio of Juigalpa.

SANTA JULIA.   Coffee hacienda in the Sierras de Managua, National District.

SANTA LASTENIA.   1) Coffee hacienda in the Jinotega department.
    2) A district of the municipio of Jinotega.

SANTA LUCIA.   1) Smallest of the municipios in the department of Boaco, is most densely populated.   Essentially agricultural, it produces sugar cane, coffee, grains, and henequen.   There is a textile production as well. The area is cool and of a highland nature.   Population, 5, 500, altitude, 2, 200 feet--within the municipio, much land is 3, 000 to 3, 500 feet high, giving an excellent climate.
    2) Cabacera of the municipio Santa Lucia, Jinotega

department.
   3) A cattle ranch in the Tipitapa municipio of Managua department.
   4) Comarca or district in the municipio of Diriamba,
department of Carazo.
   5) Comarca or district in the municipio of El Sauce,
León department.
   6) Comarca or district in the municipio of Larreynaga, León.
   7) Comarca or district of the municipio of Nagarote,
León department.
   8) A spring in the Ciudad Darío area.

SANTA MARGARITA.   A hacienda on the low southeast
   slopes of the dead volcano Mombacho, Granada department.

SANTA MARIA.   1) A mountain height in the department of
   Matagalpa, municipio of Esquipulas.
   2) Westernmost of the Nueva Segovia municipios,
   Santa María is just about two miles from Honduras.
   Population is 270.

SANTA MARIA DE LA ESPERANZA.   A location earlier
   known as Pueblo de Las Minas, in the region of Juanamostega.   (See CAMPAÑON.)

SANTA MARIA DE OSTUMA.   A district in the municipio
   and department of Matagalpa.   This is the seat of a
   delightful inn which is a popular mecca of persons wishing a lovely mountain setting at an invigorating altitude.

SANTA MARIA DE PANTASMA.   A district of the municipio
   of Jinotega.

SANTA MARIA DE TASUA.   A district of the municipio of
   Jinotega.

SANTA MARTA.   1) Comarca, valley or district in the municipio of Acoyapa, Chontales.
   2) Village on the road from Puerto Cabezas to Waspam in northern Zelaya department.

SANTA PANCHA MINE.   This mine is near the El Limón
   mine in León department, 20 miles northwest of Momotombo Volcano.   Gold and silver production; now no
   longer active.

SANTA RITA. 1) Comarca, valley or district in the municipio of Juigalpa.
2) A district of the municipio of Niquinohomo, Masaya
department.
3) See MONTE FRESCO.
4) A spring in the southern part of the municipio of
León.

SANTA RITA MINE   see   ROSITA

SANTA ROSA. 1) Municipio of León department, area 79
square miles, with 6, 000 population. Principal mountains are Ocotal, El Jicote, El Picacho, Azacualpa,
Quebrachal, Confite, and Ocotillo. Bounded on the
north by San Nicolás, south by El Jicaral, east by
Ciudad Darío, and west by El Sauce, it is a mountain-
eous section north of Lake Nicaragua. There are 11
districts other than the cabacera of the same name.
The district is significant for its mines, such as La
India, San Lucos, Dos Hermanas, El Pilar, San Juan,
El Potrero, and El Nancitol.
2) Pueblo with concentration on agriculture and mining, cabacera of the municipio of the same name.
Popularly called "Santa Rosa del Peñon. " Much of
the activity is at the La India Mine.
3) Cattle ranch of Dr. Roberto Castro Silva in Diriamba municipio of Carazo department.
4) Coffee processing plant in Jinotepe municipio,
Carazo department.
5) Comarca or district in the municipio of La Paz,
León.
6) A district of the municipio of Condega, Estelí
department.
7) A district in the municipio of San Isidro, department of Matagalpa.
8) Hacienda in the municipio of La Paz, León.

SANTA ROSA DE APAGUAJI. 1) A relatively small grant
of a hacienda, 160 acres, made January 30, 1711 to
Domingo Gómez in the Valley of Estelí.
2) A small lake in the department of Estelí.

SANTA ROSA DEL MALACO. A cattle ranch on Chontales
known as Subosa, granted to the Conquistador of Chontales, Captain Don José Antonio de Vargas in 1772.
Size, five caballerías, or 167 acres.

SANTA ROSA DEL PARRALES. Comarca or district in the municipio of Larreynaga, León.

SANTA ROSA DE TAPASKUN. A district in the municipio of Jinotega.

SANTA SARA. Cattle ranch in the municipio of El Sauce, León department.

SANTA TERESA. 1) Municipio of the department of Carazo, of 13,000 population; bounded on the north by La Paz and El Rosario, on the south by the Pacific Ocean, on the east by Rivas and Granada and on the west by Jinotega and La Conquista. Sugar cane is the principal crop with coffee second. The regional port of Escalante is located in the municipio. There are 27 districts.
2) Cabacera of the municipio of the same name, the town as 4,000 population, and was termed a "city" in 1949.
3) Coffee hacienda in the municipio of San Marcos, Carazo department.

SANTA VICTORIA. An eminence in the foothill area of the lower Río Tuma, Zelaya department, 1,700 feet altitude.

SANTA VIRGINIA. Cattle ranch of don Benjamín Gutiérrez in Diriamba municipio of Carazo department.

SANTIAGO. 1) Volcano also called Vol de Masaya, five miles west of Masaya, with four distinct craters active into the late 1950's, but presently dormant. Quite low at 1,936 feet, the volcano is impressive because of the large craters and the huge surrounding lava fields, one of them extending down into Lake Masaya, which is itself 1,100 feet above sea level.
2) Coffee processing plant in the Jinotepe municipio, Carazo department.

SANTO DOMINGO. A territory of the National District, department of Managua.

SANTO DOMINGO. A gold mine owned by the "Compañía Minera de Chontales," organized by a group of Englishmen in 1860. The manager of the company was naturalist and engineer Thomas Belt, who wrote the well-known work The Naturalist in Nicaragua.

SANTOLAR. A district in the municipio of Matiguás, Matagalpa department.

SANTO TOMAS. 1) Cabacera of the municipio Santo Tomás,
population about 1800, formerly based on the Indian town
of Loviguisca, which was moved four times. Inhabited
by Chontals, and invaded by "barbarous Indians" from
the Atlantic Coast, the town was originally eight miles
east of the present one. The final moves were in 1747
and 1861, the name Santo Tomás being adopted on the
latter date.
    2) Municipio in the department of Chontales, popula-
tion 6, 170 in 1968, area 150 square miles. Bounded on
the north by municipios San Pedro de Lovago and Santo
Domingo; on the south by municipio Villa Somoza; on the
east by El Rama in the department of Zelaya; and on the
west by Acoyapa and San Pedro de Lovago.

SAN UBALDO. Comarca, valley or district in the municipio
of Acoyapa, Chontales.

SAN VICENTE. Comarca or district in the municipio of
Diriamba, department of Carazo.

SANZ, JUAN DE. One of the captains on the expedition
which discovered Nicaragua in 1522 under the command
of Gil Gonzáles Dávila.

SAPELCOS. A Nicaraguan political party nickname, in opposition to Chapiollos (q. v.).

SAPOA. A district in the municipio of Cardenas, department of Rivas.

SARAGUASCA, CERRO DE. Part of the Guasgualf branch
of the Darien Range of mountains in Jinotega department.

SARK. A gasoline launch ("lancha de gasolina") used by
revolutionaries in the early 1900's on the San Juan River.

SARSAPARILLA. The root of this plant was early traded
on the Mosquito Coast and when sent to Europe gained
fame as a cure for venereal disease, elephantiasis, and
scrofula.

SASLAYA. Mountain on a spur of the Isabella range, for
years and in many sources listed as the highest moun-

tain in Nicaragua. It is, however, only the tenth highest mountain at an altitude of 5,414. Maps as recent
as 1955 showed the altitude as 8,500. It is in Zelaya
department, about 60 miles west of Quilali. (The more
accurate mapping was an interamerican cooperative venture of the 1950's.)

SAUCE, EL. The fourth largest municipio in the depart-
    ment of León, with an area of 27 square miles and a
    population of 12,000. Bounded on the north by Achuapa
    and Estelí, in Estelí department; on the south by Larrey-
    naga; on the east by San Nicolás and Santa Rosa; and on
    the west by Villanueva, in Chinandega department.
    There are 13 districts. Cattle raising, coffee culture,
    and general farming are principal agricultural pursuits.
    There is a rail connection to León.

SAUCE, RIO DEL. River in the vicinity of El Sauce.

SAZ, JUAN DE see SANZ

SCCS see ORGANIZATION OF AMERICAN STATES

SCHILT, CHRISTIAN FRANK. · A U.S. Marine lieutenant
    who from January 6-8, 1928, evacuated 30 wounded
    men from the Segovia town of Quilalí. There was no
    airstrip in the little mountain town, so surviving Marines
    demolished buildings along one side of Quilalí's main
    streets to allow Schilt to land. The runway was only
    250 yards long, and as his Vought O-2-U Corsair bi-
    plane landed (under severe enemy fire) Marines dragged
    on the wings; they held him back as he "revved-up" for
    take-off as well. This feat of "superhuman skill" was
    a pioneer venture in medical evacuation by air and won
    Schilt the Congressional Medal of Honor, still considered
    one of the most deserved in Marine history.

SCIEP see SERVICIO COOPERATIVO INTERAMERICANO
    DE EDUCACION PUBLICA

SEABORNE COMMERCE. The six ports of Nicaragua handled
    about 1,200,000 metric tons of cargo in 1967, but of this
    half was through the Pacific Port of Corinto, best and
    most improved of the available ports. About half that
    amount came through Puerto Somoza, and a tenth of
    that through San Juan del Sur. Only 10 percent of the
    total came to the three east-coast (Caribbean) ports of

Puerto Isabel, Puerto Cabezas, and El Bluff (near Bluefields). Puerto Somoza is principally an oil port, served
by a pipeline. Puerto Isabel deals mainly in the export
of copper concentrates. Storage facilities, berthing
space, and shallow harbors or open roadsteads are still
problems of seaborne commerce. Corinto is the only
truly modern and adequate port, and its facilities are
limited.

SEAFARERS (Middle American). Seagoing tribes seem to
have reached the Colombian Coast from Middle America
about 500 B.C. It is also probable that Florida and the
Bahamas were reached, accidentally or otherwise, by
these seafaring peoples of 25 centuries ago. We remember that Columbus saw a 70-foot vessel on his fourth
voyage in the Caribbean area (1502).

SEAL OF NICARAGUA. The great seal, used on the coinage and in many official applications, consists of an
equilateral triangle crossed by a rainbow at the apex.
Under the rainbow is a liberty cap; under that (and
springing from water at the base of the triangle), five
volcanic peaks. The symbolism of Hope and Liberty,
and the basic geography of lakes and volcanoes is clear.
In some applications the seal is surrounded by the words:
"República de Nicaragua América Central. " The seal
is used centered on the Nicaraguan flag. (See illustration.)

SEBACO. 1) A municipio of the department of Matagalpa,
area 119 square miles, 7, 000 population. Taking up the
broad Valley of Sebaco, where in aboriginal times was
a large population, the municipio is bounded on the north
by the municipios of Jinotega and La Trinidad (in Jinotega and Estelí department, respectively); on the south
by Ciudad Darío and Terrabona of Matagalpa; on the
east by Matagalpa; and on the west by San Isidro. There
are ten comarcas or districts. The great rivers of the
area are the Río Viejo and Río Grande de Matagalpa.
To the east are mountains; there are several small
lakes and ponds. Cattle, horses, mules, hogs, and
chickens are raised. There is a considerable truck
garden area with onions, tomatoes, and other vegetables
in abundance. Cotton is also a major crop. The region
has been of major agricultural importance since earliest
pre-conquest times; there are over 300 fincas or agricultural holdings.

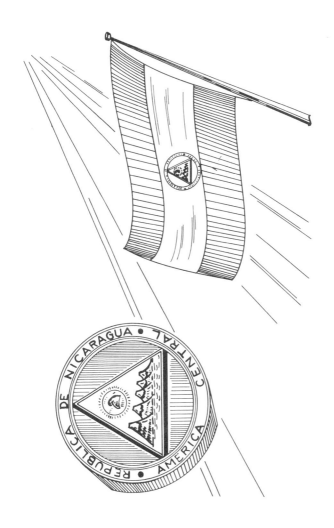

Seal of Nicaragua

2) This town is essentially of recent founding, no more than 30 or 40 years ago. The population of Sebaco has resided in four different locations; that of Tecuasnapa, recently abandoned; in the area of "Los Congos" from the year 1770; and also the ancient "Sebaco Viejo, " as well as in the present site. Now with a population of over 1, 500, the town was in 1544 made part of the Encomienda of don Rodrigo de Contreras. Legends of lost gold mines and rebellion against colonial authority abound in the region. By 1608, Sebaco was known as a base for Christian missions, but by 1693, there was an uprising against the government under Gabriel Bravo de Hayos. By 1715, Sebaco was the cabacera of the region. However, this ancient urban area had disappeared by the 20th century. The present population of the relatively new town is 2, 500. Truck farming and raising of poultry are important activities of the area. The name comes from Chorutegan words cihoa, "mother, " and coatl, "serpent"; hence, "mother-serpent. " The name derives from an ancient legend of the area.

SECOND NICARAGUA CAMPAIGN. Official terminology for the conflict of 1927-1932, so similar to the recent Vietnam conflict, in which U. S. Marines fought inside the country against the elusive Sandino. Some say that military aviation "came of age" in this war. The participants here proved to be leaders over a decade later in the World War II conflict in the Pacific theatre.

SECRETO DEL ESTRECHO. The "secret of a strait" was a well-kept one until the opening of the Panama Canal in 1914, since there was no natural strait from Atlantic to Pacific waters in the hemisphere from Point Barrow, Alaska to the Strait of Megallan. From Columbus' time onward the idea of such a strait, natural or man-made, was an obsession of many and various people. The "nearest" to a strait was the great valley across Nicaragua, with its San Juan River system and Lake Nicaragua, and the 12-mile long, low isthmus from the lake to San Juan del Sur.

SEGOVIA, PARTIDO DE. One of the nine districts of the country under the Constitution of April 8, 1826, when it was one of the United Provinces of Central America. (See PARTIDOS DE NICARAGUA.)

SEGOVIA, RIO. The Río Coco is often called the Río Segovia, as the northern departments of Nicaragua are called Las Segovias, after Segovia in Spain.

SEGOVIAS, LAS. The northern departments of Nicaragua, in general the north country in the Río Coco area, named for Segovia in Spain and after the towns called Nueva Segovia which were established successively in at least three locations not far from the Río Coco and near the present town of Quilalí.

SEGUNDO, EL. A periodical developed in Boaco in 1915.

SEGUNDOS. The middle class in Nicaragua, also called "los medio acomodados"--hence the "second ones" or the "medium wealthy." Applied to smaller landowners, minor government officials, lesser merchants, and to some artisans, these levels depend upon the community. "Segundos" might comprise the "sociedad," with only the obrero or jornalero as a lower class in a town.

SELVA, BENEVENTURA see HISE, ELIJAH

SELVA, SILVESTRE. A senator who followed José Montenegro (q. v.) in the turbulent 1843-1845 period, during Nicaragua's first decade as an independent nation.

SEMANA. The Week, a weekly publication from Managua.

SEMANA-COMICA, LA. A weekly magazine of political satire.

SEMENAL DE CARAZO. Weekly periodical in Diriamba, founded in 1895 by Alejandro Miranda of Masaya.

SEMENAL NICARAGUENSE, EL. This "Weekly Nicaraguan" of Managua, 1874-1875, picked up the name of the Walker English-Spanish paper of two decades before.

SENATE see LEGISLATURE

SEQUEIRA, FRANCISCO. Commander of an irregular liberal force which harassed the Granada-Managua-Corinto railroad in 1927. Best known as "Cabulla," Sequeira was never able to mount a direct attack. "General Cabulla" was killed by Marine Captain Richards in May, at his home in El Viejo.

SERPIENTE EMPLUMADA. A feathered (or, "plumed")
serpent called by the Mexicans "Quetzalcoatl." On Lake
Asososca five miles from Managua, a painting of such a
coiled serpent has been known since the conquest times.
(See illustration.)

SERRANIAS AMERISQUE. Low mountains paralleling the
northern shore of Lake Nicaragua, in the range known
as the Cordillero Chontaleña, and in the department of
Chontales; the name figures in the theory that the name
"America" for the new world did not derive from Amerigo Vespucci. (See AMERICA, def. 3.)

SERVICIO COOPERATIVO INTERAMERICANO DE EDUCACION
PUBLICA. (The Cooperative Public Education Service.)
A function of international cooperation agreements under
the U. S. Foreign Operations Administration (FOA) in the
1950's. Cooperative funding was provided, with Nicaragua providing more than 50% for some projects. In
this period Nicaragua had two major projects under
SCIEP: a Vocational-Technical Institute, and an elementary teacher's normal school at Estelí. Nathan Barlow
was director of the whole education effort and the normal school; Harvey K. Meyer directed the Technical
Institute and industrial and home-making education
throughout the country. (See INSTITUTO NACIONAL
TECNICO VOCACIONAL.)

SERVICIO GEODESICO INTERAMERICANO. The Interamerican Survey, carried out in cooperation with the countries
concerned and with the assistance of U. S. Army engineers, consisting of triangulation and accurate astro-
nomical establishment of position, as well as 30, 000-
foot-altitude air-photography (with other supplemental
data and accurate ground classification of detail). The
survey operations were carried out in Nicaragua during
the 1950's and 1960's, with the result that accurate topographical maps are now available for most of the country other than some east coastal areas. The Dirección
General de Cartografía in Managua has published a number of map series (including some three-dimensional
sheets in the volcanic zone)--among them, 1:10, 100;
1:250, 000; 1:150, 000; and 1:50, 000 in scale.

SERVILES. Conservative party favoring a strong centralized
government at the time of the establishment of the
United Provinces of Central America (1822). Serviles

415

Serpiente Emplumada

The feathered serpent emblem (left) as found on the walls of
Asososca crater lake near Managua, compared to a Mexican
example (right).

were opposed by the Radicals.   The center of the Servile group was Guatemala City, hoping to continue the aristo-cratic, conservative domination of colonial days.

SESAME   see   AJONJOLE

SESAN.   Coffee hacienda in the Sierras de Managua, National District.

SETENTRION.   One of the four departments created by the basic document of the Federated States of Central Ameri-ca in 1838.   The Setentrión comprised two districts, Segovia and Matagalpa.   Many Nicaraguans still use the terms "the Setentrión" or "the Segovias" to denote re-spectively these portions of the country.   The depart-ment was created by action of the first constituent as-sembly of the free state of Nicaragua in the law of De-cember 21, 1838.

SET NET.   A village on the point of the same name, the only one on 60 miles of Caribbean Coast between Tasba-pawnie and Bluefields Bluff.

SEVILLA (Spain).   Port which from the settlement of Nica-ragua until 1774 was the only authorized Spanish port to receive the commerce of Nicaragua.   Until 1663 when an earthquake changed the bed of the San Juan River, the traffic was direct from Granada (on Lake Nicaragua) to Seville.

SEVILLA, ANDRES.   Early encomendero from the Granada area following the 1548 acts of imposition of tribute on the Valley of Nicaragua.

SEVILLA SACASA, GUILLERMO   see   SACASA, GUILLERMO SEVILLA

SEVILLA SOMOZA, GUILLERMO ANASTASIO.   Bearing the combined names of his distinguished relatives, the 28-year old [1972] business executive is the son of the dean of the Washington diplomatic corps, Guillermo Sevilla-Sacasa, and the nephew of the President of Nicaragua, Anastasio Somoza Debayle; his mother is Lillian Somoza, daughter of Anastasio Somoza Garcia.   Like his uncle the President, Sevilla Somoza is a West Point graduate and also holds a master's degree in urban administra-tion from American University.   As executive director

of the Somoza family's Lanica Airlines, the young busi-
nessman figured in 1972 negotiations with the Howard
Hughes interests, and represents the type of well-educated young Somoza family member who could be thought
of in the sequence of the presidential "dynasty."

SHAFENFER. A German engineer who with the chemist
Shoenberg attempted to harness the power of the Volcãn
de Masaya (q. v. , def. 7) in 1926-1927.

"SHARK AND THE SARDINES, THE" see AREVALO, JUAN
JOSE

SHELTON, TURNER. U. S. ambassador to Nicaragua in the
1970's. Of particular interest was the fact that Shelton
was U. S. legate in Nassau, Bahamas, when the billionaire recluse Howard Hughes (q. v.) went there in 1970.
Hughes' relocation in Managua in February 1972 was
thought by some to be related to Shelton's presence in
Nicaragua. Both men are former motion picture producers.

SHICK GUTIERREZ, RENE. In following the reforms and
liberalizations instituted by engineer President Luis
Somoza, President Schick had experience as close personal assistant to Anastasio Somoza García during a
number of years of his presidency, as well as having
held portfolio as Minister of Education. He continued
the liberalized Luis Somoza policies and died in office
to be succeeded by Anastasio Somoza DeBayle.

SHIPPING see SEABORNE COMMERCE

SHIPPING COMPANIES. The following lines serve Nicaragua
in addition to the locally owned company MAMENIC:
Italian, French, Hamburg-American, Norddeutscher
Lloyd, K. Line, Daido, All American, Royal Mail,
Grace Line, Royal Netherlands, Mitsubishi, Johnson
Line, Transatlantique, Independence, Moller Line,
Standard Fruit Company, and United Fruit Company.

SHIP-RAILWAY, TEHAUNTEPEC. Significant to Nicaragua
in that this plan, to carry fully-loaded sea-going ships
across the Mexican isthmus on a multi-track railroad,
was one of three rival plans considered viable about
1880: the deLesseps Sea-Level Canal Plan for Panama;
the Tehauntepec Railway; and the Nicaragua Lock-Canal

and Lake-River Route.   Famed engineer Eads had lent
his approval to the railway plan which had been first
proposed by Dr. William F. Channing of Providence,
Rhode Island, 30 years before, and patented in 1865.
It was to have been effected originally across Honduras
by the British-Honduras Interoceanic Railway Company.

SHOENBERG.   A German chemist who, with his associate
Shafenfer placed a device over the vents of Santiago or
Volcán Masaya (q. v. , def. 7) in 1920-1927.

SHOREMEN.   Term applied to the English squatters on the
"Mosquito Shore" who were interested principally in
dealing in contraband in the Spanish colonies.   Generally thought by the Spanish to be encouraging the Sambo-
Miskito Raids, they probably were not doing so, for to
them the contraband trade was more profitable than
booty.   However, the Sambo-Miskitos served almost as
a standing army for the shoremen, as they kept the
Spanish on the defensive.

SHRIMP BOATS.   A new industry developed in the last ten
years to make up more than 5% of all Nicaraguan exports.   A colorful interlude is the story of the "Copper
Mariner, " an experimental 67-foot shrimper, the world's
first built with a copper hull, 90% copper and 10% nick-
el, using 17 tons of the alloy.   Compared to three identi-
cally shaped steel vessels, the copper boat has 10%
more speed and consumes 22. 5% less fuel.   While
operating out of San Juan del Sur in 1971, it was stolen
by three piratical adventurers.   When the vessel put in
to Manta, Ecuador, for repairs the port captain noted
its conspicuously shiny copper bottom, took the crew
into custody, and soon the "Copper Mariner" was back
at work off the Nicaraguan coast.

SIARE.   1) A district in the municipio and department of
Matagalpa.
        2) A mountain height in the municipio of Matagalpa.

SIATEPE.   A district in the municipio of Santa Lucía, department of Boaco.

SIDRAS, LAS.   A district in the municipio of San Isidro,
department of Matagalpa.

SIERO, JOSE.   A lieutenant at the Battle of San Jacinto
        (q. v.).

SIERRA DE LAS MESAS. Heights of Terrabona municipio.

SIERRAGUAS. 1) Comarca or district in the municipio of Santo Tomás, Chontales.   .
2) Mountain in the municipio of Santo Tomás, Chontales.

SIERVAS DE NUESTRO SEÑOR. A Catholic religious order of Nicaraguan women, founded within the past two decades, serving in hospitals, schools and orphanages.

SIERVAS MISIONERAS DE CRISTO REY. A women's religious order, Catholic in provenance, founded since 1950.

SIETE ESQUINAS. The "seven corners" in Masaya, a center of convergence of traffic, uncommon in Nicaragua, where most street layouts are based on ancient Spanish rectangular grids.

SIGLO XX. This "Century 20" publication was established in Managua in 1900 under the direction of several Chileans; Calderón, Rivera, and Oyarzún.

SIKIA PAKIA, LAGUNA. A coastal lagoon in Zelaya department south of Cabo Gracias a Dios.

SIKSIKWAS, RIO. A tributary of the Río Wawa, in northern Zelaya department.

SILENCIO, EL. Comarca, valley or district in the municipio of Juigalpa.

SILICO, LAGUNA. A small lake to the southeast of San Juan del Norte.

SILVA, DON NICOLAS. An ecclesiastic who was one of the secretaries of the independence movement (q. v.) in Rivas in 1811.

SIMOO. Alternative spelling of Sumu or Sumo.

SINAI, EL. Comarca or district in the municipio of El Rosario, Carazo department.

SINDICATO DE REPORTEROS Y INTELLECTUALES DE PRENSA. A trade union of newspaper workers, located in Managua.

SINECAPA. District in the municipio of Altagracia on Omotepe Island in Lake Nicaragua, department of Rivas.

SINFONIA DE LAS AMERICAS. A symphony composed by
Carlos Ramírez Vásquez of Masaya.

SINIMULI. Lands granted in 1883 to Pablo Moreno and
others, in Estelí department--an aboriginal name.

SINKITA. Village on the Laguna Sinkita just north of the
Río Grande River mouth on the Caribbean Coast, Zelaya
department.

SINTIOPE. District in the municipio of Altagracia on Omotepe Island in Lake Nicaragua, department of Rivas.

SIPPI-SAPA. Reported name of "Tipitapa" (q. v.) in Leslie's
Illustrated Newspaper, July 25, 1857, during the reporting of events following the National War.

SIRENA. A village upstream on the Río Grande de Matagalpa in the department of Zelaya.

SISTERS OF THE ASSUMPTION. Women's Catholic missionary order serving in Nicaragua, in education, hospitals,
etc.

SISTERS OF CHARITY OF THE BLESSED VIRGIN MARY.
Women's Catholic order serving in Nicaragua, in hospitals and similar service.

SITIO DE APOMPUA. A cattle hacienda of 420 acres granted
in Matagalpa department to don Feliciano de los Ríos in
1761.

SITIO DE CUAPA. Also called San Francisco de Cuapan.
Cattle ranch in Chontales granted in 1713 to the Chief
Sacristan of the Cathedral of Guatemala, Presbyter
Francisco de Mojica y Buitrón. Size, 39 cabellerías,
or 1, 000 acres.

SITIO DE NAMOTIVAS. Name given to the cabacera of
Catarina (q. v.), related to the "pueblos Namotivas"
(q. v.).

SITIO DE QUEBRADA HONDA. A cattle hacienda of 560
acres granted to don Ramón Herrera in 1722 in the
Matagalpa department.

SITIO DE SAN PEDRO DE METAPA. With only 58 acres, a cattle ranch granted in Matagalpa department to don Pedro de Cáceres in 1716.

SITIO DE SAN SEBASTIAN. A cattle ranch granted in 1716 to Alfárez Real (chief ensign) don Tomás del Castillo, of Acoyapa in Chontales. Size, ten caballerías, or about 334 acres.

SITIO DE SUSULI. A cattle hacienda of 335 acres granted in Matagalpa department to don Manuel Montoya in 1759.

SITIO DEL VALLE DE METALAPAN. A cattle hacienda of 304 acres granted in 1719 to don Manuel Gross de Montalvan in the department of Matagalpa.

SIUNAWAS. A district just east of Siuna.

SMOKEY LANE, LAGUNA. A coastal lagoon attached to the swampy Río Escondido estuary at the north end of Bluefields Bay.

SNYDER BANANA COMPANY. An early firm shipping bananas from Nicaragua in the early 1900's.

SOBADOR. A folk medicine man.

SOCIALIST YOUTH. A seemingly Communist-dominated political organization among students.

SOCIEDAD, LA. "The society"--term used for the top levels of Nicaraguan society, perhaps less restrictive than "La Primera" (q.v.).

SOCIEDAD ANONIMA. A corporation or "anonymous society," one of the five commercial company types recognized under Nicaraguan law.

SOCIEDAD COOPERATIVA. A cooperative, one of the five commercial company types to be recognized under Nicaraguan law. These organizations are frequently consumer cooperatives, credit unions, mutual building associations, producer cooperatives, and profit-sharing cooperatives linking capital and labor.

SOCIEDAD DE LA PURISIMA CONCEPCION. The "Society of the Immaculate Concepción" is a group of single women dedicated to church welfare activities.

SOCIEDAD EN COMANDITA POR ACCIONES. One of the five commercial type companies to be recognized under Nicaraguan law, this is a stock-issuing limited partnership. In most respects it is like a corporation, and is subject to most of the legal provisions therefore.

SOCIEDAD EN COMANDITA SIMPLE. A simple limited partnership, one of five types of company recognized under Nicaraguan law.

SOCIEDAD ESFUERZO EDUCACIONAL PRIVADO DE DIRIAMBA. Society responsible for the founding of the Instituto Pedagógico in Diriamba, under the direction of the Christian Brothers. Diriamba became known as an educational center throughout Central America.

SOCIEDAD FILARMONICA DE MANAGUA. Founded in 1863, this Philharmonic Society continued until 1897, when it became submerged until the formation of the "Band of the Supreme Power" which flourished from 1910-1928.

SOCIEDAD EN NOMBRE COLECTIVO. One of five types of company under Nicaraguan law, a collective partnership. This partnership may be limited in liability to the extent of a partner's contribution; hence "limitada."

SOCORRO, EL. Cattle ranch in the municipio of León, León department.

SOCORRO MINE. One of the old Spanish mines found near Amatillo in Nueva Segovia department. A 70-foot tunnel and several prospect shafts remain, as well as another tunnel of 25 feet with some further workings.

SOILS. Mature soils of Nicaragua are of the lateritic type, which reduce by weathering to mixtures of iron and aluminum oxides with some residual silica and clay. Such soils tend to be infertile, and underlaid by hardpan. Only in areas of relatively new alluvial deposits are these Nicaraguan soils more fertile. The newer soils derived from new lavas and ashes in the Great Rift are much better, but in older agricultural areas around the lakes, even these have been depleted through centuries of intensive agriculture.

SOLEDAD. District in the municipio and department of Rivas.

SOLENTINAME ISLANDS. An Archipelago in the southeasternmost part of Lake Nicaragua, and part of Río San
Juan department. There is a recent move to revive
and develop many handcrafts by the island population.

SOLIS, ADAN. A lieutenant at the Battle of San Jacinto.

SOLORZANO, CARLOS. Conservative President of Nicaragua
who followed Bartolomé Martínez and who took over in
1925. Solórzano faced revolt under Emiliano Chamorro,
who took over the Tiscapa fortress and proclaimed himself President. U.S. diplomacy opposed the move because of the coup, and ultimately prevented Chamorro
from serving in a recognized capacity. The Moncada
Revolution proclaimed Vice President Juan Baptists Sacasa as legitimate President. This was the revolution
which resulted in U.S. troops being brought in, and ultimately in the long interventionist Sandino War of 1927-
1933.

SOMOTO. Cabacera of the department of Madriz, Ciudad
Somoto derives its name from words of the "Pipiles"
or Nahuatl-speaking peoples who first came into the
area from Mexico in pre-conquest times. (See Xomotepelt.) The town has 4,000 population. In 1753, there
was a principal population of Indians when visited by
Bishop don Pedro Augustín Morel de Santa Cruz. Somoto is 135 miles from Managua along the Panamerican
Highway, and near the Honduran border and frontier
crossing of El Espino. There is a good airfield and
the cuartel is a reinforced concrete fortification built
in the 1950's, planned as a near-border strongpoint.
There are both lumber and mineral resources in the
area all the way from placer gold to rock quarries,
and both pine and tropical hardwood lumber.

SOMOZA. A district of the municipio of Nandasmo, Masaya
department.

SOMOZA, BERNABE. Colorful Nicaraguan rebel leader of
the 1840's, who was caught, court-martialed, and shot
in San Jorge in July, 1849, by forces under General
Muñoz. Somoza's general base was in and around Rivas.

SOMOZA, LUIS. President of Nicaragua from late 1956 until 1963, Luis Somoza filled out his father's unexpired
term after the elder Somoza's assassination in Septem-

ber, 1956, and then was elected for a six-year term, which he completed. According to official count, he was Nicaragua's 31st President. A graduate electrical engineer, Somoza was educated in the United States (University of Southern California). He had served for some time in the Nicaraguan senate, and was known for mild and liberal views, which as President he put into practice to liberalize internal affairs, improve relations with other Central American countries, and to improve the economy. It is generally recognized that during his incumbency, Nicaragua advanced along modern lines. He died of a massive heart attack at age 44 in 1967 while his brother, Anastasio Jr., was President-elect, after the death of René Schick Gutiérrez in office, and during the office-filling venture of Lorenzo Guerrero.

SOMOZA DEBAYLE, ANASTASIO (Hijo).   Thirty-fourth President of his country, and third of the name and family to hold that high office, Anastasio is a graduate of the U.S. Military Academy at West Point under a policy whereby two students from each of the sister American republics may be attending each of the service academies at any one time. At the time of this writing (1971), Somoza was the incumbent President. Continuing the liberal policies of his brother and predecessor Luis, Somoza hijo, 41 when he took office, has weathered some conflicts such as student protests and minor guerrilla activities, but has also as an experienced business man led the country to further participation in the Central American Common Market. He has preserved the order which has been characteristic of the Somoza regime, and has apparently eased some of the repressive tendencies which seemed to appear much earlier. There is still vigorous opposition, but also much support, and the national progress has been marked. Señora Somoza (see Hope Portocarrero) is a charming hostess and civic leader. The two Somoza brothers, Luis and "Tachito" (Anastasio) determined to institute social reforms and "phase out the old dictator image," as one author put it. Somoza has not only been instrumental in running family businesses such as a shipping line, but also has introduced new strains of rice and tobacco to help in increasing Nicaraguan productivity. The present President is the latest of the "Somoza era," now almost four decades old.

SOMOZA GARCIA, ANASTASIO.   Longtime power in Nica-

ragua, Anastasio Somoza García was born in Carazo department in the coffee-producing town of San Marcos, in
1895. Early experience in the automobile business in
Philadelphia, Pennsylvania, gave him a colloquially excellent command of English which stood him in good
stead over his long and colorful career. Valuable to
the U. S. Marines during the period 1927-1933 of the
long Nicaraguan intervention, Somoza was not only a
good interpreter but became an alert military leader.
He distinguished himself in handling the troubles attendant to the 1931 earthquake and fire which destroyed
much of Managua. Of medium height, light in complex-
ion, Somoza was the man of action as well as of intellect. He challenged President Figueres ("Don Pepe") of
Costa Rica to a duel in 1955. He had flair as well as
acumen, and while roundly condemned and lambasted by
the conservative opposition, held the admiration and
even the love of many of the common people. He was
elected President in 1937 and served two terms until
1947. Brief terms of Argüello, Sacasa, and Román y
Reyes left Somoza as President again in 1951 until his
death in 1956, when his son Luis took over. The Somoza rule is sometimes called a dynasty because Luis
served until 1963, Anastasio's secretary Schick from
1963 until his death in 1967, when "Tachito" (Anastasio,
Jr.) became presidential candidate and took office in
1968. Reputed to have owned many properties in Nicaragua (some estimates go to as high as 10 to 15 percent
of the total), Somoza is quoted as having said "Nicaragua
es mi finca"! (Nicaragua is my farm.) He is known
for having brought order to the country, for heading an
efficient and tough little army (the National Guard) and
for developing labor relations and a plan of social security. Nicaragua has built more and better roads than
several of the neighbor nations.

Somoza sr. was assassinated in León on September
21, 1956, and he lived a week before his death in a
Panamanian hospital. Besides the two sons, each of
whom became President, he left his widow, Doña Salvadorita, of the distinguished DeBayle family and a
leader in society and religious endeavors, and a daughter who is married to Dr. Guillermo Sevilla Sacasa,
Nicaraguan ambassador to the U. S. Somoza was leader
of the liberal party, and always claimed to believe in
democracy, but he felt that many of his people, being
illiterate and locked into old colonial and pre-conquest
patterns, were not ready for it. He was considered a

staunch ally of the United States. He often rode in his blue official Cadillac with a big white ten-gallon hat and a holstered pistol, accompanied by an impressive entourage, an elite guard, and frequently, aircraft flying overhead. In the palace grounds he kept a pet black panther (a color phase of the jaguar in this case).

SOMOZA REYES, ANASTASIO. Senator of Carazo who was instrumental in elevating San Marcos to the status of a city in 1916. Anastasio Somoza García, later President, was from San Marcos.

SOMPOPERO. A district in the municipio of Jinotega.

SOMSAPOTE, EL. Cattle ranch in the municipio of San Juan del Sur, Rivas department.

SONNENSTERN, DON MACIMILIAN see ROMAN, DON J. A.

SOTA CABALLOS. A district in the municipio of Cardenas, department of Rivas.

SOTACABALLOS. District in the municipio and department of Rivas.

SOUTHERN BANANA COMPANY. During the first third of the 20th century, a firm shipping Nicaraguan bananas.

SPECIAL SERVICE SQUADRON. This unit of the U. S. fleet led by the ancient ram-bowed cruiser Rochester (q. v.) as flagship was stationed on both sides of the Nicaraguan Coast during the Sandino War of the late 1920's and early 1930's, and was also known as the "Central American Banana Fleet. "

SPENCER, SYLVANUS. An American hired by Commodore Vanderbilt (q. v.) to help defeat William Walker. Spencer had navigated the transit steamers, knew the San Juan River well, had long been employed by Vanderbilt. Accompanied by a Britisher, William R. C. Webster, Spencer went in November, 1856, to President Mora of Costa Rica to plan Walker's downfall. He later took part with Colonel Cauty (q. v.) in the final acts which severed Walker's lifeline, the Accessory Transit. Webster and Spencer had agreed to help Mora hold the transit route while the other Central American armies destroyed Walker's land forces.

SQUIER, EPHRAIM GEORGE.   Squier is remarkable for having written an almost "timeless" classic: Nicaragua;
Its People, Scenery, Monuments, and the Proposed Interoceanic Canal (1852) in two volumes.   More than a
century after publication, much of the description and
observation is still valid.   Squier was born in Bethlehem, New York, on June 17, 1821.   Self-educated, he
became a civil engineer and in 1846 he was made clerk
of the Ohio House of Representatives.   Interested in
American Indians, he was soon recognized as a self-
taught ethnologist and archaeologist.   By his death in
1888 he had been recognized by membership in many
learned societies, and from the time of the U.S. Civil
War to 1881 he was the editor of Frank Leslie's Illustrated Weekly.   His Nicaraguan significance extends beyond authorship, however, for in 1849 he was appointed
U.S. chargé d'affaires to the government of Central
America.   He left New York on the Brig Francis in
May, 1849, and later landed at San Juan del Norte.
His diplomatic ventures included a tussle with British
agents over Tigre Island in the Bay of Fonseca.   Under
the pen-name of Samuel A. Bard he recorded a second
trip to Nicaragua in 1855 in the form of a factual-his-
torical novel, Waikna, Adventures on the Moskito Shore.
He was a remarkable observer; students of Nicaragua
are indebted to Squier.

STATE OF SIEGE.   In times of crisis or emergency as
judged by the President, all constitutional guarantees
are suspended, curfew and other restriction imposed.
This power is less frequently used than a generation
ago, but can still be experienced in any of the Central
American republics.   In older days the state of siege
was used as a technique for an administration to stay
in power beyond its normal time.

STEPHENS, JOHN LLOYD.   As an agent of the U.S. government, Stephens was sent to Central America by President Van Buren in 1839.   In his official capacity, Stephens recommended the Nicaraguan Canal route in strong-
est terms, and advised that surveys made by Mr. Bailey
should be continued.   He estimated the cost of the canal
to be $25,000,000.   However, the revolutionary activities
in the countries concerned caused him to recommend that
capitalists should be cautious.   Stephens arrived in Central America just as the republics were breaking up and
he was personally exposed to open warfare in El Salva-

dor.   Stephens is perhaps best known for his incidental
activities, because in his considerable travels through
Central America he published two works of two volumes
each, which have become classics.   He is considered
the father of Mayan archaeology, and his accompanying
artist, Catherwood, did a great deal to assure the opening up of Mayaland.   Stephens was later active in the
building of the cross-Panama railroad.   Stephens in his
Incidents of Travel in Central America, Chiapas, and
Yucatan gave detailed distances and elevations on the
canal route, and added much interesting information on
Nicaragua.   An earlier travel saga, to Petra and through
Russia, had already established the remarkable Stephens
in the literary world.

STIMSON, HENRY L.   Emissary of U.S. President Coolidge
during his second administration, sent to attempt peace
in Nicaragua.   He was educated at Yale and Harvard,
and was a Republican, a New York lawyer, and Secretary
of War under President Taft.   He was also a World War
I artillery colonel.   Stimson and representatives of Sacasa's government forces met at Tipitapa on neutral
ground under a cease-fire May 4, 1927, with General
Moncada of the Constitutionalists.   The resultant peace
was agreed to by all liberal generals except Agusto
Sandino.   Temporarily the war was ended.

STUDENT.   The educational system of Nicaragua has been
constantly increased in the number of students at its
several levels.   In three recent years a comparison
may be made:

	1962-1963	1966-1967	1967-1968
Primary	197, 565	234, 685	250, 141
Secondary (Bachillerata)	9, 526	20, 661	26, 885
Normal (Teacher Training)	2, 669	4, 774	3, 292
Vocational	463	950	815
University	1, 916	-0-	5, 144
Other (Business, etc.)	-0-	3, 357	1, 072
TOTAL	212, 139	264, 427	287, 349
(At Higher Levels)	13, 374		37, 308

Obviously opportunities are increasing rapidly at the higher levels. (In 1956 there were only 322 secondary gradu-
ates, and only 1/8 as many secondary students as 12
years later.)

STUDENT PROTEST, 1945. One of the major tests of the first Somoza regime, when 500 or more students appeared before the Casa del Partido Liberal in protest against the regime. "Tacho" considered resigning, but General Moncada told him to face the people and go ahead, which he did, seeming to go ahead without faltering after that time.

STUDENT PROTEST, 1970. Seemingly in sympathy with student protest movements worldwide, yet with particular Nicaraguan overtones, groups of students occupied the cathedrals in Managua and León on September 28, 1970. Many arrests were made, presumably of F. S. L. N. adherents (the Sandinista front).

SUBA. A district on the lower Río Tuma.

SUBITERRANEO, EL. A district in the municipio of Jinotega.

SUBTIABA. A residual Indian group near León, essentially ladino, Spanish-speaking.

SUBTIAVA. 1) The oldest section of the city of León, with its famous 16th-century church and its pre-Columbian history, is one of the portions of the city which antedated its founding in the present location. One of seven barrios listed in 1811.
    2) Partido de Subtiava, one of the nine districts of the country under the Constitution of April 8, 1826, when it was one of the United Provinces of Central America. (See PARTIDOS DE NICARAGUA.)

SUBTIAVA CHURCH. (St. John the Baptist). Begun in mid-16th century and completed in the 17th it is believed that Bartolomé de Las Casas preached in this church prior to his 1547 departure from America. Now in partly dilapidated condition, this oldest church in Nicaragua in the old Indian town which later became a suburb of "new" León in 1810, has an unusual facade of engaged columns, only two of the original statues remaining. Most remarkable are the 40-foot high interior columns of single "royal cedar" timbers. Construction is typically Mudéjar. (See drawing.)

SUKIA. Title of priests of the Bocay-Pantasma region in pre-conquest times. They presided over a religion

430

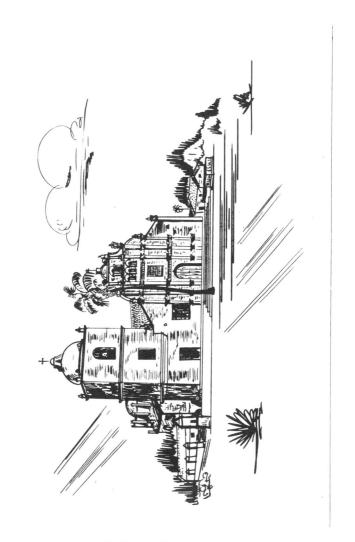

Subtiaba Church

Oldest complete and original 16th-century church in Nicaragua.

which had among other divinities the Wulasha and the
Lewire. The Sukia was soothsayer, doctor, wizard,
and intermediary with the gods.

SUKYA. Sambo name for a shaman or medicine man who
was consulted about such matters as making raids on
the Spanish settlements. See preceding entry.

SULTAN, DAN I. Lieutenant-Colonel Sultan was sent to
Nicaragua in 1929 to survey once more the trans-isthmian canal route. The survey field work was substan-
tially completed by July 1, 1931, and a favorable report
submitted December 10, 1931. The Sultan survey was
carried on in the midst of the Sandino trouble, and during the great Managua earthquake and fire. Colonel
Sultan distinguished himself in helping Nicaraguan authorities during the tragedy on March 31, 1931.

SULTANA, LA. Coffee hacienda in the Jinotega department.

"SULTANA DEL NORTE." A term sometimes applied to the
city of Ocotal, comparing it to historic Granada.

SUMO. Dialect or language of the present descendants of
the Bocay group of Chorutegans. Where their original
language was undoubtedly "Chontal," there is now in the
Sumo area a mixture of archaic Spanish, English, Miskito, and the basic indigenous tongue.

SUNIE GRANDE, LAGUNA. A lake five miles in diameter,
up the Río Sunie from Pearl Lagoon.

SUNIE PEQUENA, LAGUNA. A small lake upstream on the
Río Sunie from Pearl Lagoon, linked to Laguna Sunie
Grande.

SUPA. A palm growing in Chontales, eastern Nicaragua.

SUPRENANT, EDWARD J. A second lieutenant of the U.S.
Marines who discovered that Adolfo Cockburn (q. v.) was
a secret Sandinista General and whose sergeant aid killed
Cockburn on October 3, 1931.

SURVEYS OF 1880-1885. While the de Lesseps Panama Canal project was in its heydey and anticipating the Fre-
linghuysen-Zavala Treaty (q. v.), the Maritime Canal
Company sent A. G. Menocal, previously experienced

in the area, Lieutenant Robert E. Peary (later the polar explorer) and Ensign W. I. Chambers (later a distinguished Admiral) to refine route surveys. They did so, submitting a comprehensive report in November, 1885.

SUSULI.   1) A district in the municipio and department of Matagalpa.
2) A flowing spring in the municipio of San Ramón, Matagalpa department.
3) A mountain height in the municipio of Matagalpa.

SWEET SEA.   An early Spanish term for Lake Nicaragua. (See MAR DULCE.)

-T-

TABACO Y EL BOTE, EL.   A district in the municipio of Jinotega.

TABLAS, LAS.   1) Comarca or district in the municipio of Achuapa, León.
2) A district in the municipio of La Trinidad, department of Estelí.
3) A district in Zelaya department on the Llanos Makantaka.

TABLAZO.   A district in the municipio of Jinotega.

TABOADA, IGNACIO see GAMECO, LUIS

TABURETE.   A leather chair, found in more modest homes.

TACACHO.   A dialect of basic Chorutegan (q. v.) (or Nahuatl-derived) language, of Mexican origin.   Spoken by the Chorutegans of Yacocoyagua.

TACHITO.   Related to his father's nickname "Tacho, " this diminutive was previously applied to Anastasio Somoza DeBayle, hijo (junior).   Now that he is President (1971) the more appropriate "Tacho" is also applied to him.

TACHO.   Affectionate and otherwise nickname for Anastasio Somoza García, effective caudillo of the country 1933-1956.   Also now applied to A. Somoza hijo.

TAGUE.   Comarca or district in the municipio of El Jicaral, León.

TALANQUERA, LA. Cattle ranch in the municipio of San
Juan del Sur, Rivas department.

TALNITES, LOS. A district in the municipio of Santa Lucía,
department of Boaco.

TALPETATE. A district in the municipio of Ciudad Darío,
department of Matagalpa.

TAMAGASTAD. (Also, Tamugostad.) One of the creators
of the heavens, a God of the Nicaraos, original tribal
group found in the area of Rivas by Gil González Dávila. (See CIPALTONAL.)

TAMARINDO, EL. 1) Comarca or district in the municipio
of La Paz, León.
2) A district of the municipio of Sebaco, Matagalpa
department.

TAMARINDO DE ORO. A legendary or lost (or both) gold
mine in the region of Sebaco. Supposedly in the heights
of Tatascome in the western portion of the department,
but there seems to be no reference among early colonial
writers to a real mine of this type.

TAMARINDO DE SUBTIABA. A historic tree extant in the
León suburb of Subtiava, where tradition has it that the
cacique Adiact was hanged.

TAMARINDO, RIO. A river in the department of León,
which runs a swift course to its estuary where Puerto
Somoza, a roadstead port and oil-pipeline terminus, is
located. In 1955 it was still necessary to ford the
Tamarindo on the main highway to León from Managua.

TANQUE, EL. 1) District of the municipio of Masatepe,
department of Masaya.
2) A district of the municipio of Tipitapa, department of Managua.
3) Sugar cane plantation in the municipio of León,
León department.
4) Comarca or district of the municipio of Santa
Rosa, León.

TAPACALES, RIO. A short southern tributary of the Río
Coco in Madriz department, paralleling and close to
the Honduran border.

TASBAPAWNIE. The only village along 45 miles of Caribbean Coast, Zelaya department, from the Río Grande estuary to Punta Set Net.

TAXATION. There are four basic taxes in Nicaragua: income tax (q. v.) on internally derived income; sales tax: 2% per 1, 000 córdobas (C$) on cash and credit sales over 1666 C$ per month--also, 1% to municipalities and 1% to the Commission for Social Welfare; capital and property tax, houses over C$ 10, 000 pay a 1% annual tax, and houses over C$ 30, 000 pay a 0. 5% annual tax; and transfer tax, levied at 3% on taxable real estate value. These are greatly reduced by certain exemptions granted by law for the promotion of industrial development.

TAYLOR (Schooner). A vessel which in 1860 took William Walker (q. v.) to Cozumel and Honduras on the trip where he was finally executed.

TECOMAPA. Comarca or district in the municipio of Jinotepe, Carazo department.

TECOMAPA, RIO. River in Carazo department.

TECOMPA. A spring in the Ciudad Darío area.

TECPATL. A month festival observed by the Nicaraos of pre-conquest days. The word means "flint" or any very hard object.

TECUANAME. Comarca or district in the municipio of La Paz, León.

TECUANTEPE, RIO DE. A river in the department of Masaya, really a spring which gathers flow from the heights in the department.

TEJAS, LAS. A district in the municipio and department of Matagalpa.

TEJERA. A district in the municipio of Jinotega.

TEJERINA. A district in the municipio and department of Matagalpa.

TELEGRAFO, EL. Under the direction of General Isidro

Urtecho, don Irêneo Delgadillo, and don Francisco Padilla; this periodical was founded in Rivas in the 1870's.

TELEGRAPH SERVICE. There are 5,000 miles of telegraph
   wire, like the phone service principally available in the
   western or Pacific side of the country. The service is
   a government monopoly. Communication with the sparsely settled East Coast (Caribbean side) is by National
   Guard radio.

TELEPHONES. Telephones are like postal and telegraph
   services, a government monopoly. Growth of telephone
   service has grown in a rapid series of leaps since 1948,
   as this table will attest: 1948, 2,275 phones; 1958,
   6,332 phones; 1962, 9,261 phones; 1965, 12,320 phones.
   Phones per 100 population are average for Central America, at 0.74, but phone conversations per capita at 13.6
   are low for the region. Most phone service is on the
   Pacific side of the country, and only in Managua are
   automatic exchanges in use.

TELEVICENTRO DE NICARAGUA.   Owner of Channel 2
   television station in Managua.

TELEVICENTRO DE NICARAGUA.   Located at Los Nubes in
   the Carazo highlands, a television production company
   operating in 1968.

TELEVISION. From beginnings with the first commercial
   station in 1955, Nicaraguan TV expanded to two stations
   in 1964, and three more for a total of five in 1967. In
   1964 there were approximately 10,000 receivers; by 1967,
   around 25,000. There is a network among the Central
   American Countries and Panama. Set up with the aid of
   the United States ABC International Net, there were live
   program exchanges as early as 1961. All the stations
   are in Managua, with channels 2, 3, 6, 8, and 12.

TELEVISION DE NICARAGUA, S.A.   One of two television
   production companies in the country in 1968, located in
   Managua.

TELEVISION OF NICARAGUA, S.A.   Owner of two channels
   of the five operating in Managua--numbers 6 and 8.

TELICA.   1) Municipio of the department of León, 144 square
   miles in area, and with a population of 11,400, it is

bounded on the north by Villa Nueva and Chinandega; on
the south by the municipio of León; on the east by Larrey-
nega; and on the west by Quezalgueque and Posoltega, as
well as by the department of Chinandega. Several of
Nicaragua's long line of volcanoes, Los Marabios, are
located in the municipio, among them are Télica, Santa
Clara, and San Jacinto. One river, the Télica, is found
in the area. Many judicial controversies have arisen
over lands within Télica, due to title problems originating before 1704. Principal economic activities are agriculture, with corn, coffee, cattle and cane the major
products. Cotton gins are the "ANSCA, " San Jacinto,
and Quezalsa. Weaving and ceramics are lesser enterprises. The name Télica comes from "tlili, " meaning
"black, " and "con, " "place"--an obvious reference to the
extensive lava beds in the area. Télica became a villa
in 1871. There are 14 districts.
    2) The town or villa, cabacera of the municipio of
Télica in León, has about 2, 000 population, a small
business district, a grade school, and a library.

TELICA, RIO.   A small river, the only one in the municipio
    of the same name, León department.

TELLEZ, FRANCISCO.   Encomendero of the Managua area,
    following 1548.

TELPANECA.   Village in eastern Madriz department on the
    Río Coco.   (See   CITELPANECA.)

TELPANECA, RIO.   A northern tributary of the Río Coco
    also misused to denote the Río Coco (q. v.).

TELPOCHAPA.   A district of the municipio of San Francisco,
    Managua department.

TEMPISQUE, EL.   District in the municipio of San Dionisio,
    Matagalpa department.

TENDERI   see   NINDIRI

TEOSINTAL.   A district in the municipio of Jinotega.   (Note:
    Teosinte is the original grass from which it is presumed
    corn was developed in the valley of Mexico.)

TEPANO.   Comarca or district in the municipio of Diriamba,
    department of Carazo.

TEPESOMOTO.   An alternate name to Xomotepelt (q. v.).

TEPETATE.   Village and district just north of Granada on the shores of Lake Nicaragua.

TERAN, TORIBIO.   This director of Nicaragua was aided by Benito Rosales, holding office at the end of the 1840's decade.   They were followed by Norberto Ramírez.

TERCERO.   Comarca or district in the municipio of Larreynaga, León.

TERMOMETRO, EL.   A periodical founded in 1878 by the important Nicaraguan historian José Dolores Gámez, in the city of Rivas.   It was published until 1893, when Gámez removed to León.   (Its title derives presumably from taking the "temperature" or temper of the times.)

TERRABONA.   1) Cabacera of the municipio of the same name in the department of Matagalpa, Terrabona is partially abandoned.   During some parts of the year the town is isolated by flood waters.   The population is 700. The ruins of the ancient hacienda of San Juan de Cocolistagua y la Picata are in the environs.
        2) A municipio of the department of Matagalpa, about 110 square miles area, population 8, 500.   Bounded on the north by Sebaco, south and west by Ciudad Darío, and east by San Dionisio, it is entirely surrounded by municipios of Matagalpa.   There are 19 districts or comarcas.   The pursuits are entirely agricultural, with emphasis on poultry, sorghum, egg production (daily 4, 000 eggs) and cattle.

TERRA ROSA.   A weathered limestone soil, fertile like the volcanic soils; relatively good.

TERRERO, EL.   1) Comarca or district in the municipio of La Paz, León department.
        2) A district in the municipio of Esquipulas, Matagalpa department.

TERREROS, LOS.   1) Coffee hacienda in the municipio of Yalí, Jinotega department.
        2) District in the municipio of Yalí, Jinotega department.

TERRITORIO IN LITIGIO.   This "disputed territory" matter

was finally settled between Nicaragua and Honduras in 1963, after a brief armed clash over the territory in 1957, and a rejection of a World Court decision by Nicaragua, backed by military forces which entered the Gracias a Dios territory in question in 1961, (north of the Río Coco and near the Caribbean). The Court had supported Honduras' claim in 1960. The 1963 bilateral agreement finally confirmed the decision of the commission appointed by the International Court of Justice, and diplomatic relations since have been normal.

TERROCARRIL. Paraphrasing "ferrocarril" (railroad), this "land" train consisted of a steam tractor pulling several wagons and was a unique effort of the year 1903 to provide transportation from La Paz through Momotombo to Matagalpa. The trip took five days in spring and eight to ten days in "winter" (the wet season). Cargo and passengers were carried. A major purpose was to get the Matagalpa and Jinotega coffee crops to the railhead in La Paz and thence to Corinto port and hence to market.

TERRY, JEREMIAH. A North American by birth who had spent many years on the Mosquito Shore, and who was appointed Indian agent by the Spanish following contact with the Marquis of Almodióvar in 1777. The London embassy recommended Terry to Madrid; he went there and received his appointment, then went on at the express initiative of José de Gálvez, Minister of the Indies since 1776. Gálvez managed to provide a frigate, the Atlantico, to take Terry and a load of gifts to the Sambo-Miskitos. This was intended to undermine the British hold on the area. The ship sailed in 1778. Terry and the crew, following the apparent signing of an agreement or treaty in August, 1778, were massacred, leaving only two survivors, a short time after being on station. The Sambo-Miskitos thus proved more loyal to their British masters.

TERTULIA, LA. A Masaya periodical published for less than two years (1875-1877) under the direction of Jerónimo Pérez (q. v.).

TEUSTEPE. Municipio in the department of Boaco, ten miles· west-southwest of the departmental cabacera. The town of the same name, cabacera of the municipio, was founded over 200 years ago, but because of repeated floods was moved in 1776 to the present site, a place called previously Camoapilla. Population, 1, 500, area, 160 square miles. Entirely agricultural, there are several cattle ranches of significance. There are 18 districts.

"TEXAS WILDCATS. " Chosen name of a unit of Texans who fought for William Walker in the "National War, " 1855-1857.

TEZOATEGA 1) (see AGATEYTE). A substitute name used for the Chorutegan chieftaincy. Probably also the name of the capital city.
    2) Cacicazgo or chieftaincy of the area of the Nicaraguan lakes in pre-conquest times.
    3) Capital city of the cacicazgo of Agateyte, which seems to have disappeared following 1529; by 1540 it was a part of an encomienda of María de Peñalosa, nearby cacicazgos of Nicoya and Chira likewise going to Señora Peñalosa; by 1548 it had disappeared.

THEATRUM see ORTELIUS

THEOBROMACACAO. Scientific designation of cacao, first taken to Europe from the Rivas area of Nicaragua and labelled "Drink of the Gods. " Exports of "Cacao Nicaragua" in 1777 was over 8, 000 quintales (over 400 tons).

THEOCRATIC FORMATIVE. A period of formative cultures in the Americas which is characterized by evidence of organized politico-religious social organization and control such as is shown by mound, pyramid, and temple structures. The time is 1200 B. C. to 400 B. C. , thus following colonial Formative (q. v.).

TIANQUEZ. A market or the market-days, used in Mexico and also in the Philippines, and applied to pre- and post-conquest markets in the area of the Nicaraos. (Singular: Tianqui or Tianque.)

TICOMO. A territory of the National District, department of Managua.

TICOS. A nickname for Costa Rican natives, much used in Nicaragua.

TICUANTEPE. A territory of the National District, depart-

ment of Managua. Essentially a village or town, due to
the suburban buildings of the area.

TIE CUT. A guerrilla practice whereby bodies of dead enemies were mutilated, the subject's throat being cut and
the tongue pulled through the slit by Sandinista guerrilleros during the 1927-1932 War. See also CORTE DE...

TIERRA BLANCA. 1) Comarca or district in the municipio
of Santo Tomâs, Chontales.
2) A district in the municipio of Matiguâs, Matagalpa
department.

TIERRA CALIENTE. The hot tropical lowlands characteristic of much of Pacific Coastal Nicaragua. Here was
heavy population in contrast to Guatemala where population developed in areas of higher altitudes. Nicaragua
in this respect more resembles Panama, from which it
was colonized by the Spaniards.

TIERRA COLORADA. Comarca or district in the municipio
of Nagarote, Leôn department.

TIERRA FRIA. Occasional high portions of the central highlands area have the cool climate which is thus termed.
Fireplaces are used on the Casa Colorada heights during
much of the year after sundown.

TIERRA PINOLERA. A Managua radio station, call letters
YNPT, power 500 watts, frequency 1500 kilocycles.

TIERRA TEMPLADA. Term in Spanish used for the mild
climate to be found in higher elevations of the central
highlands.

TIGRE, EL. 1) A territory of the National District, department of Managua.
2) Comarca or district in the municipio of Diriamba,
department of Carazo.

TIGRE DE AGUA. Mountain in the municipio of El Jicaral,
Leôn department.

TIGUILOTAL, EL. A height in the area to the east of Sebaco. A very old pre-conquest name.

TILQUE. District in the municipio of Altagracia on Omotepe
Island in Lake Nicaragua, department of Rivas.

TIMBUCOS. One of the two major Nicaraguan political parties in the 1840's. The Timbucos were the government
party in 1849 as reported by Ephraim Squier. See also
CALANDRACAS.

TINCO, EL. A dance of the prehistoric Managuans, dignified
and majestic in movement, done in elaborate costumes.

TINGNI. A Miskito word for stream. In the stream-laced
high jungle Bocay region of the Río Coco Valley the word
appears dozens of times in proper names.

TIPILMA. Comarca or district in the municipio of La
Libertad, Chontales.

TIPISCAYAN. A height near the town of San Juan de Limay,
Estelí department.

TIPITAPA. 1) Spa on the stream and waterfall between
Lakes Managua and Nicaragua, the name being an example of derivation from the Nahuatl sources originating
in Mexico. Tepiton, meaning "small," and opantli,
"river," make Tepitapantli, "a small river." An alternate may derive from tetl, or "stone," and the special stone pestle or petate;--hence, Tetl-petatep-apan,
or "river of the petates." Best known for the fish
there served from fresh tanks and cooked to order, as
well as for the meeting (see Tipitapa Agreement) between Secretary Stimson of the United States and Nicaraguan General (later President) Moncada under a Tipitapa thorn-tree on May 4, 1927.
2) This municipio of the department of Managua has
an area of over 580 square miles, a population of 15, 500.
Just to the east of Lake Managua, it is bounded on the
north by the departments of Boaco and Matagalpa; on the
south by Masaya; on the east by Boaco, Masaya, and
Granada departments. and on the west by the Lake, and
by San Francisco del Carnicero municipio and the Managua National District. There are 13 comarcas or
districts. It is an agricultural area, emphasizing cotton, cattle, and grain. There are several big haciendas.

TIPITAPA AGREEMENT. In April, 1927, Henry L. Stimson
of the United States was sent to Nicaragua by the second
Coolidge administration to effect peace in the civil war
then in progress. United States intervention for much
of the preceding 15 years had caused relations with Latin

America to deteriorate. The agreement made May 4, 1927 under a thorntree at the little spa of Tipitapa near Managua was a prelude to nearly six years of interventionist war. Conditions surrounding the agreement were interesting. Constitutionalist President Sacasa did not adhere to the agreement--General Moncada, head of a Liberal army seriously threatening Managua, was the representative of the Constitutionalist Government, who was party to the agreement. Stimson accepted the Díaz or conservative position as a base for negotiation. The pact was not subject to U. S. Senate advice and consent-- Coolidge kept it as an executive device. There was not a military deadlock at the time. A liberal (Moncada) victory was quite possible, but Moncada did not wish to fight U. S. forces. Latin American help in the dispute was rejected. Stimson threatened Moncada with defeat by U. S. forces unless he accepted the imposed agreement. The agreement was that all troops would lay down their arms and that Díaz would remain president. Several of Moncada's men were given positions in the Díaz government. Each soldier turning in a weapon would receive ten dollars from the Nicaraguan treasury, U. S. Marines would occupy the country and supervise elections. The Marines, however, were not responsible to the U. S. Ambassador. Agusto Sandino refused to disarm, and the six-year war began.

TIPITAPA, RIO DE. One of the rivers in the department of Masaya which runs a 22-mile course from the town of Tipitapa and hence, between the Lakes Managua and Nicaragua. The lower part of the river flowing into Lake Nicaragua is broad and navigable.

TIPOTANI. A god of the Matiari Indians pre-conquest.

TISAY. Mountain in the municipio of Estelí. Altitude 5, 080 feet.

TISCAPA, LAGUNA. Crater lake near the center of Managua, on whose high northern rim is the "acropolis" of the capital--the Presidential Palace, the "Residencia, " the Club Militar, the military hospital, various walls and ramparts, a heliport, cover for assorted military vehicles, etc. A picturesque use of the deep lake is by the "lavanderas" or washer-women who wash clothes there by hand in daily hundreds. The hill of Tiscapa, "La Loma, " represents power to Nicaraguans.

TISMA. A municipio of the department of Masaya, of 4,000 population, in an area of 29 square miles. Bounded by Managua department and the Río Tipitapa on the north; on the south and west by the municipios of Masaya and Oriente; and on the east by Granada department. There are six districts or comarcas. It is an important area for cotton and cattle raising; there are several large cattle ranches.

TISMA, LAGUNA DE. This lake is a widened area of the lower Tipitapa River before it enters Lake Nicaragua. The lesser of two large areas of the lake, which totals about 15 square miles, is called "Charco del Genízaro." The whole is commonly called "Charco de Tisma."

TISTE. A drink of fresh parched corn ground with chocolate and sugar and mixed with water to a thin gruel-like consistency. The fresh parallel to "pinolilla" (q. v.).

TITULO DE VILLA. An example of an award of title as "villa" is in the document which awarded such designation to the Villa de la Purísima Concepción de Rivas de Nicaragua. (See Rivas, def. 1.) The document is of about 3,000 words, and deals with the early petitioner and the royal governor, don Francisco Rodríguez de Rivas, who was addressed on behalf of 500 Spanish families, about 2,500 people, in 1717. The fact that the city of Granada is 12 leagues away is given to indicate the difficulty of such jurisdiction, to which the desired villa was formerly attached. Officials were designated; two alcaldes (mayors), a royal "Alférez" (or chief ensign of the town), an alguacil mayor (high constable), a treasurer, and two regidores (aldermen or magistrates). Early in the document is mentioned the building of a church. Various decrees are cited, and previous efforts described. The title as awarded is to be subject to all privileges, immunities, franchises, and prerogatives, and the title is to be placed on all writings, instruments, and public places. Then the use of the title is commended to (and required of) dukes, princes, prelates, marquises, counts, rich men, mayors, viceroys, presidents, regents, gentlemen, officials, and others. The dating is San Ildefonso, September 19, 1783, signed "Yo, El Rey" (I, the King), and countersigned by various officials the endorsements, finally completed on October 9, 1783.

TIZATE, EL. Coffee hacienda in the Sierras de Managua, of the National District.

TOAKAS. Tribe identified in the 1880's in the Eastern portion of the then-large department of Matagalpa.

TOCHTLI. A month-festival day (and god) of the pre-conquest Nicarao. Meaning: "rabbit."

TOLA, RIO. One of the rivers in the municipio of San Juan de Tola which empties in the Pacific, and which would figure in a canal route as projected for Nicaragua.

TOLAPA. Comarca or district in the municipio of Larreynaga, León.

TOLOGALPA. The province of Tologalpa was delineated in a 1691 chronicle by Fray Francisco Vásquez as the region from northwestern Nicaragua to the Caribbean and as far south as the Río San Juan. It is essentially within this ancient province of the Guatemalan kingdom that most of the department of Jinotega lies.

TOLOLAR, EL. Comarca or district of the municipio of León, León department.

TOLOLO. Comarca or district in the municipio of Larreynaga, León.

TOLOLOS, LOS. Comarca or district in the municipio of El Sauce, León department.

TOLONDRON, EL. A place of historical meaning in the city of Rivas, as there General Bosque made a stand during the June 29, 1855, battle against the William Walker filibusters. An elevation, it was opposite the Espinosa house where Walker's men were headquartered. The ruined building whose walls served as parapets for Bosque was torn down in 1858 to make way for a street, Calle de Tolondrón.

TOMABU. 1) A district in the municipio and department of Estelí.
2) A high tableland in Estelí department at a general level of 3,900 feet.
3) Mountain in the municipio of Estelí. Altitude 4,750 feet.

TOMATOYITA. A district in the municipio of Jinotega.

TOMAYES. A subtribal group of the Chontales branch of
the "Kiribies. "

TOMAYUNCA. A district in the municipio of Jinotega.

TONALA. Pueblo or town existing in the valley of Nicaragua during the 16th and 17th centuries.

TONATIUH IXCO. The East was called by the ancient Nicaraos of the Rivas area, rather poetically, "the place
of the face of the sun. "

TOP LOCK, LAGUNA. A coastal lagoon on the lower Río
Karinwas where it enters Pearl Lagoon, Zelaya department.

TOQUEZAL, EL. Comarca or district in the municipio of
Diriamba, department of Carazo.

TORERA, LA. Comarca or district of the municipio of
Santa Rosa, León.

TORO, EL. 1) A district in the municipio of Matiguás,
Matagalpa department.
2) Hill near the pueblo San Juan de Limay, Estelí
department.

TORO-GUACA, BAILE DE see TOROGUACO

TOROGUACO. Typical dance as seen at the fiesta of San
Sebastián in Diriamba. Also called Danza del Toro
del Cementerio. Needs 40 dancers and 17 costumed
actors.

TORONDANO, RIO. A river in the department of Chinandega, part of the border between Nicaragua and Honduras.

TOROVENADO. 1) Typical dance among those which seem
to come from Chiapanecan sources (the Mexican State
of Chiapas).
2) A district four miles south of Granada.

TORO Y VENADO see TOROVENADO (def. 1).

TORREZ, BRUNO.   First prefect of the newly-created department of Managua in 1875.   Prefects became jefes
polfticos at a later time.

TORRES, JOSE   see   COLEGIO DE LA UNION

TORTILLA.   A thin flat baked cake of cornmeal and water,
usually prepared as a pliable dough called "massa, "
and then slapped into the desired thinness with great
skill.   A pre- and post-conquest Meso-American staple.
Nicaraguan tortillas tend to be thicker than Mexican
ones.

TORTUGA, LA.   District in the municipio of San Juan del
Sur, Rivas department.

TOTOGALPA.   A small town just south of Ocotal and in the
northern part of Madriz department.   There is an interesting colonial church.   (The name comes from Nahuatl
Totolfn, bird, and calli, "place. ")

TOTUMBLA.   1) A district in the municipio of Ciudad Darfo,
department of Matagalpa.
    2) A mountain height in Matagalpa department, mu-
nicipio of Ciudad Darfo.

TRABAJADOR, EL.   A labor periodical of intermittent issue
and small circulation relative to the various daily journals.

TRADE PRE-CONQUEST.   The evidences of trade in ceramics and metal items exist for the period 600-800
A. D. , in the isthmus area from Nicaragua to Panama.
Early "formative" (q. v.) period evidence is ample if
not conclusive.   See also   METALLURGY.

TRANSPORTATION.   Other than roads and highways (q. v.)
principal transport forms are the Ferrocarril del Pacif-
ico, a narrow gauge railroad on the Pacific side of the
country, serving Corinto, Chinandega, León, Masaya,
Granada, Diriamba, El Sauce, and Puerto Morazân.
There is about 450 miles of railroad.   The government-
owned shipping line (see MAMENIC) carries 70% of the
country's imports and exports.   Corinto, San Juan del
Sur, Puerto Somoza, and Puerto Morozân are ports on
the Pacific, with El Bluff and Puerto Cabezas on the
Caribbean.   Air service is provided by the Nicaraguan

airline (see LANICA) and by Pan American Airways,
Transportes Aéreos Centro-Americanos (TACA), KLM
(Royal Dutch Airlines) and the Transportes Aéreos Nacionales of Honduras (TAN). There are 30 airfields,
five of them modern, with an international airport at
Managua, "Las Mercedes. " It should be noted that in
the many remote and rural sections of the country the
two- or four-ox team and solid-wheeled cart are still a
major form of transport, and in the jungle mountains of
eastern and northern Nicaragua, transport is along jungle rivers in variants of the dugout canoe.

TRANSPORTES DE MATAGALPA. A company formed in the
1890-1900 decade to transport Matagalpa products to the
rail-head in La Paz, León department. They built a
road and ran the steam-tractor "train" called terrocarril (q. v.). As many as 15 wagons were towed by
the tractor, a plan which must have been unique in
transportation annals.

TRAPICHE, EL. 1) A cattle ranch in the Tipitapa municipio
of Managua department.
      2) Comarca or district of the municipio of León,
León department.
      3) A mountain eminence in the municipio of Matiguás,
Matagalpa department.

TRAVERTINOS. The travertine marble is quarried in the
Miraflores section of Estelí department.

TREATY OF FRIENDSHIP.... This instrument, the Treaty
of Friendship, Commerce and Navigation, and Protocol,
signed at Managua, in 1956, expresses cordial relations
between the Nicaraguan and United States governments
and peoples and also recognizes implicitly that the old
days of intervention (so soundly denounced by such authors as Arévalo of Guatemala) are presumed to be at
an end.

TREATY OF MADRID. This 1814 treaty between England
and Spain was influenced by confusion in Spanish affairs
introduced during the Napoleonic regime. England and
Spain were allies in the final campaign, and when the
Peninsular War was over, certain matters were left un-
settled about the Nicaraguan Coast. The Treaty of
Madrid confirmed all conventions of 1783 and 1786 between the two powers, which interestingly left the Carib

Indians occupying the Bay Islands of Honduras (where they had been transported from the Island of St. Vincent), the Mosquitos still in control of that Nicaraguan Coast, and the settlers in Belize confirmed in their original seizure. The Mosquito question was finally settled in the late 1880's; the Belize question still burns for Guatemala, and the Caribs have assimilated. So wash the tides of empire. The coveted Nicaraguan Canal route was left in the hands of Spain, but the old Spanish monopoly was broken forever, and seven years after the treaty, the colonies seized independence. Meanwhile, British possessions ringed the Eastern Caribbean.

TRELAWNEY-ANSELL, EDWARD C. see JOSEPH CRAD

TRIBUNA, LA. A newspaper of the 1920-1930 era in Managua.

TRIDENTINE COLLEGE OF ST. RAMON. Established in León, 1675, with professorships in law and medicine. A predecessor of the present university.

TRIGEÑO. "Dark brown" to denote a dark mestizo.

TRIGUERO. A district of the municipio of Moyogalpa on Omotepe Island, Lake Nicaragua, Rivas department.

TRINIDAD, LA. 1) Comarca or district in the municipio of Diriamba, department of Carazo.
2) Comarca or district in the municipio of Nagarote, León department.
3) A district of the San Rafael del Sur municipio, Managua department.
4) A municipio of Estelí department, area 91 square miles, population 12,500. Bounded north by Estelí and San Rafael del Norte (of Jinotega department); east by Sebaco and San Isidro of Matagalpa; west by San Nicolás of León. There are thirty-three districts, the Lake "Las Espejos" is in the area; corn, beans, plantains, bananas, and cattle are raised. There is the Cave of Ollanca, and many ceramics and idols are found near La Cañada.
5) A territory of the National District, department of Managua.
6) Rice processing plant in the municipio of Jinotepe, Carazo department.

TRINIDAD, RIO DE LA. A tributary of the Río Viejo, this stream is one of the principal rivers in Estelí department, and is partially located in the municipio of the same name.

TRINITARIA, LA. A cattle ranch or hacienda in the municipio of Nindirí, Masaya department.

TRIONFO DE LA CRUZ. Modified form of "San José del Triunfo, " presently called "La Cruz" at confluence of Pantasma River with the Coco; there is an airfield called "La Vigía" on the north side of the Coco at this point where the Pantasma flows in from the south.

TRIUNFO, EL. A cattle ranch in the Tipitapa municipio of Managua department.

TROMPICON, EL. Coffee hacienda in the municipio of Yalí, Jinotega department.

TRONCA, LA. A district and a mountain height in the municipio and department of Matagalpa.

TRONCO SOLO. District in the municipio and department of Rivas.

TRONCOSO Y MARTINEZ DEL RINCON, BERNARDO. Appointed Captain-General of Guatemala, he governed 1789-1794, but as an octogenarian brigadier at the outset and ill much of the time, he represented the decadence of Spanish policy and control. No further efforts of significance were made to pacify or subdue the Sambo-Miskitos of the coast.

TROPICAL (Ship). Under Mexican registry, this ship was carrying arms from La Unión in El Salvador to Coseguina Point in Nicaragua in 1926--reportedly 32 machine guns, small arms and ammunition. Interestingly, the ammunition seized by Chamorro forces after it was landed, had F. N. C. markings from the National Cartridge Company of Mexico, and rifles with the Russian coat of arms. These had been manufactured in the U. S. for Russia, rejected, and then sold to filibusters.

TROPICAL RADIO COMPANY. In the 1920's this company had a million-dollar investment in Managua. Foundations of the old radio towers still exist.

TRUCK TRANSPORT. With the development of good roads
(see highways), many miles of paved road throughout
the Pacific area and connecting major centers, and with
the coming of the Central American Common Market,
truck transportation has assumed a major role, con-
venience taking frequent precedence over cheaper forms
of transportation. The foreign trade at the Pan-American Highway, northern border crossing was 9, 770 metric
tons in 1961, and by six years later had increased tenfold to 99, 254 metric tons. The south border went from
7, 093 tons in 1961 to 89, 121 tons in 1967. During the
same six-year period value of foreign trade by truck
had increased from $3, 900, 000 to $62, 500, 000. In
1967 Nicaragua had about 1, 500 buses and 3, 700 trucks,
half of the latter five tons or over.

TRUCUSAN. A district in the municipio of Jinotega.

TRUESDALE, DONALD L. Lieutenant of U.S. Marines,
second in command to Frisbie (q. v.) in action against
Sandinistas in December, 1931.

TRUJILLO. 1) A district in the municipio of Ciudad Darío
in the department of Matagalpa.
2) A spring in the Ciudad Darío area.

TRUXTUN, M. S. see WORDEN

TULE, EL. Comarca or district in the municipio of El
Jicaral, León.

TUMA. 1) A district in the municipio and department of
Matagalpa.
2) El Tuma, a district in the municipio of Jinotega.
3) El Tuma, a district of the municipio of San Ramón,
Matagalpa department.

TUMA, RIO. The Tuma River has its source in Jinotega
department near San Rafael del Norte, and is 120 miles
long. It is a tributary of the Río Grande de Matagalpa.
This river has assumed major importance in Nicaraguan
development because of the dam recently constructed by
the National Power and Light Company. This Mancotal
Dam has created Lake Apanas, the first artificial lake
of any extent in Nicaragua. The development provides
a major source of hydro-electric power.

TUMA, VALLE DE.   This valley is distinguished by the recent hydro-electric project.   In the Jinotega department,
it is much smaller than the Bocay, Pantasma, and
Guamblón valleys, and is characterized by the narrow
defile where the Mancotal Dam was constructed.

TUNEL, EL.   A district of the municipio and department of
Masaya.

TUNOSA, LA.   1) A district in the municipio and department of Estelí.
2) One of several large springs in the department of
Estelí.

TWEED (Frigate).   A British naval vessel involved in occupation of the Bay Island of Roatán in 1841, and in the
incident at San Juan del Norte when a Nicaraguan officer
defied the British and their Mosquito "allies." (See
QUIJANO.)

-U-

UBI.   A district in the municipio of Matiguás, Matagalpa department.

UDCCA   see   UNION DEMOCRATICA CRISTIANA DE CEN-
TROAMERICANA

ULLOA, ANTONIO DE   see   CONDAMINE, LA

ULLOA Y CASTILLA, DON ALONSO DE.   An early surveyor
of lands in the Managua area, under orders of Captain
General don Antonio Peraca de Ayalla y Rojas, Conde
de Gómera, in 1569.   The survey was begun in the city
of Managua, and went in both directions toward León
and Granada.   "Cruz Divisora," or crosses marking
divides, were placed.

ULUA   see   CULHUA AND WOOLWA

ULUSE.   A district of the municipio of San Ramón, Matagalpa department.

UMALI   see   UMARI

UMANZOR, JUAN PABLO.   Colonel of Sandino guerrillas

initially under Ortez (q. v.) in May, 1931. At the death
of his chief, this Honduran figher took over the unit.
He had charge of the Eighth Column. (See DEFENDING
ARMY....)

UMARI. In the valley of the same name in Estelí department, property of Sergeant don Miguel Chevarría in
1734. An aboriginal Indian name.

UMURE. A mountain height in the municipio of Matagalpa.

UNCTAD. An acronym for the world-wide conference on
commerce and development under the auspices of the
United Nations, with its first conference in Geneva,
Switzerland, in 1964. The organization is of particular
meaning to developing countries such as Nicaragua.
The purpose is to present pertinent problems of development and to propose and initiate appropriate measures.

UNION, LA. 1) Cattle hacienda in the municipio of San
Juan del Sur, Rivas department.
2) Important finca in the municipio of La Concepción,
department of Masaya.

UNION DEMOCRATICA CRISTIANA DE CENTROAMERICANA.
The UDCCA is a general movement to establish Christian Democratic Parties throughout Central America,
pressing for basic reforms of a social, political, and
economic nature. Nicaragua's "PCSN, " the Partido
Social Cristiano Nicaragüense, is affiliated with UDCCA.

UNION MEMBERSHIP. Total union membership in Nicaragua
represents around 6 percent of the total paid labor force;
so far, around 25, 000 people.

UNION NACIONAL OPOSITORA. The UNO was formed in
1966 to unite all opposition forces against the PLN
party.

UNION RADIO. A radio station in Managua, call letters
YND, frequency 675 kilocycles, one of the three most
powerful in the country at 15, 000 watts each.

UNITED FRUIT COMPANY. Once having the reputation for
making and breaking Central American governments,
this ubiquitous corporation was formed in 1899 by M.

O. Keith, to produce and ship bananas from the growing
belt on the low Caribbean littoral. Nicaragua banana
lands of United Fruit were centered in the Bluefields
area. The Panama disease, and sigatoka (banana leaf-
spot) decimated crops in the 1920's and 1930's, and the
operation has never reopened in Nicaragua. Originally,
a major fiscal force as well as behind-the-scenes political power, United Fruit has lost much of its picturesque influence along with its bananas. The white-
painted United Fruit steamers used to be a major form
of access to the banana coast, and United Fruit has
been the center and subject of much "banana republic"
literary effort.

UNITED STATES OF CENTRAL AMERICA. Name of the
"República Major" chosen under a Constitution of November 1, 1898 for the three countries of El Salvador, Honduras and Nicaragua. This union, while short-lived,
was the basis for the "Partido Unionista" which developed.

UNIVERSIDAD DE GRANADA. An 1879 creation of law.
(See UNIVERSIDAD DE NICARAGUA.)

UNIVERSIDAD DE LEON. An 1879 creation of law. (See
UNIVERSIDAD DE NICARAGUA.)

UNIVERSIDAD DE MANAGUA. An 1879 creation of law.
(See UNIVERSIDAD DE NICARAGUA.)

UNIVERSIDAD DE NICARAGUA. The University of Nicaragua
was initiated under Spanish rule in the city of León, as
the "Seminario Tridentino o Conciliar de San Ramón
Nonñato. " In December, 1677, Brother Andrés de Las
Navas y Quevedo, of Guadiz, Spain, became bishop of
Nicaragua and in 1678 proceeded to the episcopal seat
in León. On December 15, 1680, Bishop Navas founded
the seminary and personally formulated its constitution
and the attendant regulations. The first class had eight
students. The original curriculum consisted of such
studies as grammar, the Spanish language, theology,
and the arts. In 1787, Don Agustín Ayesta was named
rector. It was he who applied to the king of Spain for
permission to grant degrees in León, without following
the previous practice of sending students for examination
to Guatemala. The chairs of Latin, moral theology,
philosophy, and canon and civil law were established

at this time. By 1802 further chairs including medicine and surgery were established. In 1812 the proper establishment of the University of Nicaragua took place, under Bishop Nicolás García Jérez, the last of the colonial bishops. Decreed by the Cortés de Cádiz under Manuel de Villafañe, it was yet two years before the University became organized, and in the meantime the dissolution of the Cortés de Cádiz effectively disestablished the University of Nicaragua in 1814.

By May 5, 1815, however, the Captain-General of Guatemala conveyed confirmation from King Ferdinand the VII of the establishment of the university. Actually the act of establishment and installation of officers took place in León on August 24, 1816, with Bishop García as chancellor, Dr. Ayerdi as rector, and nine others listed as faculty. The University was closed upon the declaration of independence in 1821. However, in 1822 Juan Francisco Aguilar y Villar became the first Nicaraguan rector, and the first nonecclesiastical head. In 1823 degrees were reestablished by act of the assembly in Granada, and again in 1835 the University was reestablished after closing during the War of Cerda and Argüello. In 1869, war again closed the university but studies were maintained in the old San Ramón Seminary, under title of "Academia Científica," and under the direction of Dr. José Rosa Rizo.

In 1879 a law created Universities of Managua, León, and Granada to perpetuate the work of the Academias Científicas. The Universidad Nacional de Nicaragua, however, opened in 1887, with deans appointed for the first time to direct the various faculties. A brief closing in 1896 was followed by reopening and an 1898 reorganization with changes in the faculties of Law, Medicine, and Pharmacy. The year 1899 saw the opening of the present University building in León. In 1941 a faculty of Physical Sciences was established in Managua. In 1947, the University became the National University, headed by the distinguished Dr. Crisanto Sacasa, later Minister of Education in Nicaragua, and the same year a faculty of Chemistry was formed, as was a faculty of Humanities and Philosophy in 1948. In 1958 President Luis Somoza decreed that the University should be in perpetuity an Autonomous Institution, the "Universidad Nacional Autónoma de Nicaragua." Some branches (such as civil engineering) are now established in Managua.

UNIVERSIDAD PRIVADA DE MASAYA   see   COLEGIO DE LA UNION

UNO   see   UNION NACIONAL OPOSITORA

URBAN-RURAL CONTRAST.   There is a sharp differentia-
   tion between rural and urban cultures and segments of
   society in Nicaragua, which is due partly to wealth and
   political power centered in the cities, and partly to differing rates of economic and social change.   In some
   senses, Nicaragua resembles the Renaissance city-states
   of Northern Italy, with, of course, many modern overtones.

URBAYTE.   District in the municipio of Altagracia on Omotepe Island in Lake Nicaragua, department of Rivas.

URTECHO, ISIDRO   see   TELEGRAFO, EL

URTECHO, DON JOSE ANTONIO.   One of the Spanish colonial families established in Masaya by 1800 and extant
   today.

URTECHO, JOSE CORONEL.   Born in Granada in 1906, poet
   and novelist, and a prolific writer.   His talent has also
   extended to historical, sociological, and political expression.

UTAZTECAN.   A language family among American Indians
   which extends into North America and of which the Nicaraguan Nicaraos and Siguas are southernmost examples.

UVA, LA.   A district of the municipio of Santo Tomás,
   Chinandega department.

-V-

VADO ANCHO.   A district of the municipio of Santo Tomás,
   Chinandega department.

VAINILLA, LA.   Comarca or district in the municipio of
   Santa Teresa, Carazo department.

VAINILLA, RIO EL.   A stream flowing north into Lake Nicaragua from heights in the northeast of Carazo department.

VALIENTES.   An Indian tribe as described by Orlando Roberts in 1827, presumably on the Nicaraguan and Honduran
   east coast hinterland.

VALLE, EL. Cattle ranch in the municipio of San Juan del Sur, Rivas department.

VALLE DE GOTHEL. A territory of the National District, department of Managua.

VALLE DE LAS ZAPATAS. Comarca or district in the municipio of Larreynaga, León.

VALLE DE LUMOR. A district of the municipio of Santo Tomás, Chinandega department.

VALLE NORTE FRIO. Comarca or district in the municipio of Achuapa, León.

VALLE DE TICAUNTEPE. A district of the municipio of Nindirí in Masaya department.

VALLEJO, GONZALES. Captain and second commissioner sent by the Spanish government to Central American in 1785-1786. He was in command of the corvette San Pío. The Spanish did not venture south of Cabo Gracias a Dios as they took possession of the coast following war with England. Robert Hodgson, the younger (q. v.), was appointed Spanish Governor at Bluefields.

VANAJI see VINALI

VANDERBILT, CORNELIUS. Best known as "Commodore," the able financier who once ran ferryboats saw at an early date, following 1849, the advantage of assuring a route to the California Gold Rush by going through Nicaragua on a lake-river route. Sealing a contract to provide cross Nicaragua transit (which was intended by the Nicaragua signatories to assure an eventual canal), Vanderbilt made it possible to establish the "Accessory Transit Company" (q. v.) which had the shortest route in time from New York to San Francisco. When his engineers cited the San Juan River rapids as preventing steamer traffic, Vanderbilt towed a small river steamer the Director, down to the San Juan mouth from New York, and then demonstrated the feasibility of the route by literally driving the vessel upriver over rocks and rapids. The Accessory Transit Company provided steamer passage from New York to San Juan del Norte, then shallow-draft paddle-wheel river steamers from San Juan upriver to El Castillo; then other steamers

for the remaining 40 miles or so of river and across
Lake Nicaragua to the port La Virgen.   From here
Vanderbilt constructed a stage road, and in comfortable
blue and white fleets of carriages took the passengers
to San Juan del Sur, where other oceangoing vessels
took them to San Francisco.   The fare through Nicaragua from New York to San Francisco was $300, half
the existing $600 fare.   He carried 25,000 passengers
a year.   Other claims indicate an occasional 20,000
passengers per month.

When William Walker decided to take over assets of
the Accessory Transit Company, Vanderbilt cut off the
supplies of men, munitions, and provisions he had been
sending Walker, and also worked with Costa Rica to defeat the arrogant filibuster.   Vanderbilt finally won out,
although he also got out of the transit business.   When
in 1853, Vanderbilt decided to go abroad in a steam
yacht, North Star (of 2,500 tons, 270 feet long), he
sold the Nicaragua Transit Company.   Two men, Cornelius Garrison and Charles Morgan took over to manage
the line.   Vanderbilt still had an interest, and when during his extended yachting voyage the two attempted to
oust him permanently, and even took commissions the
Commodore regarded as his, Vanderbilt seethed and
sought revenge.   On his return Vanderbilt addressed to
Morgan and Garrison a famous letter: "You have undertaken to cheat me.   I won't sue you, for the law is too
slow.   I'll ruin you.   Yours truly, C. Vanderbilt."
Garrison relied on William Walker to tip the balance.
But in the end Vanderbilt won, even though it was generally conceded Garrison ran the line well.   Walker's
seizure of the property was too much for Vanderbilt,
who was really responsible also for ruining Walker and
his dreams of empire.

VANGUARDIA.   A theatre and literary magazine founded in
1928, which caused a surge of little theatre groups, of
plays with local themes and often with social messages.

VANKES see COCO, RIO

VARA.   A length measure of about 33 inches (2.76 feet),
used in square measure as well as in distance.   (A manzana is 100 varas square, or 10,000 square varas.)
The vara in colonial days and earlier, was a linear
measure of 32 to 33 inches, derived from a rod or
staff used as a symbol of office and also for measurement.

VARELA. Comarca or district in the municipio of Achuapa, León.

VARGAS, MIGUEL DE. Alguacil Mayor, one of the two men (with Marcos de Las Navas) who established an oligarchy in Rivas in the 18th century. Partly because of distance from the Captaincy-General (in Guatemala) they were able to create a veritable dictatorship, and thus to set a pattern not unknown since. The two men enriched themselves and families at the cost of misery for their neighbors.

VARILLAL, EL. A village along the Granada-Nandaime Highway, four miles from the former.

VASCONCELOS, DON GASPAR INESTROSA. Maestre de Campo in rank, Vasconcelos was named as first commandant of El Castillo Viejo (q. v.) by Escobedo in 1672.

VASQUEZ, LOS. A district of the municipio of La Concepción, department of Masaya.

VEGETATION. There is a great variety of growth in Nicaragua, the whole country looking like a giant emerald following the onset of the rains after mid-May of each year. Among the types are tall, straight, broadleaf evergreen (rain forest) trees over 100 feet high, with trunks up to four to six feet in diameter and buttress roots spreading 40 foot spans. Low crooked evergreen trees also abound. Pine savannahs stretch over the northeast of the country. Evergreen oak and pine forests abound with virgin pines especially large (five foot diameter, 75 feet to first limbs.) Grassland, where burned annually, has small spiny trees and shrubs. Coconuts flourish near the sea; mahogany and other valuable hardwoods dot the high jungle. Mangrove swamps border the coasts. Crops include corn, cotton, beans, rice, tobacco, cassava, sugar cane, bananas, plantains, melons, gourds (jicaros), etc. Flowers grow profusely-- lilies, orchids of myriad varieties, many bromiliads, and so on. There is a wealth of vegetation in both quantity and variety.

VEHICLES. In 1955 Nicaragua had approximately 6, 000 automobiles, 5, 000 to 6, 000 tractors, and about 6, 000 four-wheel-drive vehicles ("jeep" types) and trucks. By 13 years later, there were over 30, 000 autos, buses, and trucks alone.

VELASQUEZ, LA. A district of the San Rafael del Sur municipio, Managua department.

VALASQUEZ, CARLOS RAMIREZ. A Masayan composer of the "Symphony of the Americas" and the "Symphony of Managua. "

VELEZ, MIGUEL. A lieutenant at the Battle of San Jacinto.

VENADO, EL. Comarca, valley or district in the municipio of Juigalpa.

VENECIA. A coffee hacienda or plantation in Condega municipio, Estelí department.

VENTANA. A student publication in León; a literary magazine.

VENUS. An ill-starred transport vessel which took away Spanish prisoners from the capture of Fort Inmaculada by the British in April, 1780. Loading the prisoners at San Juan's River mouth May 17, 1780, the transport took a southerly route via Cartagena, heading towards Santiago de Cuba through the passage between Haiti and Jamaica. Struck by heavy storms, the pilot returned (presumably with the prevailing winds) to the San Juan River mouth. The delay caused such a tragic shortage of provisions that scurvy broke out with resultant death for 55 prisoners and 17 English sailors. During six weeks ashore more prisoners died, and by mid-August when they left again for Cuba, nearly 90% of the prisoners had died from thirst or scurvy. English sailors died with them. When added to the English losses from fever and dysentery, the 1780 campaign was a tragic defeat for both sides.

VERACRUZ. 1) A district of the municipio of Nindirí in Masaya department.
2) District in the municipio and department of Rivas.

VERACRUZ DE ACAYO (o Paso Soleras). Comarca or district in the municipio of Santa Teresa, Carazo department.

VERDELETE, FRAY ESTEBAN. Missionary priest assassinated by Indians in the Tologalpa area in 1612. His companion Fray Juan de Monteagudo was also killed.

VERGEL, EL. Hacienda in the municipio of Rivas.

VERO. A small stern-wheel steamer "of the Western type, " boilers forward, engines aft, wood piled on deck. She is described by Admiral Walker in a canal commission survey in 1897, and was used in the survey operations.

VESTA (Brig). The vessel which in 1855 transported William Walker and his 58 "immortals" to Nicaragua. It was an unseaworthy old brig, and took six weeks for the voyage. It was used subsequently to transport Walker's early scanty forces along Nicaragua's Pacific Coast.

VESUBIO MINE. One of the Bonanza (q. v.) group of mines.

VICE-PRESIDENCY. There are two vice-presidents elected on the same ballot as the president. If the president dies, resigns, or is incapacitated, Congress appoints a "designado" or provisional president who fills out the interim of the term. The vice-presidents must have the same qualifications as the president. (See PRESI-DENCY.)

VICEROY. As a direct representative of the Spanish crown, the "vice-king" represented the king in a direct manner, and was the loftiest of colonial officials. Nicaragua, under the viceroyalty of New Spain and the "Kingdom of Goethemal" (Guatemala) was somewhat remote from the vice-regal center in Mexico, yet was also subject to the vice-regal prerogatives of appointing officials (even to very minor posts) and of granting encomiendas, most significant function during the colonial era. At the termination of an incumbency, the viceroy was subject to a review of his acts in office by a residencia, and to some limitations during his office by the advisory group known as an audiencia. Conversion of Indians, tax collection, law enforcement, and general adminis-tration were the vice-regal functions.

VICTORIA. Perhaps the best known of Nicaraguan steam vessels, the old screw steamer Victoria plied Lake Nica-ragua for around 70 years. Built by Pusey and Jones, Wilmington, Delaware in 1882, she steamed down the Atlantic and across the Caribbean to the mouth of the San Juan; thence, up that treacherous stream to the lake. She was warped up the rapids. She was de-scribed further by Colonel Dan Sultan of a U. S. canal

survey group in the 1930's as "twin-screw, fast (ten or
more knots." Iron-hulled, single-stacked, broad-
beamed, she was rescued from breaking up by General
Somoza, the president. The hull was still extant in
1969. The hull and superstructure were pockmarked
with bullet holes, from the various revolutions she had
weathered or in which she had actively participated.

VIEJO, RIO DE. The Viejo River originates near San Rafael
del Norte and has a course of 104 miles to its mouth in
Lake Nicaragua. Tributaries are the Isiqui, La Trinidad, and Quebrada Honda.

VIENTICUATRO. District in the municipio of Tisma, department of Masaya.

VIGIA, LA. An airfield on the Coco River near and just
above the mouth of the Pantasma River. Area of "La
Cruz." See TRIUNFO DE LA CRUZ.

VIJAGUA, LA. A district of the municipio of San Pedro,
Chinandega department.

VIJAGUAL. 1) A district in the municipio of Matiguás,
Matagalpa department.
2) El Vijagual, a district in the municipio of Santa
Lucía, department of Boaco.

VILAMPI. A district in the municipio of Matiguás, Matagalpa department.

VILCHEZ Y CABRERA, JUAN. A native of Nueva Segovia,
Vilchez y Cabrera was instrumental as dean and later
bishop in finishing the León cathedral, by importuning
the Captain-General in Guatemala and donating his own
funds. He died in 1774, just before the building was
consecrated in 1780.

VILLA DE LA PURISIMA CONCEPCION DE RIVAS. Full
name of the city of Rivas (q. v. , def. 1) on the site of
the principal town of the ancient Valley of Nicaragua.

VILLA DEL LIMON. Comarca or district in the municipio
of Achuapa, León.

VILLA HERMOSA. Comarca or district in the municipio of
La Libertad, Chontales.

VILLA, LUIS ANGEL. A suicide at age 21 in 1907, this
   follower of Darío shared the tragic fate of several who
   were influenced by the immortal Rubén.

VILLA SOMOZA. Municipio in the department of Chontales,
   created in 1942 in honor of then President Anastasio
   Somoza. Bounded by Santo Tomás on the north, Morrito on the south (of the department of Río San Juan);
   to the east, Rama, and to the west, the municipios
   Santo Tomás and Acoyapa. Area, 296 square miles,
   population in 1968, 12,000. Characterized by numerous
   waterfalls and cascades in the streams, the municipio
   straddles the important Rama Road to the Caribbean
   Coast area.

VILLA SOMOZA DE RIO GRANDE. Comarca or district in
   the municipio of El Sauce, León department.

VILLATORO, TERESA. Young woman from El Salvador who
   became Agusto Sandino's mistress during his stay on El
   Chipote mountain in 1928. Early in 1931 Sandino broke
   with Teresa and brought his wife into the hills with him
   in March.

VILLA VIEJA DE ESTELI. Occurring between 1680 and
   1690, where previously the whole area was called the
   "Valle of Estelí, " under the Central government in León,
   and considered attached to the "city" of Nueva Segovia.
   The engineer Navarro in 1744 spoke of the Province of
   Nueva Segovia and said that it was a frontier against
   the enemies (pirates and Sambo-Miskitos) to the east.
   There were few people.

VILLA VIEJA, RIO DE   see   RIO AGUEQUESPALA

VILLEGAS, JUAN FELIX DE. Bishop of Nicaragua from
   1785 on through the attempt to settle and Christianize
   Mosquitia by the Spanish. Formerly prosecutor of the
   inquisition in Cartagena, Villegas was a man of vigor
   and imagination. His plan to work through Colville
   Breton (q. v.) and others was foiled by the duplicity,
   sagacity, and rapacity of some of the other Sambo-Miskitos.

VINALI. A property in Estelí department of doña Manuela
   Centeno, who was given title to it by grant in 1721. An
   aboriginal Indian name.

VIRGEN, LA.   1) A district in the municipio of Jinotega.
      2) District in the municipio and department of Rivas.
      3) A district of the municipio of San Juan de Tola,
      Rivas department.
      4) This placer mining area of the northeast district
      is one of several considered to have an average value
      of $3.75 in gold per cubic yard.
      5) A quinta (country house) in the environs of Masaya.
      6) La Virgen, a sidewheel paddle steamer on Lake
      Nicaragua during the Accessory Transit Company and
      filibuster-war era, 1852-1857.   One of few side-wheel-
      ers, this steamer may have been the old Director re-
      named.   Captain Gruder commanded her.
      7) Formerly, a lake port near Rivas.

VIRGEN DE FATIMA, LA.   One of the most frequently
      found saints as patrons of Nicaraguan homes.

VIRGIN DEL PERPETUO SOCORRO.   Object of reverence in
      home shrines, one of the familiar ones revered on
      Saint's Days.

VIRREY.   This is an abbreviated form of the word.   See
      VICEROY.

VISCAINO, EL.   A territory of the National District, de-
      partment of Managua.

VISTA ALEGRE.   A district of the municipio of Nandasmo,
      Masaya department.

VIVA LEON.   A "carrera, " or fast musical favorite of Nica-
      raguans, eulogizing the beauties of "mi linda ciudad co-
      lonial, " and with a spirited chorus.   In some situations
      of political tension, it has a special significance.   An
      example of much original Nicaraguan music, popular and
      otherwise.

VIVA MASAYA.   A ballad, "carrera, " concerning the beauties
      of Masaya and the glories of the Mena-Chamorro War of
      1912.

VIXEN (Ship).   One of two British warships which participated
      in the seizure of San Juan del Norte on January 1, 1848,
      when the city was renamed "Greytown. "   A Mosquito
      sloop, flying the flag of Mosquitia, accompanied the two
      British ships.   The other vessel was the Alarm.   The

job had to be done over by the same little fleet February
8, 1848. Captain Lock of the <u>Alarm</u> followed Nicaraguan
forces upstream to Serapiqui, capturing their stronghold
there. He continued upriver and through the lake to
Granada, besieging it. Nicaragua was forced at the
points of Lock's British bayonets to relinquish the rights
to Mosquitia "forever. " She finally won them back in
1894.

VOLADOR. A game played by aboriginal inhabitants of Managua, probably as a part of religious ceremonies, and
similar to the "fliers" or voladors in various remote
parts of Mexico today.

VOLCAN, EL. Coffee hacienda in the municipio of San
Rafael del Norte, in Jinotega department.

VOLCAN BLUE. An unusual recent volcanic cone, part of
a group of three cones from 400 to 500 feet altitude.
Covered with large trees, the existence of these cones
is sure evidence of their relative recency (a few thousand years) for in this rainforest area any sharp features
are commonly levelled or dulled by alluvial action. The
feature is found in the deep "selva" or forest of the Wawashan, in Zelaya department.

VOLCAN GRANDE. A height of the Datanlí spur of the
Darien mountains in Jinotega department.

VOLCAN VIEJO. A mountain eight miles north of Ocotal,
second highest in Nicaragua at 6, 132 feet. This is not
to be confused with the volcano in the Los Marabios
range, San Cristóbal, which is more familiarly called
El Viejo. The department is Nueva Segovia.

VON HUMBOLDT, ALEXANDER. The great Humboldt needs
no biography here; the spate of data on his life and remarkable work being a flow almost like the Humboldt
current which bears his name. As to a canal route
across Nicaragua, the magnificent work throughout Spanish America of the man for whom the Pacific's Humboldt Current was named, and in particular his knowledge of the Otrato River route in Colombia, make his
views of the Nicaraguan route worth quoting exactly as
follows: (from his "personal" narratives of travels):
"The isthmus of Nicaragua and that of Cupica have always appeared to me the most favorable for the forma-

tion of canals of large dimensions. " (The Cupica is the
Atrato-Napipi Route.) Published in 1811, this dictum
(and related views) of Humboldt's caused the Cortes of
Cádiz to pass a formal decree providing for a canal for
the "largest vessels" to go through Central America.
Reestablishment of the Spanish monarchy quashed this
ebullient evidence of Spanish liberalism. The canal had
to wait for the development of capitalistic enterprise.

VOZ DE AMERICA, LA. A Managua radio station, call letters YNAJ, power 10, 000 watts, frequency 1430 kilocycles.

VOZ DE CHINANDEGA, LA. A radio station in Chinandega,
power 370 watts, 1300 kilocycles. Call letters YNRA.

VOZ DE LA VICTORIA, LA. A Managua radio station, call
letters YNQ, 750 watts power, 1100 kilocycles frequency.

VOZ DE PUEBLO, LA. One of a number of periodicals developed in Boaco during 1915-1937.

-W-

WABASH (Ship). American Naval frigate engaged in the cap-
ture of William Walker's second expeditionary force to
Nicaragua at San Juan del Norte in November, 1857.
(See HORNSBY.)

WAGES. Under social security coverage in 1967, the average
weekly wage for commercial employees was 234 córdobas
($33. 40); for construction workers, 177 córdobas ($25. 30)
and for manufacturing, 160 córdobas ($23. 00). Qualifica-
tion of personnel tends to be related to educational opportunities, which are more prevalent in commercial than
in agricultural or industrial occupations.

WALKER, WILLIAM, 1824-1860. Born in Nashville, Tennes-
see, this slightly built, grey-eyed little man became one
of the spectacular figures of the turbulent 19th century
in the United States. (Five feet, five inches tall, 120
pounds, his name became synonymous with "filibuster"
and manifest destiny.) A graduate of the University of
Nashville at age 14, he completed studies for a degree
in medicine from the Medical College of the University
of Pennsylvania at 19, to become one of the youngest

qualified physicians in the nation. He went to the Sor-
bonne in Paris, and soon after gave up medicine following a brief practice. Two years after reaching New
Orleans he was admitted to the bar, and with a partner
he opened a law office. Disillusioned by law as by
medicine, he became in 1848 a foreign editor for the
new newspaper Crescent. By 24 he had engaged in
three careers. The death of his only love, Ellen Martin, sent him to California where he again became a
newsman as well as a somewhat celebrated duellist. In
1853, Walker led an abortive expedition to attempt to
take over Mexican territories in Baja California and
Sonora as an independent "Republic of Lower California."
Just 30 on May 8, 1854, he was chased back across the
border into California by Mexican outlaws.

All this was the incredible prelude to an even more
unbelievable Nicaraguan adventure. Invading Nicaragua
with 58 men (later called the "Immortals") Walker soon
had an army of thousands and made himself President
of Nicaragua. Helped by Cornelius Vanderbilt (q. v.)
and the Accessory Transit Company (q. v.), his campaigns received world-wide attention and acclaim. Men
flocked to the filibuster army from all over America.
As President of Nicaragua by rigged elections in 1856,
Walker issued bonds, made English the official language
of the Spanish-speaking country, and finally alienated
Commodore Vanderbilt, which proved his downfall.
Meanwhile all of the other Central American countries
united against Walker, fielding a considerable army.
The last battle was April 11, 1857, when 700 of 2, 000
attackers under General Zavala (q. v.) were killed by
Walker forces. Walker surrendered to Commander Davis
(q. v.) of the U. S. Navy on May 1, 1857. Under him,
2, 500 fighting men had served in Nicaragua, opposed by
17, 000 Central Americans. It was a major instance of
united action among the otherwise nonfederated countries.
One-thousand Americans had died during the war and
700 deserted; about 5, 800 Central Americans were killed
in battle.

New Orleans gave the defeated Walker a hero's welcome in May, 1857, and by November he had landed
again in Greytown, Nicaragua. Taken into custody by
U. S. Commodore Paulding (q. v.) he was again returned
to trial and acquitted in the States. In 1859 he published a book which is remarkable in its third-person
impartiality, The War in Nicaragua. In 1860, another
venture in Central American warfare found Walker and

companions attacking an old Spanish fort in Truxillo,
Honduras. Ordered to surrender by British Captain
Norvell Salmon (q.v.) of the warship <u>Icarus,</u> Walker
did so, and was turned over to Honduran authorities.
He was executed before a firing squad on September 12,
1860, age 36. One writer said concerning Walker's
drive to unite Central America and attach it to the South
of the United States as a slave-holding entity: "Had he
been successful, the [U.S.] Civil War might have been
postponed, might never have been fought, or might have
had another result." Perhaps this unrealized possibility
in the delicate scale of global events was Walker's most
significant contribution (in the negative sense). His
ability to attract able and educated followers was marked,
as a study of his lieutenants will attest.

WALKER, WILLIAM (Literature). Many books and articles
have been written about Walker's Sonora and Nicaragua
campaigns, but perhaps it is most remarkable that from
the ranks of Walker's own soldiers of fortune came six
books, numerous articles, and much poetry. Chief
among these productions is the third-person account by
Walker himself. <u>The War in Nicaragua</u> is considered
an amazingly accurate and impartial exposition (even by
Walker's enemies) and <u>The Filibuster War</u> in Nicaragua
by C. W. Doubleday (1886), is a spirited first-hand account. The well-educated and sensitive men who followed
Walker were legion, which seems remarkable especially
when the outcomes and the later judgments of history
are considered.

"WALKER'S RANGERS" see FALANGE AMERICANA, LA

WALPASIKSA. Village on the Caribbean Coast. (See CAÑO
WALPASIKSA AWALE).

WANGKS see COCO, RIO

WANKARLAYA, LAGUNAS DE. A series of tiny lakes, one-
fourth to one-half mile across, in a swampy area 30 or
more miles upstream from the mouth of the Río Grande
de Matagalpa. The whole coastal area of this part of
Zelaya department tends to be swampy lowlands for 30
miles or more from the Caribbean.

WANKS see COCO, RIO

WANX see COCO, RIO

WARD, FREDERICK TOWNSEND. One of William Walker's
lieutenants in 1855 who later became a General in the
Chinese Army, only one of many of Walker's Nicaraguan
veterans who later distinguished themselves in military
careers.

WASALLAMA. A district on the Río Grande, a lower Río
Tuma tributary.

WASPAN. A municipio along the banks of the Río Coco in
Zelaya department, Waspan has been whimsically called
the "New York of the Río Coco." While the municipio
has 12,000 inhabitants, only about 1,000 live in the cabacera. A chicle-gathering enterprise over many years
has given one inhabitant the title "Chicle-King of the Río
Coco." The type of chicle found here is used in making
bubble-gum. The pilot project Educación Fundamental
carried on by UNESCO in the lower Río Coco had headquarters here. Near the cabacera is Bilwas-karma
where a Moravian hospital and small tubercular sani-
torium have rendered service for years.

WASPOOK, RIO see WASPUK, RIO

WASPUK, RIO. (Also, Waspook or Huaspuc.) This river
was a major means of opening out the rich gold mines
of the Bonanza (q.v.) area soon after the turn of this
century. Later, air transport was used, but the original heavy mining machinery and myriad other supplies
and equipment were transported, frequently dismantled,
in dugout canoes (pipantes) up the Waspuk. Numerous
rapids and cascades had to be portaged around. The
tasks were frequently immense, but this was the only
mode of entry to the rich mining region. The Waspuk
enters the parent Río Coco at Cocal, a few miles below
Sang Sang. It is still wild and unmapped country. Sev-
en major rapids are identified on the Waspuk.

WAWA, RIO. A northeast coastal river in Zelaya department entering the sea just south of Puerto Cabezas. A
major stream, navigable by dugout, the river enters the
sea through Laguna Yulu over the Barra de Wawa.

WAWASHAN. A village on the lower part of the river of
the same name, two miles above its mouth in Pearl
Lagoon.

WAWASHAN, RIO.   A river in the east coastal area of Nica-
    ragua, emptying into Pearl Lagoon from the west.   It
    has justly earned literary fame through Archie Carr's
    perceptive and definitive book on Nicaragua and Hon-
    duras, High Jungles and Low.

WEBB, WILLIAM H.   see   CENTRAL AMERICAN TRANSIT
    COMPANY

WEBSTER, WILLIAM R. C.   see   SPENCER, SYLVANUS

WEIGHTS AND MEASURES.   The following list of weights
    and measures gives an idea of the blend of old and new
    in the current usage of Nicaragua: cuarta (one-fourth a
    vara), 8. 3 inches; vara, 2. 76 feet; cuadra, 91. 9 yards;
    legua, 3 miles; manzana, 1. 75 acres; caballería, 27. 9
    acres; legua cuadrada, 9 square miles; fanega, 500 cu-
    bic inches; arroba, 25 pounds; libra, 1. 014 English
    pounds; galón, . 888 English gallons; and quintal, 101. 44
    English pounds.

WERWEER, GENERAL.   An officer of the Netherlands who
    was sent to Nicaragua on behalf of the King of Holland
    in 1826, to the Panama convention, and as a result of
    whose work a contract was signed on December 18,
    1830, which gave a very liberal concession to the Dutch
    for the exclusive right-of-way across Central American
    Territory for the building of a canal.   A monopoly of
    the coasting trade was also granted.   The United States
    took a dim view of the contract, on Monroe Doctrine
    bases, and the U. S. Minister to the Netherlands was
    told to secure a majority of the stock of the Holland
    Canal Company.   A Belgian revolution which erupted
    caused Holland to abandon the project.

WEST, P. C. F.   A captain of the United States Coast Survey
    who was employed by the Central American Transit Com-
    pany in the mid-1860's to survey once again the San
    Juan River and the port at its mouth, with an eye to
    making the shallow and rapids-interrupted stream navi-
    gable for light-draft vessels, and the harbor, then ra-
    pidly silting up, accessible to ocean steamers.   Che-
    valier's (q. v.) activities put a temporary end to this
    plan.

WESTERN DESIGN.   A bold expansionist plan undertaken by
    England's Oliver Cromwell and one which envisioned the

seizing and cutting of the Spanish Empire in the isthmian area, either in Panama or Nicaragua. While Cromwell was unable to carry it out, his large Caribbean expedition of 1655 being turned back at Santo Domingo, nevertheless the idea remained in the plans and actions of Jamaican governors and English coastal colonists throughout the next century, until it had to be relinquished finally in the 1780's, following the disastrous result of the major thrust at "El Castillo" or St. John's Fort by British forces under Dalling, Nelson, and others.

WESTERN REGION. One of four major Nicaraguan regions, the West includes the heavily populated Pacific highland area as well as the two large lakes, many small lakes, and the broad lowlands of the Great Rift which crosses the country (and the basic American Cordillera) from east to west. This is the heart of the country in both population and economic activity, and in effect is turned toward the Pacific.

WHEELER. A shallow-draft paddle steamer of the San Juan River, captured at El Castillo in 1856 by Captain George F. Cauty, and stranded later to be found a wreck in 1860 at the mouth of the San Juanillo.

WHELEN, THOMAS. U.S. Ambassador to Nicaragua in the 1950's, and at the time of Anastasio Somoza's assassination in 1956. Whelen was a confidant of Somoza's, and accused by the opposition of too much intimacy. The U.S. Embassy building was constructed in 1954 on "La Loma, " the presidential fortress on the rim of Tiscapa crater lake in Managua. In 1960 Whelen was burned in effigy in León, much to his puzzlement and distress. During his incumbency the educational, agricultural, military, medical, and survey assistance programs by the U.S. to Nicaragua were greatly advanced, under the Foreign Operations Administration and the International Cooperation Administration.

WHIPPLE, M. S. see WORDEN, M. S.

WILIKE GRANDE, RIO. A tributary of the lower Río Tuma.

WISCANAL. A district or valley in the municipio of La Concordia, department of Jinotega.

WISKILI. Comarca or district in the municipio of Achuapa, León.

WIWILI.   A district in the municipio of Jinotega.

WONKS   see   COCO, RIO

WOOD, JOHN C.   A U.S. Marine captain who moved on
April 13, 1931, to rescue Darrah's (q.v.) party during
the Logtown (q.v.) encounter.   His force was responsible
for killing Sandinista General Pedro Blandón, after which
the guerrillas were routed.   Eighteen of them died in
the encounter.   On April 14, 1931, Wood carried out a
spectacular return to Puerto Cabezas by an old electric
banana launch.

WOODWARD, CLARK K.   Rear Admiral of the U.S. Navy
who was appointed by President Hoover to head an electoral mission to Nicaragua in 1932.   Woodward was
guest of honor at a historic dinner when the old enemies
José María Moncada (q.v.) and Emiliano Chamorro (q.v.)
both were present.

WOOLWAS.   An Indian tribe of the interior of the eastern
Caribbean slopes of Nicaragua.   They were on the upper
branches of the Nueva Segovia, Río Grande, and other
rivers by the early 1880's.   It was the custom of the
coastal Misquitoes to capture these Indians and sell them
as slaves.   Orlando Roberts purchased a Woolwa lad in
about 1820.   It is probable they were of the Chorutegan
group, originally from Mexican sources.   (Note the fortification "San Juan de Ulua" or "Ulloa" in Vera Cruz,
Mexico.)

WORDEN, M. S.   A former U.S. destroyer, DD-16, one of
the first series built, used as a banana boat because of
high speed and shallow draft, under the Nicaraguan flag.
Refitted with Diesel engines, the Worden and two sisters,
the Truxtun (DD-15) and the Whipple (DD-15), became
motorships (hence the M.S. designation); the latter pair
had Atlas diesels and the Worden had two 400 horsepower six-cylinder Wolverines.   All three vessels were
in use for over 50 years each, testimony to the quality
of their construction.

WORKERS' CONFEDERATION OF NICARAGUA   see   OR-
GANIZED WORKERS OF NICARAGUA, and COMMUNIST
PARTY

WOUNTA, LAGUNA.   A coastal lagoon in Zelaya department

ten miles long, seven miles wide, the entrance being 12 miles north of Prinzapolka.

WULASHA. The evil spirit of the Bocay-Pantasma group of Chorutegans; but probably post-conquest and derived from the Miskitos of the Caribbean Coast.

-X-

XALTEBAS. One of the Chorutegan tribal groups found pre-conquest in the area near Granada--the appellation of modern barrio "Jalteva" is derived from this name.

XALTEVA see JALTEVA

XAQUATUR. Amerindian aboriginal name of the San Juan River, as reported by Hakluyt in 1601, who had translated Antonio Galvaô's 1555 book The Discoveries of the World.

XICARA. A Nahuatl word now spelled differently but pronounced similarly, and with the same meaning. (See JICARO.)

XILOA see JILOA

XIQUIPIL see CONTLES

XOCHITL. 1) Daughter of the cacique Adiact in León, who having fallen in love with a Spanish captain soon after the city was transferred to its present site, was the proximate cause of the false accusation and hanging of the chief her father and members of his council.
    2) A word, meaning flowers, from the Nahuatl root xochi. One of the month festivals of the Nicaraos.

XOLOTL. Chichimec leader. The Chichimecs were Mesoamerican barbarians. It is an interesting circumstance that the name of Lake Managua was originally "Xolotlán." Chichimec invasions finally closed out the effectiveness of the Maya-Toltecs.

XOLOTLAN. One of Managua's two airfields, originally used by the U.S. Marine aviation detachment during the War of 1927-1933. Presently occupied by the Fuerza Aérea Nicaragüanese, "El Fan," the Nicaraguan air force.

XOLOTLAN, LAGO. The ancient name of Lake Managua, still used a great deal among the people and in such public forms as brand names. The name comes from the Mexican-based Nahuatl language of the Chorutegans, and refers to a small amphibian called <u>xolotli</u>, which was fished for and eaten by the primitive population. Another version is that it means "coast of the mountain turkey." Either would be a reasonable interpretation. The lake's surface is about 400 square miles. There is a volcanic island, Momotombito, a near-perfect cone over 1,000 feet high, wooded, and a refuge for deer. The first steamer on the lake, the <u>Amelia</u>, arrived in 1881, followed by the <u>Isabel</u> in 1882 and the <u>Progreso</u> in 1886. The <u>Managua</u> came in 1891, and finally the <u>Angela.</u> Steamer service ended when the León to Managua rail line was opened. The first sea-planes appeared on the lake January 15, 1927.

XOMONTLI. Small birds with feathers like the Quetzal; this Nahuatl name was used in forming the name Xomotepetl (q. v.).

XOMOTEPETL. Aboriginal name of the dead volcano near Somoto which gave the town its name (Madriz department.) Meaning (Nahuatl): "hill of the small birds. "

-Y-

YACALGUAS. A district in the municipio of Jinotega.

YACOYA, RIO. A stream tributary to the Prinzapolka west of Alamikamba.

YAGUALICA. A district in the municipio of Jinotega.

YALAGUA, RIO. A river in the Muy Muy municipio of Matagalpa department.

YALAGUINA. A small town in Madriz department; the name derived from pre-conquest Mexican sources, <u>yali</u> meaning "fish," and <u>guina</u> meaning "people";--hence, town of fishermen. It is five miles east of Somoto and five miles south of Totogalpa.

YALE. A district in the municipio of San Ramón, Matagalpa department.

YALI. 1) A municipio of the department of Jinotega, north-westernmost in the department, area 135 square miles, with 8,076 population. It is bounded on the north by Nueva Segovia and Madriz departments; on the south by the municipios San Rafael del Norte and La Concordia; on the east by San Rafael; and on the west by Condega municipio of the department of Estelí. There are 13 districts. El Volcán de Yalí is the principal mountain, and the Lake Cerro Colorado crowns the mountain of the same name. The area abounds in cafe "fincas" or farms, and cattle are also raised.

2) Volcan de Yalí, a mountain in the Isabella range, a dormant volcano, altitude of 5,100 feet, in the department of Jinotega.

YANQUE, EL. A district in the municipio of Jinotega.

YANQUI. A nickname or "apodo" given to North Americans (specifically, citizens of the United States of America). The word probably originated with the Dutch name "Jan Kees." Idiomatically the English-Americans applied it to Hollanders, then to the Dutch pirates of the 16th and 17th centuries, finally to the Dutch colonials in New York, and by association to the English colonials in Connecticut and New England, whence "Yankee Doodle" and the Latin American almost universal application.

YAOCA. A district in the Río Tuma in Zelaya department.

YAOSCA. A mountain height in the municipio of Matagalpa.

YARE see COCO, RIO

YARI see COCO, RIO

YARRINCE, CARLOS ANTONIO. Chief of the Yarrinces (q. v.), an Indian tribe who in León, in 1768, offered to supply 500 warriors to fight the English. Issued the title "Captain and Governor of the Caribs" by Governor Domingo Cabello.

YARRINCES. A family-led tribe of Indians near Boaco during the border troubles of the 18th century. Considered a Carib tribe. The Yarrinces thought of themselves as warriors under the Sambo "King."

YASICA. A pass in the frontier mountains during Spanish

colonial days, when the pirates and their Sambo-Miskito allies were a continual threat from the east.

YASICA NORTE. 1) A district in the municipio and department of Matagalpa.
    2) A district of the municipio of San Ramón, Matagalpa, department.

YASICA SUR. 1) A district in the municipio and department of Matagalpa.
    2) A district of the municipio of San Ramón, Matagalpa department.

YAYULE. A district in the municipio and department of Matagalpa.

YAYULI ARRIBA. A district in the municipio and department of Matagalpa.

YELUCA. (Also spelled Yuluca.) A district in the municipio of Yalí, department of Jinotega.

YN see CALL LETTERS, RADIO

YORO see COCO, RIO

YRIGOGEN, POLICARPO. Padre Yrigoyen in 1814 was parish priest of the area of Managua. An ardent monarchist, he was loyal to the king and maintained that loyalty among his Managua parishioners for a time. This led to the designation of Managua as a "loyal town."

YSASI. Surname of a Spanish engineer who assisted in the survey of a route of canal transit across Nicaragua. The 1779 survey was in cooperation with engineers Cramer and Muestro. It is remarkable that the first of these survey parties were accompanied by the English agents Hodgson of Bluefields and Lee of Belize. They wished, of course, to capture the depression of the great Nicaraguan Lakes for the British Crown. Their reports (and maps) led to the enthusiasm of Jamaican authorities for the British attack in 1780. One of the maps undoubtedly prepared from these surveys is published in the Kemble Papers regarding that ill-fated expedition against El Castillo.

YUCUL. A district of the municipio of San Ramón, Matagalpa department.

YULU, LAGUNA. One of twin coastal lagoons along the
Wawa River near its mouth, in northern Zelaya department just south of Puerto Cabezas.

YULUCA   see   YELUCA

YUPALI. A district or valley in the municipio of La Concordia, Jinotega department.

-Z-

ZABALETE, EL. A district of the municipio of San Ramón,
Matagalpa department.

ZACALI. A property owned by don Juan Castellón in Estelí
department in 1743, from an aboriginal Indian name.

ZACUALAPA. Pueblo or town existing in the valley of Nicaragua during the 16th and 17th centuries.

ZAMARIA. A mountain, ninth highest in Nicaragua, altitude
5, 496 feet, located in Jinotega department about five
miles north of San Rafael del Norte.

ZAMBRANO. A district of the municipio of Tipitapa, department of Managua.

ZANATE   see   ROSITA MINE

ZANCUDAL, EL. Coffee hacienda in the municipio of Yalí,
Jinotega department.

ZANCUDO, EL. 1) Comarca, valley or district in the municipio of Juigalpa.
2) A weekly developed in Boaco in the period following 1915.

ZANCUDOS. Conservatives who are "Somozista, " or in
general in close collaboration with the successive Somoza
regimes 1933-1970. These "conservatives" are the ones
who are given minority representation. There have been
large groups of conservatives who have no such concession.

ZAPATA. Used in Nicaragua to denote the shoe-shaped
burial ceramics which are found in sizes varying from

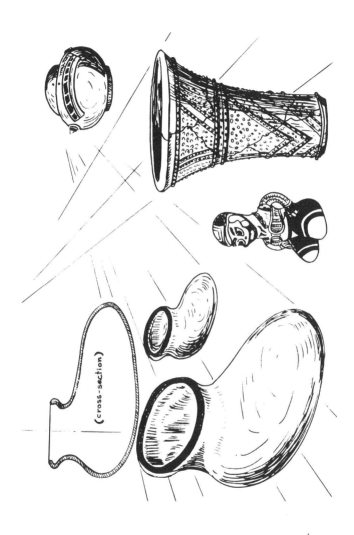

(cross-section)

Zapata (or Zapatera) and Other Ceramics

The shoe-shaped pre-conquest burial urn found in many sizes.

infant (12") to adult (30") and which are very characteristic. Also called "zapateras, " probably from the island
in Lake Nicaragua where many of them are found. (See
drawings.)

ZAPATERA see ZAPATA

ZAPOTAL. A district in the municipio of Jinotega.

ZAPOTAL, EL. 1) Comarca or district in the municipio of
Jinotepe, Carazo department.
2) A district in the municipio of Esquipulas, department of Matagalpa.
3) Mountain in the municipio of Santa Tomás, Chontales.   .
4) Comarca or district in the municipio of Santo Tomás, Chontales.

ZAPOTE, EL. 1) A district in the municipio and department of Matagalpa.
2) A district of the municipio of San Juan de Tola,
Rivas department.

ZAPOTE OCCIDENTAL. Comarca or district in the municipio of La Libertad, Chontales.

ZAPOTE ORIENTAL. Comarca or district in the municipio
of La Libertad, Chontales.

ZAPOTE Y LAS NUBES, EL. Coffee haciendas under single
ownership in the municipio of Yalí, Jinotega department.

ZARABANDA. A dance introduced in the city of León to the
society of that capital in 1765.

ZARAGOZA. A district of the city of León.

ZARAYAL. A district in the municipio of Jinotega.

ZARCETAS. Local name for widgeons, which frequent the
Tisma Lake.

ZARZALES, LOS. Comarca or district in the municipio of
Larreynaga, León.

ZARZALES, RIO LOS. A small river in the municipio of
Larreynaga.

ZAVALA, GENERAL. Guatemalan commander of Central
American forces arrayed against William Walker's men
under Henningsen (q. v.) when the latter destroyed Granada. Zavala wiped out the force of 27 men guarding the
docks at Granada, but could not follow-up his advantage
and prevent Henningsen from burning the city.

ZAVALA, JOACHIM. A Nicaraguan special commissioner
who was sent to the United States for direct canal negotiations in 1884 and who was party to the Frelinghuysen-
Zavala Treaty (q. v.).

ZAVALA, JOAQUIN. As president of Nicaragua 1879-1883,
Zavala was instrumental not only in the matter of a canal treaty, but also in such significant events as the expulsion of the Jesuits in 1881. Zavala developed the
National Library and the House of Fine Arts. An energetic idealist, he typified the highest in Nicaraguan culture.

ZELAYA. This, the largest department in Nicaragua, extends almost the whole length of the country on the Atlantic side. Almost 22,000 square miles in area, it is
nearly as big as the state of West Virginia in the United
States, and is larger than Delaware, Vermont, and New
Hampshire put together. There are only about 80,000
inhabitants in this vast area. Zelaya includes the significant gold mining areas of Siuna, La Luz, and Bonanza in its western reaches, and the area along the
Caribbean Coasts between the low-lying lagoons that
were once extensive banana plantations which a generation ago fell to blight. In the north the Standard Fruit
Company carried on large pine timber-cutting operations.
A new industrial enterprise is the copper mining up the
Prinzapolka River from the new Port Isabel. The terrain of the department is low, frequently swampy, laced
with saltwater lagoons quite a distance inland from the
Caribbean Coast. The uplands are found in the western
third of the department. There are few roads. Only
one all-weather road leads from the Pacific Coastal area
into Rama. There are roads from the Río Grande Port
of Makantaka to Alamicamba, Siuna, and Rosita. There
is a road from Puerto Cabezas to Waspam. Otherwise,
transport in this vast area is by dugout canoe, other
small craft, and by airplane. Six major rivers are
navigable for small craft, the Punta Gorda, Escondido,
Grande de Matagalpa, Prinzapolka, Kukalaya, and Coco.

The people are principally Miskito and Negro, descendants of the "Sambo-Miskitos" of two centuries ago. English, Miskito, and Spanish are spoken in that order of importance.

ZELAYA, JOSE SANTOS. Controversial and energetic President of Nicaragua, Zelaya took over by force of arms in 1893 from the Roberto Sacasa administration and ruled Nicaragua until 1909. A new constitution was promulgated by the Zelaya regime on December 10, 1893, which clearly separated church and state, a moot question for the previous decade which had even caused an 1881 rebellion in Matagalpa. Mosquitia was permanently incorporated in Nicaragua during Zelaya's time, after three centuries of British involvement, and there was a war with Honduras. Zelaya suffered continual coup attempts, one in February, 1896, which failed. Zelaya was interested in the formation of the Republic of Central America with El Salvador and Honduras, but the union was short-lived. During his terms, railway service was instituted from Corinto to Granada, Masaya, and Diriamba. In 1904, a more serious garrison revolt erupted, and in 1905, the "Rebellion of the Great Lake" (q. v.). The final anti-Zelaya revolution was led by the President's old friend Juan José Estrada. Through some U. S. intervention, Zelaya was forced to leave the country in 1910. He wrote a short book from exile entitled The Revolution in Nicaragua and the United States, an early commentary on intervention. José Madriz succeeded the tenacious Zelaya, whose name lives on in the huge Atlantic coastal department, by far the largest in the country.

ZELAYISTA. Adherents of Zelaya, actually a "party" during the dictatorship of José Santos Zelaya.

ZELEDON, BENJAMIN F. One of Nicaragua's heroes, General Zeledón was born in 1870 in La Concordia, Jinotega department. Becoming a lawyer, he held successive government offices, and during the war with Honduras in 1907, was named Auditor de Guerra, and on the battlefield of Namasigüe was named a colonel. Under the Madriz administration he became Minister of War, and followed Madriz into exile in Mexico. In 1912 he took part in the Revolution of Mena, and in opposition to forces of President Díaz aided by United States Marines, on October 4, 1912 he fell during a part of the fighting

near Masaya around Forts La Barranca and El Coyotepe,
actually in the village of Catarina, while attempting to
gather reinforcements.

ZEPATA, ANTONIO. A contemporary Nicaraguan composer
who writes concert music as well as popular songs.

ZOAGALPA. Pueblo or town existing in the Valley of Nicaragua during the 16th and 17th centuries.

ZONA DE LAS LLANURAS. The zone of "plains" of Managua
department is in two parts--those surrounding Lake Managua (Lago Xolotlán) and those on the Pacific side
around San Rafael del Sur, Masachapa, etc. The "Otro
Lado del Lago" has on the "other side of the lake"
broad plains, to the north as well as to the northwest
of Managua, where cotton is raised. The agriculture,
industry, and commerce of Managua are highly significant as the economic activity of the nation centers here.
There is varied agriculture, but much coffee, cotton,
and cane. Ten-million pounds of coffee is the annual
production. Almost 60,000 acres of cotton are planted.

ZONA DEL MUNICIPIO DE ESQUIPULAS. A significant
coffee-raising area of Matagalpa department.

ZONA DEL MUNICIPIO DE MATAGALPA. One of the significant coffee-raising areas in the northern part of the
country on heights in the eastern part of the Matagalpa
municipio.

ZONA DEL MUNICIPIO DE SAN RAMON. A significant coffee-raising area of Matagalpa department.

ZONA DE RIEGO. An area of irrigation. Especially applied to a governmental project in the department of
Rivas.

ZONA MONTANOSO. An area of the large department of Managua which is in the hills of Managua to the west of
the city and which has altitudes up to 2,000 feet. There
is a charming residential area at the summit, called
Casa Colorada, along the Panamerican Highway between
Managua and Diriamba. Casa Colorada is a cool area
with a spectacular view to both the Lake and Pacific
sides. This zone is sometimes considered to include
the Chiltepe Peninsula and the heights near San Jacinto,
the Meseta de Estrada.

ZOPILOTA, LA. Comarca or district in the municipio of Nagarote, León department.

ZOPILOTES. One of the two major forms of buzzard found in Nicaragua; neither is very like the Southern turkey buzzard of the United States.

ZORRA, LA. A hacienda six miles due south of Nandaime.

ZUNI. A district or valley in the municipio of San Rafael del Norte, Jinotega department.

ZUÑIGA, FRAY PEDRO DE. The designated first bishop of Nicaragua when following 1527 the Province was designated as a diocese. Dying before he left Cádiz, Zuñiga never took up his duties on Nicaraguan soil.

ZURRON, EL. Comarca or district in the municipio of Santo Tomás, Chontales.

Bibliography [see also List of Maps, page 500]

Abbot, Willis J. Panama and the Canal. New York: Syndi-
cate Pub. Co. , 1913.

Aid Resources Inventory Center. Nicaragua--inventorio nacional de recursos fisicos. Primera edición. Agency
for International Development, November, 1966.

Alden, John D. "Banana Boats and Blockade Runners,"
U. S. Naval Institute Proceedings, vol. 97, no. 4/818,
April, 1971.

Anderson, Dr. C. L. G. Old Panama and Castilla de Oro.
New York: North River Press, 1911, 1938, 1944.

Andrist, Ralph K. Making of the Nation. New York:
American Heritage Pub. Co. , 1968.

Arévalo, Juan José. The Shark and the Sardines. Trans.
by June Cobb and Dr. Paul Osegueda. New York:
Lyle Stuart, 1961.

Argüello y Argüello, Alfonso. Historia de León Viejo.
León, Nicaragua: Editorial Antorcha, 1969.

Ashe, Geoffrey. Land to the West. London: Collins, 1962.

Aspinall, Algernon. Pocket Guide to the West Indies. New
York: Brentano's, 1927.

Austin, Oliver L. , Jr. Birds of the World. Illus. by
Arthur Singer. New York: Golden Press, 1961.

Bacon, Edward. Vanished Civilizations of the Ancient World.
London: McGraw-Hill, 1963.

Bagrow, Leo Shelton, R. A. Ed. History of Cartography.
Cambridge, Mass. : Harvard University Press, 1966.

Bailey, Thomas A. The American Pageant. Boston: D. C.
Heath and Co. , 1956.

Banco Central de Nicaragua. Informe anual 1968. Consejo
Directivo Banco Central de Nicaragua, 1969.

Bancroft, Hubert Howe. History of Central America. 3
vols. San Francisco: A. L. Bancroft and Co., 1882-
1887.

Bard, Samuel A. (Ephraim G. Squier). Waikna; (or,) Adventures on the Mosquito Shore. (Facsimile of 1855
edition). (Latin American Gateway Series.) Gainesville:
University of Florida Press, 1965.

Beals, C. "In Quest of Sandino, Imperialism Still Rides."
Nation, September 20, 1965.

Belly, F. A travers l'Amérique Centrale. Paris: 1860.

Bendala Lucot, Manuel. Seville. 2nd ed. León, Spain:
Editorial Everest, 1970.

Bengoechea G., Adolfo J. Boletín del Servicio Geologico Nacional No. 7, Distrito Minero del Noroeste. Managua:
Ministerio de Economía, 1963.

Bettex, Albert. The Discovery of the World. New York:
Simon and Schuster, 1960.

Blacker, Irwin R. Cortés and the Aztec Conquest. New
York: American Heritage Pub. Co., 1965.

Boddam-Whetham, J. W. Across Central America.
London: Hurst and Blackett, 1877.

Borhek, Mary Virginia. Watchmen on the Walls. Bethlehem, Pa.: Society for Propagating the Gospel, Kutz-
town, Pa., 1949.

Bovallius, Carl. Nicaraguan Antiquities. Stockholm: Kongl.
Boktryckeriet, 1886.

Brandon, William. The American Heritage Book of Indians.
Ed. by Alvin M. Josephy. New York: American Heritage Pub. Co., 1961.

Bruun, Geoffrey. The World in the Twentieth Century.
3rd ed. Boston: D. C. Heath and Co., 1957.

Bureau of the American Republics, 1892 Nicaragua, Washington, D. C. : Bur. of Amer. Rep. , Bulletin No. 51, 1893.

Carles, Rubén Darío. Arquitectura colonial en Panama. Panama: Editorial Litográfica, 1966.

Carr, Albert. The World and William Walker. New York: Harper and Row, 1963.

Carr, Archie. High Jungles and Low. Gainesville: University of Florida Press, 1953.

Castillero R. , Ernesto J. Lecciones de historia patria. Panama: Librería Cultural Panameña, Editora Aleyda, 1967.

Cela, Camilo José, Avila. 4th ed. Trans. by John Forrester. Barcelona: Editorial Nogüer, 1964.

Chamorro, Pedro Joaquín. Estirpe sangrienta los Somoza. Mexico City: Impresora Juan Pablos Donato Guerra No. 5, 1957.

_____. Los pies descalzos de Nicaragua. Managua: "La Prensa" 1970.

Charnock, John, Esq. Biographical Memoirs of Lord Viscount Nelson. Boston: Etheridge and Bliss, 1806.

Cochran, Hamilton. Pirates of the Spanish Main. New York: American Heritage Pub. Co. , 1961.

Cohen, Benjamin A. , ed. -in-chief. The Worldmark Encyclopedia of the Nations. New York: Worldmark Press, 1960.

Consejo Nacional de Economía. El desarrollo económico de Nicaragua, vol. III, No. XXVII, Managua: Editorial "San José, " 1956.

Cortés, Alfonso. Las coplas del pueblo. Managua: Editorial Alemana, 1965.

Cortina, José Manual. Caracteres de Cuba. Habana: Molina y Co. , Editorial Lex, 1945.

Cottrell, Leonard. Lost Worlds. Ed. by Marshall B. Davidson. New York: American Heritage Pub. Co. , 1962.

Cramer, Floyd. Our Neighbor Nicaragua. New York: Stokes, 1929.

Craton, Michael. A History of the Bahamas. London: Collins, 1962-1969.

Crow, John A. and Crow, G. D. Panorama de las Améri-cas. Rev. ed. New York: Henry Holt and Co. 1956.

Crowther, Samuel. The Romance and Rise of the American Tropics, Garden City, N. Y. , Doubleday, Doran and Co. , 1929.

Cuadra Downing, Orlando. Seudónimos y apodos nicara-güenses. Managua: Editorial Alemana, 1967.

Cuadra, Pablo Antonio. El nicaraguense, vol. I, Managua: Ediciones Populares de Bolsillo Editorial Unión, 1968.

Cummins, Lejeune. Quijote on a burro. Mexico City: La Impresora Azteca, 1958.

Darío, Rubén. Poesías Completas. Madrid: Ediciónes Aguilar, 1952.

Davis, Richard Harding. Three Gringos in Venezuela and Central America. New York: Harper and Brothers, 1896.

Denny, Harold N. Dollars for Bullets; The Story of Ameri-can Rule in Nicaragua, New York: Dial Press, 1929.

Díaz Solís, Lucila. La flor calendríca de los Mayas. Mérida, (Yucatan) Mexico: Díaz Massa, 1966, 1968.

De Leeuw, Hendrik. Crossroads of the Buccaneers. Lon-don: Arco Publishers, 1957.

Dockstader, Frederick J. Indian Art in America. Green-wich, Conn. : New York Graphic Society, 1958.

Donald, David. Charles Sumner and the Coming of the Civil War. New York: Knopf, 1961.

Donavan, Frank. River Boats of America. New York: Thomas Y. Crowell, 1966.

Doubleday, Charles William. Reminiscences of the "Fili-buster" War in Nicaragua. New York: G. P. Putnam, 1886.

DuBois, Jules. Operation America. New York: Walker and Co., 1963.

Durant, Will and Ariel. The Lessons of History. New York: Simon and Schuster, 1968.

Duval, Miles P. Cádiz to Cathay. Palo Alto, Calif.: Stanford University Press, 1940.

Engels, Dr. Peter Bruno, et. al., Boletín del Servicio Geológico Nacional de Nicaragua. Resumen del estudio geológico sobre la tectónica interna de la región esquis-toso de Nueva Segovia, Nicaragua, Managua: Ministerio de Economia, 1964.

Espinosa Estrada, Jorge. Nicaragua, cuna de América. Managua: Editorial Alemana, 1969.

Farb, Peter. Man's Rise to Civilization as Shown by the Indians of North America from Primeval Times to the Coming of the Industrial State. New York: E. P. Dut-ton, 1968.

Floyd, Troy S. The Anglo-Spanish Struggle for Mosquitia. Albuquerque: University of New Mexico Press, 1967.

Ford, James A. A Comparison of Formative Cultures in the Americas. Washington, D.C.: Smithsonian Institu-tion Press, 1969.

Foster, Harry L. A Gringo in Mañana Land. New York: Dodd Mead and Co., 1924.

Gage, Thomas. Travels in the New World. Norman: University of Oklahoma Press, 1958.

Gallegos, Paco. Nicaragua, tierra de maravillas. Primera Edición (Cámera Nacional de Comércio y Indústrias), Managua: Editorial y Litografía San José, 1964.

Gámez, José D. Historia de Nicaragua (hasta 1860). Pri-mera Edición. Managua: Tipografía de "El Pais," 1889.

Giardini, Cesare. The Life and Times of Columbus.
Trans. by Frances Lanza. New York: Curtis Publishing Co., 1967.

Gordon, Arthur. American Heritage History of Flight. Ed.
by Alvin M. Josephy, Jr. New York: American Heritage Pub. Co., 1962.

Grau Sanz, Mariano. Segovia. León, Spain: Editorial
Everest, 1967.

Greene, Laurance. The Filibuster (The Career of William
Walker), Indianapolis: Bobbs-Merrill, 1937.

Griffin, Paul F., ed. Geography of Population. 1970 Year-
book of the National Council for Geographic Education.
Palo Alto, Calif.: Fearon Publishers, 1969.

Griffin, Paul F. and Chatham, Ronald L. Introductory College Geography. 2nd ed. Belmont, Calif.: Fearon Publishers, 1971.

Guerrero C., Julián N. Geografía e historia de Nicaragua,
Librería Cultural Nicaragüense, 1963.

_____, and Soriano, Lola. Boaco (geografía y historia).
Collección Nicaragua No. 1. Managua: Editorial
"Artes Gráficas, " 1964.

_____. Carazo (Monografía). Collección Nicaragua No.
2. Managua: Editorial "Artes Gráficas, " 1964.

_____. Chinandega (Monografía). Collección Nicaragua
No. 3. Managua: Editorial "Artes Gráficas, " 1964.

_____. Chontales. Collección Nicaragua No. 11. Ma-
nagua: Editorial "Artes Gráficas, " 1969.

_____. Estelí (Monografía). Collección Nicaragua No. 9,
Managua: Editorial "Artes Gráficas, " 1967.

_____. Jinotega (Monografía). Collección Nicaragua No.
6. Managua: Editorial "Artes Gráficas, " 1966.

_____. León (Monografía). Collectión Nicaragua No. 10.
Managua: "Artes Gráficas, " 1968.

_____. Managua (Monografía). Collección Nicaragua No.

4. Managua: Editorial "Artes Gráficas, " 1964.

_____. Masaya (Monografía). Colleción Nicaragua No. 5. Managua: Editorial "Artes Gráficas, " 1965.

_____. Matagalpa (Monografia). Colleción Nicaragua No. 8. Managua: Editorial "Artes Gráficas, " 1967.

_____. Nueva Segovia (Monografía). Colleción Nicaragua No. 12. Managua: Editorial "Artes Gráficas," 1969.

_____. Rivas (Monografía). Colleción Nicaragua No. 7. Managua: Editorial "Artes Gráficas, " 1966.

Gunther, John. Inside Latin America. 1st ed. New York: Harper and Brothers, 1941.

Hale, John R. Age of Exploration. New York: Time, Inc., 1966.

Halftermeyer, Gratus. Historia de Managua. Cuarta edicion. Managua: Talleres Nacionales, 1965.

Hanna, Kathryn Abbey and Hanna, Alfred Jackson. Florida's Golden Sands. Indianapolis: Bobbs-Merrill, Co., 1950.

Hannau, Hans W. Islands of the Caribbean. Munich: Wilhelm Andermann Verlag, 1962.

Harbaugh, William Henry. Power and Responsibility (The Life and Times of Theodore Roosevelt). New York: Farrar, Straus, and Cudahy, 1961.

Harold, J. Christopher, and Davidson, Marshal B., ed. The Age of Napoleon. New York: American Heritage Pub. Co., 1963.

Hedrick, Basil Calvin. Historical Dictionary of Panama. Metuchen, N.J.: Scarecrow Press, 1970.

Herring, Hubert. A History of Latin America. 2nd. ed., rev. New York: Knopf, 1961.

Hitchcock, H. R., et al. World Architecture--An Illustrated History. New York: McGraw-Hill, 1963.

Howarth, David. The Golden Isthmus. London: Collins, 1966.

Hydrographic Office, U. S. Navy. Naval Air Pilot; Central America. Washington, D. C. : Government Printing Office, 1937.

Incer, Jaime. Nueva geografía de Nicaragua. Managua: Editorial Recalde, 1970.

INFONAC, Division de Estudios Económicos. Guía del inversionista. Managua: Litografía San José, 1967.

Innes, Hammond. The Conquistadors. New York: Knopf, 1969.

Jane, Cecil. The Journal of Christopher Columbus. New York: Bramhall House, 1960.

Johnson, Haynes, et. al. The Bay of Pigs. New York: W. W. Norton, 1964.

Johnson, Thomas Crawford. Did the Phoenicians Discover America? London: James Nisbet and Co. , 1913.

Jones, Virgil Carrington. The Civil War at Sea. Vol. I. New York: Holt, Rinehart, and Winston, 1960.

Josephy, Alvin M. , Jr. The Indian Heritage of America. New York: Knopf. 1968 (And Bantam Books, 1968.)

Joyce, Thomas A. Central American and West Indian Archaeology. London: Philip Lee Warner, 1916.

Juarros, Br. D. Domingo. Compendio de la historia de la Ciudad de Guatemala. Guatemala City: Tómos I and II, Tercera Edicion. Tipografía Nacional, April, 1937.

Kagan, Hilde Heun (editor). The American Heritage Pictorial Atlas of United States History. New York: American Heritage Pub. Co. , 1966.

Kamman, William. A Search for Stability; United States Diplomacy Toward Nicaragua, 1925-1933. Notre Dame, Ind. : University of Notre Dame Press, 1968.

Keasbey, Lindley Miller. The Nicaragua Canal and the Monroe Doctrine; A Political History of Isthmus Transit, with Special Reference to the Nicaragua Canal Project and the Attitude of the United States Government Thereto. New York: G. P. Putnam, 1896.

Kelemen, Pál. Baroque and Rococo in Latin America.
New York: Macmillan, 1951.

_____. Medieval American Art. Vols. I and II. New
York: Macmillan, 1946.

Laganá, Tito. Boletín del Servicio Geológico Nacional de
Nicaragua, No. 4. Observaciones sobre la actividad de
los volcáns Santiago (Masaya) y Cerro Negro (León).
Managua: Ministerio de Economía, 1960.

Lamb, Robert A. Coins of Nicaragua. Tucson, Ariz.:
Published by Lamb, 1965.

Leonard, Jonathan Norton. Ancient America. New York:
Time, Inc., 1967.

Leslie, Robert C. Life Aboard a British Privateer (The Journal
of Captain Woodes Rogers). London: Conway Maritime
Press, 1889. Reprinted by Lewis Reprints Ltd., 1970.

Levy, Pablo. Nicaragua--Her History, Topography, Climate,
etc. Paris: Libreria Española de E Denné Schimtz,
1873.

Lieuwen, Edwin. Arms and Politics in Latin America. New
York: Praeger, 1961.

Lothrop, S. K. Treasures of Ancient America. Cleveland:
World Pub. Co., 1964.

McCauley, Rose, and Beny, Roloff. Pleasure of Ruins.
Norwich, England: Thames and Hudson, 1964.

MacKendrick, Paul. The Iberian Stones Speak. New York:
Funk and Wagnalls, 1969.

Macauley, Neil. The Sandino Affair. Chicago: Quadrangle
Books, 1967.

Mallin, Jay. "Che" Guevara on Revolution--A Documentary
Overview. Coral Gables, Fla.: University of Miami
Press, 1969.

Mantica, Carlos Abaunza. "The Güegüence." A comedy
ballet in El Pez y la Serpiente, Managua: Editorial
Unión, 1969.

March, Francis A. History of the World War. Philadelphia: United Publishers of the U.S. and Canada, 1919.

Marco Dorta, Enrique. Cartagena de Indias puerto y plaza fuerte. Madrid: Gráficas Condor, 1960.

Martz, John D. Central America, The Crisis and the Challenge. Chapel Hill: University of North Carolina Press, 1959.

Megee, Vernon E. "Genesis of Air Support in Guerrilla Operations." U.S. Naval Institute Proceedings, Vol. 91, No. 6, Whole No. 748. Annapolis, Md.: U.S. Naval Institute, June, 1965.

Menocal, A. G. Report of the U.S. Nicaragua Surveying Party--1885. Washington, D.C.: Government Printing Office, 1886.

Meyer, Harvey K. Technical Education in Nicaragua. Columbus, Ohio, Epsilon Pi Tau, Inc., 1958.

Miller, Hugh Gordon. The Isthmian Highway. New York: Macmillan, 1929.

Ministerio de Relaciones Exteriores. Situación jurídica del Río San Juan. Managua: Impresa Editorial "San Enrique," September, 1954.

Minter, John Easter. The Chagres--River of Westward Passage. (Rivers of America Series.) New York: Rinehart and Co., 1948.

Miranda, Dr. Ernesto. Folklore médico nicaragüense. León, Nicaragua: Editorial Hospicios, 1967.

Montross, Lynn. Cavalry of the Sky. New York: Harper and Brothers, 1954.

Moore, Richard E. Historical Dictionary of Guatemala. Metuchen, N.J.: Scarecrow Press, 1967.

Moore, W. G. A Dictionary of Geography. 3rd ed. Baltimore: Penguin Books, 1963.

Moravian Missionary Atlas, New Edition. London: Moravian Church and Mission Agency, 1908.

Morison, Samuel Eliot. The Caribbean as Columbus Saw It. Boston: Atlantic-Little, Brown, 1964.

_____. Admiral of the Ocean Sea. Vols. I and II. Boston: Little, Brown and Co., 1942.

_____. The Oxford History of the American People. New York: Oxford University Press, 1965.

Morrison, John H. History of American Steam Navigation. New York: Stephen Daye Press, 1958.

Mueller, Karl A. Among Creoles, Miskitos and Sumos. Bethlehem, Pa.: Christian Education Board, 1932.

Nesmith, Robert I. Dig for Pirate Treasure. New York: Bonanza Books, 1958.

New York Historical Society. Kemble Papers. Vol. II, Vol. XVII, New York: 1885.

Oficina Nacional de Urbanismo. Plan regulador de Managua. Managua: Ministerio de Fomento, 1956.

Palma Martínez, Ildefonso. La guerra nacional. Mexico, Impresa "Aldina," 1956.

Pan American Union. Nicaragua. American Republics Series No. 15. Washington, D. C.: Organization of American States, 1967.

Páiz Castillo, Ricardo. Historia de Nicaragua. (Collección LaSalle.) Managua: Editorial Hospicio, 1967.

Palmer, Mervyn G. Through Unknown Nicaragua. London: Jarrolds Publishers, 1920.

Parker, Franklin D. The Central American Republics. New York: Oxford University Press, 1964.

Parry, J. H. The Spanish Seaborne Empire. New York: Knopf, 1966.

Pataky, Laszlo. Nicaragua desconocida. Managua: Editorial Universal, 1956.

Paz Rivera, Narciso. Boletín del Servicio Geologico Nacional de Nicaragua. No. 6, Reconocimiento geológico

en la cuenca hidrográfica de los Ríos Coco y Bocay.
Managua: Ministerio de Economía, 1962.

Peterson, Harold L. Forts in America. New York:
Scribner, 1964.

Pim, Bedford. The Gate of the Pacific. London: Lovell,
Reeve and Co., 1863.

Quijano, José Antonio Calderón. Historia de las fortifica-
ciones en Nueva España. Sevilla: La Escuela de Estudios Hispano-Americanos, 1953.

Quintana Orozco, Dr. Ofsman. Apuntes de historia de Nicaragua. Cuarta Edición. Managua: Editora Mundial,
1968.

Roberts, Orlando W. Narrative of Voyages and Excursions
on the East Coast and in the Interior of Central Ameri-
ca; Describing a Journey up the River San Juan, and
Passage Across the Lake of Nicaragua to the City of
León. (Facsim. of 1827 ed.). Gainesville, Fla.:
University of Florida Press, 1965.

Robertson, Donald. Pre-Columbian Architecture. New York:
George Braziller, 1963.

Rodríguez, Mario. Central America. Englewood Cliffs,
N. J.: Prentice Hall, 1965.

Rovirosa, José N. Estado de Tabasco. Mexico City:
Oficina Típ de la Secretaria de Fomento, 1888.

Ruz, Alberto. Palenque. Mexico City: Talleres de Edi-
mex, 1960.

Ryan, John Morris, et. al. Area Handbook for Nicaragua.
Washington, D. C., Government Printing Office, 1970.

Schattschneider, Allen W. Through Five Hundred Years.
(A Popular History of the Moravian Church). Bethlehem,
Pa.: Comenius Press, 1956.

Schott, Joseph L. Rails Across Panama. Indianapolis:
Bobbs-Merrill, 1967.

Scroggs, William O. Filibusters and Financiers; The Story

of William Walker and His Associates. New York: Macmillan, 1916.

Sheldon, Henry I. Notes on the Nicaragua Canal. 3rd ed. Chicago: A. C. McClurg and Co. , 1902.

Silva, Fernando. El comandante. Managua: Editorial y Distribuidora Cultural Centro-Americana Editorial Unión, 1969.

Skelton, R. A. Decorative Printed Maps of the 15th to 18th Centuries. London: Staples Press, 1952.

Smith, Bradley. Mexico--A History in Art. New York: Harper and Row.

Somoza, Anastasio. El verdadero Sandino o el calvario de las Segovias. Managua: Tiopgrafía Robelo, 1936.

Southey, Robert, The Life of Nelson. 41st ed. London: Gibbings and Co. , June, 1911. (From 1813-1910: forty editions.)

Squier, E. G. Nicaragua, Its People, Scenery, Monuments ...., Vols. I and II New York: D. Appleton and Co. , 1852.

Stephens, John L. Incidents of Travel in Central America, Chiapas, and Yucatan. Ed. by Richard L. Predmore. Vols. I and II (1841), New Brunswick, N. J. : Rutgers University Press, 1949.

_____. Incidents of Travel in Yucatan. Vols. I and II (repub. of Harper and Brothers Work of 1843). New York: Dover Publications, 1963.

Stout, Peter F. , Esq. Nicaragua: Past, Present, and Future. Philadelphia: John E. Potter and Co. , 1859.

Strode, Hudson. The Pageant of Cuba. New York: Random House, 1934.

Stuart, George E. and Gene S. Discovering Man's Past in the Americas. Washington, D. C. : National Geographic Society, 1969.

Swain, Frederick M. Boletín del Servicio Geológico Nacional de Nicaragua No. 5. Reporte preliminar de los sedimentos del fondo de los lagos Nicaragua y Managua. Managua: Ministerio de Economía, 1961.

Sykes, Percy. A History of Exploration. New York: Harper and Brothers, 1961.

Szulc, Tad. The Winds of Revolution. Rev. ed. New York: Praeger, 1965.

Teilhet, Darwin Le Ora. The Lions Skin. New York: W. Sloane Assoc. , 1955.

Ugarte, Francisco. Que hace el Crefal. Mexico City: Editorial Muñoz, 1956.

UNESCO--Educación Fundamental. Español - Miskito - Inglés (A Vocabulary). Managua: UNESCO - Río Coco Project, Mimeo. , 1955.

Urtecho, José Coronel. Reflexiones sobre la historia de Nicaragua. León, Nicaragua: Editorial Hospicio, 1967.

U. S. Air Force--U. S. Navy. Flight Information Publication Terminal (Low Alt.) Caribbean and South America. Washington, D. C. , U. S. Armed Forces, 1 February 1964.

Vaillant, G. C. The Aztecs of Mexico. Baltimore: Doubleday Doran, 1944; Penguin Books, 1960.

Van Alstyne, Richard W. The Rising American Empire. Chicago: Quadrangle Books, 1960.

Velásquez de la Cadena, Mariano; Gray, Edward and Iribas, Juan. Velásquez' Spanish and English Dictionary. Chicago: Wilcox and Follett Co. , 1954.

Velie, L. "New Time Bomb in the Caribbean, " Readers Digest, January, 1962.

Verrill, A. Hyatt. Old Civilizations of the New World. New York: Tudor Pub. Co. , 1938.

Vivas Benard, Pedro Pablo. "Genealogía de la familia Quadra, Revista Conservadora del Pensamiento Centroamericano. Vol. 17-83. Managua: Editorial Alemena, Agusto, 1967.

Von Hagen, Victor W. The Aztec, Man and Tribe. New York: New American Library, 1961.

Walker, J. W. G. , U. S. N. Ocean to Ocean; An Account Personal and Historical of Nicaragua and Its People. Chicago: A. G. McClurg and Co. , 1902.

Walker, J. G. Report of the Isthmian Canal Commission 1899-1901. Washington, D. C. : Government Printing Office, 1901.

Walker, William (General). The War in Nicaragua. Mobile, S. H. Goetzal and Co. , 1860.

Wallace, William N. The Macmillan Book of Boating. New York: Macmillan, 1964.

Warner, Oliver. Victory--The Life of Lord Nelson. Boston: Little, Brown and Company, 1958.

_____. Nelson and the Age of Fighting Sail. New York: American Heritage Pub. Co. , 1963.

Watkins, T. H. , et al. The Grand Colorado. Palo Alto, Calif. : American West Pub. Co. , 1969.

Wells, William V. Walker's Expedition to Nicaragua. New York: Stringer and Townsend, 1856.

Whitaker, Arthur P. The Western Hemisphere Idea--Its Rise and Decline. Ithaca, N. Y. : Cornell University Press, 1954.

Wilgus, A. Curtis and D'Eça, Raul. Latin American History. New York: Barnes and Noble, 1969.

Wilgus, A. Curtis, ed. The Caribbean at Mid-Century. Series One, Vol. I. Gainesville: University of Florida Press, 1951.

_____. The Caribbean: The Central American Area. Series One, Vol. XI. Gainesville: University of Florida Press, 1961.

_____. The Caribbean: Contemporary Education. Series One, Vol. X. Gainesville: University of Florida Press, 1960.

_____. The Caribbean: Contemporary International Relations. Series One, Vol. VII. Gainesville: University of Florida Press, 1957.

_____. The Caribbean: Contemporary Trends. Series One, Vol. III. Gainesville: University of Florida Press, 1953.

_____. The Caribbean: Current U.S. Relations. Series One, Vol. XVI. Gainesville: University of Florida Press, 1966.

_____. The Caribbean: Its Culture. Series One, Vol. V. Gainesville: University of Florida Press, 1955.

_____. The Caribbean: Its Economy. Series One, Vol. IV. Gainesville: University of Florida Press, 1954.

_____. The Caribbean: Its Health Problems. Series One, Vol. XV. Gainesville: University of Florida Press, 1965.

_____. The Caribbean: Its Hemispheric Role. Series One, Vol. XVII. Gainesville: University of Florida Press, 1967. .

_____. The Caribbean: Its Political Problems. Series One, Vol. VI. Gainesville: University of Florida Press, 1956.

_____. The Caribbean: Natural Resources. Series One, Vol. IX. Gainesville: University of Florida Press, 1959.

_____. The Caribbean: Peoples, Problems, and Prospects. Series One, Vol. II. Gainesville: University of Florida Press, 1952.

Williams, Jay. The Spanish Armada. New York: American Heritage Pub. Co., 1966.

Ypsilanti de Moldavia, George. Los Israelitas in América precolumbina. Managua: Talleres Nacionales, 1962.

Zarur, Jorge. Geography and Cartography for Census Purposes in Latin America. Washington, D.C.: Inter-American Statistical Institute, June, 1948.

Zelaya, José Santos. <u>La revolución de Nicaragua y los Estados Unidos.</u> Madrid: Imprenta de Bernardo Rodriguez 1910.

List of Maps

Appended here is a representative group of modern maps, some of which have been used in the compilation of this dictionary. Most are quite recent. Nicaragua should be completely and very adequately mapped during the decade of the 1970's.

Some few of the maps have no publishing agency or point of issuance listed.

Esso Touring Service, Foreign Department, Mapa--La República de Nicaragua, 1:1,000,000, prior to 1955, American Geographical Society, New York.

Geographic Branch, Military Intelligence Division, (G-2) General Staff, Granada, Nicaragua; Costa Rica, Map No. 107-C-16-N-111, U.S.A. 1930, Series E-501, Edition 1-AMS, Printed by Army Map Service, Corps of Engineers

Hydrographic Office, 4th Edition, Central America and Panama, No. V-30-48, 1:2,188,800, March 1951, U.S. Navy Hydrographic Office, Washington, D.C.

Iberia, S.A., Mapa de la República de Nicaragua.

Juigalpa, Nicaragua, Hoja ND-16-16, Series E-503, 1:250,000, January 1964, Impreso por Litografía Robelo, Managua.

Junta Nacional de Turismo, 1952, Nicaragua (Mapa), "Welcome to Nicaragua," 1952, National Tourist Board, Managua.

La Palma, Nicaragua, 1:50,000, Hoja 3050-III, Series E-751, March 1961, Impreso por el Servício, Cartográfico Militar, Cuerpo de Ingenieros.

Ministerio de Fomento, Bluefields, Nicaragua, Hoja ND-17-13, Series E-503, 1:250,000, November 1962, Impreso por Litografía, Pérez Sucrs., Managua.

_____. Chinandega, 1:250, 000 Hoja, ND-16-15, October 1967, Impreso por la Dirección General de Cartografía, Managua.

_____. El Castillo, Nicaragua; Costa Rica, Hoja 3349-III, Series E-751, 1:50, 000, March 1966, Impreso por la Dirección General de Cartografía, Managua.

_____. Granada, Nicaragua; Costa Rica, Edición 2-DGC, Series E-503, Hoja NC-16-3, 1:250, 000, Impreso por la Dirección General de Cartografía, Managua.

_____. Granada y Vecindad, Hoja de Granada, 1:5, 000, December 1967, Dirección General de Cartografía, Printed by (U. S.) Army Map Service, Corps of Engineers.

_____. Los Chiles, Nicaragua; Costa Rica, Hoja 3249-II, Series E-751, 1:50, 000, April 1966, Impreso por la Dirección General de Cartografía, Managua, Nicaragua.

_____. Managua, Nicaragua, 1:250, 000, Hoja ND 16-15, Series E-503, February 1969, Impreso por la Dirección de Cartografía, Managua.

_____. Managua y Vecindad, 1:10, 000, Hoja de Managua, (Data to 1962), Impreso por Dirección General de Cartografía, Managua.

_____. Mapa Hipsográfico de Nicaragua, September 1966, Impreso por la Dirección General de Cartografía, Managua.

_____. Masaya, República de Nicaragua, Edición 1-DGC, Hoja de Masaya, 1:5, 000, August 1967, Dirección General de Cartografía, Managua.

_____. Momotombito, 1:50, 000, Hoja 2953-III, Series E-752, Second Edition, October 1967, Impreso por la Dirección General de Cartografía, Managua.

_____. Monkey Point, Nicaragua, Hoja NC-17-1, Series E-503, 1:250, 000, October 1966, Impreso por la Dirección General de Cartografía, Managua.

_____. Puerto Cabezas; Nicaragua, Honduras, Edición 2-DGC, Hoja ND-17-5, Series E-503, 1:250, 000, July 1968, Impreso por la Dirección General de Cartografía, Managua. 501

_____. República de Nicaragua Mapa Oficial, Edición Preliminar, 1:500,000, (no date), Dirección General de Cartografía.

_____. San Carlos, 1:250,000, Hoja NC 16-4, Series E-503, Impreso por la Dirección General de Cartografía, Managua.

_____. San Carlos, Nicaragua: Costa Rica, Hoja 3249-III, Series E-751, 1:50,000, April 1966, Impreso por la Dirección General de Cartografía, Managua.

Ministerio de Fomento y Obras Públicos, Departamento de Chinandega, Nicaragua, 1:150,000, Hoja No. 1, Serie Departamental, February 1967, Impreso por Litografía Robelo, Managua.

_____. Departamento de Masaya, 1:50,000, Hoja No. 04, Serie Departamental, August 1967, Dirección General de Cartografía.

Ministerio de Fomento, Oficina de Geodesia, La Paz Centro, Nicaragua, 1:50,000, Hoja 2853-II, Serie, (no date), Impreso por Litografía, C. J. Pérez Susc., Managua.

Ministerio de Obras Públicas, Bocay, Nicaragua; Honduras, 1:250,000, Segunda Edición Prelimnar, Hoja ND-16-8, Series E-503, July 1970, Dirección General de Cartografía, Managua.

_____. Cerro Kilambé, Nicaragua, 1:50,000, Hoja 3056-I Series E-751, April 1968, Impreso por la Dirección General de Cartografía, Managua.

_____. Corn Island, Primera Edición, Hoja de Corn Island, Nicaragua, 1:10,000, March 1969, Impreso por la Dirección General de Cartografía, Managua.

_____. Estelí, Nicaragua: Honduras, 1:250,000, Hoja ND 16-11, Series E-503, November 1968, Impreso por la Dirección General de Cartografía, Managua.

_____. Granada, Nicaragua: Costa Rica, 1:250,000, Edición 2-DGC, NC 16-3, Series, E-503, January 1968 Impreso por la Dirección General de Cartografía, Managua.

_____. Prinzapolka, Nicaragua, Hoja ND-17-9, Series

E-503, 1:250,000, September 1968, Impreso por la Dirección General de Cartografía, Managua.

_____. Puerto de Corinto y Vecindad, 1:5,000, June 1968, Impreso por la Dirección General de Cartografía, Managua.

_____. Siuna, Nicaragua, 1:250,000, Hoja No. 16-12, Series E-503, Segunda Edición, November 1969, Impreso por la Dirección General de Cartografía, Managua.

Texaco, America Central--La Carretera Interamericana, 1959, Rand McNally and Company.

Volcán Concepción, Nicaragua, 1:50,000, Hoja 3051-I, Series E-751, April 1961, Impreso por El Servicio Cartográfico Militar, Cuerpo de Ingenieros.

Volcán Maderas, Nicaragua, 1:50,000, Hoja 3050-II, Series E-751, March 1961, Impreso por el Servicio Cartográfico Militar, Cuerpo de Ingenieros.

Worldwide Surveys, Rivas, Nicaragua, 1:100,000, Hoja 3050, 1956, Oficina de Geodesia, Managua.

For Reference

Not to be taken from this room